Communications in Computer and Information Science 991

Commenced Publication in 2007
Founding and Former Series Editors:
Phoebe Chen, Alfredo Cuzzocrea, Xiaoyong Du, Orhun Kara, Ting Liu,
Dominik Ślęzak, and Xiaokang Yang

More information about this series at http://www.springer.com/series/7899

Slimane Hammoudi · Luís Ferreira Pires
Bran Selic (Eds.)

Model-Driven Engineering and Software Development

6th International Conference, MODELSWARD 2018
Funchal, Madeira, Portugal, January 22–24, 2018
Revised Selected Papers

 Springer

Editors
Slimane Hammoudi
Université d'Angers/ESEO
Angers, France

Bran Selic
Malina Software Corp.
Nepean, ON, Canada

Luís Ferreira Pires
University of Twente
Enschede, The Netherlands

ISSN 1865-0929 ISSN 1865-0937 (electronic)
Communications in Computer and Information Science
ISBN 978-3-030-11029-1 ISBN 978-3-030-11030-7 (eBook)
https://doi.org/10.1007/978-3-030-11030-7

Library of Congress Control Number: 2018968442

This Springer imprint is published by the registered company Springer Nature Switzerland AG
The registered company address is: Gewerbestrasse 11, 6330 Cham, Switzerland

Preface

The present volume contains extended versions of selected papers from the 6th International Conference on Model-Driven Engineering and Software Development (MODELSWARD 2018), held in Funchal, Madeira, Portugal, during January 22–24, 2018.

The purpose of the 6th International Conference on Model-Driven Engineering and Software Development (MODELSWARD 2018) was to provide a platform for researchers, engineers, academics as well as industrial professionals from all over the world to present their research results and development activities in using models and model-driven engineering (MDE) techniques for software development. Model-driven development (MDD) is an approach to the development of IT systems in which models take a central role, not only for purposes of analysis and documentation but also for their construction. It has emerged from a number of modelling initiatives, most prominently the model-driven architecture (MDA), which has been fostered by the object management group (OMG).

With the ever-increasing demand for more sophisticated functionality and more complex software systems, traditional (i.e., code-centric) development methods are proving less and less capable of supporting these developments. Consequently, in recent years there has been a significant uptake of MDD in industrial practice. This has, in turn, inspired an increased interest and investment in MDD-focused research, both in academia and industry. This trend is clearly reflected in the high-quality papers selected for inclusion in this volume.

The papers were selected by the event chairs, based on the evaluation and comments provided by the MODELSWARD Program Committee members, the session chairs' assessments, as well as the program chairs' review of all papers included in the technical program. The authors of the selected papers were then invited to submit a revised and extended version of their papers with at least 30% additional new material.

The topics covered in this volume represent highly relevant research directions in MDD, including, among others, innovative methods for MDD-based development and testing of Web-based applications and user interfaces, support for development of domain-specific languages (DSLs), MDD-based application development on multi-processor platforms, advances in MDD tooling, formal semantics and behavior modeling, and MDD-based product-line engineering.

We would like to thank all the authors for their contributions, and also the reviewers, who have helped ensure the high quality of this publication.

January 2018

Slimane Hammoudi
Luís Ferreira Pires
Bran Selic

Organization

Conference Chair

Bran Selic   Malina Software Corp., Canada

Program Co-chairs

Slimane Hammoudi   ESEO, MODESTE, France
Luis Ferreira Pires   University of Twente, The Netherlands

Program Committee

Silvia Abrahão	Universitat Politecnica de Valencia, Spain
Achilleas Achilleos	University of Cyprus, Cyprus
Hamideh Afsarmanesh	University of Amsterdam, The Netherlands
Ludovic Apvrille	LTCI, Télécom ParisTech, Université Paris-Saclay, France
Keijiro Araki	Kyushu University, Japan
Ethem Arkin	Aselsan, Turkey
Omar Badreddin	University of Texas El Paso, USA
Mira Balaban	Ben-Gurion University of the Negev, Israel
Bernhard Bauer	University of Augsburg, Germany
Martin Becker	Fraunhofer IESE, Germany
Frédérick Benaben	Ecole de Mines Albi-Carmaux (EMAC), France
Luca Berardinelli	Vienna University of Technology, Austria
Lorenzo Bettini	Università di Firenze, Italy
Paolo Bocciarelli	University of Rome Tor Vergata, Italy
Antonio Brogi	Università di Pisa, Italy
Manfred Broy	Technische Universität München, Germany
Achim Brucker	SAP Research, Germany
Matthias Brun	ESEO Group, France
Philipp Brune	University of Applied Sciences Neu-Ulm, Germany
Christian Bunse	University of Applied Sciences Stralsund, Germany
Håkan Burden	Viktoria Swedish ICT, Sweden
Renata Carvalho	Eindhoven University of Technology (TU/e), The Netherlands
Rui César das Neves	Directorate-General of Health, Portugal
Hassan Charaf	BME, Hungary
Olena Chebanyuk	National Aviation University, Ukraine
Yuting Chen	Shanghai Jiaotong University, China
Dan Chiorean	Babes-Bolyai University, Romania
Antonio Cicchetti	Malardalen University, Sweden
Nebut Clémentine	LIRMM, Université de Montpellier, France

Jean-Sébastier Sottet   Luxembourg Institute for Science and Technology, Luxembourg
Alin Stefanescu   University of Bucharest, Romania
Arnon Sturm   Ben-Gurion University of the Negev, Israel
Hiroki Suguri   Miyagi University, Japan
Massimo Tivoli   University of L'Aquila, Italy
Andreas Tolk   MITRE Corporation, USA
Naoyasu Ubayashi   Kyushu University, Japan
Andreas Ulrich   Siemens AG, Germany
Matias Urbieta   LIFIA, UNLP, Argentina
Mark van den Brand   Eindhoven University of Technology, The Netherlands
Gianluigi Viscusi   EPFL Lausanne, Switzerland
Shuai Wang   Simula Research Lab, Norway
Layne Watson   Virginia Polytechnic Institute and State University, USA
Michael Whalen   University of Minnesota, USA
Hao Wu   National University of Ireland, Maynooth, Ireland
Husnu Yenigun   Sabanci University, Turkey
Chunying Zhao   Western Illinois University, USA
Kamil Zyla   Lublin University of Technology, Poland

Additional Reviewers

Gerardo Barraza   University of Texas at El Paso, USA
Jessie Carbonnel   LIRMM, CNRS and University of Montpellier, France
Sebastian Feld   LMU Munich, Germany
Rahad Khandoker   University of Texas at El Paso, USA

Invited Speakers

Franck Barbier   University of Pau, France
Bernhard Rumpe   RWTH Aachen University, Germany
David Harel   The Weizmann Institute of Science, Israel

Contents

Executable Modeling for Reactive Programming

Franck Barbier[✉] and Eric Cariou

Univ. of Pau, Av. de L'Université, 64000 Pau, France
Franck.Barbier@FranckBarbier.com,
Eric.Cariou@univ-pau.fr

Abstract. After thirty years, it is reasonably time to critically look at Model
Driven Software Development (MDSD). Who may nowadays claim that MDSD
has been massively adopted by the software industry? Who may show numbers
demonstrating that MDSD allowed/allows massive cost savings in daily software development, but, above all, software maintenance? This paper aims at
investigating executable modeling as a balanced articulation between programming and modeling. Models at run-time embody the promising generation
of executable models, provided that their usages are thought and intended to
cost-effective software development. To envisage this not-yet-come success, this
paper emphasizes expectations from the software industry about "reactive programming". Practically, executable modeling standards like the SCXML W3C
standard or the BPMN OMG standard are relevant supports for reactive programming, but success conditions still need to be defined.

Keywords: Model driven software development · Executable modeling ·
Models at run-time · Reactive programming

1 Introduction

Since the rise of MDSD, "executable modeling" refers to the possibility of interpreting
models via an "execution engine" [1, 2, 3]. Roughly speaking, from industrial experience, models as "abstractions" are not as readable (and thus understandable) as it
appears. In other words, "abstraction" pushed forward as a panacea in the literature [4]
rather means "approximation". So, as incomplete representations of systems, models
hide second-class details (the good), but fail in providing fully controllable software
assets from requirements engineering to programming/testing (the bad).

Executable models essentially are more intuitive models that express structures and
behaviors of systems with greater clarity. In a nutshell, at design time, execution of
models is simulation of behaviors. As for structures, simulation informs us about the
evolution, for example, of object links over time. So what? Executable modeling is just
programming (*e.g.*, Java and its *Java Virtual Machine* as "execution engine"). Or, from
another perspective, programming is a subtype of modeling when programs (as
models) include implementation details. This seeming overlapping raises a worrying

© Springer Nature Switzerland AG 2019
S. Hammoudi et al. (Eds.): MODELSWARD 2018, CCIS 991, pp. 1–8, 2019.
https://doi.org/10.1007/978-3-030-11030-7_1

question: has MDSD reinvented "traditional" software development with no-value complication, no more? Indeed, it is extremely important to prove that MDSD provided/provides added value over competing software development "methods".

1.1   Back to Jurassic Programming?

By copying and adapting Winston Churchill's maxim, I may write: "Indeed it has been said that *MDSD* is the worst form of *Software Development* except for all those other forms that have been tried from time to time..." Translation: despite defects, MDSD is a true engineering progress in software development. In fact, programming and (executable) modeling are not so confusing notions in spite of some "theoretical" overlapping (see prior paragraph). To justify this opinion, let us go into further detail through the concise analysis of four executable modeling frameworks:

- The Papyrus UML/SysML integrated modeling environment supports the *Action Language for Foundational UML* (ALF) for model execution. Models are classical UML/SysML models endowed with executable parts written in ALF. In this logic, there is, *a priori*, **no use at all** of any programming language (*i.e.*, ALF acts as a neutral "programming" language). Moreover, in the spirit of model transformation, code is derived from models without any tricky model adjustment when deployment concerns occur about specificities of the targeted platforms (Web, real-time...). This (open-minded) idealistic (even naïve) vision omits the reuse of software libraries that require significant imbrication between models and *Application Programming Interfaces* (APIs). To that extent, a key ALF evangelist recently told me that perspectives of ALF take-up (and thus take-off) are poor due to the misunderstood "sophistication" behind the systematic use of ALF. In short, nobody really wants to use ALF!
- jBPM (standing for *Java Business Process Management*) is an integrated BPMN (*Business Process Model and Notation*) modeling environment that supports Java (or JavaScript) as "action language". BPMN 2.x as executable modeling language plus Java as action language for expressing the content of BPMN (routing) gateways and tasks, makes jBPM a complete platform for executable modeling. Indeed, jBPM is a simplified form of MDSD in the sense that the target platform is *Java Enterprise Edition* (Java EE) only, and more precisely the WildFly application server, a Java EE-compliant deployment middleware. jBPM perfectly illustrates the fact that programming and executable modeling **occur at the same time**. Compared to ALF, there is no intrinsic complication (and investment) associated with the use of Java because, simply, everybody knows Java.
- SCION is the JavaScript support of *State Chart XML* (SCXML). Client-side (browser) or server-side (Node.js platform) Web applications benefit from being designed from Harel's Statecharts for which SCXML provides its own (rational) execution semantics. While SCION allows the graphical or textual (a devoted *XML Schema Definition* or XSD) expression of SCXML models, SCION-CORE acts as execution engine for SCION. The actions associated with state entries, exits and transitions must be written in JavaScript (to interact with the *Document Object Model* or DOM, for instance, in the browser). Again, programming and executable modeling appear as totally complementary **and not alternatives**.

- PauWare is similar to SCION apart from supporting the execution semantics of both SCXML and UML State Machine Diagrams. PauWare is an API and a self-contained Java library only. Developers may organize their code from complex state machines in the style of reactive programming [5].

So, it is time to admit that MDSD is not the way of making software that, as much as possible, dismisses programming activities. The later ones cannot be ignored because models cannot encapsulate all of the APIs and software libraries (in varied programming languages), which are the single access to modern deployment platforms. As an illustration, a BPMN script task is a suite of Java statements within jBPM. It is naturally expected to call any "external" code within such a task.

1.2 The Economy of Executable Modeling

Model production is time-consuming and thus costly. In this logic, MDSD is a software engineering "method" (*i.e.*, "a way of making software") whose goal is, indubitably, fighting against code-only approaches, say, having no method at all, preferring DevOps or stressing agility (test driven software development that is often opposed to MDSD in the literature).

In a nutshell, from an economical viewpoint, one has to demonstrate that the return on investment is better with models. In other words, the time **lost** when constructing models definitely leads to the reduction of software cost prices **in all conditions**. Indeed, significant engineering efforts occur earlier with MDSD. Thus, models as software artifacts must accelerate software finalization later on: the only way of "getting our money back".

From experience, is it really observed? In other words, nowadays, considering 1000 (randomly chosen and sizeable) starting software projects in any kind of business sector and any kind of technological context (Enterprise (payroll, shipping, supply chain...), Web, safety-critical...), how many will use MDSD? I would bet 10. A missing link therefore exists in the economy of MDSD...

1.3 Executable Modeling in Action

As written before, as approximations, models (Fig. 1, car sketch) do not conform to (generated) code (Fig. 1, real car) while the contrary is true. Inevitable code adaptation at maintenance time (Fig. 1, repairers) breaks the initial mapping created at code generation (a.k.a. derivation) time. This is the main factor of MDSD failure because there is (and will be in the future) **no** MDSD tool capable of managing such mapping **at an industrial scale** when software masses pervade computers and above all clutter up developers' minds.

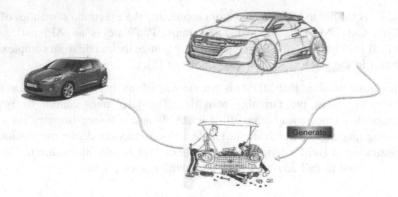

Fig. 1. MDSD recurrent pitfall.

In its very deep nature, executable modeling does not impose model transformation. Instead, executable modeling looks for the better composition of code and models. Both are expressed in different languages, but these languages have precise well-defined roles, inner workings and dependencies. Practically, Harel's Statecharts with their high-end expressiveness may be coded in JavaScript (SCION) or Java (PauWare). Data transformations only require algorithms and/or external calls that are encapsulated in actions triggered in Statecharts models. Models exist and persist at run-time [6]. There is no model transformation provided that model execution engines operate on the top of common programming languages compilers/interpreters.

As an illustration, Figs. 2, 3 and 4 show how to coordinate in PauWare any mobile app. with the Android battery management system.

Figure 2 shows the connection with the Android API. Using models here creates **no value**. Worst still, models may be considered as crippling.

```
class EventSniffer extends android.content.BroadcastReceiver {
    @Override
    public void onReceive(android.content.Context arg0, android.content.Intent arg1) {
        if (arg1 != null && arg1.getAction() != null) {
            android.content.Intent    intent    =    new    android.content.Intent(arg0,    An-
droid_energy_management_example.class);
            intent.setAction(arg1.getAction());
            arg0.startService(intent);
        }
    }
}
```

Fig. 2. Android battery management (notification subscription).

Figure 3 is the realization of a model at run-time. Instead of having cluttering Java if-then-else control code, Harel's Statecharts formalism allows rational code organization required for processing Android battery management system events.

```
public class Android_energy_management_example extends android.app.Service {
    EventSniffer _event_sniffer; // Link to the Java class in Fig. 2
    AbstractStatechart _Nominal_Energy_Level;
    AbstractStatechart _Critical_Energy_Level;
    ... // Other states here...
    AbstractStatechart_monitor _Android_energy_management_example_state_machine;
    ...
    public void start() throws Statechart_exception {
        _Android_example_state_machine.fires(android.content.Intent.ACTION_BATTERY_LOW,
    _Nominal_Energy_Level, _Critical_Energy_Level);
        _Android_example_state_machine.fires(android.content.Intent.ACTION_POWER_CONNECTED,
    _Critical_Energy_Level, _Critical_Energy_Level);
        ... // Etc.
```

Fig. 3. Android battery management (notification reaction).

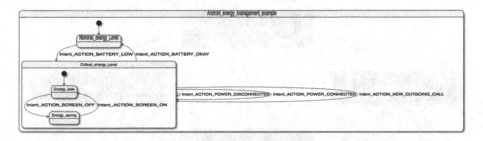

Fig. 4. Android battery management (model at run-time).

From a graphical viewpoint, Fig. 4 is totally equivalent to the model in Fig. 3. This graphical model may automatically be derived from the Java code in Fig. 3. Indeed, executable modeling with models at run-time create a true bijection between models and code. In terms of efforts and elapsed phases, models may be created first ("classical" MDSD)... or may not. While the model in Fig. 4 is an appropriate tool for test (simulation through graphical animation and execution trace) at design time, it may also be an ideal support for the (remote) administration of an energy-aware Android mobile app. when in production (*i.e.*, in users' hands). In contrast with model transformation, models at run-time are not substituted by code. **They are code**, but they cannot support and express all of the requirements and functionalities. So, the extra code that is not "models" is similar to that in Fig. 2.

As an intermediate summary, I may write that modeling and programming are brothers-in-arms. The vision that uses modeling as means for code "burying" led to the unsuccessful spreading of MDSD in the past thirty years. Instead, modeling succeeds when developers do not distinguish modeling and programming activities: this is executable modeling with direct and smart integration of programming stuff in models. In this context, beyond a human adhesion to MDSD and its inherent tools, there are economical spinoffs as well; these are the basic expectations of a general-purpose software development "method" when facing the recent "event bombing" challenge.

2   Executable Modeling for Reactive Programming

There is a great opportunity for MDSD to bounce back from the idea of "reactive programming" promoted, in particular, by *The Reactive Manifesto* (Fig. 5). In this figure, the **entailing** principle is "Message Driven" meaning that contemporary computing views applications' content as complex message exchange and coordination rather than monolithic data transformation.

Messages are point-to-point event communication and processing with data brought by events. Of course, events also are the foundational abstraction paradigm that makes the idea of "Message Driven" viable at modeling time.

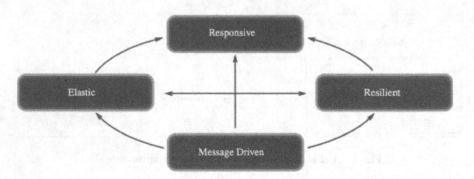

Fig. 5. The Reactive Manifesto four principles.

2.1   Reactive Programming at a Glance

Intuitively, the Internet/Web of Things moves us to some unencountered asynchronicity by which software components in applications have to re-create (*i.e.*, to create in a postponed way, at run-time probably) unanticipated synchronization through very intensive event communication and processing, *i.e.*, the "event bombing" (Fig. 6).

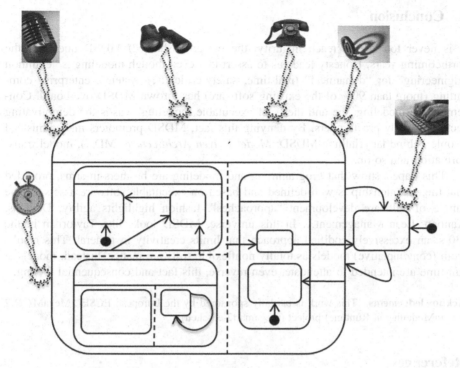

Fig. 6. Event bombing.

The key idea in Fig. 6 is that "Message Driven" middleware is/will be the norm through products, say, the famous Node.js software development framework or any other recognized similar computing infrastructure like ReactiveX. Namely, Fig. 6 shows that "Message Driven" software development imposes a strict internal organization of the inside of software components. As a complex (modeled) state machine, this organization is then capable of creating components that can serve client requests ("events", "messages", whatever…) on a concurrent and reliable basis.

So, reactive programming refers to computing frameworks that manage event production and distribution (queuing, routing, fault recovery…). Nonetheless, it is also **a programming style** in which event communication and processing benefit from having a direct and smart support. In this scope, behaviors of software components may then be instrumented by concrete models at run-time as illustrated in Figs. 2, 3 and 4. While the model is these three figures is somehow trivial, Fig. 6 adds the idea that models may express very complex behaviors imposed by the intrinsic idea of event bombing (great variation of event types, great flow rate of event occurrences…). For example, the core parallelism offered by Harel's Statecharts (a.k.a. "state orthogonality") may wisely replace multithreading statements that would surely lead to a nightmare at maintenance time: remind the initial point of this paper about the MDSD incapacity of offering truly maintainable models.

3 Conclusion

It is never too late to reach maturity, the (accomplishable?) MDSD quest for the forthcoming years. Honesty leads us to assert that even though modeling is "common engineering" for "dynamical" (real-time, safety-critical…) systems, enterprise computing (more than 90% of the existing software) has thrown MDSD overboard. Contemplative modeling, the anti-thesis of executable modeling, was/is the demotivating factor for daily practitioners. By denying this fact, MDSD promoters misled/mislead people behind labyrinthine MDSD: *Model Driven Architecture* (MDA), model transformation and so on.

This papers show that programming and modeling are brothers-in-arms, provided that their relationship is well-defined and based on executable software assets. In the jungle of software development "approaches", fashion highlights agility, DevOps, Kanban, Lean Management… In this universe, MDSD looks like Taylorism in the '30 s: an excessively codified approach that limits creativity in general. This results from (contemplative) models as totally nonflexible software matter. Instead, models at run-time are intended to attenuate, even reverse, this fact and consequential feeling.

Acknowledgements. This work is partially sponsored by the European ECSEL MegaM@Rt2 (MegaModelling at Runtime) project (megamart2-ecsel.eu).

References

1. Harel, D., Gery, E.: Executable object modeling with statecharts. IEEE Comput. **30**(7), 31–42 (1997)
2. Riehle, D., Fraleigh, S., Bucka-Lassen, D., Omorogbe, N.: The architecture of a UML virtual machine. In: Proceedings of the 2001 Conference on Object-Oriented Programming Systems, Languages, and Applications, pp. 327–341 (2001)
3. Mellor, S., Balcer, S.: Executable UML – A Foundation for Model-Driven Architecture. Addison-Wesley, Boston (2002)
4. France, R., Rumpe, B.: The evolution of modeling research challenges. Softw. Syst. Model. **12**(2), 223–225 (2013)
5. Barbier, F.: Reactive Internet Programming – State Chart XML in Action. Morgan & Claypool, New York (2016)
6. Blair, G., Bencomo, N., France, R.: Models@run.time. IEEE Comput. **42**(10), 22–27 (2009)

A Model-Driven Method for Fast Building Consistent Web Services from OpenAPI-Compatible Models

David Sferruzza[1,3]([⊠]), Jérôme Rocheteau[1,2], Christian Attiogbé[1], and Arnaud Lanoix[1]

[1] LS2N - UMR CNRS 6004, 44322 Nantes Cedex 3, France
{david.sferruzza,christian.attiogbe,arnaud.lanoix}@ls2n.fr
[2] ICAM, 35, avenue du Champ de Manœuvres, 44470 Carquefou, France
jerome.rocheteau@icam.fr
[3] Startup Palace, 18, rue Scribe, 44000 Nantes, France
david.sferruzza@startup-palace.com

Abstract. Lots of software companies rely on web technologies to test market hypotheses in order to develop viable businesses. They often need to quickly build web services that are at the core of their Minimum Viable Products (MVPs). MVPs must be reliable whereas they are based on specifications and hypotheses that are likely to change. Web services need to be well documented, to make it easy to develop applications that consume them. Model Driven Engineering approaches have been proposed and used to develop and evolve web services on one hand, and document them on the other hand. However, these approaches lack the ability to be suitable for both (*i*) rapid prototyping, (*ii*) model verification, (*iii*) compatibility with common programming languages and (*iv*) alignment between documentation and implementation. Here we propose a meta-model to express web services, the related tool to verify models consistency and an integration of this approach into the OpenAPI Specification. We adopt a shallow verification process to allow rapid prototyping by developers who are not formal methods experts, while still offering design-time guarantees that improve product quality and development efficiency. Web services are defined using parametric components which enable to express and formally verify web service patterns and to safely reuse them in other contexts. We built a tool to check consistency of extended OpenAPI 3.0 models and associated components implementations in order to generate corresponding web services. This allows us to give flexibility and verification support to developers, even in the context of an incremental development, as illustrated by a case study.

Keywords: Web applications · Web services · Model-Driven Engineering · Formal verification · Code generation · OpenAPI 3.0

© Springer Nature Switzerland AG 2019
S. Hammoudi et al. (Eds.): MODELSWARD 2018, CCIS 991, pp. 9–33, 2019.
https://doi.org/10.1007/978-3-030-11030-7_2

1   Introduction

Context. Web agencies are software companies that often work with their customers to help them develop new projects involving the web. Most of these customers need web applications to bring value to their own customers. These web applications are built iteratively to limit their cost while allowing startups to converge toward a viable market. This approach begins by building a Minimum Viable Product (MVP). In this context, it is a web application with a high level of quality but a limited set of features. MVPs (among other kinds of web applications) need to be functional, reliable, usable and designed with users' emotions in mind, with only the features required to test market hypotheses. In this perspective, it is common to develop standalone web services that will be consumed by one or several applications which may provide user interfaces (UIs). For example: one instance of web services can be simultaneously used by several UIs, such as several mobile applications (Android, iOS, ...) and a web application. This allows separation of concerns and centralization of data and process logic, even in the case where there is only one consumer application. Therefore, for *Startup Palace*[1], a web agency that evolves in this context, the process of designing, building and evolving web services is important, because it is at the center of the MVP approach. When developing a MVP it is important to focus on features that really bring value to users, also called *game-changers*. Other features, called *show-stoppers*, do not bring value directly but are required to make the application functional, reliable or usable. *Show-stopper* features are often tedious to implement and so error-prone. Furthermore, because of the iterative process and the purpose of MVPs, specifications are likely to evolve, which can introduce bugs.

Moreover, it is important to design web services in a way that makes them actually usable. This implies providing a good documentation that can be used by developers writing consumer applications or by these consumer applications if they can adapt their behavior dynamically. While this kind of documentation can take many forms, some standards such as OpenAPI [1] and RAML [2] are widely used by the industry. These standards define specifications which describe HTTP APIs of web services and are the center of ecosystems of tools. This article focuses on OpenAPI 3.0 because it is the standard used at *Startup Palace*.

Motivation. Developers need abstractions to be able to safely express, isolate, reuse and evolve features. Some programming languages do provide such abstractions, along with modern type checkers that are able to statically verify consistency of programs. But this is not practicable in our context because we would like to leverage existing expertises of developers instead of forcing them to learn a new programming language and its ecosystem from scratch. We need to master the development of *show-stoppers*. We want to fix a common issue related to the tools around OpenAPI which rises when the process of evolving the web services occurs. These tools can be used in two main ways. First, with a forward

---

[1] https://www.startup-palace.com.

engineering process, developers create manually an OpenAPI model, and use a tool to transform it. For example: a one-time generation of an implementation skeleton in a given technology. Second, with a reverse engineering process, a tool is used to extract an OpenAPI model from a working implementation (which can be enhanced by annotations). While the second process is useful to document existing web services, it cannot leverage the benefits of building web service using a top-down approach: from a high-level (model) to a low-level (implementation). Yet [3] shows the advantages of using different languages for programming-in-the-large and for programming-in-the-small. The first process makes possible to partially leverage these advantages, but the issue is that it lacks the ability to keep the OpenAPI model and the implementation aligned throughout the life of the project. Indeed, implementation is often obtained by a projection of the model that is then manually modified to implement business logic. Any following model evolution needs to be projected again which would require manual modifications to be re-applied from the beginning.

Contribution. This work is an attempt to solve the problem of building web services using safe abstractions on top of an existing programming language in order to ease development and reuse of *show-stopper* features, while keeping the web services in sync with their documentation (i.e. an OpenAPI model).

We introduce a meta-model to express web services and a corresponding semantics for verification. This leverages existing theory in Model Driven Engineering (MDE) [4–6] and a component-based approach in order to provide an expressive and language-agnostic solution to build web services. This meta-model does not allow to completely specify web services but is rather limited to a high-level representation in order to provide support while keeping models simple.

In [7] we have proposed a tool *(i)* to check models consistency and *(ii)* to generate working web services from a given valid model. As example, every component preconditions must be fulfilled in their instance contexts in order for a model to be consistent. This mechanism, coupled with the consistency checking, gives developers means to quickly and safely write and use components, and to reuse them in a reliable way.

We integrate the proposed approach in a top-down design process that relies on extended OpenAPI models. Extensions contain the parts of our meta-model that do not have any equivalent in the OpenAPI specification: the business logic. Because the OpenAPI 3.0 meta-model and ours are merged, the resulting models provide single sources of truth for building both web services and their documentation.

This article is an extended version of [8], published in the proceedings of MODELSWARD 2018[2]. It differs by the following aspects:

1. the meta-model was slightly improved in order to add the possibility to better specify service parameters, to improve the type system and to make reusability easier by adding a mechanism to bind parameters in component definitions and in their arguments in instances' contexts;

---

[2] http://www.modelsward.org/?y=2018.

2. the whole approach was redesigned as part of a more practical top-down work-flow based on tools such as OpenAPI instead of being completely standalone;
3. this workflow is tested in a two-steps case study, showing how it works in the context of incremental development.

The article is structured as follows. Section 2 presents related work. Section 3 describes the meta-model of web services. Section 4 defines consistency of compliant models and shows how they can be checked. Section 5 shows how this approach can be integrated with OpenAPI. Section 6 introduces a tool to generate actual implementations from models. Section 7 shows a two-steps case study that illustrates our approach. Finally, Sect. 8 concludes the article with some lessons and future work.

2   Related Work

The use of MDE for development and automatic generation of web services or web applications is not a new topic [4,6,9]. Indeed, this work is built on top of the approach of SWSG [8] and REIFIER [5].

SWSG shares the meta-modeling approach with tools such as *M3D* (introduced in [4] and extended in [9]) that also focus on building web services using MDE. One of the main differences between SWSG and *M3D* is that SWSG was developed with a focus on design-time support. For example, it allows to automatically verify some properties about the structural consistency of models. Even if SWSG is definitely related to existing standards such as BPEL [10] or WSDL, our approach differs on several aspects. First, we want to avoid the shortcomings described in [11], that is WSDL models contain too much technical details and are difficult to understand for humans. Indeed our meta-model is simpler and less expressive than WSDL or BPEL. Second, this allows SWSG to provide more support to users; the balance between flexibility and support is discussed in [12]. Finally, SWSG now relies on OpenAPI.

OpenAPI [1] that is also involved in various research areas. In [13], it was chosen for its popularity over WADL and other industry standards in order to automatically transform plain HTML documentations of web services to a machine-readable format. Moreover, [14] provides a great state of the art of service description formats that brings out OpenAPI as the most promising choice at the moment and enriches it with semantic annotations. It seems to be an updated version of the work proposed in [15, Sect. 3.2]. [16] shows an approach that is agnostic to service description formats but uses OpenAPI in the article. The popularity of OpenAPI is also highlighted by its use in other domains. For example [17] describes a case where OpenAPI 2.0 is used in combination of other tools from the life sciences community and points out that the specification extension mechanism of OpenAPI 3.0 (that we use in this article) might be an interesting opportunity of improvement. Another example in the telecommunication domain is presented in [18] which provides a section to emphasizes the trade-offs of Model-Driven Engineering and argues that they can be overcome "with increased investment in the tools that support the development process"; we share the same vision in the present proposal.

One of the tools featured in the OpenAPI ecosystem is *Swagger Code Generator* [19]. It aims at generating client librairies, server stubs or documentations from an OpenAPI model. The server stubs generation supports many languages and frameworks, but, as its name states, only generates stubs. This helps developers to write new services by generated boilerplate code, which is a tedious task, but they still need to add a lot of code on top of it. Moreover, when services evolve, developer need to manually propagate evolutions into the codebase because *Swagger Code Generator* isn't able to merge them automatically. Our approach solves this issue because it gives flexibility to developers before the code generation step, making useless editing generated code. It is worth mentioning that the code generators in themselves are based on similar model-to-text mechanisms: *Swagger Code Generator* uses the mustache[3] or the Handlebars[4] (depending on the version) template format whereas SWSG uses Twirl[5]. Finally, SWSG supports OpenAPI 3.0 models which is not the case of *Swagger Code Generator* at the time of writing[6].

3   A Meta-model to Express Web Services

We introduce a meta-model of web services. This meta-model is voluntarily simple in order to provide two advantages: *(i)* to give developers good abstractions to write reusable code while giving them a good flexibility and *(ii)* to allow tools to provide support to developers, such as design-time consistency verification (see Sect. 4). This is obtained with a trade-off on a lower verification aspects.

3.1   Preliminary Notations

Union.   The union or sum type of two types T_1 and T_2 is denoted $T_1 \uplus T_2$.

Tuple.   A tuple T is a product type between n types T_1 to T_n, with $n \geq 2$. It is denoted $T \equiv T_1 \times \ldots \times T_n$. A value t of type T is written as $t = (t_1, \ldots, t_n)$ where $t_1 \in T_1, \ldots, t_n \in T_n$. The notation $t(x)$ is also used to designate t_x, where $x \in \{1, \ldots, n\}$.

Record.   A record R is a tuple with labeled elements. It is denoted $R \equiv \langle label_1 : T_1, \ldots, label_n : T_n \rangle$. It is syntactic sugar over a tuple $T_1 \times \ldots \times T_n$ and n functions $label_1 : R \rightarrow T_1, \ldots, label_n : R \rightarrow T_n$. As for tuples, a value r of type R is written as $r = (t_1, \ldots, t_n)$ where $t_1 \in T_1, \ldots, t_n \in T_n$. Associated functions can also be written $r.label_1, \ldots, r.label_n$. For example, for a record $person = ("Batman", 35) \in \langle name : String, age : Int \rangle$ we have $name(person) = person.name = "Batman" \in String$.

---

[3] https://mustache.github.io/.
[4] https://handlebarsjs.com/.
[5] https://github.com/playframework/twirl.
[6] The unstable version 3.0.0-rc0 does support OpenAPI 3.0 but is not yet finished and handle only a few languages and frameworks.

Set. A set whose elements are all of type T has the type $\mathcal{P}(T)$.

List. A sequence or list of type T is a set of elements of type T which are ordered. It is denoted $List(T)$. It is similar to a function from indexes I to values of T, that is $List(T) : I \rightarrow T$ where I is a 1..N and $N = card(List(T))$. It can also be written as $List(T) \equiv [t_1, \ldots, t_n]$ where $t_1, \ldots, t_n \in T$.

Projection. The projection of a set or list of tuples S on the ith element of a tuple is written $Prj_i(S)$. Similarly, the projection of a set or list of records S on one of the elements of a record $label_i$ is written $Prj_{label_i}(S)$. For example, for a set of records $S \in \mathcal{P}(\langle name : String, age : Int \rangle)$ where $S = \{(\text{``Batman''}, 35), (\text{``Robin''}, 26)\}$, $Prj_{name}(S)$ has type $\mathcal{P}(String)$ and is equal to $\{\text{``Batman''}, \text{``Robin''}\}$.

3.2 A Meta-model of Web Services

A meta-model of web services is defined by the BNF grammar given in Fig. 1. Figure 2 shows a slightly simplified version of this grammar in the form of a UML class diagram, to provide a quick glance.

model ::=	⟨*entities* : **entity***, *components* : **component***, *services* : **service***⟩
identifier ::=	[A-Za-z] [A-Za-z0-9_] *
entity ::=	⟨*name* : **identifier**, *attributes* : **variable***⟩
term ::=	**variable** I **constant**
variable ::=	⟨*name* : **string**, *type* : **type**⟩
constant ::=	⟨*type* : **type**, *value* : **object**⟩
type ::=	**string** I **boolean** I **integer** I **float** I **date** I **datetime** I **entity-ref**
	I **seq-of** I **option-of**
entity-ref ::=	⟨*entity* : **identifier**⟩
seq-of ::=	⟨*seqOf* : **type**⟩
option-of ::=	⟨*optionOf* : **type**⟩
component ::=	**atomic-component** I **composite-component**
atomic-component ::=	⟨*name* : **identifier**, *params* : **variable***, *pre* : **variable***,
	add : **variable***, *rem* : **variable***⟩
composite-component ::=	⟨*name* : **identifier**, *params* : **variable***,
	components : **component-instance***⟩
component-instance ::=	⟨*component* : **identifier**, *bindings* : **binding***, *aliases* : **alias***⟩
binding ::=	⟨*param* : **variable**, *argument* : **term**⟩
alias ::=	⟨*source* : **variable**, *target* : **variable**⟩
service ::=	⟨*method* : **method**, *path* : **path**, *params* : **service-parameter***,
	component : **component-instance**⟩
method ::=	[A-Z] +
path ::=	. +
service-parameter ::=	⟨*location* : **parameter-location**, *variable* : **variable**⟩
parameter-location ::=	**query** I **header** I **path** I **cookie** I **body**

Fig. 1. Meta-model BNF grammar.

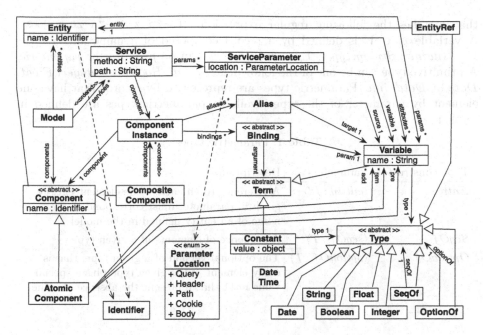

Fig. 2. Meta-model diagram.

This meta-model does not aim to replace existing standard meta-models like for instance the OpenAPI Specification [1] or RAML [2], but rather to be compatible and complementary with them (see Sect. 5). These meta-models allow to define programming language-agnostic interface descriptions for HTTP APIs (i.e. informal contracts) in order to be able for both humans and computers to discover and understand their capabilities, while our meta-model allows to express actual implementations of such HTTP APIs. Precisely, our meta-model is designed in order to match needs and requirements about verification (see Sect. 4), generation and ease of writing (see Sect. 6). For these reasons, and to be more accessible to practitioners, our approach does not rely on existing standards such as BPEL [10] or WSDL [11].

Model. A model of web services $m_i \in M$ is specified as a record of three elements: a set of entities of type E that stands as data model, a set of components of type C that stands as process model and an ordered list of services of type S that exposes component to the outer world: $M \equiv \langle entities : \mathcal{P}(E), components : \mathcal{P}(C), services : List(S) \rangle$.

Entity and Type. Entities are non-primitive data types. An entity $e_i \in E$ is represented by a record of two elements: a name and a set of variables that represent attributes: $E \equiv \langle name : Id, attributes : \mathcal{P}(V) \rangle$. An attribute of an entity can be another entity, making it a recursive type. An identifier $id_i \in Id$ is a string

that matches the following regular expression: `^[A-Za-z][A-Za-z0-9_]*$` .
A variable $v_i \in V$ is defined by a record composed of a name and a type:
$V \equiv \langle name : String, type : T \rangle$. A type $t_i \in T$ can be *primitive* or *parametric*.
A primitive type can be one of the followings: *String*, *Boolean*, *Integer*, *Float*,
Date or *DateTime*. Parametric types are represented by records that have one
element by parameter of the type; available parametric types are defined in
Table 1.

Table 1. Parametric types.

Type constructor	Parameters	Description
Entity	$\langle entity : Id \rangle$	A reference to an entity. The element `entity` given in parameter must correspond to the name of an entity defined in the model
SeqOf	$\langle seqOf : T \rangle$	A sequence of elements of a given type
OptionOf	$\langle optionOf : T \rangle$	The optional version of a given type, that is every element of the given type plus a special value `null` that represent the absence of value

Components. Components are units of processes and computations that occur
inside web services. Their execution happens in an isolated context, that can contain variables. They can mutate this context by adding and removing variables.
A component $c_i \in C$ is defined as the union type of atomic components AC and
composite components CC: $C \triangleq AC \uplus CC$. Both types of components are defined
by a name and a set of variables that express components' parameters. Because
they have parameters, we call them parametric components. An atomic component $ac_i \in AC$ is represented by a record of the following elements: name, parameters, preconditions (a set of variables that might be needed in the execution context), additions (a set of variables that will be added to the execution context)
and removals (a set of variables that will be removed from the execution con-
text): $AC \equiv \langle name : Id, params : \mathcal{P}(V), pre : \mathcal{P}(V), add : \mathcal{P}(V), rem : \mathcal{P}(V) \rangle$.
The last three elements are sometimes referred to as the component's contract.
A composite component $cc_i \in CC$ is represented by a record of the following elements: name, parameters and an ordered list of component instances:
$CC \equiv \langle name : Id, params : \mathcal{P}(V), components : List(CI) \rangle$. A component
instance $ci_i \in CI$ is represented by a record of three elements: a component,
a set of bindings used to instantiate the component by associating arguments to
its parameters and a set of aliases that allow to rename variables of the component's contract on the instantiation context: $CI \equiv \langle component : C, bindings :$
$\mathcal{P}(\langle param : V, argument : Term \rangle), aliases : \mathcal{P}(\langle source : Id, target : Id \rangle) \rangle$.
Terms can be variables or constant literal values (*Const*): $Term \triangleq V \uplus Const$.
Atomic components are meant to be along with an implementation written using
a programming language whereas composite components are not. Components
can be seen as an abstraction to encourage separation of concerns and reusability
by leveraging two mechanisms: composition and parametrization.

Service. Services are the entry points of web services. A service $s_i \in S$ is represented by a record of four elements: a HTTP method, a path, a set of expected input parameters and a component instance: $S \equiv \langle method : M, path : P, params : \mathcal{P}(\langle location : L, variable : V \rangle), component : CI \rangle$. A method $m_i \in M$ is a valid HTTP method name, as defined by RFC 7231[7]. A path $p_i \in P$ is a relative URL that can contain parameters whose names are to be placed inside braces; for example: `/user/{id}`. A location $l_i \in L$ represents where a given service parameter can be found in a HTTP request: $L \equiv \{query, header, path, cookie, body\}$. In a model of web services, services are gathered in an ordered list. This abstraction is very common in web frameworks and is often called *router*. Instead of considering a web application as a huge function of HTTP requests to HTTP responses, a router allows to dispatch HTTP requests to several such functions by filtering them declaratively by method and by path. That is to reduce complexity of the whole application by encouraging separation of concerns.

3.3 Concrete Syntax for Models of Web Services

We previously presented a mathematical definition of our meta-model in Sect. 3.2 and an equivalent BNF grammar in Fig. 1. These notations are meant to introduce formal definitions that are used to define properties on the meta-model, which we do in Sect. 4. But they are cumbersome to read or write actual models.

We also introduce a concrete syntax that is more compact and readable. Because it is equivalent to BNF grammar in Fig. 1, we won't define it formally here but only provide some intuition on it.

A model is represented, with respect to its formal definition, as an unordered list of definitions, each on its own lines. A definition starts with an element identifier: `e` for entity, `s` for service, `ac` for atomic component and `cc` for composite component. Element's properties are placed on their own indented line and prefixed with the property name (or a short alias). Listing 1 gives an example of a service declaration.

Listing 1. Definition of a service using the concrete syntax.

```
1  s
2    method POST
3    path /getName/{email}
4    param path email: String
5    ci GetName
```

For readability reasons, every item of a service parameters set must be written on its own line. For example line 4 of Listing 1 shows a `param` item instead of the whole `params` set.

---

[7] https://tools.ietf.org/html/rfc7231.

The concrete syntax of the other structures of the meta-model is defined in a similar way. A full example is available in the repository of SWSG[8].

3.4   Evaluating a Model of Web Services

Our meta-model gives helpful abstractions to develop web services but the built models need a rigorous evaluation semantics. The following successive steps describe how web services based on an instance of this meta-model could handle incoming HTTP requests.

Routing. First, the application receives a HTTP request. Its list of services is sequentially scanned until a service matches the request; that is, the HTTP method is the same and the URL matches the path. If no service matches, then a static 404 HTTP response is sent back.

Flattening. The component instance contained in the service is reduced to a flattened ordered list of instances of atomic components. Arguments passed to the different components (through bindings in component instances) are resolved so that they become only constants (no more variables), and aliases are propagated to instantiated components and their subcomponents. Instances of composite components are then recursively replaced by their subcomponents. We define by cases a function $flatten(m, c)$ (with $m \in M$) that flattens a given component:

$$flatten(m, c) = \begin{cases} [c] & \text{if } c \in AC \\ \bigcup_{ci \in c.components} flatten(m, ci) & \text{if } c \in CC \\ flatten(m, c.component) & \text{if } c \in CI \\ flatten(m, resolve_c(m, c)) & \text{if } c \in Id \end{cases} \tag{1}$$

The function $resolve_c$ used in Formula (1) takes two parameters: a model and a component name. It outputs the definition of the component with the given name in the given model. It is of type $M \times Id \to C$. When called on a model that verifies the consistency rules defined in Sect. 4 and on a component name extracted from such a model, this function returns a deterministic result.

Evaluating Components. An initial evaluation context is created by extracting parameters (if present) from the request URL and putting them into an empty context. This flattened list is then evaluated: every atomic component is executed given the previous context as an input and produces a new context as an output. This behavior is very similar to state monads (see [20, Sect. 2.5]).

---

[8] https://gitlab.startup-palace.com/research/swsg/blob/master/examples/ registration/registration.model.

Responding. Finally, a HTTP response is built. There are two cases to consider. If one of the evaluated components returned a HTTP response instead of a new context, the following components are not evaluated and this response is returned to the client. Otherwise, the context is serialized and encapsulated into a HTTP response of code 200.

4   Consistency of Web Services

Section 3 showed that our web services meta-model uses components as an abstraction to improve separation of concerns and reusability. In order to allow developers to safely use this abstraction we propose a way to do verification of models. This verification checks if a model is consistent. It can happen at *design-time* – outside any evaluation context – so that inconsistent models won't be run in production.

Definition. A model of web services $m \in M$ is consistent if it verifies all the following properties identified by Formulas (2) to (22).

Component Name Unicity. Every component in a model has a unique name.

$$\forall c, c' \in m.components \cdot (c.name = c'.name \Rightarrow c = c') \tag{2}$$

Entity Name Unicity. Every entity in a model has a unique name.

$$\forall e, e' \in m.entities \cdot (e.name = e'.name \Rightarrow e = e') \tag{3}$$

Attribute Name Unicity. Every attribute of an entity has a unique name.

$$\forall e \in m.entities, \forall a, a' \in e.attributes \cdot (a.name = a'.name \Rightarrow a = a') \tag{4}$$

Service Parameter Name Unicity. Every parameter of a service has a unique name.

$$\forall s \in m.services, \forall p, p' \in s.params \cdot (p.name = p'.name \Rightarrow p = p') \tag{5}$$

*Parameters of Location **Body** Unicity.* There is a maximum of one parameter per service that has its location equal to **body**.

$$\forall s \in m.services, \forall p, p' \in s.params \cdot$$
$$(p.location = p'.location = \text{body} \Rightarrow p = p') \tag{6}$$

Table 2. Exhaustive list of reference locations.

Referenced element	References locations
Component C	$refs_{c1} = Prj_{components.component}(m.components \cap CC)$
	$refs_{c2} = Prj_{component.component}(m.services)$
Entity E	$refs_{e1} = Prj_{entity}(Prj_{attributes.type}(m.entities) \cap EntityRef)$
	$refs_{e2} = Prj_{entity}(Prj_{params.type}(m.components) \cap EntityRef)$
	$refs_{e3} = Prj_{entity}(Prj_{pre.type}(m.components \cap AC) \cap EntityRef)$
	$refs_{e4} = Prj_{entity}(Prj_{add.type}(m.components \cap AC) \cap EntityRef)$
	$refs_{e5} = Prj_{entity}(Prj_{rem.type}(m.components \cap AC) \cap EntityRef)$
	$refs_{e6} = Prj_{entity}(Prj_{params.variable.type}(m.services) \cap EntityRef)$

Reference Consistency. Table 2 describes the reference locations in a model. It gives formulas to extract from a model every possible set of references to entities or components.

Every reference to a component designates an element that exists in the model.

$$\forall ref \in (refs_{c1} \cup refs_{c2}), \exists c \in m.components \cdot (c.name = ref) \qquad (7)$$

Every reference to an entity designates an element that exists in the model.

$$\forall ref \in (refs_{e1} \cup refs_{e2} \cup refs_{e3} \cup refs_{e4} \cup refs_{e5} \cup refs_{e6}),$$
$$\exists e \in m.entities \cdot (e.name = ref) \quad (8)$$

Component Context Variable Name Unicity. Variables in atomic components cannot have the same name if they are not identical.

$$\forall c \in (m.components \cap AC), \forall v, v' \in (c.pre \cup c.add \cup c.del) \cdot$$
$$(v.name = v'.name \Rightarrow v = v') \quad (9)$$

Composite Component Non Emptiness. Composite components must have sub-components.

$$\forall c \in (m.components \cap CC) \cdot (c.components \neq \emptyset) \qquad (10)$$

Alias Source Unicity. The source name of an alias is unique in its component instance.

$$\forall ci \in (Prj_{components}(m.components \cap CC) \cup Prj_{component}(m.services)),$$
$$\forall a, a' \in ci.alias \cdot (a.source = a'.source \Rightarrow a = a') \quad (11)$$

Alias Target Unicity. The target name of an alias is unique in its component instance.

$$\forall ci \in (Prj_{components}(m.components \cap CC) \cup Prj_{component}(m.services)),$$
$$\forall a, a' \in ci.alias \cdot (a.target = a'.target \Rightarrow a = a') \quad (12)$$

Recursive Reference Consistency. An entity is not referenced by its transitive attributes.

$$\forall e \in m.entities \cdot (EntityRef(e.name) \notin deps_e(m, EntityRef(e.name))) \quad (13)$$

where the function $deps_e : M \times T \to \mathcal{P}(T)$ returns the set of transitive dependencies of a given type. $deps_e(m, t)$ is defined as follows:

$$deps_e(m, t) = \begin{cases} deps_e(m, t') & \text{if } t = OptionOf(t') \\ deps_e(m, t') & \text{if } t = SeqOf(t') \\ t'' \cup \bigcup_{t_i \in t''} deps_e(m, t_i) & \text{if } t = EntityRef(name) \\ deps_e(m, t) = \emptyset & \text{otherwise} \end{cases}$$

$$\text{with } t'' = Prj_{type}(resolve_e(m, name).attributes)$$

where the function $resolve_e : M \times Id \to E$ returns the definition of the entity that as the same name as the one given in the second parameter.

The same is true for composite components that are not referenced from their transitive subcomponents.

$$\forall c \in (m.components \cap CC) \cdot (c.name \notin deps_c(m, c)) \quad (14)$$

where the function $deps_c : M \times C \to \mathcal{P}(Id)$ returns the set of transitive dependencies of a given component. $deps_c(m, c)$ is defined as follows:

$$deps_c(m, c) = \begin{cases} \emptyset & \text{if } c \in AC \\ Prj_{name}(c.components) \cup \\ \quad \bigcup_{ci_i \in c.components} deps_c(m, resolve_c(m, ci_i)) & \text{if } c \in CC \end{cases}$$

where the function $resolve_c : M \times Id \to C$ returns the definition of the component that has the same name as the one given in the second parameter, as defined in Sect. 3.4.

Alias Source Validity. The source name of an alias corresponds to the name of a variable of the contract of the instantiated component.

$$\forall ci \in (Prj_{components}(m.components \cap CC) \cup Prj_{component}(m.services)),$$
$$\forall a \in ci.alias \cdot (c = resolve_c(m, ci.component)$$
$$\Rightarrow a.source \in Prj_{name}(c.pre \cup c.add \cup c.rem)) \quad (15)$$

Alias Target Validity. The target name of an alias corresponds to the name of a variable that will be added to the execution context by the instantiated component.

$$\forall ci \in (Prj_{components}(m.components \cap CC) \cup Prj_{component}(m.services)),$$
$$\forall a \in ci.alias \cdot$$
$$(c = resolve_c(m, ci.component) \Rightarrow a.target \notin Prj_{name}(c.add)) \quad (16)$$

Service Path Validity. The set of names of service parameters that have a `path` location is exactly the same as the set of parameter names declared in the path string of a service.

$$\forall s \in m.services \cdot (\{p \in s.params | p.location = \texttt{Path}\} = extract(s.path)) \quad (17)$$

where the function $extract : P \to \mathcal{P}(V)$ extracts parameter names from a path; that is, for a given path, it returns the contents of the first matching parenthesis of the regular expression $\backslash\{$ ([A-Za-z0-9_] +) $\backslash\}$.

Component Context Immutability. Components don't override existing variables of the context. Every atomic component does not add a new variable to its output context if there is already a variable with the same name in its input context.

$$\forall c \in (m.components \cap AC) \cdot (c.add \cap c.pre = \emptyset) \quad (18)$$

Component Precondition Exhaustivity. Components depend on the variables they remove. Every atomic component has each variable it will remove from the context in its preconditions.

$$\forall c \in (m.components \cap AC) \cdot (c.rem \subseteq c.pre) \quad (19)$$

Component Instance Bindings Consistency. Component instances have bindings that associate a term to a variable. Every binding associates a term to a variable of the same type.

$$\forall ci \in (Prj_{components}(m.components \cap CC) \cup Prj_{component}(m.services)),$$
$$\forall b \in ci.binding \cdot (b.variable.type = b.argument.type) \quad (20)$$

Component Instance Parameters Exhaustivity. Component instances provide values for every parameter of the instantiated component. Every component instance provides exactly as much arguments as the component it instantiates needs parameters. Names and types of the arguments match those of the parameters.

$$\forall ci \in (Prj_{components}(m.components \cap CC) \cup Prj_{component}(m.services)),$$
$$\exists c \in m.components \cdot$$
$$(c.name = ci.component \Rightarrow Prj_{param}(ci.binding) = c.params) \quad (21)$$

Context Validity. Components are instantiated in contexts that fulfill their preconditions. When building flat ordered lists of atomic components for each service (see Sect. 3.4), every atomic component of these lists has its preconditions fulfilled by its input context:

$$\forall s \in S \cdot (flatten(s.component) \blacktriangleleft s.params) \quad (22)$$

where $\blacktriangleleft$ is a function of $List(AC) \times \mathcal{P}(V) \rightarrow Boolean$ in infix notation[9] that is true when applied to a component and a context that satisfies the component's preconditions. It is defined by the following semantic rules:

$$\frac{ctx_0 \in \mathcal{P}(V)}{[\,] \blacktriangleleft ctx_0}$$

$$\frac{ctx_0 \in \mathcal{P}(V) \quad c_0.pre \subseteq_\triangleleft ctx_0 \quad ctx_1 = ctx_0 \cup c_0.add \setminus c_0.rem}{\forall i \in [0, n], c_i \in CI \quad [c_1, \ldots, c_n] \blacktriangleleft ctx_1}$$
$$\frac{}{[c_0, \ldots, c_n] \blacktriangleleft ctx_0}$$

$$\frac{pre, ctx \in \mathcal{P}(V)}{\forall v \in pre \cdot v \in ctx \vee (\exists v' \in ctx, v.name = v'.name}{\wedge v'.type = OptionOf(v.type))}$$
$$\frac{}{pre \subseteq_\triangleleft ctx}$$

$pre \subseteq_\triangleleft ctx$ means that the component's preconditions pre are satisfied by the context ctx. We use $\subseteq_\triangleleft$ instead of $\subseteq$ because $\subseteq$ requires the types to be strictly identical, which we do not want in order to handle optional types.

5   Development Process Integrated to OpenAPI

In Sect. 3 we introduced a meta-model of web services, along with rules to check its consistency in Sect. 4. In Sect. 5.1 we introduce a common development process involving OpenAPI. This gives some background on OpenAPI and prepares to the merger of our approach in OpenAPI's in Sect. 5.2.

---

[9] $cs \blacktriangleleft ctx$ is equivalent to $\blacktriangleleft (cs, ctx)$.

5.1   A Common Usage of OpenAPI

The OpenAPI Specification [1] defines a standard to express interfaces to HTTP APIs in a language-agnostic way. It aims at allowing "both humans and computers to discover and understand the capabilities of the service without access to source code, documentation, or through network traffic inspection" [1]: that is a meta-model. As in MDE, the point of having meta-models is to have tools that can rely on them in order to safely manipulate models and offer support to developers. Indeed, an ecosystem of tools was developed around OpenAPI by various actors. Such tools have several purposes, including but not limited to: providing an interactive graphical user interface from a model [21,22], generating functional tests from a model [23] or generating a model from an annotated implementation [24].

The Petstore Example. To ease the development of tools, some official examples of OpenAPI models are shipped with the specification. In this article, we focus on the *Petstore* example [25]. It describes a simple application that exposes four services to list, show, add and remove data records representing animals. We assume that we are in the context of a company such as *Startup Palace*; that means the goal is to develop these web services in order for them to be consumed by user interface applications; for example, desktop and mobile applications for the owner of the store.

Development Process. The common top-down development process follows. First, developers make several iterations on writing an OpenAPI model. This model must match the functional specifications and describe web services that are fully exploitable by consumer applications. For example, the description of one of the Petstore services is shown in Listing 2. It references schemas that are defined in another part of the model, as shown in Listing 3.

When this OpenAPI model is stable enough, developers can use it as a specification to start building web services and consumer applications. There are some kinds of tools that can take the OpenAPI model as input and help to build compliant web services; for example, by generating a skeleton of application using a given technological stack [26], or by generating automated tests that can be used to check if the web services are conformant [23].

But all these tools have a major limitation: they require humans to manually update the OpenAPI model whenever the web services evolve. This is a very common situation: specifications must evolve either because business requirements have changed or new constraints have been discovered while developing. Even if some tools can mitigate this issue, it is likely that developers will eventually stop maintaining the OpenAPI model after the web services reach production, making the two diverge over time. In long-term projects, this means giving up on every advantage provided by OpenAPI and its MDE approach.

Listing 2. A service in the Petstore example.

```
1   /pets/{id}:
2     get:
3       description: Returns a user based on a single ID
                 , if the user does not have access to the
                 pet
4       operationId: find pet by id
5       parameters:
6         - name: id
7           in: path
8           description: ID of pet to fetch
9           required: true
10          schema:
11            type: integer
12            format: int64
13      responses:
14        '200':
15          description: pet response
16          content:
17            application/json:
18              schema:
19                $ref: '#/components/schemas
                      /Pet'
20        default:
21          description: unexpected error
22          content:
23            application/json:
24              schema:
25                $ref: '#/components/schemas
                      /Error'
```

Listing 3. Schemas in the Petstore example.

```
1   components:
2     schemas:
3       Pet:
4         allOf:
5           - $ref: '#/components/schemas/
                  NewPet'
6           - required:
7             - id
8             properties:
9               id:
10                type: integer
11                format: int64
12      NewPet:
13        required:
14          - name
15        properties:
16          name:
17            type: string
18          tag:
19            type: string
20      Error:
21        required:
22          - code
23          - message
24        properties:
25          code:
26            type: integer
27            format: int32
28          message:
29            type: string
```

To fix this shortcoming, we present in Sect. 6 an improved version of this process that leverages a meta-model of web services we introduced in [8]. However, in order for this new approach to be feasible, we first need to extend the OpenAPI 3.0 Specification.

5.2 Extending OpenAPI 3.0

Recall that the OpenAPI Specification describes a meta-model to express an interface to web services. But, unlike our approach, it does not describe how web services are implemented. To get the best of both our approach and OpenAPI's, we propose a way to merge the latter with our meta-model of web services.

To preserve tools compatibility we make use of *Specification Extensions*, as defined in OpenAPI 3.0 [1]. This mechanism allows to add data to models without breaking their compliance to the specification or their ability to be used by tools designed to be compatible with it. The details of the extensions to OpenAPI 3.0 can be found in [27]. The following paragraphs present the nature and the main lines of these extensions for each aspect of our meta-model.

Because an OpenAPI model can be seen as a tree (before references are resolved) that has the OpenAPI object as root, we make use of the notion of *paths*. The components path designate the child of the root named components. Sub-children are separated using a > symbol; the components > requestBodies designates the requestBodies child of the components child of the root.

Data Model. An OpenAPI 3.0 model can contain a set of `Schema` objects[10]. A `Schema` object defines a data type for input or output data, which can then be referenced from elsewhere in the model. This mechanism provides more expressiveness than ours and was made for the same purpose. Thus it is a good fit for the *entities* of our meta-model.

Processes. On purpose, there are no equivalent of our component system in OpenAPI 3.0, because it describes processes that are internal to the web services which is out of OpenAPI's scope. Accordingly we add two properties in the `Components` object of OpenAPI. They contain sets of atomic and composite component definitions[11]. Exact schemas of these components follow on from their definition in our meta-model.

Services. Describing services is the main feature of OpenAPI. As such they can be specified in a quite expressive way. Yet the service meta-model in OpenAPI is not a superset of ours because of two lacks that require it to be extended. First, each service must be associated to a component instance that describes its behavior[12] Second, if a service has a `requestBody` property (that describes the type of the data required in the request body), the `RequestBody` object must contain a variable name[13]. When generating the web services code, this is used to include the request body contents in a variable of the execution context.

From now on, we consider OpenAPI 3.0 extended with the process and service parts of our meta-model. OpenAPI's data model is not extended as it was already powerful enough for our needs.

6   A Tool to Generate Consistent Web Services

To support the approach of automatically building web services from an extended OpenAPI model (see Sect. 5), we propose a tool named *Safe Web Services Generator* (SWSG) [7] that automates both consistency verification (see Sect. 4) and code generation. This tool takes two inputs: a model file (both extended OpenAPI models and our own concrete syntax are supported), and a path to a directory which contains implementations of atomic components.

As shown in Fig. 3, our tool follows four sequential steps:

1. **Model Parsing.** Input model is parsed as concrete syntax of the meta-model (see Sect. 3.3) or as an extended OpenAPI model (see [27]).
2. **Model Transformation.** If the parsed model was an OpenAPI model, it is transformed to match our meta-model.
3. **Model Consistency Verification.** The model is checked in order to establish its consistency (see Sect. 4).

---

[10] In the `components > schemas` path.
[11] Their paths are `components > x-swsg-ac` and `components > x-swsg-cc`.
[12] In the `x-swsg-ci` property of the service.
[13] In a `x-swsg-name` property.

4. Code Generation. The model and the implementations of atomic components are used to generate an implementation of the web services they represent.

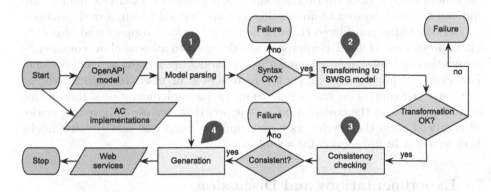

Fig. 3. SWSG process.

Model Transformation. Transforming extended OpenAPI models to SWSG models is quite straightforward, except for schemas/types. OpenAPI defines some primitive types and relies on a modified version of the *JSON Schema Specification* [28] for complex types. There are two issues; first, the *JSON Schema Specification* is more expressive than SWSG's type system. For example, it allows to define refined types, e.g. to add a minimum length to a string. Second, it supports both literal and referenced definition of attribute types. Moreover, references are quite expressive and can target many places in the OpenAPI main document or even in another one. In comparison, SWSG only supports literal primitive types or references to other *entities*.

While the second issue is more a technical problem, the first would require to alter SWSG's type system in order for it to support expressing every possible OpenAPI type. Yet, for the sake of simplicity of both our meta-model and our prototype we choose to not address them; they are not essential to test and validate our approach. Therefore our prototype might return errors when working with some OpenAPI models that contain these unsupported types or references in schemas.

Code Generation. The process defined by Fig. 3 is generic: it does not rely on a specific language or technology. Yet the language and technologies used to implement atomic components must be identical or compatible with those of the code generation target. Because we experiment in *Startup Palace*'s context, our prototype targets the PHP programming language [29] with the *Laravel* web framework [30], which is a common tool stack.

Many similar tools (see Sect. 2) take the approach to generate and output a standalone web application that includes everything necessary to operate it. We took another approach by generating code that should never be manually edited; the generated code does not override any existing files in a *Laravel*'s architecture and can be easily hooked to an existing web application through configuration.

Because of the considered trade-off between provided support and flexibility left to developers, this MDE approach was designed to allow shallow consistency verification and most inconsistencies in the model are caught at compile-time. This does not prevent developers to create flawed or insecure applications, as they have full control on the atomic components implementations. Indeed this flexibility comes at the cost of a bit of support. However, we believe this trade-off is crucial when the developers have to quickly build web services that might grow and stay in production for a while.

7   Experimentations and Discussion

Process. We derive a new process from the common OpenAPI process explained in Sect. 5.1. *Step 1:* design a stable OpenAPI model. *Step 2:* design SWSG components using the extensions we introduced in Sect. 5 to write them inside the OpenAPI model. Every atomic component defined in the model must be provided with an implementation. *Step 3:* use SWSG to check the model and generate working web services if the verification is successful.

Case Study #1. Step 1: we take the Petstore example [25] presented in Sect. 5.1. The example service defined by Listing 2 is a part of a standard OpenAPI model. *Step 2:* we need a component that will handle the response generation when this service will receive requests. We create a composite component called `FindPet` and reference it from the service, as shown in lines 26–27 in Listing 4. This composite component has two children that are atomic components. The first takes an ID as input, uses it to query the database and adds the `Pet` result to the context. The second takes a `Pet`, serializes it in JSON and put it in an HTTP response. These three components are defined in Listing 5. Implementations are written for every atomic components. Listing 6 shows the implementation of the `GetPetById` component as an example[14].

---

[14] The PHP class in Listing 6 depends on the `Component` interface and on the `Ctx` and `Params` classes. They are defined in code output by the code generator and are just implementation details of the SWSG specification in this specific code generator. Different code generators could require different constraints on implementations of atomic components.

Listing 4. A service in the SWSG Petstore example.

```
1   /pets/{id}:
2     get:
3       description: Returns a user based on a single ID
              , if the user does not have access to the
              pet
4       operationId: find pet by id
5       parameters:
6         - name: id
7           in: path
8           description: ID of pet to fetch
9           required: true
10          schema:
11            type: integer
12            format: int64
13      responses:
14        '200':
15          description: pet response
16          content:
17            application/json:
18              schema:
19                $ref: '#/components/schemas
                      /Pet'
20        default:
21          description: unexpected error
22          content:
23            application/json:
24              schema:
25                $ref: '#/components/schemas
                      /Error'
26      x—swsg—ci:
27        component: FindPet
```

Listing 5. Components in the SWSG Petstore example.

```
1   components:
2     x—swsg—cc:
3       - name: FindPet
4         components:
5           - component: GetPetById
6           - component: RenderPet
7     x—swsg—ac:
8       - name: RenderPet
9         pre:
10          - name: pet
11            type:
12              entity: Pet
13        - name: GetPetById
14          pre:
15            - name: id
16              type: String
17          add:
18            - name: pet
19              type:
20                entity: Pet
```

Step 3: we run SWSG on these inputs and get a *PreconditionError*. This verification error indicates that a component's precondition is not fulfilled in a given instanciation context. In the current case, we learn that the `GetPetById` component misses a string named `id` when instanciated by the `FindPet` component in the `GET/pet/{id}` service. Indeed, we voluntarily introduced an error in Listing 5: the `GetPetById` component is given an integer (by the service) whereas it requires a string. In this particular example, it should require an integer `id` variable in order to be consistent with the service parameter. Nevertheless, in more complex projects, this component might have been used inside several other composite components and services. Thus, it might not be a good solution to just change the component's definition because it might break other workflows. This is the kind of mistakes SWSG can prevent us to make: because they are reported very early at compile-time, instead of runtime which is too late. Developers can study the problem and decide if they have to build a better implementation or if the process model was badly designed.

When running SWSG on a fixed model, the code generation can proceed. The *Laravel* code generator generates four kinds of files: one file per atomic components (identical to those written manually by the developers; see Listing 6), one file per composite components, a router file and several static files (that do not depend on the model; for example the `Component` interface definition).

Case Study #2. After it was successfully implemented, we want to extend the Petstore example and add a new service to handle PUT/pets/{id} requests. These requests set a pet with the given attributes and the given ID, by creating it or by updating the attributes of an already existing pet that has the same given ID. This is very similar to the POST/pets service; the difference is that the latter does not receive any ID, thus it only creates pets, whereas the new service can be used to edit them as well.

To implement this, we follow the same process as earlier. *Step 1:* we extend the OpenAPI model by adding a new service that matches our needs. *Step 2:* we need to attach it to SWSG components. Because of the similarity between this service and the POST/pets one, we choose to reuse and extend existing components. The CreatePet atomic component is thereby renamed to CreateOrUpdatePet, given a boolean parameter createOnly and a new precondition on an optional integer id variable. When instanciated for the POST service, createOnly is given the value true, whereas it is false when the same component is instanciated from the PUT service. Then, the implementation of this atomic component is modified so that it adds or updates pets depending on the value of the createOnly parameter and the one of the id context variable. Listing 7 shows how the new service instantiates a composite component (defined in Listing 8) that in turn calls the CreateOrUpdatePet and passes it the right value for its createOnly parameter. *Step 3:* we run SWSG.

Discussion. Our approach has several advantages over a regular development process, for example writing the whole application using a programming language and a web framework such as Laravel. First, the model-driven approach forces developers to think of their design or design evolutions at a macroscopic scale before writing low-level implementations. Along with the automatic model verification, this provides them an easy way to spot design mistakes early-on in the process, therefore saving some of their time. In a regular process, developers could only rely on the quality tools offered by the language or the framework. Because there is no static verification step in PHP, for example, and because lots of developers do not write any automated tests, they would often be tempted to skip checking the consistency of their design, especially when making small evolutions on it. Second, because the extended OpenAPI model is used to generate both implementation and documentation, both will stay aligned during the life of the project. In a regular process, this property relies on the will of the developers; they might stop maintaining the OpenAPI model and still make evolutions to the implementation.

Listing 6. Implementation of the GetPetById atomic component.

```php
1  <?php
2  namespace App\Components;
3  use App\SWSG\Component;
4  use App\SWSG\Ctx;
5  use App\SWSG\Params;
6  use DB;
7
8  class GetPetById implements Component
9  {
10     public static function execute(Params $params, Ctx $ctx)
11     {
12         $pet = DB::table('pet')
13             ->where('id', $ctx->get('id'))
14             ->first();
15         $ctx->add('pet', $pet);
16         return $ctx;
17     }
18 }
```

Listing 7. Extract of the new service.

```
1  /pets/{id}:
2    put:
3      ...
4      x—swsg—ci:
5        component: AddOrEditPet
6        bindings:
7        - param:
8            name: addOnly
9            type: Boolean
10         argument:
11           type: Boolean
12           value: false
```

Listing 8. The AddOrEditPet component.

```
1  x—swsg—cc:
2  - name: AddOrEditPet
3      params:
4      - name: addOnly
5          type: Boolean
6      components:
7      - component: CreateOrUpdatePet
8          bindings:
9          - param:
10             name: createOnly
11             type: Boolean
12             argument:
13               name: addOnly
14               type: Boolean
15      - component: RenderPet
```

As illustrated by the second step of our case study, these advantages are especially valuable for incremental development. Indeed they enforce several forms of consistency at different levels of the projects, for a low cost in term of flexibility and productivity. In contexts such as ours where we need to build and evolve web services for MVPs, incremental development is crucial. *The model and code of this case study are available in the repository of SWSG[15].*

8   Conclusion

We proposed a method integrated to OpenAPI 3.0 to build web services. It is fast, simple, robust and flexible. It is based on a meta-model that allows developers to define implementations of web services, starting from the corresponding

---

[15] https://gitlab.startup-palace.com/research/swsg/tree/master/examples/petstore.

high-level contract as expressed by a standard OpenAPI model. Consistency of models can be verified using an operational semantics so that code generated from these models is safe. We built a tool, SWSG, that leverages this process in the technological context of a web company, *Startup Palace*. The whole approach was illustrated on a two-steps case study to show its advantages. Even if one of the motivations was to develop MVPs applications, the approach is not limited to this scope and is suitable to most applications based on web services.

We have several main prospects. First, the type system used to describe component parameters, preconditions and model's entities (among others) is at the core of the consistency verification, yet it is not flexible enough. Making it more expressive, by allowing subtyping in component preconditions for example, while keeping at least the same level of verification might be necessary to reach a good reusability on bigger projects. Another perspective is to allow and ease safe model composition, so that developers can reuse concepts between projects when it makes sense. Model composition is theoretically handled by OpenAPI but not currently supported by SWSG. Then, the developer experience could be improved if there were tools able to automatically check the compliance of atomic components to their contract in the model. Finally, the whole approach needs to be evaluated on more realistic and larger case studies. This evaluation must rely on metrics that have a good correlation with the benefits of our approach, such as easing new developers to onboard on projects and reuse of existing code. This may take several months of practice and reviews.

References

1. Open API Initiative: OpenAPI Specification (2017). https://github.com/OAI/OpenAPI-Specification/blob/master/versions/3.0.1.md
2. RAML Workgroup: RAML (2016). https://raml.org/
3. DeRemer, F., Kron, H.: Programming-in-the large versus programming-in-the-small. In: ACM SIGPLAN Notices, vol. 10, pp. 114–121. ACM (1975)
4. Bernardi, M.L., Cimitile, M., Di Lucca, G., Maria Maggi, F.: M3D: a tool for the model driven development of web applications. In: Proceedings of the Twelfth International Workshop on Web Information and Data Management, pp. 73–80 (2012)
5. Rocheteau, J., Sferruzza, D.: Reifier: Model-Driven Engineering of Component-Based and Service-Oriented JEE Applications (2016)
6. Scheidgen, M., Efftinge, S., Marticke, F.: Metamodeling vs metaprogramming: a case study on developing client libraries for REST APIs. In: Wąsowski, A., Lönn, H. (eds.) ECMFA 2016. LNCS, vol. 9764, pp. 205–216. Springer, Cham (2016). https://doi.org/10.1007/978-3-319-42061-5_13
7. Sferruzza, D.: Safe Web Services Generator (2017). https://gitlab.startup-palace.com/research/swsg
8. Sferruzza, D., Rocheteau, J., Attiogbé, C., Lanoix, A.: A Model-Driven Method for Fast Building Consistent Web Services in Practice (2018)
9. Bernardi, M.L., Cimitile, M., Maggi, F.M.: Automated development of constraint-driven web applications. In: Proceedings of the 31st Annual ACM Symposium on Applied Computing, pp. 1196–1203. ACM (2016)

10. Fu, X., Bultan, T., Su, J.: Analysis of interacting BPEL web services. In: Proceedings of the 13th International World Wide Web Conference. Citeseer (2004)
11. Gronmo, R., Skogan, D., Solheim, I., Oldevik, J.: Model-driven web services development. In: e-Technology, e-Commerce and e-Service, pp. 42–45. IEEE (2004)
12. van der Aalst, W.M.P., Pesic, M., Schonenberg, H.: Declarative workflows: balancing between flexibility and support. Comp. Sci. Res. Dev. **23**, 99–113 (2009)
13. Cao, H., Falleri, J.-R., Blanc, X.: Automated generation of REST API specification from plain HTML documentation. In: Maximilien, M., Vallecillo, A., Wang, J., Oriol, M. (eds.) ICSOC 2017. LNCS, vol. 10601, pp. 453–461. Springer, Cham (2017). https://doi.org/10.1007/978-3-319-69035-3_32
14. Cremaschi, M., De Paoli, F.: Toward automatic semantic API descriptions to support services composition. In: De Paoli, F., Schulte, S., Broch Johnsen, E. (eds.) ESOCC 2017. LNCS, vol. 10465, pp. 159–167. Springer, Cham (2017). https://doi.org/10.1007/978-3-319-67262-5_12
15. Tsouroplis, R., Petychakis, M., Alvertis, I., Biliri, E., Askounis, D.: Community-based API builder to manage APIs and their connections with Cloud-based Services. In: CAiSE Forum, pp. 17–23 (2015)
16. Schwichtenberg, S., Gerth, C., Engels, G.: From open API to semantic specifications and code adapters. In: 2017 IEEE International Conference on Web Services (ICWS), pp. 484–491. IEEE (2017)
17. Willighagen, E., Mélius, J.: Automatic OpenAPI to Bio.tools Conversion (2017)
18. Pugaczewski, J., Cummings, T., Hunter, D., Michalik, B.: Software engineering methodology for development of APIs for network management using the MEF LSO framework. IEEE Commun. Stand. Mag. **1**(1), 92–96 (2017)
19. SmartBear Software: Swagger Code Generator (2018). https://github.com/swagger-api/swagger-codegen/
20. Wadler, P.: The essence of functional programming. In: Proceedings of the 19th ACM SIGPLAN-SIGACT Symposium on Principles of Programming Languages, pp. 1–14. ACM (1992)
21. SmartBear Software: Swagger Editor (2018). https://github.com/swagger-api/swagger-editor
22. SmartBear Software: Swagger UI (2018). https://github.com/swagger-api/swagger-UI
23. Apiary: Dredd (2017). https://github.com/apiaryio/dredd
24. van der Lee, M.: PHPSwaggerGen (2017). https://github.com/vanderlee/PHPSwaggerGen
25. Open API Initiative: The Petstore Example (2017). https://github.com/OAI/OpenAPI-Specification/blob/3.0.1/examples/v3.0/petstore-expanded.yaml
26. Lopes, P., Guardiani, F.: Slush-vertx (2017). https://github.com/pmlopes/slush-vertx
27. Sferruzza, D.: Specification of SWSG extensions for OpenAPI (2018). https://gitlab.startup-palace.com/research/swsg/tree/master/openapi-extensions-specification/1.0.0.md
28. Internet Engineering Task Force: JSON Schema: A Media Type for Describing JSON Documents (2016). https://tools.ietf.org/html/draft-wright-json-schema-00
29. The PHP Group: PHP (2016). https://php.net/
30. Otwel, T.: Laravel (2016). https://laravel.com/

Reuse and Customization for Code Generators: Synergy by Transformations and Templates

Robert Eikermann[✉], Katrin Hölldobler, Alexander Roth,
and Bernhard Rumpe

Software Engineering, RWTH Aachen University, Ahornstrasse 55, Aachen, Germany
{eikermann,hoelldobler,roth,rumpe}@se-rwth.de
http://www.se-rwth.de

Abstract. Engineering languages for model-driven development (MDD) highly rely on code generators that systematically and efficiently generate source code from abstract models. Although code generation is an essential technique, there is still a lot of ad hoc mechanisms in use that prevent an efficient and reliable use and especially reuse of code generators.

The first part of the paper focuses on general mechanisms necessary to really allow reuse of flexible code generators. Based on these general considerations, we present a code generator infrastructure, that allows to easily develop a generator, but especially allows to adapt existing generators to different technology stacks and thus widely supports reusability, customizability, and flexibility.

In the second part of the paper, we present an integrated template- and transformation-based code generation approach. It enables efficient code generation of object-oriented code and retains the benefits of both approaches. Even more, its synergetic use improves usability beyond using just a single approach. Internally, an intermediate representation (IR) and a separation of the code generation process into three main steps is used. First, the input model is processed and transformed to the IR. Second, elements in the IR are manipulated by source and target language independent transformations. Target language specific implementations are added by templates, which are attached to IR elements. Third, the resulting IR is used by a template engine to generate code with a predefined set of default templates for a particular target language. The overall goal of this paper is to show how to address necessary code generator considerations to effectively and efficiently use engineering languages in MDD.

Keywords: Code generation · Model-to-model transformation · Code generator development

© Springer Nature Switzerland AG 2019
S. Hammoudi et al. (Eds.): MODELSWARD 2018, CCIS 991, pp. 34–55, 2019.
https://doi.org/10.1007/978-3-030-11030-7_3

1   Principles of Code Generation

Model-driven development (MDD) relies on code generation as an essential ingredient to systematically generate source code from an abstract representation of a software system. To generate source code, each concept of the input language has to be mapped to concepts of the target language [6,35]. The most used approaches that have been proposed to perform this mapping are template-based [4,36] and transformation-based approaches [6,9,10,20].

However, there is much more to say about good code generators. It is therefore worthwhile to first look at the important principles for a good code generator:

- *Code generation facilitate the reuse of models and the generator.*
  Ideally, a code generator is independent of any model and thus can be reused for many different models. Reuse, however, also works, when one model is mapped to different target platforms and operating systems or evolving hardware and software technology stacks.
- *Within a project, code generation must be re-doable at each time and by any developer.*
  As a consequence, generated code cannot be manipulated by hand. However, handwritten code and generated code interact with each other and fine-grained interaction patterns are necessary.
  Another consequence is to not version control generated code, because re-doing the generation in parallel may lead to conflicts (even if its only the generation time stamp).
- *Generated and handwritten code are strictly separated in different artifacts.*
  Some build processes (e.g. Apache Maven [39]) even separate these artifacts into different hierarchies. The generation-gap problem can be overcome with a variety of mechanisms, some of which are assisted by object-orientation, such as subclass building. An interesting approach is for example the generation of classes that are embedded in a "sandwich", namely a handwritten super-interface to allow function extensions and a handwritten subclass for overriding [18].
  The need of embedding all code into classes complicates the interaction between handwritten and generated code, but higher order functional abstractions, partial classes and similar approaches further improve a conceptual integration while keeping the code separate.
- *Code generators needs to be flexible to adapt to different, and evolving technology stacks.*
  Pure development of a code generator is always more work than directly implementing the system by hand. Code generators become interesting, when they are reusable. That includes a given code generator can easily be adapted to a new or evolving technology stack. Flexibility of the code generator includes the possibility to adapt the generation result without having to know all details of the generator. Templates for example are a good technology to adapt a generator, without going into its code.

Flexibility is potentially also necessary within the project, where some parts of the model are mapped to different target stacks than other parts. Sometimes the target code needs to be enhanced by additional functionality, etc.

– *Maintainability of the generator is important.*
Maintaining a generator is necessary, when the technology stack of generator changes, or when the generation has to be adapted. Thus maintainability is to some extent covered by flexibility of the generator. If however, the designated flexibility doesn't suffice anymore, it is important to have access to the generators source, e.g. from an open-source project, and the generator architecture is well structured and the code readable.

– *The generation process needs to be reliable and potential error messages understandable.*
It is necessary, that the generation process doesn't terminate with internal errors – at least the user needs to get an understandable explanation and should be able to act accordingly.
On the contrary, it's also necessary that erroneous models are detected early in the generation process and communicated to the developer. It is mandatory, that only correct code is generated. This includes that the generated code is compilable, but also behaves well.

– *The generated code needs to be reliable.*
The generated code should be pretty robust against incorrect forms of usage. Depending on the form of use, it should on the other hand either be very robust (e.g. in airplanes) or early and quickly give errors and exceptions, when detecting a misuse (e.g. when the generated code is itself used in a batch tool).
Reliability also includes, the code uniformly behaves in the same way, or that generated data structures are by construction correct and their data cannot be corrupted. The DEx generator e.g. has taken deep efforts to ensure correctness of generated classes and association codes at all (interesting) times [28].

– *A generator should be compositional.*
Composition comes in several flavors: (1) Several different models are fed into one generator, that internally is composed of several sub-generators, contributing to the same artifacts. (2) Several individual generators take the same model and produce artifacts that can be composed (in the product). (3) Several individual generators take individual models, but again produce composable artifacts.
This task is difficult to achieve, because it either enforces that generators exchange information about the targets they create, or the developers of generators have an agreement, how the interfaces of the generated artifacts interact. Sometimes, both is necessary.

– *A generator should be smart.*
One could even say, that a generator could be intelligent. That would mean that some of the domain or technology knowledge is neither part of the model, nor part of the hand written code that the generator generates against. E.g. if a class diagram contains certain classes, such as *Person*, the generator knows what kinds of attributes and functions should be embedded, where to store the objects in the data base, etc.

A smart generator could allow much more concise and abstract models. That would also mean that the purely mechanical view on generators (mentioned above an in [6,35]) would not be completely valid anymore.

It could be that it's not the generator itself, but its customization through templates, predefined models and code that are woven into the generated code, which make a generator smart. However, from the users point of view it's the generator that bears smartness.

- *A generator should assist agile development.*

  In principle a project agility becomes more agile, when we can use abstract models instead of more detailed hand written code [29,31].

  However, agility also very much lives from early and immediate feedback. If the generation process takes to long, the number of build script executions goes down considerably, the feedback gets later and thus error finding more complex. Furthermore, developers get bored and start doing other things, which leads to an interruptions of the developer "flow".

  As a consequence, a generator must be quick when generating and incremental, that means should detect, what really needs to be re-generated.

We can also observe, that round-trip engineering, i.e., generating code from models and retrieving models from code either only works for structurally equivalent models, such as class diagrams and object-oriented programs. The other alternative only was to embed the original model as an (unreadable) comment and retrieve the model not from the code, but from the comment. While having merits in some situations, both approaches are not really that helpful in normal projects.

1.1   An Example for Code Generation

After having discussed so many general principles, we have to admit that these principles to some extent conflict. For example reliability of the generated code very much depends on how much flexibility of generator is actually used. The more and deeper adaptations are made to the generator, the riskier it is that a generator doesn't fulfill all required goals anymore.

Even though, we don't have answers for all needs, we would like to demonstrate in the following, how a combination of a template- and transformation-based approach improves the situation with respects to several of the goals. These ideas go back to several projects, including the MontiCore language workbench [21,22] itself, where this combination is widely used. Especially for *data-centric applications* [25] practice has shown that using transformation- or template-based code generation in isolation restricts flexibility when generating source code for the presentation layer and the application layer (cf. [20]) and has disadvantages in realizing code generator modularity (cf. [41]).

Our approach targets object-oriented output languages and is subdivided into three steps. First, after parsing the input model, an initial step applies a sequence of transformations including a model-to-model transformation that translates the input model to an *intermediate representation (IR)*, which abstracts from object-oriented programming languages and allows to describe structural aspects of the generated code. Second, different transformations can be applied to the IR to enrich the representation, e.g., by additional classes, methods, etc. that should be generated. Flexibility of this code generation approach is achieved by allowing to switch between both approaches, i.e., transform the IR or attach templates to IR elements. Third, the transformed IR including the attached templates is used as input for a template engine, which uses a default set of templates for a target language to generate code based on the IR. The default templates are used whenever there is no template attached to an element of the IR. Integrating transformation- and template-based code generation and employing an IR allows for target language independent transformations with additional target language specific templates. The contribution of this paper are as follows:

- Flexible integration of transformation- and template-based code generation
- Proposal for a object-oriented domain-specific language for an IR
- Customization approach for code generation via template attachments.

Hence, we first give an example in Sect. 2 to demonstrate the challenge in MDD of data-centric applications. Afterwards, we form an understanding of a code generator and template- and transformation-based code generation in Sect. 3. Then, we present and discuss our approach for code generation using templates and transformation in combination (Sect. 4). Next, we present a use case, where we applied our approach in Sect. 5. Finally, an overview of current research in this field is given in Sect. 6 and the paper is concluded in Sect. 7.

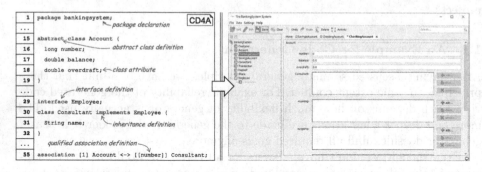

Fig. 1. Generation of data-centric applications from analysis models.

2   Motivating Example

As a motivating example, we consider the MDD of data-centric applications. Each data-centric application offers management functionality for structured and consistent information described by a model [28]. On the left-hand side in Fig. 1, the model is an instance of the class diagram for analysis (CD4A) domain-specific language (DSL) to describe class diagrams created during the analysis phase (*analysis model* [31]). This model is systematically transformed to the executable data-centric application, which offers SCRUD (search, create, read, update, and delete) functionality shown on the right-hand side (Fig. 1).

Due to varying user requirements, a data centric application has to be customizable. In this example, the developer has to change the user interface generated for each class in the input model. Since no additional models are used and adapting the generated source code in not practical, because it requires a suitable approach for handwritten code integration (cf. [17,18]) and customization of each generated artifact, the developer aims to design a customizable code generator.

In addition, the developer aims to reduce the development time of future code generators by reusing parts of the data-centric code generator, e.g., the part to generate the source code representing the data structure (i.e., Plain-Old-Java-Objects). However, a code generator my use a different input and output model (i.e., conforming to a different DSL). Hence, to make parts of the code generator reusable, the developer plans to realize this part of the code generator independent of the input and target language.

Besides customization and reuse concerns, the developer needs to choose a code generation approach. However, generating data-centric applications has multiple challenges. First, generating an application core requires the code generation to traverse the representation of the model and generation of mainly changing code. Second, generation of a graphical user interface requires the generation of mainly static source code and from dedicated parts of the input models, e.g., classes. Hence, the developer wants to mix both code generation approaches to avoid unmaintainable templates and complex transformations.

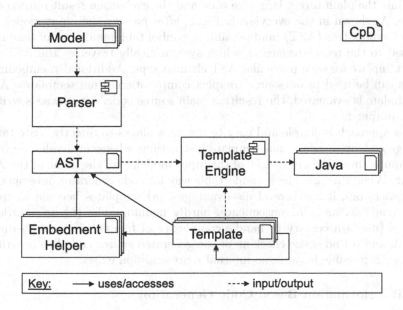

Fig. 2. Overview of a template-based generation process.

3   Transformation- and Template-Based Code Generation

In model-driven development a software system that produces an implementation from a higher-level description of a (part of a) software is regarded as a generator [6]. A code generator is a special kind of a generator that creates an implementation in a programming language from a set of input artifacts, which are, typically, models. Such code generators that always terminate and generate at least one output artifact are build on top of existing compilers for programming languages and consists of a front-end (*language processing*) and a back-end (*code generation*) [28].

Language processing is concerned with parsing the models, checking language constraints and creating an internal representation (*abstract syntax tree* and *symbol table*). Code generation systematically transforms the internal representation to concrete code, which is stored in generated artifacts. The most dominating technical realizations of code generation are *template-based* and *transformation-based* code generation. Subsequently, both approaches are explained in more detail.

3.1   Template-Based Code Generation

The prerequisite for template-based code generation is a template language and a corresponding template engine. A template forms the main artifact of interest and consists of plain *target language code*, which is the source code that is generated, and additional template language instructions. Each template is processed by a template engine, which evaluates the template language instructions and prints the plain target language code and the evaluation result into an output file. As shown in the overview in Fig. 2, after parsing the input model, the abstract syntax tree (AST) (and possibly a symbol table) and a set of templates is passed to the template engine, which systematically traverses the AST and calls a template for each particular AST element type. Additionally, embedment helpers can be used to outsource complex computations from templates. After the template is evaluated, the resulting plain source code, e.g., Java, is written into an output file.

This approach is simple and easy to use as it allows to directly write target language code with additional template instructions whenever a value needs to be computed from the given AST of the input model, e.g., the name of the AST element. While this provides a comfortable way for code generator developers to write generators, it has several disadvantages: (a) templates become complex, hardly readable, and, in consequence, hardly maintainable; (b) an additional infrastructure is necessary to handle complexity of templates (see embedment helpers); and (c) no static checking of the generated source code before writing into a file is possible because no internal representation exists.

3.2   Transformation-Based Code Generation

In transformation-based code generation, transformations are the central artifact. In this approach, an input model is parsed and an arbitrary number of transformations is applied to the AST of the input model to create an output model [20], i.e., an abstract syntax tree of the target language (cf. Fig. 3). Note that transformations can also be applied to the output model AST. Finally, the output model AST is systematically transferred into a textual representation, which conforms to the syntax of the output language, by using a pretty printer.

Transformations in this process are a sequence of endogenous transformations modifying the input model and conform to the source modeling language [7] followed by an exogenous transformation translating the input model to an IR-AST. Within the generation process a structured representation is present that can be checked for errors and processed by further transformations.

This approach has the advantage that calculations on and traversal of the input model can be replaced by pattern matching. When domain-specific transformations [1,30,34] are employed, the concrete syntax of the output language can be used to describe the output [20]. In addition, the AST representation allows for syntactic checks and extensibility of the generation by applying further transformations before transferring the result into a code. This benefit implies (a) the need for a grammar or meta model of the output language that precisely defines its structure. Furthermore, (b) transformations my become to complex and unmaintainable demanding for transformation development guidelines and additional frameworks to compose transformations. Large plain target language code fragments for single model element can more easily be created with templates [26].

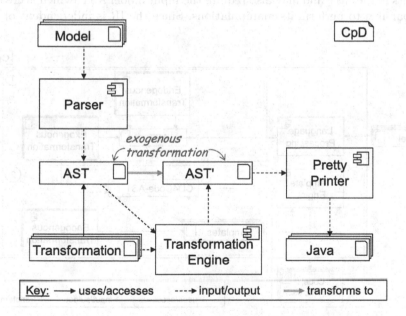

Fig. 3. Overview of transformation-based generation.

4   Synergetic Transformation- and Template-Based Code Generation

To support reusable, customizable, and flexible code generator design, we propose an approach based on the conjunction of transformation- and template-based code generation. As both approaches have their advantages and disadvantages (cf. Sect. 3), we have combined both in a way that retains their advantages and minimizes their disadvantages.

An overview of a generation process is shown in Fig. 4. The integration of transformation- and template-based code generation results in a partitioning of the overall code generation process into three steps (numbers in the figure).

Preprocessing. First, after the parser has created the abstract syntax tree of the input model ((1) in Fig. 4), it is transforms into an abstract syntax tree of an IR, which may either be completely built from scratch or may be based on an existing AST that is adapted. In this step, the input model AST may be manipulated by transformations before it is eventually transformed to the IR.

Transforming. In the second step, the IR-AST is consecutively transformed by a sequence of transformations to enrich the intermediate AST with elements that will be generated ((2) in Fig. 4). Each transformation adds, removes, or updates elements in the AST and may also require the input model AST, which is created after parsing, to perform its manipulations. Since the IR is independent of the

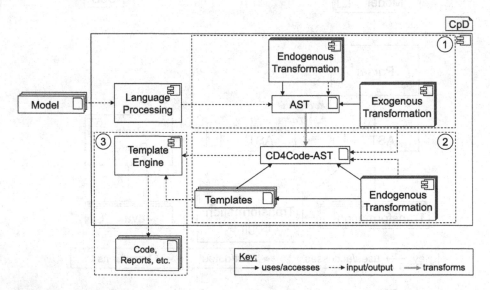

Fig. 4. Integration of template- and transformation-based code generation consists of three consecutive steps: *pretransformation, intermediate transformation,* and *template-based code generation.*

output language, additional output language specific templates can be attached to elements of the intermediate AST.

Generating. Finally, in the last step ((3) in Fig. 4) a template engine is used to generate code by passing the transformed AST including the attached templates and a set of default templates for the output language and the AST of the IR.

4.1 Intermediate Representation

As the IR forms the core for the transformations and the abstract representation of the generated code, it should provide an abstraction of the output language but should also be as input language independent as possible. As most software systems are implemented using object-oriented programming languages, we decided to choose a representation that provides an abstraction of the most common object-oriented programming concepts. As a consequence, this approach is limited to generate source code that use the object-oriented programming paradigm [11].

A natural choice to describe an IR is a DSL representing UML class diagrams [37], which provide most of the concepts found in object-oriented languages. Thus, our IR is a restricted version of UML class diagrams called *class diagram for design (CD4D)*. It only contains the most relevant parts including classes, interfaces, abstract classes and enumerations. A class may extend another class and implement interfaces. In addition, associations with navigation directions and cardinalities are supported. An association as well as each of its role ends may have names and can be ordered or qualified. Classes may have attributes with associated types. From our choice of the IR, a second limitation to our approach emerges: the IR can only describe structural aspects of the generated code. Behavioral aspects have to be added using additional language specific templates.

An example that can be described with the IR is shown in Fig. 5. Note that we use concrete syntax rather than the abstract syntax for presentational purpose. The example shows an excerpt of the Java source code (left-hand-side) that is generated for the CD4A model shown on the left-hand side in Fig. 1. It shows the interface `Account` (ll.1-50) and the implementation `AccountImpl` (ll.62-266). On the right-hand side, the textual notation of the CD4D DSL describing the object-oriented structure of the Java source code on the left-hand side. The CD4D model uses the same keywords as the Java source code to denote the corresponding UML class diagram concepts (inheritance, classes, interfaces, etc.). It also contains visibility, e.g., `private` in l.44 and `public` in l.10 on the right-hand-side. However, no method bodies are present in the IR (l.70 right-hand side).

The IR serves as the abstract representation of the source code that is to be generated. Model-to-model transformations successively enriched the IR with relevant information regarding the generated code, e.g. additional technical classes or methods. However, to make use of this language independent representation, the input model needs to be mapped to the IR.

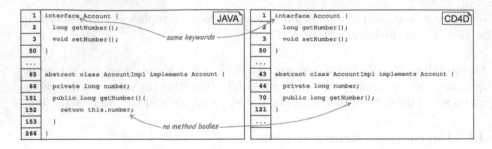

Fig. 5. Example of the IR (right-hand-side) for Java code (left-hand-side).

4.2 Model-To-Model Transformations

The first two steps, i.e., the transformational part, of our approach illustrated in Fig. 4, rely on model-to-model transformations [8]. Two types of transformation can be distinguished within our approach, *endogenous* and *exogenous* transformation. After the model has been parsed and, thus, is available in its AST representation our approach allows to manipulate the model *endogenously*, i.e., apply transformations that change the model but do not change the language it belongs to. This initial transformations are helpful to reduce the high-level concepts used in the model, i.e., normalizing [24] the input model, such that the model only uses the core concepts of the source language. By first normalizing the input model the subsequent transformations are simplified as only the core concepts of the source language needs to be considered. By allowing normalization first our approach is robust regarding newly introduced syntactic sugar as this can be handled by adding further normalizing transformations.

After the input model is normalized an *exogenous* transformation translates the input model to the IR. This transformation maps concepts of the input language to concepts of the IR. Even though depicted as a single transformation there is no need to construct the complete IR in one huge step. Our approach allows to further transform the IR endogenously. Thus, this step just needs to do minimal mapping of the input model to the internal representation.

Finally, the transformational part of our approach allows to stepwise extend the created IR and attach templates to elements of the internal representation as explained in the next section. Within this transformation the "final" IR is constructed that serves as the basis for the template-based part of our code generation. To ease the construction of the "final" IR each transformation step is allowed to add, remove and update model elements as well as attach one or several templates to specific elements and can even consider a former state of the input model, e.g. the AST after the model has been parsed. The code generator developer is free to add as much information as she likes to the IR using transformations and can even have recourse to results of arbitrary former transformation steps. The final IR AST used for the template-based code generation does not necessarily has to be too detailed about the generated structure, because the templates can add missing details. However, by switching to template-based code generation as the back-end of our approach there is no need for a pretty printer for the output language. Furthermore, switching to templates provides a simple way to merge the information stored in the IR, e.g. merge different parts of a class or method generated by different templates without relying on output language concepts such as partial classes that are present in C# but missing in Java.

4.3   Template Attachment

Transformations on the IR allow to manipulate generic object-oriented programming concepts, e.g. classes, attributes, and are target language independent. However, in case target language specific code is needed a purely transformation-based approach requires an abstract representation of the target language. To avoid this and address customizability concerns (cf. Sect. 2), we allow to attach templates to IR elements.

For instance, assume a transformation added a new method and the method body should be defined. Rather than creating a new method body by using an abstract representation and attaching it to the IR (which would make the IR target language dependent), we attach a template for the new method. This template contains the method implementation and may use the IR to access values, e.g., the method name and parameters. To efficiently manage the template attachments, we use an infrastructure that maps a template to a particular AST element. It is, therefore, possible to attach multiple templates to one AST element as shown in Fig. 4 or even to attach one template to multiple AST elements.

Besides attaching one or multiple templates, it is also possible to define the order in which templates of a AST element are executed in the code generation phase. The order of template execution is evaluated for each individual IR-AST node. To modify template execution, the following operations are provided:

- **Replace Operation:** to replace a particular template from the template extension.
- **Add-Before Operation:** to add a template at the beginning of the template extension.
- **Add-After Operation:** to append a template at the end of the template extension.

If multiple templates are marked to be executed first, last, or before a template, the template registered first is executed. The operations for template attachments may result in conflicting operations. For example, consider two replace operations for the same template; or a cyclic replacement. Hence, conflicts are handled as shown in Fig. 6.

Cyclic add and replace operations, i.e., (a) and (b) in Fig. 6, are resolved by avoiding a transitive resolution of these operations and only resolve to depth one, i.e., only one operation. For example, in (a) the first operation (execution order is from top to bottom) is the replacement of template A with template B.

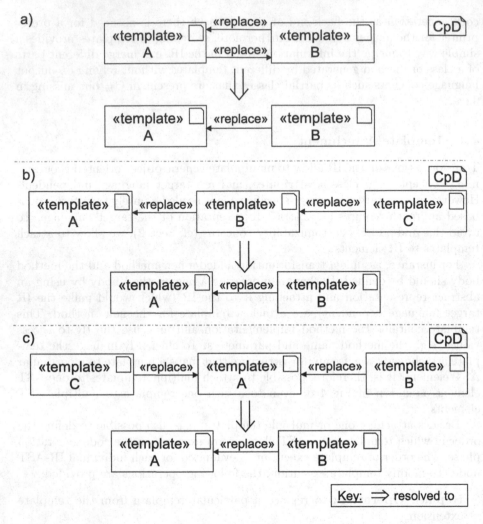

Fig. 6. Conflict resolution is done by only executing the first replace operation (a, c) in a non-transitive manner (b).

As a result, only the first operation is executed. Another example is shown in (b) (execution order is from left to right and top to bottom), where only the replacement of template A with template B is executed. Note that if a template is replaced, all before and after templates of the replacing template are added.

However, operations on template attachments are executed sequentially, thus run-time errors may occur. For example, when two *replace operations* sequentially replace the same template, i.e., (c) in Fig. 6, the latter replace operation will fail, because the template has previously been replaced. In aspect-oriented programming this is considered as the *"fragile point cut"* problem [32]. An approach to detect such errors is to process and analyze the sequence of template attachment operations a priori to detect conflicts. However, this will involve processing the complete code generator's source code. Alternatively, another approach is to detect such conflicts at run-time of the code generator and inform the developer but do not stop code generation.

The strong bond between templates and the IR AST demands for handling template attachments, when the IR AST is transformed. For example, assume a template tmpl is attached to the class C in the IR, then another transformation changes C and attaches another template tmpl2. With one exception - AST element deletion -, the result of this will be that the AST element will have both templates attached tmpl and tmpl2. In the case, when the AST element is deleted, we also delete the attachment.

4.4   Generating Code

After all transformations have successfully been applied and templates have been attached to AST elements, the resulting IR needs to be mapped to concrete code. The essential requirements for such a mapping is a clear understanding of how to map each element of the IR to the output language source code and a set of default templates for the output language that realizes this mapping.

As the main goal of the IR was to abstract from specific output language concepts and provide only relevant object-oriented programming concepts, mapping the IR to an object-oriented language is straight forward. This means classes, interfaces, enumerations, and attributes can easily be mapped to object-oriented programming languages. Association and composition are the only two concepts with varying semantics, since different approaches have been proposed on how to perform this mapping, e.g. [14,15]. However, the most simplest approach is to add a variable storing the associations links to the source class of the association and add corresponding mutators and accessors for each association direction. This simple mapping is realizable by every object-oriented programming language.

Having a mapping of the IR AST to an output language, a set of templates that realizes this mapping is needed. Indeed, this has to be done for each output language that is to be generated. However, it allows for exchangeability of the output language, as the IR AST structure is not changed. However, it needs to be considered that attached templates are written in the output language and need to be exchanged as well.

As shown in Fig. 4, the template engine is called with the transformed IR AST and the default set of templates. The template engine traverses the input AST and for each visited AST node the attached templates are called. If no template is registered for an AST element, then a default template for this type of AST element is used from the default template set. The output is either written to a file or returned as a result to be embedded in another output.

4.5   Discussion

Since this approach merges templates and transformation it needs to be discussed in which cases to use templates and in which cases to use transformations. Certainly, this cannot be answered in general. However, in current literature [26] it is proposed to use templates for code that does not require much computation and is primarily static. For instance, graphical user interface code calls methods from libraries. In contrast, transformations should be used whenever static checking is required for certain elements. For example, by adding a class to the IR, certain properties can be checked. Moreover, changes that affect the overall code generation, e.g., name of classes, and, thus, require changes that regard different output files should be realized as transformations.

A disadvantage of the simplified IR is the lack of output language specific concepts, e.g. Java annotations. While for most cases it is sufficient to neglect them (e.g. @Override), they are of essential importance when generating e.g. J2EE applications. However, the IR can be extended with additional stereotypes. Each stereotype can then be used to define output language specific annotations. Besides stereotypes, other output language specific concepts that cannot be represented using the IR. In this case, either the IR has to be extended or already existing concepts of the IR have to be reused. Perhaps, output language specific templates can be used to resolve this issue.

As code generators are software systems on their own, they have to address issues such as maintainability and complexity as well. In our approach we do not particularly address these issues. Instead, we provide an approach to structure the code generation as a whole. We try to tackle these challenges by providing signatures for templates, i.e., templates have signatures such as methods and can simply be invoked with different arguments. In addition, guidelines have to be designed in order to prevent transformations and templates to become too complex.

Another challenge that has to be addressed results from the operations on template attachments, which can introduce syntax errors in the generated source code. A typical cause for such syntax errors is the use of incomplete target language statements in templates that combined with other templates produce syntactically correct source code but if these templates are executed in the wrong order or are replaced, the resulting source code may contain syntax errors. A restriction of templates to only syntactically correct target language statements has been proposed in [40,41] to address this issue. However, this approach is not of practical use because it restricts the flexibility of the proposed code generation approach. Hence, the proposed approach is not restrictive and demands for a methodological approach to handle this challenge.

5   Use Case

To demonstrate the proposed approach, we provide an example that extends the motivating example from Sect. 2 with Statecharts. In Fig. 7, two different representations of the input models are shown. On the left-hand side is the graphical notation and on right-hand side is the condensed parsed form as an AST. The class diagram provides the static part of a data-centric application, i.e., the class `Account` with one single attribute `overdraft` (condensed model from Sect. 2). This attribute stores the maximum possible amount of overdraft for a specific account.

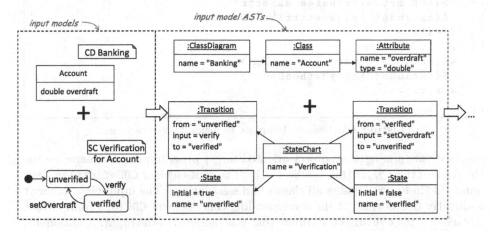

Fig. 7. Graphical notation of input models and corresponding abstract syntax (continued in Fig. 8).

The presented application in Fig. 1 provides functionality to load and store data. However, this data is not validated. We use the flexibility of the presented approach to extend this with behavioral aspects using Statecharts. It is important to verify all changes on the overdraft attribute, thus we use a Statechart to keep track if the current overdraft is verified (by an internal process of the bank).

The Statechart `Verification` is bound to the class `Account` using the `for Account` tag. It defines two states for the corresponding class `unverfied` and `verified`, meaning each instance of `Account` gets it's own associated state. The state `unverified` is the initial state. Each new account needs verification of the overdraft. Two stimuli are defined which handle the transitions between states during lifetime of an `Account`. The internal verification process is encapsulated in the stimulus `verify`. The process is designed in such a way, that it always ends with a verified account, but may include adjustment of overdraft. Every time the overdraft changes the state switches to `unverified`.

Both input models are parsed (separately) into independent ASTs as shown in Fig. 7. Parsing of the models and creation of the AST is easily possible with the MontiCore Language Workbench [22]. The AST of the Banking class diagram consists of the class `Account` and has the attribute `overdraft` of type `double` attached. The Statechart AST consists of the two states `verified` and `unverfied` and two connecting transitions `verify` and `setOverdraft`. Since no initial transformations have to be performed (but could be if e.g. the Statechart would have hierarchical states), the next step is to build up the IR from both ASTs, as shown in Fig. 8 (cf. Sect. 4).

```
                                                          FreeMarker
1  public class ${ast.getName()}{
2   <#list ast.attributes as attr>
3    ${include("PrivateAttributeDecl")}
4   </#list>
5   //...
6   <#list ast.methods as method>
7    ${include("EmptyMethodBody")}
8   </#list>
9  }
```

Listing 1.1. Default Template to generate a Java Class.

As we are aiming at an object-oriented target programming language, we use the AST of the *CD4D* DSL (cf. Sect. 4.1). The root element CDDefinition (left-hand-side in Fig. 8) bundles all classes and associations. The input class Account is directly transformed in the corresponding class element CDClass from *CD4D*. Attached is the overdraft attribute that was modeled in the input. Additionally, the Statechart AST is transformed into three classes implementing the Statechart pattern [12] and an association. The class VerificationState is the abstract super class for the two states, which are implemented by the classes Unverified and Verified. The Statechart Verification is bound to the Account class and thus an association connecting each Account. Its actual state is the class VerificationState, which is attached to the CDDefinition root element. Note that the *SC* tag in the IR-AST denotes the elements created from the Statechart input model, whereas the *CD* tag denotes the elements created form the class diagram input model.

In a next step, the IR is transformed by endogenous transformations to lift the stimuli into the Account class by creating a method for each stimulus: verify and setOverdraft (right-hand-side in Fig. 8). Via template attachment, the corresponding method body is attached as shown for the verify method. For the method setOverdraft, we attached (a) setter functionality from the input class diagram and (b) the Statechart transition handling. Further transformations on the IR can add persistence functionality, builders for all classes, or a GUI.

Finally, in the last step, the IR needs to be mapped to Java code. A default set of templates is required to perform this mapping. Having such a default set, code is generated by traversing the IR-AST and calling a template, which is either attached or defined as a default template for this particular type of AST elements. An example of a default template to generate a Java class from the IR is shown in Listing 1.1. It shows that classes of the IR can directly be mapped to Java classes. It also defines that for all attributes, which will become global variables in the Java source code, the PrivateAttributeDecl template is called if no attachment is defined. For methods, the EmptyMethodBody template is used. With respect to the above example, for the `verify` method, this default template is neglected and the attached template is called.

This use case shows two of the main benefits of the approach: (a) generating Java code from the IR is straight forward, and (b) default templates are small and maintainable (the generator consists of 8 templates only to generate arbitrary Java classes).

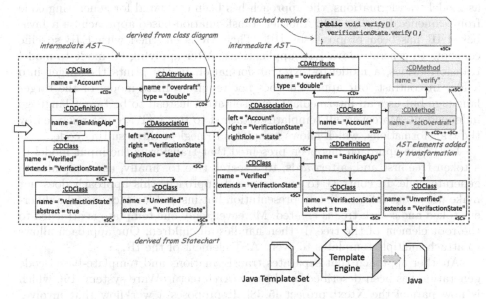

Fig. 8. Constructing an IR from the input models (left-hand-side) and attaching templates to methods (right-hand-side).

6   Related Work

Code generation as an integration of transformations and templates, is based on several approaches that have been proposed in order to improve code generation. Additionally, there are approaches used in reverse engineering that involve transformations and code generation such as [3]. However, their main focus is on model extraction instead of a flexible combination of transformation- and template-based code generation.

An approach to integrate template-based code generation into graphical model transformations has been proposed in [16]. It allows to graphically model endogenous transformations and use a template language to generate strings to define method bodies. A similar approach has been presented in [2]. As opposed to these approaches, our approach is broader as it allows for endogenous and exogenous transformations by employing an IR. Moreover, our approach regards templates as the primary artifact to generate concrete source code. Templates may not only be used to generate method bodies but also complete target language constructs such as classes with methods.

A fully transformation-based approach that systematically transforms the input model into concrete source code has been proposed in [20]. It is based on a meta-model of the target language that is extended with additional concepts to allow merging the generated code, e.g. partial classes. By using transformations the target language meta-model is consecutively transformed and the result is pretty printed to an target file. To explain practical use of code generation as model transformations, the approach has been evaluated for generating code from sequence diagrams [23]. Another transformation-based approach for a Java-based IR has been proposed by [10]. Their IR is enriched with EJB specific concepts to generate Java EJB applications. After applying all mode-to-model transformations, a model-to-text transformation pretty prints the target into a file. In contrast, our approach does not require a meta-model of the target language but uses an intermediate representation instead to be target language independent. Moreover, all templates attached to the AST are not regarded by the transformations, which allows templates to neglect the resulting code.

In [13] an approach has been presented that transforms the input model to a token tree first and, afterwards, to a search tree to, finally, use templates to generate code. In contrast to our proposed approach, this approach does not make use of one intermediate representation but instead for each model a different token and search tree is created. Moreover, only one template is attached to the root element of the tree. It then handles all children. Our approach allows to attach multiple templates to every AST element of the IR.

Another approach that separates transformations and template-based code generation has been described by the openArchitectureWare system [19], which is now part of the Xtext project [5, 38]. It proposes a workflow that involves a transformation step prior to the code generation step. The basic idea of our approach is similar but we extend it to allow a set of default templates, an intermediate representation, and allow template attachments to instances of AST elements rather then types of AST elements.

The Clearwater code generation approach uses an XML-based IR [33]. Although the IR is not restricted to an input or a target language, because it accepts arbitrary new tags, this IR hampers well-formedness checking due to its XML basis.

In [27], an IR for template-based code generation to separate the input model and the target source code from the code generation process and achieve flexibility has been proposed. However, the IR is restricted to class diagrams as input and mixes AST and additional symbol related information.

Additionally, a meta-model transformation-based approach, which uses the target language's meta-model as an IR, has been proposed in [20]. A similar approach based on a Java IR with additional EJB extensions to generate Java EJB applications is described in [10]. Both meta-model-based approaches use target language meta-models, which makes them target language dependent and reduces developers flexibility because it contains every detail of the generated code.

7 Conclusion

Code generation in model-driven development targets generation of source code from abstract models. Even though approaches exist for performing this transformation, they mainly focus on code generation and neglect aspects as flexibility, reusability, and maintainability. In the introduction, we have therefore discussed the main principles necessary for a good code generator.

Afterwards we have presented an approach that integrates template- and transformation-based code generation to address those principles. As a result, a user of this approach is able to flexibly choose how much of the generation process is done by transformations and at which point templates are better suited for the remaining generation process. For this purpose, we separated the code generation process into three phases. First, as a preparation the abstract syntax tree can be normalized and once this is done, be mapped to an intermediate representation (IR). It represents an abstraction from object-oriented programming languages and forms a lightweight version of UML class diagrams. With this abstraction the whole code generation is output language independent. In the second phase, the IR can be refined and output language specific templates can be added to add detailed output dependent information. In the last phase, we employ a template engine and a set of templates for an output language to generate concrete source code. The template engine traverses the IR AST and calls the attached templates. If no template is attached, a default template defined for the particular AST type is used.

It is, however, difficult to decide without much empirical evidence, whether this form of combined code generation will be appropriate to get more every-day developers and especially agile developers towards using abstract models and code generators, instead of handcoding. However, in our projects, a number of them are industry relevant, we experienced that this form of code generation is really of help and improves the overall productivity. However, we are somewhat biased and thus don't count as empirical evidence. It would be nice, if others can comment on these principles and the presented approach, to get more knowledge about what does work well and what needs to be changed.

References

1. Baar, T., Whittle, J.: On the usage of concrete syntax in model transformation rules. In: Virbitskaite, I., Voronkov, A. (eds.) PSI 2006. LNCS, vol. 4378, pp. 84–97. Springer, Heidelberg (2007). https://doi.org/10.1007/978-3-540-70881-0_10
2. Balogh, A., Varró, D.: Advanced model transformation language constructs in the VIATRA2 framework. In: ACM Symposium on Applied Computing. ACM (2006)
3. Brunelière, H., Cabot, J., Dupé, G., Madiot, F.: MoDisco: a model driven reverse engineering framework. Inf. Softw. Technol. 56(8), 1012–1032 (2014)
4. Chared, Z., Tyszberowicz, S.S.: Projective template-based code generation. In: CAiSE 2013 Forum at the 25th International Conference on Advanced Information Systems Engineering, vol. 998. CEURS-WS.org (2013)

5. ekkes corner: Mobile && IoT, October 2015. https://ekkescorner.wordpress.com/2009/07/16/galileo-openarchitectureware-moved-to-eclipse-modeling-projects-oaw5/
6. Czarnecki, K., Eisenecker, U.W.: Generative Programming: Methods, Tools, and Applications. Addison-Wesley, Boston (2000)
7. Czarnecki, K., Helsen, S.: Classification of model transformation approaches. In: 2nd OOPSLA 2003 Workshop on Generative Techniques in the Context of MDA (2003)
8. Czarnecki, K., Helsen, S.: Feature-based survey of model transformation approaches. IBM Syst. J. **45**(3), 621–645 (2006)
9. Di Ruscio, D., Eramo, R., Pierantonio, A.: Model transformations. In: Bernardo, M., Cortellessa, V., Pierantonio, A. (eds.) SFM 2012. LNCS, vol. 7320, pp. 91–136. Springer, Heidelberg (2012). https://doi.org/10.1007/978-3-642-30982-3_4
10. El Beggar, O., Bousetta, B., Gadi, T.: Automatic code generation by model transformation from sequence diagram of system's internal behavior. Int. J. Comput. Inf. Technol. **1**(02), 129–146 (2012)
11. Eliens, A.: Principles of Object-Oriented Software Development. Addison-Wesley Longman Publishing Co. Inc., Boston (1994)
12. Gamma, E., Helm, R., Johnson, R., Vlissides, J.: Design Patterns: Elements of Reusable Object-Oriented Software. Addison-Wesley Professional, Boston (1995)
13. Geiger, L., Schneider, C., Reckord, C.: Template- and modelbased code generation for MDA-tools. Technical report (2005)
14. Génova, G., Del Castillo, C.R., Llorens, J.: Mapping UML associations into Java code. J. Object Technol. **2**(5), 135–162 (2003)
15. Gessenharter, D.: Implementing UML associations in Java: a slim code pattern for a complex modeling concept. In: Workshop on Relationships and Associations in Object-Oriented Languages (RAOOL 2009). ACM (2009)
16. Girschick, M.: Integrating template-based code generation into graphical model transformation. In: Modellierung 2008, Berlin (2008)
17. Greifenberg, T., et al.: A comparison of mechanisms for integrating hand-written and generated code for object-oriented programming languages. CoRR abs/1509.04498 (2015)
18. Greifenberg, T., et al.: Integration of Handwritten and Generated Object-Oriented Code. In: Desfray, P., Filipe, J., Hammoudi, S., Pires, L.F. (eds.) MODELSWARD 2015. CCIS, vol. 580, pp. 112–132. Springer, Cham (2015). https://doi.org/10.1007/978-3-319-27869-8_7
19. Haase, A., Völter, M., Efftinge, S., Kolb, B.: Introduction to openArchitectureWare 4.1. 2. In: MDD Tool Implementers Forum at TOOLS Europe (2007). http://www.dsmforum.org/events/mdd-tif07/oAW.pdf
20. Hemel, Z., Kats, L.C.L., Groenewegen, D.M., Visser, E.: Code generation by model transformation: a case study in transformation modularity. Softw. Syst. Model. **9**(3), 375–402 (2010)
21. Krahn, H., Rumpe, B., Völkel, S.: MontiCore: modular development of textual domain specific languages. In: Paige, R.F., Meyer, B. (eds.) TOOLS EUROPE 2008. LNBIP, vol. 11, pp. 297–315. Springer, Heidelberg (2008). https://doi.org/10.1007/978-3-540-69824-1_17
22. Krahn, H., Rumpe, B., Völkel, S.: MontiCore: a framework for compositional development of domain specific languages. Int. J. Softw. Tools Technol. Transfer (STTT) **12**, 353–372 (2010)
23. Kundu, D., Samanta, D., Mall, R.: Automatic code generation from unified modelling language sequence diagrams. IET Softw. **7**(1), 12–28 (2013)

24. Mens, T., Czarnecki, K., Gorp, P.V.: A taxonomy of model transformations. In: Language Engineering for Model-Driven Software Development. Dagstuhl Seminar Proceedings. Internationales Begegnungs- und Forschungszentrum (IBFI) (2005)
25. Mir Seyed Nazari, P., Roth, A., Rumpe, B.: Mixed generative and handcoded development of adaptable data-centric business applications. In: Proceedings of the Workshop on Domain-Specific Modeling. ACM (2015)
26. Mohan, R., Kulkarni, V.: Model driven development of graphical user interfaces for enterprise business applications – experience, lessons learnt and a way forward. In: Schürr, A., Selic, B. (eds.) MODELS 2009. LNCS, vol. 5795, pp. 307–321. Springer, Heidelberg (2009). https://doi.org/10.1007/978-3-642-04425-0_23
27. Reiß, D.: Modellgetriebene generative Entwicklung von Web-Informationssystemen. Ph.D. thesis, RWTH Aachen University, Aachen (2015)
28. Roth, A., Rumpe, B.: Towards product lining model-driven development code generators. In: 3rd International Conference on Model-Driven Engineering and Software Development. Springer, Cham (2015)
29. Rumpe, B.: Modeling with UML. Springer, Cham (2016). https://doi.org/10.1007/978-3-319-33933-7
30. Rumpe, B., Weisemöller, I.: A domain specific transformation language. In: Workshop on Models and Evolution, vol. 11 (2011)
31. Rumpe, B.: Agile Modeling with UML: Code Generation, Testing, Refactoring. Springer, Cham (2017). https://doi.org/10.1007/978-3-319-58862-9
32. Störzer, M., Koppen, C.: PCDiff: attacking the fragile pointcut problem. In: European Interactive Workshop on Aspects in Software (2004)
33. Swint, G.S., et al.: Clearwater: extensible, flexible, modular code generation. In: 20th IEEE/ACM International Conference on Automated software engineering. ACM (2005)
34. Visser, E.: Meta-programming with concrete object syntax. In: Batory, D., Consel, C., Taha, W. (eds.) GPCE 2002. LNCS, vol. 2487, pp. 299–315. Springer, Heidelberg (2002). https://doi.org/10.1007/3-540-45821-2_19
35. Voelter, M., et al.: DSL Engineering - Designing, Implementing and Using Domain-Specific Languages (2013). dslbook.org
36. Wachsmuth, G.: A formal way from text to code templates. In: Chechik, M., Wirsing, M. (eds.) FASE 2009. LNCS, vol. 5503, pp. 109–123. Springer, Heidelberg (2009). https://doi.org/10.1007/978-3-642-00593-0_8
37. www: OMG UML Specification, October 2015. http://www.omg.org/spec/UML/2.5/
38. www: openarchitectureware, October 2015. https://web.archive.org/web/20140225123932/http://www.openarchitectureware.org/index.php
39. www: Apache maven project, August 2017. https://maven.apache.org/
40. Zschaler, S., Rashid, A.: Symmetric language-aware aspects for modular code generators. Technical Report TR-11-01, King's College, Department of Informatics (2011)
41. Zschaler, S., Rashid, A.: Towards modular code generators using symmetric language-aware aspects. In: Proceedings of the 1st International Workshop on Free Composition. FREECO 2011, pp. 6:1–6:5. ACM, New York (2011)

Model-Based Programming
for Multi-processor Platforms
with TTool/DIPLODOCUS and OMC

Andrea Enrici[1]([✉]), Julien Lallet[1], Renaud Pacalet[2], Ludovic Apvrille[2],
Karol Desnos[3], and Imran Latif[1]

[1] Nokia Bell Labs, Centre de Villarceaux, 91620 Nozay, France
{andrea.enrici,julien.lallet,imran.latif}@nokia-bell-labs.com
[2] LTCI, Télécom ParisTech, Université Paris-Saclay, 75013 Paris, France
{renaud.pacalet,ludovic.apvrille}@telecom-paristech.fr
[3] INSA Rennes, IETR, UBL, CNRS UMR 6164, 35708 Rennes, France
karol.desnos@insa-rennes.fr

Abstract. The complexity of today's multi-processor architectures
raises the need to increase the level of abstraction of software development paradigms above third-generation programming languages (e.g.,
C/C++). Code generation from model-based specifications is considered
as a promising approach to increase the productivity and quality of software development, with respect to traditional paradigms where code is
used as the main artifact to develop software. In this context, powerful
and robust tools are needed in order to accomplish the transition from
code-based programming to model-based programming. In this paper
we propose a novel approach and tools where system-level models are
compiled into standard C code while optimizing the system's memory
footprint. We show the effectiveness of our approach with the model-
based programming of UML/SysML diagrams for a 5G decoder. From
the compiled C code, we generate both a software implementation for a
Digital Signal Processor platform and a hardware-software implementation for a platform based on hardware Intellectual Property (IP) blocks.
Our optimizations achieve a memory footprint reduction of 80.07% and
88.93%, respectively.

Keywords: Model-based engineering · MPSoC programming ·
UML/SysML

1 Introduction

In order to support the data need of Internet of things and cloud computing, 5G
networks are expected to provide a 10x higher data-rate with regards to 4G networks. Future architectures supporting 5G networks will probably be based on
both dedicated circuits in base stations and on more flexible computing solutions

© Springer Nature Switzerland AG 2019
S. Hammoudi et al. (Eds.): MODELSWARD 2018, CCIS 991, pp. 56–81, 2019.
https://doi.org/10.1007/978-3-030-11030-7_4

such as cloud systems equipped with both programmable and configurable components (CPUs, Digital Signal Processors - DSPs, Field Programmable Gate Arrays - FPGAs). Because of the high complexity and heterogeneity of these architectures, developing signal-processing application will become a nightmare for engineers. Thus, a new programming paradigm is needed in order to increase the quality (e.g., scheduling, memory footprint) and productivity (e.g., correct-by-construction code generation) of application software development.

Model-Driven Engineering (MDE) [1] is widely accepted as a promising software development paradigm to answer the above-mentioned issues. MDE combines domain-specific modeling languages to abstract the structure, behavior and requirements of a system under design, with transformation engines and generators. The latter analyze models and produce artifacts such as source code, simulation, verification inputs or alternative model representations. In the context of MDE, model-based code generation is incorrectly seen as a replacement for programming. On the contrary, it actually *is* an alternative programming paradigm, where the languages aim at abstracting software systems rather than hardware computing mechanisms [2]. Similarly to programming languages, also modeling languages have features (e.g., UML relationships) that are well suited to described certain things (e.g., relations among functions or classes) and are not suited to describe some other things (e.g., indexing of arrays).

The process of creating models from existing software systems is, as of today, well understood. However, the reverse process of compiling model-based specifications into executable implementations still remains an open issue. Here, multiple challenges arise from the desire to generate code for different architecture topologies (e.g., IP-based platforms, Multi-Processor Systems-on-Chip - MPSoC), implementations (i.e., software, hardware and mixed hardware-software) and execution units (e.g., DSPs, CPUs, Hardware Accelerators).

In this paper we propose tools and a methodology to enhance the application software development for MPSoC platforms from system-level models. Our approach for model-based programming is centered around a model development environment, TTool/DIPLODOCUS [3,4] and the Optimizing Model Compiler [5] (OMC). TTool/DIPLODOCUS allows the creation, editing and debugging of UML/SysML diagrams, while OMC is a model-to-code compiler that takes as input system-level models (i.e., application, communications and architecture). It converts them into Intermediate Representations (IRs) and attempts to optimize the system's memory footprint. OMC produces as output standard C code for the memory allocation and scheduling of signal-processing operations, regardless of the system's final realization technology (e.g., FPGA, Application Specific Integrated Circuit - ASIC). As a practical case study we propose the model-based design of a 5G datalink-layer decoder. The C program compiled from the decoder's models is transformed into executable implementations for (i) a DSP-based platform (software executable file further compiled with GNU/gcc) and (ii) a hardware IP-based platform (FPGA bitstream) by a traditional software compiler and a SoC design tool (Xilinx SDx).

The rest of the paper is organized as follows. Section 2 positions our work with respect to related contributions. The overall methodology for model-based programming is presented in Sect. 3. This is followed by the structure of a generic model compiler in Sect. 4. The model development environment that we selected, TTool/DIPLODOCUS, is briefly described in Sect. 5. The Optimizing Model Compiler (OMC) is presented in Sect. 6. Section 7 shows how TTool/DIPLODO-CUS and OMC are applied to program the 5G decoder. Section 8 concludes this paper.

2   Related Work

From a code generation perspective, the relationship between UML models and text code can be classified as one of two types: one-to-one (UML specifications are translated in one output language) or one-to-many (specifications in multiple languages are generated from a UML diagrams) [6].

Code generators that fall in the category of the one-to-one relationship disambiguate the semantics of UML models for a specific executable language via extension mechanisms (e.g., stereotypes, constraints, tagged values) that are defined by the user or available in a given profile. Many works propose one-to-one mapping rules for SoC languages such as C [7], C++ [8], Verilog [9], VHDL [10] and SystemC [11–13]. Our work can also be classified as a one-to-one code generator, where mapping rules are defined by the compiler's frontend and backend implementations (Sect. 6).

As opposed to one-to-one, one-to-many code generators do not necessarily preserve a correspondence between the structure of the input UML models and the structure of the generated code. Only the system's behavior is preserved (behavioral code generation). In terms of semantics, the transition between input UML diagrams and multiple outputs is performed by relying on additional textual specifications in dedicated languages.

A representative hardware/software co-design framework that employs one-to-many translation rules based on MARTE [14] is Gaspard2 (Graphical Array Specification for Parallel and Distributed Computing) [15,16]. Here, thanks to the notion of *Deployment*, an Elementary Component (a resource or a functionality in a MARTE model) can be related to implementation code that specifies low-level behavioral or structural details in programming languages (e.g., C/C++) for formal verification, simulation, software execution and hardware synthesis.

One-to-many code generation is also possible from xUML and fUML-Alf. When programming in executable UML (xUML) or *executable and translatable UML* (xtUML) [17,18], a system's application is captured in the metamodel. The model compiler comprises some library code and a set of rules that are interpreted against the metamodel to produce text for a target SoC (e.g., C++ classes, C structs; VHDL specifications for hardware registers).

The Foundational Subset for Executable UML Models (fUML) [19] and the Action Language for fUML (Alf) [20] standard were created to go beyond xUML and specify a reasonable subset of UML with a precise semantics, in order not to be specific to any executable modeling methodology. The syntax of Alf is borrowed from Java, C, C++ and C#.

xUML and fUML-Alf aim to reduce the complexity of UML to a minimum semantically well-defined subset, that is independent of any implementation language. In terms of code generation, this permits to reach the highest abstraction level and degree of independence with regard to implementation details. To the best of our knowledge, no compiler exists that attempts to optimize the performance of code generated from xUML/fUML-Alf as implemented by our UML-to-C compiler.

Prominent examples of commercial tools that allow the generation of SoC implementations are National Instruments LabVIEW Communications System Design [21] and MATLAB (MAtrix LABoratory) [22]. With respect to UML-/SysML/MARTE, which are generic, the languages in use by these tools are specific to signal-processing systems and, by construction, have a narrower but more precise semantics. The latter is accompanied by constructs that feature high simplicity (e.g., possibility to not declare data types) and hide information about the underlying platform (e.g., absence of explicit allocation of memory banks). While this permits for higher productivity and fast development cycles, the resulting executables may have poorer performance than those generated from lower-level languages (e.g., ANSI C, Embedded C [23]). From a compiler perspective, such high-level features require more complex analysis to be disambiguated and produce efficient optimizations.

The MPSoC Application Programming Studio (MAPS) [24,25] is a work that shares many commonalities with our approach. MAPS is a compilation framework for heterogeneous MPSoCs that targets streaming applications. The most important difference between our contributions and MAPS is the input formalism. MAPS takes as input specifications written in the CPN (C for Process Networks) programming language. The latter is an extension of the C language that adds features to describe the modeling constructs (processes and channels) of Kahn Process Networks [26]. MAPS' core component is the CPN-to-C compiler. It scans and parses CPN input files and first builds an Abstract Syntax Tree (AST) for each processor in the target platform. The AST is transformed to produce plain C code, where the CPN extensions are transformed into platform-specific API calls (e.g., FIFO primitives). In the case of our compiler, Synchronous Data Flow graphs, that are semantically equivalent to KPNs, are used as intermediate representations rather than in input specifications.

3   Model-Based Programming Flow

In the embedded systems community, nearly 90% of the software developers nowadays use C and C++ [27] that have an underlying sequential programming model. Nevertheless, multi-processor platforms cannot be efficiently programmed with the constructs proposed by classical sequential programming languages (e.g., functions in C, methods in C++, arrays in C/C++). The reason being that, such constructs have a low level of abstraction that is not sufficient to tackle the complexity of the services and hardware computing paradigm offered by multi-processor architectures. These constructs cannot be translated

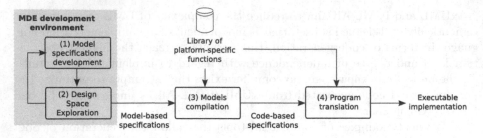

Fig. 1. The software development flow of executable implementations from system-level models.

by compilers into executable instructions in a way that improves the quality and productivity of software, from the user perspective. For these reasons, we advocate that modeling languages (e.g., UML/SysML/MARTE, SDF, KPN, AADL, Simulink) that provide higher-level abstractions (e.g., channels, actors) are more suitable to the task of programming structural aspects (e.g., memory footprint, scheduling) of multi-processor platforms.

Figure 1 illustrates the methodology that we propose to develop executable implementations from system-level specifications expressed in a modeling language. These specifications are written in a MDE development environment, step (1) in Fig. 1, such as those described in [28]. Here, the system under design is described in a modeling language where models are used to capture the system's functionality (i.e., behavior) and the target platform (i.e., the behavior and structure of the available resources). In this phase, models are used as the primary artifact for software development. Models are created, edited and debugged (e.g., formal verification, simulation, profiling) until legal specifications are obtained. Such specifications respect the syntax and semantics of the modeling language and design constraints. This is similar to the way code is created, edited and debugged in traditional Integrated Development Environments (IDE) such as Eclipse [29]. Subsequently, step (2) in Fig. 1, a Design Space Exploration (DSE) phase takes place, where alternative partitions (i.e., mappings) of the system's functionality onto the available resources are explored until a solution that satisfies some desired requirements (e.g., power consumption, latency, throughput) is found to be realized.

Next, model-based specifications for the best mapping are compiled into code, step (3) in Fig. 1, expressed in a programming language (e.g., C/C++). From this point, code becomes the primary artifact for software development as in traditional software engineering methodologies. Further development may take place where, for instance, the program produced by the model compiler is manually completed with code from an external library (e.g., I/O specific code, platform-specific code for OS or middleware).

A final implementation is produced by means of a further translation step, (4) in Fig. 1. This implementation can be realized entirely in software (e.g., an application that runs on top of an Operating System onto a general-purpose control processor) or in hardware (e.g., a hardware IP-based design) or both (e.g., some functionalities are executed by a general-purpose control processor and some are accelerated in hardware). In the case of implementations that require some functionality to be realized in hardware, the translation is performed by a Computer Aided Design (CAD) toolsuite (e.g., Xilinx Vivado High Level Synthesis). In case of pure software implementations, the translation occurs by means of a traditional programming-language compiler (e.g., GNU/gcc/g++, clang, TurboC). In the next section, we describe the generic structure of a system-level model compiler.

4   The Structure of a Model Compiler

As shown in Fig. 2, the structure of the compiler that we propose in this paper is inspired by those of classical compilers [30] for programming languages. The main difference lies in the level of abstraction at which our compiler operates, known as *system-level* [31]. Classical compilers target uni-processor platforms centralized around a single processing element (e.g., a general-purpose control processor, a specialized Digital Signal Processor - DSP) that is connected via a bus to a memory unit. On the contrary, the scale at which a model compiler operates is the one of an entire multi-processor platform that is composed of several computation, communication and storage units. For instance, the backend in a programming language compiler generates code that allocates array pointers to CPU registers. In evolution with this, code produced by the backend in a model compiler, allocates data arrays to entire memory areas (e.g., banks in a DRAM memory).

In the following, we present an overview of such a model compiler, regardless of the input modeling language. We conclude this section with a discussion about the impact of modeling languages and programming languages onto the implementation of a multi-processor compiler.

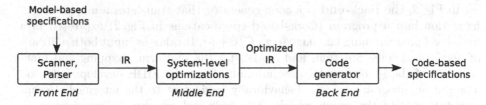

Fig. 2. The structure of a system-level model compiler.

4.1   Overview

The front-end in Fig. 2 is dedicated to "understanding", with scanning and parsing techniques, input specifications denoted in a specific modeling language. Knowledge about the structure and behavior of the system under design (e.g., dependencies between functions, mapping constraints) is encoded into Intermediate Representations, IR in Fig. 2 (e.g., a directed graph). By definition, in programming-language compilers, an Intermediate Representation is an abstraction of the given source code. In the context of modeling-language compilers where the input specifications are models themselves, also IRs are models. The IR's structure or the modeling language used to express such an IR thus becomes the IR's metamodel. It follows that the process of producing IRs from input models is a model-to-model transformation.

The purpose of the **middle-end** in Fig. 2 is to attempt to rewrite IRs in a way that is more convenient to optimize the performance of the final implementation in terms of memory management, power consumption, throughput, etc. Such a rewriting results in a second intermediate representation, Optimized IR in Fig. 2. This optimized IR must respect the partitioning of functions onto resources defined by the Design Space Exploration phase (Fig. 1), in order to comply to the DSE's design constraints (e.g., latency, throughput, power consumption). For instance, if this partitioning is static, a function f that has been allocated to unit u_1, f cannot migrate to a different unit u_2 at run-time. Examples of optimizations that can be performed at this stage are: optimizations that reduce the memory occupancy of storage units, scheduling optimizations that minimize the workload of processing and communication units. To perform these optimizations, as shown in Fig. 2, the middle-end also takes as input models of the system's platform and mapping. This is not the case of middle-ends for uni-processor compilers, where only the back-end takes as input information about the target platform.

In terms of the granularity level of optimizations, working at system-level of abstraction allows to focus on parallelism patterns (e.g., task-level) that are more coarse-grained than those in classical programming-language compilers (e.g., basic blocks). As a consequence, the compiler benefits from managing smaller IRs with respect to equivalent IRs produced from input specifications based on programming languages. In turn, this enables the compiler to implement more aggressive performance evaluation, data-flow analysis (e.g., global analysis) and program transformations.

In Fig. 2, the **back-end** is a code generator that translates a mapping configuration into a program (Code-based specifications in Fig. 2) expressed in a high-level programming language (e.g., C/C++). It takes as input both a library of platform-specific functions and models for the platform, mapping and functionality of the system under programming, from the MDE development tool. The output program must be behaviorally equivalent to the intermediate representations and the input models. The back-end schedules the execution of computation and communication operations, manages the allocation of physical memory regions and selects constructs of the output program's language that correspond to those in the IRs.

In multi-processor platforms, processing units are typically provided with dedicated tool-chains (e.g., C compilers, linkers and assemblers). The model compiler's back-end generates code that is further translated by these processor-specific tool-chains (Program translation in Fig. 1). In this sense, a model compiler can be seen as a *meta-compiler* that coordinates standard uni-processor compilers.

4.2   Discussion

Generally speaking, the input specifications' formalism impacts a compiler's intermediate representations and the functionality implemented by each building block (front-end, middle-end and back-end). Three types of formalisms can be used to program multi-processor platforms: modeling languages (e.g., UML/SysML/MARTE, SDF, KPN, AADL, Simulink), parallel programming languages (e.g., POSIX threads [32], Message Passing Interface - MPI [33], OpenMP [34]) and sequential programming languages (e.g., C/C++). In this subsection we address two aspects that have the most profound impact: (i) how parallelism is expressed and (ii) the granularity level of a formalism's constructs. For a more in-depth discussion we refer the reader to [35].

How parallelism is expressed influences the functionality implemented in the compiler's front-end. In this context a marking line can be drawn between sequential and parallel formalisms. When sequential programming languages are used, the compiler's front-end must implement dedicated techniques to extract parallelism from sequential code (i.e., static analysis, dynamic analysis, speculative execution). Conversely, this added complexity is absent with formalisms that naturally express parallelism.

The second most important criteria that impacts a compiler's implementation is the granularity level offered by a formalism's constructs to manipulate data and control instructions (e.g., data structures and operations on these data structures). This impacts the size and expressiveness of the compiler's intermediate representations, the optimizations that can be performed on these IRs as well as the source code that can be generated by the compiler's back-end. In this context, a marking line can be drawn between modeling and programming languages. Modeling languages typically abstracts away the low-level constructs used by programming languages to manipulate data and control instructions (e.g., pointers, variable initialization). As such, intermediate representations that are derived from modeling languages are lighter (e.g., graphs of smaller size) and can be used to perform more aggressive optimizations (e.g., global data-flow analysis). The implementations of these optimizations in the compiler's middle-end is significantly facilitated by the absence of pointers in modeling languages. However, the abstractions offered by modeling languages often prevent the compiler's back-end to generate complete software implementations. These implementations must be either manually completed by the user, or require the user to accompany the input models with specifications written in programming languages that are then used by the compiler's back-end to produce a complete implementation (e.g., Alf for fUML). In either case, the additional specifications correspond to low-level operations that manipulate and access data structures (e.g., arrays, structs, lists).

5   Model-Based Development in TTool/DIPLODOCUS

In the context of our research on the efficient programming of signal-processing systems for MPSoC platforms, we selected UML/SysML as modeling language and TTool/DIPLODOCUS as a development environment for model-based specifications.

The choice of using UML/SysML as modeling language is motivated by the following reasons. First, it is widely used in the software development community where it was initially created as a specification language to abstract large software systems. Here, UML/SysML Activity diagrams have become an established notation to capture control and data-flow at various level of abstractions. Their semantics makes them particularly suited to describe the behavior of the systems we target. With respect to sequential programming languages, UML/SysML diagrams express parallelism explicitly and offer richer constructs than other concurrent modeling languages such as SDF [36] and KPN [26]. The latter do not express the internal behavior of processing and communication operations that are modeled in terms of black-boxes interconnected by data dependencies. Instead, such an internal behavior can be expressed by means of UML/SysML Activity diagrams that a compiler's middle-end can analyze in the attempt to optimize the system's behavior.

TTool/DIPLODOCUS [37] is a framework for the hardware/software co-design of data-flow systems from UML/SysML diagrams. It was selected as it is open source, lightweight and offers system-level modeling and debugging features that are unavailable in concurrent tools for UML design of embedded systems. More precisely, TTool [3] is the name of the toolkit that allows to create, edit and validate UML/SysML diagrams for different profiles (e.g., Avatar [38], SysMLSec [39]). DIPLODOCUS [4] is the profile dedicated to the hardware/software co-design of data-flow systems.

Figure 3 shows the model development methodology (called Ψ-chart [40]) that is supported by TTool/DIPLODOCUS to design source models for the compiler OMC, Sect. 6. In TTool/DIPLODOCUS, the functionality of the system under design (Application model, 1.1 in Fig. 3) is denoted with SysML Block Definition and Block Instance diagrams that are composed by a set of blocks interconnected by data and control dependencies via ports and channels. The internal behavior

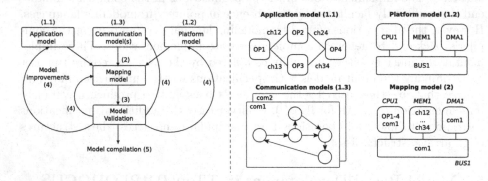

Fig. 3. The Ψ-chart development methodology (left side) and a graphical visualization of its constituent models (right side) that are supported by TTool/DIPLODOCUS.

of each block is described by a SysML Activity Diagram. An application model is based on the two following abstraction principles:

- Data abstraction: only the amount of data exchanged between application blocks is modeled. Internal decisions that depend on the value of data are expressed in terms of non-deterministic and static operators (i.e., conditional choices based on the value of random variables).
- Algorithmic abstraction: algorithms are abstracted with cost operators that express the complexity of processing items in terms of the number of operations required to transform data (e.g., number of integer operations).

The above abstraction principles have been defined as TTool/DIPLODOCUS targets early design and DSE, when not all the details about a system's application (e.g., value and type of data) and platform (e.g., Operating System, size and policy of cache memories for a CPU) are known. The validation of the effectiveness of these abstractions has been described in [Jaber 2011], where TTool/DIPLODOCUS was used for the design of the physical layer of a LTE base station jointly with Freescale Semiconductors.

The resources of the system under design (Platform model, 1.2 in Fig. 3) are denoted with a UML Deployment Diagram that represents a set of interconnected resources, e.g., bus, CPU and its operating system, DMA, memory. These resources are characterized by performance parameters (e.g., the scheduling policy and the number of cores for a CPU) that are used for validation and debugging purposes (simulation and formal verification).

The communication protocols (e.g., DMA transfers) are captured with dedicated diagrams (Communication models, 1.3 in Fig. 3) separately from the application and platform [41]. UML Activity Diagrams capture the steps that compose a communication protocols (e.g., configuration, acknowledgement) while UML Sequence diagrams denote message exchanges among master and slave components.

A partitioning of the system's functionality onto the available resources (Mapping model, 2 in Fig. 3) is created from a platform model where dedicated UML artifacts are added to map the computations and their dependencies. The abstract cost operators are assigned a value according to the performance characteristics (e.g., operating frequency) of the platform's units.

Designs in TTool/DIPLODOCUS can be validated (step 3 in Fig. 3) by simulating the workload of computations and data-transfers [42]. A formal verification engine [42] is also available to verify system properties (e.g., liveness, reachability, scheduling). Validation can be performed both manually via the tool's GUI or automatically via a set of scripts that configure the simulation and formal verification engines to evaluate different mapping alternatives. The simulator's GUI also provides a rich set of debugging features that allow the user to animate and execute UML/SysML diagrams step-by-step, inspect variables' values, save and load execution traces, etc.

Models are iteratively debugged, validated and improved (steps 3–4 in Fig. 3), until legal specifications can be compiled into implementations (step 5 in Fig. 3).

6   OMC: The Optimizing Model Compiler

In this section, we describe an implementation of the model compiler in Fig. 2 that results into OMC (Optimizing Model Compiler), Fig. 4. The current implementation is the result of a continuous research work that first started with the code generation engine in [40]. With respect to the latter, OMC's middle-end has been extended with memory allocation optimizations and the back-end has been extended with the capability to target any platform whose architecture can be designed in TTool/DIPLODOCUS. Similarly to Integrated Development Environments for programming languages (e.g., Eclipse), TTool/DIPLODOCUS allows to select OMC as model compiler by means of a plugin.

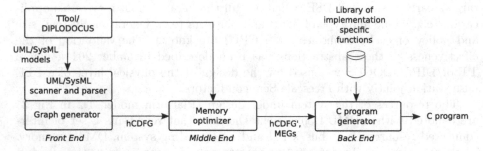

Fig. 4. The structure of OMC, the Optimizing Model Compiler.

6.1   Front-End

The front-end in Fig. 4 converts UML/SysML models that describe a system's functionality into a first intermediate representation: hCDFG, a hierarchical Control and Data Flow Graph. The latter is defined as a directed multigraph $G = <N, E>$. N is a set of nodes derived from a DIPLODOCUS Block Definition diagram that capture both data and control operations; each node $n \in N$ is itself a graph that describes the internal behavior of an operation (derived from DIPLODOCUS Activity diagrams). E is a set of edges that capture the data and control dependencies among operations (relations among DIPLODOCUS Blocks). This intermediate representation is derived from UML/SysML diagrams which have a data-flow execution semantics. As a consequence, the hCDFG's has the execution semantics of a Synchronous Data-Flow (SDF) graph [36]. In a SDF graph, nodes (actors) represent processing entities interconnected by a set of First-In First-Out (FIFO) data queues. An actor starts execution (firing) when its incoming FIFO(s) contains enough tokens, it cannot be preempted and produces tokens onto its outgoing FIFO(s). The number of tokens consumed/produced by each firing is a fixed scalar that is annotated with the graph edges. As actors have no state in the SDF Model of Computation (MoC), if enough tokens are available, an actor can start several executions in parallel. For this reason, SDF graphs naturally express the parallelism of signal-processing applications and can be statically analyzed during compilation for memory allocation optimizations.

6.2   Middle-End

In OMC's middle-end, Fig. 5, we propose a system-level memory optimizer that minimizes the footprint of the *logical* buffers associated to edges in the hCDFG. We differentiate between *logical* and *physical* buffers. A physical buffer defines a range of memory addresses of a physical memory device (e.g., a Random Access Memory - RAM). A logical buffer, instead, is a virtual address space that can be mapped onto one or multiple physical buffers.

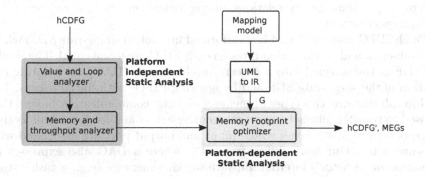

Fig. 5. The Optimizing Model Compiler's middle-end.

Value and Loop Analyzer. Value analysis in traditional program analysis attempts to determine the values in a processor's registers for every program point and execution context [30]. Similarly, in OMC, in OMC, this step aims to assign a value to the control variables that determine the size and direction of the data-flows among signal-processing operations, for every execution scenario. The analyzer starts from the hCDFG source vertex' graph. The latter is traversed and a value is assigned for all its variables. This determines a value to the consumption and production rates of hCDFG edges as well as to the number of initial tokens that the source vertex exchanges with its neighbors. The latter are iteratively examined and the variables' values are propagated to their neighbors until the hCDFG sink vertex is reached. In case these values cannot be determined exactly (e.g., presence of random operators in the input models), the analyzer attempts to determine a lower and an upper bound.

Memory and Throughput Analyzer. The results of the Value and Loop analyzer are used to determine the memory footprint and the throughput of each hCDFG vertex. The throughput is given by the amount of data that is exchanged on the edges of a hCDFG node. As edges in the hCDFG are associated to logical First-In-First-Out (FIFO) buffers, the throughput of all edges of a hCDFG node determines its memory footprint. The throughput and the memory footprint is computed by multiplying the tokens exchanged on input/output edges by the size of the tokens' data type that is specified in the input DIPLODOCUS models (e.g., int16, cpx32).

The values determined by the Value and Loop analyzer and by the Memory and Throughput analyzer are annotated to the hCDFG graph that results into hCDFG'.

Memory Footprint Optimizer. Our optimizer implements the allocation techniques presented in [43] that we adapted to allow the sharing of input/output buffers of actors, similarly to the memory reuse techniques presented in [44]. Essentially, the optimizer performs a series of graph transformations to deduce a set of graphs that specify relations among logical buffers that can or cannot share physical memory.

The hCDFG graph in Fig. 4 is transformed first into a single-rate SDF, where the production and consumption rates on each FIFO are made equal. The single-rate SDF is transformed into a Direct Acyclic Graph (DAG) by isolating one iteration of the single-rate SDF and by ignoring FIFOs with initial tokens. The DAG graph contains two types of memory objects: communication buffers that are used to transfer tokens between consecutive actors and feedback buffers that correspond to feedback edges whose input and output port are associated with the same actor. Our work differs from [43], where a DAG also expresses an estimation of an actor's internal software working memory (e.g., a task's stack space allocated by an Operating System onto a general-purpose CPU). This is because we target platforms composed of hardware IP blocks (Sect. 7) whose internal memory is defined by the hardware design of a IP block itself and cannot be controlled with software.

From the mapping model, scheduling information is added to the DAG. Subsequently, a Memory Exclusion Graph (MEG) is derived. Nodes in the MEG represent logical memory objects: FIFO buffers whose size is equal to the number of tokens in the single-rate SDF. Edges in the MEG link logical FIFO buffers that cannot be allocated to overlapping physical buffers. The MEG is then updated with mapping information from the input models that specifies the execution constraints (scheduling) for each signal-processing operation. This allows to remove edges (exclusion relations) between nodes in the MEG. The purpose of this operation is to merge logical buffers so that physical buffers in the executable code can share common memory regions, thus reducing the total footprint of the software application produced by OMC.

At this point, the heuristics proposed in [43] is applied to compute a lower bound for the memory of the physical buffers. This bound is defined in [45] as the weight of a Maximum Weight Clique (MWC). A *clique* is a subgraph of MEG vertices within which each pair of vertices is linked with an edge. As the memory objects of a clique cannot share memory space because they mutually exclude each other, the weight of a clique gives a lower bound to the amount of memory that must be allocated for all of the clique's buffers. This amount is equal to the sum of the sizes of all clique's buffers.

The pseudo-code of the heuristics proposed in [43] is shown in Algorithm 1. In each iteration of the main loop (lines 6–13) in Algorithm 1, minimum cost vertices v^* are removed from C (line 8). If multiple vertices have the same cost,

---

Algorithm 1. The MWC heuristics.

```
/* C = the clique                                              */
/* nb_edges = number of edges in C                             */
/* cost(·) = cost function of C                                */
/* v = generic vertex in C                                     */
/* w(v) = weight of vertex v                                   */
/* N(v) = neighbor vertices of v                               */
/* |N(v)| = lowest number of v's neighbors                     */
```

1 $C \leftarrow V$
2 $nb_{edges} \leftarrow |E|$
3 **foreach** $v \in C$ **do**
4 $\quad | \quad cost(v) \leftarrow w(x) + \sum_{v' \in N(v)} w(v')$
5 **end**
6 **while** $|C| > 1$ **and** $\frac{2 \cdot nb_{edges}}{|C| \cdot (|C|-1)} < 1.0$ **do**
7 $\quad$ *Select v^* from V that minimizes cost(·)*
8 $\quad$ $C \leftarrow C \backslash \{v^*\}$
9 $\quad$ $nb_{edges} \leftarrow nb_{edges} - |N(v^*) \cap C|$
10 $\quad$ **foreach** $v \in \{N(v^*) \cap C\}$ **do**
11 $\quad \quad | \quad cost(v) \leftarrow cost(v) - w(v^*)$
12 $\quad$ **end**
13 **end**
14 *Select a vertex $v_{random} \in C$*
15 **foreach** $v \in \{N(v_{random}) \backslash C\}$ **do**
16 $\quad$ **if** $C \subset N(v)$ **then**
17 $\quad \quad | \quad C \leftarrow C \cup \{v\}$
18 $\quad$ **end**
19 **end**

---

the vertex v with the lowest number of neighbors $|N(v)|$ is removed. If the number of neighbors is equal, then the vertex v with the smallest weight $w(v)$ is removed. If there are still multiple vertices with equal properties, a random vertex v_{random} is selected. The loop iterates until the vertices in C form a clique. This condition is verified, line 6, by comparing the edge density of a clique with the edge density of the MEG subgraph formed by the remaining vertices in C. The edge density of a clique is defined as the ratio between existing exclusions and all possible exclusions. Such density is equal to 1.0 in the case of the complete MEG. The number of edges, nb_{edges}, is decremented at line 9 by the number of edges in L that link the removed vertex v^* to vertices in C. Lines 10–12 update the costs of the remaining vertices for the next iteration. The complexity of the heuristic algorithm is of the order of magnitude of $O(|V|^2)$, where $|V|$ is the number of vertices of the MEG subgraph.

This MEG is further split into separates MEGs, one for each memory unit in the target platform onto which physical buffers must be allocated. This split is performed according to the algorithm described in [44], where FIFO buffers whose producer and consumer are mapped onto different processors are duplicated in different MEGs.

6.3   Back-End

OMC's back-end, Fig. 6, translates hCDFG' and the MEGs into a C program that can run as a user-space application on top of a general-purpose Operating System. The back-end is composed of three code generators. The Memory Manager code generator generates a static memory allocation for the buffers in the Memory Exclusion Graph. Buffers whose lifetimes overlap are assigned to dedicated memory areas, whereas buffers whose lifetimes do not overlap are assigned to shared memory areas. The Scheduler code generator produces a static scheduling of operations that corresponds to the scheduling used by the middle-end to produce the MEG graphs. The Operation code generator translates each operation in hCDFG' with 3 C routines for initialization, execution and clean-up purposes (Fig. 4). Initialization and clean-up routines are called once, when the program starts and terminates, respectively. These routines manipulate the software data structures that are needed by processing units in the target platform to prepare and clean up the execution of a node in hCDFG'. Execution routines (implementation-specific functions in Fig. 4) are added to each actor from an external library. They trigger the execution of an operation on the hardware.

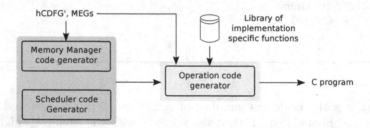

Fig. 6. The Optimizing Model Compiler's back-end.

In the current implementation of the compiler, the body of execution routines must be manually written by a user and included in the final source code via dedicated C header files. These execution routines specify, at a lower level of abstraction, the implementation details of the signal-processing algorithms that are described, at system-level, by the input UML/SysML diagrams. Given the real-time nature of the systems that we aim to program, it is mandatory to specify these algorithms with a less abstract language (i.e., C) that offers constructs which match more closely the characteristics of the underlying hardware execution platform (e.g., memory alignment of struct fields to accelerate DMA transfers). In analogy with traditional C programs that embed assembly code for functionalities that are time-critical, our UML/SysML programs embed C code for functionalities that are time-critical at system-level of abstraction.

6.4   Discussion

In this OMC implementation, we did not include any environment for the analysis of the IRs' models and their transformations as this goes out of the scope of our current research interests. As described in [46], techniques such as generative approaches, model mapping, Domain Specific Languages and metamodel instrumentation exist to guarantee the correctness and maintainability of IR transformations. However, due to scalability reasons, their use is difficult to apply to research compilers. It is, however, a practically surmountable problem that can be solved by developing additional features to the model compiler. In the context of the case study of Sect. 7, we manually verified the equivalence between (i) the relations in graphs hCDFG and hCDFG' (ii) the scheduling of operations in the output C program and (iii) the inter-operation dependencies in the input models.

Portability. This implementation of the model compiler addresses platforms where the scheduling of operations is centrally executed by a single general-purpose control processor. The latter configures and dispatches the execution of operations to a set of physically distributed units (e.g., DSPs, DMAs, IPs), according to events generated upon the consumption/production of data by computation and communication operations. For each platform, a dedicated library of implementation-specific functions must be provided by re-using those from other projects as templates. To target designs where the control code of an application is fragmented into separate executables that each run onto different CPUs, OMC must be extended to produce multiple executables, include synchronization primitives among multiple units, etc.

In order to use this OMC's implementation with a MDE tool other than TTool/DIPLODOCUS, the user needs to write a new plug-in for the front-end's scanner and parser. The existing plug-in can be used as a template to reduce development efforts.

Debugging. In our model-based programming approach, debugging is done at different locations: in TTool/DIPLODOCUS, in the output C program (OMC's output, Fig. 6) and the library's implementation-specific functions (e.g., Valgrind, gdb). Transformations of the Intermediate Representations can be manually debugged by comparing the data-flow relations among nodes in hCDFG, hCDFG' and those between SysML blocks in the input models. Also, simulation and formal verification techniques in TTool/DIPLODOCUS can be used to guarantee the correctness of the input UML/SysML models with respect to design requirements.

7   Case Study

According to the methodology in Fig. 1, we used TTool/DIPLODOCUS and OMC to develop software from the UML/SysML models of a 5G decoder for the uplink (SC-FDMA), single antenna case, Physical Uplink Shared channel (xPUSCH), based on the specifications in [47].

The algorithm of the signal-processing operations that compose the 5G decoder is shown in Fig. 7.

We captured this algorithm with a SysML Block Definition diagram containing 11 SysML Composite Block Components (1 for each signal-processing operation in Fig. 7 as well as one source and one sink components). Each Composite Block Component contains 2 SysML Primitive Block Components that are, in turn, each associated to a UML Activity diagram. Figure 8a shows the UML/SysML diagrams of operation 64QAM Demodulation. These diagrams are representative of the models for all the 5G decoder's operations. Here, the primitive block F_QAMDemod determines the amount of samples that the block X_QAMDemod must process. The latter transforms input samples into demodulated output samples. Figure 8b shows the the UML Activity diagrams of the primitive block X_Demod. Here, the amount of input and output samples is received from F_QAMDemod, operator (1) in Fig. 8b. Subsequently, a for-loop (2 in Fig. 8b) iteratively reads numBitsPerSampleIN samples from an input channel (3 in Fig. 8), processes them (4 in Fig. 8) and writes numBitsPerSampleOUT samples to an output channel (5 in Fig. 8). In Fig. 8, variables numBitsPerSampleIN and numBitsSampleOUT model 32-bits samples. The algorithm of the demodulation operations in Fig. 8 is abstracted by means of the cost operator EXECC($i\cdot$). The latter captures the complexity of an algorithm in terms of its number of operations onto complex data.

Table 1 lists the data produced and consumed by operations in Fig. 7, for an input subframe composed of 14 OFDM symbols and 41 LDPC code blocks.

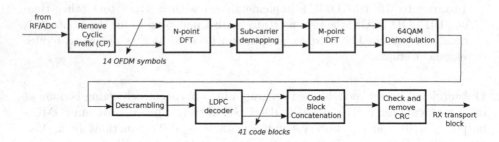

Fig. 7. The 5G decoder block diagram, as represented in [5].

In this case study we programmed two **target platforms**. One is **Embb** [48], a generic baseband architecture dedicated to signal-processing applications. Embb is composed of a Digital Signal Processing (DSP) part and a general purpose control part. The DSP part is composed of a set of Digital Signal Processing Units (DSPUs) interconnected by a crossbar. Each DSP unit is equipped with a Processing Sub-System (PSS) as computational unit, a Direct Memory Access controller (DMA) and a local memory called the Memory Sub-System

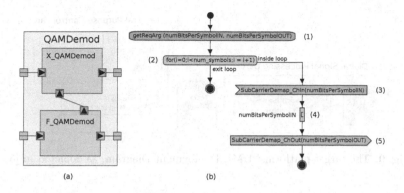

(a)   (b)

Fig. 8. The SysML Block diagram (a) and UML Activity (b) diagram for `64QAM Demodulation`, as illustrated in [5].

Table 1. Input/Output data of the decoder operations.

Operation	Input	Output
Remove CP	30720 samples (14 OFDM symbols)	2048 samples (1 OFDM symbol)
DFT	2048 samples	2048 samples
Sub-carrier demapping	2048 samples	1200 samples
IDFT	1200 samples	1200 samples
Demodulation	1200 resource elements	7200 soft bits
Descrambling	7200 soft bits	7200 soft bits
LDPC decoder	1944 soft bits	1620 hard bits
Code Block Concatenation	1620 hard bits	66416 hard bits
Remove CRC	66416 hard bits	66392 hard bits

(MSS). These DSPUs can be seen as programmable IPs that are more flexible than traditional fully hard-wired accelerators. The general purpose control part is composed of a RAM memory and of a CPU that configures and controls the processing operations performed by the DSPUs and the data transfers.

The architecture of the second target platform, a hardware **IP-based plat-form**, is composed of a programmable and of a configurable subsystem. The programmable subsystem executes control functions as well as signal-processing operations whose performance are not time critical. It is composed of a CPU and a RAM memory. The configurable subsystem accelerates performance-critical operations onto a dedicated hardware IP block. An IP block includes a processing core, a local memory and a DMA engine, similarly to a DSPU in Embb.

Thanks to the similarities in the structure of the two target platforms, we captured their architecture in the UML Deployment diagram of TTool/DIPLO-DOCUS in Fig. 9. In Fig. 9, the left-hand part describes the subsystem where the processing of data is accelerated. Here, a PE (Processing Element) block models

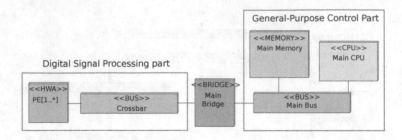

Fig. 9. The target platforms' UML Deployment Diagram, as depicted in [5].

the architecture of a DSPU in Embb or a hardware IP block. The TTool/DI-PLODOCUS model of a PE's internal architecture is depicted in Fig. 10. The right-hand side of Fig. 9 captures the control part of our two target platforms: a CPU and a memory units interconnected by a bus unit.

To program the two platforms, we instantiated a model such as the one in Fig. 9 that contains two Processing Elements for Embb and one Processing Element for the IP-based platform. The mapping information that results from the Design Space Exploration phase (Fig. 1) for each platform is listed in Table 2.

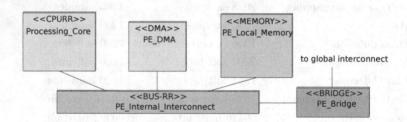

Fig. 10. The UML Deployment Diagram for a PE's in Fig. 9, as shown in [5].

7.1   The Model Compilation

The optimization techniques used by OMC reduce the memory footprint by sharing the physical buffers among the logical buffers of operations that are mapped to a given execution unit. To understand this optimization, Table 2 also shows the memory footprint of the logical buffers for the 5G decoder operations.

In the case of Embb, in Table 2, three sets of logical buffers can be identified, $\mathcal{B}_0$, $\mathcal{B}_1$, $\mathcal{B}_2$, that are associated to operations mapped onto the Main CPU, the FEP DSPU and the LDPC DSPU, respectively. For the Main CPU the logical buffers are $\mathcal{B}_0$ = {RemoveCP-DFT, Demodulation-Descrambling, Descrambling-LDPCDecoder, LDPCDecoder-CodeBlockConcatenation, CodeBlock-Concatenation-RemoveCRC}. For unit FEP DSPU, the buffers are $\mathcal{B}_1$ = {RemoveCP-DFT, DFT-IDFT, IDFT-Demodulation, Demodulation-Descram-bling}. For unit LDPC DSPU the buffers are $\mathcal{B}_2$ = {Descram-bling-LDPCDecoder, LDPCDecoder-Descrambling}.

Table 2. Memory footprint of the 5G decoder logical buffers and mapping configuration.

Operation	Memory footprint [bytes]		Mapping	
	Input	Output	Embb	IP-based platform
Remove CP	122880	14 × 8192	Main CPU (sw)	Main CPU (sw)
DFT	8192	8192	FEP DSPU (hw)	Main CPU (sw)
Demapping	//	//	Data transfer	Main CPU (sw)
IDFT	4800	4800	FEP DSPU (hw)	Main CPU (sw)
Demodulation	4800	7200	FEP DSPU (hw)	Main CPU (sw)
Descrambling	7200	7200	Main CPU (sw)	Main CPU (sw)
LDPDC Decoder	1944	202.5	LDPC DSPU (hw)	IP block (hw)
Code Block Concatenation	202.5	8302	Main CPU (sw)	Main CPU (sw)
Remove CRC	8302	8299	Main CPU (sw)	Main CPU (sw)

For the IP-based platform, based on the mapping in Table 2, we identify 2 sets of logical buffers, $\mathcal{B}_3$, $\mathcal{B}_4$, that are associated to operations mapped onto the Main CPU and the IP block, respectively. For the Main CPU the logical buffers are $\mathcal{B}_3 = \{$RemoveCP-DFT, DFT-Demapping, Demapping-IDFT, IDFT--Demodulation, Demodulation-Descrambling, Descrambling-LDPCDecoder, Code-Block-Concatenation-RemoveCRC$\}$. For the IP core, the logical buffers are $\mathcal{B}_4 = \{$Descrambling-LDPCDecoder, LDPCDecoder-CodeBlockConcatenation$\}$.

For each set of buffers, the middle-end produces a Memory Exclusion Graph. As mentioned in Sect. 6, the middle-end duplicates, in the Memory Exclusion Graphs, buffers whose producer and consumer operations are mapped onto different execution units. For instance, buffer Descrambling-LDPCDecoder is present in both $\mathcal{B}_0$ and $\mathcal{B}_2$, when compiling for Embb, and in both $\mathcal{B}_3$ and $\mathcal{B}_4$, when compiling for the IP-based platform.

When programming Embb, the back-end allocates 8192 bytes for $\mathcal{B}_1$ to the local memories of the FEP DSPU, which is equal to the size of RemoveCP-DFT. It allocates 1944 bytes for $\mathcal{B}_2$ to the local memory of the LDPC DSPU, which is equal to the size of buffer Descrambling-LDPCDecoder, and 8302 bytes for $\mathcal{B}_0$ to the Main CPU memory, which is equal to the size of buffer CodeBlockConcatenation-RemoveCRC. Assigning separate physical buffers to each of the logical buffers would have allocated 50976 bytes to the FEP local memory (the size of all logical buffers in $\mathcal{B}_1$), 2147 bytes to the LDPC processor's local memory (the size of all logical buffers in $\mathcal{B}_2$) and 39399 bytes to the main CPU memory (the size of $\mathcal{B}_0$). Compilation reduces the memory footprint of 83.88%, 9.46% and 78.93% for each of these three units, respectively. Overall, it reduces by 80.07% the memory used by the final executable code, with respect to pure translation-based approaches.

For the IP-based platform, the back-end allocates 8302 bytes for $\mathcal{B}_3$ to the main CPU memory (the programmable system), which is the size of buffer

CodeBlockConcatenation-LDPCDecoder, and 1944 bytes for $\mathscr{B}_4$ to the hardware IP-core memory (configurable system), which is the size of buffer Descrambling-LDPCDecoder. A pure translation-based approach would have reserved 90375 bytes (the size of $\mathscr{B}_3$) and 2147 bytes (the size of $\mathscr{B}_4$) to the main CPU and the hardware IP-core memories, respectively. Our compilation achieves a memory footprint reduction equal to 90.81% and 9.46%, respectively, for these two units. Overall, this reduces by 88.93% the memory used in the mixed hardware-software implementation.

These advanced memory optimizations were possible thanks to two types of analysis performed by the compiler's middle-end. First, thanks to the lifetime analysis of buffers, that is derived from the data dependencies and the scheduling information as described in Sect. 6. Secondly, thanks to the static analysis performed on the UML Activity diagrams that allows to retrieve information about the data dependencies that are *internal* to operations. More in details, if the input and output buffers of an operation have disjoint lifetimes (i.e., the input buffer is read before an output buffer of equal size is first written), these buffers can be allocated in the same physical memory space. For instance, the behavior described by the UML Activity diagram in Fig. 8 for the demodulation operation is representative for the models of all the 5G decoder operations. Here, numBitsPerSymbolIN data from the input channel (operator 3 in Fig. 8b) is always read before numBitsPerSymbolOUT data are written to the output channel (operator 5 in Fig. 8b). Hence, a subrange in the input logical buffer of size numBitsPerSymbolIN/4 bytes can be shared with the output logical buffer, when allocated to physical memory[1]. Similar techniques that take advantage of internal data dependencies are presented in [49,50].

The middle-end in OMC also optimizes an application's memory footprint by accounting for the mapping information of SDF actors onto a platform's execution units. This scheduling update does not impact the overall **timing properties** of the final executable. Specifically to this 5G decoder, its real-time properties are limited by two factors. First, by the lack of parallelism between operations that is inherent to the application in Fig. 7. Secondly, by the absence in the target platforms of multiple units capable to process different OFDM symbols in parallel. Because of the limited size of the FPGAs onto which we prototyped our platforms, it was only possible to instantiate one Front-End Processor unit and one LDPC processor in Embb as well as one hardware IP-block in the second platform (Design Space Exploration constraints). For instance, in Embb, the availability of only one FEP unit does not allow to pipeline the execution of operations DFT, Demapping, IDFT and Demodulation for consecutive OFDM symbols.

7.2　The Target Program Translation

In the case of Embb, the target C program is translated into an executable with GNU/gcc v.5.4.0 cross-compiled onto Ubuntu v.16.04.4. This executable (a

---

[1] In our DIPLODOCUS models, the number of data associated to I/O channels is expressed in terms of 32-bits samples.

pure software implementation of the input models) runs on the main CPU in Fig. 9 as a user-space application for Linux v.4.4.0-xilinx. In terms of the library of implementation specific functions that are necessary to produce a complete source C program, 371 functions were included in the source C program produced by OMC.

In the case of the IP-based platform, we translated the target C program with Xilinx SDx [51] into a mixed hardware-software implementation. The output of the Xilinx SDx translation process are a Linux image and an .elf file for the software part of the implementation, to be executed by the CPU of the programmable subsystem. The executable for the hardware part of the implementation is a FPGA bitstream. The latter is loaded into the target FPGA's configurable fabric by a Linux image that runs onto the FPGA's control processor (not represented in our models). The number of functions included to the source C program produced by OMC amounts to 33.

7.3 Discussion

With respect to code-generation approaches based on un-optimized translations of model (Sect. 2), we showed that optimizing non-functional properties (i.e., memory footprint) of models can result in significant performance improvement. These improvements do not alter the semantics of the source models. In this case study, models do not require to be accompanied by additional specifications for their semantics to be correctly translated by the compiler. The reason for this is that an invertible mapping relation exists between the constructs of a SysML Block Definition diagram (i.e., blocks and relationships) and structural constructs in C (i.e., functions and arrays in C). This mapping relation, also called *interpretation* [52], gives models a meaning with respect to the system under design that a model abstracts away. The latter is, ultimately, the software (e.g., C code) and not the signal-processing operations (e.g., a Fast Fourier Transform) of a system under design [53].

However, when this mapping relation is not invertible, code cannot be generated from models without the support of an external formalism that precisely specifies the models' semantics. This is the case for the Action Language Alf [20] and the Foundational Subset for Executable UML, fUML [19]. In our case study, this can be seen if attempting to produce code that implements the internal behavior of signal-processing operations from DIPLODOCUS Activity diagrams (Fig. 8). The DIPLODOCUS profile abstracts away operations that manipulate data and control instructions with a cost operator $EXEC(\cdot)$ [4]. The latter is a natural number that expresses the amount of operations on integer, $EXECI(\cdot)$, or custom $EXECC(\cdot)$ numbers. For instance, given two arrays of integers $\bar{A}$ and $\bar{B}$ of size n and m, respectively, the element-wise multiplication of $A \times B$ would be abstracted as $EXECI(n \times m)$. However, the same cost operator may as well represent the element-wise sum $\bar{A} + \bar{B}$, or the element-wise difference $\bar{A} - \bar{B}$. This formally explains the reason why source code produced by OMC from DIPLODOCUS models, must be manually completed by the user with calls to operation-specific functions that contain the C code modeled by DIPLODOCUS Activity diagrams.

8   Conclusion

This paper proposes a software development flow to program parallel platforms (e.g., Multi-Processor Systems-on-Chip) from system-level models. The flow we proposed produces application software specified in a third-generation language (i.e., C). It combines the UML/SysML toolkit TTool/DIPLODOCUS [3], as model development environment, with OMC (the Optimizing Model Compiler [5]) as a source-to-source compiler that translates UML/SysML diagrams into C code. Our contributions were applied to program a 5G decoder onto a multi-processor platform and onto an IP-based platform. In future work, we will extend our case study with the complete design of an encoder chain and we will extend the middle-end with other optimizations (e.g., power consumption).

As mentioned in Sect. 1 and discussed in Subsect. 7.3, we conclude that model-based code generation does not always replace software development based on programming languages. More in details, model-based code generation is an advantageous paradigm when the mapping relation between constructs in the modeling and programming languages is invertible. Because modeling languages abstract the software implementation of a system under design, invertible mappings exist between *structural* constructs (e.g., blocks in a SysML Block Definition diagram map to C functions and vice-versa, classes in a UML Class diagram map to Java classes and vice-versa). These constructs can be efficiently translated into compiler's IRs and analyzed to optimize structural properties of the system under design. This is exemplified by the memory footprint optimizations that we presented in this paper. Another structural property that can be optimized while increasing the software quality and productivity is the scheduling of the operations executed by the system under design.

Conversely, modeling constructs that capture the *behavioral* aspects of a system under design (e.g., UML Activity diagrams) cannot be invertibly mapped to equivalent constructs in programming languages. Additional languages (e.g., Alf for fUML) must then be used to fill the semantic gap between an input model and its output program.

For these reasons, it is our belief that the quality and productivity of software development for multi-processor embedded systems cannot be improved by relying only on the high-level abstractions (e.g., UML/SysML blocks and channels) offered by modeling languages. The latter must be efficiently integrated by tools and methodologies to the constructs that already exist in programming languages to abstract the manipulation of data and control instructions (e.g., operations on arrays and structs in the C language). We believe that the tools and approach proposed in this paper are a good starting point for further research in this direction.

References

1. Schmidt, D.C.: Model-driven engineering. Computer **39**, 25–31 (2006)
2. Lee, E.: Model-based code generation is not a replacement for programming (2003). http://chess.eecs.berkeley.edu/pubs/621.html
3. TTool (2017). http://ttool.telecom-paristech.fr
4. Apvrille, L., Muhammad, W., Ameur-Boulifa, R., Coudert, S., Pacalet, R.: A UML-based environment for system design space exploration. In: ICECS, pp. 1272–1275 (2006)
5. Enrici, A., Lallet, J., Latif, I., Apvrille, L., Pacalet, R., Canuel, A.: A model compilation approach for optimized implementations of signal-processing systems. In: Modelsward, pp. 25–35 (2018)
6. Vanderperren, Y., Mueller, W., He, D., Mischkalla, F., Dehaene, W.: Extending UML for electronic systems design: a code generation perspective. In: Nicolescu, G., O'Connor, I., Piguet, C. (eds.) Design Technology for Heterogeneous Embedded Systems, pp. 13–39. Springer, Dordrecht (2012). https://doi.org/10.1007/978-94-007-1125-9_2
7. Nicolas, A., Penil, P., Posadas, H., Villar, E.: Automatic synthesis over multiple APIs from UML/MARTE models for easy platform mapping and reuse. In: Euromicro DSD, pp. 443–450 (2014)
8. Ciccozzi, F., Cicchetti, A., Sjodin, M.: Full code generation from UML models for complex embedded systems. In: STEW (2012)
9. Bazydlo, G., Adamski, M., Stefanowicz, L.: Translation UML diagrams into Verilog. In: HSI, pp. 267–271 (2014)
10. Moreira, T.G., Wehrmeister, M.A., Pereira, C.E., Petin, G.F., Levrat, E.: Automatic code generation for embedded systems: from UML specifications to VHDL code. In: INDIN, pp. 1085–1090 (2010)
11. Mischkalla, F., He, D., Mueller, W.: Closing the gap between UML-based modeling, simulation and synthesis of combined HW/SW designs. In: DATE, pp. 1201–1206 (2010)
12. Xi, C., JianHua, L., Zucheng, Z., Yaohui, S.: Modeling SystemC design in UML and automatic code generation. In: ASP-DAC, pp. 932–935 (2005)
13. Tan, W.H., Thiagarajan, P.S., Wong, W.F., Zhu, Y., Pilakkat, S.K.: Synthesizable SystemC code from UML models (2004)
14. OMG: UML Profile for MARTE: Modeling and Analysis of Real-time Embedded Systems. http://www.omg.org/omgmarte/. Accessed Apr 2018
15. Gamatie, A., et al.: A model driven design framework for high performance embedded systems (2008). http://hal.inria.fr/inria-00311115/en
16. DaRTteam: Graphical Array Specification for Parallel and Distributed Computing (GASPARD2). http://www.gaspard2.org/. Accessed Apr 2018
17. Mellor, S.J., Balcer, M.J.: Executable and translatable UML. http://www.omg.org/news/meetings/workshops/UML_2003_Manual/Tutorial4-Balcer. Accessed Apr 2018
18. Mellor, S.J., Balcer, L.: Executable UML: A Foundation for Model-Driven Architecture. Addison Wesley (2002)
19. fUML. http://www.omg.org/spec/FUML/1.2.1/. Accessed Apr 2018
20. OMG: Action Language for Foundational UML (ALF). http://www.omg.org/spec/ALF/. Accessed Apr 2018
21. Labview: Labview communications system design. http://www.ni.com/labview-communications/. Accessed Apr 2018

22. Mathworks.   https://www.mathworks.com/solutions/model-based-design.html. Accessed Apr 2018
23. Beemster, M., Sugiyama, Y.: Embedded C for high performance DSP programming with the CoSy compiler development system. http://www.jnovel.co.jp/content/files/pdf/pr/2005/EmbeddedCv2.pdf. Accessed Apr 2018
24. Leupers, R., Aguilar, M.A., Eusse, J.F., Castrillon, J., Sheng, W.: MAPS: a software development environment for embedded multicore applications. In: Ha, S., Teich, J. (eds.) Handbook of Hardware/Software Codesign, pp. 917–949. Springer, Dordrecht (2017). https://doi.org/10.1007/978-94-017-7267-9_2
25. Sheng, W., et al.: A compiler infrastructure for embedded heterogeneous MPSoCs. In: PMAM, pp. 1–10 (2013)
26. Kahn, G.: The semantics of a simple language for parallel programming. In: IFIP Congress, pp. 471–475 (1974)
27. Collette, T.: Key Technologies for Many-Core Architectures (2008). http://www.mpsoc-forum.org/previous/2008/slides/8-4Collette.pdf
28. Gerstlauer, A., Haubelt, C., Pimentel, A.D., Stefanov, T.P., Gajski, D.D., Teich, J.: Electronic system-level synthesis methodologies. IEEE TCAD 28, 1517–1530 (2009)
29. Eclipse. http://www.eclipse.org. Accessed Apr 2018
30. Torczon, L., Cooper, K.: Engineering a Compiler, 2nd edn. Morgan Kaufmann Publishers Inc., San Francisco (2007)
31. Gerstlauer, A., Gajski, D.D.: System-level abstraction semantics. In: ISSS, pp. 231–236 (2002)
32. IEEE: IEEE Std 1003.1, 2004 Edition. http://www.unix.org/version3/ieee_std.html. Accessed Apr 2018
33. Snir, M., Otto, S., Huss-Lederman, S., Walker, D., Dongarra, J.: MPI-The Complete Reference: The MPI Core. MIT Press Cambridge, MA, USA (1998)
34. OpenMP: The OpenMP specification for parallel programming. http://www.openmp.org. Accessed Apr 2018
35. Leupers, R., Sheng, W., Castrillon, J.: In: Handbook of Signal Processing Systems, pp. 1215–1257 (2010)
36. Lee, E.A., Parks, T.M.: Dataflow process network. Proc. IEEE 83, 1235–1245 (1995)
37. TTool/DIPLODOCUS (2017). http://ttool.telecom-paristech.fr/diplodocus.html
38. TTool/Avatar (2017). http://ttool.telecom-paristech.fr/avatar.html
39. TTool/SysMLSec (2017). http://sysml-sec.telecom-paristech.fr
40. Enrici, A., Apvrille, L., Pacalet, R.: A model-driven engineering methodology to design parallel and distributed embedded systems. ACM TODAES 22, 34:1–34:25 (2017)
41. Enrici, A., Apvrille, L., Pacalet, R.: A UML model-driven approach to efficiently allocate complex communication schemes. In: Dingel, J., Schulte, W., Ramos, I., Abrahão, S., Insfran, E. (eds.) MODELS 2014. LNCS, vol. 8767, pp. 370–385. Springer, Cham (2014). https://doi.org/10.1007/978-3-319-11653-2_23
42. Knorreck, D.: UML-Based Design Space Exploration, Fast Simulation and Static Analysis. Ph.D. thesis, Telecom ParisTech (2011)
43. Desnos, K., Pelcat, M., Nezan, J., Aridhi, S.: Memory analysis and optimized allocation of dataflow applications on shared-memory MPSoCs. J. VLSI Sig. Proc. Syst. Signal Image Video Tech. 80, 1–19 (2015)
44. Desnos, K., Pelcat, M., Nezan, J.F., Aridhi, S.: Distributed memory allocation technique for synchronous dataflow graphs. In: SiPS 2016 (2016)

45. Fabri, J.: Automatic Storage Optimization. Courant Institute of Mathematical Sciences, New York University, New York (1979)
46. Floch, A., et al.: Model-driven engineering and optimizing compilers: a bridge too far? In: Whittle, J., Clark, T., Kühne, T. (eds.) MODELS 2011. LNCS, vol. 6981, pp. 608–622. Springer, Heidelberg (2011). https://doi.org/10.1007/978-3-642-24485-8_45
47. Verizon: 5G specifications. http://www.5gtf.org/. Accessed Apr 2018
48. Embb (2017). http://embb.telecom-paristech.fr/
49. de Greef, E., Catthoor, F., de Man, H.: Array placement for storage size reduction in embedded multimedia systems. In: ASAP, pp. 66–75 (1997)
50. Desnos, K., Pelcat, M., Nezan, J., Aridhi, S.: On memory reuse between inputs and outputs of dataflow actors. ACM TECS **15**, 30 (2016)
51. Xilinx: SDx Development Environment. https://www.xilinx.com/products/design-tools/all-programmable-abstractions.html. Accessed Apr 2018
52. Seidewitz, E.: What models mean. IEEE Softw. **20**, 26–32 (2003)
53. Selic, B.: The pragmatics of model-driven development. IEEE Softw. **20**, 19–25 (2003)

Evaluating Multi-variant Model-To-Text Transformations Realized by Generic Aspects

Sandra Greiner$^{(\boxtimes)}$ and Bernhard Westfechtel

Applied Computer Science I, University of Bayreuth, 95440 Bayreuth, Germany
{Sandra1.Greiner,bernhard.westfechtel}@uni-bayreuth.de

Abstract. The discipline *model-driven product line engineering (MDPLE)* aims at increasing the level of productivity when realizing a family of related products. Relying on *model-driven software engineering (MDSE)* seeks to support this effect by using models raising the level of abstraction. In MDSE model transformations are the key technology to transform in between different (model) representations. By now, model transformations are mature and successfully applied in many use cases. In annotative approaches to MDPLE model elements are typically augmented with *variability annotations* controlling in which products the elements are visible. For delivering products, source code is generated from the configured models in model-to-text (M2T) transformations. Applying a state-of-the-art model transformation on an annotated model, however, does not regard the annotations since such *single-variant model transformations* (SVMTs) are unaware of annotations and not able to transfer them to the output. In the present work we evaluate our solution which *reuses* the already existing SVMT support and propagates annotations *orthogonally*. In particular, a generic aspect, supporting any kind of input metamodel, augments the outcome of SVMTs with annotations. Comparing the transformation with the state-of-the-art approach of manually adding the annotations to the target model reveals not only 100% accuracy regarding the similarity of the derived products. It also states a significant reduction of the user effort compared to the laborious task of manually annotating the target source code. In this way our approach helps to really increase the productivity in MDPLE.

1 Introduction

Model-driven software engineering (MDSE) aims to increase productivity by generating source code from models residing on a higher level of abstraction than the pure text [21]. Different kinds of models with well-defined syntax and semantics come into play during the process of establishing a software system. A *metamodel* defines the abstract syntax to which a model conforms. The Eclipse Modeling Framework (EMF) [16] is the de facto standard for realizing domain specific metamodels based on the Ecore (meta-) metamodel.

© Springer Nature Switzerland AG 2019
S. Hammoudi et al. (Eds.): MODELSWARD 2018, CCIS 991, pp. 82–105, 2019.
https://doi.org/10.1007/978-3-030-11030-7_5

Based on the principles of *organized reuse* and *variability*, model-driven software product line engineering (MDPLE) [13] seeks to reduce the user effort when realizing a set of similar products. In *annotative* approaches [1] the elements of domain models, capturing the whole functionality of the product line, are decorated with variability *annotations*, controlling in which products the model elements are visible. The set of features can be designed in *feature models* [10]. Given a *feature configuration*, which assigns boolean values to the features of the feature model, the final product should easily be derived (*filter*) by removing all elements the annotation of which evaluates to false.

On the other hand, *model transformations* are the key technology used in MDSE. While *model-to-model (M2M)* transformations allow to transform in between two (or more) models, e.g., for refining them, *model-to-text (M2T)* transformations are frequently used to automatically generate source code as output for a given model (input). A transformation considering only one direction is called *unidirectional* whereas languages specifying not only the *forward* direction but also treating the *backward* transformation are called *bidirectional*. While in *in-place* transformations the input model gets refined, a separate output is created (*batch*) or modified (*incremental*) in *out-place* transformations.

By now, model transformations in various forms are mature and frequently applied in MDSE. In MDPLE, however, annotations of domain model elements are (usually) not foreseen in aforementioned *single-variant model transformation (SVMT)*. With a multi-variant model including all variants as input to the transformation the output model also contains representatives for these variants but the annotations are lost. The straightforward solution of annotating the target model manually, is a rather laborious and error-prone process. Automatically transferring annotations instead, calls for *multi-variant model transformations* (MVMT) propagating annotations to the target model.

Recently, MVMTs have gained attention in research: One approach provides the means to lift single-variant rules to the whole product line in in-place graph-based transformations [14]. A formalization for in-place transformations based on category theory is proposed in [19] and a proof when combined with transformations rules containing varying parts in [17]. In [7] the authors automatically transfer annotations after executing SVMTs written in ATL in an *a posteriori* approach whereas annotations are propagated by relating source and target elements in a separate specification in [3]. In Sect. 8 we elaborate and categorize the different approaches in greater detail.

Aforementioned solution approaches all deal with M2M transformations. In contrast, we contribute a specific solution which is able to transfer annotations in the common use case of M2T transformations by enriching single-variant transformations with a generic aspect. Since thereby we can *reuse* already written transformation specifications independently of the metamodels, we support a wide variety of M2T use cases. In particular, this article is an extension to a conference contribution [8] which is extended here w.r.t. the following points: We include

- a rough categorization of MVMT transformations and characterize our approach with respect to these criteria
- an quantitative evaluation of commutativity and
- discuss our approach based on the results of our work in greater detail.

We like to highlight especially the results of the evaluation in which we compared the outcome of the SVMT and the MVMT regarding the final products. They exhibit not only 100% similarity but also a significant reduction of the user effort.

The remainder of this article is structured in the following way: At first, we motivate the need for MVSC based on a concrete example. Then, the paper provides an overview on the contribution and, next, a description of the technical realization. Finally, it presents an example transformation and the evaluation results followed by a short discussion. The article concludes with related work and a short summary giving an outlook on future work.

2   Background

This section motivates why we need MVMTs and what characteristics they should expose.

2.1   Motivation for Annotated Multi-variant Source Code

Our motivating example is based on an annotated Ecore model for the Graph SPL. As depicted in Fig. 1, the Graph consists of Egdes and Nodes which are mandatory features of the feature model located in the upper right corner of the figure. Edges might be Directed and/or Weighted. Moreover, nodes might be Colored.

With state-of-the art MDPLE tools supporting annotative approaches, so far, products are derived by filtering the annotated multi-variant domain model

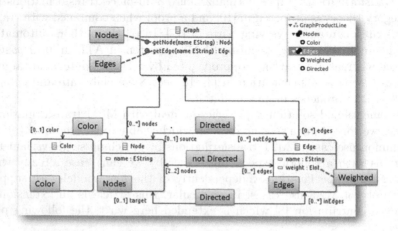

Fig. 1. Graph domain model annotated with features from the feature model placed in the upper right corner. (Reproduced from [8]).

by a given feature configuration. From the filtered model (Java) source code is generated resulting in *single-variant source code (SVSC)*. Selecting, for instance, only the features Edges and Nodes results in three classes. The class Node contains a field edges and a corresponding field nodes is included in the class Edge. For both fields respective accessor methods are generated. Since for the omnipresent Graph class only the method stubs for the operations getNode() and getEdge() are created, the engineer implements their method bodies *manually* in the final product. The whole code, however, is completely *unaware* of features and the manual modifications are unique to this single product.

In the meantime, more products are derived – all of them missing the two method bodies implemented in the first derived product. As the manual implementation should be present in all products, the developer copy-and-pastes the manual modifications to all other derived products. Despite the increased effort – contradicting the promise of increased productivity when using MDPLE –, a high risk to forget one product or to slightly modify the implementations inadvertently remains.

This problem could be solved by generating the MVSC first and adding manual implementations there. Although it is possible to generate the source code including all variants from elements present in the domain model, the default Ecore code generation is not able to integrate annotations in the generated text. A link to the feature(s) a single source code fragment is realizing is missing. As a consequence, it is not possible to derive products from this code base automatically, instead it would be necessary to associate the annotation belonging to a source code fragment with the corresponding code fragment.

As deducted from this scenario, having annotated MVSC, hence provides the following benefits:

- Products can be derived automatically from the MVSC without generating a single-variant model first.
- Derived products may include manually added source code fragments concerning them, *increasing the degree of automation and productivity.*

Please note: This kind of problem can hardly be solved by designing more detailed domain or feature models. Even if behavior was modeled and source code for method bodies was automatically derived, still most commonly manual extensions would be required. If such extension was associated with a feature, it would be best having it in all corresponding products automatically upon derivation.

2.2   Consequences

In order to be beneficial, we postulate basic requirements on (text producing) MVMTs, transforming a multi-variant source model mv_s consisting of a pair of a domain model m_s, realizing the product line, and a mapping model, map_{F,m_s} holding annotations (which are boolean expression over the features stated in the feature model F) for the elements contained in the domain model:

Reuse. Existing SVMTs should not be meaningless but ideally *reused* as they are. This can be achieved by propagating annotations separately and automatically. At the most, such solution offers the following advantages:

- no new language constructs need to be learned and
- no new tools need to be developed from scratch
- the cognitive complexity of the transformation remains on the same level
- already written transformation specifications can still be used.

Orthogonality. Annotations should be propagated *orthogonally* to the reused SVMT. Having the links transferred in an orthogonal step, strictly separates the concerns of transforming the models from treating the annotations.

Tracelink. The kind of annotations realized in the input must be translated into a form understood by the output. In particular, the transformation outcome, here: the MVSC, should compile and should still be readable and understandable.

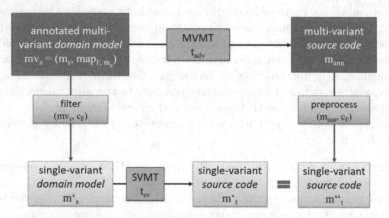

Fig. 2. Commutatitvity cirterion of SVMT and MVMTs: the final products m'_t and m''_t should be equal.

Commutativity. As depicted in Fig. 2 an MVMT should *commute*: The source code m'_t generated for a single-variant model m'_s which was filtered from the multi-variant domain model by specifying a feature configuration c_F should be the same as the source code m''_t resulting from preprocessing the annotated MVSC m_{ann} by the same configuration c_F. Deriving the source code from the MVSC achieves the same goal but based on a higher degree of automation – as motivated in Sect. 2.1.

Transformation Engine. Furthermore, an MVMT engine is needed that fulfills the following criteria:

- **generic:** support any kind of variability representation as input and produce generic output based on the reused transformation
- **reuse of** already present SVMTs.

Accordingly, such engine is able to support the heterogeneity of MDPLE. Usually, they rely on different tools and languages for realizing SVMTs. Ideally, they should be seamlessly extended to MVMTs with the help of the engine.

On the whole, we postulate MVMTs which are automatically executed based on the reuse of unchanged SVMTs. Commutativity should be achieved by propagating tracelinks orthogonally to the reused SVMTs.

3   Multi-variant Model Transformations

3.1   Classification of Solution Approaches

The following descriptions serve to categorize certain MVMT approaches and to delimit the Xpand realization from others.

Solutions towards MVMT may be characterized regarding (1) the level of *abstraction* about the transformation internals and (2) the *scope* of the solution.

Firstly, *black-box* solutions – situated at the highest level of abstraction – require no knowledge about the transformation internals at all. The only information exploited are the source and target instances (and their metamodels). Although ideally knowing only source and target of the transformation should suffice, more likely at least some other transformation artifacts, e.g., a trace, might be necessary. We refer to these approaches as *grey-box* solutions. In contrast, in a *white-box* approach all internals are known and exploited, i.e., concrete transformation specifications might lay the ground for the MVMT realization.

Secondly, the scope can be classified from the most specific solution to the most general: Having no MVMT at all requires to manually propagate annotations from every source model to the corresponding target model (*instance specific*). The next stage works for a single transformation definition. In such *transformation-specific* solutions the tool builder manually provides the means for propagating the annotations. This effort is omitted from the end user. *Tool-specific* solutions propagate annotations for all executed transformations with a certain tool whereas *language-specific* approaches support all definitions written in one language, independent of the transformation tool. On the highest level, the solution should work *language and tool independent*, i.e., regardless of the transformation language and tool annotations can be transfered from the source to the target of the transformation.

3.2   MVMT Approach

In general we seek for an MVMT solution reusing already existing SVMTs. Thereby it should realize the highest level of scope, i.e., working language and tool independent. In this way the MVMT can be deployed to arbitrary MDPLE tools, especially to those supporting heterogeneous artifacts, like the tool FAMILE [4].

Our present work supports the widely spread use case of generating source code. The source code should be automatically annotated without adapting the SVMT. The presence of annotations in the target model provides the means to derive products from the multi-variant code base. Additionally, the source code may comprise manual implementations which, thus, can be part of final products.

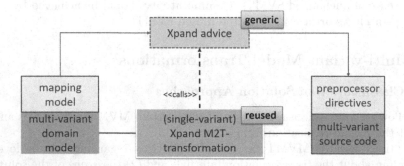

Fig. 3. Reuse-based MVMT approach with Xpand language using the generic aspect. (Reproduced from [8]).

Figure 3 sketches the realized approach: An SVMT should be *reused* (branch on the bottom) and annotations should be translated separately into preprocessor directives (branch on the top). Since the SVMT should not have to be altered, the approach demands for an M2T transformation language generating artifacts or providing mechanisms to work with, orthogonally to the executed base transformation. We have picked the M2T language Xpand because it allows to adapt the behavior of existing model transformations with an aspect-oriented approach. More details on the language are given in the remainder of this section.

As shown in the aforementioned figure, the annotation transfer relies on a generic implementation supporting arbitrary model transformations written in Xpand: annotations (c.f., Sect. 3.5) are translated into preprocessor directives and integrated in this form into the resulting source code. As Java does not support a preprocessor, the directives are translated into JavaDoc comments and will be processed by a separate tool, which is roughly explained in Sect. 3.4. Thus, source code fragments belonging to a specific feature are embraced with comments in the multi-variant Java source code resulting from the SVMT.

Please note: The reused SVMT is single-variant as it does not cover annotations, being *unaware* of the variability. Nevertheless, the input domain model is multi-variant because it captures the whole product line. Additionally, the model elements are as well unaware of the variants they belong to. The annotations associated with them are stored alongside the domain model in a separate *mapping model* (Sect. 3.5). Finally, generating source code from the multi-variant domain model with a plain SVMT results in MVSC including representatives for all input elements. The MVSC, too, is unconscious of the different features it is realizing.

To this end, we provide a tool-independent but language-specific solution towards MVMTs. Regardless of the issued tool, extending an existing Xpand SVMT by our advice should produce annotated source code in the case the annotations are stored in a mapping model as described below (Sect. 3.5). Moreover, our proposal is a black-box solution because no transformation contents are necessary at all. Rather the end user solely needs to integrate the provided advice.

3.3 Xpand

Xpand stems from the openArchitectureWare (oAW) project where it serves as a template-based M2T transformation language. Extensive documentation can be found in [5].

Xpand projects typically consist of templates, extensions and an MWE(2) workflow. In the *templates* a DEFINE block specifies how a metamodel element is converted into text. In these blocks plain text can be intermingled with other Xpand directives, e.g., the FILE or EXPAND directives, where the first one creates a file located at the given path and the latter invokes the execution of another DEFINE block. Moreover, complex instructions can be written in *extensions* which provide a subset of the Xtend language. Additionally, extensions may call Java methods that could be used for any instruction which is not (or only restrictively) expressible with Xtend.

Most importantly for the present work, the language allows to extend or rewrite template definitions with an aspect-oriented component: *advice* templates define AROUND blocks specifying a generated element that they might (almost) arbitrarily alter. Quite like a DEFINE statement, they, first, state a fully qualified element that should be modified and, second, the type of this element. *Wildcards* (*) inside the fully qualified name allow to scan different directories and/or to match arbitrary element types of DEFINE blocks.

In addition, in order to preserve manually added source code when executing the transformation repeatedly, Xpand supports such incremental transformation with the concept of protected regions. The user needs to provide the type of comment symbols being used to integrate the regions in the generated source code and an ID with which those regions can be distinguished. Especially the ID plays a key role for the success of the transformation. Only if the ID of the protected block surrounding a text fragment is unique in the target source code, the regions will remain untouched after executing the transformation again.

Finally, MWE(2) workflows[1] are used to execute the transformation. Workflows are given a name and consist of different components. They are interpreted

---

[1] http://www.eclipse.org/Xtext/documentation/306_mwe2.html.

as normal Java classes. When executing model transformations, a workflow usually specifies a reader component which receives the path to the input model/s and its/their metamodel/s and an Xpand generator component. The latter expects the entry point to the transformation (corresponding with the root element of the input) and a path the output is written to. The generator component may receive advices which can be realized for templates and extensions alike.

3.4   Java Preprocessor

As the present work should create Java source code annotated with preprocessor directives, some facility is needed to cope with preprocessor directives in Java. In the past, some approaches have been proposed but they are mostly not compatible with current Eclipse projects, e.g., *Prebop*[2], or require a manual adaptation of the build process, e.g., when using the *Java Comment Preprocessor*[3]. Thus, we introduce a different preprocessor, which we developed in a model-driven way, realized as Eclipse plugin. The preprocessor is *configurable* with respect to

- the files that should be preprocessed by their file-ending,
- the kind of comment signs that open and close the directives inside these files,
- the names/signs for the opening, closing and possible branching directives.

Furthermore, the preprocessor expects a set of flags with boolean values or a feature configuration being translated into such set of boolean flags. All source code fragments surrounded with directives evaluating to false are turned into comments by the preprocessor.

3.5   Feature to Domain Mapping Model

Last but not least, model elements need to be associated with annotations. We choose the form provided by the tool FAMILE [4], which is an annotative approach residing in the Eclipse Modeling Framework (EMF) [16]. While feature models capture the variability, a single product is derived by providing a feature configuration setting the features to true or false.

Furthermore, *annotations* are boolean expressions over the features and can be assigned to arbitrary domain model elements. In FAMILE the mapping of a domain model element and its associated annotation is stored in a separate mapping model, the *feature to domain mapping model (F2DMM)*. The mapping model resembles the structure of the domain model it belongs to and, thus, stores an *object mapping (OM)* for all EObjects contained in the domain model. For example, every instance of an EClass or an EOperation, etc., is referenced by an OM and may be visible just for a specific expression over the features. Based on feature configurations, final products are derived by filtering all objects the annotations of which evaluate to false.

---

[2] http://prebop.sourceforge.net/.

[3] https://github.com/raydac/java-comment-preprocessor.

4   Realizing the Multi-variant Source Code Generation

In the following we provide details on how annotations stored in a mapping model of the tool FAMILE (F2DMM) are propagated in order to annotate the source code resulting from arbitrary Xpand transformations. We assume the Xpand SVMTs already exist. They should be *reused* without any modification.

For realizing the MVMT with Xpand two components are decisive: A generic *advice* to modify the existing SVMT and a *second MWE(2) workflow* executing the workflow of the SVMT augmented with the provided advice. Now we illuminate both Xpand artifacts.

4.1   Preprocessor Directives

First of all, the automatic transfer of annotations requires a generic instruction to associate source code fragments with the annotations of their corresponding model elements. The text produced for the annotation should open the preprocessor directive before writing the actual text for the model element and close the directive afterwards. Thereby the directive must mention the annotation. Since in our use cases we generate Java source code, the preprocessor directives must be turned into comments, i.e., they should not hinder the source code from compiling properly. As seen in Listing 1 – in our original contribution to realizing MVMTs with Xpand the opening and closing comments not only stated the annotation of the actual element text was generated for but also closed and opened the preprocessor directive of the containing element. Choosing this comment style is caused by the capabilities of the preprocessor. A preprocessor not supporting nested comments assumes a opening directive is immediately closed after opening it. Thus, two consecutive opening directives, without a closing one in between, might lead to erroneous behavior.

```
1  /** #ENDIF Edges */
2
3     /** #IFDEF Weighted # */
4     // @ID: _TACGEFc3Eeetfr4BhVYAxQ
5     protected int weight;
6     /** #ENDIF Weighted*/
7
8  /** #IFDEF Edges # */
```

Listing 1. Example of a field declaration. The JavaDoc comments are added by the generic advice.

However, with a preprocessing tool capable of handling nested directives it is possible to simply put one opening and one closing directive, stating the annotation only. Accordingly, the employed strategy for the comments must always correspond with the used preprocessor. Moreover, the style of the annotation depends on the validity of the feature configuration which is discussed in greater detail in Sect. 7.2.

4.2   Advice Template

The functionality of the generic aspect can be described as follows: If an model element of the input model is annotated, this annotation should be integrated in the source code. The integration must be such that all source code fragments generated for the object can only be present when the annotation is satisfied given a feature configuration.

Our generic advice – presented in a simplified version in Listing 2 – implements aforementioned behavior: By using wildcards in the AROUND statement (l. 1), the following procedure is executed for any Object text is generated for inside a file located in a directory called *templates*. Due to the fact that FAMILE only supports Ecore-compliant domain models, EObjects are the only elements, text is generated for. Additionally, the mapping model of FAMILE ensures exactly one mapping is present for every object and that there are mappings for each of its structural features.

Thus, firstly, the algorithm searches the corresponding OM (l. 2) with the help of an extension. In the background the mapping model is loaded upon the first invocation of getOM. The function, then, searches the mapping, OM, referencing the given object in the mapping model. If the OM contains an annotation (l. 3), the actual text production is surrounded by comments mentioning the annotation as presence condition (l. 4–7). The comment is constructed in another function provided in the extensions (l. 4 and 7). As explained above, the style of the comment may vary with the capabilities of the preprocessor. We follow a conservative approach and include the container expressions as well. Finally, by invoking the function targetDef.proceed() (l. 6 and 10) the original text production of the SVMT is triggered.

```
1  «AROUND templates::*::* FOR Object»
2    «LET getOM((EObject)this) AS o»
3      «IF om.isSetFeatureExprStr()»
4        «getOpeningComment()»
5        // @ID: «getID()»
6        «targetDef.proceed()»
7        «getClosingComment()»
8      «ELSE»
9        // @ID: «getID()»
10       «targetDef.proceed()»
11     «ENDIF»
12   «ENDLET»
13 «ENDAROUND»
```

Listing 2. Advice annotating the source code generated for a single EObject.

By adding the comments, it is possible to relate the text surrounded with comments to its annotation and, hence, to inject the variability information in the pure text. Furthermore, in any case a unique ID is generated for the EObject (l. 5 and 9) and put before the generated text. This way we keep a unique trace information, which might be used to support later evolution processes.

Please note: the overall success of annotating each element depends on the contents of the single-variant transformation. Only around text productions for the EObjects matching a DEFINE block the preprocessor directives can be written. Other elements are not considered by the advice. In particular, this subsumes the attributes of objects and anything that is written in other language constructs, like being verbatim included in a FILE block.

4.3 Workflow

The second part needed to realize the annotations is the MWE2 workflows. As depicted in Fig. 3, the Xpand project providing the advice template calls the reused SVMT. Thereby it adds the generic advice template to the Xpand generator executed in the single-variant workflow. Accordingly, the advice project provides a workflow that executes the SVMT and adds the previously presented advice. Without the loss of generality[4], technically, we assume that the single-variant code generation is initiated by an MWE2 workflow providing a slot to add an advice template. This slot is filled by adding our advice in a second Xpand project that injects the advices into the original single-variant text generator.

Altogether the MVMT behaves as follows. First of all, the SVMT is executed. During this execution the advice, overriding the single-variants behavior, is triggered for each object of the input instance matching a DEFINE block. Accordingly, if the object is annotated, it will receive a preprocessor directive, stating the annotation, otherwise the ID only. Finally, to derive products, the preprocessor needs to be invoked on a given feature configuration. The overall process is presented in the next section based on two concrete execution scenarios.

5 Example

Now we demonstrate a product generation workflow in our MVMT. Based on two independent transformations, we show the genericity of the provided advice: We produce multi-variant Java source code for annotated Ecore models and for annotated MoDisco models based on the same advice we are providing. MoDisco [2] is an extensible model-driven framework supporting different use cases of software modernization. It provides an Ecore-compliant metamodel resembling the Java AST and offering discoverers that, for example, translate Java source code into valid instances of this metamodel.

Both transformations, Ecore to Java and MoDisco to Java, are partially reimplemented in Xpand for the purpose of this evaluation because the EMF and MoDisco code generators are implemented in different template languages (JET and Acceleo, respectively, both do not natively support aspect-orientation).

Below, we demonstrate the transformation process for one concrete model element: Remember the class Edge being part of the Graph product line introduced in Sect. 2 in the case the feature Edges is selected. It may have an attribute

---

[4] The procedure is quite similar for a simple MWE workflow.

weight (Weighted) and a source and target node when the feature Directed is selected. If it is not selected, exactly two nodes will be part of the Edge. For simplicity and space reasons, we focus on showing the interface only (not the created class).

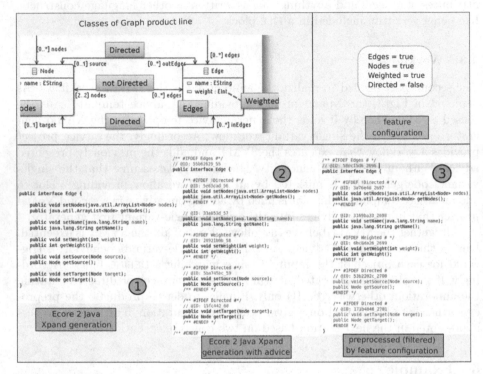

Fig. 4. Generated Edge interface when applying the Xpand transformation without (1) and with (2) our generic advice on the Ecore model (top) as input. On the right (3) the result of the preprocessor run – given the above stated feature configuration – is depicted.

Ecore To Java Source Code. The first transformation receives an annotated Ecore model of the Graph product line [12] as input. The plain Xpand transformation creates source code partially resembling the default Ecore code generation: For instance, for every EClass an interface and a class are created. Additionally, for the structural features fields and accessor methods are included.

Figure 4 depicts the different target classes created from executing the plain Xpand transformation (1) and the same transformation extended by the provided advice (2). Running the *SVMT* only (1) on the multi-variant edge class results in a class and an interface where all modeled elements – independent of the associated features – are visible. The connection to the features is lost. Executing the same transformation *with our generic advice* (2), generates the same source code but adds the annotations in form of preprocessor directives. For instance, the methods setWeight and getWeight are embraced by the "# IFDEF Weighted#" comment and the closing "# ENDIF" comment.

Independent of a present annotation, each element created in a DEFINE block receives the ID corresponding with the EObject it was created from. Moreover, if it is annotated, it is embraced by a preprocessor directive stating the annotation. Accordingly, while the attribute name inside the edge class only receives its corresponding ID, the other text fragments are additionally embraced by preprocessor directives. Consequently, the resulting source code resembles the mapping model and allows to associate manual modifications with a feature.

Finally, products can be derived from the MVSC. In Fig. 4 the rightmost located interface represents the outcome of running the preprocessor on the feature configuration depicted in the top right corner of the figure. The result consists of nodes with weighted edges: All source code annotated with deselected features is turned into JavaDoc comments, hence, making it invisible in the resulting product. For the final delivery of the product all directives can be removed. However, in this case all connections to the associated model elements are lost. We keep the comments in the figure in order to demonstrate the differences between the different development stages.

MoDisco To Java Source Code. To illustrate the same advice allows to annotate the outcome of Xpand transformations for arbitrary metamodels, we have used it in the transformation generating source code for the Java MoDisco metamodel.

Input to the transformation are the Java MoDisco model resulting from discovering the source code generated for the Graph metamodel in the default Ecore code generation and a mapping model for this Java MoDisco instance. The mapping model is annotated such that it is semantically similar to the mapping model for the Ecore Graph model. In contrast to the Ecore model, the Java model, resulting from discovering the source code, contains significantly more model elements. For instance, the accessor methods and their parameters created for a field (one single element, i.e. one annotation) in the Ecore code generation are all distinct model elements in the Java model. Accordingly, the mapping model for the MoDisco instance includes distinct object mappings not only for each accessor method but also, e.g., for their parameters.

Figure 5 depicts the outcome of the MVMT for the annotated Java model representing the Graph product line as input. The source code almost equals the one generated with the Xpand Ecore code generation (number 2 of Fig. 4). However, the Xpand implementation generating Java from Ecore in the first scenario does not include all details of the Ecore standard code generation. Rather it uses the standard Java libraries (e.g., using an ArrayList instead of the EList). As a consequence, the discovered model resulting from the default Ecore code generation (which is input to this scenario) includes EMF-specific types which are, thus, included in the text produced with the MoDisco to Java Xpand transformation.

Summary. The examples above illustrate that our generic advice allows to propagate annotations automatically in Xpand transformations. They demonstrate the success of the advice for two considerably different metamodels and show in

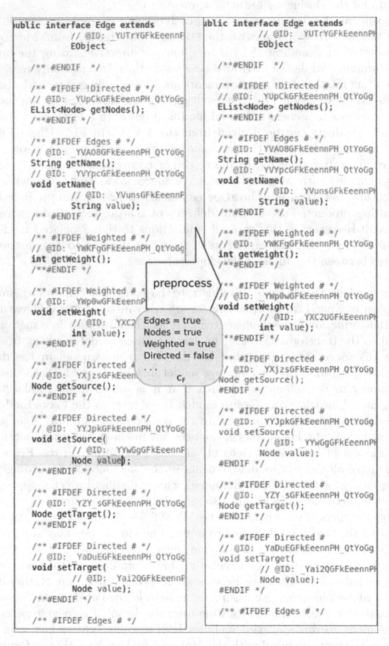

Fig. 5. The annotated Edge interface after the MVMT (left) and after running the preprocessor (right) on the Java model as input. (Reproduced from [8]).

the ongoing how the MVSC is modified in order to derive products. The success of transferring the annotations, however, depends on whether the text for some EObject is created in a separate DEFINE statement as mentioned in Sect. 4. Despite showing the genericity, it still needs to be evaluated whether the MVMT fulfills the criteria of commutativity which is evaluated in the next section.

6   Evaluation of Commutativity

In order to be purposeful, our basic Xpand advice for achieving an MVMT needs to fulfill its two main characteristics: working generically for arbitrary transformations, i.e., independent of the source metamodel and its instances, and it needs to achieve commutativity. The first property has been investigated in the example presented in the last section. The evaluation of the second criteria is sketched in this section. By extending the Graph product line, introduced in Sect. 2, we evaluated the transformation against the latter property. Following two criteria are of interest:

1. *User effort:* the user should not be confronted with the straightforward approach of manually adding annotations to the MVSC. Likewise, repeatedly filtering and transforming the single-variant product should be more laborious than transforming once and running a preprocessor on a given feature configuration thereafter.
2. *Accuracy:* According to Fig. 2, products derived from the MVSC (m_t'') should resemble the corresponding result from the state-of-the-art approach of transforming each product individually (m_t') with the highest possible *accuracy*. Thus, the diagram depicted in Fig. 2 must *commute*.

Below we describe, first of all, the applied methodology followed by presenting the results of the evaluation. The outcome reveals our approach fulfills both expected criteria.

6.1   Evaluation Strategy

Input Product Line. We conduct a quantitative evaluation similar to the one introduced in detail in [7] being based on the *Graph* product line. Accordingly, the Graph domain model is extended by a class Algorithm being necessary to provide Search operations. Adjacency stores the connection of nodes and edges and Cycles may be detected. The feature model is extended by an optional feature Algorithm and a mandatory feature Search which can either be BFS or DFS. As opposed to the mapping model in [7], annotations associated with structural features of the model elements are removed. In concrete, the property weight of the class Edge should be a derived attribute only when the feature Weighted is selected. Our input mapping model lacks this information, thus, all the code fragments generated for the EAttribute weight, including the field declaration, are annotated with the feature Weighted as stated in the input mapping model.

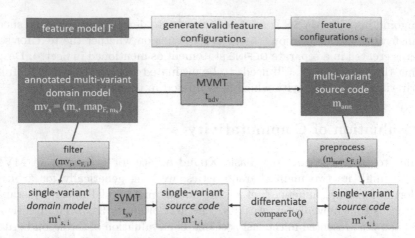

Fig. 6. Evaluation methodology: First, creating all feature configurations, then running the branches, MVMT-preprocess and filter-SVMT, in competition and comparing the outcome.

Evaluation Procedure. The employed methodology, outlined in Fig. 6, consists of the following steps: In a first step, all valid feature configurations $c_{F,i}$ – the cardinality of which is denoted as n in the following – are created from the feature model F. Then, we execute the two execution branches:

1. **MVMT.** First, the multi-variant source model mv_s is transformed in the transformation with our advice, t_{adv}. From the resulting MVSC (m_{ann}) repeatedly the target products $m''_{t,i}$ are derived by providing the feature configurations to the preprocessor ($preprocess(m_{ann}, c_{F,i})$).
2. **Repeated SVMT.** Form the multi-variant source model mv_s all n source products are created by filtering the multi-variant source model mv_s by the different feature configurations ($filter(mv_s, c_{F,i})$). Thereafter, repeatedly the Xpand transformation without the advice (t_{sv}) is applied resulting in target source code $m'_{t,i}$.

The results are then compared and evaluated in the following way:

We estimate the *user effort* saved from the number of lines of code (LOC), i.e., the annotations automatically added to the MVSC. It can be measured by counting all lines that are additionally integrated with our provided advice. We also count the ID generated for non-annotated elements because it is an artifact that might be necessary for incremental transformations and, moreover, not present in the single-variant code base.

For *accuracy*, we compare each product $m''_{t,i}$ resulting form the preprocessor with its corresponding partner $m'_{t,i}$ resulting from the SVMT. In order to differentiate both products, for each file contained in the respective product we build a string of its contents. Before invoking a lexicographical comparison on the pairs of strings, we remove all white spaces, including line breaks (since the advice writes line breaks not present in the targets of the plain SVMT).

Please note: In contrast to the example presented in the last section, all (!) annotation artifacts generated by the advice – including the ID statements – are removed from the delivered products m_t'' in a postprocessing step.

Thus, after removing all white spaces, we expect 100% equality as outcome of the comparison since the order of executing the transformation is deterministic, i.e., in every execution run all code fragments are written in the same order.

6.2 Key Figures and Results

The results of running the evaluation claim reduced user effort and the expected accuracy of 100% for MVMT when compared to repeated SVMT. Detailed quantities are given now.

Input. In total, the Ecore-based Graph product line comprises 49 model objects (packages, classes, attributes, references, operations, and parameters).

Secondly, the feature model consists of 14 features, eleven of which are optional. Out of $2^{11} = 2048$ possible variants, $n := 180$ conform to the constraints of the feature model (parent/child and group constraints, requires/excludes relationships). The mapping model contains 32 annotations for elements of the multi-variant source model.

User Effort. In the course of the MVMT annotated source code was created. Differentiating the lines of codes from the multi-variant source code basis (334 LOC) and the annotated one m_{ann} (784 LOC) results in a total of 450 lines of code, in form of comments, automatically added. Thus, even more lines of code are produced than there were present before running the MVMT. Accordingly, the user saves a significant amount of effort, if there is no need to manually integrate all annotations in the source code.

Additionally, it must be remarked that the user needs to execute one operation per product less: After deriving a product by applying the preprocessor, no further work is required whereas after filtering the source model in the state-of-the-art way a subsequent transformation is necessary. However, the saved effort is hard to measure.

Taken together, the user effort (cf. evaluation criterion (1)) is significantly reduced when compared to a manual transfer of variability information. The saved time can be used to further modify the source code platform, e.g. for implementing the bodies of methods.

Accuracy. After preparing the files by omitting the white spaces, all literal comparisons between $m_{t,i}'$ and $m_{t,i}''$ yielded an accuracy of 100%. As a consequence, we fulfill our main evaluation criterion to our full satisfaction. From this result we can deduce that the two branches, repeated SVMT vs MVMT, commute.

6.3 Threats to Validity

Despite the positive result regarding commutativity, it must be stated that the evaluation is based on specific input on the level of the metamodel (Ecore) and on the instance level (Graph product line). For other inputs results may vary. Regarding the commutativity, the evaluation is no general proof for commuting execution branches.

In addition, in order to achieve similarity, mappings for structural features of the model objects had to be removed since the advice cannot handle them correctly yet. However, most of the MDPLE tools do not foresee to annotate such features at all. Thus, this might only restrict the accuracy in the rare case such mappings are present.

Likewise, achieving commutativity also depends on the contents of the SVMT: Although, naturally each model type should be considered in a separate DEFINE block, this property cannot be guaranteed. If this assumption is violated, some source code fragments might not be annotated though associated with a mapping.

7   Discussion

Although we successfully support genericity with our advice, as seen in Sect. 5, and have achieved 100% accuracy regarding commutativity, some further points regarding the MVMT need to be discussed.

7.1   Cognitive Complexity

Regarding the level of complexity, the MVMT itself is rather simplistic. Once the end user provides a slot for the advice in the SVMT, automatically, the annotations are propagated. Deriving products by applying a feature configuration is an automated task as well.

However, it must be stated that adapting the MVSC might become complex. While implementing the body of an already annotated method should easily be accomplished, adding new code fragments that should be annotated requires to adapt exactly the same preprocessor directive style as used in the advice. This is a rather error-prone process, e.g., when forgetting a closing directive. Additionally, being confronted with different variants in a single code base might be confusing.

In order to avoid these issues, tools, like the one presented in [11], have been developed to hide or display single variants, reducing the cognitive complexity. Moreover, the benefits of tracelinks present in their corresponding artifacts has been justified only recently in [9].

7.2   Style and Contents of Preprocessor Directives

As described in the last sections, generating compilable MVSC and final compilable products depends on the capabilities of the preprocessing tool and on the given feature configuration.

Style. First of all, the annotations must be integrated in the source code, on the one hand, in a way that guarantees a compiling result, on the other hand, such that they can be distinguished from the "normal" source code.

Regarding the first point, i.e., the annotations should be syntactical correct in the target language. In Java and other GPLs without preprocessors, like Python, this leads to the solution of turning them into comments.

Regarding the second point of being distinguishable, while the comments must be written such that the preprocessing tool recognizes annotations and removes or includes the associated text fragments in a preprocessor run, "normal" comments must remain untouched.

Contents of Comments. Different strategies can be followed for realizing annotations in comments:

1. adding an ID on every element
2. stating only the annotation of the corresponding element
3. combining the annotation from all elements the target element is depending on

In our advice implementation we add a unique ID corresponding with the EObject for every created element, regardless whether it is annotated or not. In this way, we may keep track which element is associated with some text fragments. This information is valuable when thinking of incremental transformations. It might be argued that the ID is necessary in protected regions and does not have to be part of the advice then. This point of view neglects that in general not all text fragments are put into protected regions. Thus, not all of them receive an ID which could be needed in the case of incremental or even bidirectional transformations.

In its current version our advice surrounds the actual text production only with the annotation it its associated with in the mapping model. Consequently, at first glance it is clear to which variants one fragment belongs. However, first of all, this is only possible if the preprocessing tool and the target language support nested directives, i.e., for instance, one closing comment sign should not close all previously opened comments but only the last one. Secondly, the feature configuration must be satisfiable. Given some selection of features c_F, after preprocessing the multi-variant source code, the resulting product is only runnable if c_F was valid w.r.t. dependencies in the domain model. For instance, one element should just be selected if its container is selected as well. When stating only the annotation of each element, dependencies must be resolved before transforming otherwise pending references might lead to uncompilable source code.

Alternatively, in the most conservative approach the annotation of a target element could be built from its source element and all annotations attached to elements it is dependent on. All of these annotations should then be conjuncted. In this case even an unsatisfiable c_F should result in compilable source code. On the downside, the annotations might not be readable anymore. Furthermore, without applying conventions it is hard to defer which one of the combined annotations was the original one associated with the source element. This information, however, might also be necessary in evolution processes, like incremental or bidirectional transformations. Last but not least, this is a task that should be accomplished by the MDPLE tool since invalid feature configurations play a key role in the whole process an can lead to problems throughout the development and of product lines.

8   Related Work

Work related to the present approach comprises the following contributions:

Most of the provided approaches to realize multi-variant transformations follow the same paradigm as we do: to *reuse* already existing single-variant transformation tools and transformations.

An *a posteriori* integration of annotations is proposed in [7]. We evaluate the two artifacts of an SVMT, a trace and an execution model, in order to propagate annotations in out-place M2M transformations. It is an language-dependent grey-box approach since it works only – but independent of the transformation specification – for ATL transformations executed by the EMFTVM [22] and relies on evaluating the contents of each transformation in form of the given execution model. In our current contribution we take up the idea of reusing existing model transformations but add annotations with the help of aspects. Thus, we do *not* have to evaluate the transformation artifacts *a posteriori* and do not rely on a persisted trace. Rather we integrate annotations based on the capabilities of the transformation language and provide a generic implementation that, however, also allows to reuse existing transformations without modifying them.

Another way to realize MVMTs *lifts* the transformation [14]. This work proposes an algorithm for graph-based transformations where the single-variant rules are interpreted with variability semantics. The approach was not only successfully applied to in-place graph transformations but also to out-place M2M transformations with a graph-oriented DSL that was slightly modified for this purpose [6]. Due to the fact that the contents of each transformation specification are needed, the proposal can be considered as white-box approach.

Instead of changing the execution semantics of the SVMT, our approach executes the single-variant transformation without adaptations. We rather exploit the existing capabilities of the engine without changing the SVMT to propagate annotations seamlessly. Furthermore, we produce source code instead of models as it increases the degree of automation to deliver a final product. Manual modifications required in the annotated MVSC may be automatically integrated in all products in that way.

Another *a posterori*, but *not reuse-based*, approach is presented in [3]. Given the source and target (meta)models of the single-variant transformation, propagation is achieved by providing a correspondence specification in an ATL-like DSL. Based on the specifications, the annotations of the source elements are automatically attached to the enumerated target elements. Since no internals of the single-variant transformation must be considered, it is a black-box solution.

In contrast to our solution using the aspect, for different transformations the mapping script of corresponding metamodel elements must be provided, thus, being transformation-specific but language-independent.

In contrast, in [18] the transformation rules themselves are variability-aware. Although the proposed tool allows filtered editing on the rules which reduces the cognitive complexity, it is necessary to consider variability in the transformation rules themselves. This base concept rather solves different problems, like the transformation in between platform independent and platform specific models.

The idea of combining variability-based rules with the lifting of product lines was only recently presented in [17]. Latter contribution, however, can only support very basic in-place algebraic graph transformations. Since the whole set of rules is necessary for its success, it must be considered as a white-box approach being independent of the transformation but only working for the restrictive kind of in-place graph transformation languages.

In [15] the authors are, likewise, changing the transformation rules by introducing new syntax to ATL transformations. The new language constructs are maintained in *higher-order transformations*. Again, this approach rather addresses variability in transformations than in models.

Technically, Xpand has already been used to enrich existing transformations with source code fragments belonging to different features [20]. In contrast to our contribution, a different approach is applied. As with aspect-oriented approaches, each feature that could be added to a common code base is realized in a separate aspect and provided in a second workflow. We, instead, provide only one single aspect that annotates source code containing realizations for all features. Thus, our approach is tailored for negative rather than for positive variability.

On the whole, our approach is unique with respect to the following aspects: First, it addresses M2T transformations rather than M2M transformations. Second, unlike in [15,18] the approach deals with multi-variant input rather than with multi-variant transformation specifications. Finally, unlike in [3,7,14], the already existing functionality of the transformation engine is exploited, relying on aspects which extend reused transformation definitions in a modular way.

9   Conclusion and Future Work

On the whole, we presented a successful approach to propagate variability annotations by reusing single-variant model transformations. Based on a generic aspect provided to Xpand transformations we are able to correctly implement such multi-variant transformation.

Evaluating the approach reveals that a considerably amount of user effort can be saved regarding the amount of transfered annotation to the multi-variant source code. Additionally, we achieve 100% accuracy comparing the target products created in a single-variant and in a multi-variant transformation run. Moreover, to the best of our knowledge, the Xpand transformation is the first M2T solution automatically creating annotated multi-variant source code by reusing a single-variant transformation.

In the future we like to investigate the incremental behavior in greater detail and extend the evaluation of commutativity to more complex metamodels and instances thereof.

References

1. Apel, S., Janda, F., Trujillo, S., Kästner, C.: Model superimposition in software product lines. In: Proceedings of the 2nd ICMT, pp. 4–19, July 2009
2. Bruneliere, H., Cabot, J., Jouault, F., Madiot, F.: MoDisco: a generic and extensible framework for model driven reverse engineering. In: Proceedings of the IEEE/ACM International Conference on Automated Software Engineering, ASE 2010, pp. 173–174. ACM, New York (2010). http://doi.acm.org/10.1145/1858996.1859032
3. Buchmann, T., Greiner, S.: Managing variability in models and derived artefacts in model-driven software product lines. In: Proceedings of the 6th International Conference on Model-Driven Engineering and Software Development - Volume 1: MODELSWARD, pp. 326–335. INSTICC, SciTePress (2018)
4. Buchmann, T., Schwägerl, F.: FAMILE: tool support for evolving model-driven product lines. In: Joint Proceedings of the Co-located Events at 8th ECMFA, pp. 59–62. CEUR WS, Lyngby, Denmark, July 2012
5. Efftinge, S., et al.: Xpand documentation. Technical report, 2004–2010 (2004)
6. Famelis, M., et al.: Migrating automotive product lines: a case study. In: Kolovos, D., Wimmer, M. (eds.) ICMT 2015. LNCS, vol. 9152, pp. 82–97. Springer, Cham (2015). https://doi.org/10.1007/978-3-319-21155-8_7
7. Greiner, S., Schwägerl, F., Westfechtel, B.: Realizing multi-variant model transformations on top of reused ATL specifications. In: Pires, L.F., Hammoudi, S., Selic, B. (eds.) Proceedings of the 5th International Conference on Model-Driven Engineering and Software Development (MODELSWARD 2017), pp. 362–373. SCITEPRESS Science and Technology Publications, Portugal, Porto, Portugal, February 2017
8. Greiner, S., Westfechtel, B.: Generating multi-variant java source code using generic aspects. In: Proceedings of the 6th International Conference on Model-Driven Engineering and Software Development - Volume 1: MODELSWARD, pp. 36–47. INSTICC, SciTePress (2018)
9. Ji, W., Berger, T., Antkiewicz, M., Czarnecki, K.: Maintaining feature traceability with embedded annotations. In: Proceedings of the 19th International Conference on Software Product Line, SPLC 2015, pp. 61–70. ACM, New York (2015). http://doi.acm.org/10.1145/2791060.2791107
10. Kang, K.C., Cohen, S.G., Hess, J.A., Novak, W.E., Peterson, A.S.: Feature-oriented domain analysis (FODA) feasibility study. Technical report CMU/SEI-90-TR-21, Carnegie-Mellon University, Software Engineering Institute, November 1990
11. Kästner, C., Trujillo, S., Apel, S.: Visualizing Software Product Line Variabilities in Source Code. Ph.D. thesis, San Francisco, CA, USA, September 2008
12. Lopez-Herrejon, R.E., Batory, D.: A standard problem for evaluating product-line methodologies. In: Bosch, J. (ed.) GCSE 2001. LNCS, vol. 2186, pp. 10–24. Springer, Heidelberg (2001). https://doi.org/10.1007/3-540-44800-4_2
13. Pohl, K., Böckle, G., van der Linden, F.: Software Product Line Engineering: Foundations, Principles and Techniques. Springer, Germany (2005)

14. Salay, R., Famelis, M., Rubin, J., Sandro, A.D., Chechik, M.: Lifting model transformations to product lines. In: 36th International Conference on Software Engineering, ICSE 2014, Hyderabad, India, 31 May–07 June, 2014, pp. 117–128 (2014)

15. Sijtema, M.: Introducing variability rules in ATL for managing variability in MDE-based product lines. In: Proceedings of the MtATL 2010, pp. 39–49 (2010)

16. Steinberg, D., Budinsky, F., Paternostro, M., Merks, E.: EMF Eclipse Modeling Framework. The Eclipse Series, 2nd edn. Addison-Wesley, Boston (2009)

17. Strüber, D., Peldzsus, S., Jürjens, J.: Taming multi-variability of software product line transformations. In: Russo, A., Schürr, A. (eds.) FASE 2018. LNCS, vol. 10802, pp. 337–355. Springer, Cham (2018). https://doi.org/10.1007/978-3-319-89363-1_19

18. Strüber, D., Schulz, S.: A tool environment for managing families of model transformation rules. In: Echahed, R., Minas, M. (eds.) ICGT 2016. LNCS, vol. 9761, pp. 89–101. Springer, Cham (2016). https://doi.org/10.1007/978-3-319-40530-8_6

19. Taentzer, G., Salay, R., Strüber, D., Chechik, M.: Transformation of software product lines. In: Tichy, M., Bodden, E., Kuhrmann, M., Wagner, S., Steghöfer, J.P. (eds.) Software Engineering und Software Management 2018, pp. 51–52. Gesellschaft für Informatik, Bonn (2018)

20. Völter, M., Groher, I.: Handling variability in model transformations and generators. In: 7th OOPSLA Workshop on Domain-Specific Modeling (2007)

21. Völter, M., Stahl, T., Bettin, J., Haase, A., Helsen, S.: Model-Driven Software Development: Technology, Engineering, Management. Wiley, UK (2006)

22. Wagelaar, D., Iovino, L., Di Ruscio, D., Pierantonio, A.: Translational semantics of a co-evolution specific language with the EMF transformation virtual machine. In: Hu, Z., de Lara, J. (eds.) ICMT 2012. LNCS, vol. 7307, pp. 192–207. Springer, Heidelberg (2012). https://doi.org/10.1007/978-3-642-30476-7_13

Definition and Visualization of Virtual Meta-model Extensions with a Facet Framework

Jonathan Pepin[1,2]($\boxtimes$), Pascal André[1]($\boxtimes$), Christian Attiogbé[1]($\boxtimes$), and Erwan Breton[2]($\boxtimes$)

[1] LS2N CNRS UMR 6004, University of Nantes, 44322 Nantes, France
{jonathan.pepin,pascal.andre,christian.attiogbe}@univ-nantes.fr
[2] Mia-Software, 11 rue Nina Simone, 44000 Nantes, France
ebreton@sodifrance.fr

Abstract. Model-driven engineering (MDE) provides gainful solutions to software development, maintenance and evolution. Model based standards and techniques emerged and proved useful to develop new applications but also for re-engineering legacy systems. Unfortunately MDE is subject to frequent new standards and upgraded releases which lead stakeholders to proceed costly maintenance operations of the software modules they depend on. The existing techniques suffer from limitations and require new solutions to ensure a better adaptability and flexibility of the tooling. We propose a solution to modify meta-models already in use without rebuilding completely the software product with graphical facilities. This solution includes an improved technique of virtual extension of meta-models with Facets and end-users facilities to handle the model mappings. An open-source implementation, including user graphical interactions, is available on-line.

Keywords: Meta-model · Weaving · Model mapping · EMF · Facet · Automation · Sirius

1 Introduction

Model Driven Engineering (MDE) emphasizes the use of models and meta-models to improve the software quality and the software construction process productivity. The key role of modelling in software engineering and the popularity of the UML notation result in the dissemination of model-based tools and the emergence of a modelling language industry based on the model-driven approach (MDA) [1]. The Meta-Object Facility (MOF) language, as well as the Ecore for Eclipse, became then the foundation for an ecosystem of Domain Specific Languages (DSL) [2]. Some of them are standards like BPMN, BMM, SoaML, SysML, UPDM while others are specific. MDE techniques have proven useful not only for developing new software applications but for re-engineering

© Springer Nature Switzerland AG 2019
S. Hammoudi et al. (Eds.): MODELSWARD 2018, CCIS 991, pp. 106–133, 2019.
https://doi.org/10.1007/978-3-030-11030-7_6

legacy systems and dynamically configuring running systems [3]. There are a growing number of companies which have successfully applied MDE [4].

Software maintenance covers the major part of software life cycle and concerns amply more evolution issues than bug corrections. Unfortunately, the source code (or even worse the binary code) remains the lone reliable information, because the design models are out-of-date or even lost. In the context of model-driven (reverse) engineering of a legacy system, we face challenges related to model evolution, model composition, multi-generation models and multi-layered models.

- Meta-models are a key concept in MDE since model processing is mainly described at the meta-model level through transformation rules or operations. This is also a pitfall because both models and meta-models evolve separately. In particular, modelling languages depend on standards that continuously evolve making the related models evolve too leading to maintain dependency chains. **Model evolution** is even more complex when (meta-)models are parts of larger models.
- MDE promotes the separation of concerns to deal with the complexity and maintainability of software design [5]. This current practice implies to create several heterogeneous models using different (domain specific) languages and subsequent meta-models. While the semantics of each individual model is limited, their consistency and completeness are easier to prove but the difficulty is postponed to the composition of these individual models. **Model composition** is the symmetric paradigm of separation of concerns [6]. It is necessary to compose models to reason on the overall designed system for many purposes such as: checking the global consistency of the models, understanding the interactions between models, generating code, etc. We are particularly interested in the kind of compositions that do not interfere with the individual models.
- **Multi-generation** happens when different releases of one model (or meta-model) are maintained e.g. for different customers or different branches of a company. This may occur also in software product lines or software customization.
- **Multi-layering** happens when we need to maintain links between models at different levels of abstraction (traceability, refinement...). Examples are the CIM-PIM-PSM stack or the enterprise architecture alignment stack [7].

From a software provider point of view, a *typical scenario* is to deliver customised releases to various customers. Customisation leads to tricky maintenance problems when models and meta-models evolve. These include the case of legacy code built with various development methods and tools at different levels of abstraction (from implementation code up to business processes). In order to represent specific (or customised) aspects we extend meta-models with new concepts, attributes and relations. This is always possible to create new meta-models with references to the initial meta-model but every modification requires to rebuild the delivery product. This problem also happens when the modelling language evolves; the new release requires tool adaptation.

A primary requirement to handle the above issues is to find techniques to build new models without modifying the source models (to preserve source property), we call them **non-intrusive model mappings**. The existing approaches are not fully satisfying because they are either intrusive, volatile or too generic. Let us argue in the following. Paige et al. mentioned several challenges of evolving models in MDE [8]. The work presented in this paper is a practical contribution to the *dependency heterogeneity* challenge. We focus on model mappings supporting various semantic links (1), models (or meta-models) evolution (2), persistence (3), while staying non-intrusive by preserving their parts (4). More precisely our contribution is fourfold:

- A mapping definition enabling to connect models without breaking their legacy semantics and without rebuilding the associated software tool support.
- A mapping technique compliant with the existing MDA tools. Taking an industrial point of view, the question is not only to find a mapping meta-model, which is usually depending on the context (the models we work with), but also to implement mapping techniques which are compliant with the existing MDA tools (*e.g.* tools based on the Eclipse EMF Frameworks) and efficient for large-scale applications.
- A mapping tool that can be reused by others (*e.g.* published in a public repository) and customised to similar model transformation in practice. At the implementation level, maintaining the links between model elements require a robust algorithm engine to maintain the constraints imposed by the multiplicities.
- A visual support that enables user friendly model definition and mapping. End-users demand now human interaction facilities.

The core ideas and concepts of this paper were introduced at the MODELSWARD conference [9]. This paper presents a more detailed contribution which includes new facilities related to graphical modelling and assistance, new material for beginners (starter kit and tutorial example) and a new eclipse plugin proposal. The previous paper examples are replaced by new examples that illustrate the tool extensions. The article is structured as follows. In Sect. 2 we review model mapping techniques and motivate our choices. Section 3 overviews EMF Facet and introduces our improvements. Persistence, navigation and testing issues are discussed in Sect. 4. New user interface facilities are presented on the illustrating example in Sect. 5. The new graphical facilities with Sirius are detailed in Sect. 6. The application field is detailed in Sect. 7 including a beginner's guide, user stories and a return on experience of larger case studies. Finally, Sect. 8 summarises the contribution and draws open perspectives.

2   Model Mapping Requirements

This section defines the background and requirements for model mapping. We overview the core concepts and basic requirements, then we compare with related works to finally set the contribution requirements.

2.1 Basic Requirements for Model Mapping

A software system sustains several releases that can even co-exist for different users with different hardware. The definition of models needs enhancements: new attributes, new entities, new classifications, new links... Thus the real life systems generally handle more than one model that may co-exist with different semantics *i.e.* as defined by their meta-models. To capture this reality, we need a particular *model mapping* technique that owns the following criteria:

1. **Non-intrusiveness:** the mapping must not modify the individual models because they evolve independently.
2. **Semantics:** the mapping is not simply a set of links, it supports a semantic relation to connect differently the concepts with an equivalence class of interpretation (an ontology of the concepts and links).
3. **Link Resolution:** the mapping techniques must provide a mechanism to navigate by mapping links directly from the source model to the target model and reciprocally.
4. **Serialization:** the mapping links must be persistent to store the working environment for future updates.

These properties come from lessons learned during model maintenance activities. They build the basis for finding an adequate *"mapping semantics"*.

2.2 A Semantics for Model Mapping

Clavreul identified 88 model composition techniques for different purposes in his systematic review [10]. Consequently our first goal was to find the adequate semantics and an associated operational technique. Considering our basic requirements, we reduce the research field to **model mapping**.

Model Mapping is a model composition that preserves the components. It is called the *"model-based correspondence"* by Clavreul. Model mapping belongs to the *"Model manipulation and management challenges"* of [11] and in particular to the points (2) and (3) mentioned by France et al.: *(2) maintaining traceability links among model elements to support model evolution and round trip engineering and (3) maintaining consistency among viewpoints*. Model mapping techniques are useful for model composition, decomposition or synchronization [11]. We retain five approaches: extension, merging, annotation, weaving and DSL. We detail these approaches.

Model Extension or Merging. The meta-model is either extended with the concepts of another one or merged with another to make a single big model. In both case, the meta models loose their independence and they can hardly evolve (flexibility loss). The Clavreul's mapping language is a merging approach and requires to learn a DSL. We opted for a mechanized approach by providing a simple tool which applies at both compile and run time. Currently, model compositions are done in ad-hoc ways. El Kouhen [5] proposed an unified methodology to compose models based on meta-model extensions. The composition operators are symmetric (commutative *e.g.* merge, parallel) or asymmetric (weaving -see below-, sequential integration). His work is largely inspired by [12] who gave a formal semantics for weaving and merging through morphisms of a category theory. Our approach can be seen as an *ad hoc* model composition in their classification since our mapping uses semantic information of the source models while their approach is a model mapping in our classification. Their mapping approaches enable the separation of concerns, but the merging and weaving do not preserve the legacy models (and the existing related tool support) because their result is a new model. Model merging or extension are intrusive techniques because the source models disappear in the target model.

Model Annotation and Weaving. Model mapping is close to model weaving as defined by [13] which was inspired by Aspect Oriented Modelling. *"Model weaving operations are performed between two or more meta-models, or between models. They aim to specify the links, and their associated semantics, between elements of source and target models"* [13]. Models are woven by establishing different kinds of links denoting the semantics of weaving: merge operations, traceability links, data translation mappings, text to graphical representation, etc. Atlas Model Weaver (AMW) includes a transformation mechanism with ATL[1] to create an automatic weaving. Virtual EMF [14] provides a visual assistant to edit two models from different meta-models and to create links between concepts with *drag and drop*. Unfortunately, editors are not supported since the 4.x versions of Eclipse. The existing tools did not suit to our requirements but we got inspired by them to create our own weaving assistant, including improvements and new features (see Sect. 5.3). Didonet et al. [15] propose an approach that uses matching transformations and weaving models to semi-automate the development of transformations, which is not our goal. In that case, weaving can implement transformations but cannot map models, which is our goal. Our automated mappings implementation has been inspired by this work.

DSL. Model mapping has also been explored in the context of Domain Specific Languages (DSL) to define new languages from existing ones in a non-invasive way without re-creating the tool support. Bruneliere et al. [16] define a textual DSL with extension operators to extend meta-model semantics. It is independent from modelling tooling. Similarly, Greifenberg et al. propose DSL-specific tag language [17]. Kolovos et al. [18] propose decorator extraction and injection operators based on GMF notes to ensure the non-invasive property but it requires manual transformations and conflicting specializations of GMF notes may appear. Langer et al. [19] propose EMF profiles, a lightweight adaptation of UML profiles to extend meta-models with annotations, constraints and stereotypes. An advantage is to add new information. These DSL extension approaches have in common to work on the (binary) inheritance relation (one model is more specialised than another) while we target any kind of n-ary relations between models such as aggregation, composition, inheritance, dependency e.g. traceability... However they are complementary.

---

[1] http://eclipse.org/atl/.

2.3   Requirements for Non-intrusive but Persistent and Semantic Model Mapping

The requirements criteria of the beginning of this section are refined.

- Mapping meta-models in a unique meta-model usually breaks the evolution lifecycle: when the individual models change, the mapping becomes inconsistent and the associated tools obsolete. We need a technique to map meta-models **without intrusion** and **without version dependency**.
- The weaving and annotation techniques are non-intrusive but use only generic links while the end-user model transformation tools need specific information to proceed adequate transformations according to the meta-model relations and multiplicities. The mapping technique must include **semantic information** for these relations.
- Last, the technique must **serialize** the mapping links to support persistence in a way that loading model mappings enables the **navigation** between the original model elements and the new one without disturbing the end-user experience. This ensures the ascending compatibility and enables the preservation of existing tool suites which are industrial concerns.

In summary, we require an equipped *Non-intrusive but Persistent and Semantic Model Mapping* technique (NIPS-MM for short).

In a previous work [20], we compared the above detailed model mapping techniques and we showed that they do not support properly the four above mentioned mandatory criteria for model maintenance and evolution. In practice, it's common to use tools based on the Eclipse EMF Frameworks. EMF enables to define meta-models, load, persist and manipulate the compliant models. We choose the EMF Facet approach, the closest answer to our requirements, except persistence and navigation facilities which are not supported.

3   Toward an Improved EMF Facet for NIPS-MM

The EMF Facet tool is based on EMF to extend virtually a meta-model. This solution answers to the non-intrusiveness and the semantics criteria. However the existing EMF Facet tools do not fulfil all requirements: they have no persistence support for the mapping links (the values are computed by queries only) and few navigation and semantics support. Nevertheless this was the closest approach conforming to our requirements so we decided to improve EMF Facet to draw links between models and manage them in conformance to the defined multiplicities. In this section we overview the EMF Facet features, its interest and limitations and we introduce improvements.

3.1   The Base EMF Facet

Eclipse EMF Facet is a runtime meta-model extension framework composed of four parts: Facet, Customization, Widgets and Query. The Facet part offers the

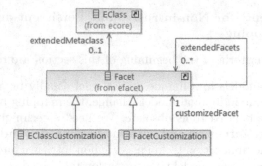

Fig. 1. Facet and customization [9].

possibility to virtually extend (at runtime) existing meta-models and models. The Customization part adds UI enhancements on a meta-model. The Widgets part can be used to apply customizations to model editors. The Query part enables to compute attribute, reference and operation value. The queries are written in Java or OCL. Facet and Customization are the two useful parts for mapping models: one can **extend models** by adding virtual features to existing models and also **weave models** by linking their concepts (Fig. 1). This paper is mainly concerned with the *Facet* part; we dealt with customizations when handling specific meta-models editors in [20].

A Facet provides a new viewpoint on a model which is helpful to categorize model elements with new classifications, to add information on model elements, to navigate easily between model elements with new derived links. A facet provides a virtual mechanism to add new attributes, references or operations on a model without modifying the initial meta-model. Several facets can co-exist and be loaded/unloaded on demand without re-opening the model instance. Under the hood, the Facet meta-model extends the meta-class (EClass) from the EMF Ecore meta-model. Facet applicability is checked by optional conformance rules.

As illustrated by Fig. 2, the meta-model of a Facet may contain FacetAttribute (extend EAttribute in Ecore), FacetReference (extend EReference in Ecore) and FacetOperation (extend EOperation in Ecore) which return values based on query evaluation. Facets are contained in a FacetSet (extend EPackage in Ecore, and FacetSet can be contained in an another FacetSet hierarchically.

3.2   Facet Usage and Limitations

In practice, Facet is an answer to different situations. Next we illustrate three current use cases.

- Facet can be used to implement UML *derived features i.e.* those attributes or associations that are not implemented but computed from other features (also called daemons in programming). For example, the age is computed from the date of birth. Facet enables one to represent them as attributes or references[2] without storing redundant informations.

---

[2] References are the way to represent associations at the implementation level.

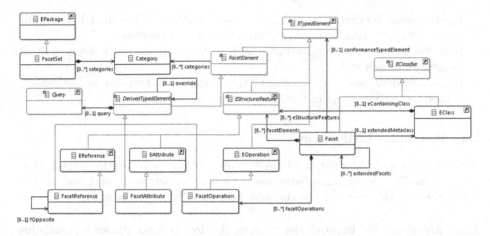

Fig. 2. Facet class diagram [9].

- Facet can be used to customise instances of a meta-model for GUI (user interface) facilities (labels, icons, color...). Facet enables to customize Eclipse SWT components like trees, arrays, lists, etc. As an example, Fig. 3 shows a software component classification (components and applications). We modify the GUI by separating components and application types and the associated icons in Fig. 4.
- Facet can be used to add new data in a model; new features (attributes or references) which are not computed but stored as standard features.

▷ ⬛ Application Component SAFIG
▷ ⬛ Application Component ASPHERIA
▷ ⬛ Application Component MIKROS
▷ ⬛ Application Component PN_ContratsIARD
▷ ⬛ Application Component 128 Consultation RAQVAM 1ere Generation

▷ ⬛ Component SAFIG
▷ ⬛ Component ASPHERIA
▷ ⬛ Application MIKROS
▷ ⬛ Application PN_ContratsIARD
▷ ⬛ Application 128 Consultation RAQVAM 1ere Generation

Fig. 3. Before custom applied [9].   **Fig. 4.** After custom applied [9].

As illustrated by these examples, Facet improves the practice of model (and meta-model) maintenance and evolution but also model transformation. New information can be added without breaking the source meta-models and without requiring a migration to a new meta-model.

The base EMF Facet is a great candidate to NIPS-MM but it suffers from some limitations to cover all the NIPS-MM requirements. We remind the limitations of the Facet approach for NIPS-MM:

- A new feature of the Facet systematically calls a query. However the queries cannot access to the model to map. It is necessary to store the values.

- Queries must be executed during the model loading. If the model is voluminous, the computation times can impact the response time.
- New features cannot be valued manually, as the attributes or references of an ordinary meta-model.
- In independent model composition, the mapping links must be persistent, consequently the values of the features is to be serializable.

3.3   Revisiting EMF Facet

We revisited Facet to fix the above limitations. We first improve the meta-model, then we modify the existing Facet manager and serialization mechanisms. We detail them in this section. We also add visual facilities (see Sect. 6).

Facet Manager. We improve the meta-model by allowing dynamic structures instead of the static one. We add *FacetAttribute* and *FacetReference* getters and setters instead of recomputing systematically the attached query (Fig. 5). Since the meta-model constraints have an impact on the behaviour of the current Facet manager, we upgraded its implementation to support the new behaviour.

Technically, enabling the access of values turns to weakening the multiplicity of *FacetAttribute* and *FacetReference* which extend *DerivedTypeElement*. Thus the multiplicity of the query *eReference* on *DerivedTypedElement* is changed from 1..1 to 0..1. This feature will permit to get the values of *FacetReference* and *FacetAttribute* without using a query. Furthermore we add a new *eReference* named *fOpposite* to create a reflexive reference mechanism like *eOpposite* on *EReference* in the Ecore meta-model. The improved EMF Facet enables now to manually extend and weave models. As a matter of fact, we fulfil the criterion of Sect. 2.1: the serialization makes the improved Facet be the most effective approach among all the mapping techniques of Sect. 2. This corresponds to contribution 1 of page 2.

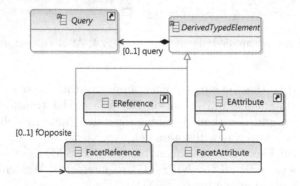

Fig. 5. EMF facet meta-model modifications [9].

We submitted our proposal of extended EMF meta-model as a contribution to the open-source Eclipse EMF Facet[3]; this has been approved. This is a public part of contribution 3 of page 2.

Serialization Mechanisms. Once we modified the meta-model, we turned to the Java implementation of the new behaviour of the Facet engine called *FacetManager*. At first, we supported the two simplest multiplicities of the bi-directional references type: one-to-one and many-to-many. But, this was not sufficient to cover all the cases so we proceeded with all the possible cases.

In the next section, we present the different multiplicity cases and how to implement them in order to obtain a complete weaving engine.

4 Adding Persistent Mapping and Navigation to EMF Facet

Until now, one can create *FacetReference* links to map concepts from different meta-models. In this section, we describe the mechanism that supports bi-directional mappings and a two-way navigation to browse models and mappings.

Mappings are represented here by UML associations, which are bi-directional by default. An association end multiplicity (or cardinality) is an interval of value represented by a lower and an upper bound. An association between classes is represented by a set of links at the instance level. At the implementation level, maintaining a link between elements is an *object relation mapping* (ORM) problem [21] where the link multiplicities and bi-directional navigation are ensured. This problem needs a robust algorithm engine to maintain the constraints imposed by the multiplicities. A (bi-directional) association is represented by a pair of uni-directional (one-way) associations as shown in the Human/City example of Fig. 6.

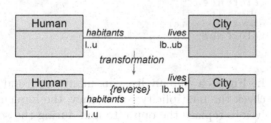

Fig. 6. Bi-directional link example.

4.1 The Four Mapping Cases

Thus any (instance) link modification must be propagated to the opposite link. Depending on the multiplicity values, four cases are distinguished: **one to one**

---

[3] Available since version 1.0: https://bugs.eclipse.org/bugs/show_bug.cgi?id=463898.

(an instance is linked to one instance only), **one to many** (an instance can be linked to several instances), **many to one** (several instances can be linked to one instance), **many to many** (several instances can be linked to several instances). Note that *one to many* and *many to one* cases are not symmetric because the relation is oriented. Then, these two cases have different algorithms to preserve the multiplicity.

A core issue is to preserve the symmetry constraint (`lives.reverse() = habitants`) of the opposite association ends. Updating only one side usually leads to a symmetry constraint violation. In the following, we illustrate each case by giving a figure and the algorithm we implemented in FacetManager[4].

One to One. In Fig. 7, a human lives in only one city, and city have only one habitant. To check the multiplicity consistency, the implementation in the FacetManager involves to keep only one opposite link during the *set* operation.

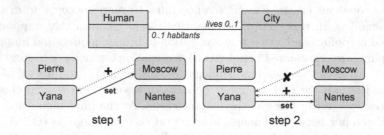

Fig. 7. One to one relation.

```
1  delete old reference
2  delete old opposite reference
3  create new opposite reference
4  create new reference
```

One to Many. In Fig. 8, a human lives in many city, and city have only one habitants. To check the multiplicity consistency, the implementation in the FacetManager involves to replace the opposite link during the *set* operation.

```
1  remove old reference from existings
2  delete old opposite reference
3  create new opposite reference
4  add new reference into existing
```

---

[4] Available since version 1.1: https://bugs.eclipse.org/bugs/show_bug.cgi?id=510039.

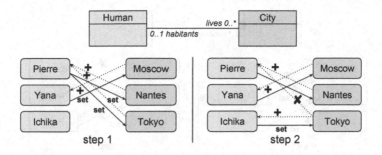

Fig. 8. One to many relation.

Many to One. In Fig. 9, a human lives in only one city, and city have many habitants. To check the multiplicity consistency, the implementation in the FacetManager involves to delete the old and to add the new opposite link during the *set* operation.

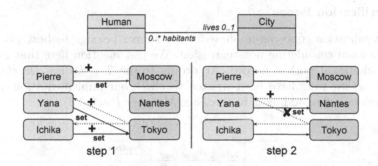

Fig. 9. Many to one relation.

```
1   delete old reference
2   remove old opposite reference from existings
3   add new opposite reference into existing
4   create new reference
```

Many to Many. In Fig. 10, a human lives in many city, and city have many habitants. To check the multiplicity consistency, the implementation in the FacetManager involves to delete the old and to add the new opposite link during the *set* operation.

```
1   remove old reference from existings
2   remove old opposite reference from existings
3   add new opposite reference into existing
4   add new reference into existing
```

Thanks to the automatic management of bi-directional links, the instance mapping is transparent for users. Our implementation allows one to weave the

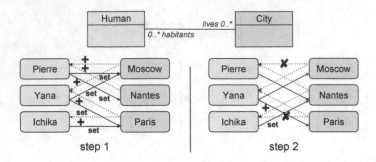

Fig. 10. Many to many relation.

instances without a slave-master semantics. The user can draw a link in any order: from the source to the target or reverse. This corresponds to contribution 2 of page 2.

4.2 Verification Issues

Adding verification concerns in shared open source belongs to best practices, especially when considering non-regression. We just mention here that interest because additional work is needed. According to the *Test-Driven Development* approach, *JUnit* tests have been written to check our implementation and its code coverage before adding it to the *FacetManager* (Sect. 3.3).

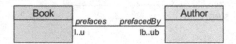

Fig. 11. Library example.

For sake of compatibility with the previous committed contribution in Facet project (see page 9), the following *JUnit* tests are illustrated with the `Library` example of Fig. 6. Indeed it is embedded in Facet Framework. It includes meta-model and models. The `Library` case study has been presented in detail in the precedent paper [9] and will naturally be reused it for our new Junit tests. We illustrate them with two simple examples of the `Library`.

For each multiplicity case, we set *facetReference* between different instances of books and writers, then we check if the reference setting conforms to the reference and its opposite.

Example 1. In the many-to-one case, `writer1` and `writer2` write the preface of `book1`. The test case of Listing 1.1 assigns the value, establishes the mapping and checks the reverse link. It succeeds.

Listing 1.1. Many-to-one: the direct preface reference.

```
FacetReference preface = getFacetRef(MANY_TO_ONE, WRITER_EXT,
    PREFACE);
Book book1writer1 = this.facetMgr.getOrInvoke(writer1, preface,
    Book.class);
Assert.assertEquals(book1, book1writer1);
Book book1writer2 = this.facetMgr.getOrInvoke(writer2, preface,
    Book.class);
Assert.assertEquals(book1, book1writer2);
```

Example 2. The test case of Listing 1.2 checks the automatic setting of the opposite reference prefaced: **book1** is prefaced by **writer1** and **writer2**. Its execution also led to success.

Listing 1.2. Many-to-one opposite: the prefaced reference.

```
FacetReference prefaced = getFacetRef(MANY_TO_ONE, BOOK_EXT,
    PREFACED);
List<Writer> writers1and2 = this.facetMgr.
    getOrInvokeMultiValued(book1, prefaced, Writer.class);
Assert.assertEquals(Arrays.asList(writer1, writer2),
    writers1and2);
```

The above examples are specific to the **Library** case study. Next step will be to write generic tests, written at the meta-model level, that can be shared by all applications. Henceforth EMF Facet enables one to create links between any models following a definition at the meta-model level.

We present additional tools to handle the mapping links at the instance level in Sect. 5.

5   Actual End-User Running Tools

The previous sections introduced the mapping framework and its implementation. This section illustrates the implemented tools associated to the mapping framework. This corresponds to contribution 3 of page 2. The support example is again the **Library** case study presented in a previous paper [9].

In this example, we extend *Book* and *Writer* meta-classes by creating new *FacetSet* for each link mapping cases containing all facets which define the new virtual references with the specific multiplicity: *prefaces* and **prefaced**. A usual mapping process includes the following activities: *facet mapping definition, instance valuation, instance linking, mapping navigation and evaluation.*

5.1   Defining Mappings with Facet

At least each facet defines a name and the meta-class type. A facet can extend an existing Facet. The extended facet refers to the original meta-class by its absolute *Universal Resource Identifier* (URI). A facet defines three kinds of features: FacetAttribute, FacetReference and FacetOperation. One can create as many new features as required. We focus only on reference and attribute. A FacetReference defines at least a name, a multiplicity, a type and an opposite reference if the association is bidirectional. The type is a meta-class from any Ecore reachable meta-model or another predefined FacetReference in the current FacetSet. A FacetAttribute defines at least a name, a multiplicity and the meta-class type as in FacetReference.

Example. Let the previous practical example of books and authors. Assume a *Book* meta-model describing the books and a *Writer* describing authors. In Fig. 12, we create four FacetSets, one for each mapping multiplicity: many to many (MToM), many to one (MToO), one to many (OToM), and one to one (OToO). For each case, a new reference *preface* links 'writers to books' and the opposite reference *prefaced* links 'books to writers'. The multiplicity differs through the upper and lower bound. In the example of Fig. 12, -1 represents the 'many' upper bound value. The purpose of this new definition is to extend the existing classification of a library of books and authors to obtain an enriched catalog.

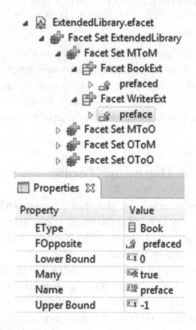

Fig. 12. FacetSet definition example [9].

5.2   Setting Links by Property Value

We use `Property editors` to set attributes and references values that will be used by queries.

Example. We experiment the different multiplicity links, by creating a library with books and writers. We apply a specific FacetSet at a time: MToM, MToO, OToM, or OToO. In Fig. 14 the FacetSet OToM is applied, the book "2001 Space Odyssey" have two prefaced writers "Isaac Asimov" and "Arthur C. Clarke". The property field varies according to the multiplicity: a pop-up menu selector (one) or a double selector (many). We can check that the opposite link is correctly set in Fig. 13: *"Isaac Asimov" preface "2001 Space Odyssey"*, and *"Arthur C. Clarke" preface "2001 Space Odyssey"*.

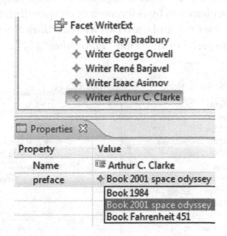

Fig. 13. Editing mono-valued references [9].

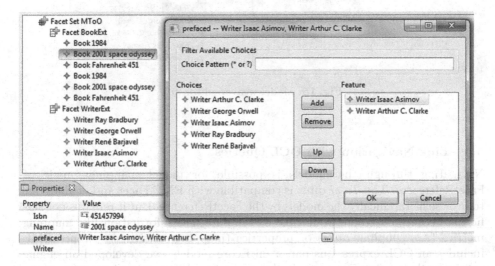

Fig. 14. Editing multi-valued reference [9].

5.3   Setting Links by Model Weaver

Setting manually many links between instances by the property values is quite fastidious and editors are really useless in this case. To assist users we developed a specific weaving editor with multiple views (drag-and-drop).

Example. An outline displays the different models to weave on the right part of Fig. 15: a first model 'library with books' and a second model 'library with writer'. On the left part of Fig. 15, a specific view organizes the weaving result by facets. The MToM facet is loaded here. This design allows us to drag and drop elements from right to left to link elements by references corresponding to the FacetSet definition. In this example, we drag and drop two writers *"Ray Bradbury"* and *"George Orwell"* on reference *prefaced* of the book *"Fahrenheit 451"*.

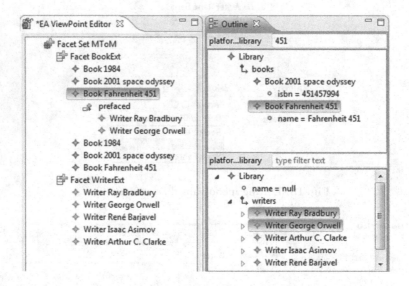

Fig. 15. Model weaver editor [9].

5.4   Link Navigation with OCL Queries

Navigating through the models is possible for model mappings made of FacetReferences. The *TreeEditor* is compatible with EMF Facet and enables one to browse hierarchically the models by the FacetReference. But it remains not sufficient because designers would like to compute new information like mapping metrics (*e.g.* coupling rates) or properties (mapping consistency). Since EMF includes an OCL expressions parser on Ecore models, we developed an engine extension that makes Facet compatible with virtual features to be used as properties in OCL statements. OCL queries are a flexible means to write assertions or computations. This extension has also been integrated in our plug-in to the EMF Facet project.

Example. In Fig. 16, we use the previous model weaving result. We open the model 'library with books' and write an OCL query in the console to know all writers who prefaced the books: "*self.books.prefaced*". The query writing is assisted with auto-completion and the result appears in the console.

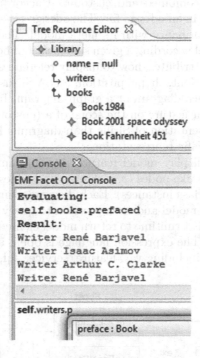

Fig. 16. OCL facet console [9].

In previous screen captures, we saw that Facet is compatible with tree editor to navigate in extended model by Facet. To value the different facet features, properties view helped, and drag drop is possible between different trees. The console is another batch working way to navigate and query facet models. But we have no specific graphical mode driven by the behaviour and semantic from a meta-model. A diagram editor would be a good practical to create this modelling workbench. We will present a solution based on a Sirius and Facet compatibility in the next section.

6 New Diagram Representation with Sirius Compatibility Implementation

Sirius is an open source framework to create a graphical modelling workbench that fits to specific requirements. Sirius follows model-driven architecture principle and engineering methods. The specifier can create viewpoints for end-users with functional behaviours that conform to a meta-model. Sirius is very popular in the Eclipse community and is mainly used by the modelling community. It replaced old (fastidious) ways to create diagram representations with GMF and GEF frameworks.

Sirius provides a set of customizable and dynamic representations. These representations can be combined and customized according to the concept of Viewpoint. It is specified in an odesign file. The odesign reference meta-model will display a model in conformance with its meta-model. The representations show instances from the model according a given specification: how to display instance classes, how to display attributes, how to display references... Graphical features are given such as colour, font, shape, position, etc. A Sirius representation can be a table, a tree, a sequence diagram or a graph diagram. In this paper, the goal is display facet extension feature on the scope of a (customizable) diagram. We do not test other representation of Sirius than diagrams but our compatibility does not depend on specific representations.

To specify how to display model features by diagrams, the specifier must create diagram elements like nodes (*e.g.* classes) and edges (*e.g.* associations for the references between class instances). Each diagram element defines a concept mapping from the meta-model and an expression to query the meta-model. The expression is interpreted at runtime to return model elements or to produce texts (*e.g.* label in diagram). The expression language is open, it can be an extension of the default standard including var, feature, service, aql, acceleo and raw ocl.

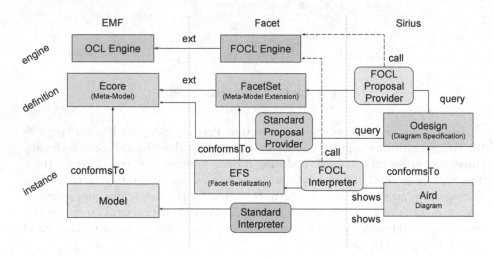

Fig. 17. Sirius and facet compatibility mechanism overview.

One goal of our current contribution was to provide a custom language compatible with facets. The new language must have a prefix to distinguish its own expressions and must provide an evaluation engine. We implement an extension point[5] with an implementation conform to the IInterpreter interface. Optionally,

---

[5] Eclipse mechanism to contribute functionality to specific open API plug-ins.

an auto-completion support can be provided by another extension point which implementation conforms to IProposalProvider interface. Figure 17 presents the main mechanism and interaction to state the compatibility between Sirius and Facet. The diagram includes visual information (special layering and sizing of shapes). Mapping references to the models are stored in an Aird file. The Aird behaviour is specified in the odesign file. The odesign expressions interpreter evaluates facet features (new extension of the original meta-model) defined in facetset to return values from the facet model.

Next section we present the implementation proposal, a representation definition and its usage with the facet support. This corresponds to contribution 4 of page 3.

6.1 Evaluating FOCL Expressions

A previous work [9] introduced an extension for the OCL Ecore engine to be compatible with Facet. This is a fine opportunity to reuse and adapt our facet ocl language to write Sirius expressions (*cf.* Fig. 17). The extension mechanism offered by Sirius allows us to define a new query expression interpreter language based on our OCL Ecore engine. We name the new query protocol with the prefix focl *i.e.* for facet ocl. To provide new focl interpreter, we implement the extension point *org.eclipse.sirius.common.ex- pressionInterpreter* and implementation class is named *FacetOCLInterpreterProvider*.

The new interpreter implements methods of the interface *org.eclipse.sirius.common. tools.api.interpreter.IInterpreter*. First, the method *evaluate* includes string expressions and context as parameters. The values are transmitted to Facet Ocl engine for evaluation. Second, we added compatibility to the Sirius session (*i.e.* the working context of a loaded instance representation) to attach the FacetManager (facet execution and support engine). Last, at runtime the evaluator must know the facets managed in its current context *i.e.* which facetsets are applied on model and where the facets values are stored for the opened diagram editor instance. We added command buttons in the tool bar ⚙ 📂 to apply facets and open a facet serialization file (efs).

Now, we are able to evaluate expression containing facet features with our new focl interpreter. In next section, we implement an assistant to write focl expressions.

6.2 Writing Specification Queries

A second extension point *org.eclipse.sirius.common.proposalProvider* offered by Sirius enables to define an auto-completion support for new expression language. We wrote an extension point and a *FacetOCLProposalProvider* implementation. The proposal of Fig. 18 is really user friendly, the queries writing is greatly helped by auto-completion, for those that do not know well the focl language.

We are ready to specify representation and use diagram with extended information from facet. In next section, we describe an example step by step.

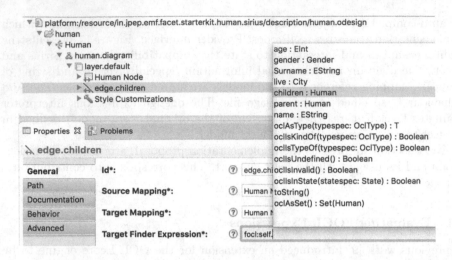

Fig. 18. Auto-completion help writing Focl expression.

6.3   Illustration

We reuse the toy example presented in Sect. 4 which is already available in the starter kit on our gitlab repository.

The definition of the representation in the odesign file is very simple. We define (i) a node to map the original human class from the meta-model (*cf.* Fig. 20) and (ii) an edge to map the children extended relation from the faceset definition (*cf.* Fig. 19).

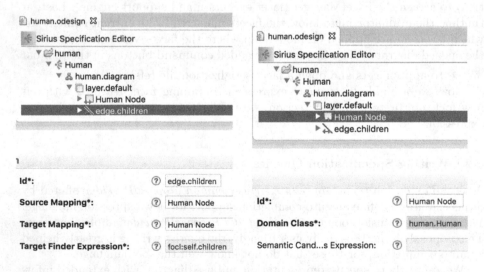

Fig. 19. Node for original human class.

Fig. 20. Edge for facet children relationship.

According to Facet compatibility, the relationship between Human appears on the diagram at execution time (*cf.* Fig. 21).

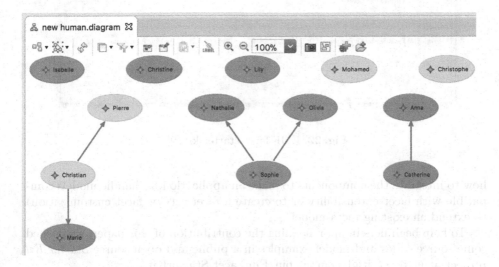

Fig. 21. Diagram result with facet relation values between humans.

Our contribution demonstrates that Facet is compatible with Sirius. It is a major enhancement to extend existing graphical workbench without changing the meta-model. Our current implementation accepts the focl query language in a read mode only. The next step will be to override the implementation to set the values corresponding facet references and attributes by the FacetManager instead of the standard Ecore mechanism. When implementation will be complete and stabilized, including junit tests, we will propose and submit our contribution to Facet Eclipse community project for the review and acceptance process. We expect our contribution will be accepted.

Section 7 draws experimentations of the above tools and wizards.

7 User Tutorial and Applications

As mentioned in the previous sections the improved Facet tooling is available at the open-source Eclipse EMF Facet https://wiki.eclipse.org/EMF_Facet. In this section we provide materials to potential users.

7.1 Beginner's Guide

EMF Facet is not standalone but remains a framework to be integrated by developers in their applications. This project has no introductory examples to show

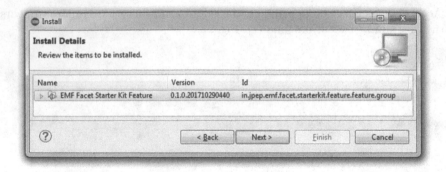

Fig. 22. EMF facet starter kit [9].

how to integrate the components to make an application, to handle models compatible with facet extensibility or to create a facet set (or facet customization) to extend an existing meta-model.

To help beginners in apprehending the contribution of this paper, we pushed some source codes and model examples in a public and open source *Starter Kit* project at https://gitlab.com/jpepin/EmfFacet_StarterKit/.

Eclipse users can use the *Update Site* to install easily the example in Eclipse installations (compatibles with the Kepler or more recent versions).

1. In Eclipse '*Help > Install New Software*', enter the update site url https://gitlab.com/jpepin/EmfFacet_StarterKit/raw/master/in.jpep.emf. facet.starterkit.updatesite/.
2. As illustrated by Fig. 22, select *EMF Facet Starter Kit Feature* and next...
3. After the plugin installation, create the example project with '*File > New > Example*'.
4. Choose *Models Example* from the *EMF Facet Starter Kit* category.

Figure 23 illustrates the given tiny example that includes two models: *human* and *city*. Three testing scenarios are proposed as follows.

S1 *Intra model facet extension.* You can open and compare the files *example.human* and *example.mset*. This *mset* is opened with an editor compatible with Facet and the facet definitions are enabled at the beginning. You can see through the *Properties* view, that the facet extension adds a new attribute 'Surname' and a new bidirectional reference 'parent'/'children' of *John*. The values of the two new features can be assigned and stored in the data file.

S2 *Inter model facet extension.* The *human* and *city* models are clearly independent. This example shows a new facet extension to add bi-directional references 'lives' and 'habitants'. Similarly to the 'intra' scenario, the values can be updated with the *Properties* view, and saved with result serialized in *data.efs*.

S3 *Customization.* By default the *human* meta-model does not distinguish the gender man and woman. To add the visual distinction of Fig. 23, that improves the navigation ergonomics, open the file *example.mset*, press the button 'Load/Unload Customizations' from the tool bar 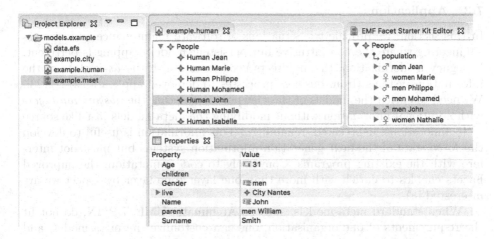 ▼ and choose *Family Custo* definition. Now, men and women are displayed with different prefix label and icon.

Fig. 23. EMF facet starter kit models example [9].

If you are a software developer, you can download the example sources code from the *EMF Facet Starter Kit* Git repository. It shows how to implement an editor with facet compatibility integration: extended property view, load/unload facet and customization buttons, set/load facet serialization file. Facet and customization definitions for meta-models Human and City are available too for example and can be widen. Two query examples are given in the customization definition, one in Java and the other in OCL.

The above tiny example shows that the facet persistence and navigation contribution is already available in the Eclipse open source project for developers to create simple tools without complex configuration for end-user. Moreover, the example demonstrates that EMF Facet is adapted to different use cases: to add attributes and association in a model; to link two different and independent models; or to customize the user interface. This example can be adapted and extended to larger and real case studies.

7.2 Sirius Compatibility

The source code to add EMF Facet compatibility described in Sect. 6 is in a single plugin named *in.jpep.emf.facet.ext.util.efacet.ocl.sirius*. The source code is entirely open and available in new repository at:
https://gitlab.com/jpepin/EmfFacet_OCLSiriusExt

The Starter Kit project has been updated to add Sirius compatibility. The examples of Sect. 6.3 are also added in Starter Kit repository which includes also the *odesign* file representation definition of the `Human/City` meta-model in the new plugin and the *aird* example file diagram to test our compatibility at runtime. Note that once the diagram is opened, do not forget to open the serialization file *data.efs* to load the facet values. The result is shown in Fig. 21.

7.3   Applications

In this section, we provide two situations of software maintenance and reverse-engineering where the non-intrusive but persistent model mapping is pertinent. In legacy modernization, the architects need to establish the *as-is* state of the information systems (from business processes to deployed applications) [22,23]. We need to enrich the models of the viewpoints denoting the *abstraction layers* with additional information without modifying the meta-models just like source code annotations: deprecated, renaming... This information is useful to develop the *to-be* state of the next generation information systems but must not interfere with the existing programs. Conversely to code annotation, the improved Facets enables to enrich with more than one layer (one layer by aspect we are interested in).

When standard meta-models, such as Archimate, UML, BPMN, do not fit the requirements of one organisation, one can customize the meta-models and create a family of extensions that is consistent with the standard releases, as far as a new release of one standard does not impact too many concepts (like the transition from UML 1.x to UML 2.x). The maintenance of the customizations follow their own life cycles.

Next section reports large scale experimentations.

7.4   Return on Experience

The `Human/City` and `Library` examples are toy case studies that are simple enough to illustrate our contributions. We lead experimentations of our improved Facet in the context of Business-IT alignment of Enterprise Architecture. This context covers a wider field than the scope of this paper. We just briefly report here this experimentation but the reader will find more details in [20].

In the context of Information System maintenance, Business-IT alignment (BITA) means to align models coming from different enterprise architecture points of view. This is a tricky problem [7]. Alignment can be seen as traceability links when the models represent different abstraction layers produced along the information system development.

We proposed an operational vision of BITA to provide tools and assistance to help enterprise architects during their analysis activity. We defined different meta-models for the different points of view (business process, functional, application). We implemented techniques to feed the corresponding models from legacy information: reverse engineering to abstraction the implementation information (*e.g.* source code, data) and extraction from enterprise repository models when they exist. The general problem was then reduced to align concretely the models produced for each viewpoint, which is a model mapping problem.

The mapping support, as defined in this paper, was the core technique to establish the concrete alignment links between models.

We experimented real size case studies provided by insurance companies with heterogeneous information supports: lots of java source files, MEGA repositories, documents, databases... The experiments showed that big mappings are hardly manageable by humans; tool assistance is mandatory. Our tool support handled efficiently big models. More generally the alignment technique is generic, adaptable, efficient and scalable. Even in bulky case with manual mapping, our Weaving Editor (cf. Fig. 15) provides an advanced user interface with search engine to find and highlight concepts matching. However additional tools are needed to visualize big mappings, to evaluate the mapping properties (consistency, completeness) and quality (misalignment, evolution). Our Facet query engine was a first step to reach this last goal.

8   Conclusion

MDE support is subject to frequent new standards and upgraded releases. Stakeholders have to proceed regularly maintenance periods to maintain their models and applications to keep compatibility with their providers dependencies. As an answer to the problem of upgrading legacy model driven application and the related tool support, we propose an equipped technique that enables one to modify meta-models already in use by software, without rebuilding completely the legacy tool support. This solution emerged from the comparison of existing techniques of model composition against the NIPS-MM requirements (Non-intrusive but Persistent and Semantic Model Mapping).

This technique, based on EMF Facet, enables the virtual extension of meta-models with persistence and model navigation. The extension is called virtual because it does not directly impact the initial meta-models which can be EMF meta-models or already extended meta-models. Our extension takes into account the various multiplicities of the associations between entities and considers two-way references between the involved entities. We implemented this technique and the associated tool including the end-users facilities is compliant with the EMF and is integrated to the open-source Eclipse EMF Facet project. Thanks to Sirius, graphical facilities have been implemented to make the model weaving activity and result more user friendly. The graphical add-on is on the way to be integrated to EMF Facet. We illustrated the approach on toy examples but we experimented it on various real case studies to fix its applicability. We have then contributed to solve an true model and software evolution issue.

This work also opens new perspectives. One of them to is provide more intelligent user assistance. We target heuristics to propose a list of possible model mappings to the modeller, he can then choose the desired ones. Those heuristics will depend on the nature and the semantics of the model mappings. For example, when mapping two releases of the same model, it is usually easier to detect equality mapping. In specific cases, one can detect patterns or naming conventions.

Another perspective is to propagate model change to other models which are mapped to the changing model. This may also depend on the semantics of the mapping links. For example, suppose a design software model mapped to an analysis model (functional requirements) and a technical model (target infrastructure). Changing functional or technical requirements will impact the design model. The mapping structure will help to delimit the impact measure and the design parts that are subject to changes.

References

1. Ruscio, D.D., Paige, R.F., Pierantonio, A.: Guest editorial to the special issue on success stories in model driven engineering. Sci. Comput. Program. **89**, 69–70 (2014)
2. Brambilla, M., Cabot, J., Wimmer, M.: Model-Driven Software Engineering in Practice. Synthesis Lectures on Software. Morgan & Claypool, San Rafael (2012)
3. Cuadrado, J.S., Izquierdo, J.L.C., Molina, J.G.: Applying model-driven engineering in small software enterprises. Sci. Comput. Program. **89**, 176 (2014)
4. Hutchinson, J., Whittle, J., Rouncefield, M.: Model-driven engineering practices in industry. Sci. Comput. Program. **89**, 144–161 (2014)
5. El Kouhen, A.: Panorama: a unified framework for model composition. In: 15th International Conference on Modularity, Malaga, Spain (2016) MODULARITY 2016
6. Atlee, J.M., France, R., Georg, G., Moreira, A., Rumpe, B., Zschaler, S.: Modeling in software engineering. In: Companion to the Proceedings of the 29th International Conference on Software Engineering, ICSE COMPANION 2007, Washington, DC, USA, pp. 113–114. IEEE Computer Society (2007)
7. Clark, T., Barn, B.S., Oussena, S.: Leap: a precise lightweight framework for enterprise architecture. In: Proceedings of the 4th India Software Engineering Conference, ISEC 2011, New York, NY, USA, pp. 85–94. ACM (2011)
8. Paige, R.F., Matragkas, N., Rose, L.M.: Evolving models in model-driven engineering: state-of-the-art and future challenges. J. Syst. Softw. **111**, 272 (2016)
9. Pepin, J., André, P., Attiogbé, C., Breton, E.: Virtual extension of metamodels with facet tools. In: Proceedings of the 6th International Conference on Model-Driven Engineering and Software Development, vol. 1, MODELSWARD, INSTICC, pp. 59–70. SciTePress (2018)
10. Clavreul, M.: Model and metamodel composition: separation of mapping and interpretation for unifying existing model composition techniques. Ph.D. thesis, Université Rennes 1 (2011)
11. France, R., Rumpe, B.: Model-driven development of complex software: a research roadmap. In: 2007 Future of Software Engineering, FOSE 2007 (2007)
12. Marchand, J.Y., Combemale, B., Baudry, B.: A categorical model of model merging and weaving. In: Proceedings of the 4th International Workshop on Modeling in Software Engineering, MiSE 2012 (2012)
13. Jouault, F., Vanhooff, B., Bruneliere, H., Doux, G., Berbers, Y., Bezivin, J.: Inter-DSL coordination support by combining megamodeling and model weaving. In: Proceedings of the SAC 2010 (2010)
14. Brunelière, H., Dupé, G.: Virtual EMF - transparent composition, weaving and linking of models. In: EclipseCon Europe 2011 (2011)

15. Del Fabro, M.D., Valduriez, P.: Semi-automatic model integration using matching transformations and weaving models. In: Proceedings of the 2007 ACM Symposium on Applied Computing (2007)
16. Bruneliere, H., et al.: On lightweight metamodel extension to support modeling tools agility. In: Taentzer, G., Bordeleau, F. (eds.) ECMFA 2015. LNCS, vol. 9153, pp. 62–74. Springer, Cham (2015). https://doi.org/10.1007/978-3-319-21151-0_5
17. Greifenberg, T., Look, M., Roidl, S., Rumpe, B.: Engineering tagging languages for dsls. CoRR (2016)
18. Kolovos, D.S., Rose, L.M., Drivalos Matragkas, N., Paige, R.F., Polack, F.A.C., Fernandes, K.J.: Constructing and navigating non-invasive model decorations. In: Tratt, L., Gogolla, M. (eds.) ICMT 2010. LNCS, vol. 6142, pp. 138–152. Springer, Heidelberg (2010). https://doi.org/10.1007/978-3-642-13688-7_10
19. Langer, P., Wieland, K., Wimmer, M., Cabot, J.: EMF profiles: a lightweight extension approach for EMF models. J. Obj. Technol. 11, 1–29 (2012)
20. Pepin, J., André, P., Attiogbé, C., Breton, E.: An improved model facet method to support EA alignment. CSIMQ 9, 1–27 (2016). https://doi.org/10.7250/csimq.2016-9.01
21. Ambler, S.W.: Building Object Applications That Work: Your Step-by-Step Handbook for Developing Robust Systems with Object Technology. Managing Object Technology. SIGS (1998)
22. Clark, T., Barn, B.S., Oussena, S.: A method for enterprise architecture alignment. In: Proper, E., Gaaloul, K., Harmsen, F., Wrycza, S. (eds.) PRET 2012. LNBIP, vol. 120, pp. 48–76. Springer, Heidelberg (2012). https://doi.org/10.1007/978-3-642-31134-5_3
23. Lankhorst, M.: Enterprise Architecture at Work: Modelling, Communication and Analysis. TEES. Springer, Heidelberg (2013). https://doi.org/10.1007/978-3-642-29651-2

Automated Recommendation of Related Model Elements for Domain Models

Henning Agt-Rickauer[1]([envelope]), Ralf-Detlef Kutsche[2], and Harald Sack[3]

[1] Hasso Plattner Institute for IT Systems Engineering, University of Potsdam,
Potsdam, Germany
`henning.agt-rickauer@hpi.de`
[2] Database Systems and Information Management Group,
Technische Universität Berlin, Berlin, Germany
`ralf-detlef.kutsche@tu-berlin.de`
[3] FIZ Karlsruhe, Karlsruhe Institute of Technology (KIT), Karlsruhe, Germany
`harald.sack@fiz-karlsruhe.de`

Abstract. Domain modeling is an important activity in the early stages
of software projects to achieve a common understanding of the problem
area among project participants. Domain models describe concepts and
relationships of respective application fields using a modeling language
and domain-specific terms. Creating these models requires software engineers to have detailed domain knowledge and expertise in model-driven
development. Collecting domain knowledge is a time-consuming manual process that is rarely supported in current modeling environments.
In this paper, we describe an approach that supports domain modeling through formalized knowledge sources and information extraction
from text. On the one hand, domain-specific terms and their relationships are automatically queried from existing knowledge bases. On the
other hand, as these knowledge bases are not extensive enough, we have
constructed a large network of semantically related terms from natural
language data sets containing millions of one-word and multi-word terms
and their quantified relationships. Both approaches are integrated into a
domain model recommender system that provides context-aware suggestions of model elements for virtually every possible domain. We report
on the experience of using the recommendations in various industrial and
research environments.

Keywords: Domain modeling · Recommender system ·
Semantic network · Information extraction · Knowledge-based modeling

1 Introduction

1.1 Motivation

Model-driven engineering (MDE) suggests the systematic use of models as
primary development artifacts for software system building [1]. These models

© Springer Nature Switzerland AG 2019
S. Hammoudi et al. (Eds.): MODELSWARD 2018, CCIS 991, pp. 134–158, 2019.
https://doi.org/10.1007/978-3-030-11030-7_7

describe various aspects of a system at a higher level of abstraction using particular modeling languages (e.g., UML, entity relationship diagrams, or domain-specific languages). MDE aims to continuously refine models and generate source code. As a result, the effort of manually creating code with programming languages is reduced and recurring tasks are automated.

An important activity in early phases of model-driven software development is domain modeling [2,3]. Its goal is to create models that reflect the conceptual structures of a business domain. These models include domain-specific terms and their relationships to improve the understanding of the problem area among stakeholders [4].

Domain modeling requires knowledge in model-driven software development, e.g., finding the right abstractions, creating meta-models, and the correct use of generalizations, specializations and aggregations. Assuming that software engineers have these skills, these techniques are typically applied to different areas of application and industries. Engineers must have detailed knowledge of the domain to build domain-specific models and derive corresponding refined implementation models. Building domain knowledge is a time-consuming manual process (such as talking to domain experts and reading specific documentation). Recent modeling environments (e.g., Eclipse Modeling Project, MagicDraw) provide sophisticated assistance for the correct use of modeling languages and verification of models, but support for the actual content and meaning of the model elements is very limited [5,6].

1.2 Problem Statement

Domain modeling was and still is a challenging task [7,8]. It involves gathering a lot of information that comes from different types of people, documents, and other sources of knowledge. Domain modeling is a knowledge-intensive process and requires intensive collaboration between engineers and domain experts. Automation of domain modeling was addressed by research [9], but support for this activity is still an open problem [10]. The key challenges of domain modeling and knowledge acquisition are as follows.

Solutions based on reusable domain information libraries such as Domain Engineering [11] suffer from a cold start problem. Reusable domain knowledge will only be available if enough solutions have already been developed using this methodology, while new projects already want to benefit from this domain knowledge. In the end, domain models often have to be developed from scratch [12].

Collaborations between technical stakeholders (modeling experts) and non-technical stakeholders (domain experts) require a time-consuming learning phase during a project [13]. Domain experts are often unfamiliar with modeling notations, and modeling experts usually need to develop a deeper understanding of domain concepts and terms in order to properly organize them into domain models. The greatest effort is at the modeler's desk, as it is usually more time-consuming to find, understand, and process all available domain information than to learn a few visual modeling concepts.

Domain information is contained in arbitrary sources. Structured information sources (e.g., databases, XML documents, knowledge bases, models) may be available, but unified access to all sources is in most cases not available and can only be facilitated by building additional search engines. Unfortunately, the amount of structured information sources is negligible compared to unstructured information. It is estimated that 80% of existing data is unstructured[1]. Domain information is often contained in natural language documents (e.g., textbooks, manuals, requirement specifications). Relevant facts must first be manually located and then interpreted.

Finally, the availability of large conceptual knowledge bases containing domain information is very limited. There are few handcrafted semantic databases (e.g., WordNet, ConceptNet, Wikidata) that are far from covering the diversity of possible domains. Most approaches of information extraction [14] and automatically created knowledge bases (e.g., DBpedia, YAGO) focus on factual knowledge at the instance level, which can not be used for domain modeling at the conceptual level. In addition, the core of many works (e.g., YAGO, BabelNet, DBpedia) is based on only one source of information: extraction from structured parts of Wikipedia (e.g., info boxes, categories).

1.3   Contributions and Outline

In this article, we present a domain modeling recommender (DoMoRe) system that contains a ready-to-use, extensive knowledge base of domain-specific terms and their relationships. DoMoRe also uses a set of existing knowledge bases to retrieve domain information, and is easily extensible with additional knowledge databases. Connected knowledge sources are automatically used during modeling to provide context-sensitive suggestions for model elements. The recommender system is integrated with a widely used modeling tool, the Ecore Diagram Editor of the Eclipse Modeling Project.

The rest of the paper is organized as follows. Section 2 introduces the general approach and details the model refinement steps that our system supports. In Sect. 3 we describe how existing knowledge sources are used and how the knowledge base of related terms was created. Section 4 describes in detail the implementation of the recommender system and how the delivery of contextual information and search-based suggestions works. In Sect. 5 we report on experiences with DoMoRe in different domains and scenarios. Related work can be found in Sect. 6, and Sect. 7 concludes the article and describes future work directions.

This paper extends [15], originally published in the proceedings of the MODELSWARD 2018 conference. In this extended version, we provide more detailed descriptions and examples of the semantic network, additional details on the recommendation generation and on the implementation of the recommender system, as well as additional related work.

---

[1] https://www.forbes.com/sites/forbestechcouncil/2017/06/05/the-big-unstructured-data-problem/. (Last accessed April, 2018).

2   Semantic Modeling Support

In this section we introduce the concept of semantic modeling support and detail our approach. *Modeling*: The activity of creating and refining models. In our case these models are domain models that focus on concepts and relationships of various application areas. *Support*: Modeling activities are assisted with context-sensitive pieces of information. Tool support is completely automated in contrast to guidelines or methodologies. *Semantic*: Modeling support focuses on the domain-specific terms and their relationships in domain models in contrast to syntactic modeling language assistance.

2.1   General Support Procedure

The semantic modeling support works as follows: (1) At some point of time during domain modeling a manual change in the model is made. This is usually referred to as model refinement, the activity in which a developer creates, modifies or deletes a model element (e.g., a new class). We concentrate on supporting the modifications that add new content to the model. All detailed scenarios are described in the next paragraph. (2) Based on the current state of the model, domain knowledge is acquired automatically. Knowledge acquisition is based on the terms that are used to name the elements (e.g., class names or association names). We pursue **two strategies**: First, we exploit existing structured knowledge sources to acquire the required domain terms and their relations. We employ mediator-based querying for a uniform access to this knowledge. Secondly, it is a well known problem [16] that existing knowledge bases (often created manually) do not contain enough information or do not exist at all for respective target domains. We address this issue by the automated creation of own semantic terminology networks from natural language datasets that cover a variety of domains. Section 3 details both approaches. (3) Acquired knowledge is transformed automatically into appropriate suggestions (e.g., related classes, possible sub- or super-classes) and presented to the user. It is the goal to present semantically related model elements that support the developer's decisions on what to include in the model and how to connect the elements. After that the procedure starts all over again.

2.2   Modeling Support Scenarios

Many opportunities exist to create and manage domain models. Domain modeling is not necessarily bound to using one specific modeling language. For example, UML class diagrams, ER models, and ontologies can be used. All approaches have in common that the respective modeling language is used to express conceptual structures of a domain using specific terms to improve understanding of the problem field. Since our semantic modeling support concentrates on the terms in domain models, the methods presented in this paper are applicable to several modeling languages. Nevertheless, we had to exemplarily choose one approach to illustrate our work, namely UML-like class diagrams, because they are the most widely used modeling paradigm in industry [17,18].

During domain model development the user has several options to change the model. In the following we itemize for which modeling activities what kind of support will be accomplished. We distinguish between two different kinds of support. First, contextual information will be provided if an element of a domain model is selected by the developer (Scenarios 1 and 2). Context information includes possible related model elements with all kinds of relationships the modeling language offers. Second, if a new element is created, automated suggestions will be provided on how to name the element (Scenarios 3 to 9). The support depends on the type of connection between the new element and existing elements of the model.

Scenario 1 – Selection of a Class. The goal of providing contextual information is the recommendation of possible connected model elements together with their types of relations for a selected domain model element. In case a class is selected (c.f., Fig. 1) possible generalizations/specializations, aggregations (containers and parts), and associations are shown. Related classes are either unconnected classes or classes that are connected with an association that has no name.

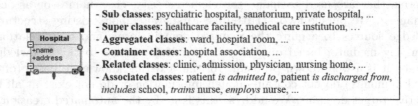

Fig. 1. Contextual information for a selected class [15].

Scenario 2 – Selection of an Association. If an association is selected, alternative association names, and possible other connected classes for each association end will be shown (c.f., Fig. 2). Note that if nothing is selected, contextual information for every element of the model will be shown in a summarized form.

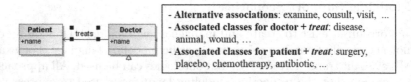

Fig. 2. Contextual information for a selected association [15].

Scenario 3 – Creation of a Class (no connection). Modeling tools usually offer the creation of new classes in a model without any connection. Typically, this happens, when classes are added to the diagram and the respective connections are drawn afterwards (c.f., Fig. 3). In this case, class name suggestions are dependent on all existing class names in the model. Particularly, in the list of suggestions class names should appear that are related to all of the existing classes ordered by relevance.

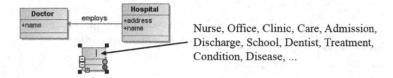

Nurse, Office, Clinic, Care, Admission, Discharge, School, Dentist, Treatment, Condition, Disease, ...

Fig. 3. Suggestions of related class names when adding a class without a connection [15].

Scenario 4 – Creation of a Sub Class. A sub class will be created, when the developer uses the specialization link starting from an existing class to empty space in the diagram (c.f., Fig. 4). In this case, class name suggestions are dependent on the linked super class. In the example, different types of doctors are shown (different kinds of medical specialists).

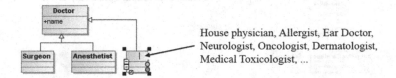

House physician, Allergist, Ear Doctor, Neurologist, Oncologist, Dermatologist, Medical Toxicologist, ...

Fig. 4. Suggestions of sub class names when adding a specialization [15].

Scenario 5 – Creation of a Super Class. Analogous to the sub class creation, a super class will be created when using the generalization link. The example shows the recommendation of more general terms for doctor (c.f., Fig. 5).

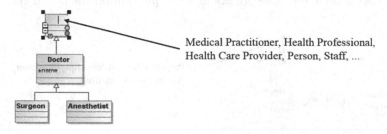

Medical Practitioner, Health Professional, Health Care Provider, Person, Staff, ...

Fig. 5. Suggestions of super class names when adding a generalization [15].

Scenario 6 – Creation of an Aggregated Class. In case the developer uses a composition or aggregation link starting from an existing class, an aggregated class will be created in the diagram. The example in Fig. 6 shows possible parts of a hospital.

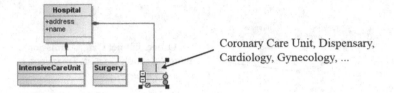

Coronary Care Unit, Dispensary, Cardiology, Gynecology, ...

Fig. 6. Suggestions of aggregated class names when adding an aggregated class [15].

Scenario 7 – Creation of a Container Class. If the opposite direction of a composition or aggregation relation is used, a container class will be created. In the example used in Fig. 7, suggestions are provided what a hospital can be part of.

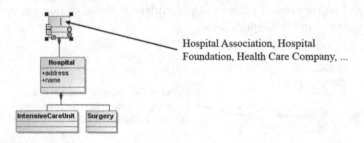

Hospital Association, Hospital Foundation, Health Care Company, ...

Fig. 7. Suggestions of container class names when adding a container class [15].

Scenario 8 – Creation of an Associated Class. An associated class will be created, if the developer draws an association link from a class to empty space in the diagram (a new class and an association without a name will be created). Names for the new related class will be recommended (c.f., Fig. 8). This scenario is very similar to Scenario 3, but the suggestions are dependent on the linked class only.

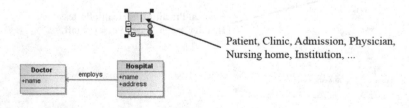

Patient, Clinic, Admission, Physician, Nursing home, Institution, ...

Fig. 8. Suggestions of associated class names when adding an associated class [15].

Scenario 9 – Creation of Association. If the developer creates an association link between two classes, association names (verbs) will be provided. The suggestions are dependent on both class names. In case the association does not have a direction, verbs are suggested that apply to both directions (Fig. 9).

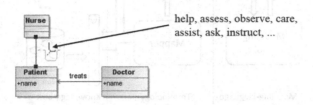

Fig. 9. Suggestions of association names when adding an association [15].

3 Domain Knowledge Sources

Our intended modeling support requires a large body of background knowledge in order to provide model element suggestions for nearly every possible domain. Since the support focuses on the terms used in the models, we concentrate on knowledge sources that provide lexical information.

We pursue two strategies: First, we exploit existing structured knowledge sources to acquire the required domain knowledge. Knowledge bases and ontologies are automatically queried for terms of a model to retrieve related terms. Secondly, we target the lack of conceptual knowledge bases by the automated creation of a semantic network of terms from natural language datasets.

3.1 Mediator-Based Knowledge Base Querying

As described in the introduction, only a few knowledge bases exist that contain conceptual knowledge. WordNet [19] is the most widely used lexical database for the English language. Other important resources are BabelNet [20], a multilingual encyclopedic dictionary, and Cyc [21] and ConceptNet [22], both common sense knowledge bases. Most of the other large publicly available knowledge bases (e.g., DBpedia, YAGO, Wikidata) consist of a relatively small ontology schema describing the model of the data and a large body of factual knowledge. These facts describe entities on instance level, hence, most of the content cannot be used for domain modeling. Nevertheless, the schemata of these knowledge bases can be used for modeling suggestions.

The greatest challenge in using these knowledge sources is the unavailability of uniform access to lexical information. Heterogeneous data models prevent querying the knowledge bases in a consistent way. Lexical information of terms and their relationships exist on schema level, intermediate proprietary data models and on instance level.

Our approach proposes a mediator-wrapper solution. A mediator allows the interaction of a user or system with heterogeneous data sources in a uniform

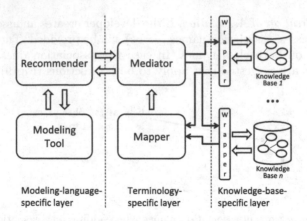

Modeling-language-   Terminology-   Knowledge-base-
specific layer   specific layer   specific layer

Fig. 10. Three layer mediator-wrapper architecture to retrieve terminological information from heterogeneous knowledge bases [15].

way [23]. Knowledge bases remain as they are, a wrapper is responsible for content translation, and the mediator provides a single point of access to the information for the modeling recommendations. Figure 10 shows the architecture of our approach. We differentiate between three different layers.

In the *modeling-language-specific level*, the developer uses the modeling tool and interacts with the recommender. This layer treats elements such as classes and associations, and the recommender proposes these types of elements based on the content of a model.

The mediator and the mapper are in the *terminology-specific level*. Domain-specific terms used in a model are relevant in this layer (e.g., nouns and their related terms). The mediator is responsible for translating terminology-specific content into the modeling layer and vice versa. It also manages a set of knowledge bases and their corresponding wrappers and sends queries to them as needed. The mapper collects and integrates results of the wrappers and provides the information to the mediator.

In the *knowledge-base-specific layer*, the wrappers communicate with the knowledge bases. Each wrapper must handle different query languages and formats (such as OWL, RDF, SPARQL, JSON) and different types of modeling (e.g., graphs, concepts, synsets). The DoMoRe recommender system supports the **automated integration** of these types of data models without any development effort:

- Ontology schemata: concepts and relationships modeled using OWL or RDFS classes and object properties.
- SKOS-based vocabularies: terms modeled with concepts and broader, narrower, and related relationships [24].
- Lemon-based knowledge bases: a specific vocabulary for modeling lexicons of ontologies [25].

If none of these data models are present, we support **semi-automatic integration** of any knowledge base that offers a SPARQL endpoint. The effort to add a new knowledge base to the system is relatively small, it is only necessary to specify a small set of queries for taxonomic, part/whole, related and verbal relationships.

3.2   Extraction of Semantically Related Terms

The automated proposal of related model elements requires a comprehensive lexicon that covers almost all possible domains and their domain-specific terms. On the one hand, existing conceptual knowledge bases are valuable sources of structured information, but on the other hand they are not extensive enough to do that. For this reason, we use natural language processing techniques on a large textual dataset to identify conceptional terms and their relationships.

The approach relies on syntactic properties of sentences and statistical features of text corpora to perform a *domain-independent* extraction. Large collections of texts contain a lot of redundancy and paraphrases [26]. That is, the same facts are repeated in several documents and formulated differently. In addition, natural language has the property that certain lexical elements tend to co-occur more often than others. This implies that words with similar meanings occur in similar contexts known as the distribution hypothesis [27].

We use these features to automatically create a large database of semantically related terms. Our methods are applied to Google Books N-Gram Corpus [28], a dataset derived from 5 million books with over 500 billion words. It covers a wide range of domains because it contains scientific literature from many areas as well as fiction and non-fiction.

The dataset provides the information on how often words and phrases occurred within the original text corpus (an n-gram is a sequence of n consecutive words). For example, *"the doctor and the patient – 8,339"* is one of the 700 million 5-grams in the dataset (c.f., Fig. 11a). We apply part-of-speech (POS) tagging on all n-grams to identify technical terms [29] and sum up how often concept terms co-occur in different contexts (e.g., *doctor – patient – 418,711 times*, c.f., Fig. 11b). We exclude proper nouns and named entities (e.g., city names, people). With this information, we obtain related terms and their frequencies for each term and build a semantic network (c.f., Fig. 11c).

The first version of SemNet was published in [30]. In the following, we describe several improvements that have been made in comparison to the original version. SemNet contains binary **noun-noun relationships** as shown in the previous paragraph. Besides that, the semantic network now features **verbal relationships**. That means, the analysis also records how often noun terms co-occurred with verbs (e.g., *doctor – consult – 173,786 times*). These relationships allow to suggest association names for domain models. SemNet now also includes **ternary relationships** for nouns and verbs (e.g., *obesity – hypertension – diabetes – 4,372 times/pregnancy – induce – hypertension – 2,365 times*). Ternary noun relationships record simultaneous occurrence of three technical terms. This information allows improved suggestions of related class names for multiple input

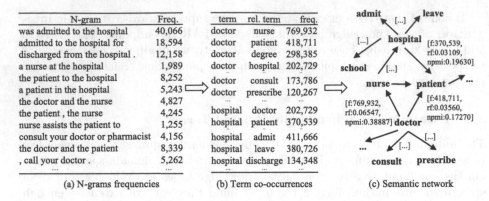

N-gram	Freq.
was admitted to the hospital	40,066
admitted to the hospital for	18,594
discharged from the hospital .	12,158
a nurse at the hospital	1,989
the patient to the hospital	8,252
a patient in the hospital	5,243
the doctor and the nurse	4,827
the patient , the nurse	4,245
nurse assists the patient to	1,255
consult your doctor or pharmacist	4,156
the doctor and the patient	8,339
, call your doctor .	5,262
...	...

(a) N-grams frequencies

term	rel. term	freq.
doctor	nurse	769,932
doctor	patient	418,711
doctor	degree	298,385
doctor	hospital	202,729
doctor	consult	173,786
doctor	prescribe	120,267
...	...	...
hospital	doctor	202,729
hospital	patient	370,539
hospital	admit	411,666
hospital	leave	380,726
hospital	discharge	134,348
...	...	...

(b) Term co-occurrences

(c) Semantic network

Fig. 11. Information extraction procedure to construct a large-scale semantic network from co-occurring terms in n-gram natural language datasets (f – absolute frequency, rf – relative frequency, $npmi$ – normalized point wise mutual information) [15].

terms. Ternary noun-verb relationships record the connection of one verb with two technical terms. These relationships are used to recommend names for classes connected with an association. Finally, for the current version of SemNet several heuristics were applied to extend the limited five word context of the Google N-gram dataset. As a result, we were able to extract terms consisting of more words and almost five times more relationships.

Table 1 shows examples of SemNet divided into the respective types of relationships. Three terms where queried: *pregnancy*, *software*, and *movie*. Each category shows the two strongest relationships of the respective query term.

In essence, the semantic network is a large-scale graph in which each term is a node and each directed edge denotes a weighted relationship between the terms. SemNet includes 5.7 million unique one-word terms and multi-word expressions and 222 million relationships. Each relationship is quantified by the absolute frequency of co-occurrence, a calculated relative frequency, and the pointwise mutal information (PMI) measurement (see Sect. 4.4 for more details on this associativity value between terms). While the text analysis and extraction requires sophisticated hardware and runtime, the semantic network only needs 14 GB of storage space and can therefore be used on standard PC hardware. We provide an online web interface to browse and query SemNet: http://www.bizware.tu-berlin.de/semnet.

4   Recommender System

In this section we describe in detail the implementation of the Domain Modeling Recommender (DoMoRe) system. We describe how domain information from a set of knowledge bases and our self-created semantic network of terms are used and transformed into recommendations of model elements according to our nine modeling support scenarios.

Table 1. Examples of automatically identified binary and ternary relationships for the terms "pregnancy" and "software". Each paragraph shows the top two relationships with the highest degrees of relatedness.

Noun-noun relationships			Noun-verb relationships		
pregnancy	lactation		pregnancy	terminate	
pregnancy	childbirth		pregnancy	occur	
software	hardware		software	use	
software	piece		software	install	
movie	television		movie	see	
movie	TV		movie	watch	
Ternary noun relationships			Ternary noun-verb relationships		
pregnancy	delivery	labor	pregnancy	carry	term
pregnancy	nausea	vomiting	pregnancy	feed	breast
software	hardware	data	software	require	hardware
software	hardware	system	software	allow	user
movie	television	radio	Movie	watch	television
movie	magazine	book	movie	win	award

In essence, the task of the recommender system is as follows. For a given model element, it is necessary to determine a set of related model elements associated with a particular relationship type (e.g., all possible subclasses of the class "Doctor" or all related classes of "Doctor" and "Hospital"). In the following, we first provide a mapping of semantic relationships between different representations of knowledge. Then the architecture of the recommendation system is presented. After that we explain the features of the recommendation system and how the proposals are ranked by relevance.

4.1   Semantic Relationships

Domain models describe concepts and relationships of an application domain using a modeling language. Although the modeling community still discusses [31, 32] how real-world concepts can be represented correctly using modeling languages, UML class diagrams are the most commonly used modeling paradigm in the industry to do that [17,18]. In this section, we analyze the semantic relationships of UML class diagrams from a lexical perspective and their representations in other knowledge sources (see Fig. 10 for the three levels).

We reviewed literature from database research [33], linguistics [34,35], information systems [36,37], and semantic web research [38,39] and relate the various types of relationships. Table 2 provides an overview, details are given below.

Specialization and Generalization are hierarchical abstraction mechanisms in UML to refine abstract classes to more specific ones and to group specific classes to more abstract ones. In lexical semantics these conceptual relationships are referred to as *hyponymy* and *hypernymy* between words or phrases. They are

Table 2. Corresponding semantic relationship types of different modeling paradigms [15].

Modeling language relationship	Lexical-semantic relationship	Knowledge source relationship
Specialization	Hyponymy	Subclass, Narrower term
Generalization	Hypernymy	Subclass (inv.), Broader term
Aggregation (Part)	Meronymy	HasPart (SPW), *Meronym (WN)*
Aggregation (Whole)	Holonymy	PartOf (SPW), *Holonym (WN)*
Association (named)	Agent-action	Object property
Association (unnamed) or group of classes	Semantic relatedness	Related term

mapped to *subClassOf*-relationship (and its inverse) in RDF/OWL ontologies and to the *broader term* and *narrower term* relation in thesaurus specification (e.g., based on ISO 25964).

Specialization and Generalization are hierarchical abstraction mechanisms in UML to refine abstract classes to more specific ones and to group specific classes into more abstract classes. In lexical semantics, these conceptual relationships are referred to as *hyponymy* and *hypernymy* between words or phrases. In RDF/OWL ontologies and in thesaurus specifications (e.g., based on ISO 25964), they are referred to the *subClassOf*-relationship (and their inverse) and to the relationships *broader term* and *narrower term*.

Aggregation is used to specify a part-of relationship between two UML classes. We summarize both aggregation (parts can exist independently of each other) and composition (parts can not exist independently of each other) under the term aggregation. In linguistics, part-whole relationships are called meronymic relationships (meronyms are the parts and holonyms are the wholes). Part-whole relationships are not supported directly in the thesaurus definition nor in the RDF/OWL ontology specification. There is a W3C Best Practice specification "Simple Part Whole" (SPW) that includes *hasPart* and *partOf* relationships. However, there are knowledge bases that contain part-whole relationships but use a non-standard vocabulary (such as WordNet).

Association is the third kind of conceptual relationship that we have analyzed in terms of other representations. We distinguish two types: unnamed associations, to express a simple dependency between two domain model classes and named associations that further specify the kind of association (usually with a verb). In linguistics, named dependencies fall into the category of case relationships [35], more specifically in our case in *agent-action* relationships. To a certain extent, RDF/OWL *object properties* with domain and range constraints can be compared with named associations. In lexical semantics, the unnamed association is referred to as *semantic relatedness*, an associative relationship that describes any functional relationship between two words. The relation *related term* of thesauri is assigned to this relationship. From a lexical point of view, the unnamed association is similar to a group of classes (the diagram is the container).

In summary, taxonomic relationships in domain models can be well mapped to other structured knowledge sources such as thesauri and ontologies. Other domain model relationships are not fully represented in these resources. As a result, they are a good source for acquiring knowledge for our modeling support, but they are not enough. All domain model relationships and their inherent conceptual relationships are rooted in various linguistic theories. Thus, the combination of knowledge base queries and natural language analysis allows retrieving related domain model elements for all our modeling support scenarios (see Sect. 2.2).

4.2 Components of the Recommender System

Figure 12 shows the architecture of the DoMoRe recommender system. DoMoRe is integrated into the Eclipse environment with a number of plug-ins. The *Model Listener* monitors changes in Ecore models developed with the Ecore Diagram Editor. When a change is made to a model, the current content of the model is retrieved along with the newly added or changed model element and its relationships.

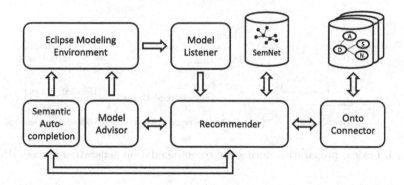

Fig. 12. Architecture of the DoMoRe recommender system [15].

The *Recommender* is notified and coordinates all subsequent steps of the modeling suggestions. First, the domain model is transformed into a lexical-semantic representation using the domain-specific terms and semantic relationship mappings (c.f., Table 2). Based on this representation, the *Semantic Network* is queried for related terms and directly provides ranked lists with related terms. The *Ontology Connector* manages the set of linked knowledge bases and is also queried. It contains the mediator and the mapper (see Fig. 10) and runs the translation of the terminological queries into knowledge-base-specific queries and the integration of results. The recommender controls two components that the user interacts with. The *Model Advisor* is a view in the Eclipse environment that displays contextual information about the model elements. It shows possible generalizations, specializations, aggregations, associations and related elements. The developer can use this view to easily add new content to a domain model by dragging suggested elements into the diagram. The corresponding relationships are created automatically. *Semantic Autocompletion* is triggered when a new element is named in the model or the name of an existing element is changed. This function behaves like a search engine. A context-sensitive pop-up list of names for the item will be displayed and suggestions will be filtered as you type.

4.3   Recommendation Generation

This section provides an insight into the features of the recommender system using examples. In the following, we demonstrate the retrieval of knowledge and the generation of recommendations for Scenario 3: A few classes already exist in a diagram, and in this diagram, a new unconnected class is created. Figure 13a shows the domain model that contains two classes connected with a named association. After creating the new class, the model listener triggers the recommender, and the lexical representation of the domain model is created (see Fig. 13b). The information need depends on the model refinement step. In this case, the unconnected class requires the system to retrieve nouns that are semantically related to both *Hospital* and *Doctor* (c.f., Fig. 13c).

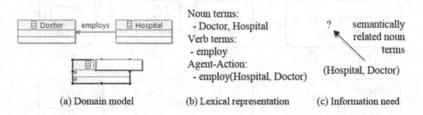

(a) Domain model   (b) Lexical representation   (c) Information need

Fig. 13. Lexical preparation during the recommendation generation process [15].

In the following, the information need is broken down into separate lexical queries for each term and relationship type (c.f., Fig. 14a). The main reason for separately retrieving the information is that there is virtually no conceptual knowledge base that contains n-ary relationships. In contrast, our semantic network directly supports ternary relationships that allow more accurate results for pairs of terms. First, ternary relationships are retrieved from SemNet. Second, separate binary relationship queries are executed for each term (c.f., Fig. 14b). Each connected knowledge base is also queried for each term (see Fig. 14c).

Up to now, separate lists of related terms were determined for each term of the original domain model and for each relationship type and for each knowledge

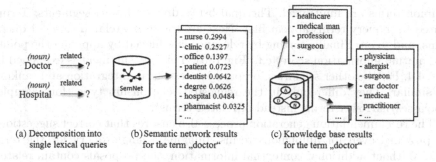

Fig. 14. Retrieval during the recommendation generation process [15].

source[2]. Results from the knowledge bases are integrated based on the following principle. First, for each query term, it is recorded in how many knowledge bases (e.g., WordNet, BabelNet, ConceptNet) each related term occurred. Second, the distinct union of all intermediate results is generated for each query term (c.f., Fig. 15a). The resulting lists have a tentative order indicating that more important terms appear first.

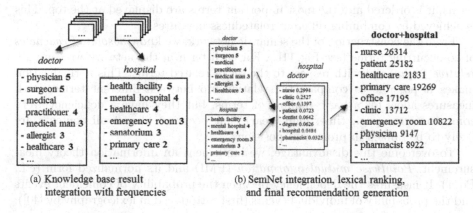

Fig. 15. Integration and ranking during the recommendation generation process [15].

In the final step, the presorted knowledge base results are integrated into the semantic network results. First, the knowledge base result and the respective semantic network result are joined for each term. The occurrence frequencies ensure that terms found in many knowledge bases occupy a more prominent position in the final ranking. In our example, this results in one list of related terms for *Doctor* and one for *Hospital*. Second, a final list of recommended terms is created. Separate results are intersected and the relative frequencies of

---

[2] For instance, for two terms, one relationship type and five connected knowledge bases, 10 intermediate result lists are generated.

common terms are multiplied. The final list is divided into n segments: Terms related to n query terms appear first. Next are the terms related to $n-1$ query terms, and so on. Finally, sorting by relevance is achieved by applying the pointwise mutual information score (c.f., Fig. 15b). This measurement is explained in Sect. 4.4. For the other scenarios, preparation, retrieval, integration and ranking are similar. They differ only in the requested relationship type (for example, subclasses/narrower terms instead of related terms).

The recommendation generation process also ensures that correct suggestions are provided even for ambiguous terms. Imagine a single query for the term *table*. Without additional contextual information, the proposals contain related terms for both the furniture and tabular array meaning. If there is a second term *database* in the domain model, the result integration ensures that all terms related to furniture are ranked low.

4.4   Ranking

It is likely that queries to our semantic network and connected knowledge bases will yield many related terms (up to a few thousand for each request). The ranking implemented in the recommendation component is responsible for presenting the most relevant model elements first. Thus, when retrieving a list of related terms, it is ordered and the most important terms are displayed at the top. This is achieved by combining different relatedness measures.

From the construction of the semantic network, we know *absolute frequencies* of co-occurring terms (see Fig. 11b). For each term in the network we compute *relative frequencies* with respect to the set of related terms. This normalization makes it possible to compare the relationship between different terms. Both measures allow for a basic ranking of terms, but they have a deficiency: very common terms (e.g., time, man, year) that occur in almost all contexts are likely to be ranked in prominent positions.

To overcome this disadvantage, we implement an information theory measurement: *Pointwise mutual information* (PMI) and its normalized form (c.f., Eq. 1). It measures the dependency between the probability of coincident events and the probability of individual events (first introduced in lexicography by [40]).

$$pmi(x,y) = \log\left[\frac{p(x,y)}{p(x)p(y)}\right] \quad npmi(x,y) = \frac{pmi(x,y)}{-\log\left[p(x,y)\right]} \tag{1}$$

The application of PMI to the semantic network means that x and y are terms and PMI relates the probability of their coincidence $p(x,y)$ with the probabilities of observing both terms independently $p(x)p(y)$. PMI is an associativity score of two terms that takes into account their individual corpus frequencies, so very common and general terms get lower values. Unfortunately, this measurement also has a drawback: although very general terms are ranked lower, very rare terms that co-occur with other terms only a few times tend to get high values.

Finally, to achieve a balanced ranking, our recommendation system uses the lexicographer's mutual information (LMI), which is the NPMI score multiplied by the absolute co-occurrence frequency [41].

4.5   Eclipse Plug-Ins

Two extensions for the Eclipse Ecore Diagram Editor have been implemented to allow the user to interact with the recommender system. The *Semantic Autocompletion* function of the recommender system relies directly on the ranked lists of terms that are generated based on the current content of a domain model. When the name of a class or association is edited, the user can trigger the display of a context-sensitive pop-up list of related terms that contains the most relevant terms at the top. It behaves like a search engine and provides filtering as you type (c.f., Fig. 16).

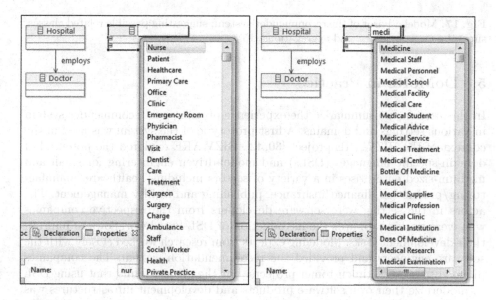

Fig. 16. Semantic autocompletion of the recommender system: context-sensitive name prediction and infix search [15].

The second extension, the *Model Advisor*, is a view plug-in that displays contextual information about the currently selected model element. It queries the semantic network and knowledge bases for just one term, but with multiple relationship types. The information is aggregated and grouped into related elements, possible generalizations, specializations, aggregations, and associations (c.f., Fig. 17).

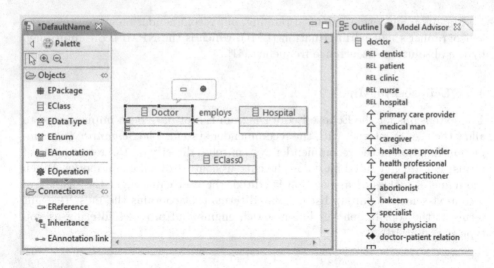

Fig. 17. Model advisor of the recommender system: suggesting possible related classes, superclasses, subclasses, and aggregations [15].

5   DoMoRe in Practice

In this section, we summarize the experience of using our recommender system in various settings and domains. A first prototype of the system was used in the context of the BIZWARE project [30,42]. BIZWARE explored the potential of domain-specific languages (DSLs) and model-driven engineering for small and medium-sized enterprises in a variety of sectors including healthcare, manufacturing/production, finance/insurance, publishing and facility management. The actors in the setting were software developers from the respective companies who were working towards the introduction of DSL-based workflows to improve their development tasks. Modeling experts from research worked closely with the software engineers and provided the recommendation system. The companies planned to use DSL in customer projects, but the project found that using DSL to modernize their own software products and development infrastructures was more effective. Because the software engineers had little experience with DSLs, DoMoRe mainly supported the domain analysis phase to identify and agree on domain-specific terms that were later used in DSL's meta-models. In particular, the suggestions in the abstraction process helped to correctly distinguish between class and instance levels. The analysis of the modeling sessions showed that the ranking had to be improved (too general terms in the top positions) and that the software engineers missed suggestions for relationships between domain-specific terms (extraction of verbal relationships was not available at the time).

DoMoRe has also been used in the dwerft project [43], a collaborative research effort to apply Linked Data principles for metadata exchange across all stages of the media value chain. The project successfully integrated a number of film production tools based on the Linked Production Data Cloud, a technology platform for the film and television industry, to enable the interoperability of software in the production, distribution and archiving of audiovisual content. One of the key tasks of the project was to develop a common data model that would convey all the metadata from the different production steps (e.g., screenplay, production planning, on-set information, post-production, distribution). The actors in the environment were domain experts of the respective tasks (most of them with no technical background) and modeling experts who created the domain models and metadata schemas. Many interviews with domain experts had to be conducted to gather domain-specific knowledge and to discuss drafts of domain models. DoMoRe mainly supported post-meeting modeling and interview preparation with more extensive models that allowed for more efficient agreement on the necessary metadata. For these tasks, the recommender system was adapted to ontology schema development to use it in a Linked Data context.

Currently, DoMoRe is being used as part of the AdA project[3], an interdisciplinary research group in which film scholars collaborate with computer scientists to support empirical film studies using tool-based semantic video annotation and automated video analysis. The goal of the project is to reduce the burden of elaborate, manual annotation routines in order to accelerate the film-scientific analysis of audiovisual motion patterns at the level of larger data sets. All annotation data and analysis results are published as Linked Open Data using the project's semantic vocabularies. Collaboration on domain modeling is similar to the project mentioned above. We expect similar support by using the recommender system for the domain expert interviews. One of the main findings so far has been that the recommender system requires more complex support for concept-value relationships (e.g., Recording Playback Speed – slow motion, timelapse, freeze).

6   Related Work

Modeling Assistance. Modeling support systems provide additional information and functionality during the modeling process to help model development. They typically focus on two areas: (1) creating model libraries or similar content; and (2) developing assistance frameworks and functions using these libraries. The largest known *model repository* of UML models and meta models is the Lindholmen UML dataset [44]. It contains links to over 93,000 UML diagrams collected from GitHub repositories. A similar effort, the Gothenburg UML Repository contains over 20,000 models crawled from the Internet, images and GitHub (only a collection of nearly 1,000 models is publicly searchable). Not surprisingly, most of the models are implementation models rather than domain models (for example, the search for "hospital" or "doctor" yielded 7 models, while a search for "interface" returned 90 models). Other important resources are ReMoDD [45], MOOGLE [46], the AtlanMod Metamodel Zoos[4] (containing a total of several

---

[3] http://www.ada.cinepoetics.fu-berlin.de/.
[4] http://web.emn.fr/x-info/atlanmod/index.php?title=Zoos.

hundred models). EMFStore[5] and the Eclipse Model Repository[6] are tools for maintaining model repositories. There are works that propose certain *recommendation features*: SmartEMF [47] uses reasoning in Prolog for consistency checking in DSL development. Kuhn proposes a concept for recommending method names in source code and UML models [6].

The HERMES project a framework for creating model *recommendation systems* to support the reuse of software models [48]. The main objective is to provide tool support for building model libraries and providing the deployment infrastructure to create recommenders that use the contents of these libraries. The EXTREMO assistant [5] is a similar tool to facilitate meta-model development with unified model element search in a model repository. We share the same goals, but both systems are facing a cold start problem: Reusable content will only be available if enough solutions have already been developed or converted to the repository, but new projects already want to benefit from domain knowledge. To some extent, this challenge is solved by using WordWeb/WordNet, which we also use, but these databases contain about 150,000 concepts, in contrast to our semantic network of 5.7 million terms.

Knowledge-Based Modeling. There is a variety of work on how model-driven engineering can benefit from formalized knowledge. At the *conceptual level* there are approaches to unify ontological and software modeling paradigms [49], approaches to adopt modeling concepts from each other [31], and to extend MDE languages with ontological foundations [37].

The OntoDSL framework [50] uses *ontology technologies* at the meta-model level (such as reasoning) to help DSL users identify model-level inconsistencies. The CoCoViLa tool [51] generates metamodels of domain-specific languages from OWL descriptions and [52] use ontologies in the analysis phase of DSL development, but both works require manual development of the respective ontologies.

There are several *knowledge sources* from other research areas that can be used for domain modeling. The most popular resource is WordNet [19], a lexical database for the English language that most other knowledge-based approaches also use (as we do). It contains about 82,000 noun synsets and 100,000 noun relationships. OpenCyc [21] is a common sense ontology with around 230,000 classes and 300,000 relationships. ConceptNet [22] is a multilingual semantic graph containing approximately 415,000 English concepts and 900,000 relationships. Linked Open Vocabularies[7] is a data set that stores vocabulary specifications. To the best of our knowledge, BabelNet [20] is the largest semantic dictionary available with 3 million concepts. It is based on WordNet, integrates several other dictionaries and uses machine translation to achieve multilingualism. Our DoMoRe recommender system uses all of them to retrieve terms and domain information.

---

[5] http://www.eclipse.org/emfstore/.

[6] http://modelrepository.sourceforge.net.

[7] http://lov.okfn.org/dataset/lov/.

7   Conclusion and Future Work

We presented DoMoRe, a recommender system that automatically suggests model elements for domain models. The system is based on a large semantic network of related terms that has 5.7 million distinct nodes and 222 million binary and ternary weighted relationships. DoMoRe also integrates multiple existing knowledge bases using mediator-based information retrieval of lexical information. This allows context-sensitive information to be provided during domain modeling (Model Advisor) and to propose semantically related names for model elements ordered by relevance (Semantic Autocompletion).

In our future work, we'll cover more modeling support scenarios (such as suggesting attributes, operation names, relationship types) that require other types of information extraction. We will also examine how lexical information can be used to detect semantic inconsistencies in domain models.

Currently we are working on a controlled experiment to quantitatively measure the efficiency of our recommender system as opposed to the qualitative feedback we received during the practical application of DoMoRe. Participants are introduced to a modeling tool and asked to perform multiple domain modeling tasks. Subjects are randomly subdivided into a treatment group using the tool with recommendation of related model elements and a control group modeling without the system. It is planned to measure the outcome variables time on task and model completeness.

Acknowledgment. This work is partially supported by the Federal Ministry of Education and Research under grant number 01UG1632B.

References

1. Whittle, J., Hutchinson, J., Rouncefield, M.: The state of practice in model-driven engineering. IEEE Softw. **31**, 79–85 (2014)
2. Evans, E.: Domain-driven Design: Tackling Complexity in the Heart of Software. Addison-Wesley Professional, Boston (2004)
3. Fowler, M.: Domain-Specific Languages. Pearson Education, Boston (2010)
4. Atkinson, C., Kühne, T.: Reducing accidental complexity in domain models. Softw. Syst. Model. **7**, 345–359 (2008)
5. Segura, Á.M., Pescador, A., de Lara, J., Wimmer, M.: An extensible meta-modelling assistant. In: 2016 IEEE 20th International Enterprise Distributed Object Computing Conference (EDOC), pp. 1–10. IEEE (2016)
6. Kuhn, A.: On recommending meaningful names in source and UML. In: Proceedings of the 2nd International Workshop on Recommendation Systems for Software Engineering, pp. 50–51. ACM (2010)
7. Mylopoulos, J., Borgida, A., Jarke, M., Koubarakis, M.: Telos: representing knowledge about information systems. ACM Trans. Inf. Syst. (TOIS) **8**, 325–362 (1990)
8. Störrle, H.: Structuring very large domain models: experiences from industrial MDSD projects. In: Proceedings of the Fourth European Conference on Software Architecture: Companion Volume, pp. 49–54. ACM (2010)

9. Reinhartz-Berger, I.: Towards automatization of domain modeling. Data Knowl. Eng. **69**, 491–515 (2010)
10. Frank, U.: Multi-perspective enterprise modeling: foundational concepts, prospects and future research challenges. Softw. Syst. Model. **13**, 941–962 (2014)
11. Reinhartz-Berger, I., Cohen, S., Bettin, J., Clark, T., Sturm, A.: Domain engineering. Springer, Heidelberg (2013). https://doi.org/10.1007/978-3-642-36654-3
12. Frank, U.: Domain-specific modeling languages: requirements analysis and design guidelines. In: Reinhartz-Berger, I., Sturm, A., Clark, T., Cohen, S., Bettin, J. (eds.) Domain Engineering, pp. 133–157. Springer, Heidelberg (2013). https://doi.org/10.1007/978-3-642-36654-3_6
13. Ionita, D., Wieringa, R., Bullee, J.-W., Vasenev, A.: Tangible modelling to elicit domain knowledge: an experiment and focus group. In: Johannesson, P., Lee, M.L., Liddle, S.W., Opdahl, A.L., López, Ó.P. (eds.) ER 2015. LNCS, vol. 9381, pp. 558–565. Springer, Cham (2015). https://doi.org/10.1007/978-3-319-25264-3_42
14. Banko, M., Cafarella, M.J., Soderland, S., Broadhead, M., Etzioni, O.: Open information extraction from the web. IJCAI **7**, 2670–2676 (2007)
15. Agt-Rickauer, H., Kutsche, R., Sack, H.: Domore - a recommender system for domain modeling. In: Proceedings of the 6th International Conference on Model-Driven Engineering and Software Development, MODELSWARD 2018, Funchal, Madeira, Portugal, 22–24 January 2018, pp. 71–82 (2018)
16. Colace, F., De Santo, M., Greco, L., Amato, F., Moscato, V., Picariello, A.: Terminological ontology learning and population using latent dirichlet allocation. J. Vis. Lang. Comput. **25**, 818–826 (2014)
17. Reggio, G., Leotta, M., Ricca, F.: Who knows/uses what of the UML: a personal opinion survey. In: Dingel, J., Schulte, W., Ramos, I., Abrahão, S., Insfran, E. (eds.) MODELS 2014. LNCS, vol. 8767, pp. 149–165. Springer, Cham (2014). https://doi.org/10.1007/978-3-319-11653-2_10
18. Hutchinson, J., Whittle, J., Rouncefield, M.: Model-driven engineering practices in industry: social, organizational and managerial factors that lead to success or failure. Sci. Comput. Program. **89**, 144–161 (2014)
19. Fellbaum, C.: WordNet : An Electronic Lexical Database. The MIT Press, Cambridge (1998)
20. Navigli, R., Ponzetto, S.P.: Babelnet:the automatic construction, evaluation and application of a wide-coverage multilingual semantic network. Artif. Intell. **193**, 217–250 (2012)
21. Lenat, D.B.: Cyc: a large-scale investment in knowledge infrastructure. Commun. ACM **38**, 33–38 (1995)
22. Speer, R., Havasi, C.: Representing general relational knowledge in ConceptNet 5. In: Proceedings of the Eight International Conference on Language Resources and Evaluation (LREC 2012), Istanbul, Turkey (2012)
23. Wiederhold, G.: Mediators in the architecture of future information systems. Computer **25**, 38–49 (1992)
24. Miles, A., Bechhofer, S.: SKOS simple knowledge organization system reference. W3C recommendation, W3C, 18 2009
25. McCrae, J., et al.: Interchanging lexical resources on the semantic web. Lang. Resour. Eval. **46**, 701–719 (2012)
26. Banko, M.: Open Information Extraction for the Web. PhD thesis, University of Washington (2009)
27. Turney, P.D., Pantel, P.: From frequency to meaning: vector space models of semantics. J. Artif. Int. Res. **37**, 141–188 (2010)

28. Michel, J.B., et al.: Quantitative analysis of culture using millions of digitized books. Science **331**, 176–182 (2011)
29. Williams, S.: An analysis of pos tag patterns in ontology identifiers and labels. Technical report, Technical Report TR2013/02, Department of Computing, The Open University, UK (2013)
30. Agt, H., Kutsche, R.-D.: Automated construction of a large semantic network of related terms for domain-specific modeling. In: Salinesi, C., Norrie, M.C., Pastor, Ó. (eds.) CAiSE 2013. LNCS, vol. 7908, pp. 610–625. Springer, Heidelberg (2013). https://doi.org/10.1007/978-3-642-38709-8_39
31. Henderson-Sellers, B., Gonzalez-Perez, C., Eriksson, O., Ågerfalk, P.J., Walkerden, G.: Software modelling languages: a wish list. In: 7th IEEE/ACM International Workshop on Modeling in Software Engineering, MiSE 2015, Florence, Italy, 16–17 May 2015, pp. 72–77 (2015)
32. Atkinson, C., Kühne, T.: In defence of deep modelling. Inf. Softw. Technol. **64**, 36–51 (2015)
33. Storey, V.C.: Understanding semantic relationships. VLDB J. **2**, 455–488 (1993)
34. Maroto García, N., Alcina, A.: Formal description of conceptual relationships with a view to implementing them in the ontology editor protég. Terminol. Int. J. Theor. Appl. Issues Spec. Commun. **15**, 232–257 (2009)
35. Chaffin, R., Herrmann, D.J.: The similarity and diversity of semantic relations. Mem. Cogn. **12**, 134–141 (1984)
36. Olivé, A.: Conceptual Modeling of Information Systems. Springer, New York (2007)
37. Guizzardi, G.: Ontological foundations for structural conceptual models. CTIT, Centre for Telematics and Information Technology (2005)
38. Almeida, M., Souza, R., Fonseca, F.: Semantics in the semantic web: a critical evaluation. Knowl. Organ. **38**, 187–203 (2011)
39. Huang, C.: Ontology and the Lexicon: A Natural Language Processing Perspective. Cambridge University Press, Cambridge (2010)
40. Church, K.W., Hanks, P.: Word association norms, mutual information, and lexicography. Comput. Linguist. **16**, 22–29 (1990)
41. Milajevs, D., Sadrzadeh, M., Purver, M.: Robust co-occurrence quantification for lexical distributional semantics. In: ACL 2016, vol. 58 (2016)
42. Agt, H., Kutsche, R.D., Natho, N., Li, Y.: The bizware research project. In: 15th International Conference on Model Driven Engineering Languages and Systems-Exhibition Track, MODELS (2012)
43. Agt-Rickauer, H., Waitelonis, J., Tietz, T., Sack, H.: Data integration for the media value chain. In: International Semantic Web Conference (Posters & Demos) (2016)
44. Hebig, R., Quang, T.H., Chaudron, M.R., Robles, G., Fernandez, M.A.: The quest for open source projects that use UML: mining github. In: Proceedings of the ACM/IEEE 19th International Conference on Model Driven Engineering Languages and Systems, pp. 173–183. ACM (2016)
45. France, R.B., Bieman, J.M., Mandalaparty, S.P., Cheng, B.H., Jensen, A.: Repository for model driven development (remodd). In: 2012 34th International Conference on Software Engineering (ICSE), pp. 1471–1472. IEEE (2012)
46. Lucrédio, D., Fortes, R.P.M., Whittle, J.: Moogle: a metamodel-based model search engine. Softw. Syst. Model. **11**, 183–208 (2012)
47. Hessellund, A., Czarnecki, K., Wąsowski, A.: Guided development with multiple domain-specific languages. In: Engels, G., Opdyke, B., Schmidt, D.C., Weil, F. (eds.) MODELS 2007. LNCS, vol. 4735, pp. 46–60. Springer, Heidelberg (2007). https://doi.org/10.1007/978-3-540-75209-7_4

48. Dyck, A., Ganser, A., Lichter, H.: On designing recommenders for graphical domain modeling environments. In: 2014 2nd International Conference on Model-Driven Engineering and Software Development (MODELSWARD), pp. 291–299. IEEE (2014)
49. Kühne, T.: Unifying explanatory and constructive modeling: towards removing the gulf between ontologies and conceptual models. In: Proceedings of the ACM/IEEE 19th International Conference on Model Driven Engineering Languages and Systems, pp. 95–102. ACM (2016)
50. Walter, T., Parreiras, F.S., Staab, S.: An ontology-based framework for domain-specific modeling. Softw. Syst. Model. **13**, 1–26 (2014)
51. Ojamaa, A., Haav, H.-M., Penjam, J.: Semi-automated generation of DSL meta models from formal domain ontologies. In: Bellatreche, L., Manolopoulos, Y. (eds.) MEDI 2015. LNCS, vol. 9344, pp. 3–15. Springer, Cham (2015). https://doi.org/10.1007/978-3-319-23781-7_1
52. Tairas, R., Mernik, M., Gray, J.: Using ontologies in the domain analysis of domain-specific languages. In: Chaudron, M.R.V. (ed.) MODELS 2008. LNCS, vol. 5421, pp. 332–342. Springer, Heidelberg (2009). https://doi.org/10.1007/978-3-642-01648-6_35

An Integrated Framework to Develop Domain-Specific Languages: Extended Case Study

Bahram Zarrin[1(✉)], Hubert Baumeister[1], and Hessam Sarjoughian[2]

[1] DTU Compute, Technical University of Denmark, 2800 Kgs Lyngby, Denmark
{baza,huba}@dtu.dk
[2] School of Computing, Informatics, and Decision Systems Engineering,
Arizona State University, Tempe, AZ 85281, USA
hessam.sarjoughian@asu.edu

Abstract. In this paper, we propose an integrated framework to formally specify the syntax and the semantics of domain-specific languages. We build this framework by integrating the Microsoft DSL Tools, a framework to develop graphical domain-specific languages, and an extension of the ForSpec, a logic-based specification language. The motivation for proposing this framework is the lack of a formal and rigorous approach by DSL Tools for semantics specifications. We combine the aforementioned technologies under the umbrella of Microsoft Visual Studio IDE to facilitate the development of graphical DSLs within a single development environment. We use the Microsoft DSL Tools to specify the metamodel and graphical notations for DSLs, and our extension of the ForSpec, offering better support for semantic specifications. As a case study, we develop a modeling language to design domain-specific flow-based languages.

Keywords: Domain-specific languages · Formal languages ·
Semantics specification · Microsoft DSL Tools · FORMULA ·
ForSpec · Flow-based programming

1 Introduction

Domain-specific languages (DSLs) are specialized languages tailored to a particular application area, which use the terms and concepts established in the domain. Therefore, they enable domain experts to directly use their domain knowledge about what a system under development should do. DSLs improve the readability and understandability of the problem specifications and also increase the productivity of the domain experts to define a problem domain in a manageable and analyzable way. Additionally, they employ the domain rules as constraints to disallow the specification of illegal or incorrect models in the problem domain.

There are a number of language tools and frameworks to develop DSLs such as EMF, MetaEdit+, Microsoft DSL Tools, Onion, Rascal, Xtext, SugarJ, and

© Springer Nature Switzerland AG 2019
S. Hammoudi et al. (Eds.): MODELSWARD 2018, CCIS 991, pp. 159–184, 2019.
https://doi.org/10.1007/978-3-030-11030-7_8

MPS. Most of these tools and frameworks provide sufficient support for defining the abstract and concrete syntax of DSLs. According to these specifications, they build graphical or textual editors automatically with a set of IDE features, e.g. syntax coloring, synthetic compilation, for the DSL under the development.

Abstract syntax and concrete syntax of a language do not provide any information about what the concepts in a language actually mean. Therefore, it is essential to capture the semantics of the language in a way that is precise and useful to the user of the language. Formal methods provide the required rigidity and precision for semantic specifications [9]. They can provide an unambiguous and precise specification of the language and support a certain level of reasoning about the properties of the language by employing the tools of mathematical logic. Additionally, formal specifications can facilitate an automated generation of language editors, interpreters, compilers, debuggers and other related tools. Although most of the aforementioned tools provide generative approaches, e.g., model-to-model and model-to-text transformation, to specify the semantics of DSLs, they do not provide a rigorous or formal approach for semantics specifications.

In this work, we propose an integrated framework to formally specify the syntax and the semantics of DSLs. We combine the Microsoft DSL Tools and our extended version of the ForSpec [31], a logic-based specification language which is an extension of the FORMULA [12] developed at Microsoft Research, under the Visual Studio umbrella.

This paper is an extended version of our previous papers [34] and [35]. In [34], we presented our integrated framework to specify DSLs using a simple example. In [35], we proposed the idea of utilizing model-driven engineering (MDE) for designing domain specific flow-based language (DSFBL). Our contribution in this paper is developing a meta-modeling language to specify flow-based languages within our integrated framework. This meta-modeling language on one hand demonstrates a realistic case study for our integrated framework presented in [34], and on the other hand it provides a formal framework to develop domain-specific flow-based languages.

The remainder of this paper is organized as follows: in Sect. 2, we give a brief introduction to some of the approaches and existing formal languages for specifying the semantics of domain-specific languages. Afterwards, in Sect. 3, we present our extension of the ForSpec which is used as the basis for semantics specifications language in our approach. In Sect. 4, we propose our integrated framework to design domain-specific modeling languages. Finally, in Sect. 5, we briefly introduce the flow-based programming and we propose a modeling language to specify flow-based languages as a case study. We evaluate and conclude the paper in Sect. 10.

2   Formal Approaches for Semantics Specifications of Modeling Languages

Formal approaches proposed for specifying the semantics of modeling languages can be categorized into weaving, rewriting, and translational approaches. In the weaving approaches [8,9,18,20,27], the behavioral semantics of a modeling language are defined directly in the metamodel of the underlying language by adding operations to the meta-classes and employing a meta-language, e.g. xOCL [20], QVT [24], for the behavioral specification of these operations. These meta-languages are normally a set of primitive actions, e.g. assignment, declaration, conditions, loops, and object manipulations, to define the behavior of the language. The advantage of this approach is that syntactical and semantical specifications of the language are encapsulated. Its main drawback is that some of these meta-languages are simplified versions of traditional programming languages. Therefore the semantic specifications written using these languages have similar complexity as the specifications written in a conventional programming language [9].

Rewriting approaches [1,3,15,32], describe the semantics of a modeling language by a set of rewriting rules, which define a mapping from the left-hand side of the rule to its right-hand side. Matching a specification phrase with the left-hand side of a rule triggers substituting it with the right-hand side of the rule. This substituting ends when there are no more applicable rules. The advantage of rewriting approach is that the semantics specification is directly specified in terms of the metamodel. This approach is more suitable for modeling languages where their behavior can be specified in the operational semantic style.

Translational approaches [5,6,9,25,26,29,30], describe the semantics of a modeling language as a mapping from the metamodel of the underlying language to a metamodel of another language which already has a well-known semantics, e.g. abstract state machines [10]. The advantage of this approach is that the available tools of the target language can be used for performing formal analysis. Its drawback is that the DSL designer should have knowledge of the target language in order to define and understand the semantics of the underlying language.

The semantics specification approach used in this paper is the continuation of [2,29,30], in which the metamodel of the underlying modeling language is translated into a formal specification language, e.g. FORMULA and ForSpec, and its behavioral semantics are defined using the constructs of the specification language. In the following, we briefly introduce our extension of ForSpec which we use as the semantics specification language in our integrated framework. A detailed description of FORMULA and ForSpec languages can be found in [13, 14] and [31].

3   Extending ForSpec Language

ForSpec [29], proposed by Simko [29], supports the structural and behavioral semantics specifications of modeling languages for cyber-physical systems. It extends FORMULA with functional terms, semantic functions, and semantic equations to provide support for operational, denotational, and translational style specifications. ForSpec has been used to specify the denotational semantics of a bond graph language, which is a physical modeling language [30], and to specify the structural and behavioral semantics of a cyber-physical system modeling language [31]. Although ForSpec provides essential means for the structural and behavioral specifications of DSLs, it has some limitations for specifying the semantics of the DSL proposed in our experience paper [33]. In this section, we address these limitations and extend ForSpec to overcome them.

3.1   List Data Types and Set Comprehensions

ForSpec does not support *List* data types explicitly. Although we are able to define a list structure implicitly, this will require more effort when we need to apply operations on the lists, e.g. add or remove elements. To this end, we extend the ForSpec syntax to support *List* as a primitive data type. The following example shows how a list can be defined using our explicit list construct in ForSpec. It specifies a domain which includes a type called *Substance* and a list called *SubstanceList*. The elements of the list are *Substance* types. A model is defined as an instance of this domain, and it describes three substances and one list that includes them.

```
domain Material {
  Substance ::= new (name:String, value:Real).
  SubstanceList ::= list < Substance >. }
model material of Material {
  CO is Substance ("CO", 0.23).
  H2 is Substance ("H2", 2.44).
  CH4 is Substance ("CH4", 1.03).
  SubstanceList <CO, H2, CH4> }
```

Head and tail of a list can be obtained by accessing the structural fields of the list, e.g. *hd* and *tail*. We also extend the built-in functions of ForSpec with the list operation functions *append (list1, list2)*, *count (list)*, and *isin (element, list)*.

```
NoSubstanceListForCO ::= new ( Integer ).
NoSubstanceListForCO ( n ) :-
  n = count ( { sl | sl is SubstanceList , isin ("CO", sl[name]) } ).
```

Set comprehensions in ForSpec is defined as {*head* | *body*}, and its elements are used by built-in functions *count* and *toList*. *Count* computes the number of elements in the set and *toList* stores the items in the set in a list data structure as presented earlier. We extend the *toList* function to accept the data type of the *list* as the arguments. The extended function stores the elements of the set comprehension in an instance of the given list, and it uses constant value *Nil* to represents the end of the list. For example, the following example specifies a list of all the substances which have positive values.

```
PositiveSubstance ::= new ( SubstanceList ).
PositiveSubstance (sl) :-
 sl = toList ( SubstanceList , { s | s is Substance , s.value > 0 } ).
```

Furthermore, we extend ForSpec by providing syntax to iterate the list elements within the set comprehensions. This extension allows ForSpec to support some list operations, e.g. *filter()*, *map()*, and *reduce()*, which are quite useful in functional programming. The following specifications defines a function that rescales a *SubstanceList*. It maps each element of a given *SubstanceList* to the rescaled element in the list, called result. The list iterator is defined as $e \leftarrow sl$ where *sl* is the given list, and *e* is a variable representing an element of the list.

```
RescaleSubstanceList ::= [ SubstanceList , Integer ⇒ SubstanceList ].
RescaleSubstanceList (sl, n) ⇒ (result) :-
result = toList (SubstanceList, {Substance(e.name, e.value * n) | e   ←
sl}).
```

We also provide support for *union* and *intersection* operators for the set comprehensions. The following example specifies a function that merges two substance lists.

```
MergeSubstanceList ::= [SubstanceList , SubstanceList ⇒ SubstanceList
+ {Nil}].
MergeSubstanceList ( l1 , l2 ) ⇒ ( l3 ) :-
 l3 = toList ( SubstanceList ,
 { Substance ( e1.name , e1.value + e2.value ) | e1 ← l1 , e2 ← l2 ,
e1.name = e2.name}
 union {e1 | e1 ← l1 , e1.name ∉ l2[name]}
 union {e2 | e2 ← l2 , e2.name ∉ l1[name]}).
```

3.2 Reduce Function

Reduce, in functional programming, relates to a function that performs on a list or any recursive data structure to collapse or accumulate its elements into a single element or value by employing the same computation to each element. In this paper, we extend ForSpec to allow modelers to specify the *reduce* function. The following example defines a *reduce* function called *MergeSubstanceLists* to aggregate the substances of a list of *SubstanceList*:

```
SubstanceLists ::= list < SubstanceList >.
MergeSubstanceLists ::= [SubstanceLists >> MergeSubstanceList >>
SubstanceList].
```

The following example defines a *reduce* function called *Sum* to calculate the sum of the numbers in the given list:

```
NumberList ::= list <Real>.
Add ::= [ Real , Real ⇒ Real ].
Add ( x , y ) ⇒ ( z ) :- z = x + y.
Sum ::= [ NumberList >> Add >> Real].
```

3.3 Typed Union Type

ForSpec does not provide any mechanism to define constraints on the elements of a union type. This is required when a union type should be extended from other domain modules by using union type extension since any arbitrary types can be appended to the elements of the union type. To support this, we introduce a new built-in type to ForSpec that allows defining a type for the union types.

The syntax to define a typed union is the same as the syntax to define a composite type. The main difference is using ":;=" instead of "::=". This helps us to distinguish between the definition of these two built-in types. A typed union is a particular union type which can declare the *new* keyword and a set of named fields. It enforces a set of type checking rules to ensure that all of the components of the typed union match this common declaration. The rules of the type checking is as follows:

- If the typed union has the *new* keyword in its definition, then all of its components should have the *new* keyword in their declaration.
- Every field defined in the typed union definition should have a unique name.
- For each field specified in the typed union declaration, all the components of the typed union should have the same field with the same type (not necessarily the same order) in their declarations.

Union type extension "+=" can be used to add a type component to a typed union type. It can be used both within the same domain that contains the declaration or within other domains extending the domain.

A typed union type cannot be used to generate a fact either via rules or constructors within a model of a domain. But its signature can be used as a composite type to match the facts of the type of its components in the knowledge base of the ForSpec interpreter. There is a difference between matching a composite type and a typed union type. For the composite type, the matching is done by comparing the arguments of the fact and matching terms in the sequence, and comparing the type of the fact with the type of matching term. While in the typed union the argument matching is done according to the name of the fields and not their position in the constructor (same fields should have the same value and the type matching is done according to the type of component.

The following example utilizes a typed union type to define an interface for a type of *Component*. This type has been extended with a type of *Network* using a union type extension operator in another domain called "Network". The typed union type is also used to match the facts of the type of *Component* to check if they have ports with duplicated name.

```
domain Core {
InPort ::= new (id: String, type: String).
OutPort ::= new (id: String, type: String).
Port ::= InPort + OutPort.
PortList ::= list < Port >.
Component :;= new (id: String, ports: PortList).
...
InvalidComponent ::= ( String ).
InvalidComponent ( id ) :-
 Component ( id , ports ),
 no { x | x ← ports , y ← ports , x != y , x.id = y.id }. }
domain Network extends Core {
Component += Network.
Network ::= new ( id : String , ports : PortList, ... ).
... }
```

4   Integrating the Extended ForSpec into the Microsoft DSL Tools

The Microsoft DSL Tools is a framework to develop graphical domain-specific languages that can be integrated into the Microsoft Visual Studio. The framework uses a DSL definition diagram for defining both the metamodel and the graphical notations of a DSL. The definition diagram is used to generate a graphical editor for the DSL, so that modelers can edit or view the whole or part of the model [19].

Our work is inspired by [17]. The authors utilize FORMULA [14] for specifying the semantics of DSLs, and they provide a transformation tool to convert metamodels and models specified within Generic Modeling Environment [16] to FORMULA for analyzing the semantics of the models. A drawback of this approach is switching between different programming tools and development environments.

In this paper, we combine the aforementioned technologies under the umbrella of Microsoft Visual Studio IDE to facilitate the development of DSLs within a single environment. Furthermore, we employ our extension of ForSpec instead of FORMULA that offers better support for semantic specifications. We also provide some language tools, as Visual Studio's extensions for ForSpec, such as code editor, command window, and LATEX generator for pretty-printing specifications, which has been used to generate the specifications presented in this paper. In the following, we explain our approach for integrating the Microsoft DSL Tools and the proposed extension of ForSpec in this paper.

4.1   Generating ForSpec Specifications

Based on a DSL definition file (.dsl), the Microsoft DSL Tools automatically generates the required code for domain classes, connectors, shapes, diagram editor, model explorer, validations, and other artifacts. This is done by utilizing a set of text templates files (.tt) located within the DSL project. We employ the same method to generate the ForSpec specifications for the metamodel specified within the DSL definition file and its corresponding models. Accordingly, we adopt the DSL project template to include two additional text template files in the DSL project, for whenever a DSL developer creates a new DSL project. These text template files, along with the other templates, generate the required code whenever the DSL definition file is changed. One of these files is used to generate the ForSpec specification for the metamodel of the DSL. Therefore, the specifications are available at the design time of the DSL, and the DSL developer can extend these specifications with the DSL semantics.

We generate the ForSpec specification according to the following rules: For each non-abstract domain class, a data type with the same name will be generated. The parameters of the data type include all the domain properties explicitly defined for the domain class and its base classes. In addition, for each domain relationship with which a source is associated, a parameter will be generated for the domain class or its base classes. The type of parameter is defined according to the multiplicity of the relationship. For one to one relationships, the type is the same as the type of the domain class associated with the target of the relationship. For the one to many relationships, the type is defined as a list of the type of the domain class targeting the relationship. For each abstract class, depending on its domain properties, a union type or a typed union type is generated. The former is generated if the class does not have any domain property. The later is generated if the class or its base class has one or more domain properties. In both cases, the classes inherited from the abstract class are added to the union definition.

The other template is used for generating ForSpec specifications for the model instances of the DSL. To this end, it generates, e.g. C#, VB, code for an adapter that can transfer the model instances of the DSL to ForSpec. This adapter can be used by applications or within another text template file in the Visual Studio IDE.

As a case study, in the following sections, first we introduce the flow-based programming paradigm and then we develop a modeling language within our integrated framework to specify flow-based languages.

5   Flow-Based Programming

Flow-based programming (FBP) [22] was first introduced in the early 1970s by Morrison [21] and it has recently become an active topic again in computing science [4,7,11,22,23]. FBP decomposes an expensive computation into a directed graph with processing nodes that communicate via message passing. Each processing node computes part of the main computation, and edges represent data-flow dependencies between the nodes. Computation in a node is triggered upon data arrival. Parallelism is realized when nodes can execute concurrently. FBP is a visual programming language at first level. The network definition is diagrammatic, and it will be transformed into a connection list in the lower-level languages. Processing nodes in the network are instances of components which are either atomic or composites. The atomic components are defined using non-visual languages and their instances can be connected in a sub-network to define a composite process. This helps FBP to support a hierarchic structure of processes that reduce the complexity in the network's level and it provides encapsulation for process definitions [22].

In FBP, components are reactive systems that produce outputs once they receive data on their input channels. A component can be in one of the following states at any time; not-started, active, inactive, terminated, suspended-on-send, or suspended-on-receive. It starts in the not-started state, which means that the component is not initialized yet, and it requires initialization once it is activated. As soon as a data-packet arrives at any input port of a component, its state changes to active, which means the entry point of the component will be triggered by the FBP scheduler. If a component does not have any input ports, then its state changes to active immediately. After the component leaves its entry point, its state may change to either inactive or terminated. Inactive means that the component is done with execution and it can be activated again once new data arrives on its input ports. If a component is in an inactive state and all of its input ports are closed, then its state will change to terminated. This means that it can not be activated anymore. When an output channel of a component is full, and the component sends more data to this channel, its state changes to the suspended-on-send state. It will remain in the same state until the channel receives more data. In the same manner, the state of a component will change to suspend-on-receive if the component is demanding to receive data on an empty channel.

6   Metamodeling Framework

Figure 1 presents our proposed metamodels for specifying domain-specific flow-based languages (DSFBL) as an UML diagram. These metamodels are domain neutral and they should be extended by the DSL designer in order to be tailored to a specific domain. In the following, we give an overview of each metamodel, and then we provide the syntax, the structural and behavioral semantics of the metamodels in ForSpec.

At the core of the framework, there is a package called "DSFBLCore". This package provides the set of *DesignElements* required to design a DSFBL. An abstract metamodel called *Component* is used to represent the component model. This element has a set of *ModelElement* which are *InPort* and *OutPort*, and parameter definitions (*ParameterDef*) to describe the interface of the component models. Ports and parameter definitions have a reference to *DataType* which is an abstract element for defining the required data-types for the models. *Component* and *DataType* elements are the extension points of the metamodel and they provide means to incorporate different domains within the framework. We provide parameter definitions as primitive and composite data types. *PrimitivePa-rameter* is proposed to define parameters with primitive data types, e.g. string,

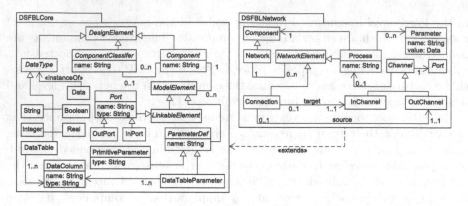

Fig. 1. The metamodel for specifying domain-specific flow-based languages.

integer, etc. and *DataTableParameter* is proposed to define a two-dimensional list structure, where each item of the list has a list of named values called *DataColumn*. We called these structures *DataTables* and *DataColumns* since the domain experts are more familiar with these terms.

A package called "DSFBLNetwork" contains the metamodel of the FBP network language which supports hierarchical composition of the atomic or composite models. As presented in the UML diagram, we extend the composite language from the core language. In this metamodel, a *Network* is defined as an extension of *Component*. Therefore, it has the set of ports and parameter definitions we described earlier. Additionally, it has a set of *Process* and *Connection* elements classified as *NetworkElements*. Processes are the computational nodes of the network and they are the proxy models of the components. They specify a unique name and parameter values of the components within a network. The *InChannels*, *OutChannels*, and *Parameters* of a process should correspond to the *InPorts*, *OutPorts*, and *ParameterDefs* of the referenced component. Channels are ports that are associated with the processes of a network or the network itself. They uniquely specify the ports of a network. Connections are model elements that provide message passing from an *OutChannel* to an *InChannel*.

In the following section, we provide the concrete syntax and the formal specification for the structural and behavioral semantics of the metamodels presented above.

7   Concrete Syntax

In this section, we define the concrete syntax of the proposed metamodels for specifying DSFBL within our integrated framework as presented in Sect. 4. To this end, we define a DSL definition diagram for each metamodel. Microsoft DSL Tools provides *DSLLibrary* projects to share a set of domain classes with the other DSL projects. Therefore, we define the metamodel of the core language as a DSLLibrary project to provide the base domain classes for the languages

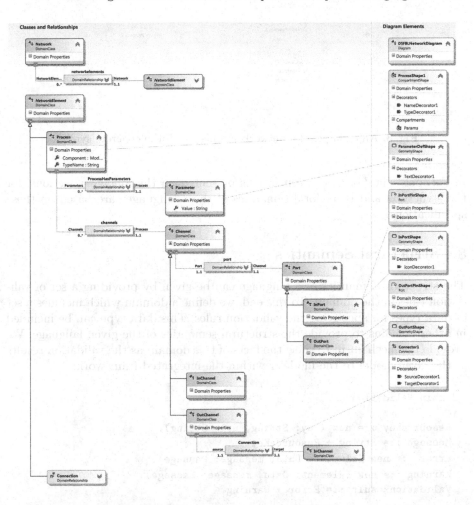

Fig. 2. DSL definition of the DSFBLNetwork Microsoft DSL Tools.

which extend DSFBLCore metamodel. This library should be imported into the DSL project of the other languages e.g. network language, to define the concrete syntax for the language. Since this language is abstract, we do not associate any notation to the model elements of this language.

We import this library into the DSL project for the network language and we extend the domain classes according to the DSFBLNetwork metamodel. Finally, as presented in Fig. 2, we map the domain classes to the shape classes in order to provide the concrete syntax for the language.

To present the structural and behavioral semantics of the metamodels, we need to specify the abstract syntax of the metamodels in ForSpec. This can be done automatically within our integrated framework presented in Sect. 4. We map each metamodel presented in this paper to a domain with the same name

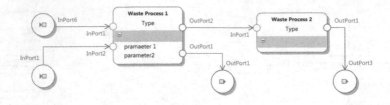

Fig. 3. An example of a network specified with the concrete syntax.

in ForSpec. The ForSpec specifications presented, in the following sections, for the structural and behavioral semantics of these languages are based on these specifications.

8   Structural Semantics

The structural semantics of a language can be given by providing a set of validation rules in the domain. To this end, we define a domain which includes a set of data types for specifying the validation rules. This data type can be included in other domains to provide the structural semantics of the given language. We provide the mechanism to show the facts of this domain as the validation results of the given model to the modeler within the integrated framework.

```
domain Validation
{
  ResourceKey ::= new (key: String, url: String).
  Message ::= String + ResourceKey.
  Error ::= new (element: Data, message: Message).
  Warning ::= new (element: Data, message: Message).
  ValidationResult ::= Error + Warning.
}
```

The domain contains two data types called *Error* and *Warning* to specify the validation result. Finding an *Error* makes the validation fail, while *Warning* are considered alerts. Both data types have the arguments of *model* and *message*. The first argument refers to the element of the model which is subjected to the validation result and the second argument provides a description of this validation. The description can be given by either a string or by providing a resource key within a resource dictionary file. This provides the means to localize the validation messages for different domains by using different resource files.

8.1   DSFBLCore

The structural semantics of this metamodel are given by providing the rules to check that the named elements, such as *Component, Port, ComponentClassifer*, have a unique name. The following specifications can verify this:

```
Validate the components.
Error (X, "The component should have a unique name") :-
X is Component,
Y is Component,
X != Y, X.name = Y.name.
Validate the classifiers.
Error (X, "The classifier should have a unique name") :-
X is ComponentClassifier,
Y is ComponentClassifier,
X != Y, X.name = Y.name.
Validate the ports.
Error (X, "The port should have a unique name") :-
Component (_, elements, _),
X ← elements, Y ← elements,
X: Port, Y: Port, X != Y, X.name = Y.name.
Validate the parameters.
Error (X, "The parameter should have a unique name") :-
Component (_, elements, _),
X ← elements, Y ← elements,
X: ParameterDef, Y: ParameterDef, X != Y, X.name = Y.name.
```

Since we use *String* data types for specifying the name of the references to *DataType* and *ComponentClassifier* elements, we therefore need to validate these reference names by matching these elements with the given names.

```
Validate the component's classifier.
Error (X, "The component should have a valid classifier") :-
    X is Component,
    no ComponentClassifier (X.classifier).
Validate the data type of ports.
Error (port, "The port should have a valid data type") :-
    Component (_, elements, _),
    port ← elements, port: Port,
    type = rflFindType (port.datatype),
    type != Nil,
    rflIsSubtype(type, DataType) = FALSE
; Component (_, elements, _),
    port ← elements, port: Port,
    rflFindType (port.datatype) = Nil.
Validate the data type of parameters.
Error (param, "The parameter should have a valid data type") :-
    Component (_, elements, _),
    param ← elements, param: PrimitiveParameter,
    type = rflFindType (param.type),
    type != Nil, rflIsSubtype(type, DataType) = FALSE
```

```
; Component (_, elements, _),
    param ← elements, param: PrimitiveParameter,
    rflFindType (param.type) = Nil.
; Component (_, elements, _),
    param ← elements, param: DataTableParameter,
    datacolumn ← param.columns,
    type = rflFindType (datacolumn.type),
    type != Nil, rflIsSubtype(type, DataType) = FALSE
; Component (_, elements, _),
    param ← elements, param: DataTableParameter,
    datacolumn ← param.columns,
    rflFindType (datacolumn.type) = Nil.
conforms no Error (_, _).
```

In the above specification, the built-in reflection functions *rflFindType* and *rflIsSubtype* are used to validate the data type associated with the ports and the parameter definitions. The first function returns a data type associated with the given name. If a data type with the given name is not defined in the domain, it returns *Nil*. The second function specifies whether the first given data type is a subtype of the second data type or not. At the end of the domain we use *conforms* to determine that the model can not contain any *Error* fact.

8.2   DSFBLNetwork

We apply the same approach for specifying the structural semantics of the "DSF-BLNetwork". The following rules define the well-formedness of a network model. Each process in a network should have a unique name:

```
Error (X, "The process should have a unique name") :-
Network (_, _, _, elements),
X ← elements, Y ← elements,
X: Process, Y: Process, X != Y, X.name = Y.name.
```

The component names referenced by the processes of a network should exist within the components of the model:

```
Error (process, "The process has an invalid Component") :-
Network (_, _, _, elements),
process ← elements, process: Process,
no Component (process.component, _, _).
```

The parameters of a process in a network should correspond to the parameters defined for the component which is referenced by the process:

```
Error (process, "The process has an invalid parameter") :-
Network (_, _, _, elements),
```

```
process ← elements, process: Process,
param ← process.parameters,
Component (process.component, com_elements, _),
no {e | e ← com_elements, e: ParameterDef, e.name = param.name}.
```

The following rules validate the well-formedness of the connection elements of the model. The source and target channels of each connection should refer to a valid process name if they are not associated with the network itself:

```
Error (conn, "The connection has invalid process") :-
Network (_, _, _, elements),
conn ← elements, conn: Connection,
conn.source.process != Nil,
no {e | e ← elements, e: Process, e.name = conn.source.process}.
; Network (_, _, _, elements),
conn ← elements, conn: Connection,
conn.target.process != Nil,
no {e | e ← elements, e: Process, e.name = conn.target.process}.
```

The ports of the channels associated with the processes must match the defined ports of the corresponding component associated to the process:

```
Error (conn, "The connection has invalid port") :-
Network (_, _, _, elements),
conn ← elements, conn: Connection,
conn.source.process != Nil,
process ← elements, process: Process,
process.name = conn.source.process,
Component (process.component, com_elements, _),
no {e | e ← com_elements, e: OutPort, e.name = conn.source.port}
; Network (_, _, _, elements),
conn ← elements, conn: Connection,
conn.target.process != Nil,
process ← elements, process: Process,
process.name = conn.target.process,
Component (process.component, com_elements, _),
no {e | e ← com_elements, e: InPort, e.name = conn.target.port}.
```

The ports associated with the source and target channels of a connection should have a same data type. In order to validate this, we first need to define the following function in order to determine the type of a port associated to a channel:

```
ChannelDataType ::= [Network, Channel ⇒ String].
ChannelDataType (network, channel) ⇒ (type) :-
channel.process = Nil,
port ← network.elements, port: Port,
```

```
port.name = channel.port, type= port.type
; channel.process != Nil,
process ← network.networkelements, process: Process,
process.name = channel.process,
Component (process.component, com_elements, _),
port ← com_elements, port: Port,
port.name = channel.port, type= port.type.
```

Then we use this function to match the data type of the source and target channels of each connection in a network:

```
Error (conn, "The data type of source and target of the connection are
not compatible") :-
net is Network,
conn ← net.networkelements, conn: Connection,
ChannelDataType (net, conn.source) ⇒ (source_type),
ChannelDataType (net, conn.target) ⇒ (target_type),
source_type != target_type.
```

Finally, we check that the model should not have any fact of type *Error*.

9   Behavioral Semantics

In this section, we provide the behavioral semantic specifications of the proposed meta-
models. In our FBP metamodeling framework, the communication between a component with its channels is done through a set of *IOActions*. This helps to abstract away the complexity of handling the connection related issues, i.e. the channel's capacity constraints from the component and delegate it to the scheduler. Furthermore, it allows extending the communication between the FBP scheduler and the components by introducing a new type of actions, i.e. time-related actions.

As presented in Fig. 4, *IOAction* data type is defined in a package called "DSFBLIO". There are two type of *IOActions* which are *ClosePort* and *DataActions*. A component can receive or send a *ClosePort* action. It receives this action when one of its input ports should be closed and it sends this action when one of its output ports should be closed. If a port is closed, it can not receive or send data. *DataActions* are *Read*, *Write*, and *Drop* actions. A component receives a *Read* action for each *DataPacket* available in the buffer of the related input channels, and it can send *Write* and *Drop* actions to write a *DataPacket* to its output channels, or remove a *DataPacket* from its input channels. In the following sections, we specify the behavioral semantics of "DSFBLCore" and "DSFBLNetwork".

9.1   DSFBLCore

In order to define the behavioral semantics of the components, we must first formalize the execution environment of the components, and then we provide

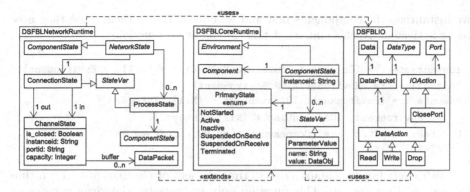

Fig. 4. The run-time models of DSFBLCore and DSFBLNetwork.

the mechanisms to map a component from the design time environment to the execution environment. Afterwards, we provide the mechanism to trigger the entry point of a component. The execution environment of components is presented in Fig. 4. An abstract class called *ComponentState* is used to specify the execution environment. This is comprised of a reference to the corresponding component, a *PrimaryState* and a set of *StateVars* including *ParameterValues*, and an instance name to store the actual status of a component. *Instance-id* is an auto-generated unique identifier that specifies this particular instance of the component. *StateVars* are the dynamic structures of the component which need to be stored. The *PrimaryState* indicates the execution state of the component as we discussed earlier. We can formalize the execution environment as the following data types:

```
domain DSFBLCoreRuntime extends DSFBLCore, DSFBLIO
{
  Environment ::= ComponentState.
  ComponentState :;= new (instanceid: String, component: Component,
    primary_state: PrimaryState,
    statevars: StateVarList + {Nil}).
  PrimaryState ::= { NotStarted, Active, Inactive,
    Suspended_on_receive, Suspended_on_send, Terminated}.
  StateVarList ::= list <StateVar>.
  StateVar ::= ParameterValue.
  ParameterValue ::= new (name: String, Value: DataObj).
  ParameterValueList ::= list <ParameterValue>.
}
```

As we mentioned earlier, the only components in a network that will be activated are the ones that either receive data on their input ports or do not have any input ports. Therefore, there are some components which will never be activated and, consequently, initializing these components is useless. Thereby, we instantiate the components first and we only initialize them when they need to be activated. To this end, we define the following functions:

```
Instantiate ::= [Component, ParameterValueList + {Nil} ⇒ Environment].
Initialize ::= [Environment ⇒ Environment].
Execute ::= [Environment, IOActionList + {Nil}, Integer
   ⇒ Environment, IOActionList + {Nil}, Integer].
UpdatePrimaryState ::= [ComponentState, PrimaryState ⇒
ComponentState].
```

Instantiate function maps a design time element of *Component* to a run-time element of *Environment*. This function only instantiates the given component by generating a unique Instance-id and returns it within an initialized environment. This function does not load the component. The *Initialize* function maps an initialized environment which only contains instantiation information, e.g. instance-id, to other environments which contain the information of the component in the initialized state. This function loads the component by initializing all the elements of the component. The function called *UpdatePrimaryState* updates the primary state of a component. *Execute* is the function that specifies the entry point of a component. When the component is in the active state, the scheduler will call this function. This function has three input arguments which are types of *Environment*, *IOActionList*, and Integer. The first parameter specifies the current state of the component at which it can be the initialized environment generated by calling the *Initialize* function or the environment produced by the last call to this function. The second argument specifies a list of *IOActions* generated according to the current state of the input channels of the component, and the last arguments indicate the activation-id. Since a component can be activated multiple times, in order to distinguish the different execution traces of the execution function, we assign a unique id to each execution. The function as output returns: the updated state of the component, a list of *IOActions* that should be applied on the input channels or output channels of the component, and the activation-id which should be the same as the activation-id given as the input argument.

The FBP scheduler calls the *Execute* function of the component to produce the outputs. The function does not have direct access to the channels. Instead, it receives and generates actions to be applied to the channels. This allows the component to generate as many actions as required each time it gets activated and the scheduler eventually applies these actions to the channels by considering the capacity constraint of the bounded channels.

9.2 DSFBLNetwork

In this section, we provide the behavioral semantics of a *Network* according to the runtime protocol implemented for the C# implementation of FBP (C#FBP). For reasons of brevity, we only provide the important parts of the specifications here. As presented in Fig. 4, we extend the execution environment of a *Network* from the execution environment of *Component*. A *NetworkState* is representation of a *Network* in run-time environment. This extends *ComponentState* with two more state variables which are *ConnectionState* and *ProcessState*. These are necessary to store the run-time environment of a network. *ProcessState* is used to store the execution state of the processes of a network within a *ComponentState*. *ConnectionState* is used to store the state of the connections of the network. This stores the state of its channels by utilizing two *ChannelStates*. Each *ChannelState* is comprised of the following; a *buffer*, which is a FIFO list to store the data packets arriving in the associated channel, a referencing name for the associated port called *portid*, the *instanceid* of the process associated with the channel, and *capacity* to specify the buffer's size of the channel.

In the previous section, we provided three abstract functions to specify the operational semantics of the components in our framework. Since we extend *Network* from *Component*, in order to specify the operational semantics for networks, we need to specify the operational rules for these functions as follows:

```
Instantiate (component, params) ⇒ (env) :-
  component: Network,
  statevars = params,
  net_instance_no = count ({ X | Instantiate (X, _, _), X: Network }),
  instanceid = strJoin (component.name, net_instance_no),
  env = NetworkState (instanceid, component, NotStarted, statevars).
```

In order to instantiate a network, we first need to generate an instance id by concatenating the component name and the number of times that the *Instantiate* function has been triggered for components of type *Network*. Afterwards, we construct a *NetworkState* as the initial environment with the following arguments; the generated instance-id, the given component, *NotStarted* as the primary state, and the list of the given parameter's values as the state variables.

We initialize a network by initializing the processes and connections of the network. To this end, first, we initialize the network processes by calling *IntializeProcesses* function. Afterwards, we initialize the network's connections by utilizing a function called *IntializeConnections*. At the end, we generate a new *NetworkState* as the updated environment and we set the primary state of the network to *Active*. We specify this function as follows:

```
Initialize (env) ⇒ (env''') :-
  env: NetworkState,
  IntializeProcesses (env) ⇒ (env'),
  IntializeConnections (env') ⇒ (env''),
  env''' = NetworkState (env.instanceid, env.component, Active,
    env''.statevars).
```

After we map the design-time elements of the network language to the elements of the execution environment, we are ready to specify the big-steps and the small-steps of the behavioral semantics for the network language. To this end, we specify the execution rules for *Execute* function for the network language as three big-steps. Firstly, we apply the input *IOActions* to the associated input channels of the network. This maps the given execution environment *env* to an updated environment *env'*. Afterwards, we call the *ExecuteProcesses* function which maps the updated environment *env'* to the final environment *env"*. This executes the network through several small-step execution rules and it ends when there are no more active processes in the network. Finally, we call a function called *WriteActions* to generate the output actions according to the state of the input and output channels of the network. We formalize the *Execute* function as follows and we specify the other functions afterwards:

```
Execute (env, in_actions, actid) ⇒ (env'', out_actions, actid) :-
    env: NetworkState,
Read the input actions and load the data on the input ports of the network.

    LoadActions (env, in_actions) ⇒ (env'),
Execute the processes in the network, until all input channels are empty.

    ExecuteProcesses (env', actid) ⇒ (env''),
Convert the output channels of the network to IOAction list as the output.

    WriteActions (env'', in_actions) ⇒ (out_actions).
```

We utilize *LoadActions* function to load the input data to the input channels of the network. To this end, we iterate the connections of the network and we apply the given input actions to the network input channels. Finally, we update the environment with the updated channels. After loading the data into the input channels of the network, the connections of the network should be executed to transfer the data-packets from the source channels to the target channels of the connections. This activates the processes connected to the target channels. The next step is to execute these active processes and update their output channels accordingly. This can be done by repeating these steps. *ExecuteProcesses* formalizes these rules as a big-step, which maps the updated environment from the last step to the final environment of executing the network. This function calls itself until no more processes can be executed. It also uses a new activation id for each execution trace. We specify this function as follows:

```
ExecuteProcesses ::= [NetworkState, Integer ⇒ NetworkState, Integer].
ExecuteProcesses (env, actid) ⇒ (env''', actid) :-
Execute the connection of the network.

    ExecuteConnections (env) ⇒ (env'),
Extracts the active processes in the network.

    active_processes = toList(ProcessStateList, Nil,
    {proc_state | proc_state ← env'.statevars,
    proc_state: ProcessState,
    proc_state.primary_state = Active}),
Verifies if there are any active process in the network.

    active_processes != Nil,
```

Execute the active processes.

```
  ExecuteActiveProcesses (active_processes, env', actid)
  ⇒ (env'', actid),
Repeat these steps with the updated environment.
  ExecuteProcesses (env'', new_actid)
  ⇒ (env''', new_actid),
  new_actid = actid+1
; active_processes = toList(ProcessStateList, Nil,
  {proc_state | proc_state ← env.statevars,
  proc_state: ProcessState,
  proc_state.primary_state = Active}),
  active_processes = Nil,
  UpdatePrimaryState (env, Inactive) ⇒ (env''').
```

ExecuteConnections formalize the execution rules for the connections of a network as two small-steps which are propagating the connections and updating the process states of the network.

```
  ExecuteConnections ::= [NetworkState ⇒ NetworkState].
  ExecuteConnections (env) ⇒ (env'') :-
    PropagateConnections (env) ⇒ (env'),
    UpdateProcessStates (env') ⇒ (env'').
```

PropagateConnections propagates each connection in the given network by transferring the data-packets from the source channels to the target channels of the connection and it returns the updated environment. After propagating the connections, we need to update the state of the network's processes. To this end, we update the state of each process by calling *UpdateProcessState* which updates the state of the network processes according to the following rules:

- If the state of the process is *NotStarted* and the buffer of at least one of its input channels is not empty, initialize the process.
- If the state of the process is *Inactive* and the buffer of at least one of its input channels is not empty, update the process state to *Active*.
- If the state of the process is *Suspended_on_receive* and the buffer of at least one of its input channels is not empty, update the process state to *Active*.
- If the process has unconsumed data-packets on at least one of its output channels, update the process state to *Suspended_on_send*.
- If the state of the process is *Suspended_on_send* and the process has no unconsumed data-packets on all of its output channels, update the process state to *Active*.
- If all the input channels of the process are closed, update the process state to *Terminated*.
- Otherwise, keep the state of the process.

ExecuteActiveProcesses executes a list of active processes and returns the updated environment. We can execute a process within four small-steps; generating the input actions based on the current state of the input channels of the process, calling the *Execute* function for the component associated to the process to obtain the output actions, update the network environment with the updated state of the process, and finally updating the process channels by applying the output actions and obtaining the updated execution environment. *ExecutePro-cess* formalizes these rules as follows:

```
ExecuteProcess ::= [ NetworkState, ProcessState, Integer
⇒ NetworkState, Integer].
ExecuteProcess (env, proc_state, actid) ⇒ (env'', actid) :-
Generate the IO actions based on the state of the process input channels.

    GenerateActions (env, proc_state.state.instanceid)
    ⇒ (in_actions),
Execute the process.

    Execute (proc_state.state, in_actions, actid)
    ⇒ (state', out_actions, actid),
Update the environment

    UpdateStateVar (env, proc_state.state, state')
    ⇒ (env'),
Apply the outputs to the channels.

    ApplyActions (env', proc_state.state.instanceid, out_actions)
    ⇒ (env'').
```

GenerateActions function generates a list of *IOAction* based on the state of the input channels of the process with the given instance-id of the given environment. This function is called before executing an active process within a network. This generates a *Read* action for each data-packet available in the buffer of the input channel associated to the process. It also generates *Close* action for any input channels of the process which are in close state.

```
GenerateActions ::= [NetworkState, String ⇒ IOActionList + {Nil}].
GenerateActions (env, instid) ⇒ (actions) :-
    actions = toList(IOActionList, Nil,
    {act | conn ← env.statevars, conn: ConnectionState,
    conn.out.procid = instid,
    packet ← conn.out.buffer,
    act = Read (conn.out.portid, packet)} union
    {act | conn ← env.statevars, conn: ConnectionState,
    conn.out.procid = instid,
    conn.out.is_closed = TRUE,
    act = Close (conn.out.portid)}).
```

ApplyActions function updates the environment by applying the list of the given actions on the channels associated to a process with the given instance-id. This function is called after executing an active process within a network. The function utilizes another function called *UpdateChannel* for applying the *IOActions* on the buffer of the related channels as follows:

```
UpdateChannel ::= [ChannelState, String, IOActionList ⇒
ChannelState].
UpdateChannel
(ChannelState (proc_id, portid, buffer, isclosed), instid, actions)
  ⇒ ( ChannelState (proc_id, portid, buffer', isclosed)) :-
```

If the channels are not empty, the updated buffer of the channel will be calculated by appending the data-packet associated to each *Write* action in the action list, to the list of the data-packets available in the channel's buffer, excluding the data-packets associated to the *Drop* actions in the action list.

```
new_datapackets= toList (DataPacketList, Nil,
{act.data | act ← actions, act: Write, act.portid = portid}),
current_datapackets= toList (DataPacketList, Nil,
{data | data ← buffer, not isin(Drop (portid, data), actions)}),
buffer'= append (current_datapackets, new_datapackets),
proc_id = instid, buffer != Nil, actions != Nil
```

If the channels are empty, the updated buffer of the channel will be calculated by inserting the data-packet associated to each *Write* action in the action list into the channel's buffer.

```
; buffer'= toList (DataPacketList, Nil,
  {act.data | act ← actions, act: Write, act.portid = portid }),
  proc_id = instid, buffer = Nil, actions != Nil
```

If the given process instance-id does not match the instance id associated to the channel, no update will be required.

```
; buffer' = buffer, proc_id != instid
```

WriteActions function generates a list of *IOAction* which is the output of the execution of the given network. Therefore, it generates three kinds of *IOActions* as follows:

```
WriteActions ::= [NetworkState, IOActionList ⇒ IOActionList + {Nil}].
WriteActions (env, in_actions) ⇒ (actions) :-
```

For each data-packet available in the buffer of the network's output channels, generate a *Write* action:

```
actions = toList(IOActionList, Nil,
{act | conn ← env.statevars, conn: ConnectionState,
conn.out.procid = env.instanceid,
packet ← conn.out.buffer,
act = Write (conn.out.portid, packet)} union
```

For each output channel of the network which is in closed state, generate a *Close* action:

```
{act | conn ← env.statevars, conn: ConnectionState,
conn.out.procid = env.instanceid,
conn.out.is_closed = TRUE,
act = Close (conn.out.portid)} union
```

For each data-packet which is associated to the *Read* actions within the given input actions, but not available in the buffer of the network's input channels, generate a *Drop* action:

```
{act | act' <- in_actions, act':Read,
no {conn | conn ← env.statevars, conn: ConnectionState,
conn.in.procid = env.instanceid, isin (act'.data, conn.in.buffer)},
act = Drop (act'.portid, act'.data)}).
```

10   Conclusions

In this paper, we proposed an integrated framework under the umbrella of the Microsoft Visual Studio IDE to facilitate the development of graphical DSLs within a single development environment. This framework utilizes Microsoft DSL Tools to specify the metamodel and graphical notations of DSLs, and our extension of ForSpec to define their semantics.

To offer better support for semantic specifications, we have extended ForSpec with list datatypes, union operators, iterators, map and reduce functions, and typed union datatype. Since ForSpec specifications are executable, the semantic specifications of the developed DSLs can execute and validate their model instances.

As a case study, we developed a metamodeling language to specify flow-based languages. We formalized the metamodel, structural semantics, and behavioral semantics of the language within our integrated framework. We specified the behavioral semantics of the FBP network presented in this paper according to the runtime protocol implemented for the C# implementation of FBP (C#FBP). We validated the ForSpec specifications given in this paper by modeling the test cases developed for C#FBP within the network language proposed in this work.

As future work, we are going to combine this framework with other language development tools for developing textual languages such as Microsoft Irony.

References

1. Agrawal, A., Simon, G., Karsai, G.: Semantic translation of simulink/stateflow models to hybrid automata using graph transformations. Electron. Notes Theor. Comput. Sci. **109**, 43–56 (2004)
2. Balasubramanian, D., Jackson, E.K.: Lost in translation: forgetful semantic anchoring. In: Proceedings of the 2009 IEEE/ACM International Conference on Automated Software Engineering. ASE 2009, IEEE Computer Society (2009)
3. Balasubramanian, D., Narayanan, A., van Buskirk, C., Karsai, G.: The graph rewriting and transformation language: GReAT. Electronic Communications of the EASST (2007)
4. Bergius, H.: NoFlo, April 2014. http://noflojs.org/
5. Chen, K., Sztipanovits, J., Abdelwalhed, S., Jackson, E.: Semantic anchoring with model transformations. In: Hartman, A., Kreische, D. (eds.) ECMDA-FA 2005. LNCS, vol. 3748, pp. 115–129. Springer, Heidelberg (2005). https://doi.org/10.1007/11581741_10
6. Di Ruscio, D., Jouault, F., Kurtev, I., Bézivin, J., Pierantonio, A.: Extending amma for supporting dynamic semantics specifications of DSLs. Technical report, LINA Research Report (2006)
7. DSPatch: DSPatch - C++ flow-based programming library, April 2014. http://www.flowbasedprogramming.com/
8. Ducasse, S., Girba, T., Kuhn, A., Renggli, L.: Meta-environment and executable meta-language using smalltalk: an experience report. Softw. Syst. Model. **8**(1), 5–19 (2009)
9. Gargantini, A., Riccobene, E., Scandurra, P.: A semantic framework for metamodel-based languages. Autom. Softw. Eng. **16**(3–4), 415–454 (2009)
10. Gurevich, Y.: Evolving algebras 1993: Lipari guide. Specification and Validation Methods, pp. 9–36 (1995)
11. IBM: IBM InfoSphere DataStage, April 2014. http://www01.ibm.com/software/data/infosphere/datastage/
12. Jackson, E., Sztipanovits, J.: Formalizing the structural semantics of domain-specific modeling languages. Softw. Syst. Model. **8**(4), 451–478 (2009)
13. Jackson, E.K., Bjørner, N., Schulte, W.: Canonical regular types. In: ICLP (Technical Communications) (2011)
14. Jackson, E.K., Kang, E., Dahlweid, M., Seifert, D., Santen, T.: Components, platforms and possibilities: towards generic automation for MDA. In: Proceedings of the Tenth ACM International Conference on Embedded Software. ACM (2010)
15. Karsai, G., Agrawal, A., Shi, F., Sprinkle, J.: On the use of graph transformation in the formal specification of model interpreters. J. Univers. Comput. Sci. **9**(11), 1296–1321 (2003)
16. Lédeczi, Á., et al.: Composing domain-specific design environments. Computer **34**(11), 44–51 (2001)
17. Lindecker, D., Simko, G., Levendovszky, T., Madari, I., Sztipanovits, J.: Validating transformations for semantic anchoring. J. Object Technol. **14**(3), 1–25 (2015)
18. Mayerhofer, T., Langer, P., Wimmer, M., Kappel, G.: xMOF: executable DSMLs based on fUML. In: Erwig, M., Paige, R.F., Van Wyk, E. (eds.) SLE 2013. LNCS, vol. 8225, pp. 56–75. Springer, Cham (2013). https://doi.org/10.1007/978-3-319-02654-1_4
19. Microsoft: Visualization and Modeling SDK – Domain-Specific Languages, April 2014. http://msdn.microsoft.com/en-us/library/bb126259.aspx

20. Montages: xocl: executable ocl, November 2007. http://www.montages.com/xocl. html

21. Morrison, J.P.: Data stream linkage mechanism. IBM Syst. J. **17**(4), 383–408 (1978)

22. Morrison, J.P.: Flow-Based Programming, A New Approach to Application Development, 2nd Edn. CreateSpace Independent Publishing Platform, CreateSpace (2010)

23. PyF: PyF - Python FBP implementation, April 2014. http://pyfproject.org/

24. QVT: OMG MOF 2.0 query/view/transformation (qvt), OMG Document - formal/08-04-03, April 2008

25. Romero, J.R., Rivera, J.E., Durán, F., Vallecillo, A.: Formal and tool support for model driven engineering with Maude. J. Object Technol. **6**(9), 187–207 (2007)

26. Sadilek, D.A., Wachsmuth, G.: Using grammarware languages to define operational semantics of modelled languages. In: Oriol, M., Meyer, B. (eds.) TOOLS EUROPE 2009. LNBIP, vol. 33, pp. 348–356. Springer, Heidelberg (2009). https://doi.org/10.1007/978-3-642-02571-6_20

27. Scheidgen, M., Fischer, J.: Human comprehensible and machine processable specifications of operational semantics. In: Akehurst, D.H., Vogel, R., Paige, R.F. (eds.) ECMDA-FA 2007. LNCS, vol. 4530, pp. 157–171. Springer, Heidelberg (2007). https://doi.org/10.1007/978-3-540-72901-3_12

28. Action Semantics: The action semantics consortium for the UML, OMG Document - formal/2001-03-01, April 2001

29. Simko, G.: Formal Semantic Specification of Domain-Specific Modeling Languages for Cyber-Physical Systems. Ph.D. thesis, Vanderbilt University (2014)

30. Simko, G., Levendovszky, T., Neema, S., Jackson, E., Bapty, T., Porter, J., Sztipanovits, J.: Foundation for model integration: semantic backplane. In: ASME 2012 International Design Engineering Technical Conferences and Computers and Information in Engineering Conference. American Society of Mechanical Engineers (2012)

31. Simko, G., Lindecker, D., Levendovszky, T., Neema, S., Sztipanovits, J.: Specification of cyber-physical components with formal semantics – integration and composition. In: Moreira, A., Schätz, B., Gray, J., Vallecillo, A., Clarke, P. (eds.) MODELS 2013. LNCS, vol. 8107, pp. 471–487. Springer, Heidelberg (2013). https://doi.org/10.1007/978-3-642-41533-3_29

32. Wachsmuth, G.: Modelling the operational semantics of domain-specific modelling languages. In: Lämmel, R., Visser, J., Saraiva, J. (eds.) GTTSE 2007. LNCS, vol. 5235, pp. 506–520. Springer, Heidelberg (2008). https://doi.org/10.1007/978-3-540-88643-3_16

33. Zarrin, B., Baumeister, H.: Design of a domain-specific language for material flow analysis using Microsoft DSL Tools: An experience paper. In: Proceedings of the 14th Workshop on Domain-Specific Modeling, DSM 2014. pp. 23–28. ACM (2014)

34. Zarrin, B., Baumeister, H.: An integrated framework to specify domain-specific modeling languages. In: Proceedings of the 6th International Conference on Model-Driven Engineering and Software Development, vol. 1: MODELSWARD, pp. 83–94. INSTICC, SciTePress (2018)

35. Zarrin, B., Baumeister, H., Sarjoughian, H.: Towards domain-specific flow-based languages. In: Proceedings of the 6th International Conference on Model-Driven Engineering and Software Development, vol. 1: MODELSWARD, pp. 319–325. INSTICC, SciTePress (2018)

Technology Enhanced Support for Learning Interactive Software Systems

Jenny Ruiz[1(✉)], Estefanía Serral[2], and Monique Snoeck[2]

[1] University of Holguin, XX Anniversary Ave, Holguin, Cuba
jruizp@uho.edu.cu
[2] KU Leuven, Naamsestraat 69, Leuven, Belgium
{estefania.serral,monique.snoeck}@kuleuven.be

Abstract. The development of useful and usable interactive software systems depends on both User Interface (UI) design and software engineering in a complementary way. However, today, application development and UI design are largely separated activities and fields of knowledge. This separation is also present in education as can be witnessed from the common independent way of teaching of both subjects. Although the development of better interactive software systems could benefit significantly from an integrative teaching approach, there is a lack of concrete and proven approaches for such way of teaching. This paper presents technology enhanced support for filling this gap. The proposed tool supports and improves learning achievements for the development of interactive software systems. The learning support includes feedback for conceptual modeling integrated with UI design. The tool applies Model Driven Engineering principles that allows the automatic generation of a working prototype from specification models. This capability allows the learner trying out the final application while validating the requirements. An experimental evaluation with novice developers demonstrates the advantages of this didactic tool.

Keywords: Abstract User Interface Model · Presentation model ·
Feature model · Model-driven engineering · User interface design ·
User Interface Generation

1 Introduction

Nowadays, the development of useful and usable interactive software systems has become essential to guarantee the quality of the systems [1, 2]. The fields of User Interface (UI) design and software engineering complement each other to reach that goal. However, there seems to be an implicit separation between application development and the design of its UI, mainly because the two fields of knowledge are not well integrated. A gap between the two communities makes each one of them focusing primarily on their own field [3, 4]. As pointed by [5], there is a lack of harmonization between UI and application design, with both communities largely neglecting the relation to other software views.

This problem is already present in education. Due to the commonly isolated way of teaching UI design and application development, the link between both aspects is rarely made, despite the fact that the integration between UI design and application development can significantly contribute to the development of even better systems [5]. Specifically, there is a need for integrated teaching support to foster the understanding of the relationship between functional aspects of an application and its UI.

At the same time, UI design has been considered a difficult process [6, 7]. Therefore, the learning process should not be hampered by the use of tools that are difficult to use := ease of use is a critical factor for tools oriented to novice designers [8]. Different tools have been developed to enhance the learning of either software engineering or UI design. However, very few of them provide (some level of) integration with application development, and these tools are difficult to use and not tailored to learners [9].

In previous work [10] we presented a fully-implemented and integrated simulation tool for the teaching of UI design and application development at once. With this tool the learner defines conceptual models to describe the business logic behind the interactive software system, and augments it with a presentation model to capture UI requirements. The tool provides simulation by automatically generating a full working prototype of the described system in an integrated environment, that allows the learner testing the system against its requirements. In addition, teaching support is provided with two kinds of feedback: (1) to facilitate tracing the application's behavior back to its origin in the underlying conceptual models; and (2) related to the UI design, giving the learner clues according to design principles for the UI functional aspects and helping understanding the relationship between functional aspects and the UI.

This paper extends previous work [10] by providing a comparison of the related work according to the goal of the presented environment. It also presents more details of the design of the environment and the teaching support provided. A theoretical evaluation demonstrates this tool's effectiveness, its ease of use, and its level of integration towards the development of interactive software systems. Additional experimental evaluation is also provided in this paper showing the practical results of the use of the proposed environment as a didactic tool.

The remainder of this paper is structured as follows: Sect. 2 examines the related work on educational tools to teach UI design and application development. Section 3 describes the integrated learning tool for interactive software systems. Section 4 presents an evaluation of the developed tool. Section 5 discusses the limitation of the tool and Sect. 6 concludes the paper.

2   Related Work

We analyzed the approaches related to our work from different perspectives: (1) integration focused on UI design; (2) integration focused on application development and (3) teaching support for UI design and or application development.

A number of Model Driven Engineering (MDE) approaches support UI design, while giving support for integration with the application. Some approaches use models for partial integration, but it is still the developer who manually needs to make the link with the application. Examples are MASP [11], that has a service model which allows connecting backend services to application tasks, and LIZARD [12], that has a data service model used to populate UI controls. Dygimes [13] allows defining the link to the application logic by means of operations invoking web services linked to the application. Similarly, MARIA [14] generates UIs for various platforms from existing UIs, and is able to keep functioning with the rest of the application by using web services.

Approaches like WAINE [14] and TERESA [15] generate web applications where the components of the UI are defined at the highest abstraction level, which is a difficult task. These environments do not support the UI integration with persistence and functionality. Some approaches, besides generating the UI code, generate part of the code for the underlying application. DB-USE [16] generates code to create, update, delete and retrieve data. CIAT-GUI [17] generates .Net classes that work behind the UI.

Examples of Model Driven Architecture (MDA) approaches for supporting application development are OptimalJ (www.compuware.com/products/optimalj) and AndroMDA (www.andromda.org), which are code generation frameworks that generate fully deployable applications. These approaches generate the links between all the layers, including a default presentation layer, but there is no support for tailoring the UI.

Some other approaches offer partial integrated support, where the code for the integration of the different layers needs to be written by the developer. For example, ArcStyler (www.interactive-objects.com) supports application development and has a mechanism for designing sequences in the UI. ACCELEO (www.acceleo.org) allows creating templates for the generation of code from models. OO-Method [18] provides complete, integrated support for the UI design and application development. WebRatio (www.webratio.com) generates fully-functional applications, focused on Web and mobile applications [19]. However, those approaches also require detailed models which makes them difficult to use by junior developers.

The main shortcoming of the previous approaches is the lack of teaching support: it is not their core focus. For example, although some of the previous approaches offer design choices for the application and/or its UI, the novice leaner does not receive feedback that helps him during the design process. The approaches are not easy to use either. Ideally, technical hurdles should be avoided so that the learner can focus on the design aspects. Ideally, it should be possible to generate the UI code and its integrated application code through a single click. Current approaches need different tools (e.g. MASP, Dygimes and DB-USE have two and three tools respectively) or take models from external tools and require additional transformation steps (e.g. AndroMDA).

There are a number of approaches that focus on supporting the teaching of UI design. [20] proposes a hypertext module called UID tutorial which exemplifies the use of design principles through examples of good and bad UIs. The tutorial contains a major overview of design principles and includes explanations for example, of using metaphors, input devices and evaluation issues. [21] proposes a multimedia design advisor tool. The tool uses examples to give recommendations about which media is appropriate (according to the information type). UsabilityGame [22] supports the teaching of the usability engineering life cycle, requirements analysis, prototyping and heuristic evaluation. It shows examples of design of web interfaces where the student needs to select which heuristics are applied. [23] proposes an approach to address usability issues in a learning management system: ILIAS. The approach provides a taxonomy of UI components within ILIAS and guidelines for how to use them. These approaches are only focused on teaching UI design without providing support for teaching the integration between UI design and application development.

Teaching application development is also supported by tools. For instance, the JMermaid tool, based on MERODE, a method for enterprise information system engineering [24], allows generating a full functional application with a single click while embedding feedback in the application. The feedback explains the application's behavior by referring to the models it was generated from [25]. This tool has been used and successfully validated for teaching conceptual modelling [26]. However, this environment does not offer support for tailoring the UI or teaching UI design.

Table 1 shows a summary of the analyzed approaches from the different perspectives. Each approach shows to what extend the support is provided:

Table 1. Comparison of approaches.

Approach	Support for UI design	Support for integration	Support for teaching
MDE UI design			
MASP	●	◖	○
LIZARD	●	◖	○
Dygimes	●	◖	○
MARIA	●	◖	○
WAINE	●	◖	○
TERESA	●	◖	○
DB-USE	●	◖	○
CIAT-GUI	●	◖	○
MDA application development			
OptimalJ	○	●	○
AndroMDA	○	●	○
ACCELEO	○	◖	○
ArcStyler	◖	●	○
WebRatio	●	●	○
OO-Method	●	●	○
Teaching UI design/application development			
Hypertext module	○	○	◖
Multimedia design advisor	○	○	◖
UsabilityGame	○	○	◖
ILIAS	○	○	◖
Jmermaid	○	●	◖

Legend:

– Support for UI design.
  - ●: UI design can be customized
  - ◖: UI design options can be partially customized or with some effort
  - ○: UI design cannot be customized
– Support for integration
  - ●: Fully deployable applications are obtained
  - ◖: Only part of the code for the integration is provided or the developer needs to write the code for the integration of the different layers
  - ○: No support
– Support for teaching
  - ●: Support for teaching UI design integrated with application development
  - ◖: Support for teaching UI design or application development
  - ○: No support

Although the presented initiatives have their merits, they suffer from a lack of teaching support for UI design and application development integrated, which is the goal of the environment presented in this paper. Additionally, there seems to be no teaching support on how to design UIs based on practical approaches used in industry or on academic approaches for UI design. Only [20, 22] support the teaching of design principles. However, [20] does not show how the application of the principles affects the UI design and although [22] allows recognizing if a heuristic has been applied in a given interface, it is not possible for the student to check the appliance of the heuristics on their UI design, something that is possible in the environment proposed in this paper.

3 Technology Enhanced Support for Learning Interactive Software Systems

To support the teaching of interactive software systems, this paper proposes an integrated tool that allows the co-design of an application and its UI. In previous work [10] we presented the overall design of a fully-implemented and integrated simulation tool for the teaching of UI design and application development at once, with the JMermaid tool, provided by the MERODE method and the Feedback ENabled user Interface Simulation (FENIkS), extension to JMermaid, to provide support for UI design. This paper presents the detailed design and implementation of this tool. First, the MERODE method and JMermaid tool are introduced. Then, the details of the extension, FENIkS, the transformation engine for the generation process and how the teaching support is provided are explained.

3.1 MERODE Method

MERODE is an enterprise engineering approach focused on the development of a conceptual model (close to a Computational Independent Model) that is sufficiently complete to automatically generate the application's code from it. The structural view of MERODE is established through a class diagram to capture the domain classes while the functional view is defined by a collection of Finite State Machines to capture enterprise object behavior and an Object-Event Table to capture interaction aspects.

The MERODE method is supported by a proven conceptual modelling teaching environment, JMermaid, which allows model creation and checking the coherence of the different views, structural and functional [25]. This tool has a MDE-based code generator for the fast prototyping of a conceptual domain model that generates a fully functional prototype Java application [27]. The use of JMermaid as a teaching conceptual modelling tool has been successfully validated for more than 5 years [26].

While MERODE and JMermaid support application development, they do not provide specific support for UI design. The prototypes generated by JMermaid have a default UI with always the same kind of representation format for the input and output services. It does not provide options for designing the UI. The teaching support for the UI design is not provided either. Although the tool automatically provides the link between the UI with the underlying application, it doesn't provide any specific teaching support for the integrated teaching of UI design and application development. By the fact that the possibility of changing the UI is lacking, understanding the link between the UI and the application development process is not actively supported. For a complete analysis of limitations of JMermaid in terms of support for UI design the reader is referred to [28].

Not visualizing the behavior of the application through a UI makes it really difficult for the learner to check the behavior of the domain model: the interaction with the system would then have to be simulated in the mind of the learner to imagine what would happen while interacting with the system. Testing the functional aspects of the UI and the responses that the system would provide would be also difficult without application logic because the effect of an action cannot be verified. It would also be hard for the learner to find the missing functional aspects he did not incorporate in the UI design.

The well-defined conceptual models used by the MERODE method allow extending them with separated, but, at the same time, integrated UI models. The UI and application models make the integrated environment useful for modeling and simulation, including the enhancements with feedback that facilitate a process of model validation by novice learners. All the components that compose the UI and the possibility of checking their behavior through the simulation, help to foster the understanding of the link between the UI and the application logic.

3.2   FENIkS

Feedback ENabled user Interface Simulation is the extension to JMermaid that provides an integrated approach for UI design and application development of interactive software systems. In order to guarantee the integration with application development it is necessary that the generation of the UI and the application code are based on the same set of integrated models. The overall approach is shown in Fig. 1.

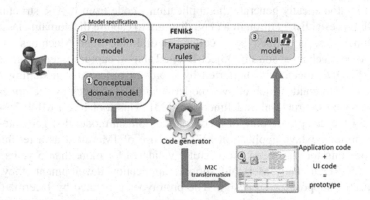

Fig. 1. FENIkS generation architecture.

The basic required input models are: (1) a domain model to capture the application's functional logic and (2) a presentation model to capture the characteristics of the interface layout and components and the user preferences. These two models are used to generate (3) an "Abstract User Interface" (AUI) which describes the UI in a technology-agnostic way. Finally, using the three mentioned models the engine generates (4) the application code and the UI code which compose the final application. The transformations are automatically done by the tool and there is no need for manual tailoring.

The following subsections describe the presentation model, the AUI model and the generation process of the final application.

Presentation Model. Before the FENIkS extension, it was possible to generate a prototype with a default UI. The generated UI was composed of: (1) default output services (or reports) that are a list of instances of a single domain object type into one window (e.g. view the lists of orders) and (2) the details of one object with all its information (e.g. view details of one order) shown in another window. Default input service is triggering the execution of a business event (e.g. create an order). FENIkS allows the definition of extra output services for showing specific information the user wants to see, for example, a list combining information from multiple domain objects (e.g. view a customer with all his orders).

Figure 2 shows the presentation meta-model that allows capturing these additional reports through the meta-object type Report and the associated meta-object types. A Report includes a selection of object types to be shown, together with a selection of their attributes and associations. The search can be configured in the same way.

The preferences related to how elements of the UI should be configured is also captured by the presentation model. The preferences have been split into two categories: Window aspects, for all the reports (default and non-default) and Input aspects, for input services. Generalizing the preferences for showing or capturing information allows applying them in a consistent way through the UI. This contributes to an important UI design principle of keeping a UI consistent.

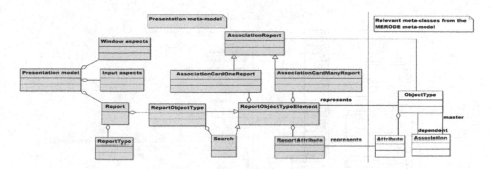

Fig. 2. FENIkS presentation meta-model [10].

The Window aspects capture the preferences about the static layout of the top level containers of the application, defining the main application window and how the information is displayed. Here it is possible to configure how to trigger the services of the domain objects, how the pagination will be, if there will be shortcuts for interacting with the system, etc.

The Input aspects capture the preferences related to how the user will input information into the application, like which kind of widgets are needed for inputting the information, how to select associated objects, the validation of the inputs or how to show the error messages when errors occur [29].

The generalization of all these aspects, allows FENIkS incorporating a set of generation options for the generation of the interactive software system from the input models. A family of prototypes with variations and commonalities in the way the information is presented and captured can be generated by the code generator. A feature model captures the various UI generation options, as such model provides an adequate visual representation that is easy to manipulate [30]. The feature model shows the relationships between a parent feature and its child features categorized as Optional or Mandatory depending on whether a child feature is optional or not, and 'Or' or 'Alternative (Xor)' depending on whether at least one or exactly one sub-feature must be selected.

The feature model of FENIkS starts from the root node 'presentation model' that is mandatorily composed of the basic elements 'Window aspects' and 'Input aspects', as also shown in the presentation meta-model. Figure 3 shows the options corresponding to the feature Window aspects. On the right side, the corresponding tab of the presentation model is shown. Here, the designer can select the values of the Window aspects for the options as presented in the feature model.

In a similar way, Fig. 4 shows the options corresponding to the feature 'Input aspects'. On the right side, the corresponding tab of the presentation model is shown. In this tab of the presentation model the designer can select the values of the Input aspects for the options as presented in the feature model.

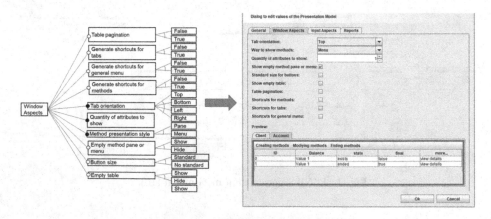

Fig. 3. Feature Windows aspects.

The majority of features of the Window and Input aspects are included for didactic purpose: they are used to generate the UI and to show the learner how to apply UI design principles. An example of such feature in the Window aspects is Generate shortcuts for tabs. An example of such feature in the Input aspects is Validate Boolean data. Section Teaching Support provides further detailed explanations of the examples.

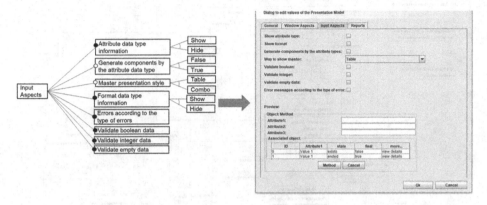

Fig. 4. Feature and Input aspects.

Some additional features are included to give flexibility to the prototype generation process. Examples of such features are mainly in the Window aspects: Tab orientation, Empty method pane or menu, Table pagination, Quantity of attributes to show and Empty table. In the Input aspects there is only one feature to give flexibility, namely the Master presentation style [10].

Abstract User Interface Model. FENIkS allows the automatic generation of an AUI from the conceptual and the presentation models. The Abstract User Interface is an UI definition that is independent of any modality of interaction.

Nowadays, when there is a variety of contexts of use, AUIs are important for the development of applications that can be used in several of these [31]. AUIs also play an important role from the teaching perspective. An AUI has the advantage of representing the UI without taking into account any modality of interaction or platform. As such it helps to foster understanding the main principles behind UI generation. Therefore, the generation of an AUI can be used to provide teaching support for novice designers for highlighting the general aspects of the UI generation (i.e., the components that constitute an UI in abstract terms) and, at the same time, while making the link between the UI and the underlying application logic.

The AUI meta-model of FENIkS is shown in Fig. 5. It is based on the AUI meta-model of the User Interface eXtensible Markup Language (UsiXML documentation version 1.4), a User-Interface Modelling language proposed by [32].

The lower part of the figure (in light blue) shows the AUI meta-model, while the upper part (in white) presents the relevant concepts of the MERODE method meta-model and presentation meta-model connected to the AUI meta-model. The domain model of the MERODE method is used for a transformation to obtain the AUI for the default output and input services. Additionally, the Report objects of the presentation model are used to generate the AUI for the user-specified output services.

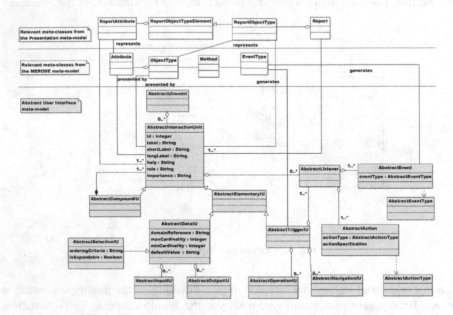

Fig. 5. FENIkS AUI meta-model [10]. (Color figure online)

The AbstractInteractionUnit is the basic unit for expressing the interaction in a recursive decomposition of an AUI. This decomposition can be related to one or many concepts like ObjectType, ReportObjectType, Attribute or ReportAttribute. An AbstractCompoundIU can be composed by one or many AbstractInteractionUnit [10].

Examples of AbstractElementaryIU are AbstractDataIU and AbstractTriggerIU. AbstractDataIU manages data input (with the meta-class AbstractInputIU) or data output (with the meta-class AbstractOutputIU). Linking the AbstractDataIU to a domain object is possible using the domain object reference in its definition, which allows ensuring data binding with the associated domain model. A special case of the AbstractInputIU is the AbstractSelectionIU, which is a way to interact with the system by selecting an item from a list.

The navigation and operation of the UI are managed by AbstractTriggerIU related to the AbstractListener, which describes the behavior of the UI. An AbstractListener is composed of an AbstractEvent (to specify the signal that triggers the action, e.g. onTriggerSelected) and an AbstractAction (which allows updating or invoking the domain model data, or modifications of the abstract entities themselves, e.g. IUOpen).

Transformation Engine. The transformation engine is the core of the model-driven process described in Fig. 1. The transformations are done in two steps: (1) transformation to the AUI model and (2) transformation to the UI and application code. The first step takes as input the conceptual domain and the presentation models. The second step additionally uses the AUI model resulting from the first step.

The code generator for the integrated support of MERODE was built using the Java language and the Velocity Templates Engine (velocity.apache.org). Template-based transformations (model-to-text transformations) are a widely supported platform integration technique in contemporary model-driven tools. The use of a template-based transformation approach allows going straight from model to code.

Figure 6 shows the components for the transformation process of the code generator. The code generator consists of three main modules: the *Input processor*, the *Generator* and the *Output processor*. It also has the necessary templates and the mapping rules.

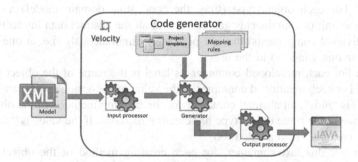

Fig. 6. Code generator transformation process.

The *Input processor* imports from the xml file, stored by FENIkS, the domain and the presentation models. The *Generator* is responsible for the transformation of the information imported from the models. First, it generates the AUI model, then the UI and application code. The *Generator* distributes the properties into template contexts and merges each context with a specified template to generate a set of files. The *Output processor* is responsible for creating the structure of the generated application and storing there the generated files to make a compiled executable application.

The code that implements the generated application has been designed according to the model-view-control (MVC) pattern having a hibernate database for the persistent layer, a handler layer and the UI layer. In order to obtain the final code, the code generator has been structured with various function objects that provide the implementation of model, view and control elements. According to this structure, the *Generator* provides the following modules:

- *generateAUICode,* for generating the AUI model.
- *generateHibernateFiles,* for generating elements of the database.
- *generateEventHandlerFiles,* for generating elements of the *control* layer.
- *generateDriverFile,* for generating the main class of the application.
- *generateUICode,* for generating elements of the *view* layer.
- *generateCode,* for managing the overall transformation.

The code generator uses mapping rules in its architecture to allow mappings between the various models. For example, a set of mapping rules exits between the domain model and the AUI model and between the presentation model and the AUI model. In addition to these mappings, an additional set of rules define the mapping between the AUI and the final UI code and between the domain model and the application code.

For the transformation to the AUI, FENIkS incorporates a set of mapping rules that allows determining a full definition of the AUI. We present here the most generic rules to obtain the Abstract User Interface from the domain model and presentation model. These are used as a starting point, and are complemented with more detailed rules:

- **Rule 1:** An abstract interaction unit (a container) is generated as the main window for the application.
- **Rule 2:** For each object type (from the conceptual domain model) an abstract interaction unit (a container) is generated with all the abstract data interaction units (the individual components) that are presented simultaneously (i.e. at one moment in time in one window) to the user.
- **Rule 3:** For each mentioned container its label is the name of the object type.
- **Rule 4:** For each mentioned container, if the value of the option *empty method pane or menu* is "hide", an abstract container for the creating methods of the object type is generated only if the object type has creating methods. If the value is "show", the abstract container is generated too.
- **Rule 5:** For this last container, for each creating method of the object type an abstract trigger interaction unit is generated.
- **Rule 6:** For each mentioned container, if the value of the option *empty method pane or menu* is "hide", an abstract container for the modifying methods of the object type is generated only if the object type has modifying methods. If the value is "show", the abstract container is generated too.
- **Rule 7:** For this last container, for each modifying method of the object type an abstract trigger interaction unit is generated.
- **Rule 8:** For each mentioned container, if the value of the option *empty method pane or menu* is "hide", an abstract container for the ending methods of the object type is generated only if the object type has ending methods. If the value is "show", the abstract container is generated too.
- **Rule 9:** For this last container, for each ending method of the object type an abstract trigger interaction unit is generated.
- **Rule 10:** For each container of each object type an abstract repetition region is generated.
- **Rule 11:** For each abstract trigger interaction unit is an abstract listener is generated.
- **Rule 12:** For each creating and modifying method an abstract interaction unit is generated with two abstract data interaction units for each attribute of the object type (one to show the name of the attribute and other to input the value of the attribute).
- **Rule 13:** For this last abstract data interaction unit that shows the name of the attribute, if the value of the option *attribute data type information* is "show", its long label includes the data type of the attribute.

- **Rule 14:** For this last abstract data interaction unit that shows the name of the attribute, if the value of the option *format data type information* is "show", its long label includes the format of the attribute.
- **Rule 15:** For each report (from the presentation model) an abstract interaction unit (a container) is generated with all the abstract data interaction units (the individual components) that are presented simultaneously (i.e. at one moment in time in one window) to the user.
- **Rule 16:** For this last container, for each report attribute of the report object type, an abstract data interaction unit (the individual components) is generated.

The rules below, corresponding to Rules 1–3 applied to the template, are shown in Fig. 7. These rules generate the AUI for the main window of the application and the containers where all the object types can be seen with their methods. AbstractCompoundIU represents the abstract interaction unit and an example of Abstract Individual Component is AbstractTriggerIU, which represents components for methods. The use of the Rules 4, 5, 11 are shown in Fig. 8. These rules generate the abstract containers for the creating methods and the corresponding triggers for the methods.

```
Rule 1
        <AbstractCompoundIU id="$id" label="MainWindow"
        longLabel="MainWindow" shortLabel="MainWindow" help="In this
        window you can find all the windows to operate with the
        objects" role="MainWindow" importance="Very high">
        #set ($id = $id + 1)
        #foreach ($object in $objects)
            <AbstractCompoundIU id="$id" label="${object.objName}"       Rule 3
        longLabel="${object.objName}" shortLabel="${object.objName}"
        help="In this tab you can find all options to operate with
        ${object.objName}" role="ObjectTab" importance="High">           Rule 2
        #set ($id = $id + 1)
        ...
        </AbstractCompoundIU>
```

Fig. 7. Fragment of the template to generate the AUI model: Rules 1–3.

```
Rule 4
        #if ($showEmptyMethodPane == show
        <AbstractCompoundIU id="$id" label="${object.objName}"
        longLabel="Creating methods" shortLabel="Creating methods"
        help="Here you can find all creating methods to operate with
        ${object.objName}" role="CreatePane" importance="Medium">
        #set ($id = $id + 1)
        #foreach ($create in $object.createMethods.entrySet())
        #set ($methodAlias = ${create.getValue()})
            <AbstractTriggerIU id="$id" label =
        "${create.getKey().toLowerCase()}" longLabel="$methodAlias"
        shortLabel="${create.getKey().toLowerCase()}" help="Option to
        ${create.getValue().toLowerCase()} ${object.objName}"
        role="Create" importance="Medium">
Rule 5
        #set ($id = $id + 1)
            <AbstractNavigationIU/>
            <AbstractOperationIU/>
            <AbstractListener>
            <AbstractEvent eventType="onTriggerSelected">
            </AbstractEvent>                                              Rule 11
            <AbstractAction actionType="IUOpen"
        actionClassification="${object.objName}${create.getKey().toLow
        erCase()}Window">
            </AbstractAction>
            </AbstractListener>
            </AbstractTriggerIU>
        #end
        </AbstractCompoundIU>
        #end
```

Fig. 8. Fragment of the template to generate the AUI model: Rules 4, 5, 11.

The template has static information and variables that needs to be substitutes from the values obtained from the models. The lines beginning with # are commands to the generator. The lines beginning with ${, are variables that need to be substituted with the information captured from the conceptual domain and presentation models. Figure 9 shows a fragment of the generated AUI model in UsiXML using the previous examples.

```
<AbstractCompoundIU id="0" label="MainWindow" longLabel="MainWindow" shortLabel="MainWindow" help="In this
window you can find all the windows to operate with the objects" role="MainWindow" importance="Very high">
  <AbstractCompoundIU id="1" label="Client" longLabel="Client" shortLabel="Client" help="In this tab you can find all
  options to operate with Client" role="ObjectTab" importance="High">
    <AbstractCompoundIU id="2" label="Client" longLabel="Client" longLabel="Creating methods" shortLabel="Creating methods"
    help="Here you can find all creating methods to operate with Client" role="CreatePane" importance="Medium">
      <AbstractTriggerIU id="3" label="me_cr_client" longLabel="Create" shortLabel="me_cr_client" help="Option to
      create Client" role="Create" importance="Medium">
        <AbstractNavigationIU/>
        <AbstractOperationIU/>
        <AbstractListener>
          <AbstractEvent eventType="onTriggerSelected"> </AbstractEvent>
          <AbstractAction actionType="IUOpen" actionSpecification="Clientme_cr_ClientWindow"> </AbstractAction>
        </AbstractListener>
      </AbstractTriggerIU>
    </AbstractCompoundIU>
</AbstractCompoundIU>
```

Fig. 9. Fragment of generated Abstract User Interface using the UsiXML language.

This fragment of the AUI model shows the main structure of the application consisting of containers (AbstractCompoundUI) in a recursive way. The first container reflects the main application that contains other abstract containers with the information of the object types existing in the domain model. There are other containers like the CreatePane that groups options for methods. Each option is linked to the container that offers the execution of the method in the AbstractListener with the actionSpecification.

The AUI is then transformed into the final UI code. This can already be done at a very early stage in the development process as long as the used models are correct. The final design of a UI reflects the design decisions. In FENIkS, design decisions are stored in the presentation model, and further used during the transformation until the final UI code is obtained. Having the options for design decisions in the presentation model avoids hard-coding the options into the model transformation rules.

These mappings rules take into consideration the information captured in the two primary models (domain and presentation models), to provide the users with a generated UI suitable to their requirements while integrated with the application logic. The code generator produces as output Java code that exploits the Swing widget set.

Teaching Support. The didactic JMermaid tool extended with FENIkS provides support for teaching the development of interactive software system. The main extended features are as follows: (1) incorporation of UI design principles, (2) runtime preview of the resulting UI according to the configured UI design, and (3) feedback for UI design and its integration with the development of the software application.

UI Design Principles. The teaching support of FENIkS is based on a set of UI design principles. There are some inherent and similar characteristics in the way the users interact with the applications as humans, independently of using different system by different users. Design principles help to design usable UIs according to the study of the human behavior with computer systems [33].

Many design principles can be found in the literature. In order to select the design principles to be applied in FENIkS we analyzed the ones proposed by important authors in the field, such as [34–38].

From the more generic design principles, more concrete guidelines have been derived. Due to the fact that UI design principles are high level concepts and beliefs, and there is a need for a concrete way to apply them, we also use guidelines associated to the principles for two purposes: (1) to check if it is possible to use the principle in a model-driven environment for the generation of the UI and (2) to translate the guidelines in testable rules that we can actually use in the environment.

We retained the principles that can be applied to the functional design of the UI and have empirically validated guidelines. The selected principles are: Prevent errors, Good error messages, Allow users to use either keyboard or mouse, Provide visual cues, Structure the UI, Offer Informative feedback, Strive for consistency and Visibility.

We analyzed the principles and their corresponding validated guidelines according to [39]. It is not possible in all cases to easily incorporate the guidelines in a didactic model-driven environment like FENIkS. However, when using a MDE environment, the application of guidelines is partially automatic.

Table 2 shows the selected UI design principles and the way they are applied in the model-driven generation process. Some of them are applied by means of UI design options, some of them are applied by default by the generation engine. Some principles can be partially applied by means of options and also partially applied by default.

Table 2. UI design principles applied in the generation process.

Principle	With UI design options	By default
Prevent errors	X	X
Good error messages	X	X
Allow users to use either keyboard or mouse	X	
Provide visual cues	X	X
Structure the UI		X
Offer informative feedback		X
Strive for consistency		X
Visibility		X

When possible, we defined options with two kinds of values: a positive value, that makes the generated interactive software system compliant with the guideline and a negative value, that boils down to violating the guideline. The possible options, related to the design principles are shown to the learners as UI design options in the presentation model, as already described. The values are stored and further used for the UI generation. The possible values for the options are related to feature model elements (see Figs. 3 and 4). For better understanding, Table 3 shows the relation between the UI design principles, the corresponding guidelines and the features in the Feature model.

Using the values for the design options stored in the presentation model, FENIkS checks for each principle if all the values selected by the learner are correct. According to this check, FENIkS informs for which principles the interactive software system is (or partially) compliant or not. For example, if the learner selects to show the data format information and the attribute data type information, he/she is selecting the values that make the system compliant with the principle Provide visual cues. This information is used to provide automatic feedback to the learner as further explained.

Table 3. UI design principles, guidelines and feature model elements.

Principles	Guidelines	Features
Prevent errors	Validation of different types of data	Validate Boolean
		Validate numbers
	Validation of empty data	Validate empty data
	Components according to the type of data	Generate components by the attribute type
Good error messages	Make the error messages as specific as possible	Generate errors according to the type of error
Allow users to use either the keyboard or mouse	Allow experienced users to by-pass a series of menu selections and make an equivalent command entry or keyboard shortcuts directly	Generate shortcuts for methods
		Generate shortcuts for tabs
		Generate shortcuts for general menu
Provide visual cues	For data entry, provide the user with the required formats and acceptable values e.g., include in a field label additional cueing of data format (e.g., Data (mm/dd/yy): - -/- -/- -)	Format data type information
		Attribute data type information

Table 4 shows the principles for which there are guidelines to be applied by default during the generation process of the interactive software system.

UI Generation Preview. To support a learner in understanding the presentation model more easily, FENIkS has included UI-GEAR: User Interface Generation prEview capable to Adapt in Real-time [29]. The presentation model is shown with different tabs according to its structure: Window and Input aspects and Reports.

At the top of each tab of the UI-GEAR component, the learner sees the options and selects the corresponding values. While developing the presentation model, and using the preview feature, the designer can play with the different options and the preview feature shows the consequences. At the bottom of the Window and Input aspects, UI-GEAR offers a preview showing how the UI will be generated in the prototype.

Table 4. UI design principles and guidelines to be applied by default.

Principles	Guidelines
Prevent errors	Protect field labels from accidental change by users
	Fields designed for information display should be protected: users should not be allowed to change the information contained in these fields
	Ensure that User Interface software will deal appropriately with all possible user errors, including accidental inputs
Good error messages	For error messages, adopt task-oriented wording
	Make error messages brief but informative
	Adopt neutral wording for error messages; do not imply blame on the part of the user, or personalize the computer, or attempt to make a message humorous
	If the user selects an invalid function key, no system action should result except a message indicating the functions appropriate for that transaction step
Provide visual cues	For each data field, display an associated label
	Provide cues on the acceptable length of entries
	Provide a title for each window
Structure the UI	Organize the options of a menu dialogue as a function of the objects to which they apply
Offer informative feedback	Display all users' entries
Strive for consistency	Window titles should always be located in the same place
	Use similar screen formats
	Use similar procedures to access menu options
	Consistent phrasing and punctuation should be used in all prompts
	Prompts for data or command entry should be displayed in a standard location
	Data entry fields should always be the same
Visibility	Provide clear visual distinction of areas having different functions (command zone, message zone, etc.)
	Provide clear visual distinction of data fields and their labels

To clarify the working of UI-GEAR, we illustrate how the different design option of the Input aspects determine the design of the UI. In this tab the UI developer chooses whether or not to show attribute data type information for each attribute, whether or not to show data format information, whether or not to generate the component for the attributes input according to the data type or not. If the class has associations with other classes, the master presentation style must be chosen to define if this association is shown as a table or a combo. This is also the place to select if the generated interactive software system will validate different kinds of inputs and how the errors will be shown. Figure 10 shows two screenshots of the Input aspects.

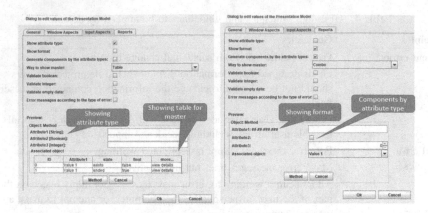

Fig. 10. Input aspects with variations.

The two variations have different values for some features. For example, in the first one the attribute data type is shown, while in the second one it is not. The format of the attribute is only shown in the second example. In the first one, all the components are generated as input boxes, while in the second one they are generated according to the attribute type. Finally, the associated objects are shown in a table in the first example, while are showing in a combo box in the second. The result of each selected value is shown in the preview, allowing to see the changes instantaneously.

Every time the learner changes a value of the Window or Input aspects, the UI-GEAR automatically adapts the preview, allowing to see how the UI will look like. The preview allows tracing changes from both conceptual domain and presentation models to their effects by testing several "what-if" scenarios. For all the options of the Window and Input aspects, the presentation model has default values that can be used for the generation process without being explicitly specified by the developer. The first time UI-GEAR is invoked, it shows the preview according to these default values.

The UI-GEAR component for the presentation model has an internal representation of the feature model that is parsed and interpreted in real-time, enabling instantaneous update of the preview. This gives the possibility to validate user requirements, and reduces the time and effort required to implement the UI [10, 29].

Automated Feedback. The proposed didactic tool allows the generation of a prototype corresponding to an interactive software system. While prototyping itself is already an efficient instrument supporting the learning process, adding feedback features can offer further support of learning [25]. Feedback has been widely recognized and proven as an important aspect in teaching to ensure that students learn [40]. Technology can support the provision of the frequent, constant and immediate feedback [41] that is usually not possible to provide by teachers.

The previous version of the tool, JMermaid, already included automatic feedback features for developing domain models [25]. The feedback features allow explaining reasons of execution failures with a graphical visualization that links the failure to the part of the model that causes it. The integrated support provided with the FENIkS extension incorporates UI design feedback features that assist the learners to validate the generated UI in a fast and easy way, while integrated with the rest of the application.

FENIkS provides two kinds of feedback related to the UI design of interactive software systems to explain: (1) why the UI is generated in a specific way tracing the application's appearance back to its origin in the presentation model and how to change it, and (2) whether the design decisions are compliant with UI design principles or not and why. This helps understanding the relationship between functional aspects and the UI.

The introduction of functional design options, as previously explained, allows making the link between the UI design principles, the features and the presentation model. These design decisions are also used to provide feedback for the design principles and the specification of the models. The feedback is presented as an UI Help in the main window of the generated interactive software system. This feedback is divided in the same structure of the presentation model and the help for the UI design principles.

The first kind of feedback can show to the designers the reasons why the UI is generated in certain way. The designer selects General, Window or Input aspects, and which option he/she wants to see the explanation for.

Figure 11 shows an example of the first kind of feedback corresponding to the Input aspects, where the learner is provided with the feedback for the option: Generate components by attribute type. The feedback is divided in three parts: what the stored values are in the presentation model according to the selected option, what the consequences are for the generated prototype explaining why the UI looks in this way, and how it is possible to change it, specifying the place in the presentation model. From this place it is also possible to see all the values of the Input aspects (in the example) or the Window aspects, and all the values of the presentation model.

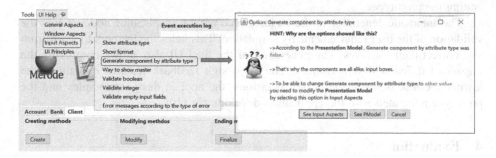

Fig. 11. Design options explanatory feedback.

The second kind of feedback is also in the UI Help with the UI principles option. Figure 12 shows a fragment of an example of the second kind of feedback.

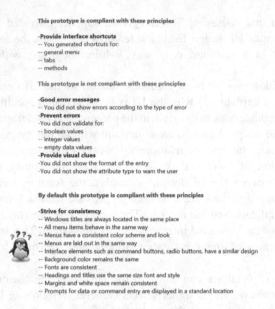

This prototype is compliant with these principles

-Provide interface shortcuts
-- You generated shortcuts for:
-- general menu
-- tabs
-- methods

This prototype is not compliant with these principles

-Good error messages
-- You did not show errors according to the type of error
-Prevent errors
-You did not validate for:
-- boolean values
-- integer values
-- empty data values
-Provide visual clues
-You did not show the format of the entry
-You did not show the attribute type to warn the user

By default this prototype is compliant with these principles

-Strive for consistency
-- Windows titles are always located in the same place
-- All menu items behave in the same way
-- Menus have a consistent color scheme and look
-- Menus are laid out in the same way
-- Interface elements such as command buttons, radio buttons, have a similar design
-- Background color remains the same
-- Fonts are consistent
-- Headings and titles use the same size font and style
-- Margins and white space remain consistent
-- Prompts for data or command entry are displayed in a standard location

Fig. 12. Checking the UI principles [10].

When developing the presentation model, the designer needs to take into account the UI design principles to select the correct values for the options. This type of feedback shows which principles the generated prototype is compliant with and which principles it is not compliant with. Besides the names of the principles that are well applied or not, the feedback explains the rationale behind it. As explained earlier, FENIkS also incorporates the application of some guidelines of principles by default by the MDE engine while generating the prototype. The feedback shows the rationale behind those principles too. Checking the UI principles is also possible before generating the prototype.

The automatic generation of the UI integrated with the application code enables the validation of the user requirements by simulation. This helps the learners to learn from and correct their mistakes. The generation of the final UI also allows comparing the impact of different design choices. The UI design feedback features explain to the learner the link between the design decisions, the applied design principles and the prototype integrated with the application development [10].

4   Evaluation

To validate the developed didactic tool we evaluated: (1) its support as an integrated approach for the teaching of interactive software systems, (2) its ease of use by learners and (3) its practical results as a didactic tool with experimental evaluation.

4.1   Evaluation of the Integration

The presented didactic tool improves the learning of the development of interactive software systems by providing support to create the domain and the presentation models, as well as generating the AUI model and the system code. The advantages include:

1. It offers an integrated tool adapted to conceptual modelling goals with the original tool and UI design goals through the extension FENIkS. This tool provides the conceptual domain model to "co-design" the application and the presentation model and the further generated AUI model for the UI design. The tool allows managing the consistency and links between all the models, while allowing the learner to easily switch between adapting the application or adapting the UI.
2. The domain model and the presentation model allow the automatic generation of an AUI model, enabling further transformation to different contexts of use. The use of templates in the transformation process allows the creation of new ways of presenting the UI for different languages, platforms, modalities of interaction.
3. Both, application code and UI code are well integrated to allow the generation of a fully functional prototype that contains the link between UI and application logic.
4. The prototype can be generated from early stages from a minimal domain model consisting of only one object type. Similarly, for the prototype generation during early stages, default values of the presentation model can be used, without needing to be specified by the developer. There is no need to have a perfect or complete set of models before being able to test the UI and the application code.
5. Iterative design is supported by FENIkS. It allows generating variations of UIs according to different options described in the presentation model. This facilitates the comparison of each variant for a best match to user preferences.
6. Feedback features link the UI design options with the generated prototype. They explain how the UI design principles are applied. The application development and the UI design, are supported with feedback that is linked to the conceptual domain and presentation models. Both kinds of feedback are embedded in the generated prototype. The feedback for the UI design can be checked before generation too, which makes the tool easier to use. The possibility of generating the prototype without needing the complete models, checking partial versions of the prototype in a faster way, also contributes to ease of use.

4.2   Ease of Use

We performed an experiment to evaluate MERODE tool extended with FENIkS from the perspective of perceived usability. We used the Computer System Usability Questionnaire (CSUQ) [42] which has been considered a reliable measure of overall satisfaction with an interface [43].

The participants were 12 novice developers with a background in informatics engineering without prior exposure of the tool. The tool was presented with an explanation of its use. The participant were asked to carry out a set of tasks in FENIkS. Using an already developed conceptual domain model as starting point, they played with the different design options to create a presentation model and to generate the prototype. After completing the tasks, the users were asked to fill the CSUQ.

The participant ranked all the items of the CSUQ with scores between 5 and 7 (the highest possible value is 7), indicating a very positive evaluation. From all the items of the CSUQ, the mode of only three items was 5, while for all the other items the mode was 6 or 7. According to the highest mean values, the participants perceived that the system helps them to complete their work and that FENIkS has all the functions and capabilities they expected. The clarity of the errors provided by the system that help to fix problems was also between the items better scored.

The experiment demonstrated that the perceived usefulness is high: the users believe the system enhances their performance. Besides measuring the overall satisfaction, CSUQ allows measuring different components of (perceived) usability: System Usefulness, Information Quality, and Interface Quality. Developers found FENIkS very satisfactory in all these areas. It is positively perceived overall and provides the functionalities the developers expected. For more details of the experimental evaluation the reader is referred to [29].

We also tested the suitability of FENIkS for novice UI designers by means of a questionnaire to measure the perceived usefulness (user acceptance). In this case, 34 students of the 4th year of Informatics Engineering program at the University of Holguín were the participants. The students took a design course where they were able to use FENIkS. At the end of the course, the participants filled the questionnaire.

The scores per item ranked well above 5 on 6, indicating a positive evaluation. The mode of only four items was 5, while for all the other items the mode was 6 or 7. The learners agree that using FENIkS was a positive experience and that it improves their understanding of UI principles which were the items with a highest mean values. The preview feature was also well perceived. The participants agree previewing the UI helps them to decide better about design options.

The results of the questionnaire gave support that the proposed simulation method is suitable for novice UI designers.

4.3   Experimental Evaluation

To assess the effects of feedback and simulation with respect to UI design principles understanding with FENIkS, we conducted an experiment with the participation of 34 students of Informatics Engineering program at the University of Holguin. While following an UI design course the students learned how to use FENIkS. After that, the students had two tests to evaluate their understanding of UI design principles: one test without the use of FENIkS and other test where they were allowed to use FENIkS.

For both tests, students were given a set of UIs were some design principles were well applied while others violated. Students were asked to evaluate the UIs by responding to a set of true/false questions, checking whether the provided UIs were compliance to the design principles or not. Students were asked to motivate their answers.

A paired t-test (see Table 5) was performed to determine if the built-in teaching support in FENIkS was effective.

Table 5. t-test: paired two sample for means (all principles).

$\overline{X}_{errorwithout}$	$\overline{X}_{errorwith}$	$\overline{X}_{difference}$	p-value
15.94	13.15	−2.79	0.000

The results shows a significant correction with the use of FENIkS, with 95% confidence interval providing evidence that FENIkS is effective in producing positive correction of UI design principles understanding.

During the tests, the students had to answer questions for the principles where there is teaching support in FENIkS (*to actively observe*) and principles without teaching support in FENIkS. We separated and compared the average improvements for the questions testing the *'to actively observe'* principles, and the questions testing the principles without teaching support. A paired t-test was performed to determine if FENIkS was effective for both kind of principles: *'to actively observe'* and without teaching support. Table 6 shows the mean error rates and t-test results for the *'to actively observe'* principles and the principles without teaching support.

Table 6. t-test: paired two sample for means (different kind of principles).

	$\overline{X}_{errorwithout}$	$\overline{X}_{errorwith}$	$\overline{X}_{difference}$	P value
To actively observe principles	5.5	3.73	1.76	0.000
Principles without teaching support	5.88	5.14	0.74	0.987

If we compare the results in both tests for the *'to actively observe'* principles with the principles without teaching support we can see that only there is an improvement for the *'to actively observe'* principles, that is also significant, p-value *'to actively observe'* vs principles without teaching support: 0.000 < 0.987.

The results suggest that the teaching support in FENIkS is effective: the students have a better performance for principles with teaching support (where they are allowed to experiment by changing options and seeing the feedback according to the changes).

5   Limitations

A first limitation of our approach is that only functional aspects of the UI are modelled: FENIkS is not focused on aesthetic appeal.

For the moment, the tool only addresses the development of enterprise information systems in one context of use. In order to adapt to the huge variety of users, platforms and environments (contexts of use) that nowadays exist, the tool needs to be further extended. However, since this approach relies on MDE, and already incorporates an Abstract User Interface Model, future versions of the tool can adapt the generation of the interactive software system for other contexts of use. Generating the prototype for different contexts use will allow also comparing and giving feedback according to the results of the design in different final UIs.

Since the original MERODE tool had no support for the UI design, it is clear that the FENIkS extension improves UI design when designing interactive software systems. Nevertheless, the presentation meta-model could be further extended to improve flexibility. Other models (e.g., user model, platforms model) could be incorporated to provide better support for users characteristics and adaptation to other environments.

6   Conclusion

This paper has presented a MDE didactic tool for improving the teaching of interactive software systems. The tool allows defining the conceptual domain and the presentation models that are used for the generation of the interactive software system, with the UI code integrated with the application logic. The tool provides teaching support that consists of simulation with prototype generation enhanced with feedback. The feedback for the conceptual modeling is provided by the JMermaid tool while the feedback for the UI design is provided by the extension FENIkS. While designing the UI the learner receives feedback about how some UI design principles are applied through the options the learner selects. The complete generation of the UI and application code allows validating user requirements against the prototype behavior and the resulting UI. Thus, necessary changes in the models can be made in less time while maintaining the link between the UI and the application.

The tool improves the UI designing and application development by letting the learner tests the models incrementally. The feedback allows understanding how the UI design principles are applied and immediately shows their effects on the final UI.

An experimental evaluation was performed. The tool was evaluated for its perceived usability, perceived usefulness and practical results as a didactic tool. The tool was positively perceived by novice developers and students. They agree the tool helps them to complete their work and has all the expected functionalities. The results of the experimental evaluation with students demonstrated that the tool improve their understanding of UI design principles.

Last, but not least, we discussed how FENIkS could be extended with more flexibility in the UI design and to support other contexts of use.

References

1. Akiki, P.A., Bandara, A.K., Yu, Y.: Adaptive model-driven user interface development systems. ACM Comput. Surv. **47**(1), 9 (2015)
2. Cayola, L., Macías, J.A.: Systematic guidance on usability methods in user-centered software development. Inf. Softw. Technol. **97**, 163–175 (2018)
3. Seffah, A., Gulliksen, J., Desmarais, M.C. (eds.): Human-Centered Software Engineering-Integrating Usability in the Software Development Lifecycle, vol. 8. Springer, Heidelberg (2005). https://doi.org/10.1007/1-4020-4113-6
4. da Cruz, A.M.R., Faria, J.P.: Automatic generation of user interface models and prototypes from domain and use case models. In: ICSOFT, no. 1, pp. 169–176 (2009)
5. Meixner, G., Paternò, F., Vanderdonckt, J.: Past, present, and future of model-based user interface development. i-com **10**(3), 2–11 (2011)

6. Nguyen, K.D., Rahman, M.A.: Identifying interface design patterns by studying intrinsic designs. In: CSCEET 2016, pp. 13–24 (2016)
7. Sboui, T., Ayed, M.B.: Generative software development techniques of user interface: survey and open issues. Int. J. Comput. Sci. Inf. Secur. **14**(7), 824 (2016)
8. Dehinbo, J.: Establishing and applying criteria for evaluating the ease of use of dynamic platforms for teaching web application development. Inf. Syst. Educ. J. **9**(5), 86 (2011)
9. Ruiz, J., Serral, E., Snoeck, M.: Evaluating user interface generation approaches: model-based versus model-driven development. Softw. Syst. Model. 1–24 (2018)
10. Ruiz, J., Serral, E., Snoeck, M.: A fully implemented didactic tool for the teaching of interactive software systems. In: Modelsward 2018, pp. 95–105 (2018)
11. Feuerstack, S., Blumendorf, M., Schwartze, V., Albayrak, S.: Model-based layout generation. In: AVI, pp. 217–224 (2008)
12. Marin, I., Ortin, F., Pedrosa, G., Rodriguez, J.: Generating native user interfaces for multiple devices by means of model transformation. Front. Inf. Technol. Electron. Eng. **16**(12), 995–1017 (2015)
13. Coninx, K., Luyten, K., Vandervelpen, C., Van den Bergh, J., Creemers, B.: Dygimes: dynamically generating interfaces for mobile computing devices and embedded systems. In: Chittaro, L. (ed.) Mobile HCI 2003. LNCS, vol. 2795, pp. 256–270. Springer, Heidelberg (2003). https://doi.org/10.1007/978-3-540-45233-1_19
14. Delgado, A., Estepa, A., Troyano, J.A., Estepa, R.: Reusing UI elements with model-based user interface development. Int. J. Hum. Comput. Stud. **86**, 48–62 (2016)
15. Mori, G., Paterno, F., Santoro, C.: Design and development of multidevice user interfaces through multiple logical descriptions. Softw. Eng. IEEE Trans. **30**(8), 507–520 (2004)
16. Tran, V.: UI generation from task, domain and user models: the DB-USE approach. In: 2nd ACM SIGCHI, pp. 353–356 (2010)
17. Molina, A.I., Giraldo, W.J., Gallardo, J., Redondo, M.A., Ortega, M., García, G.: CIAT-GUI: a MDE-compliant environment for developing Graphical User Interfaces of information systems. Adv. Eng. Softw. **52**, 10–29 (2012)
18. Pastor, O., Molina, J.C.: Model-Driven Architecture in Practice - A Software Production Environment Based on Conceptual Modeling. Springer, Heidelberg (2007). https://doi.org/10.1007/978-3-540-71868-0
19. Acerbis, R., Bongio, A., Brambilla, M., Butti, S.: Model-driven development based on OMG's IFML with WebRatio web and mobile platform. In: Cimiano, P., Frasincar, F., Houben, G.-J., Schwabe, D. (eds.) ICWE 2015. LNCS, vol. 9114, pp. 605–608. Springer, Cham (2015). https://doi.org/10.1007/978-3-319-19890-3_39
20. Barrett, M.L.: A hypertext module for teaching user interface design. ACM SIGCSE Bull. **25**(1), 107–111 (1993)
21. Sutcliffe, A.G., Kurniawan, S., Shin, J.-E.: A method and advisor tool for multimedia user interface design. Int. J. Hum. Comput. Stud. **64**(4), 375–392 (2006)
22. Benitti, F.B.V., Sommariva, L.: Evaluation of a game used to teach usability to undergraduate students in computer science. J. Usability Stud. **11**(1), 21–39 (2015)
23. Lisowska Masson, A., Lalanne, D., Amstutz, T.: A usability refactoring process for large-scale open source projects: the ILIAS case study. In: 2017 CHI Conference Extended Abstracts on Human Factors in Computing Systems, pp. 1135–1143 (2017)
24. Snoeck, M.: Enterprise Information Systems Engineering: The MERODE Approach. Springer, Cham (2014). https://doi.org/10.1007/978-3-319-10145-3
25. Sedrakyan, G., Snoeck, M.: Feedback-enabled MDA-prototyping effects on modeling knowledge. In: Nurcan, S., et al. (eds.) BPMDS/EMMSAD -2013. LNBIP, vol. 147, pp. 411–425. Springer, Heidelberg (2013). https://doi.org/10.1007/978-3-642-38484-4_29

26. Sedrakyan, G., Snoeck, M., Poelmans, S.: Assessing the effectiveness of feedback enabled simulation in teaching conceptual modeling. Comput. Educ. **78**, 367–382 (2014)
27. Sedrakyan, G., Snoeck, M.: A PIM-to-Code requirements engineering framework. In: Modelsward 2013, pp. 163–169 (2013)
28. Ruiz, J., Sedrakyan, G., Snoeck, M.: Generating user interface from conceptual, presentation and user models with JMermaid in a learning approach. In: Interaction 2015 (2015)
29. Ruiz, J., Serral, E., Snoeck, M.: UI-GEAR: user interface generation prEview capable to adapt in real-time. In: Modelsward 2017, pp. 277–284 (2017)
30. Benavides, B., Segura, S., Cortés, A.R.: Automated analysis of feature models 20 years later: a literature review. Inf. Syst. **35**(6), 615–636 (2010)
31. Engel, J., Märtin, C., Forbrig, P.: Practical aspects of pattern-supported model-driven user interface generation. In: Kurosu, M. (ed.) HCI 2017. LNCS, vol. 10271, pp. 397–414. Springer, Cham (2017). https://doi.org/10.1007/978-3-319-58071-5_30
32. Limbourg, Q., Vanderdonckt, J., Michotte, B., Bouillon, L., Florins, M.: USIXML: a user interface description language supporting multiple levels of independence. In: ICWE Workshops, pp. 325–338 (2004)
33. Mandel, T.: The Elements of User Interface Design, vol. 20. Wiley, New York (1997)
34. Norman, D.A.: Design principles for human-computer interfaces. In: SIGCHI, pp. 1–10 (1983)
35. Nielsen, J.: 10 Usability Heuristics for User Interface Design. Nielsen Norman Group, Fremont (1995)
36. Stone, D., Jarrett, C., Woodroffe, M., Minocha, S.: User Interface Design and Evaluation. Morgan Kaufmann, Burlington (2005)
37. Johnson, J.: GUI Bloopers 2.0: Common User Interface Design Don'ts and Dos. Morgan Kaufmann, Burlington (2007)
38. Shneiderman, B.: Designing the User Interface: Strategies for Effective Human-Computer Interaction, vol. 3, 5th edn. Addison-Wesley, Boston (2010)
39. Bastien, J.M.C., Scapin, D.L.: Ergonomic criteria for the evaluation of human-computer interfaces. Inria (1993)
40. Hattie, J., Timperley, H.: The power of feedback. Rev. Educ. Res. **77**(1), 81–112 (2007)
41. Merrill, M.D.: First principles of instruction. Educ. Technol. Res. Dev. **50**(3), 43–59 (2002)
42. Lewis, J.R.: IBM computer usability satisfaction questionnaires: psychometric evaluation and instructions for use. Int. J. Hum. Comput. Interact. **7**(1), 57–78 (1995)
43. McArdle, G., Bertolotto, M.: Assessing the application of three-dimensional collaborative technologies within an e-learning environment. Interact. Learn. Environ. **20**(1), 57–75 (2012)

Interactive Measures for Mining Understandable State Machines from Embedded Software: Experiments and Case Studies

Wasim Said[1,2(✉)], Jochen Quante[1], and Rainer Koschke[2]

[1] Robert Bosch GmbH, Corporate Research, Renningen, Germany
{wasim.said,jochen.quante}@de.bosch.com
[2] University of Bremen, Bremen, Germany
koschke@informatik.uni-bremen.de

Abstract. State machines are a commonly used formalism for specifying the behavior of a software component, which could also be helpful for program comprehension. Therefore, it is desirable to extract state machine models from code and also from legacy models. The main drawback of fully-automatic state machine mining approaches is that the mined models are too detailed and not understandable. In our previous work [1], we presented different measures for the interaction with the state machine extraction process, such as selecting a subset of state variables, reducing the state variable range and providing additional user constraints. These measures aimed to reduce the complexity of the mined state machines to an understandable degree. In this article, which is an extended version of [1], we evaluate the approach through a case study with twelve professional developers from the automotive supplier company Bosch. The study shows that adding our interactive measures to the model mining process leads to understandable state machines, which can be very helpful in a rich set of use cases in addition to program comprehension, such as debugging, validation and verification. Furthermore, we conduct an experiment to evaluate the required computation time of the interactive measures against the fully-automatic mining. The experiment shows that the interactive approach can drastically reduce the computation time.

Keywords: Model mining · Program comprehension ·
Software analysis · Static analysis · Reverse engineering ·
User interaction · State machines

1 Introduction

The idea of model mining is the extraction of higher-level models from existing software systems. A lot of tools extract different kinds of models from *explicit* structural information in the code and help users get an overview and understanding at a higher (design) level. Extracting *implicit* information that is not

© Springer Nature Switzerland AG 2019
S. Hammoudi et al. (Eds.): MODELSWARD 2018, CCIS 991, pp. 211–235, 2019.
https://doi.org/10.1007/978-3-030-11030-7_10

explicitly visible in code, such as a state machine model when no explicit state machine pattern can be found in the code, will be more useful for users. This is exactly the kind of state machines that we are interested in, along with the traditional state machine implementations.

Having such higher-level models can help developers in (1) program comprehension, (2) migration towards model-based software development, and (3) model-based development. (1) Program comprehension is a time-consuming activity that makes up to 70% of total software life cycle effort [2–4], where developers often try to manually reconstruct such models during maintenance tasks [5]. (2) Companies that want to switch to model-based development usually do not start from scratch, but already have a large code base. It realizes a huge amount of functionality and cannot be easily replaced by corresponding models. Model mining can support this transformation and even make it economically worthwhile. For example, model-based development tools such as ASCET[1] or Matlab Simulink[2] have been introduced at almost all automotive companies and help to save cost and time [6]. (3) Developers using model-based development do not always use the best-suited models for a given aspect. For example, control logic is sometimes modelled as a block diagram – which makes the aspect "control logic" very hard to understand. In this case, a state machine that describes the behavior of a function – with respect to control logic – will be more desirable and helpful for experts.

Let us look at a concrete example. Consider the following C code function, which realizes a bidirectional edge detection element that is often used in control software.

```c
int biEdge(int sig) {
    static int state = 0;
    if ((sig && !state) || (!sig && state)) {
        state = sig; return 1; }
    return 0;
}
```

The static variable state is the only variable that holds state in the sense that it remembers something from the last invocation which influences its behavior. It is used in the conditions state and !state. Consequently, a state machine model for this aspect of the function would distinguish between these two states and look like the model in Fig. 1.

Although simple in this example, this "manual" kind of model extraction can be very laborious with more state variables and conditions. Therefore, automation of this process is highly desired. However, fully-automatic model mining approaches – when applied to complex real-world systems – deliver too detailed or low-level models that are not useful for human understanding. This is because code alone does not contain all the necessary information to distinguish between important and not unimportant details for example. Also, a tool is not capable of introducing abstractions that a human would immediately come up with.

---

[1] https://www.etas.com/en/products/ascet_software_products.php.
[2] https://www.mathworks.com/products/simulink.html.

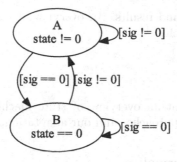

Fig. 1. The state machine model of function biEdge [1].

Consequently, effective model mining requires a combination of automation and user interaction to extract highly useful models with low manual effort.

Our interactive state machine mining approach works as follows: The user starts the mining process on the function that she wants to understand with respect to sequencing logic. Then she gets an initial state machine, which is usually far too complex to be understandable. To reduce the complexity of this model, the user can use our proposed interaction scenarios, such as selecting a subset of state variables and providing additional constraints. Then, the mining tool returns a different state machine model – one that considers this additional information. This interactive process can go through multiple iterations with changed user input, which leads to a more abstract model that is potentially closer to the domain and thus less complex. The interaction with the mining process this way enables the user to extract understandable state machines under different projections, which in combination can provide a complete picture of the relevant functionality.

Our main and new contributions in this article, which complements and extends the contributions of our previous work [1], are:

1. An experiment on industrial real-world automotive software with professional engineers of the company Bosch. The experiment evaluates (a) the understandability of state machines provided by our interactive approach [1] and (b) the usefulness of the interactively extracted state machines for developers with different levels of system knowledge.
2. A case study that assesses the impact of the interactive measures on the required time for state machine mining from real-world software, and compares the results with the fully-automatic alternative.

The article is organized as follows: Sect. 2 presents the required background about state machine formalism, the approaches of Kung [7] and Sen [8] and our adaptations and optimizations. In Sect. 3, we sum up our different techniques for interactive exploration of state machines with evaluation of their effectiveness. The case study about the understandability of the interactively mined state machines is presented in Sect. 4 and the runtime experiment in Sect. 5. In Sect. 6, we discuss the approach and results. An overview of related work is presented in Sect. 7, and Sect. 8 concludes.

2   Background

In this section, we present an overview of state machine formalism, analysis techniques, Kung/Sen's approaches and our adaptations and optimizations.

2.1   State Machine Formalism

The deterministic finite state machine in our approach is a simplified extended finite state machine (EFSM) [9]. An EFSM is a finite state machine that additionally has variables, update operations on these variables, and evaluation of variables for determining trigger conditions. In our formalism, we include variables and allow to use them in transition conditions, but do not include update operations in the model. We defer the latter to the function f (see below). This results in the quadruple (S, T, V, s_0) with:

- a finite set of states S,
- the transition function $T : S \times V \to S$,
- a set of variable valuations V, and
- the initial state $s_0 \in S$.

Each variable valuation $v \in V$ is a function $v : N \to D$, where N is a set of variable names and D is the set of values that variables can take on.

Additionally, we introduce the following definitions:

- $Inv : S \times V \to \mathbb{B}$ (with $\mathbb{B} = \{\text{true}, \text{false}\}$) is a predicate on the variables that holds while the system is in the given state, i.e., the state invariant.
- $f : V \to V$ is the function that maps a valuation $v_1 \in V$ to the corresponding valuation $v_2 \in V$ that results after execution of the subject function on v_1.

The example state machine model from Sect. 1 can be specified according to our definitions as follows:

- $S = \{A, B\}$, $Inv(A, v) = (state \neq 0)$, $Inv(B, v) = (state = 0)$
- $T(A, v) = \begin{cases} A & sig \neq 0 \\ B & sig = 0 \end{cases}, \quad T(B, v) = \begin{cases} A & sig \neq 0 \\ B & sig = 0 \end{cases}$

2.2   Symbolic Execution and Concolic Testing

Symbolic execution executes a program with symbolic values instead of concrete values. It performs path enumeration for test case generation with full path coverage [10]. At a branching point, symbolic execution explores all branches in a depth-first search manner, so that when it comes to a point where the path condition is not satisfiable, it backtracks and explores the next branch. During this process, symbolic execution delivers for each path (1) the path condition (PC) and (2) the output variable values as symbolic expressions over the input variables. This way, all possible distinct behavior of the function will be represented with just a single control condition – the path condition. For state machine mining, this provides a good basis to begin with: States are contained in path conditions, and each path corresponds to a certain transition.

Concolic testing is a more recent technique for path enumeration [11]. It differs from the traditional symbolic execution in so far as it explores paths sequentially and not by forking at the branching nodes. This happens by executing each path with concrete values and collecting the symbolic path condition in parallel. Also, the input for the next execution is inferred from the path conditions of the previous test cases by means of an SMT solver.

The major limitation of symbolic execution is constraint solving. For example, non linear constraints cannot be handled by solvers. However, these complex constraints can be solved with concrete values by concolic testing. See [12] for more information about the differences between these two techniques.

2.3   Kung/Sen Approach to State Machine Mining

Kung et al. [7] extract state machine models from a given C++ class. Sen et al. [8] add some improvements and work on Java classes. Both approaches use symbolic execution to generate the following information for each feasible path: (1) PC: path condition, i.e., the conjunction of all fulfilled branching conditions encountered on this path. (2) E : name $\rightarrow$ symbolic value: pairs of updated member variables during the execution of the path, and (3) the returned symbolic expression (if any). Then, states are generated and transitions are determined.

The following terms were defined by Kung and are necessary to explain the extraction process of states and transitions: An *atomic condition* represents either a boolean symbolic variable such as a or a relational operator over two symbolic expressions like $a + b < 5$. When atomic conditions are connected by conjunction, disjunction or negation, they create a *compound condition*, such as $(a + b > 5) \land d$. A *conditional literal* is an atomic condition or the negation of an atomic condition.

Extraction of States

Kung's state generation approach works as follows: Imagine that x is an integer variable in the conditional literals $x > 0$ and $x == 3$. Then, the state candidates of the variable x are the relevant intervals of x: $(-\infty, 0], (0, 3), [3, 3]$ and $(3, \infty)$. However, computing the intervals of the variables is only possible when the condition contains exactly one member variable. For conditions with more than one variable like $a < b$ and $a \mid b \mid x > 5$, computing the intervals is not possible. These conditions are ignored by Kung's approach.

This limitation was addressed by Sen and Mall, who presented a different way to extract states: They compute the partitions from the original conditions and create a state space for *all* member variables at once. This is done by creating all possible valuations of the conjunction of all conditional literals and then using a solver to find out which of these are satisfiable, which then results in the state candidates. For the above example, the extracted partitions are: $x > 0 \wedge x = 3$, which is equivalent to $x = 3$, $x > 0 \wedge x \neq 3$, $x \leq 0 \wedge x = 3$, which is not satisfiable and $x \leq 0 \wedge x \neq 3$, which corresponds to $x \leq 0$. This results in three partitions – less than the four intervals from Kung's technique. Obviously, it is possible to create such partitions for conditional literals with more than one variable.

Sen and Mall distinguish between three different types of conditional literals, according to the kind of variables involved (in an object-oriented program):

- *Member dependent literal (MDL):* a conditional literal in which only member variables of the class appear.
- *Parameter dependent literal (PDL):* a conditional literal in which only parameters of a class method appear.
- *Mixed literal (MXL):* a conditional literal which is neither MDL nor PDL.

In our C code and ASCET models, we do not have member variables. However, we stick to these definitions. For us, *members* correspond to *state candidates*. Because only MXLs and MDLs are practically relevant for state machine extraction, we also use the term *pure literal* for MDLs.

Kung considered only MDLs with a single variable, and Sen extended the range to consider only MDLs but with any number of variables. In our approach, the decision of including MXLs – in addition to the MDLs according to Sen – is left to the user (see Sect. 2.4).

Extraction of Transitions

Transitions are generated as follows: It is examined for each path P_k from which state it can possibly start (*pre state* s_1). This is done by using a constraint solver. It checks for which state candidates $s_1 \in S$ the condition $Inv(s_1, v) \wedge PC_k(v)$ is satisfiable for any $v \in V$. The *post state* s_2 is determined in different ways. Kung et al. use the condition $\forall v \in V : Inv(s_1, v) \wedge PC_k(v) \models Inv(s_2, f(v))$[3], which means that the target state condition on the resulting symbolic values of the path must be satisfied in *all* cases for which $Inv(s_1, v) \wedge PC_k(v)$ is true. Sen requires that $PC_k(v_1) \wedge Inv(s_1, v_1)$ is satisfiable, and that $PC_k(v_2) \wedge Inv(s_2, f(v_2))$ is satisfiable independently. In our approach, we combine these two conditions so that $Inv(s_1, v) \wedge PC_k(v) \wedge Inv(s_2, f(v))$ must be fulfilled for the same v.

2.4   Adaptations and Optimizations

In this section, we present our adaptations of Kung/Sen's approaches for our setting:

(1) Adaptation for C code: The approaches of both Kung and Sen work on object-oriented software, where state variables are simply the member variables that influence any control conditions. In C code or ASCET models, there are no natural member variables. Therefore, we have to come up with additional heuristics to determine the relevant state candidate variables. For us, any variable that

---

[3] The combination of all Es from symbolic execution defines the function f.

conforms to the following set of criteria will be considered as a state variable: It is static or global, it influences a control decision, and there is at least one path on which it is read before it is written. These criteria have been empirically determined in our previous work [13]. Note that a state variable in a classical switch-case implementation of a state machine also fulfills these criteria.

(2) Use of Concolic Testing: We use concolic testing instead of symbolic execution as used by Kung and Sen, because it better supports our interactive extensions. For example, concolic testing solves additional user constraints incrementally with every newly encountered path, which is quite efficient and makes concolic testing a more adequate choice for handling user constraints.

(3) Mixed Literals: When all conditional literals of a state variable are MXLs, the state would always be changed according to the value of an input variable or parameter. Therefore, it does not make much sense to consider them as states in this case. Furthermore, ignoring them can effectively make state machines more understandable. Sen et al. *always* ignore these mixed variables.

However, these MXLs can sometimes carry important information that may be helpful for program understanding. For example, the state machine in Fig. 2 was extracted from the test function MON (cf. Sect. 3). LmpOn is a state variable, but it occurs in mixed literals with the input variable TmMAX. The information that describes how states can change according to the input variable shows an interesting fact: Once LmpOn has become lower or equal to TmMAX, it can never raise to a value higher than TmMAX value again. For this reason and such cases, we do not ignore mixed variables. Instead, we delegate this decision to the expert as a kind of interaction. The user can then determine which input variables should be considered for state machine mining and which should not (see Sect. 3.4).

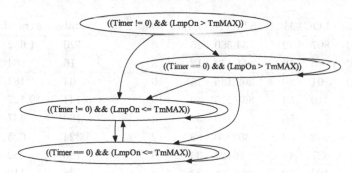

Fig. 2. Example for the potential importance of mixed literals (function MON) [1].

3 Interactive Exploration

We implemented Kung/Sen's approach for state machine mining in a prototype with the adaptations as described in Sect. 2.4. This prototype tool is based on our software analysis framework [14], which includes frontends for C and

ASCET, control/data flow analysis, concolic testing and an interface to the Z3 SMT solver. Then, we used this tool to extract state machines from complex real-world functions, which were seven C code and seven ASCET real-world functions from different automotive software systems. The C functions are part of an engine control software. For example, the SPD function is responsible for switching between different possible input signals when certain conditions apply. MON contains a timer and checks whether input signals change in a certain way within a specified time. AVG calculates several kinds of average signal values according to a clock signal. The ASCET models are taken from another automotive control unit. These functions were nominated for state machine extraction by developers because they found them to be hard to understand with respect to control logic. Table 1 summarizes their characteristics: Lg is language (A = ASCET), LOC denotes lines of code (ASCET: ESDL code), MCC is McCabe's cyclomatic complexity, NPATH is Nejmeh's static approximation of the number of paths [15], and #var is the total number of variables.

Extracting state machine models from these functions – excluding interactive measures, but including our other optimizations and both pure and mixed literals – results in state machines as shown in Table 1, where #state var. is the number of state variables, and #states and #transitions are the numbers of states and transitions, respectively. The experiments showed that the approaches of Kung and Sen have a big problem, which is the state space explosion. Their approaches quickly generate hundreds of states and transitions, which are impossible to understand [16]. For example, the function CT1 has 632 lines of code and 12 state variables which results in 324 states and 625 transitions.

Table 1. Characteristics of subject functions ([1] extended).

	Lg.	LOC	MCC	NPATH	#var.	#state var.	#states	#transitions
SPD	C	807	52	34,560	25	6	720	1,652
MON	C	75	18	41,472	12	3	16	64
AVG	C	91	20	262,145	16	6	64	184
VDA	C	410	54	863,115	39	10	6,144	19,127
HCR	C	775	56	170	32	4	160	437
CT1	C	632	52	302400	88	12	324	625
CT2	C	427	48	56724	34	6	120	382
PRK	A	104	30	284,756	33	4	36	112
RSK	A	169	27	147,480	56	5	48	170
VPR	A	110	17	10,368	17	3	1,157	5,904
SSD	A	58	16	2,816	13	2	32	160
PPR	A	49	16	86	10	3	8	16
SM1	A	67	19	98	13	4	12	21
SM2	A	59	17	84	11	3	8	18

Furthermore, the computation time is also very high. Even small functions can contain hundreds of states and transitions, which makes the models extracted from them very difficult to understand. Take the function VPR as an example: It has only 110 lines of code and 3 state variables. But it is so complex that these variables lead to a state machine model with 1,157 states. The state variables in this function depend on input variables with a large number of possible value ranges (conditions).

The majority of the fully-automatically mined models in Table 1 is too complex for human comprehension. Therefore, the interaction with experts is very necessary to reduce the complexity of these models to a degree that makes them understandable for humans. In the following, we present our interactive measures to complexity reduction and investigate their effect on the resulting models.

3.1 State Variable Subset

It is not always necessary to describe the entire functionality of a large function in a single diagram, but it is usually more useful to focus on certain aspects at once – and abstract away the rest. In other words, instead of generating a state machine model with all state variables in a program, the model can be extracted for only a subset of the relevant state variables, which obviously leads to a state machine with a lower number of states. A comprehensive group of such simplified state machines may still provide a full picture of a function's behavior.

Selecting a subset of state variables is implemented as follows: The tool presents the full list of identified *state variables* along with their relevant values/value ranges to the user, who in turn selects those variables that are potentially interesting. In Table 2, we demonstrate how this information is presented. The user interacts by selecting/deselecting an entire row in this table.

The effect of this interaction is shown in the following example: The function AVG contains six state variables, which – with only pure conditions – generate a model with 16 states and 64 transitions (see Table 3). When the user selects only the variables *ppa, ppb*, this will reduce the number of states to four and transitions to eleven. We present the models with all and with only these two variables in Fig. 3[4]. The result shows a significant complexity reduction, and the reduced model concentrates on certain aspects of the overall state. As the user can select any combination of state variables, which means a wide variety of alternatives, we show here only one example from the large number of experiments that we have done.

The variable selection in the previous example was done randomly. For new users, who do not have any idea about the considered function, it may be difficult and even not effective to determine the relevance of state variables according to the variables' names only. Those users need additional information that can give them a better direction to the relevant variables. One important aspect that we

---

[4] In all our experiments in this paper, we concentrate on the structure and complexity of the resulting state machines regarding the number of states and transitions. Therefore, we do not show transition conditions in the figures.

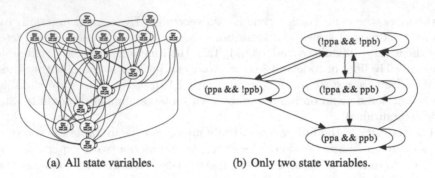

(a) All state variables.   (b) Only two state variables.

Fig. 3. The effect of reducing the set of state variables (AVG) [1].

use for this issue is the **effect size**. In our context, this means which share of statements is affected by a given state variable. When a lot of code depends on a variable, this variable is probably more important than another variable that only controls a few statements. We use program slicing [17] to determine the code that depends on a state variable. Slicing corresponds to reachability analysis on the program dependence graph (PDG) [18], which contains control and data dependencies. After doing this on our representation of a PDG [14], we count the number of PDG nodes in the slice and calculate the relation to the number of nodes of the complete PDG. Then, the variables are sorted by descending effect size, starting with the most influential one (see Table 2). This can be used by the user as an indication of relevance of each variable.

3.2 Joining States/Reducing State Variable Alternatives

In the above example in Sect. 3.1, state variables consider all possible values in the program. However, our approach also allows the expert to restrict values or ranges of values for state variables. This interaction is implemented in the same way as in state variable subset: The user is presented a list of the relevant value/range alternatives for each state variable, as shown in column *Values/Partitions* in Table 2. Then, the user can (a) ignore the irrelevant alternatives, (b) merge certain alternatives, and even (c) create her own alternatives.

Figure 4(a) illustrates the state machine of the function (SPD) with all possible states of the state variables *Ctr* and *Sync* and without additional constraints

Table 2. Information about the first three state variables, their effect size and relevant values/ranges for function SPD [1].

State variable	Effect	Values/Partitions
Ctr	0.60	=0 | =1 | =2 | =3 | other
SPD_mode	0.30	=4 | ≠4
Sync	0.27	true | false

from the user. The values/alternatives of *Ctr* in (SPD) are $\{0, 1, 2, 3\}$. In this experiment, the user has only selected the values $\{0, 1\}$. This selection generated the state machine in Fig. 4(b), which is much simpler than the original model.

Figure 4(b) presents an example of the combination between two interaction scenarios. Firstly, it contains only *Ctr* and *Sync* as a subset of the six state variables of SPD. Secondly, only the states $\{0, 1\}$ are selected from all possible values of *Ctr*. Such combinations are fully supported and desired in our approach.

3.3   Constraints

Adding user constraints to the mining process means (1) setting some variables to a fixed value, and/or (2) generating paths under general constraints, such as $x = y+1$. These constraints can reduce the number of paths, which results in reducing (a) the number of states and transitions and (b) the complexity of state invariants and transition conditions. Consequently, the resulting models become less complex and more understandable. Also, adding such constraints will allow the user to investigate arbitrary scenarios such as what-if scenarios.

This interaction is also implemented by presenting a list of *all* variables that appear in the program to the user, who in turn can (1) select the variables and their values or ranges of values in the same way, and/or (2) write her own constraints in the form of expressions on these variables (plus literals). The constraints can also contain any combination of conjunction, disjunction and negation. Feeding these constraints into the state machine mining process is done very simply by adding them to concolic testing as additional conditions.

This interaction differs from joining states in the previous section in so far as joining states is done only on state variables to let the user select the relevant states that she wants to have in the state machine. Adding user constraints covers all variables in the program – including non-state variables – which can affect not only the states, but also the transition and their conditions.

To show the effect of user constraints, we have randomly selected 12 variables from the 19 non-state variables that the function SPD has. Then, we set the 12 variables to randomly selected values or range of values. The result was that these constraints reduced the number of transitions from 35 (without constraints) to nine (with the 12 constraints). The number of states stayed at ten, because the constraints were applied only on non-state variables[5]. Table 3 shows how – randomly selected – user constraints reduce the models from all subject functions. The third column gives information about the used number of user constraints (#C) and the share of remaining transitions (%T) with pure and mixed conditions (see Sect. 3.4). The last column shows the same information – with the same user constraints – but with only pure conditions. For example, adding only two constraints reduces the number of transitions to 36% in SM2, 38% in CT2 and 75% in PPR. Adding more constraints can even result in more reduction. However, the degree of state machine reduction largely

---

[5] In the figure, we show only five states, because the other five states (with !Sync) are not connected by any transitions.

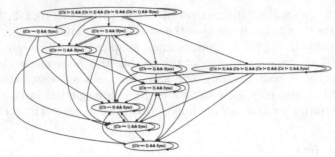

(a) with *all* states of *Ctr* and *Sync* and without constraints

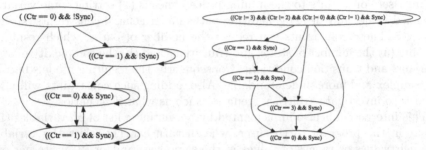

(b) With only the states {0,1} of vari-   (c) With extra user constraints and all states of
able *Ctr*   *Ctr* and *Sync*

Fig. 4. The effect of user constraints and reducing state variables' range (SPD) [1].

depends on the system under consideration and the chosen constraints. Here we have selected the constraints randomly and set them to certain values, and the result was very good. When the user had some ideas about which constraints have the highest effect on states, the result would be even better. Therefore, we plan to automatically identify the most effective constraints in our future work. Because the constraints in this experiment were applied only on non state variables, the number of states remains the same, and we only present the effect on the number of transitions (%T).

3.4   Mixed Literals

Table 3 also demonstrates how ignoring mixed literals (MXLs) in the mining process can reduce the number of states and transitions. The evaluation is done by generating state machines from all state variables of our subject functions in two variants: The first one was done including MXLs and MDLs. The number of states (#S) and transitions (#T) are shown in the first column "Pure + Mixed" of Table 3. In the second variant, we removed all MXLs and extracted the state machines again. The results are presented in the second column "only Pure" as a percentage of the original number of states and transitions from the first column, i.e., the remaining share of states and transitions. From this experiment we can conclude that removing mixed literals can reduce the number of states and transitions in the extracted state machines. However, this reduction depends on the subject functions. It depends on whether they contain mixed literals at all and on the number of used mixed literals. For example, ignoring all mixed literals in the function VPR will remove all states and transitions in the mined models, because this function does not contain any pure conditions. All the conditional literals depend on parameters. This emphasizes again that these conditions cannot always be ignored (cf. Sect. 2.4). On the other hand, this procedure (removing mixed literals) has no effect on the mined state machines from the function PRK, because it contains only pure conditions.

Table 3. Model reduction: the effect of using only pure conditions and user constraints on the number of states and transitions ([1] extended).

	Pure + Mixed		only Pure		UserCon Pure + Mixed		UserCon only Pure
	#S	#T	%S	%T	#C	%T	%T
SPD	720	1652	1%	2%	12	1%	0.5%
MON	16	64	25%	18%	6	81%	15%
AVG	64	184	25%	34%	4	69%	17%
VDA	6144	19127	2%	2%	4	45%	1%
HCR	160	437	10%	14%	3	34%	11%
CT1	324	625	6%	11%	5	42%	7%
CT2	120	382	8%	16%	2	38%	10%
PRK	36	112	100%	100%	5	49%	49%
RSK	48	170	4%	1%	3	56%	0.5%
VPR	1157	5904	0%	0%	5	35%	0%
SSD	32	160	12%	10%	4	63%	6%
PPR	8	16	25%	25%	2	75%	18%
SM1	12	21	22%	32%	3	64%	24%
SM2	8	18	9%	16%	2	36%	9%

3.5 Comparison with Kung/Sen Approach

In Sects. 2.3 and 2.4, we presented the approaches of Kung and Sen and our adaptations and optimizations. In the previous sections, we introduced our interactive extensions. In the following, we summarize and highlight the differences, improvements and new contributions between these approaches. Table 4 shows a comparison of the approaches of Kung and Sen with our interactive approach for state machine mining. The comparison includes several aspects: Targeted systems (C++/Java programs or C functions), system type (object-oriented or procedural code), approach (fully-automatic or interactive) and the used analysis techniques. In addition, the table shows how the three approaches identify state variables, states and transitions.

Table 4. Comparison between the approaches of Kung [7] and Sen [8] and our interactive approach [1].

	Kung et al.	Sen et al.	Our approach
Targeted systems	C++ programs	Java programs	C embedded software + ASCET models
System type	Object-oriented	Object-oriented	Procedural code
Approach	Fully-automatic	Fully-automatic	Interactive semi-automatic
Used techniques	Symbolic execution path enumeration	Symbolic execution path enumeration	symbolic execution concolic testing path enumeration
State variables identification criteria	Member dependent variables with only a single variable	Member dependent variables only	- global/static variables - control decision effect - read before write
Mixed literals	Always ignored	Always ignored	Ignoring/Including: expert decision
States	Intervals of a variable	Satisfiable partitions of state variables	Satisfiable partitions of state variables
Transition generation	$\forall v \in V : Inv(s_1, v)$ $\wedge PC_k(v) \models$ $Inv(s_2, f(v))$	$\exists v_1 : PC_k(v_1) \wedge Inv(s_1, v_1) \wedge$ $\exists v_2 : PC_k(v_2) \wedge Inv(s_2, f(v_2))$	$\exists v \in V : Inv(s_1, v) \wedge$ $PC_k(v) \wedge Inv(s_2, f(v))$

4   Experts Feedback

The main goal of our work is to extract state machines from code that are understandable by humans, in order to support developers in their program understanding tasks. How understandable and useful the extracted models are can only be determined by humans (experts or developers) who work with the code. For this reason, we conducted a case study to investigate whether our approach helps in providing understandable state machines and whether industrial developers can apply the interactive measures themselves and consider them useful.

Research Questions:

- **RQ1:** To what extent can the interactive measures of our approach provide understandable state machines?
- **RQ2:** How helpful and useful are the interactively extracted state machine models for developers with different levels of system knowledge?

Study Design: Quasi-experiment with subsequent discussion.

Subjects and Subject Functions: The participants were twelve professional engineers from different business units of the company Bosch. They have at least a master's degree in computer science or electrical engineering and they have all worked with state machines in industrial systems.

The subject functions were the seven industrial real-world automotive C functions from Table 1. The participants have different levels of knowledge about the subject functions. Therefore, we classify the participants according to their prior knowledge of the subject functions into three groups:

- Experts: we had three experts, who were the function responsible for three subject functions.
- Developers: We had four developers, who had at least an idea about functions which are not implemented by them, but they use these functions in their work.
- New users: We had five developers, who work in another business unit and do not have any prior knowledge about the functions.

Procedure and Tasks: We performed different tasks with each of the three above groups, as follows:

1. Experts: We asked each expert to use the interactive measures in our tool to extract a state machine from two state variables at his/her choice from his/her function, and to add some constraints, which can affect the extracted models. Then, we asked them to
   - check the correctness of all states and transitions in the extracted model.
   - write down for each state and transition whether it definitely exists, may exist or can never exist.
   - rate on a scale of one to ten (best mark) if the models contain the right level of required details that a user needs.
2. Developers: We asked the developers with an idea about the functions to
   - note down their knowledge about the control logic of the function as a state machine on paper.
   - use the prototype tool with the interactive measures to extract a model with the same variables that exist in their model.
   - identify the differences between the extracted model and their model.
   - write down if they gained any new knowledge from the extracted model about the behaviour of the function.
   - note down the time they needed to review the extracted model.
3. New users: We asked the users without any prior knowledge to
   - use our prototype tool to extract a state machine from two state variables of a function.
   - note down what they can read and understand from the state machine model of the two selected variables and draw conclusions about the behaviour of the function.
   - note down the time they needed to review the extracted model.

Each participant worked on the task independently from the others, whenever he/she had some time. After finishing the task, we had an interview with each participant, in which we explained the approach and discussed the results of his/her task. Also, we discussed the following points with all participants:

- The understandability of the extracted models.
- How they evaluate the support information about state variables, their effect size and their states, which were provided by the tool.
- Would they use the approach for their program understanding tasks?

Results: In the following, we begin with the results from each group, then we move on to the discussion points that we had with all the participants:

1. The feedback from the first group (experts) was quite interesting. All states in the extracted models (24 states in three models) were classified by the experts as "definitely exist" in the code. Seven transitions out of 38 in three models were classified as "may exist" and four as "can never exist". However, when the experts reviewed the code, it turned out that the transitions that were classified as "can never exist" do exist in the code. Therefore, we can say that these models can help in **validation and verification**. All the experts asked about transition conditions, because we did not show them in the models. We told them that the conditions at this stage of work are too complex to be understandable by humans. Making transition conditions understandable is our next goal. The experts rated the models at 8.5 on average with respect to the question whether they contain the required details that a user may need.

2. None of the developers in the second group identified all states of the variables in their models. Determining the transitions between the states was even more difficult to them, and almost all developers did not identify the transitions from a state to itself in their models. However, when they got the models from our interactive approach, they were able to return to the code and track the states and transitions between them. In the discussion, they stated that automatically extracting the states and transitions into state machine models first and then tracking them in the code strongly helps in understanding the function under consideration. Therefore, they said that the extracted models gave them valuable insights into the functions, which would be a lot of work to get from code. One expert wrote down: "The model at this level of detail is already very helpful, since I can validate the possible states and transitions with my expectations. The proposed approach of interactive scenarios and projections should help to make the complexity more manageable.". All the developers gained new knowledge from the models, especially about the existence of specific transitions. The developers needed five minutes on average to review the models, which means – given the complexity of the code – that they can understand the function's behaviour in the extracted models quickly. Therefore, we can say that the interactive measures can also reduce the required time for understanding.

3. Finally, the feedback from the last group (new users) was also interesting: They all were able to determine the main ideas in the models quickly (which states exist, what they mean and how they can be reached). When we compared these conclusions with the available information from the function authors, they were correct. For example, three developers were able to come to the fact in Fig. 2, that LmpOn can never raise to a value higher than the value of TmMAX once it becomes lower or equal to TmMAX. The required time for model review was eight minutes on average. This is quite short time in relation to the complexity of the code and the fact that the users had no idea about the functions before.

The results from the discussion with all the participants were as follows:

- The participants had models of only two state variables. Most of these models were considered **understandable** to them with respect to the number of states and transitions and the required time for review. Two models were classified as "difficult to understand" by two new users. Therefore, we asked them to extract a separate model for each of the two state variables and to evaluate the resulting models again. The models were then "completely understandable" to them.
- The information about the variables, their importance and states was considered very helpful, especially by the new users. In addition, feeding the relevant information and constraints to the state machine mining process does not seem to be a problem to the experts, who were immediately able to identify which states would be interesting and which constraints they would like to try.
- Most of the participants (8) said that they would use the approach for their program understanding tasks. The other four were not sure if they need the approach, because they work on completely different tasks.

Discussion: The participants found the interactively extracted models understandable with respect to the number of states and transitions and the required time to review (RQ1). In addition, the feedback shows that the extracted models can be helpful to developers with different levels of system knowledge (RQ2). This is true even for the experts who worked with the function for a longer time. These results are quite promising and encourage further research and refinement of our interactive approach.

In this experiment, the experts were colleagues of ours. They may have been biased to tell us what we want to hear. Therefore, we tried to ask them about concrete details, such as the existence of states and transitions in their code, the differences between the extracted models and their understandability or expectations. In addition, the number of participants (12) may be quite low. However, the participants have a very good background in state machines and reverse engineering and the typical user of state machine mining is expected to have a similar background.

All subject functions were from the automotive domain and the number of them may also be quite low. However, the selection criterion was to have real-world functions that are hard to understand with respect to control logic.

5 Computation Time

In the above study, we asked the developers about the required time to review and understand the models. In this section, we want to check the effect of user interaction on the required time for state machine mining. Therefore, we conduct the following study.

Research Questions:

1. **RQ3:** What is the required time to extract state machines with all state variables (fully-automatic), two variables, only one variable, and then with only two states of a variable?
2. **RQ4:** What is the effect of the interaction scenarios "state variable subset" and "reducing states alternatives" on the required computation time for the mining process, compared to fully-automatic state machine extraction with all state variables of a function?

Study Design: Case study.

Subject Functions: The same 14 functions from Table 1.

Procedure: In this experiment, state machine models are extracted four times: First, with all identified state variables in the function (fully-automatic without any user interaction). Second, with the two state variables that are most important according to the effect size. Third, with the most important state variable, and finally with only two states of the most important variable. Computation times are measured and compared. All the tests and measurements were carried out on a 2.4 GHz Intel CPU with 8 GB physical memory.

Results: The results are shown in Table 5 (RQ3). The first column shows how much time the fully-automatic extraction of state machines from all state variables can take ("All state vars."). The last three columns show how much time the interactive measures save compared to the fully-automatic times. Column "two state vars." means the two variable with the most effect size, "one state var." the variable with the highest effect size, and "only 2 states" means selecting only two states of the variable with the highest effect size. A value of 99% means that only 1% of the computation time remains when these interactions are used.

The interaction had a very positive impact on the extraction time (RQ4), especially for large functions (SPD, VDA, VPR). For example, extracting a complete state machine model for all six variables of SPD, which results in 720 states and 1,652 transitions, takes about seven hours. Extracting a model for only the two most important variables results in ten states and 40 transitions and requires 306 s, which is a huge reduction in computing time (reduced by 98.9%).

The table also shows that the fully-automatic extraction of state machines from large functions provides not only models with a large number of states and transitions, which are not understandable by humans, but it also costs very much time.

Discussion: Since this state machine mining approach intensively uses an SMT solver – for path enumeration, for determining feasible states, and for finding out pre and post states for each path, the computational cost is very high. However, the interactive approach also addresses this issue: By providing additional input, limiting ranges or giving additional constraints, the number of paths and states

Table 5. The required time to extract state machine models with all state variables (fully-automatic) and with applying the interactive measures of state variable subset and reducing states alternatives.

	All state vars. Time	Two state vars. Reduction	One state var. Reduction	Only 2 states Reduction
SPD	7 h	98.9%	99.2%	99.8%
MON	48 s	77%	89%	89%
AVG	16 s	84%	92%	94%
VDA	14 h	99.1%	99.7%	99.7%
HCR	5 min	82%	86%	86%
CT1	12 min	92%	94%	95%
CT2	4 min	94%	96%	97%
PRK	42 s	76%	78%	78%
RSK	56 s	79%	84%	86%
VPR	9 h	99.1%	99.4%	99.6%
SSD	46 s	0%	56%	86%
PPR	6 s	68%	74%	74%
SM1	8 s	72%	78%	82%
SM2	5 s	66%	78%	78%

is largely reduced. The number of solver calls is in $O(P * S^2)$ with P number of paths and S number of states. Therefore, specially reducing the number of states also drastically reduces the required computation time.

In comparison to Sen [8], our running times are quite high. This is probably due to several reasons: They use a time bound on the constraint solver, while we let it run to completion. Also, our transition condition is more precise and therefore requires more computations. However, further optimizations are required. One idea for optimization is utilization of a cache as in KLEE [19] to reuse previously found solutions from the solver.

We have presented several interaction scenarios, which results in a wide variety of alternatives. However, in this experiment, we applied only two scenarios "state variable subset" and "reducing states alternatives", and the runtime was drastically reduced. When the user applies more interactions in a combination, such as adding some constraints or joining states, the runtime can be even better.

The maximum number of state variables in the experiment was two. However, models with a larger number of state variables will make the models "not understandable" to users. In addition, the two selected variables were the most important ones. Selecting variables with less effect on the code will result in even shorter computation times. Therefore, the generalization appears to be permissible in this case. Finally, all subject functions were from the automotive domain and thus the results are not necessarily generalizable to other domains.

In summary, the contribution of the expert strongly affects the required time for the model mining process. In an interactive setting, the expert needs to get the desired results within a short response time and does not want to wait for information that she does not need. Our approach gives the user the possibility to direct the analysis towards the relevant information only and speed it up.

6   Discussion

Our experiment showed that the interaction with experts can strongly lead to less complex but still useful state machines. It enables the developer to control the focus and complexity of the models according to the task at hand. Each proposed interactive scenario can be applied individually and reduce the number of states and transitions. However, the combination of these techniques offers even more possibilities and reduction. The runtime case study shows that the interactive measures drastically reduce the required time for state machines mining. Given these results, the applicability of such a process on complex real-world systems appears to be feasible and realistic. However, our case studies are only the first steps towards proving the efficiency of our interactive approach. Only a controlled experiment can prove that our approach really improves the efficiency, and this will be our essential future work.

The feedback from users was also very promising: Applying the interactive measures does not seem to be a problem to them. Also, they immediately had ideas about which scenarios they wanted to investigate and which constraints could be useful. Furthermore, our approach can meet the needs of users with different levels of system knowledge. So both technically and from user perspective, our interactive approach appears feasible. To get a better picture about users feedback, our controlled experiment will be done with a larger number of users from different domains.

The experiment also showed that domain experts or users with good system knowledge can directly select the states or constraints of interest. For new users, who do not have any idea about the system, our tool gives them a ranking of all state variables according to their effect size. Providing similar information about the constraints that affect specific states at most will also be helpful for users. Therefore, we plan to automatically mine the relevant constraints from code.

We concentrated on states and transition structure so far and ignored transition conditions. The state/transition structure alone was already considered quite useful by our developers. However, transition conditions are also important for understanding. The conditions that result from the extraction process are usually complex and not understandable for humans. Also, reducing the number of states obviously makes state machine models more understandable. On the other hand, the information that was previously contained in the state invariants will not get lost, but it will move into the transitions, which may make those more complex. We are currently investigating approaches for reducing this complexity. For example, not all information in these conditions is relevant. This could lead to another interactive extension.

Finally, the case studies suggest that the interactive approach can also be helpful for validation, verification and debugging tasks. These usage scenarios make the approach even more attractive. Therefore, we plan for more experiments to assess the efficiency of the approach with respect to these challenges.

7 Related Work

Most *state machine extraction* approaches try to extract the allowed sequences of API calls, such as in the work of Ammons et al. [20], Whaley et al. [21], Lo et al. [22], Shoham et al. [23] and Eisenbarth et al. [24]. However, we are interested in extracting state machines that describe the *behavior* of an application.

Walkinshaw et al. [25] use symbolic execution to extract transitions between the states. They assume that the states have been manually identified in a prior step. In addition, they assume that all transitions correspond to functions. Our approach does not have these assumptions. In another paper [26], Walkinshaw et al. extract state machines interactively with the user. The approach uses a grammar inference technique to mine state machines from execution traces. However, the kind of interaction in this approach is very much different from ours: The user has to decide for given (generated) sequences of events whether they should be accepted by the state machine or not. Our interactive approach is rather the other way around.

In Bandera [27], state machines are automatically extracted from the source code of Java programs for model checking. The extracted models are in the input language of one of the used verification tools. The resulting models with thousands of states are useful for this use case – but for human comprehension, they are not. Xie et al. [28] extract state machines from object-oriented code based on tests. They extract object state machines (OSM), whose states are the object state of the class and transitions are the method calls of the class. Therefore, this approach is not applicable for the implicit state machines in procedural code that we are interested in. The extraction of state machines from object-oriented code is also discussed by Tonella et al. [29]. They assume that each method call on an object represents a transition, which is not true for procedural code. A different approach is followed by Dallmeier et al. [30]. They use *inspectors* to define the state space. Inspectors are methods (in object-oriented programs) that only read from an object's attributes and thus represent state. They often create an abstraction, like in the case of a Java collection's isEmpty() function, that can then be used as a basis for state candidates.

Van den Brand et al. [31] extract state machines from legacy C code. They search for state variables only in specific patterns such as nested-choice patterns (e.g., nested ifs). Also, they depend on enumerations to determine state variables. For example, enumerations that contain the word "state" in their name are considered state variables. The approach is restricted to these patterns. Another example for using specific state machine patterns is the work of Knor et al. [32].

Abadi et al. [33] extract state charts from specific patterns generated from code generators, so it cannot be applied for hand-written software.

Somé et al. [34] assume that the state is represented by only one variable, which restricts the implementation of this approach to systems with obvious state machines. Jiresal et al. [35] use static data flow analysis and heuristics based abstractions to create state charts. However, the heuristics only include some specific patterns that specifically suit the automotive case study that they had done. Furthermore, the heuristics must be chosen very carefully and by domain experts. Jiresal et al. also mentioned that better heuristics require user interaction, but they did not implement that. Industrial tools like Rhapsody[6] do only simple mapping from code to models, they do not do a real abstraction of systems. Therefore, developers cannot use the extracted models to understand and develop the system. For this reason, they also do not meet our needs.

Kung et al. [7] use symbolic execution to extract state machines automatically from C++ source code. Sen and Mall [8] extend Kung's approach for Java programs. The techniques in these approaches were presented in Sect. 2, since our interactive approach builds upon this work. Both approaches were applied to classes with a small number of states and transitions. We have adapted the approach for C code and tested it on larger functions, which resulted in hundreds of states and transitions [1], which makes the extracted models not understandable by humans.

8   Conclusion and Future Work

In this article, we evaluated the interaction measures for reducing the complexity of mined state machines from embedded software, which we have proposed in our previous work [1]. Based on the results from our experiment on industrial real-world automotive software and with professional developers from the company Bosch, we can conclude that these interactive measures are very useful to provide understandable state machines from complex real-world systems: They have the ability to reduce the number of states and transitions of the models and to extract specific projections of the models. The experiment also showed that our interactive approach can help developers with different levels of system knowledge by extracting understandable state machines that can also be useful in validation, verification and debugging. The runtime case study showed that fully-automatic approaches for state machine mining result in complex models, and that their computation time is very high. On the other hand, the study showed that our interactive measures can drastically reduce the required time for model extraction.

Our studies also showed up further opportunities for improvements, which include: (1) A comprehensive evaluation through a controlled experiment with a larger number of experts and more real-world projects. In this experiment we will assess the efficiency of our interactive approach from different aspects, such as the understandability and quality of the models and the developers' effort for applying the interactive scenarios. (2) Reducing the complexity of transition conditions to an understandable degree for humans. (3) The automatic mining of

---

[6] http://www-03.ibm.com/software/products/de/ratirhap.

constraints in code that affect specific states at most. (4) Runtime optimization for the SMT solver. (5) Adding more interaction scenarios, and (6) Extracting other kinds of models that can also be helpful in reengineering tasks.

In summary, supporting state machine mining with user interaction appears to be a realistic and scalable approach for understanding of complex real-world systems and migration towards model-based development.

References

1. Said, W., Quante, J., Koschke, R.: Towards interactive mining of understandable state machine models from embedded software. In: Proceedings of the 6th International Conference on Model-Driven Engineering and Software Development: MODELSWARD, vol. 1, pp. 117–128 (2018)
2. Fjeldstad, R.K., Hamlen, W.T.: Application program maintenance study: report to our respondents. In: Proceedings of GUIDE 48 (1984)
3. Ko, A.J., Myers, B.A., Coblenz, M.J., Aung, H.H.: An exploratory study of how developers seek, relate, and collect relevant information during software maintenance tasks. IEEE Trans. Softw. Eng. **32**, 971–987 (2006)
4. Minelli, R., Mocci, A., Lanza, M.: I know what you did last summer: an investigation of how developers spend their time. In: Proceedings of 23rd International Conference on Program Comprehension, pp. 25–35 (2015)
5. Roehm, T., Tiarks, R., Koschke, R., Maalej, W.: How do professional developers comprehend software? In: Proceedings of 34th ICSE, pp. 255–265 (2012)
6. Broy, M., Kirstan, S., Krcmar, H., Schätz, B., Zimmermann, J.: What is the benefit of a model-based design of embedded software systems in the car industry? In: Software Design and Development: Concepts, Methodologies, Tools, Applications, pp. 310–334 (2013)
7. Kung, D.C., Suchak, N., Gao, J.Z., Hsia, P., Toyoshima, Y., Chen, C.: On object state testing. In: Proceedings of 18th International Computer Software and Applications Conference (COMPSAC), pp. 222–227 (1994)
8. Sen, T., Mall, R.: Extracting finite state representation of Java programs. Softw. Syst. Model. **15**, 497–511 (2016)
9. Cheng, K.T., Krishnakumar, A.S.: Automatic functional test generation using the extended finite state machine model. In: Proceedings of 30th ACM/IEEE Design Automation Conference, pp. 86–91 (1993)
10. King, J.C.: Symbolic execution and program testing. J. ACM **19**, 385–394 (1976)
11. Godefroid, P., Klarlund, N., Sen, K.: DART: directed automated random testing. In: Proceedings of PLDI, pp. 213–223 (2005)
12. Hoffmann, A., Quante, J., Woehrle, M.: Experience report: white box test case generation for automotive embedded software. In: Proceedings of 9th International Conference on Software Testing, Verification and Validation Workshops, TAIC-PART Workshop, pp. 269–274 (2016)
13. Said, W., Quante, J., Koschke, R.: On state machine mining from embedded control software. In: Proceedings of the 34th International Conference on Software Maintenance and Evolution (ICSME). (2018)
14. Quante, J.: A program interpreter for arbitrary abstractions. In: 16th International Working Conference on Source Code Analysis and Manipulation, pp. 91–96 (2016)
15. Nejmeh, B.A.: NPATH: a measure of execution path complexity and its applications. Commun. ACM **31**, 188–200 (1988)

16. Miranda, D., Genero, M., Piattini, M.: Empirical validation of metrics for UML statechart diagrams. In: Camp, O., Filipe, J.B.L., Hammoudi, S., Piattini, M. (eds.) Enterprise Information Systems V, pp. 101–108. Springer, Netherlands (2005). https://doi.org/10.1007/1-4020-2673-0_12

17. Weiser, M.: Program slicing. In: Proceedings of 5th International Conference on Software Engineering (1981) 439–449

18. Horwitz, S., Reps, T.W., Binkley, D.: Interprocedural slicing using dependence graphs. In: Proceedings of Conference on Programming Language Design and Implementation, pp. 35–46 (1988)

19. Cadar, C., Dunbar, D., Engler, D.R.: KLEE: unassisted and automatic generation of high-coverage tests for complex systems programs. In: 8th USENIX Symposium on Operating Systems Design and Implementation, pp. 209–224 (2008)

20. Ammons, G., Bodík, R., Larus, J.R.: Mining specifications. In: Proceedings of 29th Symposium on Principles of Programming Languages, pp. 4–16 (2002)

21. Whaley, J., Martin, M.C., Lam, M.S.: Automatic extraction of object-oriented component interfaces. SIGSOFT Softw. Eng. Notes **27**, 218–228 (2002)

22. Lo, D., Khoo, S.C., Liu, C.: Efficient mining of iterative patterns for software specification discovery. In: Proceedings of 13th International Conference on Knowledge Discovery and Data Mining, pp. 460–469 (2007)

23. Shoham, S., Yahav, E., Fink, S.J., Pistoia, M.: Static specification mining using automata-based abstractions. IEEE Trans. Softw. Eng. **34**, 651–666 (2008)

24. Eisenbarth, T., Koschke, R., Vogel, G.: Static object trace extraction for programs with pointers. J. Syst. Softw. **77**, 263–284 (2005)

25. Walkinshaw, N., Bogdanov, K., Ali, S., Holcombe, M.: Automated discovery of state transitions and their functions in source code. Softw. Test. Verif. Reliab. **18**, 99–121 (2008)

26. Walkinshaw, N., Bogdanov, K., Holcombe, M., Salahuddin, S.: Reverse engineering state machines by interactive grammar inference. In: Proceedings of 14th Working Conference on Reverse Engineering (WCRE), pp. 209–218 (2007)

27. Corbett, J.C., Dwyer, M.B., Hatcliff, J., Laubach, S., Pasareanu, C.S., Robby, Zheng, H.: Bandera: extracting finite-state models from Java source code. In: Proceedings of 22nd ICSE, pp. 439–448 (2000)

28. Xie, T., Martin, E., Yuan, H.: Automatic extraction of abstract-object-state machines from unit-test executions. In: Proceedings of 28th ICSE, pp. 835–838 (2006)

29. Tonella, P., Potrich, A.: Reverse Engineering of Object Oriented Code. Springer, New York (2011). https://doi.org/10.1007/b102522

30. Dallmeier, V., Lindig, C., Wasylkowski, A., Zeller, A.: Mining object behavior with ADABU. In: Proceedings of International Workshop on Dynamic Systems Analysis, pp. 17–24 (2006)

31. van den Brand, M., Serebrenik, A., van Zeeland, D.: Extraction of state machines of legacy C code with Cpp2XMI. In: Proceedings of 7th Belgian-Netherlands Software Evolution Workshop, pp. 28–30 (2008)

32. Knor, R., Trausmuth, G., Weidl, J.: Reengineering C/C++ source code by transforming state machines. In: van der Linden, F. (ed.) ARES 1998. LNCS, vol. 1429, pp. 97–105. Springer, Heidelberg (1998). https://doi.org/10.1007/3-540-68383-6_15

33. Abadi, M., Feldman, Y.A.: Automatic recovery of statecharts from procedural code. In: International Conference on Automated Software Engineering, pp. 238–241 (2012)

34. Somé, S.S., Lethbridge, T.: Enhancing program comprehension with recovered state models. In: 10th International Workshop on Program Comprehension (IWPC), pp. 85–93 (2002)
35. Jiresal, R., Makkapati, H., Naik, R.: Statechart extraction from code - an approach using static program analysis and heuristics based abstractions. In: Proceedings of 2nd India Workshop on Reverse Engineering (2011)

Adaptation and Implementation of the ISO42010 Standard to Software Design and Modeling Tools

Maged Elaasar[1], Florian Noyrit[2], Omar Badreddin[3(⊠)], and Sébastien Gérard[2]

[1] Modelware Solutions, La Canada Flintridge, CA, USA
melaasar@gmail.com
[2] CEA, LIST, Laboratory of Model Driven Engineering for Embedded Systems, Point Courrier 174, 91191 Gif-sur-Yvette, France
{florian.noyrit, sebastien.gerard}@cea.fr
[3] CS Department, University of Texas El Paso, El Paso, TX, USA
obbadreddin@utep.edu

Abstract. Model cantered software development practices adoption remains limited to small niche domains. The broad development practices remain code centric. Modeling tool complexity is often cited as a significant factor limiting the adoption and negatively affecting user experience. Modeling and design tools complexity are due to multiple factors including complexity of the underlying language, weak support for methodologies, and insensitivity to users' concerns. This results in modeling and design tools that expose all or most of their capabilities and elements at once, often overwhelming users and negatively affecting user experience. The problem is further exacerbated when a tool supports multiple domain-specific modeling languages that are defined on top of a base language such as UML. In this case, the tool customizations and visual elements necessary to support each language often interfere with each other and further exacerbate the modeling tool complexity. In this paper, we present a novel and systematic approach to reduce the complexity of design and modeling tools by introducing an interpretation and adaptation of the ISO42010 standard on architecture description specific to the software domain. We demonstrate this approach by providing a working implementation as part of the Papyrus opensource modeling framework. In this approach, we leverage the notions of Architecture Contexts and Architecture Viewpoints to enable heterogeneous UML-based languages to be independently supported and help contextualize the exposed tool capabilities. This paper presents the ISO42010 interpretation and adaptation to software design and architecture and a case study with several definitions of architecture contexts. The implementation of this novel approach demonstrates the ability for multiple modeling languages and notations to coexist without interference and provides significant reduction in the exposed capabilities in the UI. Reducing design and modeling tool complexity has a potential to significantly broaden the adoption of modeling and design practices in the software engineering sphere.

© Springer Nature Switzerland AG 2019
S. Hammoudi et al. (Eds.): MODELSWARD 2018, CCIS 991, pp. 236–258, 2019.
https://doi.org/10.1007/978-3-030-11030-7_11

Keywords: ISO 42010 · Architecture description language · Architecture framework · UML · SysML · Software design · Model driven architecture · Model driven development · Software modeling

1 Introduction

The Unified Modeling Language (UML) is a general-purpose modeling language in the field of software engineering. The language was first adopted by the Object Management Group as a standard in 1997, and since then has become widely adopted. UML has an abstract syntax (defining its concepts) and a concrete syntax (graphical notation) to model different concerns ranging from system structure (e.g., Class Diagram and Composite Structure Diagram) to system behavioral (State Machine Diagram and Activity Diagram). The language is large and complex; it contains over 250 concepts and directly supports 14 diagram kinds.

As such, a methodology is often required to guide designers on creating meaningful and consistent models. Meanwhile, the language itself is kept agnostic so it can support several methodologies.

Furthermore, despite being a general-purpose language, UML is often used as a base to define domain-specific modeling languages (DSMLs). This is made possible by leveraging UML's profile extension mechanisms. A UML profile allows extending the language's abstract syntax (with stereotypes) and/or concrete syntax (with graphical annotations). Many DSMLs have been defined on top of UML including: for systems design [9], MARTE for real-time and embedded design [24], SoaML for service-oriented architecture [25], and for BPMN for business process modeling [13]. Multiple profiles can be applied to a UML model at the same time to address different concerns. This capability is often leveraged by domain-specific frameworks (e.g., DoDAF [14]) that integrate multiple DSMLs together. These extension mechanisms add to the complexity, and is a significant overhead that designers have to manage.

UML enjoys a wide range of tool support, including open-source, commercial, educational, and research tools [26]. These tools cater to designers with different levels of expertise (ranging from novices to experts) and needs (e.g., creating models to document a design, generating code from models, performing model-based testing, and creating executable models to simulate and analyze designs). Unfortunately, most of these tools cannot hide complexity without compromising functionality. For example, tools typically expose all possible diagram types, along with their relevant concepts, relationships and properties in the user interface. Tools often do not allow filtering of these UI items according to a specific methodology, and if they did, such filtering is globally applied and is not contextual to the model and the underlying methodology. This filtering approach often leads to further user frustration as required elements may become inaccessible (when filters are applied) or the user interface becomes too complex when such filters are absent. Moreover, when tools support DSMLs defined with UML profiles, they typically add to the UI additional elements that facilitate the creation of DSML models. Since there are no formalisms to identify relevant and/or dependent elements, the UI becomes quickly cluttered with elements from the base modeling notation (i.e. UML) and elements from DSML extensions. More importantly, many DSMLs require tooling customizations. When multiple DSMLs are applied to a model, their customizations may sometimes interfere with each other in unexpected ways. For example, one DSML may expect a newly created Class to have public visibility, while another may expect it to be private. Furthermore, tools that attempt to address these issues do not achieve this in a systematic scalable manner, making extensions to other DSMLs unpredictable and unreliable, and further complicates modeling tool development, testing, and maintenance.

The aforementioned issues are caused by two main underlying fundamental limitations. The first one is that a UML model is not characterized by a unique context, for which customizations can be formally specified. Such context cannot simply be a UML profile, since (a) multiple profiles can be applied at once, possibly leading to customization interference, and (b) many customizations do not depend on profiles at all, like ones intended to implement a framework (e.g., DoDAF) or methodology. The second limitation is the lack of methods to control UML tool UI item visibility based on a methodology, user role, or user concerns.

In this paper, we describe an approach to address the aforementioned limitations that can be applied to any UML modeling tool. Our approach is inspired by the ISO42010 Standard which specifies how architecture is described [1, 3]. In this standard, architecture description must always be associated with a context that can either be an architecture description language (ADL) or an architecture framework (AF). A context specifies a set of architecture viewpoints that define a set of permissible Model Kinds.

We make four contributions in this paper. Our first contribution is adapting and implementing the ISO 42010 standard for the Model Driven Engineering context, and in particular for the UML modeling domain. This entails an Architecture metamodel, whose instances, i.e., architecture models, can be referenced by UML models to specify their context and viewpoints. Our second contribution is a demonstration of how architecture models can be used to mitigate common concerns in UML modeling tools. One concern is the complexity of the UML tool's UI. Another concern is the ability to extend UML architecture contexts or define new contexts by extending existing ones. A third concern is migrating UML models from one architecture context to another. A fourth concern is supporting modeling methodologies. Our third contribution is an implementation of the proposed approach in the Papyrus open source modeling tool [27]. This implementation includes defining a Papyrus Architecture metamodel that extends the base Architecture metamodel. It also includes an implementation of solutions to the aforementioned concerns in Papyrus. Our fourth contribution is a case study that involves defining three architecture contexts (UML, Profile, SysML) in Papyrus. The case study demonstrated that several UML-based architecture contexts can coexist in the same modeling tool without interfering with each other. The case study also demonstrates that the approach can reduce the complexity of the UML modeling tool's UI.

This paper extends previous published work as follows [23]. First, we formally define the ISO42010 interpretation and adaptation to the Model Driven Software Engineering domain. We introduce the concept of extensibility points that enables users to contribute and extend architecture domain models. We also specify assumptions and a rule-based approach for materializing these extensibility points. Moreover, we improved the case study and included additional modeling domains.

The rest of this paper is organized as follows. Section 2 introduces the motivation and significance of this work. In Sect. 3 we present a background on the ISO 42010 standard; a description of our Architecture metamodel is given in Sect. 3; Sect. 4 discusses how architecture models can address UML tools' concerns; an implementation of the approach in Papyrus is described in Sect. 5; Sect. 6 presents a case study where several architecture contexts are defined in Papyrus; related works are presented in Sect. 7; and finally, Sect. 8 provides conclusions and outlines future research directions.

2 Motivation and Significance

Despite the near consensus on the value-added of software design and modeling using languages such as UML, adoption of model-centric methodologies remains dismal. A study that included 113 professionals reveals that modeling tools complexity is a major factor limiting adoption [12]. In the open source sphere, the majority of software development practices remains code-centric [30, 31], but recent studies show significant uptake of modeling using UML [28]. Modeling tools complexities has also been cited as a significant concern. As the adoption of Domain Specific Modeling Languages continue to increase, modeling tools complexity will continue to grow as these DSML often introduce new modeling concepts and elements. Models play a key role in communication and collaboration due to their level of abstraction and support for visual elements. Nevertheless, modeling tools are often perceived to have weak support for collaboration and communication [33]. Modeling tools that attempt to add such support often introduces additional complexities and further exacerbate the learning curve. Abrahão et al., report that extensive usability studies of modeling notations and tools is uncommon as evident by the scarcity of user experience studies in model driven engineering domain [32]. They also report that based on feedback from industry practitioners, user interface and user experience is an important factor for the dissemination and adoption.

In education, multiple researchers have identified the need for educational-specific modeling tools in order to achieve their educational goals [29]. In this study, Liebel et al. have conducted a case study and found that using industrial-level modeling tools require dedicated tool support and instructions. As such, they reiterate the need for simplified tooling for educational purposes.

Solving the challenge of modeling tools complexity is likely to impact the education and practices of broad community of practitioners and educators. Ultimately, this could significantly increase the adoption of model-centric software development.

3 Background on the ISO 42010 Standard

In our attempt to search for methods to reduce the complexity of UML and DSML tools, we broadened our search to include architectural tools at large. This lead us to the ISO42010 standard which specifies the requirements for creating an Architecture Description (AD), shown in Fig. 1, as a product of systems/software architecting. The standard provides a uniform vocabulary to specify architectures and aims at systematizing the architecting processes.

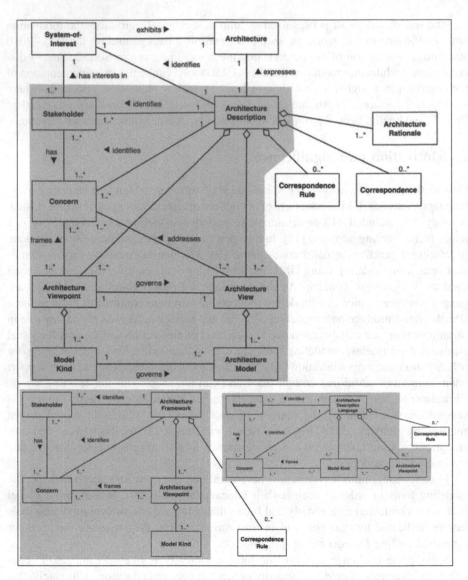

Fig. 1. Highlighted fragments of the ISO 42010 standard vocabulary on architecture description (AD) [23].

In a nutshell, the standard adheres to the concept that every system has an architecture and that AD is a specification of that architecture. It defines architecting as the "process of conceiving, defining, expressing, documenting, communicating, certifying proper implementation of, maintaining and improving an architecture throughout a system's life cycle [1], which takes place in the context of a specific organization or project. The architecture of a system, within the context of this standard, intends to convey the essence of a system. The rationale for this rather broad definition is to capture the underlying common theme of various existing definitions of architectures. This also ensures that the standard is not domain or discipline specific, but rather, a generic standard that targets complex systems architecture in general.

The standard also acknowledges that architecting a system, especially when it is a complex system, involves multiple Stakeholders that have various Concerns that are framed by Architecture Viewpoints and their referenced Model Kinds. An AD contains instances of those Architecture Viewpoints, called Architecture Views, which in turn contain instances of Model Kinds, called Architecture Models.

Furthermore, the ISO42010 standard specifies that an AD conforms to a meta (higher level) description. This meta description can be an Architecture Description Language (ADL), shown in Fig. 1 (top-right) or an Architecture Framework (AF), shown in Fig. 1 (bottom-right), which are two widely used mechanisms to describe architectures. Each mechanism establishes common practices for creating, interpreting, analyzing and using ADs within a particular domain of application or stakeholder community. ADL and AF can both contain Architectural Viewpoints. However, only ADL can contain Model Kinds, which can be referenced by any viewpoints.

4 ISO42010 Interpretation for the Software Architecture Domain

This international standard defines architectures and the architecting processes broadly and abstractly to ensure domain and discipline independence. In this Section, we present an interpretation specific for the software architecting domain. Namely, we present formal interpretation for the Conceptual Model, Architecture Description, Architecture Concerns, and Architecture Views and Viewpoints.

4.1   Conceptual Model

The presented conceptual model in Fig. 2 should serve as a context for understanding the process of architecting at a high level. An architecture is an emergence property of the system (i.e. the system-of-interest exhibits an architecture). The system-of-interest is situated in exactly one environment which may contain multiple systems.

System stakeholders, in this context, refers to those who have fundamental concerns pertaining to the architecture of the system-of-interest. This includes users, operators, acquirers, owners, suppliers, developers, builders, and maintainers of the system. Stakeholders have a set of 'concerns' that are fundamental to the system architecture. As shown in Fig. 2, the 'Purpose' of the system is one type of such concerns. Other concerns include suitability of the system for achieving its purpose, feasibility of construction and deployment, risks and hazards, and maintainability and evolvability of the system. An important aspect of this conceptual model is that the system-of-interest may exhibit zero or more Architectures. Similarly, a specific architecture may specify zero or more systems.

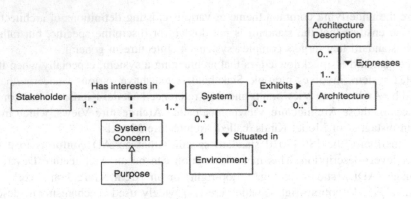

Fig. 2. Architecture conceptual model.

4.2 Architecture Description

The Architecture Description (AD) contains a set of Correspondences and Correspondence Rules (Fig. 3). A correspondence is a relationship between AD elements which are governed by correspondence rules. An element in this context is the most primitive construct, such as stakeholder, concern, architecture viewpoint, architecture view, model kind, architecture model, architecture decision and rationale. AD also contains Architecture Rationale, which records reasoning for architecture decisions, alternatives, and trade-offs, and may cite external sources for additional information on potential consequences of decisions.

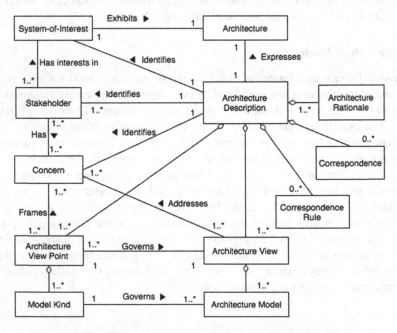

Fig. 3. Architecture decision, rationale, and concerns.

4.3 Architecture Concerns

A concern is any topic of interest pertaining to the system, which are held by the system's stakeholders. This definition is aligned with "separation of concerns" concept in software and systems engineering, first coined by Dijkstra [34]. Each architecture viewpoint frames one or more of the known concerns of the system, as shown in Fig. 4. Since the fundamental premise of separation of concerns is to enable stakeholders to reason on an individual concern independently of the others (to the extent possible), architecture viewpoints enable stakeholders to manage the underlying system complexity. In the context of this definition, concerns include, but are not limited to, risks and hazards. Concerns are framed by architecture viewpoints and are addressed by one of more Architecture views. Architecture views are governed by Architecture viewpoints, which formalizes how views are constructed. Distinction and elaboration on views and viewpoints are discussed in the next section.

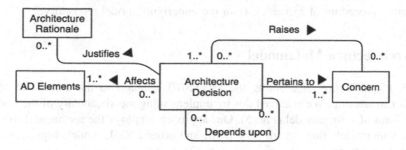

Fig. 4. Architecture concerns.

4.4 Architecture View and Viewpoint

The terms architecture view and architecture viewpoint, despite being apparently similar and are sometimes used synonymously, refer to distinctly different concepts. System architectures typically contain a wide variety of collections of models. In current practices, when a set of these models are organized together to form a cohesive group, the group is referred to as a 'view'. In practice, the view addresses a specific concern(s), and hides away unrelated models and elements. This serves the objective of separation of concerns.

However, there is no formal mechanism for constructing these views. As a result, the formation of the grouping remains implicit, resulting in weakened validation and analysis by the users of the framework. This standard, therefore, defines viewpoint as the set of conventions or formalisms for expressing an architecture with respect to a set of concerns. In a nutshell, A "viewpoint is a way of looking at systems; a view is the result of applying a viewpoint to a particular system-of-interest".

Viewpoints are treated as first class architectural elements, and the standard does not provide a pre-defined set of viewpoints. Because the standard does not target a specific domain or type of systems, it provides users of the standard with the ability to define their own viewpoints. In effect, this perspective improves the portability of the standard across different domains. This perspective of viewpoints is not novel, however. As early as in 1977, Ross has proposed treating Viewpoints as first-class entity in the Structured Analysis approach (SADT) [35].

The distinction between view and viewpoint is a source of confusion. The reported definitions of such concepts are far from being uniform. This concept of a viewpoint is not popular in practice but has been proposed in some architecture frameworks. To clarify this concept, one can think of the relationship between a view to a viewpoint similar to the relationship between a map and a legend. The legend defines the reasoning and semantics of constructing the map, and aids in the understanding of it. Similarly, the viewpoints define the rational and conventions of the contents and elements of the view. This formal distinction has the goal of promoting reuse of tools and techniques within a community, and across-communities, of the architecture frameworks that conforms to this standard. There are two common approaches to the construction of views: the synthetic approach and the projective approach. The synthetic approach is based on model correspondences, while the projection approach is based on routine procedure of extraction from the underlying model repository.

5   Architecture Metamodel

Our first contribution is adapting the ISO42010 standard to the context of Model Driven Engineering. We achieved this by implementing the vocabulary of the standard in the form of a metamodel (Fig. 5). Our approach employs the metamodel to create architecture models that govern how UML and other DSML models represent architecture descriptions.

All elements in an architecture model have types that extend *ADElement* in the architecture metamodel. This type characterizes elements by their unique id, name, qualified name, optional description and optional icon. The *Architecture Domain* type represents the root of the architecture model. This type, which is not explicitly defined in the standard, represents an application domain or a stakeholder community (e.g., Software Engineering, Systems Engineering, Automotive, Aerospace). It contains a set of Stakeholders (e.g., Software Engineers, Systems Analysts) and Concerns (e.g., Structure, Behavior, Parametrics). A stakeholder may have concerns from any domain. A domain may contain a set of Architecture Contexts. This new type (also not in the standard) is an abstract supertype of both ADL and AF and represents the context of an Architecture Description (represented by a UML or a DSML model). A context specifies a *creationCommandClass* and (optionally) a *conversionCommandClass* that can be used by a modeling tool to create a new user model in, or convert an existing user model to, that context respectively. A context also captures the capability of both ADLs and AFs to contain *Architecture Viewpoints*, which reference a set of *Model Kinds*. An ADL specifies a modeling language (e.g., UML, SysML) by defining its abstract syntax with a metamodel and an optional set of UML profiles (when the metamodel is that of UML), and its concrete syntax, or notation, by a set of Model Kinds (e.g., diagrams and tables). An AF, on the other hand, specifies a modeling methodology that involves Model Kinds from one or more ADLs.

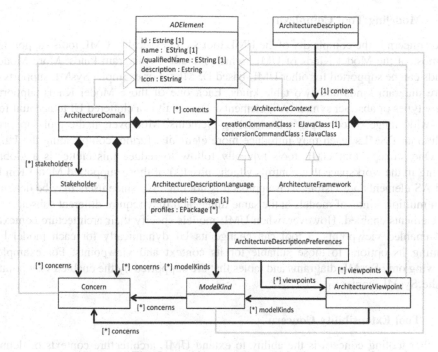

Fig. 5. Architecture Metamodel 26.

Model Kind is defined as an abstract *metaclass* in this metamodel. Instead of predefining possible representations, we assume that the Model Kind concept can be specialized to define any kind of representation and, as discussed later, our implementation allows toolsmiths to define their own.

There are two remaining types in the architecture metamodel, which are *Architecture Description* and *Architecture Description Preferences*, are not meant to be instantiated within an architecture model, but rather within a UML or other DSML model that represent an architecture description. The former references an Architecture Context that the description conforms to and is considered a characteristic of the model. The latter specifies which Architecture Viewpoints are currently enabled in the description and is considered a preference that may be stored in the description model, to share with all users of the model, or in a tool's preference store that belongs to one user or is shared with a group of users.

6   Using Architecture Models to Address UML Tooling Concerns

The architecture models that are discussed in the previous section allow UML models to specify their architecture contexts and viewpoints. This can in turn be leveraged by UML tools to address several concerns, which is another contribution of this work.

6.1   Modeling Tool Complexity

One concern is the complexity of the UML tool's UI. Typically, UML tools support all or most of the Model Kinds of UML, which include 14 diagram kinds. More Model Kinds can be supported for other UML-based DSMLs. For example, SysML supports 4 more diagram kinds and two table kinds. Each one of those Model Kinds supports many types of abstract syntax (AS) elements. The result is a cluttered UI to account for this wide range of concepts and modeling elements. Moreover, if the tool supports additional DSMLs, each may introduce more elements, further complicating the UI.

One strategy that UML tools typically follow to reduce this clutter is a global setting in the workspace that controls which subset(s) of those supported Model Kinds and AS elements are visible. This approach is not effective since users may be dealing with multiple kinds of models at the same time, each may require different subset(s) of UI elements enabled. However, when UML models specify their architecture contexts and enabled viewpoints, a tool can change its UI dynamically for each model by limiting its options to those suitable for its context and viewpoints. For example, showing only SysML diagrams and tables that are supported by the enabled viewpoints of the SysML context.

6.2   Tool Extensibility Concern

Another tooling concern is the ability to extend UML architecture contexts or define new contexts by extending existing ones. For example, some of SysML's Model Kinds (e.g., Block Definition Diagram and Internal Block Diagram) extend corresponding ones in UML (e.g., Class Diagram and Composite Structure Diagram), while including others as is (e.g., State Machine and Activity Diagram). Without formalisms to specify that, most UML tools today expose all of their supported Model Kinds. However, with architecture models, it is straightforward for an ADL or AF to define viewpoints that reference Model Kinds from other ADLs. This allows a tool to only show those Model Kinds that are supported by the visible viewpoints, while making them follow the rules of the ADL or AF in context. For example, the Profile AF has a viewpoint that includes the UML class diagram but restrict its elements to only classes, data types, associations and generalizations.

Our approach supports two types of extension mechanisms. These extension mechanisms are generic and not specific to the implementation we provide in the Papyrus modeling tool. They are discussed in this section since they are not defined as part of the ISO42010 standard. It is however important to note that one of the standard's goal is to establish coherent architecting practices, facilitate portability across different architecture frameworks, and remain domain neutral. For example, users of the standard are expected to contribute their own domain specific viewpoints. As such, providing extensibility mechanism is in strong alignment with the ISO41010 essence.

6.2.1   Extension Points for Contribution of Architecture Domain Models

The Papyrus implementation provides an eclipse extension point allowing contribution of architecture domain models. Each contribution is required to specify a path to a valid *.domain model. A second extension point is provided to allow the contribution of an implementation of an interface, which enables the application of a specific Architecture Context to and from models. This is automatically invoked when an architecture context is applied or unapplied to a model. Each architecture context with a unique ID corresponds to a GMF client context with the same ID. Therefore, contributions to the element type set configurations for a given architecture framework can also be made by extending the element type configuration extension point with the same ID.

6.3   Architecture Domain Extensibility

An architecture domain can be defined by several independent architecture models that are merged dynamically at runtime. This is demonstrated in the example shown in Table 1 where the domain systems engineering is defined more than once. These multiple definitions of the same architecture domain requires that the domain elements be merged together. This merge procedure is subject to the following two assumptions.

A1: It is expected that only one of the merge increments for each element to have a value for the description attribute. In the event that more than one increment has a description value, one of them will be randomly picked.

A2: It is expected that all merge increments of an architecture context to have the same value for the ID attribute. In the event that more than one increment has a unique ID, an error will be logged.

The semantics of the implemented merge is achieved by applying the following rules.

R1: Architecture domains with the same name will be merged.
Stakeholders with the same name will be merged
Concern references will be merged

R2: Concerns with the same name will be merged

R3: Architecture framework with the same name will be merged
Architecture viewpoint with the same name will be merged
Representation kind references will be merged
Concern references will be merged

R4: Architecture description language with the same name will be merged
Architecture viewpoint with the same name will be merged
Representation kind references will be merged
Concern references will be merged
Element type set configurations references will be merged
Representation kind references will be merged

6.4   Model Migration Across Different Contexts

A third tooling concern is the need to migrate UML models from one architecture context to another, which is usually considered as a refactoring operation. Without knowing which architecture context a model belongs to or is migrating to, performing this refactoring becomes very tricky and error prone. However, when a model references an architecture context "A" and is migrating to architecture context "B", the latter's *conversionCommandClass* can be instantiated and run to perform the conversion to "B", while taking "A" into account. For example, converting a UML model to a SysML model involves applying the SysML profile, applying the relevant SysML stereotypes to various UML elements (e.g., stereotyping all classes with SysML:: Block), and deleting all non-supported elements (e.g., UML::Component).

6.5   Support for Modeling Methodologies

A fourth tooling concern is supporting modeling methodologies. As mentioned earlier, by default, UML tools either show all their supported capabilities or allow them to be filtered globally. Unfortunately, both approaches do not allow a tool to support a modeling methodology that most often revolves around defining Model Kinds and grouping them into viewpoints that address specific stakeholders' concerns. With architecture models, a UML model can specify which architecture viewpoints, from the selected architecture context, should be enabled. These could be ones that frame the concerns of the current stakeholder's role. For example, if the stakeholder is a systems analyst that has a Specifying Requirements concern, then the Systems Analysis viewpoint, which includes the Use Case Diagram and the Requirements Diagram, would be visible. By switching roles or concerns, different viewpoints will be available and thereby, depending on the activated viewpoints, different Model Kinds can be made available. A user may also want to change the activation of the viewpoints manually to follow the steps of a methodology.

7   Implementation in the Papyrus UML Tool

We demonstrate the proposed approach by providing an implementation in the Papyrus opensource UML modeling tool. As depicted in Fig. 6, the Architecture metamodel has been extended to introduce Papyrus-specific concepts and Papyrus's Model Kinds.

The Papyrus-specific metamodel includes an extension to both the ADL and the AF that make them reference a set of Element Type Set Configurations. The latter is Papyrus's model-based mechanism (details of this mechanism is outside the scope of this paper) of configuring the editing behavior for abstract or concrete syntax model elements.

By referencing these configurations from an ADL or an AF, one can control how UML or DSML models can be edited in that context. The other extension in the Papyrus-specific metamodel is for Model Kind. The Papyrus Model Kind specifies an implementation id of an underlying model kind (diagram kind or table kind) that is supported by Papyrus. For example, the underlying Model Kinds include the 14 UML diagrams. This type has two subtypes, Papyrus Diagram Kind and Papyrus Table Kind that specify how an underlying model kind is customized (the customization details are beyond the scope of this paper) in the context of an ADL or AF. For example, a Package Diagram can be defined as a customization of the standard UML Class Diagram by limiting the elements on the diagram to UML Packages. Notice that a Papyrus Model Kind can also specify another model kind as its parent to inherit and add to its customization. For example, the UML Package Diagram can be a parent to a new version that restricts the content of the packages to Classes only.

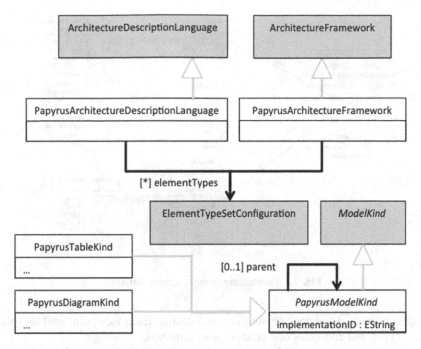

Fig. 6. Papyrus architecture metamodel [23].

Aside from the extended Architecture metamodel, we also implemented a mechanism, by which a single architecture domain can be defined across several architecture models that might be contributed by different extensions to Papyrus. To implement this, we used a composite design pattern. All the Papyrus tooling used the merged architecture elements from several architecture models. The merge required that single valued structural features (e.g., ADElement.id) have values in only one merge increment (the main architecture model), while multi-valued structural features (e.g., Architecture Domain. contexts) get their values aggregated across merge increments.

7.1 Examples

To demonstrate the impact of the approach implementation on Papyrus tool, we present two examples. The first to demonstrate the Architecture Context and the second to demonstrate the Architecture Viewpoints. At any point, users can modify their desired Context(s) and Viewpoint(s). If the UML Context is active, users will be able to create new UML relationship as shown in Fig. 7. However, if SysML context is active, then only SysML relationships will be visible. In case both contexts are active, new relationships from both UML and SysML will be visible.

Figure 8 demonstrates the implementation of Architecture Viewpoints. The

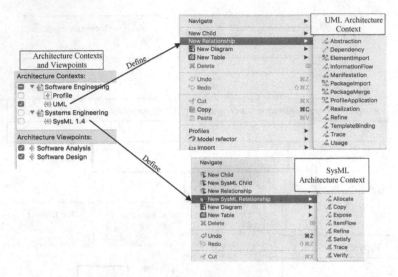

Fig. 7. Architecture context implementation.

example shows two Viewpoints; Analysis and design. Each viewpoint enables specific Model Types and addresses one or more user concerns.

Architecture Contexts and Viewpoints also defines other aspects of the UI, such as

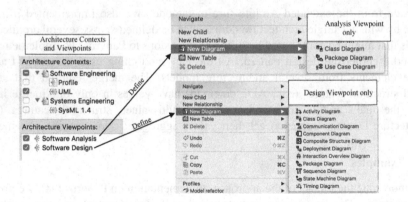

Fig. 8. Architecture viewpoints implementation.

the available elements in the pallet, as well as other tool customization (i.e. default model element visibility).

8 Case Study

Our last contribution is a case study whose objectives are to (a) show that several architecture contexts can be supported in the same tool (Papyrus in this case) without cross interference and (b) that we can reduce the complexity of a modeling tool's UI by dynamically changing the UI based on a model's architecture context and enabled viewpoints. In particular, we defined two architecture models: (a) one with one ADL (UML) and one AF (Profile), and (b) one with another ADL (SysML). Table 1 summarizes the models' contents.

8.1 Architecture Context Independence

The first objective of the case study is to allow multiple architecture contexts (UML, SysML, Profile) to coexist in Papyrus without their contributions interfering with each other, which was a source of conflicts in the model editing behavior. Using the new approach, an architecture context is defined explicitly in architecture models. These contexts directly reference their supported model elements (using the Element Type Set Configurations), which makes it possible for Papyrus to allow exactly and only those elements to be used in each context, along with their supported editing behavior. This makes it easier to avoid interference, which increase the reliability of the tool but more importantly let tool smiths design their own domain specific tooling on top of Papyrus with no concern for potential conflicts with another architecture context. In fact, after the integration of this implementation with Papyrus code base, many other Papyrus ADLs and AFs were migrated to this new solution with reports of reduced development efforts.

Table 1. A summary of the case study architecture models [23].

Context	UML	SysML	Profile
Context Kind	ADL	ADL	AF
Concerns	C1: Functions C2: Structure C3: Behavior C4: Interactions	C5: Requirements C6: Parametrics C7: Reliability	C6: UML Profiling
Stakeholders (Concerns)	S1: Software Engineer (C1, C2, C3)	S2: Systems Engineer (C1, C2, C3, C4, C5)	S3: Domain Architect (C6)

(continued)

Table 1. (*continued*)

Model Kinds	M1: Class Diagram	M15: Block Definition Diagram	
	M2: Component Diagram	M16: Internal Block Diagram	
	M3: Deployment Diagram	M17: Parametrics Diagram	
	M4: Inner Class Diagram	M18: Requirements Diagram	
	M5: Package Diagram	M19: Requirements Table	
	M6: Profile Diagram	M20: Allocations Table	
	M7: Composite Structure Diagram		
	M8: State Machine Diagram		
	M9: Sequence Diagram		
	M10: Activity Diagram		
	M11: Communication Diagram		
	M12: Interaction Overview Diagram		
	M13: Timing Diagram		
	M14: Use Case Diagram		
Viewpoints (Model Kinds)	V1: Software Analysis (M1, M5, M10, M14)	V3: Systems Analysis (M15, M5, M14, M18, M19)	V5: Profile Definition (M1, M6)
	V2: Software Design (M1–M5, M7–M13)	V4: Systems Design (M15–M17, M20, M4, M5, M8-M13)	

8.2   Reducing UI Complexity

The second objective of the case study is to reduce the complexity (clutter) of the modeling tool's UI. Much of this complexity is due to displaying all existing model contents (abstract and concrete syntax elements) or potential new contents that can be created. For example, the model explorer view typically shows all existing elements in a model. Similarly, the explorer provides a context menu that allows creating all kinds of (abstract syntax and concrete syntax) elements in a model. Similarly, a diagram or table editor has a palette and/or a context menu that allows creating all possible model elements. The property sheet view also typically displays all properties of the current selection.

The way to reduce the UI complexity is to remove irrelevant existing elements (e.g., in the model explorer) or potential elements (e.g., menu actions to create new elements) from the UI. Traditionally, there is no reliable way to check for relevance, since there is neither explicit context nor any methodological preferences associated with the model. However, with our proposed approach, an explicit architecture context

(ADL or AF), as well as a set of enabled/visible architecture viewpoints, are referenced by the model. As discussed in Sect. 5, an architecture context in Papyrus specifies the set of (abstract syntax) element types that are supported. This can be used to automatically filter both the set of existing or potential elements in the model from the UI. Similarly, architecture viewpoints, and their Model Kinds, frame stakeholders' concerns. Therefore, by identifying the user as one of the supported stakeholders, the set of existing or potential Model Kinds that need to be visible can be derived automatically. Alternatively, a user can choose the set of enabled viewpoints, which also allows the calculation of the visible Model Kinds.

Furthermore, when we defined the set of three architecture contexts in the case study, we achieved reductions in the number of visible UI items, both existing and potential. Since the reduction of existing elements can only have statistical significance when measured on a set of representative UML or DSML user models, which we do not have now (we leave it to future work), we choose to report only on the reduction of potential elements (i.e., menu actions for creating new elements). Table 2 shows the number of menu actions for creating new abstract syntax elements (e.g., UML elements) and concrete syntax elements (i.e., diagrams and tables), both before and after applying our approach, as counted in the context menu of Papyrus's model explorer by right clicking on the root package (different numbers will result when clicking elsewhere in the hierarchy). For all architecture contexts, we assume that all their viewpoints are enabled (further reduction is expected when some of those views are disabled).

The data in Table 2 suggests that before applying our approach, the number of abstract syntax element create actions, which spanned all Packageable Elements in UML and SysML equaled 88. After applying our approach, the number is reduced by $\sim 23\%$ for UML, $\sim 14\%$ for SysML (lost the subset of UML not used in SysML but gained SysML specific subset), and $\sim 72\%$ for Profile (this is not surprising given that only a few elements from UML are needed). The table also suggests that the total number of concrete syntax elements (Model Kinds) create actions before our approach was 20 (14 UML diagrams + 4 SysML diagrams + 2 SysML tables). After our approach, the number is reduced by 35% for UML, 40% for SysML, and 90% for Profile (Table 3).

Table 2. Number of new element actions in model explorer before and after the new approach [23].

Syntax	UML	SysML	Profile
Abstract Syntax Before	88	88	88
Abstract Syntax After	68	76	25
Concrete Syntax Before	20	20	20
Concrete Syntax After	13	12	2

Table 3. Percentage reduction in abstract and concrete syntax.

Complexity Reduction in	UML	SysML	Profile	Average
Abstract Syntax	23%	14%	72%	36%
Concrete Syntax	35%	40%	90%	55%

9 Related Works

Complexity of UML modeling tools is a recognized and persistent challenge. The emergence of domain specific modeling languages and architectural frameworks means that modern modeling tools must support broader set of functionalities and expose even more elements to users. Petre has conducted a large-scale study of professional software engineers in 50 companies and reported that modeling tools complexity is a key impediment [11]. Forward and Lethbridge surveyed 113 software engineers to uncover patterns in their modeling practices [12]. Among their findings, the tools' steep learning curve and complexity appear to limit the adoption of the modeling practice. Baker et al. report on their experience with MDA for over 20 years at Motorola [19]. They state multiple positive findings, including improved software quality and reduced defects rates. However, they identify key deficiencies in tool support for different languages and model exchange issues between development groups using different tools. Surveying the MDE practices in the Embedded Systems domain, Liebel et al. find that interoperability, high levels of required training, and usability to be the biggest shortcomings of all [20].

Education on modeling driven engineering in software engineering programs seems to also suffer from the complexity of UML tools. One study reports that industrial-level modeling tools can be used in education, only if a dedicated and expert tool support is available [22], a prerequisite not easily met at many academic institutions. In an investigation of MDA pedagogies at four higher-level institutions, students consistently reported that UML, and its supporting tools, are too complex, and their associated overhead does not justify the added value [21].

Lightweight modeling tools have been developed to minimize the learning curve and reduce tool complexity. Examples of such tools include Umple [15] and TxtUML [16] that enable users to create models quickly using textual editors. Other works proposed a light version of UML itself [17]. These approaches do achieve some level of complexity reduction, but typically at the cost of compromised functionality.

Existing modeling tools may provide global preferences or settings to allow users to enable and disable modeling notations and/or features. This is the case in Rational Software Architect [18]. These global sittings are not tuned to the specific model(s) being worked on. Other tools provide pre-set preferences per role. For example, for an analyst role, the tool may hide away specific modeling notations and UI elements.

Architecture description languages and frameworks have emerged around the same time as UML. Some of the early ADLs include Rapide [5], Wright [6], and [7]. These early ADLs focused on structural concerns: large-scale system organization expressed in terms of components, connectors and configurations and had varying support for framing behavioral concerns. More recently, "wide-spectrum" ADLs have been developed which support a wider range of concerns. These include Architecture Analysis & Description Language (AADL) [8], SysML [9] and ArchiMate [10].

In 2000, the Computer Society approved IEEE Standard 1471 [4] which established a consensus on desirable architectural description practices. Heescha and Hilliard have proposed a documentation for architecture decision that is based on ISO42010 standard [2]. This framework focuses on four viewpoint definitions; a Decision Detail viewpoint, a Decision Relationship viewpoint, a Decision Chronology viewpoint, and a Decision Stakeholder Involvement viewpoint. These viewpoints definitions satisfy several stakeholder concerns related to architecture decision management. Hilliard also published a template that can be used by architects and organizations to specify architecture viewpoints in accordance with the ISO42010 standard [3].

10 Conclusion

Software modeling tools are notorious for their high level of complexity which negatively affect the tool usability and user experience. This complexity often stems from the underlying modeling language as tools must support broad set of modeling notations and concepts. As an example, UML modeling language contains thirteen modeling notations. This challenge is exacerbated further when Domain Specific Modeling Languages DSML are introduced. These DSMLs often introduce additional concepts and elements, further cluttering the user interface with more elements. Current approaches rely on using filtering mechanisms to control what elements are made visible to the user. However, these approaches suffer from two fundamental limitations. First, such filtering is often applied globally and is not sensitive to the specific user concerns or the related context. Second, these filtering approaches are not sensitive to the underlying methodology. Moreover, these filters do not address the need for tool customization required for specific context and model types.

This paper introduces a novel and systematic approach for reducing the complexity of modeling tools by leveraging the concepts of architectural contexts and viewpoints. This approach is inspired by and based on the ISO42010 standard which establishes coherent practices for describing the architecture of large and complex systems.

This paper makes four contributions; (1) interpreting and implementing the ISO 42010 standard in the Model Driven Engineering domain through a new Architecture metamodel that reflects and refines the vocabulary of the standard; (2) a demonstration of how the approach addresses several modeling tools' concerns including UI complexity, extensibility to other architecture contexts, model migration between architecture contexts, and support of modeling methodologies; (3) a working implementation of the approach in the Papyrus modeling tool, and (4) a case study that includes two architecture models that define three architecture contexts (UML, SysML, Profile). The case study demonstrates (a) the proposed approach's effectiveness in easing the implementation of domain specific tooling and improving the reliability when several architecture contexts are supported, and (b) the proposed approach's ability to reduce UI complexity by filtering UI items that do not suit the model's context and enabled viewpoints.

The proposed approach has the potential to significantly improve the usability of modeling tools in general. However, several limitations have been identified throughout the paper that we plan to address in future work. One of them is the effort to standardize the Architecture metamodel at OMG. However, we will first need to define the Model Kinds in a tool-neutral way, which would open the door for better modeling tool interoperability and improve the users' experiences across different modeling tools. We also plan to investigate the limit to which we can automate model migration between architecture contexts with more declarative means. We also plan to study the impact of this approach on reducing the visible details in user models.

References

1. IEEE 2008. IEEE Std 1028-2008: IEEE Standard for Software Reviews and Audits. ISO, Systems and Software Engineering – Architecture Description. ISO/IEC/IEEE 42010, pp. 1–46, May 2011
2. van Heesch, U., Avgeriou, P., Hilliard, R.: A documentation framework for architecture decisions. J. Syst. Softw. **85**(4), 795–820 (2012)
3. Hilliard, R.: Architecture viewpoint template for ISO/IEC/IEEE 42010, June 2012. http://www.iso-architecture.org/42010/templates/. Accessed Mar 2017
4. Maier, M.W., Emery, D., Hilliard, R.: Software architecture: introducing IEEE standard 1471. Computer **34**(4), 107–109 (2001)
5. Luckham, D.C., Kenney, J.J., Augustin, L.M., Vera, J., Bryan, D., Mann, W.: Specification and analysis of system architecture using Rapide. IEEE Trans. Softw. Eng. **21**(4), 336–354 (1995)
6. Allen, R., Garlan, D.: The Wright architectural specification language. Rapport technique CMU-CS-96-TBD, Carnegie Mellon University, School of Computer Science (1996)
7. Magee, J., Dulay, N., Eisenbach, S., Kramer, J.: Specifying distributed software architectures. In: Proceedings on Fifth European Software Engineering Conference (ESEC 1995), September 1995
8. Feiler, P.H., Gluch, D.P., Hudak, J.J.: The architecture analysis & design language (AADL): an introduction. No. CMU/SEI-2006-TN-011. Carnegie-Mellon University, Pittsburgh, PA, Software Engineering Institute (2006)
9. Huang, E., Ramamurthy, R., McGinnis, L.F.: System and simulation modeling using SysML. In: Proceedings of the 39th Conference on Winter Simulation: 40 Years! The Best is yet to Come. IEEE Press (2007)
10. Lankhorst, M.M., Proper, H.A., Jonkers, H.: The architecture of the ArchiMate language. In: Halpin, T., et al. (eds.) BPMDS/EMMSAD -2009. LNBIP, vol. 29, pp. 367–380. Springer, Heidelberg (2009). https://doi.org/10.1007/978-3-642-01862-6_30
11. Petre, M.: UML in practice. In: Proceedings of the 35th International Conference on Software Engineering (ICSE 2013), pp. 722–731, San Francisco, CA, USA, 18–26 May 2013
12. Forward, A., Lethbridge, T.C.: Problems and opportunities for model-centric versus code-centric software development: a survey of software professionals. In: Models in Software Engineering workshop (MiSE 2008) at ICSE, pp. 27–32. ACM (2008)
13. Elvesæter, B., Panfilenko, D., Jacobi, S., Hahn, C.: Aligning business and IT models in service-oriented architectures using BPMN and SoaML. In: Proceedings of the First International Workshop on Model-Driven Interoperability, pp. 61–68. ACM, October 2010

14. Hause, M.: The unified profile for DoDAF/MODAF (UPDM) enabling systems of systems on many levels. In: 2010 4th Annual IEEE Systems Conference. IEEE (2010)
15. Forward, A., Badreddin, O., Lethbridge, T.C., Solano, J.: Model-driven rapid prototyping with Umple. Softw. Pract. Exp. **42**(7), 781–797 (2012)
16. Dévai, G., Kovács, G.F., An, Á.: Textual, executable, translatable UML. In: OCL@ MoDELS, pp. 3–12 (2014)
17. Wrycza, S., Marcinkowski, B.: A light version of UML 2: survey and outcomes. In: Proceedings of the 2007 Computer Science and IT Education Conference, pp. 739–749 (2007)
18. Leroux, D., Nally, M., Hussey, K.: Rational software architect: a tool for domain-specific modeling. IBM Syst. J. **45**(3), 555–568 (2006)
19. Baker, P., Loh, S., Weil, F.: Model-driven engineering in a large industrial context—motorola case study. In: Briand, L., Williams, C. (eds.) MODELS 2005. LNCS, vol. 3713, pp. 476–491. Springer, Heidelberg (2005). https://doi.org/10.1007/11557432_36
20. Liebel, G., Marko, N., Tichy, M., Leitner, A., Hansson, J.: Assessing the state-of-practice of model-based engineering in the embedded systems domain. In: Dingel, J., Schulte, W., Ramos, I., Abrahão, S., Insfran, E. (eds.) MODELS 2014. LNCS, vol. 8767, pp. 166–182. Springer, Cham (2014). https://doi.org/10.1007/978-3-319-11653-2_11
21. Badreddin, O.B., Sturm, A., Hamou-Lhadj, A., Lethbridge, T., Dixon, W., Simmons, R.: The effects of education on students' perception of modeling in software engineering. In: HuFaMo@ MoDELS, pp. 39–46 (2015)
22. Liebel, G., Heldal, R., Steghöfer, J.-P., Chaudron, M.R.V.: Ready for Prime Time,-Yes, Industrial-Grade Modelling Tools can be Used in Education (2015)
23. Elaasar, M., Noyrit, F., Badreddin, O., Gérard, S.: Reducing UML modeling tool complexity with architectural contexts and viewpoints. In: International Conference on Model-Driven Engineering and Software Development (MODELSWARD) (2018)
24. Selic, B., Gérard, S.: Modeling and Analysis of Real-Time and Embedded Systems with UML and MARTE: Developing Cyber-Physical Systems. Elsevier, Burlington (2013). https://doi.org/10.1016/C2012-0-13536-5
25. Elvesæter, B., Carrez, C., Mohagheghi, P., Berre, A.J., Johnsen, S.G., Solberg, A.: Model-driven service engineering with SoaML. In: Dustdar, S., Li, F. (eds.) Service Engineering. Springer, Vienna (2011). https://doi.org/10.1007/978-3-7091-0415-6_2
26. Agner, L.T.W., Lethbridge, T.C.: A survey of tool use in modeling education. In: 2017 ACM/IEEE 20th International Conference on Model Driven Engineering Languages and Systems (MODELS), pp. 303–311. IEEE (2017)
27. Lanusse, A., et al.: Papyrus UML: an open source toolset for MDA. In: Proceedings of the Fifth European Conference on Model-Driven Architecture Foundations and Applications (ECMDA-FA 2009), pp. 1–4 (2009)
28. Ho-Quang, T., Hebig, R., Robles, G., Chaudron, M.R.V., Fernandez, M.A.: Practices and perceptions of UML use in open source projects. In: 2017 IEEE/ACM 39th International Conference on Software Engineering: Software Engineering in Practice Track (ICSE-SEIP), pp. 203–212. IEEE (2017)
29. Liebel, G., Badreddin, O., Heldal, R.: Model driven software engineering in education: a multi-case study on perception of tools and UML. In: 2017 IEEE 30th Conference on Software Engineering Education and Training (CSEE&T), pp. 124–133. IEEE (2017)
30. Badreddin, O., Lethbridge, T.C., Elassar, M.: Modeling practices in open source software. In: Petrinja, E., Succi, G., El Ioini, N., Sillitti, A. (eds.) OSS 2013. IAICT, vol. 404, pp. 127–139. Springer, Heidelberg (2013). https://doi.org/10.1007/978-3-642-38928-3_9

31. Aldaeej, A., Badreddin, O.: Towards promoting design and UML modeling practices in the open source community. In: Proceedings of the 38th International Conference on Software Engineering Companion, pp. 722–724. ACM (2016)
32. Abrahão, S., et al.: User experience for model-driven engineering: challenges and future directions. In: 2017 ACM/IEEE 20th International Conference on Model Driven Engineering Languages and Systems (MODELS), pp. 229–236. IEEE (2017)
33. Petre, M.: UML in practice. In: Proceedings of the 2013 International Conference on Software Engineering, pp. 722–731. IEEE Press (2013)
34. Dijkstra, E.W.: On the role of scientific thought. In: Dijkstra, E.W. (ed.) Selected Writings on Computing: A Personal Perspective, pp. 60–66. Springer, New York (1982). https://doi.org/10.1007/978-1-4612-5695-3_12
35. Ross, D.T.: Structured Analysis (SA): a language for communicating ideas. IEEE Trans. Softw. Eng. 3(1), 16–34 (1977)

Generation and Validation of Frame Conditions in Formal Models

Philipp Niemann[1,2]($\boxtimes$), Nils Przigoda[3], Robert Wille[2,4], and Rolf Drechsler[1,2]

[1] Group for Computer Architecture, University of Bremen, Bremen, Germany
[2] Cyber-Physical Systems, DFKI GmbH, Bremen, Germany
[3] Siemens Mobility GmbH, Braunschweig, Germany
[4] Institute for Integrated Circuits, Johannes Kepler University Linz, Linz, Austria
pniemann@uni-bremen.de

Abstract. Operation contracts are a popular description means in behavioral system modeling. Pre- and postconditions are used to describe the effects on model elements (such as attributes, links, etc.) that are enforced by an operation. However, it is usually not clearly stated what model elements may be affected by an operation call and what shall remain unchanged—although this information is essential in order to obtain a comprehensive description. A promising solution to this so-called frame problem is to define additional frame conditions. However, properly defining frame conditions which complete the model description in the intended way can be a non-trivial, tedious, and error-prone task. While in general there are several tools and methods for obtaining formal model descriptions and also a broad variety of approaches for the validation and verification of the generated models, corresponding methods for frame conditions have not received significant attention so far. In this work, we provide a comprehensive overview of recently proposed approaches that close this gap and support the designer in generating and validating frame conditions.

Keywords: Operation contracts · Frame conditions · Validation and verification

1 Introduction

Nowadays, formal models are more and more used in the design of complex hardware as well as software systems as they allow for a precise specification of corresponding designs even in the absence of a specific implementation. The modeling of behavior plays an important role in this development. In fact, being able to simulate models might allow for the detection of design flaws in a very early stage—thereby significantly reducing the efforts and costs related to their correction.

To this end, operation contracts are a popular means for describing system behavior. The general idea of this modeling paradigm is to define which conditions need to be satisfied in order to invoke an operation in the first place

S. Hammoudi et al. (Eds.): MODELSWARD 2018, CCIS 991, pp. 259–283, 2019.
https://doi.org/10.1007/978-3-030-11030-7_12

(*preconditions*) and to describe which assumptions on the system can be taken for granted after the operation is finished (*postconditions*). Note, however, that pre- and postcondition describe the effects of an operation in a declarative way, i.e., without providing any information on how these are achieved in detail. In doing so, the descriptions often focus on the desired effects and typically omit those parts of the model that may not change. Since this does not necessarily mean that the omitted parts are indeed unaffected, e.g., when implicit dependencies or model constraints require changes, it becomes non-trivial to decide what is within the *frame* that might be modified by an operation. In fact, this can in general not be inferred automatically from the constraints themselves.

This problem of determining the precise behavior from a declarative operation contract is called the *frame problem* [4] and occurs in many (modeling) languages that use declarative descriptions like, e.g., UML/OCL, Eiffel, Z, JML, VDM, or CML. Consequently, there has been a large body of research on this problem. A common approach to cope with it is to provide additional constraints in terms of so-called *frame conditions* (this will be discussed in more detail in Sect. 3).

However, while frame conditions are indeed able to solve the frame problem, properly defining them is a non-trivial process. Similarly as the definition of the model itself, it requires a full understanding of the considered system as well as its dependencies. But while the designer is aided by several tools and methods when defining the basic model (see, e.g., [13,15,17] for UML/OCL design environments and [2,6,9–11,18,28,30,32,34,35] for corresponding methods that aim at validation and verification of the designs), almost no support exists yet for the proper definition of frame conditions. In order to close this gap, we have come up with methodologies for the

- *Generation* of frame conditions, i.e., a methodology that provides the designer with an initial proposal for frame conditions in a semi-automatic fashion [23, 24], and
- *Validation* of frame conditions, i.e., a methodology for the dedicated analysis of frame conditions in order to check whether they are indeed correct and complete the specification of the model in the actually intended way [25].

In this work[1], we provide a comprehensive overview of these methodologies. To this end, after introducing some preliminaries and a running example in Sect. 2, we first discuss the frame problem itself as well as alternative ways for the specification of frame conditions (Sect. 3). After that, we consider the problem how an (initial) set of frame conditions can be generated for a given model and present a semi-automatic approach that uses information from the basic model in order to provide the designer with proposals for frame conditions and a classification of model elements that may be affected by an operation (Sect. 4). Then, we discuss which objectives shall be used for validating a given set of frame conditions and establish a notion of *consistency*, *equivalence*, and *independence* of frame conditions. Based on that, we outline how these objectives can be

---

[1] This chapter is an extension of the work previously published at [25].

incorporated into existing approaches for model validation in order to allow for an *automated* validation of a given set of frame conditions (Sect. 6).

While the proposed methodologies are in principle not restricted to a particular modeling language, in the following we concentrate on UML/OCL models as the UML is a widely established modeling language in software as well as hardware design. Moreover, there is a variety of powerful tools (for the general design as well as the validation and verification of corresponding models) that can be built on. In fact, this allows to provide the designer with prototypical tools that implement the proposed methodologies and, thus, aid the designer in the proper definition of frame conditions.

2   Preliminaries

In this section, we introduce basic concepts and notions of UML/OCL by means of the running example that will also be later on used to illustrate the basic concepts of frame conditions as well as the proposed methodologies for their generation and validation.

The *Unified Modeling Language* (UML) [33] is one of the standard modeling languages which allows, e.g., the description of a design by means of *class diagrams*. Since UML version 1.1, the respective models can additionally be enriched by descriptions formulated in the *Object Constraint Language* (OCL) [26]—a declarative language that allows to impose additional textual constraints which further refine properties and relations between model elements.

In this work, we use as running example a slightly modified version of the access control system originally presented in [31]. In this system, access to buildings is granted based on magnetic cards as authentication method. The cards are checked at turnstiles at the buildings' entries and exits. The system is modeled in terms of the UML class diagram (enriched with textual OCL constraints) depicted in Fig. 1. Here, the pure UML part describes the structure of the system in terms of classes (e.g., *Building, MagneticCard, Turnstile*), attributes (e.g., `Building::inside`), and available operations of each class (e.g., `Turnstile::goThrough()`) as well as relationships between the classes in terms of associations (e.g., the relation between turnstiles and buildings). For the sake of a convenient reference, we will refer to the union of all attributes (of all classes) together with all associations/relations of a model as the set of *model elements*.

The kinds of constraints that can be formulated using pure UML essentially comprise *multiplicity constraints* (e.g., stating that each turnstile is associated with a unique **building** and that each building contains at least two turnstiles (**gates**) or are concerned with the inheritance of classes (which is not present in the running example).

To enforce further constraints or properties of a system, textual OCL constraints are applied. To this end, invariants are used to describe properties such as the uniqueness of a magnetic card's ID (invariant **uniqueID**), the existence of at least one entry and one exit for each building (invariants **atLeastOneEntry** and **atLeastOneExit**) or the fact that permanently either the green or the red

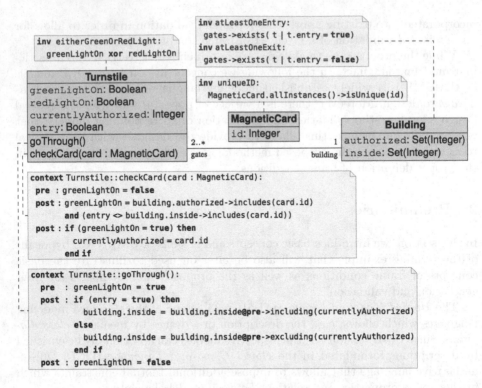

Fig. 1. Class diagram of the running example [25]

light of a turnstile is lit (invariant `eitherGreenOrRedLight`). In addition, OCL constraints are employed to formulate so-called *operation contracts* [22] which comprise *preconditions* (denoted by ◁) that describe necessary conditions to invoke an operation call in the first place as well as *postconditions* (denoted by ▷) that describe which properties can be taken for granted after the execution of the operation has been completed. For instance, the operation `checkCard()` can only be invoked on a turnstile if its green light is not on (precondition). The state of the green light after the operation has been executed depends on whether (a) the inserted card is in principle authorized to enter/leave the building (`building.authorized->includes(card.id)`) and whether (b) the card has been inserted on the "expected" side of the turnstile according to the logical state of the card owner (`entry <> building.inside-> includes(card.id)`). Note that the second part has been added in order to prevent multiple persons from using the same card to enter/leave a building one after the other. If these checks are passed, the postconditions enforce that the green light is lit and the ID of the inserted card is stored in the attribute `currentlyAuthorized`.

All these constraints determine which instantiations of the model (system states) and operation calls (transitions) are valid and which are not:

- A system state σ is a set of objects together with attribute values (instantiations of classes) and interconnecting links (instantiations of associations).

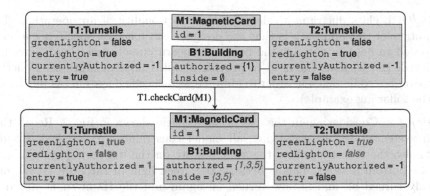

Fig. 2. A valid execution scenario for the operation `Turnstile::checkCard(..)`.

A state σ is termed *valid* if, and only if, it satisfies all UML constraints (multiplicity and inheritance) as well as all OCL invariants.

– A transition between two system states σ_1, σ_2 through an operation call ω (i.e., an operation op_ω called on some object from σ_1) is termed *valid* if, and only if, the preconditions $\lhd_\omega$ of ω are satisfied in σ_1 and the associated postconditions $\rhd_\omega$ are satisfied in σ_2[2].

A valid transition is denoted as $\sigma_1 \xrightarrow{\omega} \sigma_2$ and is termed *valid execution scenario* if, and only if, also both system states σ_1 and σ_2 are valid (which is not required in the definition of valid transitions).

Example 1. Figure 2 shows two valid system states comprising a single building with two turnstiles. In both states, all multiplicity constraints as well as invariants hold. As indicated, performing the operation call `checkCard(M1)` on turnstile T1 leads to the transition from the system state depicted on the top of Fig. 2 to the system state depicted on the bottom of Fig. 2. This transition is valid since all pre- and postconditions are satisfied. Overall, Fig. 2 shows a valid execution scenario for the operation `checkCard()`.

3   Frame Problem and Frame Conditions

In this section, we describe the frame problem in behavioral models and review different approaches for the introduction of frame conditions addressing this problem. This builds the basis for the following sections, where methods are proposed which assist the designer not only in the generation of frame conditions but also their validation.

Pre- and postconditions are frequently used as a means to describe behavioral aspects of models in general. Of course, pre- and postconditions are available in

---

[2] Note that the postconditions might also refer to the pre-state of the operation (σ_1) using the suffix @pre as, e.g., for `Turnstile::goThrough()` in the running example.

UML/OCL class diagrams to describe the functionality of an operation. The advantage of this approach is that the designer can focus on specifying *what* is supposed to happen without the need to concern oneself *how* this behavior is achieved, i.e., without the need to provide detailed implementations. Nonetheless, care has to be taken in order to obtain a well-specified system (as illustrated by the following example).

Example 2. Consider again the execution scenario shown in Fig. 2. Recall that both system states are valid, i.e., all model constraints are satisfied. Besides that, also the transition from the system state on the top to the system state on the bottom is valid. This is because the green light of turnstile T1 was previously turned off and is now turned on again and the ID of M1 is stored in the `currentlyAuthorized` attribute. This means that the preconditions of the operation `checkCard(M1)` as well as the postconditions are satisfied in the top and bottom system state, respectively.

In other words, while the transition of the system states discussed before in Example 1 is intended by the designer, it is additionally possible to turn the green light of the other turnstile T2 on or to add arbitrary IDs (e.g., 3 and 5) to the `inside` attribute of the building B1 or to change the set of `authorized` cards (highlighted in red and italics in Fig. 2). Although such a behavior is obviously not intended, it is completely in line with the postconditions.

This example illustrates a shortcoming of declarative languages like OCL and of pre- and postconditions in particular: It remains unclear or at least is made not clear enough which model elements are allowed to change during a transition. Pre- and postconditions do not comprehensively specify and—in general—do not allow to automatically infer what is within the *frame* of an operation. This means that the available description means in the model are under-specified which is usually refered to as the *frame problem* [4].

It should be noted that the frame problem does not only arise in the modeling domain but also in the context of software verification. In fact, a substantial body of research has focused on possible solutions (see, e.g., [3]) and corresponding approaches have been integrated into several verification tools like Boogie [21] or KeY [1]. Unfortunately, a direct transfer from the software verification domain to the modeling domain is not possible because there are crucial differences between both domains. More precisely:

- OCL in general allows one to access arbitrary objects via `allInstances()`.
- Associations are always bi-directional (in contrast to uni-directional pointers) such that changes to references always affect both ends.
- Object creation and deletion can be rather random as usually no precise implementation is given.

In contrast to the first two issues, many programming languages used in the software design process have `private` or `protected` attributes which, in general, prohibit arbitrary access.

Nonetheless, in the recent past different proposals have been made for addressing the frame problem in UML/OCL models by specifying so-called *frame*

```
1    context Turnstile::checkCard(card : MagneticCard):
2    ...
3    -- FrameConditions for Class Turnstile
4    post : Turnstile.allInstances()—>forAll( t |
5              t.entry = t.entry@pre
6              and t.building = t.building@pre
7              and (( self <> t ) implies
8                    (t.greenLightOn = t.greenLightOn@pre
9                      and t.redLightOn = t.redLightOn@pre
10                     and t.currentlyAuthorized = t.currentlyAuthorized@pre) )
11             )
12   post :    Turnstile.allInstances@pre() = Turnstile.allInstances()
13   -- FrameConditions for Class Building
14   post : Building.allInstances()—>forAll( b |
15              b.authorized = b.authorized@pre and b.inside = b.inside@pre )
16   post : Building.allInstances@pre() = Building.allInstances()
17   -- FrameConditions for Class MagneticCard
18   post : MagneticCard.allInstances()—>forAll( mc | mc.id = mc.id@pre )
19   post : MagneticCard.allInstances@pre() = MagneticCard.allInstances()
```

Fig. 3. Frame conditions for `checkCard(..)` using the *explicit postconditions* approach.

```
self.greenLightOn, self.building, self.building.authorized, self.entry,
card.id <—> MagneticCard.id, self.building.inside, self.currentlyAuthorized
```

Fig. 4. List of model elements referenced within the postconditions of the operation `checkCard(..)`. [25]

conditions. Of course, they are inspired by the above mentioned approaches. In the following, we will shortly review a selection of these proposals:

– **Explicit Postconditions:** A straightforward approach is to explicitly specify what is *not* in the frame by extending the postconditions with constraints like `modelElem = modelElem@pre` for all unaffected model elements. Following this approach for the operation `Turnstile::checkCard(..)` from the running example, the frame conditions as shown in Fig. 3 can be formulated. Remarkably, the *new* set of postconditions is approximately three times bigger than the original pre- and postconditions of the operation. This shows the drawback of this approach: it is time-consuming to manually create the constraints in the first place. In addition, maintaining them later in the case of design changes will also result in cumbersome tasks. A case study that clearly demonstrates this approach as well as its drawbacks can be found in [14].

– **Nothing Else Changes:** An alternative to explicitly writing down frame conditions is given by the idea to automatically derive them from the postconditions using a paradigm such as *nothing else changes* [7,8]. The working hypothesis of this paradigm is that every model element that is referenced within the postconditions is included in the frame of what may change—but nothing else. In the best case, this implicit approach requires no additional efforts by the designer. However, in general, the resulting frame conditions

```
1     context Turnstile::checkCard(card : MagneticCard):
2     ...
3     -- Implicit Dependency
4     post : redLightOn = not greenLightOn
5     -- FrameConditions for Class Turnstile
6     post : self.entry = self.entry@pre
7     post : self.building = self.building@pre
8     -- FrameConditions for Class Building
9     post : Building.allInstances()-->forAll( b |
10              b.authorized = b.authorized@pre and b.inside = b.inside@pre )
11    post : Building.allInstances@pre() = Building.allInstances()
12    -- FrameConditions for Class MagneticCard
13    post : MagneticCard.allInstances()-->forAll( mc | mc.id = mc.id@pre )
14    post : MagneticCard.allInstances@pre() = MagneticCard.allInstances()
```

Fig. 5. Additional postconditions for `checkCard(..)` required for the *nothing else changes* approach.

```
1     context Turnstile::checkCard(card : MagneticCard):
2     ...
3     -- FrameConditions for Class Turnstile
4     modifies only : self::greenLightOn
5     modifies only : self::redLightOn
6     modifies only : self::currentlyAuthorized
7
8     context Turnstile::goThrough():
9     ...
10    -- FrameConditions for Class Turnstile
11    modifies only : self::greenLightOn
12    modifies only : self::redLightOn
13    modifies only : self.building::inside
```

Fig. 6. Frame conditions for `checkCard(..)` and `goThrough()` using the *modifies only* approach [25].

are often not exactly what the designer intended and it can be non-trivial to adjust them manually—which would have to be done by rewriting the postconditions or adding further ones.

As an example, consider again the operation `checkCard(..)`. Figure 4 lists the model elements that are referenced within the postconditions. Note that including precisely these model elements in the operation's frame would still allow for most of the unwanted changes discussed in Example 2, while changes to `redLightOn` (as required to fulfill the implicit dependency that is expressed in the invariant `eitherGreenOrRedLight`) would not be permitted. To this end, Fig. 5 presents the additional postconditions that would be required in order to obtain comprehensive frame conditions for the operation `checkCard(..)`.

– **Modifies Only Statements:** A complementary approach has been suggested by Kosiuczenko [19,20]. The approach is complementary because, instead of forbidding changes of model elements, the changeability of them is explicitly allowed. More precisely, the general idea is to specify the set of variable model elements, i.e., model elements that are allowed to be changed during an operation call—together with the pre- and postconditions in terms of *modifies only* statements[3], which are of the form

`modifies only: scope::modelElement.`

For instance, the clause `modifies only: self::greenLightOn` expresses that the operation may only change the attribute `greenLightOn` of the turnstile on which the operation is called (`self`). Likewise, the complete frame conditions for the operations `Turnstile::checkCard(..)` and `Turnstile::goThrough()` are shown in Fig. 6. Note that the scope can also be more complex than just `self` and may contain navigation or collections as in Line 13. In addition, it is even possible to allow objects of a certain class to be created or deleted during an operation call using the construct `Class::allInstances()`.

Using this approach, the designer can precisely define frame conditions in a much more comfortable, understandable, and maintainable fashion compared to the other two approaches.

To sum up the results of this section, frame conditions are very important in order to address the frame problem and obtain comprehensive behavioral descriptions in UML/OCL models. Various approaches to their specification exist, each with complementary strengths and weaknesses.

4   Generation of Frame Conditions

The related work reviewed in the previous section provides various description means that enable designers to address the frame problem by precisely describing the behavior of operations. However, all these description means only provide a syntax and semantic for the definition of the frame conditions, but it remains a non-trivial task to define them properly such that they complete the model in the intended way. Even if the designer fully understands the considered model as well as its dependencies, deriving the actual frame conditions for a given model, i.e., for all its operations, remains a cumbersome task. Existing solutions for that rely on "workarounds" only, i.e., methods based on:

- *Manual definition*, i.e., methods which completely rely on a manual refinement of the model like, e.g., the approach proposed in [16]. This leaves the burden solely on the designer (who requires the respective design understanding) and, at the same time, is time consuming. A noteable case study that clearly illustrates the weaknesses and limits of this strategy can be found in [14].

---

[3] *Modifies only* statements were originally introduced as *invariability clauses* by Kosiuczenko [19]. A variation of this idea is to specify the set of variable model elements within the postconditions using an OCL primitive `modifiedOnly(Set)` [5].

– *Implicit definition,* i.e., methods which simply apply naive schemes such as enforcing all model elements which are not restricted by originally provided constraints to remain unchanged (and, hence, ignore implicit relations and side-effects of the respective model elements). Approaches such as proposed in [34] are representatives for this.

In order to avoid the problems caused by these unsatisfactory solutions, improvements in the *extraction of frame conditions* are required, i.e., solutions which neither leave the burden of the extraction entirely on the designer (avoiding the introduction of another time-consuming and expensive design step) nor are completely automatic (which, due to ambiguities and inaccuracies, will not lead to satisfactory results anyway). In the following, we present a semi-automatic approach (originally proposed in [23, 24]) that automatically extracts a preliminary set of frame conditions in terms of so-called hypotheses which is then to be approved or checked by the designer. The aim of this approach is to filter out rather definite cases and pinpoint the designer to a subset of model elements which require a more detailed consideration.

To this end, *all* model elements are considered at the beginning. For each of them, it is determined which of these elements shall be variable and, if so, for which objects, i.e., for which *scope*. These questions may not always be answered by means of automatic methods, due to the fact that the models' semantics, especially the OCL constraints, often allow for several interpretations. Consequently, the general idea of the proposed approach is an automatic model analysis to provide preliminary answers (called *hypotheses* in the following) by means of a distinction between the following categories:

– *Variable elements,* i.e., elements that are evidently meant to be modified by the respective operation since this modification is (precisely) constrained.
– *Unaffected elements,* i.e., elements that are evidently not meant to be affected by the respective operation. These elements should simply keep their current value.
– *Ambiguous elements,* i.e., elements where it remains unclear whether they are supposed to be modified by the operation or not. Hence, they have to be inspected more thoroughly by the designer.

As arbitrary changes are to be allowed for elements that are defined to be in an operations' frame of change, the classification *variable* is only to be assigned when there is strong evidence for it and precise information about the affected objects is known. Following the *"nothing else changes"* scheme (cf. Sect. 3), the focus is restricted to elements that are mentioned within the contractual scope of the current operation, while elements for which there is no clear evidence for a relation to the operation are immediately excluded. For this purpose, three sources that define the scope of operations in contractual designs are considered:

– *Postconditions* are the main source as they constrain the post-state and, therefore, describe the changes performed during an operation call in a direct manner.

– *Invariants* define further requirements that have to be satisfied at all times, in particular also in the post-state of the operation in addition to postconditions. To this end, they may establish implicit dependencies to further elements which are relevant for the frame conditions as they require additional modifications in order to reach a valid system state.
– *Preconditions* provide assured information about the pre-state of an operation call, i.e., precise values or properties that can be useful to clarify whether elements keep or change their value during the operation call.

While focusing on these constraints already gives a good approximation of the set of possibly relevant elements, definitive decisions on the elements' variability cannot always be provided automatically. Instead, a heuristic approach is applied to derive hypotheses from the respective OCL constraints, i.e., tuples composed of a model element, a scope-term (describing the set of objects on which the hypothesis applies), and a preliminary classification (variable, ambiguous, or unaffected).

Example 3. For instance, for the operation `goThrough()` the approach suggests to consider the model elements `self.greenLightOn` and `building.inside` as affected (with high probability) and to have a more thorough look at `self. currentlyAuthorized`, `self.entry`, and `self.redLightOn` (which also occur in the postconditions or may have a dependency via invariants, respectively).

Including all mentioned model elements in the frame of change (e.g., using corresponding *modifies only* statements) yields frame conditions that allow for much more changes than intended by the designer. Consequently, the impact of the individual model elements needs to be analyzed and unnecessary elements have to be dropped.

An evaluation on several example models known from the literature has shown that the obtained hypotheses often have a very good quality and only a tiny fraction are false-positives/false-negatives. Nonetheless, for generating the final set of frame conditions, the hypotheses need to be validated and ambiguities have to be clarified (see [24] for details on that).

Overall, the proposed methodology is a big improvement considering that, by default, designers are supposed to generate *all* frame conditions manually. In fact, the proposed methodology essentially boils down these efforts to a brief consideration of hypotheses out of which just a few ambiguous elements remain to be inspected in detail. Nonetheless, the approach cannot guarantee that the derived frame conditions are indeed correct or complete the model description in the actually intended way. Consequently, (automatic) methods for the validation of frame conditions would be of great help to support the designer in this design step. A corresponding method and its implementation on top of powerful reasoning engines is discussed in the following sections.

5   Validation Objectives of Frame Conditions

Once a (preliminary) set of frame conditions has been derived, e.g., using the approach reviewed in the previous section, there is a need to validate whether the derived frame conditions are correct and complete the specification of the model in the actually intended way. To this end, the frame conditions need to be analyzed with the particular aim to check their correctness and adequateness. Here, three primary objectives can be distinguished [25]:

1. Most importantly, to judge the correctness of frame conditions, it is essential to investigate their *consistency* w.r.t. the basic model (i.e., do the obtained frame conditions still allow for a valid execution of the operations?).
2. On top of that, an analysis of the effect of different sets of frame conditions, i.e., their possible *equivalence* or non-equivalence, is of interest in order to judge whether they indeed complete the model in the intended way. For instance, this analysis can be conducted to investigate the effect of different scope-terms or different classifications (variable, unaffected) for individual model elements.
3. Furthermore, for several purposes (e.g., for the sake of obtaining a small/compact set of frame conditions or for debugging inconsistent frame conditions) the designer may be interested in dependencies between different (sub-)sets of frame conditions, i.e., in analyzing *independence* of frame conditions.

In the following, the three above-mentioned analysis objectives are discussed in more detail and described in a formal way in order to allow for an automatic analysis (which will be discussed in the following section). This automation is essential as a manual analysis of the effect of frame conditions quickly becomes infeasible even for simple models.

As proposed in [25], the analysis is conducted by studying the impact of frame conditions on the set of valid *execution scenarios* (cf. Sect. 2). Recall that this set (in the following denoted by $\mathbb{S}$) is constituted by all valid transitions $\sigma_1 \xrightarrow{\omega} \sigma_2$ between valid system states σ_1, σ_2. A transition is induced by an operation call ω which consists of an object $o_\omega \in \sigma_1$, an operation op_ω that is called on o_ω and a (possibly empty) set of parameters. The transition $\sigma_1 \xrightarrow{\omega} \sigma_2$ is termed valid if, and only if, the preconditions $\lhd_\omega$ of ω are satisfied in σ_1 and its postconditions $\rhd_\omega$ are satisfied in σ_2 (see the top of Fig. 7). Note that the particular operation op_ω can be arbitrary for the transitions in $\mathbb{S}$.

Now, to focus on individual operations, the valid execution scenarios of a model are classified by the corresponding operation op_ω. This yields a partition ω of the set of all valid scenarios of a model into disjoint subsets $\mathbb{S}_{op} = \{\sigma_1 \xrightarrow{\omega} \sigma_2 \in \mathbb{S} \mid op_\omega = op\}$ for each operation op (of any class) of the model (see the center of Fig. 7). Note, however, that only pre- and post-conditions, but no frame conditions have been taken into account so far. Consequently, in order to analyze a particular set of frame conditions, a further restriction to those execution scenarios that additionally satisfy the given frame conditions (denoted by $\mathcal{F}$) is applied and the corresponding subsets $\mathbb{S}_{op}^{\mathcal{F}} \subset \mathbb{S}_{op}$ are considered (see the bottom of Fig. 7).

Using this notation, the above-mentioned objectives can be formalized as follows.

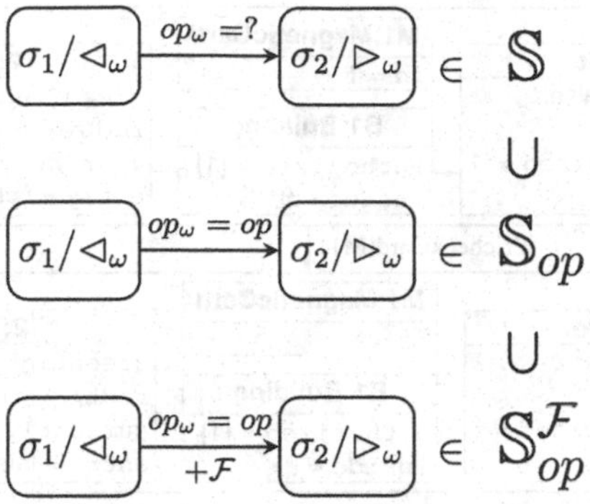

Fig. 7. Execution scenarios [25].

5.1 Consistency

The major criterion for the quality and validity of well-defined frame conditions is that they are consistent with the (original) contractual specification of the operation. More precisely, assuming that an operation contract in terms of pre- and postconditions is free of contradictions and in principle allows for an execution of the operation ($\mathbb{S}_{op} \neq \emptyset$), this property shall be preserved when additionally enforcing the frame conditions ($\mathbb{S}_{op}^{\mathcal{F}} \neq \emptyset$). In other words, frame conditions can only be considered consistent, if they are compatible with at least one execution scenario.

To strengthen the significance of this objective, the same compatibility can be required for a set of *pivot scenarios* $P \subset \mathbb{S}_{op}$ (provided by the designer) that characterize the intended behavior of the operation, i.e., it is checked whether $P \subset \mathbb{S}_{op}^{\mathcal{F}}$. In a similar fashion, one may also employ scenarios that characterize unintended behavior and, thus, shall be incompatible to well-defined frame conditions. For most significant results, the pivot scenarios shall cover the operation's functionality as comprehensively as possible, i.e., affect as many model elements as possible, be as complementary as possible, and desirably also cover corner-cases.

Example 4. Consider the operation checkCard() from the running example (Fig. 1) together with the frame conditions specified in Fig. 3. The operation contract in principle allows for an execution of the operation ($\mathbb{S}_{\texttt{checkCard()}} \neq \emptyset$), since the transition from Fig. 2 (termed ω_0 in the following) is a valid execution scenario as shown above. However, the frame conditions do not allow the changes highlighted in red: B1::inside is required to remain constant in Line 15 of Fig. 3 and switching the lights of T2 is prohibited by Lines 8–9. Overall, this means $\omega_0 \notin \mathbb{S}_{\texttt{checkCard()}}^{\mathcal{F}}$. Nonetheless, the frame conditions themselves are clearly consistent. For instance, when refraining from the changes highlighted in red, i.e., the attributes of B1 and T2 do not change, the resulting transition (shown in Fig. 8(a)) is still a valid execution scenario and is also compatible with the frame conditions. A meaningful set of complementary pivot scenarios would cover the

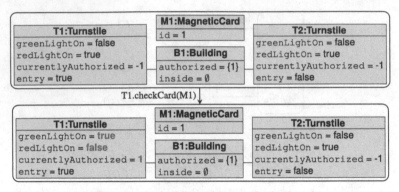

(a) Entering the building with an authorized card

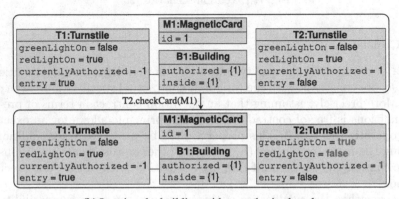

(b) Leaving the building with an authorized card

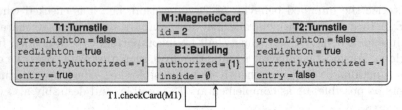

(c) Entering the building with an unauthorized card

Fig. 8. Pivot scenarios for the operation `checkCard()` [25].

cases of leaving and entering the building (cf. Figs. 8(a) and (b)) as well as checking an authorized or unauthorized card (Fig. 8(c)).

5.2 Equivalence

Aiming at the relationship between different sets of frame conditions, the first important objective is to check for equivalence. More precisely, given two sets of frame conditions $\mathcal{F}_1$ and $\mathcal{F}_2$ we are interested to know whether they lead to the same set of valid execution scenarios ($\mathbb{S}_{op}^{\mathcal{F}_1} = \mathbb{S}_{op}^{\mathcal{F}_2}$) or, if not, what the reasons for the non-equivalence are. To this end, the aim is to find scenarios that are only compatible with one set of frame conditions, but not with the other, i.e., scenarios from the symmetric difference $\mathbb{S}_{op}^{\mathcal{F}_1} \triangle \mathbb{S}_{op}^{\mathcal{F}_2} = (\mathbb{S}_{op}^{\mathcal{F}_1} \setminus \mathbb{S}_{op}^{\mathcal{F}_2}) \cup (\mathbb{S}_{op}^{\mathcal{F}_2} \setminus \mathbb{S}_{op}^{\mathcal{F}_1})$. The check can be performed on sets of frame conditions that are only slight variations of each other, but also if they are specified using different approaches/formalisms. Again, pivot scenarios can be employed to prove equivalence on a relevant subset of scenarios or to allow for a more detailed analysis of the differences.

Example 5. Consider again the operation `checkCard()` from the running example (as in the previous example). Comparing the frame conditions from Fig. 3 (specified as explicit postconditions) and Fig. 6 (specified using *modifies only* statements) shows that they are indeed equivalent. However, if the second *modifies only* statement regarding `self::redLightOn` would have been forgotten in the specification, an evaluation of the pivot scenarios from Fig. 8 shows that only the third one is still compatible, while the first two scenarios are no longer compatible. A deeper analysis of the second scenario reveals that only `T2::greenLightOn` and `T2::redLightOn` are modified which provides a hint on the missing *modifies only* statement for `self::redLightOn`.

5.3   Independence

The second objective aiming at analyzing the relationship between different sets of frame condition addresses dependencies between individual frame conditions. To this end, two sets of frame conditions $\mathcal{F}_1, \mathcal{F}_2$ are combined to a set $\mathcal{F}_1 \cup \mathcal{F}_2$ whose frame of change is essentially the union of the respective frames of $\mathcal{F}_1$ and $\mathcal{F}_2$. In other words, a model element is allowed to be modified according to $\mathcal{F}_1 \cup \mathcal{F}_2$ if, and only if, it is allowed to be modified according to at least one set of frame conditions.

Then, several different cases are possible:

- $\mathcal{F}_1 \cup \mathcal{F}_2$ is consistent ($\mathbb{S}_{op}^{\mathcal{F}_1 \cup \mathcal{F}_2} \neq \emptyset$), although neither $\mathcal{F}_1$ nor $\mathcal{F}_2$ (considered separately) are consistent. This means that $\mathcal{F}_1$ and $\mathcal{F}_2$ require each other.
- $\mathcal{F}_1 \cup \mathcal{F}_2$ and $\mathcal{F}_i$ are consistent ($i = 1$ and/or $i = 2$). This means that $\mathcal{F}_i$ is independent from the other set of frame conditions $\mathcal{F}_{3-i}$.
- $\mathcal{F}_1 \cup \mathcal{F}_2$ is not consistent ($\mathbb{S}_{op}^{\mathcal{F}_1 \cup \mathcal{F}_2} = \emptyset$), although $\mathcal{F}_1$ or $\mathcal{F}_2$ (considered separately) are consistent. This means that $\mathcal{F}_1$ and $\mathcal{F}_2$ exclude each other.
- Neither $\mathcal{F}_1 \cup \mathcal{F}_2$, nor $\mathcal{F}_1$, nor $\mathcal{F}_2$ are consistent. This only implies that $\mathcal{F}_1$ and $\mathcal{F}_2$ are not sufficient to obtain complete or consistent frame conditions.

In order to obtain more detailed information about the particular dependencies, we can go down to the level of model elements and analyze what happens if particular model elements are not only allowed to be modified, but are required to actually be subject to changes. More precisely, we consider a set of model elements $M = \{m_1, \ldots, m_k\}$ (all included in the frame of $\mathcal{F}_1$) together with another model element $m_0 \notin M$ (included in the frame of $\mathcal{F}_2$). If all elements

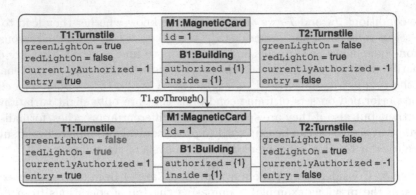

Fig. 9. Entering a building without changing the attribute `building.inside` [25].

from M are actually changed in an execution scenario, m_0 can either (a) be forced to be modified as well, (b) be forced to remain constant, or (c) be allowed to behave either way, i.e., do not have an immediate dependency to the model elements in M.

Example 6. Consider the operation `goThrough()` from the running example together with the *modifies only* statements as listed in Fig. 6. Set $\mathcal{F}_1$ to be the first *modifies only* statement (`self::greenLightOn`) and $\mathcal{F}_2$ to contain the two remaining statements (`self::redLightOn` and `self.building::inside`). Then, $\mathcal{F}_2$ requires $\mathcal{F}_1$ and vice versa. In fact, it can be shown that a modification of `building.inside` and/or `self.redLightOn` implies that also `self.greenLightOn` needs to be modified. On the contrary, a change to `self.greenLightOn` also requires `self.redLightOn` to be modified, but not necessarily also `building.inside`. In fact, if the magnetic card whose ID is stored in `currentlyAuthorized` is—by incidence—logically already inside/outside the building, a building can be entered/left with no change to `building.inside` (cf. Fig. 9). This dependency becomes apparent at the level of frame conditions if one moves the second *modifies only* statement (`self::redLightOn`) from $\mathcal{F}_2$ to $\mathcal{F}_1$. Then, $\mathcal{F}_2$ still requires $\mathcal{F}_1$, but not vice versa.

Overall, Fig. 10 summarizes the three proposed objectives for the analysis and validation of frame conditions. As already illustrated by the provided examples, the manual evaluation can be a very elaborate task. Consequently, the objectives need to be evaluated in an automatic fashion in order to be the basis of a really useful validation methodology. In the following, we outline exemplarily for UML/OCL models how this aim can be achieved.

6   Automated Validation of Frame Conditions

In order to automatically analyze frame conditions w. r. t. the objectives introduced above, it seems promising to employ approaches for automatic reasoning.

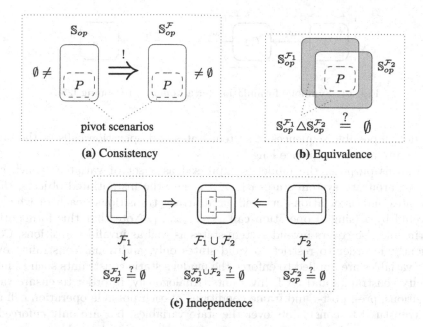

Fig. 10. Summary of analysis objectives [25].

In fact, in the domain of UML/OCL models these have shown to be very powerful tools for determining execution scenarios with a given property (or proving the non-existence of such scenarios). In the following we, thus, focus on UML/OCL models for the sake of using one of these tools as a basis for our prototypical implementation.

To this end, we first review corresponding approaches in Sect. 6.1. Afterwards, we describe in Sect. 6.2 how the analysis objectives can be formulated on top of these solutions, while Sect. 6.3 provides details about the actually implemented (prototype) tool for an automatic validation of frame conditions.

6.1 Automatic Reasoning on UML/OCL Models

In the recent past, several approaches for automatic reasoning on UML/OCL models have been proposed which aim at the validation and verification of structural as well as behavioral aspects (see, e.g., [2,6,9–11,18,28,30,32,34,35]). Here, we focus on approaches using solvers for *Boolean Satisfiability* (SAT) or *Satisfiability Modulo Theories* (SMT) problems, see, e.g., [18,30].

The general idea of these approaches is sketched by means of Fig. 11. Instead of explicitly enumerating all possible system states and operation calls, they utilize a symbolic formulation of the given UML/OCL model which allows to

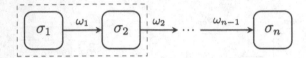

Fig. 11. Symbolic formulation for automated reasoning [25].

consider all possible sequences of system states and operation calls at the same time (up to a given sequence length n)[4].

For this purpose, the model is expressed as a set of variables which can describe arbitrary system states $\sigma_1, \ldots, \sigma_n$, i.e., the instantiated objects, their attributes and associations, as well as arbitrary transitions—each of which is triggered by a (single) operation call $\omega_1, \ldots, \omega_{n-1}$. Note that this formulation in principle also covers invalid system states as well as invalid transitions. Consequently, in order to restrict to valid states only, additional constraints over these variables are applied to enforce the model's static constraints such as multiplicity constraints and OCL invariants. Analogously, in order to ensure valid transitions, pre-, post-, and frame conditions of each possible operation call are also translated to constraints over the state variables, but are only enforced if the transition ω_i is chosen to be the corresponding operation. More precisely, the following formulation is applied[5]:

Formulation 1. For a sequence of system states $\sigma_1, \ldots, \sigma_n$, let Ω_i be the set of all operation calls that are available within system state σ_i ($i = 1, \ldots, n$). Then, for each of the transitions ω_i ($i = 1, \ldots, n - 1$) from a system state σ_i to the succeeding state σ_{i+1} it is required that

$$\bigwedge_{\omega \in \Omega_i} (\omega_i = \omega) \Rightarrow ([\![\lhd_\omega]\!] \wedge [\![\rhd_\omega]\!] \wedge [\![\mathcal{F}_\omega]\!])) \tag{1}$$

holds, where

- $[\![\lhd_\omega]\!]$ is a constraint enforcing the preconditions of ω for system state σ_i,
- $[\![\rhd_\omega]\!]$ is a constraint enforcing the postconditions of ω for system state σ_{i+1}, maybe by using σ_i as well, and
- $[\![\mathcal{F}_\omega]\!]$ is a constraint enforcing the frame conditions for the entire transition (i.e., for both system states).

Based on this formulation, afterwards the particular validation or verification objective can be formulated in terms of further specific constraints. For instance,

---

[4] In addition to limiting the sequence length, all these approaches require further *problem bounds* in order to limit the search space, i.e., they need to be provided with a fixed number or at least a range of objects that shall be instantiated as well as a finite domain for all data types.

[5] Note that, in the following, an abstract description is provided which is sufficient for the purposes of this work. For a more detailed treatment of the respective formulation, we refer to [30].

in order to check whether a certain operation `Class::op()` is executable at all, a constraint stating that $\omega_1 = o_1.op() \vee \ldots \vee \omega_1 = o_k.op()$ (where o_1 to o_k are the possibly instantiated objects of `Class` in σ_1) needs to be added. Finally, the complete problem instance is passed to a reasoning engine (solver) which is supposed to determine a *satisfying assignment* to all variables, i.e., an assignment that satisfies all of the constraints. If the solver returns SAT, i.e., a satisfying assignment has been determined, a corresponding sequence of valid system states and transitions (a so-called *witness* of the problem instance) can be extracted. Otherwise, if the solver returns UNSAT, it has been proven that no satisfying assignment exists (within the specified problem bounds)[6].

6.2 Incorporating the Validation Objectives

In the following, we utilize the reasoning scheme reviewed above for the analysis of frame conditions. For this purpose, we apply as validation or verification objective the previously proposed analysis objectives, namely consistency, equivalence, or independence of frame conditions. To this end, it is important to note that we may restrict to a single transition between two system states and also to one particular operation (as illustrated by the dashed box in Fig. 11). While all effects that we are interested in are still present in this restricted scenario, the complexity of the formulation can be reduced significantly. Taking this into account, the considered objectives and resulting decision problems can be formulated as follows.

Consistency. In order to analyze the consistency for given frame conditions $\mathcal{F}$ regarding an operation op, the formulation simply has to ask "Does there exist a valid execution scenario for operation op?" ($\mathbb{S}_{op}^{\mathcal{F}} \neq \emptyset$). As validity is ensured implicitly by the general formulation, this boils down to the question whether the operation op is executable at all. As already discussed above, no further constraints have to be applied to answer this question besides the restriction of ω_1 to the operation under consideration.

In order to check whether a pivot scenario $\omega_p \in P$ given in terms of a pair of a pre- and a poststate is valid ($\omega_p \in \mathbb{S}_{op}^{\mathcal{F}}$), the specified values of attributes, links, etc. additionally have to be enforced in the corresponding state.

Example 7. In order to enforce the pivot scenario from Fig. 8(a), the constraints listed in Fig. 12 have to be added.

If these formulations return SAT, it has been shown that $\mathbb{S}_{op}^{\mathcal{F}} \neq \emptyset$ or $\omega_p \in \mathbb{S}_{op}^{\mathcal{F}}$, respectively, and a valid execution scenario can be extracted from the satisfying assignment. If UNSAT is returned, it has been proven that no valid execution scenario exists or that the given scenario ω_p is not valid, respectively.

Note that it is possible to let the solver check a set P of multiple alternative pivot scenarios at the same time. However, in case of SAT, we would not be able

---

[6] Note that the solver will always conclude at some point due to the finite search space.

```
1  σ₁::T1::greenLightOn = false
2  σ₁::T1::redLightOn = true
3  ...
4  σ₁::T1::building = σ₁::B1
5  ...
6  σ₂::T1::greenLightOn = true
7  σ₂::T1::redLightOn = false
8  ...
9  ω₁ = σ₁::T1.checkCard(σ₁::M1)
```

Fig. 12. Constraints for the pivot scenario from Fig. 8(a) [25].

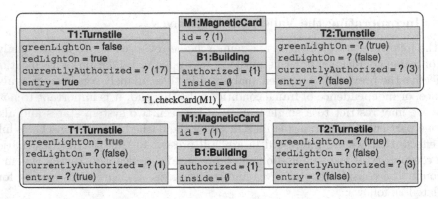

Fig. 13. Partially specified pivot scenario [25].

to deduce that P is entirely contained in $\mathbb{S}_{op}^{\mathcal{F}}$, as the found witness only implies that $P \cap \mathbb{S}_{op}^{\mathcal{F}} \neq \emptyset$.

Nonetheless, there is a useful application of this capability, namely partially specified pivot scenarios where values of model elements can be left open and will be assigned by the solver if, and only if, there is a possible assignment that belongs to a valid scenario.

Example 8. Figure 13 shows a pivot scenario where only a few attribute values are actually specified, while the majority is not specified (indicated by a "?"). For the corresponding variables, the solver determines a satisfying assignment (shown in blue color) which extends the partially specified scenario to a completely specified scenario that is valid and compatible with the given frame conditions.

Equivalence. In order to prove the equivalence of two sets of frame conditions $\mathcal{F}_1$ and $\mathcal{F}_2$, i.e. to show that $\mathbb{S}_{op}^{\mathcal{F}_1} = \mathbb{S}_{op}^{\mathcal{F}_2}$, we ask the solver to find a counterexample that would show that $\mathbb{S}_{op}^{\mathcal{F}_1} \neq \mathbb{S}_{op}^{\mathcal{F}_2}$. For this purpose, we ask the solver whether there exists an execution scenario $\omega \in (\mathbb{S}_{op}^{\mathcal{F}_1} \setminus \mathbb{S}_{op}^{\mathcal{F}_2}) \cup (\mathbb{S}_{op}^{\mathcal{F}_2} \setminus \mathbb{S}_{op}^{\mathcal{F}_1})$, i.e., a scenario that is only valid when enforcing one set of frame conditions, but not for the other. Using the standard formulation (cf. Eq. (1)), we can only enforce either $[\![\mathcal{F}_{1,\omega}]\!]$ or $[\![\mathcal{F}_{2,\omega}]\!]$ at the same time. However, as the corresponding constraints are commonly generated in an automatic fashion from the original description of frame conditions, there is no reason why one should not enforce, e.g., the logical negation $\neg[\![\mathcal{F}_{i,\omega}]\!]$ instead of $[\![\mathcal{F}_{i,\omega}]\!]$ $(i = 1, 2)$. Then, only those scenarios would be considered "valid" by the solver which are *not* compatible with the respective frame conditions. This can be exploited for our purpose by enforcing the constraint

$$((\,[\![\mathcal{F}_{1,\omega}]\!] \wedge \neg[\![\mathcal{F}_{2,\omega}]\!]) \vee ([\![\mathcal{F}_{2,\omega}]\!] \wedge \neg[\![\mathcal{F}_{1,\omega}]\!]))$$

instead of $[\![\mathcal{F}_{\omega}]\!]$ in Eq. (1).

If this formulation returns UNSAT, it has been proven that the symmetric difference $(\mathbb{S}_{op}^{\mathcal{F}_1} \setminus \mathbb{S}_{op}^{\mathcal{F}_2}) \cup (\mathbb{S}_{op}^{\mathcal{F}_2} \setminus \mathbb{S}_{op}^{\mathcal{F}_1})$ is indeed empty. This is logically equivalent to $\mathbb{S}_{op}^{\mathcal{F}_1} = \mathbb{S}_{op}^{\mathcal{F}_2}$, i.e., both sets of frame conditions are equivalent. If SAT is returned, an execution scenario can be extracted from the satisfying assignment which is valid for exactly one set of frame conditions (but not for the other). This scenario can then be analyzed further.

Example 9. Consider the frame conditions specified in Fig. 6. If one drops either of the first two *modifies only* statements (Line 4 or 5), one obtains frame conditions that are incompatible with any scenario in which the performed checks succeed and access is granted. Dropping the third statement (Line 6) makes it impossible to store the card's ID in case of success. Overall, this shows that the initial set of frame conditions is already minimal. A similar methodology using consistency and equivalence checks can be applied on any model.

Note that equivalence can either be checked for the frame conditions of a single operation or for all operations of the considered model at once. However, in the latter case, a possible witness will reveal only one of possibly multiple operations for which the frame conditions are not equivalent.

Independence. Determining dependencies between different sets of frame conditions $\mathcal{F}_1$ and $\mathcal{F}_2$ essentially boils down to performing consistency checks on $\mathcal{F}_1$, $\mathcal{F}_2$ and $\mathcal{F}_1 \cup \mathcal{F}_2$. Unfortunately, it is in general not possible to automatically derive the constraint $[\![(\mathcal{F}_1 \cup \mathcal{F}_2)_{\omega}]\!]$ for the frame conditions $\mathcal{F}_1 \cup \mathcal{F}_2$ from the constraints $[\![\mathcal{F}_{1,\omega}]\!]$ and $[\![\mathcal{F}_{2,\omega}]\!]$. In fact, only when the frame conditions are specified using *modifies only* statements, the approach presented in [27] can be employed to do this automatically. More precisely, the constraints $[\![\mathcal{F}_{1,\omega}]\!]$ and $[\![\mathcal{F}_{2,\omega}]\!]$ are constructed using so-called variability maps which store for each model element whether it may be modified or not. Then, the logical disjunction of these maps precisely gives $[\![(\mathcal{J}_1 \cup \mathcal{J}_2)_{\omega}]\!]$. In all other cases, $\mathcal{F}_1 \cup \mathcal{F}_2$ is required to be specified manually which can be a highly elaborate and non-trivial task.

In order to determine dependencies between changes to model elements from a set $M = \{m_1, \ldots, m_k\}$ and changes to a model element $m_0 \notin M$, the solver is asked to determine two different execution scenarios. In these scenarios, all elements from the set M are required to be modified using constraints like `modelElem <> modelElem@pre` or `modelElements->exists(m | m <> m@pre)` (depending on whether a single or multiple instances of the model element are included in the frame), while (1) the model element m_0 is required to be modified using similar constraints in one scenario and (2) m_0 is required to keep its value (`m0 = m0@pre` or `m0->forAll(m | m = m@pre)`) in the other scenario.

If the solver can determine a valid execution scenario in both cases, there is no dependency. If the solver can determine a valid execution scenario only in one case, it follows that m_0 is either forced to change or to remain constant, respectively. If the solver returns UNSAT in both cases (and the frame conditions are consistent in principle), one can deduce that there already has to be a dependency between the model elements of M such that not all of them may be changed at once.

6.3   Implementation

Having these problem formulations, the objectives proposed in the previous section can be evaluated automatically using approaches for automated reasoning on UML/OCL models. To this end, we implemented the presented concepts and formulations for the analysis of frame conditions on top of the model verification approach presented in [30]. The general idea of this approach is to translate the verification task into a *Satisfiability Modulo Theories* (SMT) problem. The corresponding symbolic formulation is created automatically in terms of the SMT-LIB bit-vector logic QF_BV. Then, the problem instance can be solved using so-called SMT solvers (e.g., Z3 [12]). These solvers allow for an efficient traversal of large search spaces and, hence, are suitable to determine precise assignments to the symbolic formulation and, by this, a sequence of transitions satisfying the considered verification objective. A big advantage of this particular approach regarding the analysis of frame conditions is that it natively supports the *nothing else changes* approach as well as *modifies only* statements according to the symbolic formulation proposed in [27,29]. More precisely, as already indicated above, the constraints $[\![\mathcal{F}]\!]$ that enforce a set of frame conditions within the symbolic formulation (cf. Eq. (1)) are realized as variability maps which, for each model element, store whether it may be modified by the corresponding operation call or not. By combining several of these maps for different sets of frame conditions, the required constraints for analyzing equivalence or independence can be generated in a convenient, automatic fashion.

We successfully employed this implementation for the automatic analysis of the objectives introduced above. In fact, the whole analysis presented in Examples 4 (consistency), 5 (equivalence), and 6 (independence) could be performed automatically and the absence or existence of corresponding execution scenarios could be proven formally. This is especially remarkable for the equivalence of the frame conditions provided in Figs. 3, 5, and 6 (cf. Example 5) as the required proof for the absence of a counterexample is very elaborate (if not completely infeasible) to be conducted manually. Using the deductive power of established reasoning approaches certainly helped here.

Overall, the proposed method allows for an efficient, automatic analysis of frame conditions with respect to the three primary analysis objectives of consistency, equivalence and independence, and also provides potential for a variety of further applications beyond that.

7   Conclusions

In this work, we considered the generation and validation of frame conditions in formal models with a focus on UML/OCL models. While several proposals and formalisms for specifying frame conditions exist, it remains non-trivial to define them properly. In fact, no corresponding methods or tools have been developed so far which assist the designer in deriving an initial set of frame conditions from a given model or could guarantee that the derived frame conditions indeed complete the model description in the intended way. We addressed this gap by proposing methodologies and prototypical tools that assist the designer in these tasks. Regarding the generation of frame conditions, a preliminary classification of the model elements, i.e. hypotheses on their intended variability, is automatically derived from a given model. As a consequence, the designer is pinpointed to ambiguous cases that require a more thorough consideration, while obvious cases are filtered out. To further aid the designer in this process, modeling tools such as [15] may be employed where hypotheses can be visualized by highlighting ambiguous model elements. Regarding the validation of frame conditions, we proposed a set of analysis objectives (consistency, equivalence, and independence) together with a formulation that allows for performing corresponding analyses using automated reasoning engines. Moreover, we implemented the proposed concepts on top of an established approach for model validation and verification. By this, a method and also a corresponding tool becomes available that has a similar performance as many established approaches for the validation and verification of UML/OCL models in general, but allows for the dedicated analysis and validation of frame conditions.

Overall, the presented methodologies significantly aid the designer in defining proper frame conditions and, thus, in creating more complete behavioral model descriptions.

Acknowledgments. This work was supported by the German Federal Ministry of Education and Research (BMBF) within the project SELFIE under grant no. 01IW16001 and the Deutsche Forschungsgemeinschaft (German Research Foundation, DFG) within the Reinhart Koselleck project under grant no. DR287/23-1.

References

1. Ahrendt, W., et al.: The KeY tool. Softw. Syst. Model. 4(1), 32–54 (2005)
2. Anastasakis, K., Bordbar, B., Georg, G., Ray, I.: UML2Alloy: a challenging model transformation. In: Engels, G., Opdyke, B., Schmidt, D.C., Weil, F. (eds.) MODELS 2007. LNCS, vol. 4735, pp. 436–450. Springer, Heidelberg (2007). https://doi.org/10.1007/978-3-540-75209-7_30

3. Beckert, B., Schmitt, P.H.: Program verification using change information. In: SEFM, p. 91 (2003)
4. Borgida, A., Mylopoulos, J., Reiter, R.: On the frame problem in procedure specifications. IEEE Trans. Softw. Eng. **21**, 785–798 (1995)
5. Brucker, A.D., Tuong, F., Wolff, B.: Featherweight OCL: a proposal for a machine-checked formal semantics for OCL 2.5. Archive of Formal Proofs (2014)
6. Brucker, A.D., Wolff, B.: HOL-OCL: a formal proof environment for UML/OCL. In: Fiadeiro, J.L., Inverardi, P. (eds.) FASE 2008. LNCS, vol. 4961, pp. 97–100. Springer, Heidelberg (2008). https://doi.org/10.1007/978-3-540-78743-3_8
7. Cabot, J.: Ambiguity issues in OCL postconditions. In: OCL Workshop, pp. 194–204 (2006)
8. Cabot, J.: From declarative to imperative UML/OCL operation specifications. In: Parent, C., Schewe, K.-D., Storey, V.C., Thalheim, B. (eds.) ER 2007. LNCS, vol. 4801, pp. 198–213. Springer, Heidelberg (2007). https://doi.org/10.1007/978-3-540-75563-0_15
9. Cabot, J., Clarisó, R., Riera, D.: Verification of UML/OCL class diagrams using constraint programming. In: ICST, pp. 73–80 (2008)
10. Cabot, J., Clarisó, R., Riera, D.: Verifying UML/OCL operation contracts. In: Leuschel, M., Wehrheim, H. (eds.) IFM 2009. LNCS, vol. 5423, pp. 40–55. Springer, Heidelberg (2009). https://doi.org/10.1007/978-3-642-00255-7_4
11. Choppy, C., Klai, K., Zidani, H.: Formal verification of UML state diagrams: a Petri net based approach. Softw. Eng. Notes **36**(1), 1–8 (2011)
12. de Moura, L., Bjørner, N.: Z3: an efficient SMT solver. In: Ramakrishnan, C.R., Rehof, J. (eds.) TACAS 2008. LNCS, vol. 4963, pp. 337–340. Springer, Heidelberg (2008). https://doi.org/10.1007/978-3-540-78800-3_24
13. Demuth, B., Wilke, C.: Model and object verification by using dresden OCL. In: IIT-TP, p. 81. Technical University (2009)
14. de Dios, M.A.G., Dania, C., Basin, D., Clavel, M.: Model-driven development of a secure ehealth application. In: Heisel, M., Joosen, W., Lopez, J., Martinelli, F. (eds.) Engineering Secure Future Internet Services and Systems. LNCS, vol. 8431, pp. 97–118. Springer, Cham (2014). https://doi.org/10.1007/978-3-319-07452-8_4
15. Gogolla, M., Büttner, F., Richters, M.: USE: a UML-based specification environment for validating UML and OCL. Sci. Comput. Program. **69**(1–3), 27–34 (2007)
16. Gogolla, M., Hamann, L., Hilken, F., Kuhlmann, M., France, R.B.: From application models to filmstrip models: an approach to automatic validation of model dynamics. In: Modellierung, pp. 273–288 (2014)
17. Gogolla, M., Kuhlmann, M., Hamann, L.: Consistency, independence and consequences in UML and OCL models. In: Dubois, C. (ed.) TAP 2009. LNCS, vol. 5668, pp. 90–104. Springer, Heidelberg (2009). https://doi.org/10.1007/978-3-642-02949-3_8
18. Hilken, F., Niemann, P., Gogolla, M., Wille, R.: Filmstripping and unrolling: a comparison of verification approaches for UML and OCL behavioral models. In: Seidl, M., Tillmann, N. (eds.) TAP 2014. LNCS, vol. 8570, pp. 99–116. Springer, Cham (2014). https://doi.org/10.1007/978-3-319-09099-3_8
19. Kosiuczenko, P.: Specification of invariability in OCL. In: Nierstrasz, O., Whittle, J., Harel, D., Reggio, G. (eds.) MODELS 2006. LNCS, vol. 4199, pp. 676–691. Springer, Heidelberg (2006). https://doi.org/10.1007/11880240_47
20. Kosiuczenko, P.: Specification of invariability in OCL - specifying invariable system parts and views. Softw. Syst. Model. **12**(2), 415–434 (2013)
21. Leino, K.R.M.: This is Boogie 2. Technical report (2008). http://research.microsoft.com/apps/pubs/default.aspx?id=147643

22. Meyer, B.: Applying design by contract. IEEE Comput. **25**(10), 40–51 (1992)
23. Niemann, P., Hilken, F., Gogolla, M., Wille, R.: Assisted generation of frame conditions for formal models. In: DATE, pp. 309–312 (2015)
24. Niemann, P., Hilken, F., Gogolla, M., Wille, R.: Extracting frame conditions from operation contracts. In: MoDELS, pp. 266–275 (2015)
25. Niemann, P., Przigoda, N., Wille, R., Drechsler, R.: Analyzing frame conditions in UML/OCL models - consistency equivalence and independence. In: MODELSWARD, pp. 139–151 (2018)
26. OMG - Object Management Group: Object Constraint Language (2014). http://www.omg.org/spec/OCL/2.4. Version 2.4, February 2014
27. Przigoda, N., Filho, J.G., Niemann, P., Wille, R., Drechsler, R.: Frame conditions in symbolic representations of UML/OCL models. In: MEMOCODE, pp. 65–70 (2016)
28. Przigoda, N., Hilken, C., Wille, R., Peleska, J., Drechsler, R.: Checking concurrent behavior in UML/OCL models. In: MoDELS, pp. 176–185 (2015)
29. Przigoda, N., Niemann, P., Filho, J.G., Wille, R., Drechsler, R.: Frame conditions in the automatic validation and verification of UML/OCL models: a symbolic formulation of modifies only statements. Comput. Lang. Syst. Struct. (2017). https://doi.org/10.1016/j.cl.2017.11.002
30. Przigoda, N., Soeken, M., Wille, R., Drechsler, R.: Verifying the structure and behavior in UML/OCL models using satisfiability solvers. IET Cyber-Phys. Syst.: Theory Appl. **1**(1), 49–59 (2016). https://doi.org/10.1049/iet-cps.2016.0022
31. Przigoda, N., Stoppe, J., Seiter, J., Wille, R., Drechsler, R.: Verification-driven design across abstraction levels: a case study. In: DSD, pp. 375–382. IEEE Computer Society (2015)
32. Przigoda, N., Wille, R., Drechsler, R.: Ground setting properties for an efficient translation of OCL in SMT-based model finding. In: MoDELS, pp. 261–271 (2016)
33. Rumbaugh, J., Jacobson, I., Booch, G. (eds.): The Unified Modeling Language Reference Manual. Addison-Wesley Longman Ltd., Essex (1999)
34. Soeken, M., Wille, R., Drechsler, R.: Verifying dynamic aspects of UML models. In: DATE, pp. 1077–1082 (2011)
35. Soeken, M., Wille, R., Kuhlmann, M., Gogolla, M., Drechsler, R.: Verifying UML/OCL models using Boolean satisfiability. In: DATE, pp. 1341–1344 (2010)

Analysis and Evaluation of Conformance Preserving Graph Transformation Rules

Fazle Rabbi[✉], Yngve Lamo, and Lars Michael Kristensen

Western Norway University of Applied Sciences, Bergen, Norway
{Fazle.Rabbi,Yngve.Lamo,Lars.Michael.Kristensen}@hvl.no

Abstract. Model transformation is a formal approach for modelling the behavior of software systems. Over the past few years, graph based modeling of software systems has gained significant attention as there are numerous techniques available to formally specify constraints and the dynamics of systems. Graph transformation rules are used to model the behavior of software systems which is the core element in model driven software engineering. However, in general, the application of graph transformation rules cannot guarantee the correctness of model transformations. In this paper, we propose to use a graph transformation technique that guarantees the correctness of transformations by checking required and forbidden graph patterns. The proposed technique is based on the application of conformance preserving transformation rules which guarantee that produced output models conform to their underlying meta-model. To determine if a rule is conformance preserving we present a new algorithm for checking conformance preserving rules with respect to a set of graph constraints. We also present a formal proof of the soundness of the algorithm. We apply our technique to homogeneous model transformations where input and output models must conform to the same meta-model. The algorithm relies on locality of a constrained graph to reduce the computational cost.

Keywords: Model transformation · Graph constraint ·
Metamodelling · Formal correctness of model transformations ·
Domain-specific modeling languages

1 Introduction

Model transformation is the process of transforming a model into another model and plays a key role in model driven software development. A transformation rule describes how a target model can be automatically generated from a source model. Often these models need to conform to the syntax and semantics of a metamodel. There are various applications of model transformations such as model migration, model synthesis, code generation, model simulation, model execution, and model repair. Formal development of transformation rules is an important concern since precisely defined rules can be used to verify that the

© Springer Nature Switzerland AG 2019
S. Hammoudi et al. (Eds.): MODELSWARD 2018, CCIS 991, pp. 284–307, 2019.
https://doi.org/10.1007/978-3-030-11030-7_13

automated transformations are correct [24]. Graph transformation is a formal technique to represent model transformation rules enabling reasoning and studying properties of transformation systems. Depending on the source and target language, a transformation can be homogeneous or heterogeneous. In homogeneous model transformation, input models and output models belong to the same language. Heterogeneous model transformation transforms models from one language to another. In general, the result of the application of a model transformation rule may lead to inconsistency, i.e., the target model violating constraints defined in its metamodel. Therefore, the application of a model transformation rule requires conformance checking of the target model which is time consuming. To address this problem, it is of interest to develop techniques to reduce the complexity of conformance checking. Since the application of a conformance preserving transformation rule retains the conformance of a model, it eliminates the need for conformance checking of target models. This approach is particularly suited for the development of systems where models produced in every step of a model transformation are supposed to be valid i.e., conforming with respect to a set of constraints.

Current verification approaches for model transformation rules include theorem proving and model checking. The authors in [7] proposed a relational and logical approach to graph grammars that allow the analysis of asynchronous distributed systems with infinite state spaces. They used relational structures to define graph grammars and first-order logic to model graph transformations. They provided a semi-automated process to prove structural properties of reachable graphs using theorem proving. Another theorem proving technique was presented in [19] based on translating graph grammars into Event-B specifications preserving its semantics and then using theorem provers available for Event-B for analysis. Automatic verification of model transformation is gaining popularity and several methods have already been proposed. Baresi and Spoletini [4] proposed a methodology to analyze graph transformation systems by means of Alloy. Given an initial graph of a system, the method can be used to check the configurations that can be obtained by applying a sequence of transformation rules. In [25], Wang et al. investigated the use of the Alloy analyzer for analyzing model transformation systems. A bounded verification approach was used to check if a model transformation system is correct with respect to conformance by translating a metamodel specification into a relational logic specification in Alloy. The authors in [23] presented a formal semantics of the ATL model transformation language using rewriting logic and Maude. Through the formalization it was possible to simulate and verify model transformations. Although model checking is an elegant analysis method, it requires building the complete state space. This can easily lead to the state explosion problem thereby limiting its practical applicability. Hackel and Wagner [14] presented an approach that ensures the conformance of graph transformations by automatically adding application conditions to rules. Application conditions are derived by analyzing the constraints individually which can produce an unnecessary large number of application conditions.

In our approach, we use characteristics of model transformation rules and present an algorithm to check if a transformation rule is conformance preserving with respect to a given set of constraints. We focus on homogeneous model transformation. We do not automatically modify a rule, but provide an algorithm for checking the conformance preserving property of a transformation rule that can be used to provide feedback to the modeler. The approach is illustrated by an example from the healthcare domain.

This paper is an extended version of a previously published article, Rabbi, F., Kristensen, L.M, and Lamo, Y.: Static Analysis of Conformance Preserving Model Transformation Rules, in the proceedings of the 6th International Conference on Model-Driven Engineering and Software Development. This extended version of the paper includes a report on the proof of concept implementation of the proposed algorithm and also includes an evaluation of the proposed algorithm. The rest of the paper is organized as follows. Section 2 provides background on the theoretical foundation of our approach. Section 3 presents the concept of conformance preserving rules. Section 4 presents our algorithm for checking conformance preserving rules. Section 5 presents the evaluation of the proposed technique. Section 6 concludes the paper with a discussion of related and future work. We assume that the reader is familiar with graph transformation systems [10].

2   Modelling in DPF

We use Diagrammatic Logic [8] and the Diagram Predicate Framework (DPF) [20] for the formal development of metamodel specifications. In DPF, a model is represented by a diagrammatic specification $\mathfrak{S} = (S, C^{\mathfrak{S}} : \Sigma)$ consisting of an underlying graph S together with a set of *atomic constraints* $C^{\mathfrak{S}}$ specified by a *predicate signature* Σ. A predicate signature consists of a collection of predicates, each having a name, an arity (shape graph, $\alpha^{\Sigma}(p)$), visualization and semantic interpretation (see Table 1). The underlying graph and arity of predicates specify type graphs with a data algebra as in [10]. A predicate is used to specify a constraint in a model by means of graph homomorphisms. DPF provides a general mechanism of diagrammatic modeling as it supports various kinds of graph structures. DPF provides a formalization of multi level meta-modelling by defining the conformance relation between models at adjacent levels of a meta-modelling hierarchy. DPF has a potentially unbounded number of metalevels.

There are two kinds of conformance: *typed by* and *satisfaction of constraints*. Figure 1 (top) shows a DPF metamodel specification $\mathfrak{S}$ of a Multiple Sclerosis Clinic. Multiple sclerosis (MS) is a progressive disabling disease of the brain and the spinal cord (central nervous system). In this disease, the immune system attacks the protective sheath (myelin) that covers nerve fibers and causes communication problems between the brain and the rest of the body. Eventually, the disease can cause the nerves themselves to deteriorate or become permanently damaged. The signs and symptoms of this disease vary. Treatments can

Table 1. Predicates of a signature, Σ [18].

p	Arity $\alpha^\Sigma (p)$	Visualization	Semantic interpretation
<mult(n,m)>	$1 \xrightarrow{f} 2$	$\boxed{X} \xrightarrow[\text{[n..m]}]{f} \boxed{Y}$	f must have at least n and at most m instances for each instance of X
<pre-Condition>	$1 \xrightarrow{f} 2$; $g \searrow 3$	$\boxed{X} \xrightarrow{f} \boxed{Y}$; $g \searrow \text{[pCond]}$; $\boxed{Z}$	For each instance of f there exists an instance of g with the same source node
<composite>	$1 \xrightarrow{f} 2$; $h \searrow\; g\downarrow\; 3$	$\boxed{X} \xrightarrow{f} \boxed{Y}$; $\text{-[comp]--}\; g$; $h\;\boxed{Z}$	For each composition of instances f;g, there exists an instance of h such that h = f;g
<injective>	$1 \xrightarrow{f} 2$	$\boxed{X} \xrightarrow[\text{[inj]}]{f} \boxed{Y}$	Instances of f never maps distinct elements of its domain to the same element of its codomain

help reduce the MS symptoms [3]. While some people with severe MS may loose mobility, others experience long periods of remission. It is therefore essential to monitor the progression of the symptoms of MS patients. In the DPF meta-model specification, we model an MS-application that aims to serve the following purposes:

- Patients can be registered to the MS clinic and can be assigned to medical doctors;
- Medical doctors can have appointment slots;
- Patients can be allocated to appointment slots;
- Patients with appointments to the MS clinic may participate in a survey where they can enter information about their symptoms;
- The doctor assigned to a patient can give an order to perform MRI for patients.

The metamodel specification is constrained by a set of predicates from the signature Σ. Constraints are added into the specifications by graph homomorphisms from the arity (shape graph) of the predicates to the model elements. Below is a list of constraints specified in $\mathfrak{S}$:

- **C1.** *A patient must have exactly one birthdate (specified by <mult(1,1)>)*
- **C2.** *An appointment time-slot allocated to a patient must belong to that patient's assigned doctor (specified by <composite>)*
- **C3.** *An order for MRI can only be given to a patient by that patient's assigned doctor (specified by <composite>)*
- **C4.** *An appointment time-slot cannot be allocated to more than one patient (specified by <injective>)*

– **C5.** *Only registered patients who have appointments are allowed to participate in survey (specified by <pre-condition>).*

To be a valid instance of a DPF metamodel specification, requires that the instance is typed by the shape graph of the metamodel specification and satisfies all the constraints specified in the metamodel. Formally, this means that there is a graph homomorphism $(\iota_I : I \to S)$ from the graph I to the graph of $\mathfrak{S}$, where S is the underlying graph of $\mathfrak{S}$. We use a compact notation (I, ι_I) for representing a DPF instance.

2.1   Coupled Graph Constraints

The semantics of a DPF predicate can be specified in various ways. In this paper, we use graph constraints to specify the semantics of the predicates. Typically a graph constraint $N \xleftarrow{n} L \xrightarrow{u} R$ consist of three graphs: left L, right R and an application condition N (positive or negative application condition), and two injective graph homomorphisms n and u where the graphs are typed by the underlying graph of the model [10]. We propose to use graph constraints which conforms to two syntactic formats $\forall L^p \to \exists R^p$ and $\forall L^p \to \neg \exists R^p$ where the graphs are typed by the shape graph of the predicates. Therefore we use graph constraints of the following forms where superscript p indicates that the constraint is giving the semantics of a DPF predicate, p. The graph constraints are called coupled graph constraints as they link to predicates.

– $\forall(L^p : \alpha^{\Sigma}(p)) \to \exists(R^p : \alpha^{\Sigma}(p))$, read as "for all matches of the condition pattern L^p (typed by $\alpha^{\Sigma}(p)$) in a model, there exists a match of the required pattern R^p (typed by $\alpha^{\Sigma}(p)$) in the model"
– $\forall(L^p : \alpha^{\Sigma}(p)) \to \neg \exists(R^p : \alpha^{\Sigma}(p))$, read as "for all matches of the condition pattern L^p (typed by $\alpha^{\Sigma}(p)$) in a model, there does not exist a match of the forbidden pattern R^p (typed by $\alpha^{\Sigma}(p)$) in the model".

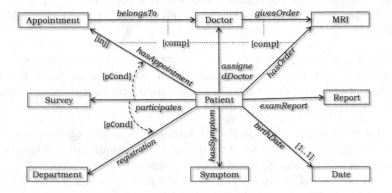

Fig. 1. Metamodel specification $\mathfrak{S}$ of an Orthopedic department.

Here L^p and R^p are typed graphs over the arity of the predicate p and there exists an inclusion graph morphism $m_c : L^p \hookrightarrow R^p$. A coupled graph constraint gc may have a post-condition $PC(gc)$ imposed on R^p. Table 2 shows the semantics of predicates from signature Σ in terms of graph constraints. The semantic of the $<mult(1,1)>$ predicate is given by two graph constraints where the patterns are typed by $\alpha^\Sigma(<mult(1,1)>)$, i.e., the arity of the $<mult(1,1)>$ predicate.

Let $gc \in GC(p)$ be a graph constraint linked to a predicate p. A match (δ, m_L) of the condition pattern $(L^p : \alpha^\Sigma(p))$ for the graph constraint gc in a model (I, ι_I) is given by an atomic constraint $\delta : \alpha^\Sigma(p) \to S$ and an injective morphism m_L such that constraint δ and the injective graph homomorphism m_L together with the typing morphisms $\iota_c : (L^p \cup R^p) \to \alpha^\Sigma(p)$ and $\iota_I : I \to S$ constitute a commuting square: $\iota_c; \delta = m_L; \iota_I$ as shown in Fig. 2(a). If gc has a required pattern $(R^p : \alpha^\Sigma(p))$, then for any match (δ, m_L) of the condition pattern in (I, ι_I), a match (δ, m_R) of the required pattern must exist, which is given by the commuting diagram in Fig. 2(b). If gc has a forbidden pattern $(R^p : \alpha^\Sigma(p))$, then for any match (δ, m_L) of the condition pattern in (I, ι_I), a match (δ, m_R) of the forbidden pattern must not exist such that it constitutes a commuting diagram as shown in Fig. 2(c). A valid model is typed by its metamodel specification and conforms to the constraints specified in its metamodel specification. Formally, it states that a valid model (I, ι_I) satisfies all the constraints defined in $\mathfrak{S}$, which is written as $I \models \mathfrak{S}$.

Table 2. A set of graph constraints giving semantics to the predicates in Σ [18].

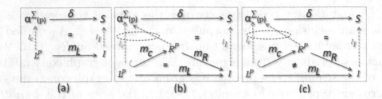

Fig. 2. (a) Match of a condition pattern; (b) match of a required pattern; (c) satisfaction of a forbidden pattern [18].

3 Conformance Preserving Rules

DPF provides functionality to specify graph-based model transformations [21]. We use the standard double-pushout (DPO) [10] approach for defining transformation rules. A model transformation rule $(r : N \xleftarrow{n} L \xleftarrow{m_l} K \xrightarrow{m_r} R)$ has a matching pattern (L), a gluing graph (K), a replacement pattern (R) and an optional negative application condition, $NAC(n : L \to N)$ where L, K, R, N are typed by $\mathfrak{S}$ and m_l, m_r, n are injective graph morphisms. We use a transformation approach where transformation rules have a set of negative application conditions as proposed by Lambers et al. in [16].

Given a model (I, ι_I), a model transformation $I \overset{r,m}{\Longrightarrow}$ I^* via a transformation rule $r : L \leftarrow K \to R$ with a set of negative application conditions NAC_r and a match $m : L \to I$ consists of the double pushout as shown in the diagram to the right. Here, the injective morphism

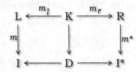

m satisfies each NAC in NAC_r, written $m \models NAC_r$. When a rule is applied, some elements from the source model are deleted and some elements are added to the target model. The rest of the source model remain unchanged in the target model. A rule is applied as long as it satisfies its negative application conditions. Negative application conditions are typically used in graph transformation to prohibit an infinite number of rule applications. Figure 3 shows a model transformation rule for allocating resources (i.e., appointment) to patients in a model of the metamodel specification from Fig. 1. The transformation rule r_1 encodes the following instructions:

- Allocate an appointment *appt* to patient pt_1 if *appt* belongs to the doctor whom pt_1 is assigned to

The typing information of a modelling element in r_1 appears after a colon (:). The green color (thick arrow) is used to represent elements that the rule is going to produce. The rule r_1 has one negative application condition to prohibit an infinite number of rule applications.

One problem with this version of the transformation rule is that it does not guarantee the conformance of constraint **C4** (an appointment time-slot cannot be allocated to more than one patient). The application of the rule may allocate an appointment time-slot to more than one patients. Figure 4 illustrates how

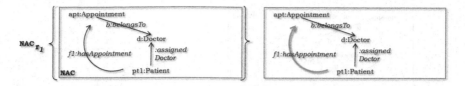

Fig. 3. Transformation rule r_1 for individual resource allocation of patients. (Color figure online)

we check the satisfaction of the atomic constraint ($<injective>, \delta_1$) over model (I^*, ι_{I^*}) by its graph constraint. Even if the rule is applied on a valid model, it does not guarantee that the result will be a valid model conforming to the metamodel specification. The portion of the model that is not conforming to the constraints are highlighted in red (thick arrow) in the figure.

The rule r_1 can be enhanced so that while matching with a model it makes sure that the result will be a valid model. Since the appointment allocation in a valid model of $\mathfrak{S}$ can possibly violate atomic constraints **C2** and **C4**, we enhance rule r_1 with an additional negative application condition to make sure that when applied on a valid model of $\mathfrak{S}$, the output does not violate any of the above mentioned constraints. Figure 5 shows rule r_2 which is conformance preserving and therefore the application of rule r_2 will not require any further conformance checking.

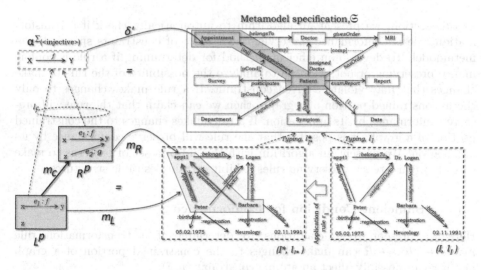

Fig. 4. Application of rule r_1 over a valid model (I, ι_I) and the checking for the satisfaction of a graph constraint (adapted from [18]). (Color figure online)

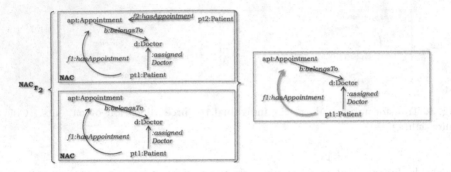

Fig. 5. Conformance preserving transformation rule (r_2) for individual resource allocation of patients.

A formal definition of conformance preserving transformation rule is given below:

Definition 1 (Conformance Preserving Rule). *Given a metamodel specification $\mathfrak{S} = (S, C^{\mathfrak{S}} : \Sigma)$. A transformation rule r is conformance preserving w.r.t a set of atomic constraints from $C^{\mathfrak{S}}$ if the application of r on any valid model $(I, \iota_I) \models \mathfrak{S}$ always results in a valid model of $\mathfrak{S}$.*

4   Analysis for Checking Conformance Preserving Rules

In this section, we present an algorithm to automatically check if a transformation rule is conformance preserving w.r.t a set of constraints specified in a metamodel. To develop an efficient method for determining if a rule is conformance preserving or not, we need to analyze the possibility of the rule to make changes that may violate a given constraint. If a rule makes changes to only the unconstrained portion of a graph, then we can claim that the rule will preserve conformance by its application. If a rule makes changes to the constrained portion of a graph, it is possible that the rule will preserve conformance by its application. We present an algorithm with the aid of a set of patterns to make sure that consistency preserving rules exhibit certain desirable structures.

4.1   A Sufficient Condition for Conformance

Here we present three conditions to determine if a transformation rule $r : L \leftarrow K \rightarrow R$ can make changes to the constrained portion of a graph i.e., if r can possibly affect an atomic constraint (p, δ):

- **Cond 1:** r creates an element x of type X where X is constrained by a predicate p and X is mapped by the condition pattern of a graph constraint $gc \in GC(p)$ via the typing morphism of L^p and the atomic constraint (p, δ), i.e., $X \in \iota_c; \delta(L^p)$;

– **Cond 2:** r deletes an element y of type Y where Y is constrained by a predicate p and Y is mapped by the elements from (*required pattern*, $R^p \setminus$ *condition pattern*, L^p) via the typing of $(R^p \cup L^p)$ and the atomic constraint (p, δ), i.e., $Y \in \iota_c; \delta(R^p \setminus L^p)$;

– **Cond 3:** r creates an element x of type X where X is constrained by a predicate p and X is mapped by the elements from (*forbidden pattern*, $R^p \setminus$ *condition pattern*, L^p) via the typing of $(R^p \cup L^p)$ and the atomic constraint (p, δ), i.e., $X \in \iota_c; \delta(R^p \setminus L^p)$;

Intuitively, **Cond 1, 2,** and **3** checks if a rule can create a new match with the condition pattern, delete an existing match of a required pattern, or create a new match with the forbidden pattern of a graph constraint, respectively.

Lemma 1. *Given a metamodel specification $\mathfrak{S}$ with a set of constraints $C^{\mathfrak{S}}$. A transformation rule r is conformance preserving if it does not satisfy any of* **Cond 1–3.**

Proof. Let (I, ι) be a valid instance of $\mathfrak{S}$ and the application of r on (I, ι) produces an instance (I^*, ι^*). There are three ways (I^*, ι^*) may violate a constraint from $C^{\mathfrak{S}}$: (i) r produces a new match with the condition pattern L^p of a graph constraint where the corresponding required pattern is missing; (ii) r deletes an existing match of a required pattern; (iii) r produces a new match with the forbidden pattern. However, it can be seen that if r does not satisfy any of **Cond 1–3**, then it does not affect any constraint from $C^{\mathfrak{S}}$ because of the following reasons:

– r does not satisfy **Cond 1**; therefore, it does not produce any new match with the condition pattern L^p of a graph constraint.

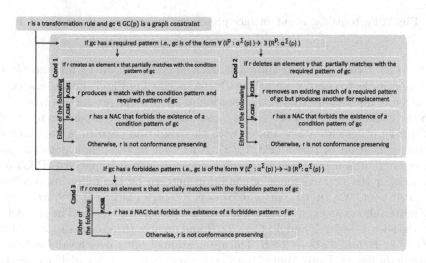

Fig. 6. Informal description of the algorithm illustrating the intuition.

- r does not satisfy **Cond 2**; therefore, it does not delete any existing match of a required pattern.
- r does not satisfy **Cond 3**; therefore, it does not produce any new match with the forbidden patterns.

4.2   Desired Patterns for Conformance

It is possible for a rule r to be conformance preserving even if it satisfies some conditions from **Cond 1–3** and complies with desired patterns described below. Figure 6 illustrates a diagram representing the intuition of the proposed method where **P.C1#1, P.C1#2, ...** indicates a pattern number.

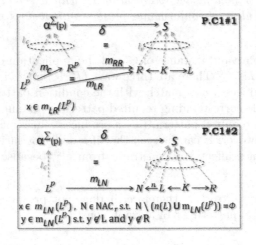

Fig. 7. Patterns for a conformance preserving rule r that satisfies **Cond 1**.

Patterns for **Cond 1** *:* In our approach, if a rule satisfies **Cond 1** for a graph constraint gc, it has to comply with the patterns specified in Fig. 7. Patterns specified in the figure makes sure that if the creation of an element produces a new match with the condition pattern of a graph constraint, the required pattern must exist (**P.C1#1**); otherwise a new match with the condition pattern is not produced by the application of rule r (**P.C1#2**). Note that in the graph patterns, solid arrows are representing injective graph homomorphisms. In pattern (**P.C1#2**), we check for the non existence of condition pattern by the following condition: $N \in NAC_r$ s.t. $N \setminus (n(L) \cup m_{LN}(L^p)) = \emptyset, y \in m_{LN}(L^p)$ s.t. $y \notin L$ and $y \notin R$.

Figure 8 shows an example of a conformance preserving rule, r. The rule deletes two edges $1 : A \rightarrow 2 : B$ and $3 : C \rightarrow 2 : B$ and creates three edges $1 : A \rightarrow 4 : D$, $4 : D \rightarrow 2 : B$, and $3 : C \rightarrow 2 : B$. The application of rule r over a valid instance is shown in the figure. The output of the transformation is a DPF model instance that produces a new match with the condition pattern, L^p. Since the transformation also produces a corresponding match with the required pattern, R^p, the output model instance is a valid DPF model. To help the reader understanding about the portion of the model being affected by the graph constraint, we show the graph constraint with the typing information using the composition $\iota; \delta$ in the left bottom part of Fig. 8.

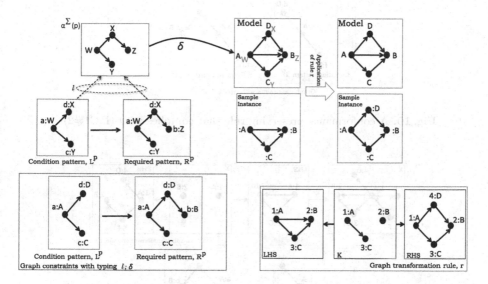

Fig. 8. Example of a conformance preserving transformation rule that complies with $P.C1\#1$.

Given the same model and graph constraint as in Fig. 8, an example of a transformation rule r' that is not conformance preserving is shown in Fig. 9. The application of rule r' produces two matches with the condition pattern L^p but it produces one corresponding match with the required pattern R^p. Hence it is not satisfying $P.C1\#1$ and therefore r' is not conformance preserving.

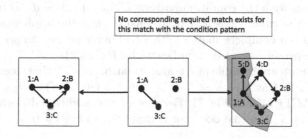

Fig. 9. A transformation rule that does not comply with $(P.C1\#1)$.

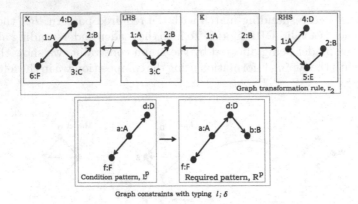

Fig. 10. A conformance preserving rule that complies with (P.C1#2).

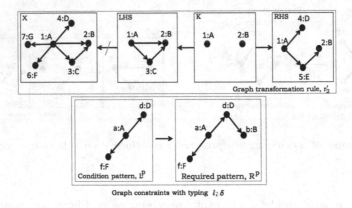

Fig. 11. A transformation rule that does not comply with (P.C1#2).

Figure 10 shows an example of a conformance preserving transformation rule r_2 that complies with $(P.C1\#2)$. Even though rule r_2 creates and edge that partially matches with the condition pattern L^p i.e., $a : A \rightarrow d : D$ matches with $1 : A \rightarrow 4 : D$, the rule r_2 has a NAC to ensure that the application of rule r_2 does not produce a complete match with L^p. Therefore we can see that rule r_2 is conformance preserving as it complies with $(P.C1\#2)$.

Figure 11 shows an example of a transformation rule r_2' that does not comply with $(P.C1\#2)$. In this rule $X \in NAC_{r_2'}$ but $X \setminus (n(LHS) \cup m_{LN}(L^p)) \neq \emptyset$ as specified in $(P.C1\#2)$ (see Fig. 7). Because of the additional elements $(7 : G, 1 : A \rightarrow 7 : G)$ in X, the rule does not comply with $(P.C1\#2)$.

Patterns for **Cond 2**. The patterns presented in Fig. 12 makes sure two of the following:

- **(P.C2#1)**: If the deletion of an element removes an existing match of a required pattern of a graph constraint, then another match of a required pattern is produced;
- **(P.C2#2)**: Deletion of an element that partially matches with a required pattern, does not remove an existing match of a required pattern.

For checking the non existence of a required pattern in **(P.C2#2)**, it is sufficient to check for the non existence of the corresponding condition pattern. If the condition pattern does not exist, we can safely remove portion of a model that partially matches with the requird pattern. Note that in pattern **(P.C2#2)**, we check for the non existence of condition pattern by the following condition: $N \in NAC_r$ s.t. $N \setminus (n(L) \cup m_{LN}(L^p)) = \emptyset, z \in m_{LN}(L^p)$ s.t. $z \notin L$ and $z \notin R$. In the rest of the section we provide some examples of transformation rules that comply with the patterns described above.

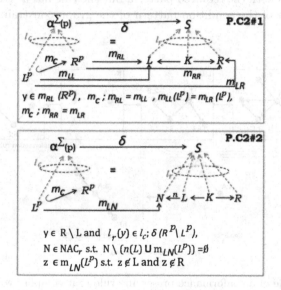

$y \in m_{RL}(R^p)$, $m_c ; m_{RL} = m_{LL}$, $m_{LL}(L^p) = m_{LR}(L^p)$,
$m_c ; m_{RR} = m_{LR}$

$y \in R \setminus L$ and $l_r(y) \in l_c; \delta(R^P \setminus L^P)$,
$N \in NAC_r$ s.t. $N \setminus (n(L) \cup m_{LN}(L^P)) = \emptyset$
$z \in m_{LN}(L^P)$ s.t. $z \notin L$ and $z \notin R$

Fig. 12. Patterns for a conformance preserving rule that satisfies **Cond 2**.

Figure 13 shows an example of a conformance preserving rule that complies with **(P.C2#1)**. The rule removes an existing match with a required pattern by deleting elements $2 : B$ and $3 : C \rightarrow 2 : B$ but produces another match of the required pattern by creating elements $4 : B$ and $3 : C \rightarrow 4 : B$.

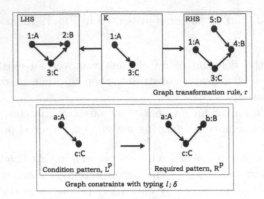

Fig. 13. Example of a conformance preserving rule that complies with (**P.C2#1**).

Figure 14 shows an example of a conformance preserving transformation rule that complies with (**P.C2#2**). The rule deletes an element $1 : A \rightarrow 6 : F$ that partially matches with the required pattern, but the rule has a NAC that ensures the non existence of the condition pattern of the graph constraint shown at the bottom of Fig. 14.

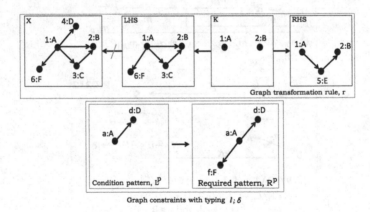

Fig. 14. Example of a conformance preserving rule that complies with (**P.C2#2**).

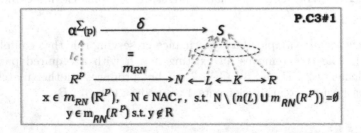

Fig. 15. Pattern for a conformance preserving rule r that satisfies **Cond 3**.

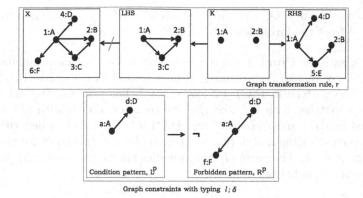

Graph transformation rule, r

Graph constraints with typing $l; \delta$

Fig. 16. Example of a conformance preserving transformation rule that complies with **P.C3#1**.

*Patterns for **Cond** 3:* The pattern **P.C3#1** presented in Fig. 15 makes sure that the creation of an element does not produce a match with the forbidden pattern of a graph constraint. We check for the non existence of the forbidden pattern by the following condition: $N \in NAC_r$ s.t. $N \setminus (n(L) \cup m_{RN}(R^p)) = \emptyset, y \in m_{RN}(R^p)$ s.t. $y \notin R$.

Figure 16 shows an example of a conformance preserving transformation rule that creates an element $1 : A \rightarrow 4 : D$ which partially matches with the forbidden pattern of a graph constraint. However, the rule makes sure that a complete match with the forbidden pattern does not exist by means of a negative application condition. Therefore, it complies with **P.C3#1**.

4.3   Algorithm for Checking Conformance Preserving Rule

Algorithm 1 provides a method for checking the conformance preserving property of a rule w.r.t a set of graph constraints.

Theorem 1 (Soundness of Algorithm 1). Let $\mathfrak{S} = (S, C^{\mathfrak{S}} : \Sigma)$ be a meta-model specification and r (typed by S) a transformation rule which is determined to be conformance preserving w.r.t $C^{\mathfrak{S}}$ by Algorithm 1. If r is applied on a valid model $(I, \iota_I) \models \mathfrak{S}$ then the result (I^*, ι_{I^*}) will be a valid model of $\mathfrak{S}$.

Proof. Let GC be a set of constraints giving semantics to the set of constraints $C^{\mathfrak{S}}$. To prove the theorem by contradiction, it is sufficient to show that there exists a $gc \in GC$ such that (I^*, ι_{I^*}) does not satisfy gc. There are three ways in which it is possible for (I^*, ι_{I^*}) to violate the graph constraint:

i gc is of the form $\forall (L^p : \alpha^{\Sigma}(p)) \rightarrow \exists (R^p : \alpha^{\Sigma}(p))$ and a new match (δ, m_{LI^*}) is produced from $(L^p : \alpha^{\Sigma}(p))$ to I^* but a corresponding match from $(R^p : \alpha^{\Sigma}(p))$ to I^* is missing.

ii gc is of the form $\forall (L^p : \alpha^{\Sigma}(p)) \rightarrow \exists (R^p : \alpha^{\Sigma}(p))$ and a required match from $(R^p : \alpha^{\Sigma}(p))$ to I is removed but a corresponding match from $(L^p : \alpha^{\Sigma}(p))$ to I still remains in I^*.

iii gc is of the form $\forall(L^p : \alpha^\Sigma(p)) \to \neg\exists(R^p : \alpha^\Sigma(p))$ and a new match is produced from the forbidden pattern $(R^p : \alpha^\Sigma(p))$ to I^*.

Case (i). r satisfies **Cond 1** since a new match for the condition pattern is produced. According to Algorithm 1, r must comply with either **P.C1#1** or **P.C1#2**. The pattern in **P.C1#2** has a *NAC* that prevents the existence of pattern that matches with $(L^p : \alpha^\Sigma(p))$. Since a new match with $(L^p : \alpha^\Sigma(p))$ is produced in (i), r must comply with **P.C1#1**. Therefore, when the rule is applied, a corresponding match (δ, m_{RI^*}) from $(R^p : \alpha^\Sigma(p))$ to I^* for the match (δ, m_{LI^*}) must exist. Therefore (I^*, ι_{I^*}) satisfies the graph constraint gc. Hence we reach to a contradiction.

Case (ii). This case is explained by considering three matches:

- $(\delta, m_{LI}) : (L^p : \alpha^\Sigma(p)) \to (I : S)$,
- $(\delta, m_{RI}) : (R^p : \alpha^\Sigma(p)) \to (I : S)$,
- $(\delta, m_{LI^*}) : (L^p : \alpha^\Sigma(p)) \to (I^* : S)$.

where m_c; $m_{RI} = m_{LI}$, $m_{LI}(L^p) = m_{LI^*}(L^p)$ and there does not exist a corresponding match $(\delta, m_{RI^*}) : (R^p : \alpha^\Sigma(p)) \to (I^* : S)$ such that m_c; $m_{RI^*} = m_{LI^*}$. Therefore $\exists\, y \in (m_{RI}(R^p) \setminus m_{LI}(L^p))$ from which we obtain $Y \in \iota_c$; $\delta(R^p \setminus L^p)$ where Y is the type of y. Hence, r satisfies **Cond 2** and according to Algorithm 1, r must comply with either **P.C2#1** or **P.C2#2**. Pattern in **P.C2#2** has a *NAC* that prevents the existence of pattern that matches with $(L^p : \alpha^\Sigma(p))$. Since in

---

Algorithm 1. Check for conformance preserving rule.

Require: a coupled transformation rule r, a set of graph constraints GC
   C := R \ L of r //set of elements created by r
   D := L \ R of r //set of elements deleted by r
   for each x in **C** do
      for each gc $\in$ GC **do**
         if gc has a required pattern R^p
           and r satisfies **Cond 1** for x and gc **then**
           if r does not comply with **P.C1#1** or **P.C1#2** for x **then**
              return ``may not be conformance preserving''
         if gc has a forbidden pattern R^p
           and r satisfies **Cond 3** for x and gc **then**
           if r does not comply with **P.C3#1** for x **then**
              return ``may not be conformance preserving''
   for each y in **D** do
      for each gc $\in$ GC **do**
         if gc has a required pattern R^p
            and r satisfies **Cond 2** for y and gc **then**
         if r does not comply with **P.C2#1** or **P.C2#2**
         for y **then**
              return ``may not be conformance preserving''
   return ``conformance preserving''

case (ii), the matching with the condition pattern remains, the rule r must comply with **P.C2#1**. However, pattern **P.C2#1** makes sure that a corresponding match for the required pattern is produced which contradicts with the second case.

Case (iii). r satisfies **Cond 3** since a new match for the forbidden pattern is produced. According to Algorithm 1, r must comply with **P.C3#1**. Pattern **P.C3#1** has a NAC that prevents the existence of pattern that matches with $(R^p : \alpha^\Sigma(p))$. Therefore we reach to a contradiction.

In all three cases we have shown that if r is applied on a valid model $I \models \mathfrak{S}$ then the result (I^*, ι_{I^*}) cannot violate the constraints specified in $\mathfrak{S}$.

Complexity of Algorithm 1. The complexity of the algorithm depends on two factors: (i) the size of graph patterns of the graph constraints and (ii) the size of graph patterns in transformation rules. The size of a graph pattern refers to the number of vertices of the graph. The performance of the algorithm depends on injective matching. Finding an injective match from an n-vertex graph (G) to a m-vertex graph (H) has complexity $2^{\mathcal{O}(n \ log \ m)}$ as finding all possible vertex subsets of H of size at most n is $m^{\mathcal{O}(n)}$ and for each subset we need to try all possible mappings from G. The algorithm avoids processing the models of a system, therefore it is expected to analyze the transformation rules fast because in a typical situation, the size of graph patterns in graph constraints and transformation rules would be very small compared to the size of models.

Theorem 2. Given a metamodel specification $\mathfrak{S} = (S, C^\mathfrak{S} : \Sigma)$ and a set of conformance preserving rules $\mathcal{R} = \{r_1, ...r_n\}$ w.r.t a set of atomic constraints $C^\mathfrak{S}$. If the rules are applied on a valid model of $\mathfrak{S}$ a finite number of times, the result will be a valid model of $\mathfrak{S}$.

Proof. The theorem can be proved by induction over the number of application of the transformation rules as the results produced in each step are valid models of $\mathfrak{S}$.

5   Evaluation

We have implemented a proof of concept (PoC) tool [1] for graph transformation, conformance checking, and detecting conformance preserving graph transformation rules. The tool takes a metamodel specification and model transformation rules as input in JSON format and provides a visualization of models and rules using a graph visualization software called 'Graphviz' [11]. The algorithm presented in Sect. 4 has been implemented in the web-based PoC tool. Figure 17 shows a screenshot of the PoC tool where the user can visualize the model, transformation rules and can select predicates from a drop-down list. The mappings of the predicates to the model (i.e., constraint) are visualized by color matching. For example, the node 'W' from the predicate is mapped to the node 'A' in the model which is represented by the same color. The user can check for

the conformance from the web-based tool. Note that the example presented in
Fig. 17 is the same as presented in Fig. 8.

To evaluate the performance of our algorithm for checking conformance we
performed experiments with models and model transformation rules of various
size. Table 3 shows the results of the experiments. The table shows the size of

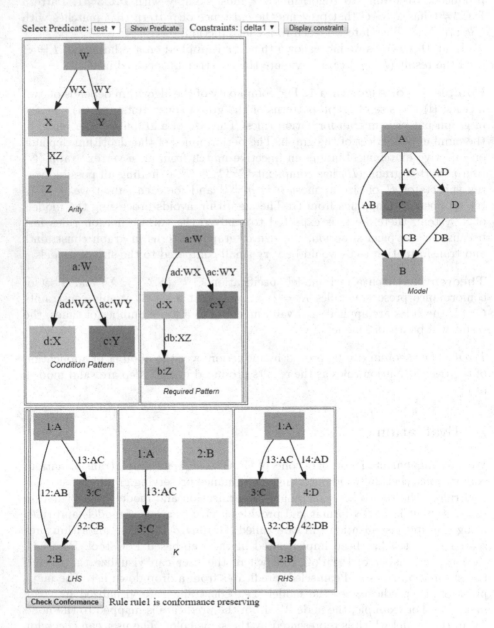

Fig. 17. Screenshot from the PoC tool.

the models and transformation rules being considered for the evaluation, and the time taken to detect conformance. Below is a description of the columns of the table:

- *Index No*: Experiment number;
- *vertex + edges*: Number of vertex and edges in the model;
- *LHS*: Total number of elements in the LHS of the rule;
- $X \cap RHS$: Number of common elements in X and RHS of the rule;
- $X \setminus (LHS \cup RHS)$: Number of unique elements in X of the rule;
- $LHS \setminus K$: Number of elements deleted by the rule;
- $RHS \setminus K$: Number of elements created by the rule;
- *time (in ms)*: Time required to determine the conformance of the rule.

In experiment number 1–7, we consider the models, graph constraints and transformation rules from Figs. 8, 9, 10, 11, 13, 14, and 16, respectively. To evaluate the performance of the algorithm, we used a Java program to produce models and model transformation rules of increasing size. The Java program takes meta information such as the number of nodes and edges in the model, and number of nodes and edges in the LHS, and RHS of the transformation rule. The program also takes input specifying the percentage of nodes and edges that will be removed and produced by the rule. From the meta information, the program produces models and transformation rules in JSON format which

Table 3. Time required for conformance checking in different settings.

Index No	Size of model vertex + edges	LHS	$X \cap RHS$	$X \setminus (LHS \cup RHS)$	$LHS \setminus K$	$RHS \setminus K$	Computation time (in ms)
1	$4+5=9$	6	0	0	2	4	12
2	$4+5=9$	6	0	0	2	6	14
3	$6+8=14$	6	4	2	4	5	11
4	$7+9=16$	6	4	4	4	5	12
5	$4+4=8$	6	0	0	3	4	12
6	$6+7=13$	8	2	2	6	3	11
7	$6+7=13$	6	4	2	4	5	12
8	$4+7=11$	3	4	2	1	5	11
9	$8+12=20$	3	4	2	2	6	12
10	$12+18=30$	3	4	2	2	6	11
11	$10+200=210$	3	4	3	2	6	11
12	$50+200=250$	3	4	3	2	6	12
13	$4+8=12$	23	18	16	10	23	23
14	$4+8=12$	23	29	16	4	23	31
15	$4+8=12$	23	49	36	4	43	145
16	$4+8=12$	43	63	36	10	43	250
17	$15+38=53$	47	71	36	6	43	61563

is compatible with the PoC tool. Experiment number 8–12 are performed over transformation rules with a small number of elements and models with increasing size; and experiment number 13–16 are performed over models with small number of elements and transformation rules with increasing size. These experiments (i.e., 8–16) are performed with one graph constraint using the predicate $<composite>$. The results indicate that the algorithm takes longer time to detect if we have transformation rule with larger size. Experiment number 17 has been performed with a graph constraint using a predicate with 23 elements in the condition pattern and 26 elements in the required pattern. The longer time (approx. one minute) required for this experiment is expected as the algorithm need to check for various injective matches from the condition and required pattern of the constraint to the transformation rule.

6 Related Work and Conclusion

In this paper, we have presented a static analysis technique for checking the conformance property of transformation rules. The static analysis technique processes the semantics of graph constraints and analyzes if a transformation rule exhibits certain structure in order to be conformance preserving rule with respect to a set of constraints. We presented the idea in the context of DPF which provides a formal framework for metamodelling. We performed performance evaluation tests suggesting that the approach is promising for analyzing model transformation rules.

There has been a great deal of research related to the formal analysis of termination, confluence, functional behaviour of model transformation systems [6,13,15,17] and tool support [2,22]. One important difference between our approach and existing approaches is that our approach rest on diagrammatic logic. Our approach is closely related to the work of Heckel and Wagner [14]. They ensured consistency of graph transformations by automatically adding application conditions to single pushout (SPO) rules. They propose a technique for deriving application conditions from SPO rules of the form $L \xrightarrow{r} R$ and constraints. Constraints are specified in the form $P \xrightarrow{c} Q$ where P and Q are directed graphs and c is an injective morphism. In their approach, a post-condition (i.e., an application condition over the right hand side of a rule) is constructed as a set of all right-sided constraints by generating all possible gluings of the premise P and the graph R. The post-condition is then used to construct a left-sided constraint (i.e., an application condition over L) by inverse decomposition of pushout diagrams. One issue with this approach is that a post-condition induced by a constraint may include a large number of right-sided constraints. A simple technique was presented in [14] to reduce the number of right-sided constraints from a post-condition. The idea of the reduction is based on the removal of right-sided constraints that is obtained from a gluing $R \xrightarrow{s} S \xleftarrow{p} P$ where the image of P in S does not depend on elements generated by rule r i.e., $p(P) \cap s(R - r(L)) = \emptyset$. This reduction technique however cannot handle situations where a rule deletes an element that matches with the required pattern Q of a constraint $c : P \rightarrow Q$ (see **Cond 2** of Fig. 6). To illustrate this issue, consider an input graph G with $c; m_q = m_p$ where $m_p : P \rightarrow G$ and $m_q : Q \rightarrow G$ are two injective morphism. Now consider a rule $L \xrightarrow{r} R$ where $p(P) \cap s(R - r(L)) = \emptyset$ which means that the reduction will disregard the constraint c and no left-sided constraint will be constructed. But it is possible for the rule to remove an element x from $m_q(Q)$ which results in an output not conforming to its metamodel.

Later on, this approach for ensuring consistency was adapted for a double pushout approaches and generalized for high level transformation systems [10]. The approach was further enhanced for nested constraints in [12]. Although the approach presented in [10,12] can deal with situations where a rule add/delete elements, the construction of application conditions do not include any reduction technique. This results in a large number of application conditions. In our approach, we rely on the modeller to develop transformation rules and automatically check conformance using our algorithm. The proposed algorithm filters out trivially conformance preserving rules as described in Sect. 4.1 before checking the existence of the desired patterns in Sect. 4.2 for optimal performance.

Becker et al. [5] developed a verification technique for structural safety property of a transformation system which is very similar to our approach in the sense that their technique is based on checking the locality of transformation rules against a set of safety properties. In their approach, the authors checked if the application of transformation rules can violate any safety property given as a set of forbidden graph patterns. Dyck and Giese [9] improved the technique for the automated verification of structural invariants for graph transformation systems by extending the expressive power. They provided support for negative application conditions in constraints and support for application conditions in transformation rules. However, both techniques only check against forbidden patterns while in our approach we support checking the conformance property of transformation rules against both required and forbidden patterns. Making sure that the application of a transformation rule does not violate any required pattern is more complex than checking against a set of forbidden patterns as it involves more scenarios to cover for the checking algorithm.

In future, we plan to adapt the algorithm to more expressive constraint language such as nested graph constraints. We also plan to enhance the proof of concept presented in this paper with more user interaction and visualization support.

Acknowledgement. The authors would like to thank the reviewers for their constructive comments on the earlier version of this paper.

References

1. Analysis of conformance preserving transformation rule (2018). https://github. com/fazlRabbi/ConformanceTxRule
2. Arendt, T., Biermann, E., Jurack, S., Krause, C., Taentzer, G.: Henshin: advanced concepts and tools for in-place EMF model transformations. In: Petriu, D.C., Rouquette, N., Haugen, Ø. (eds.) MODELS 2010. LNCS, vol. 6394, pp. 121–135. Springer, Heidelberg (2010). https://doi.org/10.1007/978-3-642-16145-2_9
3. Artemiadis, A.K., Vervainioti, A.A., Alexopoulos, E., Rombos, A., Anagnostouli, M.C., Darviri, C.: Stress management and multiple sclerosis: a randomized controlled trial. Arch. Clin. Neuropsychol.: Off. J. Nat. Acad. Neuropsychol. **27**(4), 406–16 (2012)
4. Baresi, L., Spoletini, P.: On the use of alloy to analyze graph transformation systems. In: Corradini, A., Ehrig, H., Montanari, U., Ribeiro, L., Rozenberg, G. (eds.) ICGT 2006. LNCS, vol. 4178, pp. 306–320. Springer, Heidelberg (2006). https:// doi.org/10.1007/11841883_22
5. Becker, B., Beyer, D., Giese, H., Klein, F., Schilling, D.: Symbolic invariant verification for systems with dynamic structural adaptation. In: Proceedings of the 28th International Conference on Software Engineering, ICSE 2006, pp. 72–81. ACM, New York (2006)
6. Bruggink, H.J.S., König, B., Zantema, H.: Termination analysis for graph transformation systems. In: Diaz, J., Lanese, I., Sangiorgi, D. (eds.) TCS 2014. LNCS, vol. 8705, pp. 179–194. Springer, Heidelberg (2014). https://doi.org/10.1007/978-3-662-44602-7_15
7. da Costa, S.A., Ribeiro, L.: Verification of graph grammars using a logical approach. Sci. Comput. Program. **77**(4), 480–504 (2012)
8. Diskin, Z., Wolter, U.: A diagrammatic logic for object-oriented visual modeling. Electron. Notes Theor. Comput. Sci. **203**(6), 19–41 (2008). Proceedings of the 2nd Workshop on Applied and Computational Category Theory (ACCAT 2007)
9. Dyck, J., Giese, H.: Inductive invariant checking with partial negative application conditions. In: Parisi-Presicce, F., Westfechtel, B. (eds.) ICGT 2015. LNCS, vol. 9151, pp. 237–253. Springer, Cham (2015). https://doi.org/10.1007/978-3-319-21145-9_15
10. Ehrig, H., Ehrig, K., Prange, U., Taentzer, G.: Fundamentals of Algebraic Graph Transformation. MTCSAES. Springer, Heidelberg (2006). https://doi.org/10.1007/3-540-31188-2
11. Graphviz: Graph visualization software (2018). https://www.graphviz.org/
12. Habel, A., Pennemann, K.-H.: Correctness of high-level transformation systems relative to nested conditions. Math. Struct. Comput. Sci. **19**(2), 245–296 (2009)
13. Heckel, R., Küster, J.M., Taentzer, G.: Confluence of typed attributed graph transformation systems. In: Corradini, A., Ehrig, H., Kreowski, H.-J., Rozenberg, G. (eds.) ICGT 2002. LNCS, vol. 2505, pp. 161–176. Springer, Heidelberg (2002). https://doi.org/10.1007/3-540-45832-8_14
14. Heckel, R., Wagner, A.: Ensuring consistency of conditional graph grammars - a constructive approach. ENTCS **2**(C), 118–126 (1995)
15. Hermann, F., Ehrig, H., Orejas, F., Golas, U.: Formal analysis of functional behaviour for model transformations based on triple graph grammars. In: Ehrig, H., Rensink, A., Rozenberg, G., Schürr, A. (eds.) ICGT 2010. LNCS, vol. 6372, pp. 155–170. Springer, Heidelberg (2010). https://doi.org/10.1007/978-3-642-15928-2_11

16. Lambers, L., Ehrig, H., Prange, U., Orejas, F.: Embedding and confluence of graph transformations with negative application conditions. In: Ehrig, H., Heckel, R., Rozenberg, G., Taentzer, G. (eds.) ICGT 2008. LNCS, vol. 5214, pp. 162–177. Springer, Heidelberg (2008). https://doi.org/10.1007/978-3-540-87405-8_12

17. Plump, D.: Checking graph-transformation systems for confluence. ECEASST **26**, 16 (2010)

18. Rabbi F., Kristensen L.M., Lamo Y.: Static analysis of conformance preserving model transformation rules. In: Hammoudi, S., Pires, L.F., Selic, B. (eds.) Proceedings of the 6th International Conference on Model-Driven Engineering and Software Development, MODELSWARD 2018, 22–24 January 2018, Funchal, Madeira - Portugal, pp. 152–162. SciTePress (2018)

19. Ribeiro, L., Dotti, F.L., da Costa, S.A., Dillenburg, F.C.: Towards theorem proving graph grammars using Event-B. ECEASST **30**, 16 (2010)

20. Rutle, A.: Diagram predicate framework: a formal approach to MDE. Ph.D. thesis, Department of Informatics, University of Bergen, Norway (2010)

21. Rutle, A., Rossini, A., Lamo, Y., Wolter, U.: A formal approach to the specification and transformation of constraints in mde. J. Logic Algebraic Program. **81**(4), 422–457 (2012)

22. Taentzer, G.: AGG: a graph transformation environment for modeling and validation of software. In: Pfaltz, J.L., Nagl, M., Böhlen, B. (eds.) AGTIVE 2003. LNCS, vol. 3062, pp. 446–453. Springer, Heidelberg (2004). https://doi.org/10.1007/978-3-540-25959-6_35

23. Troya, J., Vallecillo, A.: Towards a rewriting logic semantics for ATL. In: Tratt, L., Gogolla, M. (eds.) ICMT 2010. LNCS, vol. 6142, pp. 230–244. Springer, Heidelberg (2010). https://doi.org/10.1007/978-3-642-13688-7_16

24. Varró, D., Varró, G., Pataricza, A.: Designing the automatic transformation of visual languages. Sci. Comput. Program. **44**(2), 205–227 (2002)

25. Wang, X., Büttner, F., Lamo, Y.: Verification of graph-based model transformations using alloy. ECEASST **67**, 13 (2014)

Generation of Inductive Types from Ecore Metamodels

Jérémy Buisson[1](✉) and Seidali Rehab[2]

[1] IRISA, Écoles de Saint-Cyr Coëtquidan, Guer, France
jeremy.buisson@irisa.fr
[2] MISC, University of Constantine 2 - Abdelhamid Mehri,
Nouvelle ville Ali Mendjeli, Constantine, Algeria
seidali.rehab@misc-umc.org

Abstract. When one wants to design a language and related supporting tools, two distinct technical spaces can be considered. On the one hand, model-driven tools like Xtext or MPS automatically provide a compilation infrastructure and a full-featured integrated development environment. On the other hand, a formal workbench like a proof assistant helps in the design and verification of the language specification. But these two technical spaces can hardly be used in conjunction. In the paper, we propose an automatic transformation that takes an input Ecore metamodel, and generates a set of inductive types in Gallina and Vernacular, the language of the Coq proof assistant. By doing so, it is guaranteed that the same abstract syntax as the one described by the Ecore metamodel is used, *e.g.*, to formally define the language's semantics or type system or set up a proof-carrying code infrastructure. Improving over previous state of the art, our transformation supports structural elements of Ecore, with no restriction. But our transformation is not injective. A benchmark evaluation shows that our transformation is effective, including in the case of real-world metamodels like UML and OCL. We also validate our transformation in the context of an ad-hoc proof-carrying code infrastructure.

Keywords: Model-driven engineering · Model transformation · Inductive type · QVT-Operational · Ecore · Xtext · Coq

1 Introduction

In this paper, we present our work that is specifically related to the implementation of support tools for a formal architecture description language for system of systems engineering, named SosADL [1]. In this paper, we do not intend to describe this novel architecture description language. We would like to put the emphasis on difficulties that arise when we want to benefit from convenient tools like Xtext [2] and, at the same time, formally ensure language properties by means of proofs.

© Springer Nature Switzerland AG 2019
S. Hammoudi et al. (Eds.): MODELSWARD 2018, CCIS 991, pp. 308–334, 2019.
https://doi.org/10.1007/978-3-030-11030-7_14

Nowadays the creation of a language and its infrastructure becomes easier thanks to the tools that model-driven engineering offers. Among these effective tools we find MPS [3] or Xtext [2]. A complete editing environment can be generated from a combined description of concrete and abstract syntax. This can include syntax-highlighting, auto-completion and elaborated error reporting. A compilation or interpretation framework accompanies these tools in order to smoothly interact with the generated editing environment. For SosADL we choose Xtext to benefit from the mature Ecore/EMF ecosystem.

In the formal side, principled language design has been promoted by language theory. This is done using well-established techniques to specify a language in terms of, e.g., semantics and type system, and then prove that this specification is sound. Proof techniques, relevant properties and proof techniques have been proposed in the meta-theory related to language theory. And several proof assistants as Coq [4] or Isabelle/HOL [5] have been successfully used to mechanize such specifications and proofs. For SosADL we choose Coq.

The problem in our work is how to ensure the automatic transformation between the two technical spaces in order to benefit from their crossed contributions, so that the disadvantages of one can be overcome thanks to the contributions of the other. This question comes from the fact that there is a difficulty of integration between the model-driven engineering tools like Xtext or MPS and the proof assistants. Some (model-driven engineering) researches often rely on graph-based modeling, while the others (proof assistants) use inductive data types, despite some exceptions such as Rascal [6]. In other words, we need to make sure that both sides, that is, informal implementation in the Ecore/EMF technical space, and the formal specification in the Coq technical space are consistent. To overcome this problem, we base SosADL tools on the proof-carrying code approach [7]. Therefore, we aim to generate automatically large parts of the infrastructure for proof-carrying code.

In this paper, we study how to generate Coq types for the abstract syntax tree from an Ecore metamodel, such that the abstract syntax of the language is shared in the two technical spaces. Our contribution is an improved transformation in comparison to prior state of the art: constraints on the input metamodel are relaxed, especially with respect to inheritance, to the detriment of not being injective.

The work described in this paper is an extended version of our earlier publication [8]. In addition to more detailed description of the transformation, we better describe its implementation, and more specifically the transformation framework we have designed. We extend the test suite that we use to validate our transformation with real-world metamodels. And we extend the validation with some discussion of execution time.

Section 2 describes the overall context of our work. Section 3 gives a brief description of Ecore and of inductive types. Section 4 presents related work about transforming from metamodels to inductive types. Section 5 describes a running example that we use in the subsequent description of the transformation, given in Sect. 6. Section 7 discusses specific points, noticeably why we consider having an injective transformation is not that important in our case. Section 8 gives indications about implementation issues. Section 9 summarizes how we validate the transformation. Finally, Sect. 10 concludes the paper with perspectives.

2   Context and Motivations

When one wants to use model-driven techniques to implement the supporting tools for a formally-defined language, the question arises how to ensure the implementation actually conforms to the formal definition of the language. In this paper, we consider that this issue is solved by means of proof-carrying code [7].

With the proof-carrying code, the compiler (or any supporting tool for the language) not only generates compiled code. It also generate a verifiable proof of properties about the source or compiled code. By checking the validity of the

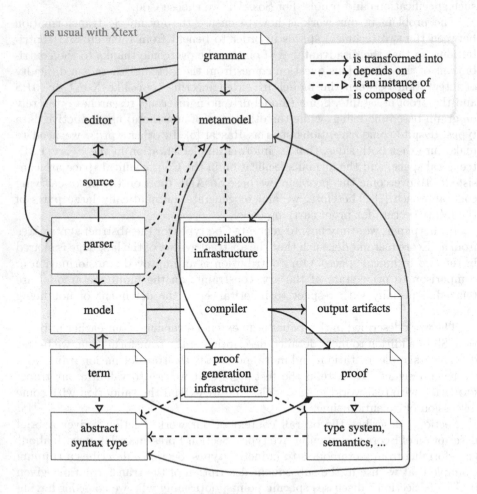

Fig. 1. The big picture of our general approach.

proof, one can easily ensure that the compiler performed correctly. For instance, the Java compiler generates annotations in the compiled byte-code such that the Java virtual machine can easily ensure that the generated byte-code has been correctly generated, without having to perform complete type checking.

Our general approach described in Fig. 1 explains the proof-carrying code approach in the way we apply it to the SosADL [1] context. This one is divided into two parts. The first (upper) part of the figure, which aims to produce at the end *output artifacts*, starts with the generation of our complete editing environment from a concrete *grammar*. This operation, which generates a *metamodel*, an *editor*, a *compilation infrastructure* and a *parser*, is performed using Xtext [2]. Thanks to this generated code, the *model* that is an instance of the metamodel is obtained from the textual *source* thanks to the parser. Then, we develop a *compiler* using the compilation infrastructure, which (the compiler) is in turn the tool for transforming the object-oriented model to the output artifacts. The second (bottom) part of the figure gives the explanation of the proof-carrying code. The *proof generation infrastructure* is used by our compiler to provide a *proof*. This proof is an instance of the language's specification, *i.e.*, of the *type system* or *semantics*. *Terms* compose this proof, which represent instances of *abstract syntax type*. In addition, these terms map with models, and thus we have to ensure a strong consistency between the metamodel and the abstract syntax type, that is, any object that is an instance of a metamodel class maps to a term whose type come from the abstract syntax, and conversely.

3   Background

In this section, we introduce Ecore and inductive types, which are the two languages which we consider to express an abstract syntax.

3.1   Ecore

An Ecore [9] metamodel is an object-oriented description of the abstract syntax of a modeling language. An Ecore metamodel consists in hierarchically-nested *packages*, where the root packages are the Ecore files. Each package contains several *classes*, which describe the types of objects that can exist in instance models. As usual in object-oriented modeling languages, Ecore supports inheritance and subtyping by means of a specialization-generalization relationship between classes. A specific kind of classes, *abstract* classes, denote classes that cannot be instantiated in models; only their concrete, i.e., non-abstract specialization classes can be.

An Ecore class contains *structural features*, namely, the fields declared by the class. In Ecore, fields can be either *attributes* or *references*. The former (attributes) denote fields whose type is a plain Java type imported as a *data type*; while the latter (references) are fields whose type is described by an Ecore type. References are further refined as either *containment* references or non-containment references, where the semantics of containment is the same as UML's composition.

An instance model, which is an instance of a metamodel, is a tree of objects (according to the containment references) whose classes are the classes described in the metamodel. Additional non-containment references allow to describe arbitrary graphs. An instance model either resides in memory or is serialized to an XMI file.

Orthogonal to the attribute/reference classification, structural features have additional properties. To transparently represent collections, each structural feature has multiplicity indication. The actual kind of collection is further refined by uniqueness and ordering properties. In addition, a feature is said *derived* when its value is computed on-demand; *transient* when it is omitted from XMI serialization; or *volatile* when it is omitted from the in-memory object.

Ecore classes also contain *operations*. But operations are not relevant in the context of this work.

Figure 2 shows an example metamodel, which contains an abstract class named `Tree` specialized by two concrete classes `Leaf` and `Node`. So only `Leaf` and `Node` can be instantiated in models. While `Leaf` has no structural feature, `Node` contains an attribute `x`, whose type is data type `EInt`, the data type that imports Java's `int` primitive type, and two containment references (containment is denoted by the diamond) named `left` and `right`. The attribute and the references all have here 1..1 multiplicity, meaning that each instance of `Node` contains exactly one `left Tree` and one `right Tree`.

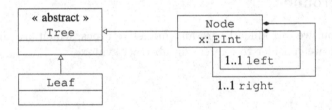

Fig. 2. Example of a simple Ecore metamodel.

3.2 Inductive Types

Inductive type is a usual approach to the definition of data types in the context of functional programming. Without lack of generality, in the following, we consider the specific case of Gallina and Vernacular, Coq's languages for terms and for module-level commands.

Each inductive type is a set of *constructors*, each of which declares a variant of the type. The data structure associated with a given constructor is specified by the formal parameters of that constructor. Types are gathered in hierarchical *modules*, where each file is a module too.

To illustrate, consider the following example in Gallina and Vernacular:

```
Inductive Tree: Set :=
| Leaf: Tree
| Node: Tree → nat → Tree → Tree.
```

This code reads as the definition of an inductive type named Tree, for which two constructors are defined:

- When a Tree is built by the Leaf constructor, its does not contain any data: the type of Leaf is Tree.
- When a Tree is built by the Node constructor, it contains a Tree, a nat (a natural integer), and another Tree. The type of Node states that it is a function that takes 3 parameters and returns a Tree.

Any value is the result of calling the constructors. A term is therefore inherently a tree that mimics the abstract syntax tree of itself, like:

```
Definition x := Node (Node Leaf 2 Leaf) 6 Leaf.
```

4   Related Works

Language theory provides background on how one specifies a language and what properties of such specification should be investigated for in order to convince that the language specification is sound. The idea to extend the theoretical approach to languages with effective tools to help in the implementation of language supporting tools has already been investigated, like witnessed by several projects. For instance, Ott [10] is a tool that, given a single description of inference rules, *e.g.*, for semantics or type systems, generates boilerplate code, as well as definitions suitable for mechanization with a proof assistant and LaTeX-based documentation. Lem [11] goes one step further and generates in addition executable functions from inductive relations encoding operational semantics or type systems. The K-framework [12] is a comprehensive approach to generate interpreters and tools from the executable semantics of a language.

More than just interpreters or tools, it may be convenient to generate compilation infrastructure, as well as full-featured editors and development environments. The idea is not new like witnessed by older projects like Centaur [13] and ASF+SDF [14]. It has been renewed in the context of model-driven engineering and domain-specific languages, that rise the issue of routinely producing supporting tools and editors for many languages. In this perspective, Xtext [2] generates a full-featured text editor and a compilation framework based on the Eclipse IDE, from a combined description of concrete and abstract syntax. MPS [3] is based on projectional editor, *i.e.*, edition is made directly at the level of the abstract syntax. MPS also provides a declarative language for executable type systems. Other language workbenches like Spoofax [15] and Rascal [16] have similar objectives of generating both compilation infrastructure and IDE services.

There is therefore a need for bridging the gap between model-driven engineering, which enables automatic generation of convenient IDE from the language definition, and formal methods that allows precise specification and analysis of the language and its semantics. To bridge this gap, one possible approach consists in generating a formal description of the language from a metamodel, or conversely in generating a metamodel from a formal language description.

Several previous work have studied how one can analyze a metamodel thanks to tools coming from formal methods, *e.g.*, [17–20]. These work usually address the question whether a metamodel is consistent, especially when the metamodel is partly specified by constraints such as OCL constraints. These work propose approaches to decide whether the metamodel is inhabited and contradiction-free, *i.e.*, whether some instance model exists and conforms to the metamodel. Since they try to prove properties of the metamodel, the main object made available in the proof assistant is the metamodel itself.

In Sect. 2 and Fig. 1, we have depicted a slightly different issue. What we are interested in is ensuring, here by means of proof-carrying code, that an analysis or a transformation conforms to its specification, and, of course, to encode this specification. In this context, the main object we would like to manipulate in the proof assistant is *instances* of the metamodel, and not the metamodel itself. So the metamodel has to be transformed into types, such that instances of this metamodel could be transformed into manipulable terms conforming to these types.

Such a transformation has already been studied in [21]. Authors have defined a bidirectional transformation between Ecore and Isabelle's inductive type: each abstract class A is mapped to an inductive type t; and each concrete class C is transformed to a constructor c of the inductive type a mapped from the super class A of C. Fields of class C are mapped to formal parameters of constructors c. Examples given in Sect. 3 illustrate this transformation scheme on a simple case. To apply this transformation, the metamodel must conform to the strict pattern of having only abstract classes without any super type nor any field, and each concrete class must specialize exactly one abstract class. The transformation is injective. But multiple inheritance, or even having a class that specializes another class that specializes yet another class is prohibited.

Rascal [6] comes with another similar transformation. Instead of restricting the metamodel, the transformation described in [6] leverages a preprocessing step of the metamodel before the scheme of [21] is used. First, structural features are pushed to concrete classes (same as our step ⑥ in Fig. 4); then references are generalized, *i.e.*, a reference to any class C is replaced with a reference to C's most general super class, hence flattening the inheritance tree to two levels. After this preprocessing step, the metamodel obviously conforms to the restrictions required by [21]. The second step of preprocessing intrinsically assumes that a most general super class exists for any class. But in presence of multiple inheritance, this assumption may not hold, unless a class implicitly generalizes all the other classes, *e.g.*, like Ecore [9]'s EObject or Java's Object classes. And if such a class exists, it turns out that the transformation issues a single inductive type for this class, to which all the constructors belong. In the end, terms manipulated in the proof assistant are therefore untyped, what is undesirable.

This last comment is the issue we address in this paper. In Sect. 6, we follow the same principles as [6,21], but without any restriction on the input metamodel. Furthermore, when multiple inheritance is not used, our transformation generates narrower types than the transformation of [6] by duplicating constructors. As counterpart, generating a term from a model is going to be harder, because the right constructor has to be selected with respect to the expected type for the term. Like in [6], our preprocessing steps break injectivity.

5   A Running Example

To illustrate the discussion in subsequent sections, we use the metamodel for λ terms of Fig. 3. A `File` is composed of `Definitions`, each containing a `Term`. A term is either an `Abstraction`, an `Application` or a `Variable`. In order to avoid issues related to naming and scopes, the abstract syntax assumes variables have already been resolved, hence `Variable` has a non-containment reference to `Binder`, which is either an abstraction or a definition. Classes are generic such that terms can be annotated, *e.g.*, with types.

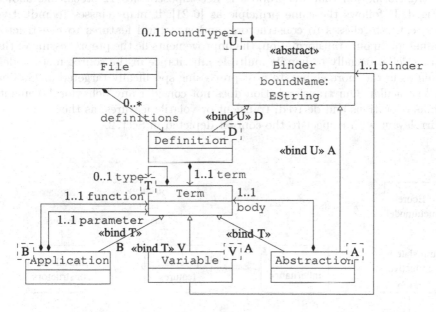

Fig. 3. Ecore metamodel of the example. Source [8].

We expect that our transformation generates the following Coq script (or equivalent), *i.e.*, inductive types such that any model that is an instance of the source metamodel can be written as a term whose type is one resulting from the transformation.

```
Inductive _Term: Type → Type :=
| Term_Abstraction: ∀ (A: Type) (type: option A) (boundName: string)
    (boundType: option A) (body: _Term A), _Term A
| Term_Application: ∀ (A: Type) (function: _Term A) (parameter: _Term A), _Term A
| Term_Variable: ∀ (A: Type) (binder: _URI (_Binder A)), _Term A
with _Binder: Type → Type :=
| Binder_Definition: ∀ (D: Type) (boundName: string) (boundType: option D)
    (term: _Term D), _Binder D
| Binder_Abstraction: ∀ (A: Type) (type: option A) (boundName: string)
    (boundType: option A) (body: _Term A), _Binder A.
Inductive _Definition: Type → Type :=
| Definition_Definition: ∀ (D: Type) (boundName: string) (boundType: option D)
    (term: _Term D), _Definition D.
Inductive _File: Type :=
| File_File: ∀ (definitions: list (_Definition _Type)), _File.
```

6   The Transformation

The transformation that we propose is decomposed into 12 steps, like shown in Fig. 4. It follows the same principle as [6,21]: it maps classes to inductive types, concrete classes to constructors, and structural features to constructor parameters. In our transformation, the improvements lie the preprocessing of the metamodel, especially to handle multiple inheritance in the source metamodel, as well as in the more elaborate post-processing specifically targeted at Gallina and Vernacular. Our transformation does not consider any behavioral element, such as operations and derived, transient or volatile features, as these elements are irrelevant with respect to the context depicted in Sect. 2.

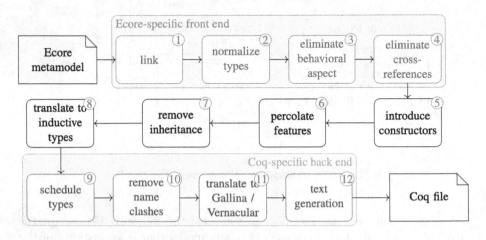

Fig. 4. Decomposition of the Ecore-to-Coq transformation.

To describe the transformation, we begin first with the Ecore-specific front-end, i.e., steps ① to ④ in Sect. 6.1. Then, in Sect. 6.2, we present the main steps ⑤ to ⑧ of the transformation. Last, Sect. 6.3 describes the Coq-specific back-end containing steps ⑨ to ⑫.

6.1 Ecore-Specific Front-End

The goal of the front-end step is to first transform the Ecore metamodel in order to normalize and simplify its representation. The first step ① erases the concept of package: all the classes are gathered in a single top-level package and a single file. Indeed, it would be tempting to map packages to modules. However, while each class can be member of any package, regardless of the relationships between classes, the situation is different in the context of inductive types. The constructors of an inductive type belong to that type, and therefore they are all members of the same module. But like explained in Sect. 6.2, constructors are mapped from classes. If the packages were not ignored, our transformation would attempt to generate the constructors of a single inductive type within several distinct modules, which is forbidden in the target language.

To illustrate more concretely, consider an abstract class A in package p1, specialized by concrete class C of package p2. In Sect. 6.2, we will see that class C maps to constructor C, which belongs to type A, itself being mapped from class A. If packages were mapped to modules, type A should be in module P1 and constructor C should be in module P2. This is impossible since constructors belong to types, not to modules.

```
 1 <LEPackage>
 2   <eClassifiers name="ecore_EString" ... />
 3   <eClassifiers name="lambda_Binder"
 4                   eSupertypes="//ecore_EObject" ...>
 5     <eTypeParameters name="U" />
 6     <eStructuralFeatures name="boundName" ... />
 7     <eStructuralFeatures name="boundType" ...>
 8       <eGenericType eTypeParameter="//lambda_Binder/U" />
 9     </eStructuralFeatures>
10   </eClassifiers>
11   ...
12 </LEPackage>
```

Fig. 5. XMI excerpt after step 1 *link*. Source [8].

To show the effect of step ①, Fig. 5 gives an excerpt of the result when applied to the metamodel of Fig. 3. The metamodel is almost unchanged. Still, classes from the Ecore metamodel are pulled into the single root package, starting with EObject because it is used as the raw type of type in Term. Because of boundName in Binder, EString is pulled too. Any other class that EObject depends on is pulled as well, and the process is repeated until all the dependencies are gathered. Like shown in the XMI excerpt of Fig. 5, the transformation encodes the name of the originating package in the class name. By using this systematic renaming scheme, the transformation avoids name clashes after all the classes are gathered in a single package.

In step ②, the transformation deals with the representation of types in Ecore. In its early versions, Ecore did not support generic classes. In this context, types and classes were confused in a single concept. Thus, the type of, *e.g.*, a reference or an attribute were given as a direct reference to the data type or to the class. Since the introduction of generic classes in Ecore, types and classes have been made two distinct concepts, yielding to the introduction of `EGenericType` to represent types. But due to backward compatibility, old-style types are still allowed when referring to non-generic data types or classes. Figure 5 contains examples of both:

- The super class of `lambda_Binder` (line 4) is given as a direct reference to the `ecore_EObject` class, which is indeed a non-generic class.
- The type of `boundType` (line 8) is given as an instance of `EGenericType`, here to represent type variable `U`.

Step ② translates all the types to a simpler uniform representation, whose abstract syntax is given in Fig. 6, regardless the types were initially given old-style or new-style. We define five kinds of types:

- `GEClassifierType` is a type built by applying effective parameters (`eArguments`) to a possibly generic classifier, *i.e.*, either a data type or a class. If the referenced classifier is not generic, *i.e.*, if it does not have any formal type parameter, then `eArguments` is empty.
- `GEVariableType` is a type variable `eTypeParameter`, *e.g.*, bound by an enclosing generic classifier.
- A `GEAnyType` represents the any-type wildcard.
- `GELowerBoundType` is a wildcard type with a lower bound.
- `GEUpperBoundType` is a wildcard type with an upper bound.

Figure 7 shows an excerpt of the resulting XMI file, in our running example. For instance, the super-class of `lambda_Binder`, which where initially given as an old-style direct reference to `ecore_EObject`, is now encoded as an instance of `GEClassifierType` (lines 5 and 6); and the type of `boundType` is an instance of `GEVariableType` referring to formal type parameter `U` of `lambda_Binder` (lines 14 and 15).

Steps ③ erases behavioral elements, that is, operations and derived, transient or volatile features. In step ④, all the non-containment references are replaced with attributes of type `_URI`. These attributes are intended to store identifiers of

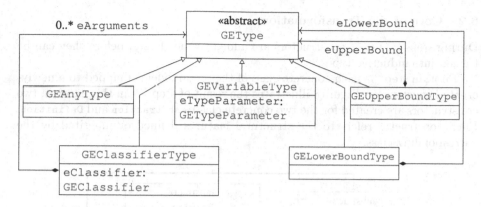

Fig. 6. Abstract syntax for types.

```
1    <GEPackage>
2     <eClassifiers  xsi:type="GEClass"
3                    name="lambda_Binder" abstract="true">
4      <eTypeParameters name="U"/>
5      <eSuperTypes xsi:type="GEClassifierType"
6                   eClassifier="//ecore_EObject"/>
7      <eStructuralFeatures  xsi:type="GEAttribute"
8                            name="boundName" lowerBound="1">
9       <eType xsi:type="GEClassifierType"
10             eClassifier="//ecore_EString"/>
11     </eStructuralFeatures>
12     <eStructuralFeatures  xsi:type="GEReference"
13                           name="boundType" containment="true">
14      <eType  xsi:type="GEVariableType"
15              eTypeParameter="//lambda_Binder/U"/>
16     </eStructuralFeatures>
17    </eClassifiers>
18    ...
19   </GEPackage>
```

Fig. 7. XMI excerpt after step 2 *normalize*.

the referred objects. Feature multiplicities are expanded to appropriate collection types at the same time, hence completing the simplification of the types:

- Features with 0..1 multiplicity are mapped to type _Option.
- Features with 1..1 multiplicity keep their original type.
- Features with $m..n$ multiplicity where $n \geq 2$ are mapped to types _List, _Set or _Bag, depending on uniqueness and ordering properties stated in the source Ecore metamodel.

In subsequent steps of the transformation, these collection types are suitably interpreted such that they are ultimately mapped to corresponding Coq types.

6.2   Core of the Transformation

During steps ⑤ to ⑦, constructors are added to the classes, before they can be
turned into inductive types.

First, in step ⑤, each concrete class of the metamodel is mapped to a newly-
created constructor. Figure 8 illustrates the result of step ⑤: in this excerpt, two
constructors are created for the two concrete classes `Abstraction` and `Definition`.
Each constructor refers to the structural features defined or inherited by the
corresponding class.

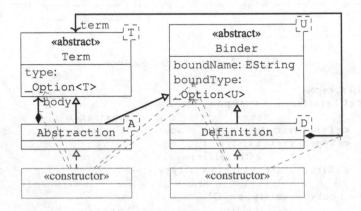

Fig. 8. Metamodel excerpt after step 5 *introduce*. Source [8].

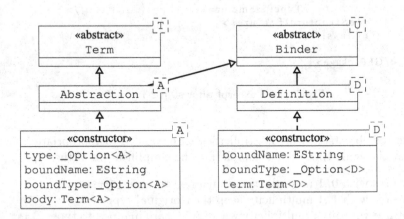

Fig. 9. Metamodel excerpt after step 6 *percolate*. Source [8].

Then in step ⑥, structural features are pulled down and cloned into the constructors, through inheritance. Like shown in the excerpt of Fig. 9, the structural
features are duplicated to all the constructors that inherit from them. Step ⑥

also ensures correct handling of generic classes by substituting type variables when the structural features are inherited, like illustrated by `type` and `boundType` in Fig. 9.

The last step that deals with constructors is step ⑦. This step duplicates constructors previously built up at each level of the generalization relation, including at abstract classes. For instance, because the `Abstraction` class inherits from the `Term` and `Binder` abstract classes, the `Abstraction` constructor is duplicated at these two classes. Because `Binder` is also a generalization of the `Definition` class, the `Binder` class is also made containing a duplicate of the `Definition` constructor. At the end of step ⑦, the generalization/specialization relation can be discarded. For each constructor duplicate, an assignment stores the precise type of the value built, hence taking into account of generic classes correctly (Fig. 10).

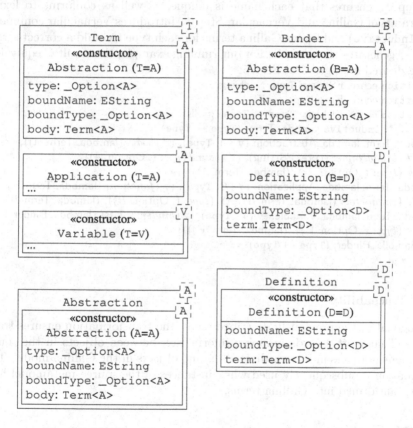

Fig. 10. Metamodel excerpt after step 7 *flatten*. Source [8].

Step ⑧ straightforwardly turns each class into an inductive types, without any further transformation.

6.3 Coq-Specific Back-End

In Gallina and Vernacular, it is forbidden that an inductive type refers to another type that is not previously defined or that does not belong to the same group of definitions. Inductive type definitions must be ordered accordingly to their dependencies. To do so, step ⑨ computes strongly connected components in the dependency graph in order to build groups of types, then this step sorts the groups according to topological order.

For instance, in the result of step ⑨, types `Binder` and `Term` shall be in the same group, since they refer each other. Indeed, constructor `Variable` (in `Term`) has a parameter of type `_URI<Binder<V>>`; and constructor `Definition` (in `Binder`) has a parameter of type `Term<D>`. This group is put before `Definition`, which refers to `Term`.

Step ⑩ ensures that each name is unique, as well as conforms to lexical constraints of Gallina and Vernacular. Step ⑪ introduces Vernacular commands (like `Inductive`) and builds Gallina terms for each type to build a correct script. Step ⑫ generates the text file. For our running example, the result is equivalent to the desired ones given at Sect. 5:

```
Definition ecore_EString: Type := string.
Definition ecore_EInt: Type := Z.
Definition ecore_EEList: (Type → Type) := list.
    (* ... *) Inductive lambda_Term: (Type → Type) :=
| lambda_Term_lambda_Abstraction: (∀ (A: Type), (∀ (body: (lambda_Term A)),
      (∀ (boundName: ecore_EString), (∀ (boundType: (_Option A)),
      (∀ (type: (_Option A)), (lambda_Term A))))))
| lambda_Term_lambda_Application: (∀ (B: Type), (∀ (function: (lambda_Term B)),
      (∀ (parameter: (lambda_Term B)), (∀ (type: (_Option B)), (lambda_Term B)))))
| lambda_Term_lambda_Variable: (∀ (V: Type), (∀ (binder: (_URI (lambda_Binder V))),
      (∀ (type: (_Option V)), (lambda_Term V))))
with lambda_Binder: (Type → Type) :=
    (* and so on *)
```

6.4 Traceability

Orthogonal to the previously described steps, the transformation ensures traceability. That is, it records mapping information between objects in the source metamodel, objects in intermediate steps and objects in the Gallina model. This information is subsequently used when instances of the source metamodel have to be transformed into Gallina terms.

7 Discussion

Our transformation restricts to metamodels that strictly conform to Ecore constraints as implemented in EMF, including constraints at the *warning* level.

In addition, the following patterns are ignored:

- When a multi-valued reference in an Ecore metamodel refers to a class that contains two features named `key` and `value`, and when this class's instance class name is `java.util.Map$Entry`, the Ecore tool chain handles this reference as a hash map. Our transformation ignores the pattern, yielding to a collection of pairs.
- When a multi-valued attribute has type `EFeatureMapEntry` and if it is suitably annotated, the attribute declares a feature map, that is, a structural feature that merges several subset structural features in a single one. Values in the collection are indexed by subset features. Because the subset features must be volatile, transient and derived, they are erased at step ③ of our transformation. But the attribute's type is not decoded to the correct type, which should be the union of the types of all the grouped subset features.

Except the above-described limitations, Ecore is fully supported. Hence the transformation cannot be injective. To illustrate the reason, consider Fig. 11: the two metamodels, despite different, result in identical Coq scripts. When the structural features are pulled from classes to constructors at step ⑥, our transformation does not track the class they originate from. By the way, this information is irrelevant in Gallina.

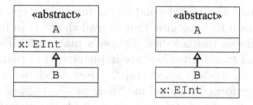

Fig. 11. Two different metamodels yielding to identical Coq scripts. Source [8].

The fact that the two metamodels yield to the same Coq script is not an issue: any model that is an instance of any metamodel of Fig. 11 is also an instance of the other one. Indeed, these models contain only instances of B that contain an integer named x, regardless x is declared in B or inherited from one of its super classes.

Still, we can further analyze what steps of the transformation are injective, and what steps are not:

- Steps ⑤, ⑧, ⑪ and ⑫ are straightforwardly injective.
- When the naming scheme is robust enough, steps ① and ⑩ are obviously injective too.
- Step ④ is not injective, mainly because multiplicities are simplified as one of 0..1, 1..1 or 0..*. Though, Gallina would allow to preserve any exact multiplicity if desired.
- Step ② is trivially not injective because Ecore's representation of non-generic types is not unique. But making the distinction between old-style representation and `EGenericType` is irrelevant as both are considered as interchangeable by the Ecore tool chain.

- Step ⑨ discards the order of metamodel elements.
- Steps ③, ⑥ and ⑦ discard information from the metamodels.

Like described in Sect. 6, the transformation is a pipeline decomposed in many steps. This approach makes each individual step simpler as each one focuses on a single issue (or few related issues). The first steps ① to ④ of the transformation are specific to Ecore, and steps ⑨ to ⑫ are specific to Gallina and Vernacular. If other source or target languages were considered, only the related steps would have to be changed. Consider MOF [22] for instance: according to [23], older versions of MOF and Ecore are convertible to one another. To adapt the transformation to MOF, step ① has to deal with nested classes, e.g., similarly to the way packages are merged; step ④ has to deal with MOF's richer reified associations; and data type mapping has to be updated, since MOF is not based on Java types. Likewise, switching to, say, Isabelle/HOL would require changing steps ⑩ and ⑪ in order to take into account the different abstract and concrete syntax.

8   Implementation

The decomposition of the transformation in multiple steps allows us to mix several implementation technologies. Our overall choice is in favor of industrial-strength freely-available technologies: Eclipse's mature EMF-and-Java ecosystem. Model-to-model transformations are implemented in plain Java and QVT-Operational. The final model-to-text step ⑫ uses Acceleo.

Steps ① to ⑩ perform only local modification. At each of these steps, when considered individually, the transformation rebuilds the overall structure of the source (meta)model into the target one, only substituting some specific sub-trees. Rather than using a general-purpose approach to model transformation, we design an ad-hoc framework that duplicates an EMF (meta)model with hooks to customize its behavior at some features of some classes. Our framework is a mixture of EMF's `EcoreUtil.copy`, ATL's refining mode [24] and Rascal's `visit` operation. But unlike these inspiring approaches, our framework is not restricted to endogeneous transformations, and therefore adopts a copy-based strategy.

The overall algorithm of our framework is given, in pseudo-Java code, in Fig. 12. At lines 2 and 3, the algorithm uses EMF's reflection to clone the object at the root of the subtree that must be transformed. The `remapClass` hook lets the transformation change the class of the object on the fly. Then at line 4, the algorithm records the mapping between source and target objects, in order to later resolve references. Each structural feature of the target class (line 5), is mapped back to a structural feature of the source class (line 6) by the `remapFeatureBack` hook.

- If the target feature is a containment feature, values are assigned immediately (line 10). By default, the `remapValue` hook calls the `clone` function in order to recursively copy model objects.

```
 1 clone(sourceObject) {
 2   targetClass = remapClass(class of sourceObject)
 3   targetObject = new object of type targetClass
 4   mapping.put(sourceObject, targetObject)
 5   for (targetFeature: targetClass.features) {
 6     sourceFeature = remapFeatureBack(targetFeature)
 7     if(targetFeature.isContainment) {
 8       for (v: remapValue(values of sourceFeature
 9                                  from sourceObject)) {
10         add v to targetFeature of targetObject
11       }
12     } else if(!sourceFeature.isContainment
13               && !targetFeature.isContainment) {
14       register (sourceObject,sourceFeature,
15               targetObject,targetFeature)
16     } else {
17       error
18     }
19   }
20   return targetObject
21 }
22
23 post-processing {
24   for(sourceObject,sourceFeature,
25       targetObject,targetFeature: registrations) {
26     for (v: remapReference(values of SourceFeature
27                                  from sourceObject)) {
28       add v to targetFeature of targetObject
29     }
30   }
31 }
```

Fig. 12. Pseudo-code of our Java-based transformation framework.

- If none of the source feature and target feature is a containment feature, the task is registered for post-processing (lines 14 and 15). After the source model has been fully handled, post-processing tasks call the `remapReference` (lines 26 and 27), which, by default, looks in the mapping table to set the reference in the target object (line 28).
- With our framework, it is non-sense when the source feature is a containment feature, while the target feature is not. Line 17, our algorithm raises an error in this case.

On top of this framework, we provide an implementation of the hook functions (`remapClass`, `remapFeatureBack`, `remapValue` and `remapReference`) based on Java reflection, yielding to simpler description of the transformation steps. Figure 13 illustrates our framework with the real source code for step ③. In the constructor at lines 3 and 4, it directs the framework to remap classes

```
 1 public class G2S extends GenericRemapper {
 2    public G2S() {
 3        super(GenericPackage.eINSTANCE, "GE",
 4              StructuralPackage.eINSTANCE, "SE");
 5    }
 6    @Rule public void eStructuralFeatures(
 7            GEClass source, SEClass target) {
 8        Function<EObject, EObject> transformer =
 9          maybeTransform(GE_CLASS__ESTRUCTURAL_FEATURES,
10                    SE_CLASS__ESTRUCTURAL_FEATURES);
11        source.getEStructuralFeatures().stream()
12        .filter((s) -> !s.isDerived() && !s.isTransient()
13                    && !s.isVolatile())
14        .map(transformer)
15        .map(cast(SEStructuralFeature.class))
16        .forEach(target.getEStructuralFeatures()::add);
17    }
18 }
```

Fig. 13. Java code for step 3 *eliminate*.

of the Generic package to classes with same name (except a prefix) of the Structural package. The rule at lines 6 to 17 implements a remapValue hook for eStructuralFeatures of a SEClass target object, when it is mapped from a GEClass source object. Lines 8 to 11 retrieve the default behavior of the hook, that is, the cloning of objects as a function named transformer. Then, the rule retrieves the eStructuralFeatures of the source object (line 11), filters those that are neither derived nor transient nor volatile (lines 12 and 13), applies the default behavior transformer to the retained objects (line 14), and put the resulting objects in eStructuralFeatures of the target object (line 16). Other structural features in any other class are just copied by the framework. By not having any structural feature named eOperations in SEClass, operations are omitted in the target (meta)model, without any further programming.

At step ⑪, QVT-Operational seems a good choice as it avoids most of the notation burden. Disjunct mapping and collection operations like iterate remind pattern-matching and higher-order functions, like usually found in functional programming. For the purpose of the comparison, we have also manually translated the QVT-Operational transformation into strictly equivalent Java code.

Our implementation records mapping information between source objects and generated ones, including intermediate ones, using a generic one-to-one correspondence metamodel. In order to deal with the size of mapping information, especially in the context of EMF's XMI serialization, our implementation produces two records:

- Summarized mapping information record only indirect mapping from each source Ecore object to the corresponding Gallina objects, hence omitting intermediate steps.
- Full mapping information is split into fragments in order to keep the size of each fragment below a fixed threshold. This trick lowers memory consumption by EMF's XMI serialization code. Synthetic objects, which do not belong to any intermediate model, are saved alongside mapping information.

Most of the transformation steps are exogeneous transformations, with the only exception of step ⑩ that is endogeneous. By making this choice, the abstract languages for target metamodels are fitted to the needs. Doing so is required to for implicit removal of objects by our framework, such as the removal of operations at step ③ like previously described. The whole transformation involves 11 different metametamodels. In the pipeline of the whole transformation, each two consecutive metametamodels must remain consistent for the elements that are not directly affected by the concerned step. Managing such 11 different metametamodels while maintaining their consistency appears to us to be a tedious and error-prone task during development, despite the small size of the metametamodels[1]. We would have appreciated lightweight mechanisms for automatic application of some editing commands to a group of several metametamodels. Using transformations engines, e.g., based on QVT or ATL, for such operations appeared inconvenient: such transformations would have had to be generic enough to be applicable to several similar-yet-different metametamodels, while not offering any reuse opportunity because editing commands are one-shot.

The Java code for steps ① to ⑩ contains 1555 SLOC, and the underlying Java-based framework contains 320 SLOC according to ohcount. The QVT-Operational script for step ⑪ is made of 218 SLOC and its Java translation contains 655 SLOC. The Acceleo template for step ⑪ contains 41 SLOC. The code is available at https://bitbucket.org/jbuisson/ecore2coq.

9   Validation

To evaluate our transformation and our implementation, we build a benchmark suite from four third-party open-source projects, in addition to the metamodels involved in our transformation itself: EMF, Eclipse's OCL, Xtext extras, and Dresden OCL. In total, we gather 80 Eclipse projects from the repositories of these projects. Like summarized in Table 1, these projects contain 279 Ecore metamodel files, of which 241 are unique files. At the completion of Eclipse's builder task, some of these metamodels are duplicated in target directories, yielding to 338 Ecore metamodel files. In this suite, 319 files pass EMF's validator

---

[1] Each metametamodel contains approximately 20 classes, 50 references, 30 attributes, and 30 data types.

Table 1. Summary of the benchmark suite.

	Ecore files (downloaded)	Ecore files (after build)	Ecore files (validated)	Coq scripts (generated)
Raw count	279	338	319	319
Unique files	241	241	226	197

without any error nor warning, of which 226 are unique files. Our transformation produces 319 Coq scripts, of which 197 are unique files, hence illustrating that our transformation is not injective.

9.1 Metrics on Source Metamodels and Generated Scripts

Table 2 summarizes some metrics about few source metamodels and generated scripts. The biggest metamodel is the UML metamodel in its version coming from the Dresden OCL project: it contains 247 classes, of which 199 are concrete and 48 are abstract. It also contains 4 data types and 13 enumeration types. Not shown on Fig. 2, the classes of the source metamodel contain 508 references and 110 attribute; increased to 554 references and 140 attributes after step ①. After step ①, additional classes are pulled in, increasing the size to 265 classes (212 abstract classes and 53 concrete classes), 15 data types and 13 enumeration types. Because one inductive type is generated for each class and for each enumeration type, 278 inductive types are generated, which altogether define 1964 constructors. The 23 generated type definitions come from the 15 data types after step ①, and 8 predefined types definitions, *i.e.*, types like _URI and _Option mentioned at Sect. 6.1.

In total, the source metamodels of our benchmark contains 3421 concrete classes and 692 abstract classes containing 5529 references and 2996 attributes, 943 data types and 210 enumeration types. After step ①, it contains

Table 2. Metrics on source metamodels and generated scripts.

File	Ecore source				After step ① *link*				Gallina target		
	classes		type	enum.	classes		type	enum.	ind.	cons.	def.
	concr.	abs.			concr.	abs.					
Ecore	20		33	0	20		33	0	20	61	41
	15	5			15	5					
UML	247		4	13	265		15	13	278	1964	23
	199	48			212	53					
...											
Total	4113		943	210	11578		4092	367	11945	43584	6675
	3421	692			8777	2801					

11578 classes (8777 concrete classes, 2801 abstract classes, 23743 references and 13589 attributes), 4092 data types and 367 enumeration types. Our transformation produces 11945 inductive types made of 43584 constructors, as well as 6675 type definitions.

The metamodels of our benchmark involve multiple inheritance. At most, one class has 8 immediate super types, increased to 9 after step ①. The depth of inheritance is up to 11 levels.

9.2 Validity of the Generated Scripts

As a first validation, we ensure that the transformation produces correct Coq scripts. To do so, we invoke the Coq compiler on each of them. Of the 319 generated scripts, 315 pass successfully compilation. Manual inspection lets us ensure that the generated scripts correspond to the source Ecore metamodels.

The remaining 4 scripts raise Coq's *non strictly positive occurrence* error. To better understand this error, consider the anti-pattern and generated script of Fig. 14. The generated type U recursively uses itself in the type of parameter x, as a parameter of generic type T. By doing so, and depending on the type of T's constructors, one can make the logic inconsistent, but, in the case of Fig. 14, this is not the case. Still Coq[2] restrict definitions of inductive types to conform to a syntactical criterion, named *strictly positive* recursive occurrences in order to ensure that any inconsistent definition is rejected. However, the syntactical criterion is a conservative one, hence ruling out some consistent definitions too. In Fig. 14, the alternate definition of T, which differs only in Coq's internal treatment, allows to work-around the criterion by moving parameter A to the inductive type itself instead of the constructor. This alternate definition shows that, in this example, our transformation generates only consistent definitions.

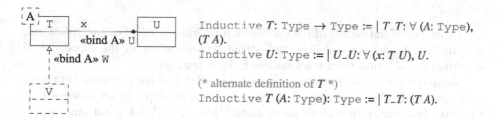

Inductive T: Type $\rightarrow$ Type := $\mid T\_T$: $\forall$ (A: Type), ($T\,A$).

Inductive U: Type := $\mid U\_U$: $\forall$ (x: $T\,U$), U.

(* alternate definition of T *)

Inductive T (A: Type): Type := $\mid T\_T$: ($T\,A$).

Fig. 14. Anti-pattern leading to Coq error.

Figure 14 is representative of the 4 failing scripts. Because the problematic parameters are type parameters of generic classes, one could think the error could be avoided by simply changing our transformation to put type parameters at the inductive type, rather than at constructors. But doing so would prevent

---

[2] Other proof assistants based on dependent types, such as Agda or Lean behave similarly.

a non-generic class, *e.g.*, V to inherit from, *e.g.*, T<W> (dashed in Fig. 14, where W is yet another class), while such a construct is perfectly permitted by our transformation and yields no error in the generated Coq script.

The error could be worked-around by specializing generic classes, that is, by doing partial application of type parameters. We have not yet included this strategy in our transformation.

9.3   Execution Time of the Transformation

Using the same benchmark, we have measured the execution time spent in the transformation with several platforms. In this perspective, we instrument the transformation in order to measure the time spent in each step, including serialization of the result but excluding XMI deserialization of the input. To mitigate intrinsic variations of execution time, each step is preceded by an invocation of the garbage collector. We also do our best to make the transformation reproduce identical artifacts regardless the execution environment, sometimes at the cost of sub-optimal implementation, *e.g.*, to ensure identical order of elements even in unordered collections. In order to avoid effects of cache and JIT, every source metamodel is transformed several times before execution time is measured.

Table 3. Execution platforms used in experiments.

Platform	CPU	RAM	OS	JDK	Heap size
A	2x Xeon L5640	48 GiB	Debian 9.4	Oracle 8_162 64-bits	16 GiB
B	4x Xeon E5-2630 v4	128 GiB	Debian 9.2	Oracle 8_162 64-bits	16 GiB
C	4x Xeon E5-2630 v4	128 GiB	Debian 9.2	Oracle 10+46 64-bits	16 GiB
D	1x i7-4702HQ	16 GiB	Windows 10 1709	Oracle 10+46 64-bits	8 GiB

Table 3 gives the details of the execution platforms we use. For each platform, we enable G1 garbage collector and string deduplication in the Java virtual machine. In each run, we use a headless Eclipse product.

Measured execution time are given in Table 4. We first use platform D to compare Java and QVT-Operational implementations of step ⑪: we observe that the Java implementation is 30 times faster than the QVT-Operational implementation.

After this first observation, we measure execution time only for the Java implementation using the other platforms, hence showing that, even with real-world metamodels, our transformation is compatible with use in interactive IDE. By comparing two runs on each platform, we evaluate variability of the execution time, here up to 2.6%, despite efforts to mitigate. Because the transformation is intended to be used in interactive environments, we do not feel necessary to have more accurate measures.

To assess the relevance of summarized mapping information, the two last lines of Table 4 give the time spent when full mapping information is saved,

Table 4. Measured execution time (seconds) of each individual step.

Step	A		B		C		D	
	Java 1	Java 2	Java 1	Java 2	Java 1	Java 2	Java	QVTo
① *link*	7.7	7.5	2.8	2.9	2.7	2.7	9.4	9.4
② *normalize*	5.8	5.7	2.1	2.1	1.9	2.0	6.9	6.6
③ *eliminate*	3.9	3.8	1.3	1.2	1.2	1.2	5.0	5.0
④ *eliminate*	4.8	4.6	1.8	1.8	1.6	1.7	5.6	5.4
⑤ *introduce*	5.8	5.6	2.2	2.2	2.1	2.1	6.4	6.1
⑥ *percolate*	14.8	15.4	6.2	6.0	5.7	5.9	10.7	10.5
⑦ *flatten*	495.4	509.4	202.1	196.6	187.3	197.9	207.6	202.9
⑧ *translate*	43.8	45.0	22.9	22.4	21.5	22.3	31.7	30.5
⑨ *schedule*	146.7	146.4	67.0	68.2	61.0	61.0	82.9	81.2
⑩ *rename*	65.5	65.9	34.3	34.0	33.5	33.5	61.6	60.9
⑪ *generate*	39.2	39.1	19.5	19.5	19.6	19.1	42.1	1332.9
⑫ *generate*	94.1	95.3	52.6	50.2	45.1	45.1	49.6	49.0
Save mapping summary	193.1	199.2	119.3	116.5	114.5	115.5	123.8	123.3
Total (transformation)	1120.5	1142.9	534.1	523.6	497.7	510.0	643.2	1923.6
Save synthetic objects	579.5	579.1	358.6	353.8	357.2	370.3	437.5	433.1
Save full mapping	2731.9	2737.4	1658.4	1727.5	1748.7	1709.9	1817.1	1792.9

including synthetic objects and intermediate objects generated at each step. We observe the time spent in these tasks is large in comparison to the time spent in the transformation. To better explain, in the case of Dresden OCL's UML metamodel, the biggest one of our suite, 59793 synthetic objects are created and 7414201 correspondences are recorded, while summarized mapping contains only 6287 correspondences. For the complete benchmark suite, 20 GiB are generated for synthetic objects and mapping, to be compared with 6.9 MiB input Ecore files, 2.5 GiB generated models and 359 MiB summarized mapping. This observation confirms that saving full mapping information should be avoided if unnecessary.

9.4   Usability in the Context of Proof-Carrying Code

To ensure that the generated scripts are actually usable in the context of proof-carrying code [7], we fully applied the approach depicted in Fig. 1 in the implementation of tools supporting SosADL [1]. This paper focuses on automating only the transformation of the Ecore metamodel towards Gallina inductive types. Hence the others tasks either involve preexisting tools such as Xtext [2] or are done by hand. Noticeably, the transformation of SosADL architectures into Gallina terms has been manually written. Then we manually instrument SosADL's type checker in order to produce proofs that witness that the architecture under consideration is actually well-typed. Last we use Coq to check the correctness of all the generated artifacts.

This experiment witnesses that the types generated by the transformation described in this paper conform to the requirements of a proof-carrying code infrastructure.

10   Conclusion

In this paper, we describe a transformation from Ecore metamodels to inductive types. This transformation allows to set up a model-driven language engineering chain, *e.g.*, involving Xtext and, at the same time, to specify the language using a proof assistant, such as Coq, and then prove properties of this specification. In comparison to previous work [6,21], our transformation has fewer constraints on the source Ecore metamodel and ensures stronger typing in the generated inductive types, but it is not injective.

To validate our proposal, we implement the transformation using QVT-Operational, Acceleo, and EMF-and-Java. We fetch of 226 Ecore metamodels from open source projects, in order to gather both synthetic and real-world metamodels for the purpose of benchmarking. For all of them, except 4 metamodels, our transformation produces valid Coq scripts. The 4 erroneous cases correspond to a specific pattern that infringes a syntactic criterion that prevents Coq from accepting potentially inconsistent type definitions. Still, this criterion is a conservative approach, and we analyze that, in our case, none of the generated type definitions may introduce any contradiction in the underlying logic. We propose to further study this point, investigating how partial application of type parameters may work-around Coq's restriction.

Our experience shows that, regardless the execution platform, our transformation scales to real-world metamodels.

In the near future, we will continue automatic generation of the proof-carrying code infrastructure from an Ecore metamodel. Our next step will be to produce a second transformation, that will generate the transformation from instance models to terms, such that the terms have the types generated by the transformation described in this paper.

References

1. Oquendo, F., Buisson, J., Leroux, E., Moguérou, G., Quilbeuf, J.: The SoS Architect Studio: toolchain for the formal architecture description and analysis of software-intensive systems-of-systems with SosADL (2016)
2. Bettini, L.: Implementing Domain-Specific Languages with Xtext and Xtend. Packt Publishing, Olton (2013)
3. Voelter, M.: Language and IDE modularization and composition with MPS. In: Lämmel, R., Saraiva, J., Visser, J. (eds.) GTTSE 2011. LNCS, vol. 7680, pp. 383–430. Springer, Heidelberg (2013). https://doi.org/10.1007/978-3-642-35992-7_11
4. Bertot, Y., Castéran, P.: Interactive Theorem Proving and Program Development: Coq'Art: The Calculus of Inductive Constructions, 1st edn. Springer, Heidelberg (2010). https://doi.org/10.1007/978-3-662-07964-5

5. Nipkow, T., Wenzel, M., Paulson, L.C. (eds.): Isabelle/HOL: A Proof Assistant for Higher-Order Logic. LNCS, vol. 2283. Springer, Heidelberg (2002). https://doi.org/10.1007/3-540-45949-9
6. Klint, P., van der Storm, T.: Model transformation with immutable data. In: Van Gorp, P., Engels, G. (eds.) ICMT 2016. LNCS, vol. 9765, pp. 19–35. Springer, Cham (2016). https://doi.org/10.1007/978-3-319-42064-6_2
7. Necula, G.C.: Proof-carrying code. In: Proceedings of the 24th ACM SIGPLAN-SIGACT Symposium on Principles of Programming Languages, POPL 1997, Paris, France, pp. 106–119 (1997)
8. Buisson, J., Rehab, S.: Automatic transformation from Ecore metamodels towards Gallina inductive types. In: Proceedings of the 6th International Conference on Model-Driven Engineering and Software Development - Volume 1: MODEL-SWARD, INSTICC, pp. 488–495. SciTePress (2018)
9. Steinberg, D., Budinsky, F., Paternostro, M., Merks, E.: EMF: Eclipse Modeling Framework 2.0, 2nd edn. Addison-Wesley Professional, Amsterdam (2009)
10. Sewell, P., et al.: Ott: effective tool support for the working semanticist. J. Funct. Program. **20**, 71–122 (2010)
11. Mulligan, D.P., Owens, S., Gray, K.E., Ridge, T., Sewell, P.: Lem: reusable engineering of real-world semantics. In: Proceedings of the 19th ACM SIGPLAN International Conference on Functional Programming, ICFP 2014, Gothenburg, Sweden, pp. 175–188 (2014)
12. Roşu, G., Şerbănuţă, T.F.: K overview and SIMPLE case study. Electron. Notes Theor. Comput. Sci. **304**, 3–56 (2014). Proceedings of the Second International Workshop on the K Framework and its Applications (K 2011)
13. Borras, P., et al.: Centaur: the system. In: Proceedings of the Third ACM SIGSOFT/SIGPLAN Software Engineering Symposium on Practical Software Development Environments, SDE 3, Boston, Massachusetts, USA, pp. 14–24 (1988)
14. Klint, P.: A meta-environment for generating programming environments. ACM Trans. Softw. Eng. Methodol. **2**, 176–201 (1993)
15. Kats, L.C., Visser, E.: The Spoofax language workbench: rules for declarative specification of languages and IDEs. In: Proceedings of the ACM International Conference on Object Oriented Programming Systems Languages and Applications, OOPSLA 2010, pp. 444–463 (2010)
16. Klint, P., van der Storm, T., Vinju, J.: EASY meta-programming with Rascal. In: Fernandes, J.M., Lämmel, R., Visser, J., Saraiva, J. (eds.) GTTSE 2009. LNCS, vol. 6491, pp. 222–289. Springer, Heidelberg (2011). https://doi.org/10.1007/978-3-642-18023-1_6
17. Barbier, F., Cariou, E.: Inductive UML. In: Abelló, A., Bellatreche, L., Benatallah, B. (eds.) MEDI 2012. LNCS, vol. 7602, pp. 153–161. Springer, Heidelberg (2012). https://doi.org/10.1007/978-3-642-33609-6_15
18. Cabot, J., Clarisó, R., Riera, D.: On the verification of UML/OCL class diagrams using constraint programming. J. Syst. Softw. **93**, 1–23 (2014)
19. Meyer, E., Souquières, J.: A systematic approach to transform OMT diagrams to a B specification. In: Wing, J.M., Woodcock, J., Davies, J. (eds.) FM 1999. LNCS, vol. 1708, pp. 875–895. Springer, Heidelberg (1999). https://doi.org/10.1007/3-540-48119-2_48
20. Lano, K., Clark, D., Androutsopoulos, K.: UML to B: formal verification of object-oriented models. In: Boiten, E.A., Derrick, J., Smith, G. (eds.) IFM 2004. LNCS, vol. 2999, pp. 187–206. Springer, Heidelberg (2004). https://doi.org/10.1007/978-3-540-24756-2_11

21. Djeddai, S., Strecker, M., Mezghiche, M.: Integrating a formal development for DSLs into meta-modeling. In: Abelló, A., Bellatreche, L., Benatallah, B. (eds.) MEDI 2012. LNCS, vol. 7602, pp. 55–66. Springer, Heidelberg (2012). https://doi.org/10.1007/978-3-642-33609-6_7
22. OMG: OMG Meta Object Facility (MOF) Core Specification (2016)
23. Gerber, A., Raymond, K.: MOF to EMF: there and back again. In: Proceedings of the 2003 OOPSLA Workshop on Eclipse Technology eXchange, eclipse 2003, Anaheim, California, pp. 60–64 (2003)
24. Tisi, M., Martínez, S., Jouault, F., Cabot, J.: Refining models with rule-based model transformations. Research Report RR-7582, INRIA (2011)

Towards Automated Defect Analysis
Using Execution Traces
of Scenario-Based Models

Joel Greenyer[1], Daniel Gritzner[1], David Harel[2], and Assaf Marron[2]($\boxtimes$)

[1] Leibniz Universität Hannover, Hannover, Germany
[2] The Weizmann Institute of Science, Rehovot, Israel
assaf.marron@weizmann.ac.il

Abstract. Modern software systems are so complex that at times engineers find it difficult to understand why a system behaves as it does under certain conditions, and, in particular, which conditions trigger specific behavior. This adds a significant burden to tasks like debugging or maintenance. Scenario-based specifications can mitigate some of the problems engineers face thanks to the scenarios' intuitiveness, executability and amenability to formal methods such as verification and synthesis. However, as a specification grows it becomes increasingly difficult to fully comprehend the interplay of all scenarios, thus again making it difficult to understand the final system's behavior. Therefore we propose a (semi-)automatic trace analysis method. It incorporates automatic techniques for identifying interesting traces, or subsequences within traces, from large sets of long execution traces. Developers are interested in knowing whether certain specification properties hold: if a property holds, what are possible executions which are evidence of this? If a property does not hold, what are examples that violate it? Scenario-based specifications are well-suited to generating meaningful execution traces due to being based on events which are meaningful in the domain of the system under design. A key observation we made was that interesting properties of a trace are often encoded in just one or very few scenarios. These concise scenarios, describing desired or forbidden behavior, are often already part of the specification or should be added to it as they encode implicitly made assumptions.

This paper incorporates and substantially extends the material of the paper published in MODELSWARD 2018 "Towards Systematic and Automatic Handling of Execution Traces Associated with Scenario-based Models" [1].

Keywords: Software engineering · System engineering ·
Scenario-based programming · Behavioral programming · Abstraction ·
Debugging · Program repair · Execution trace · Event log

© Springer Nature Switzerland AG 2019
S. Hammoudi et al. (Eds.): MODELSWARD 2018, CCIS 991, pp. 335–354, 2019.
https://doi.org/10.1007/978-3-030-11030-7_15

1   Introduction

Execution logs of complex systems often contain thousands if not millions of events. Depending on the task at hand, say, debugging an apparent problem, studying existing behavior in preparing for new developments, or making a management decision, extracting from such logs, or traces, just the relevant items can be a difficult and error-prone task. Much work has been done on trace summarization, mining, and more, towards simplifying and accelerating tasks in software and system engineering (SE) that require, or that can take advantage of, execution traces. In this paper we extend this work by observing that the properties that one finds relevant in a given trace, may change depending on the task one is working on, be it helping a customer, debugging a problem, designing a new feature, validation and verification, detecting cyber intrusions, or, demonstrating the capabilities and limitations of a system to new audiences. More generally, we propose to create a systematic arsenal of algorithms, tools, and development methodologies for using event traces in SE.

Consider, for example, the case of a model of a city-wide road system, with many autonomous and human-driven cars, and with automated traffic lights and other controls. Then, during a model-based simulation a human observer looking at a video of the system behavior notes several near-collision situations. The system's event trace, will likely contain a large number of events, including of course all car movements, traffic light changes, raw and event-based sensor data coming in from cameras, range finders and other instruments, as well as high level abstract ones such as cars reaching their intended destinations, cars having negotiated busy intersections successfully, and, sudden queues having been handled successfully. However, in analyzing each of the near-collision situations, especially for the first time, one has to filter out the vast majority of the events in the trace. Moreover, a human may be able to describe the relevant portion of the video, or the trace, which may still be quite large, with very few terms and implicit abstractions, such as: "car C_1 stopped abruptly because bicycle B_1 was quite fast, and was about to cross in front of C_1 without slowing down; and, car C_2 driving behind C_1 was barely able to brake in time and nearly collided with C_1; further, not only did C_2 not keep a safe distance at that moment, but it has been driving aggressively for some time now; this is interesting because car C_2 seems to be autonomous...".

Our context is the *scenario-based programming* approach (SBP), in which models and even final systems can be developed from components representing different aspects of desired and undesired system behavior. Here, our goal is to assist engineers working on development, debugging or maintenance of SBP models by automating the handling of simulation and execution traces, specifically, the extraction, and subsequent use of succinct sub-traces and relevant abstractions thereof.

This paper incorporates and substantially extends the material of the paper published in MODELSWARD 2018 "Towards Systematic and Automatic Handling of Execution Traces Associated with Scenario-based Models" [1]. For example, the proposed method, preliminary results, and discussion are substantially extended with technical details and examples, additional generalizable elements in the proposed methods, and new insights about defect analysis and software engineering methods in general.

In Sect. 2 we first present a small running example to be used as context for the rest of the paper; in Sect. 3 we introduce scenario-based modeling and programming; in Sect. 4 we discuss existing relevant research and tools; in Sect. 5 we present our proposed methodology; in Sect. 6 we show preliminary results and examples of applying the methodology, as well as additional reflections about processes associated with development and defect analysis; finally, in Sect. 7 we conclude with a discussion of the results and of the next steps in this research.

2 A Running Example

As a running example we use an advanced driver-assistance system using automated car-to-x communication to replace classic traffic control mechanisms such as traffic lights, towards safer and more efficient traffic flow. Figure 1 (borrowed from [1]) shows an example situation in such a system as well as a scenario that would appear in a scenario-based specification or model of that system. Roadworks block one lane of a two-lane road. Cars approach on either lane and need to communicate with the obstacle's controller in order to know what signal (either *Go* or *Stop*) to show to their driver on their dashboards. An example scenario from the system's specification could be that: (1) when a car's sensors register an obstacle coming up ahead (2) the car's driver must be shown a *Go* or a *Stop* signal (3) before the car actually reaches the obstacle.

Even experienced engineers usually need many iterations until a specification is feature-complete and defect-free. Understanding the behavior induced by a specification, including an intuitive scenario-based one, is difficult. Simple mistakes, e.g., forgetting to specify the assumption that drivers obey the signals on the dashboard, can lead to formal methods reporting that violations, e.g., car collisions, are still possible despite the expected outcome being different.

3 Scenario-Based Modeling

Scenario-based Modeling (and Programming), also termed *behavioral programming*, offers an intuitive approach for writing formal specifications. Short scenarios specify sequences of events that involve multiple objects and that define how objects/components *may*, *must*, or *must not* behave. A collection of these scenarios is a specification which, through the interplay of the contained scenarios, defines the overall behavior of an entire system. Visual and textual formalisms and languages for writing scenarios include Live Sequence Charts (LSCs) [2,3], the Scenario Modeling Language (SML) [4–6], and behavioral programming in general-purpose procedural languages like C++ or Java [7]. Figure 2 (borrowed from [1]) shows an LSC of the scenario depicted in Fig. 1.

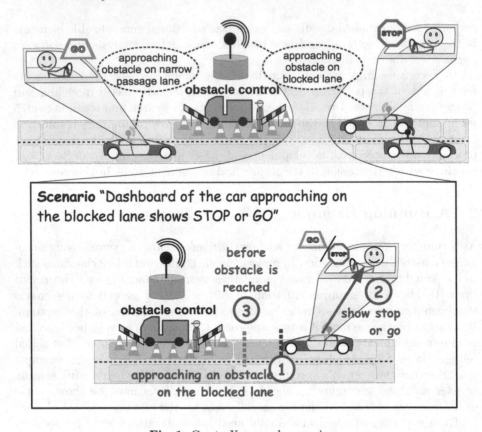

Fig. 1. Car-to-X example overview.

Key to the scenario-based approach is that execution of the specification can be done intuitively using *play-out*, namely concurrent execution of all scenarios, while complying with the constraints and possibilities defined by the entire specification and yielding cohesive system behavior. Another execution method is by synthesizing a composite automaton that reflects the desired behavior of the system under all environment behaviors; in fact, this synthesis can be seen as creating a strategy that guides event selection during play-out. Yet another approach is execution with lookahead, termed *smart play-out*, where the event selection is subject to run-time assessment of all possible upcoming execution paths, to some limited depth or horizon.

Scenarios consist of events, representing system or environment actions. Scenarios define a partial order of events and modalities encoding what events may, must, or must not occur in each system state. An event may be *requested*, *waited for*, or *blocked*. During play-out, at each state, an event that is requested by some scenario and is not blocked by any scenario is selected for triggering. All scenarios either requesting or waiting for this event are notified and can change their state and optionally change their declarations of requested, blocked, and waited-for events.

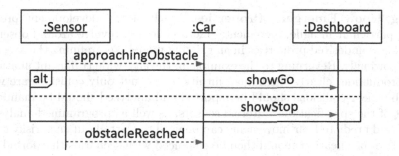

Fig. 2. LSC1: The dashboard of car approaching the obstacle must display either "go" or "stop" before the car reaches the obstacle.

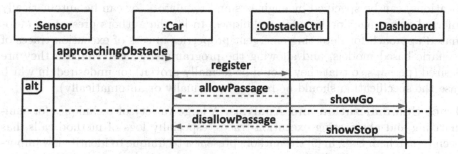

Fig. 3. LSC2: A car approaching an obstacle must first register and then wait for a go or stop signal from its dashboard.

Playing-out the scenarios in Figs. 2 and 3, after the event *approachingObstacle* both LSCs are active, but the dashboard events *showGo* and *showStop* are blocked due to the order enforced by LSC2. Thus, *register* will be executed next. Depending on the obstacle controller's reply, the car will then update its dashboard appropriately. If a car is able to reach the obstacle before the dashboard shows either *Go* or *Stop* the specification is violated.

The amenability of SBP specifications to incremental refinement is accompanied by their often being under-specified and non-deterministic: depending on the specification, multiple events may be candidates in a given state some of which may be undesirable or even lead to violations. The opposite, not all desirable events are enabled in a given state, may also be true. These situations are indicators for missing features or defects and are vital for engineers to notice and to understand their cause. However, finding and reasoning about such situations is often difficult, especially in large systems.

4 Related Work

Below we give brief examples of the kind of existing research that can be applied ad-hoc in the use of execution traces in the desired SE activities. In Sect. 5 we explain how our contribution aims to extend these capabilities.

Acting Upon Emergent Properties. Much of the development process, and in particular in agile, incremental methodologies, revolve around observing desired and undesired properties in an existing model, and refining the specification accordingly. Returning to the example in the city-wide traffic automation in the introduction, clearly the human intuition that not only collisions are violations, but near-collisions should be reported and analyzed should be manifested as part of the specification. External sensors, as well as programmed analysis of known and predicted car movements can be used to alert about such risky conditions. The specification should then be enhanced with scenarios that forbid such events from occurring. At run time, these will thus be automatically avoided where possible, and when they nevertheless occur, a violation will be reported. The detection of near-collisions in general traces (depending on velocities and locations) can be specified by engineers and regulators, or can be automatically inferred using machine learning techniques. In [8] the authors present an automated approach for detecting emergent properties in sets of execution traces of scenario-based models, and allowing the programmer to determine if they are desired (perhaps so that they should be formally proven), or undesired, in which case the specification should be repaired (manually or automatically).

Trace Summarization and Analysis. A large variety of techniques for summarizing and abstracting execution traces, especially logs of method calls, has been researched. E.g., in [9] the authors present a technique to identify low importance utility method calls by a fan-in/fan-out metric. In [10] execution traces are used to automatically generate system documentation via use case maps. The authors describe eight algorithms (some emerging from prior works on the topic) for assigning relevance or importance of methods calls. These algorithms look at call patterns, method size, etc. In other papers, such as [11], filtering of events is based on pre-designated or inferred importance of the events themselves or of the objects involved.

While the structured data of a trace can be processed using many classical techniques, including storing in databases and subjecting the information to database queries, another approach [12], treats the log data as free text and applies natural language processing techniques to summarize the raw data and distill relevant properties thereof.

Causality Analysis. In the present context of SBP we relate to causality, especially that of undesired events, as the sequence of events preceding the undesired one, where each one could occur only after one of several explicitly-specified events have occurred (triggered either by the system or the environment). This chain of events can be readily examined in a trace in which the states of all scenarios is known in addition to the identity of the events that occurred. Automated tools for problem detection (and repair) analyze traces that violate the specification or cause a crash. The tools then attempt to detect the unexpected environment event, or the undesired system decision that are the root cause for the violation, and the sequence of events leading from that root cause to the observed failure. The traces containing the problem may emanate from, e.g., execution failures (in the field or during testing) [13], and from counterexamples generated by formal verification [14]. In incremental SBP development, when an added specification scenario reflecting a valid user requirement, causes the specification to become non-realizable, the engineers then search for the unrealizable core of the specification. In this context the new scenario can be viewed both as part of the specification and as test run that violates it.

5 Proposed Method

Below we discuss in detail key elements of a proposed method for working with execution traces in the development and verification of scenario-based models. The method is outlined in Fig. 4.

The methodology is to contain the following tool capabilities and human-controlled steps:

5.1 State-Graph Generation and Analysis

Our approach assumes that the formal specification is such that one can automatically generate a composite state graph from it. The graph can be comprehensive and cover the entire behavior of the system, or, when violations are found during the generation of the state graph, a partial one can be used. Most commonly the graph will be created by a BFS or DFS play-out of all scenarios in the specification, exploring all possible event selections in each composite state. When a violation or a deadlock occurs during the play-out, the state is marked as bad, or safety violating. When a cycle is detected, that branch of the search

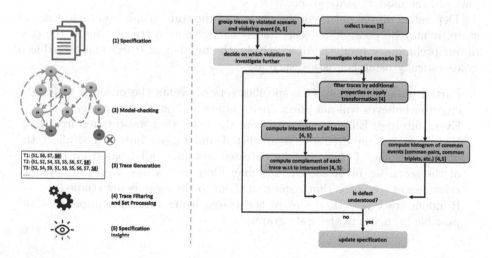

Fig. 4. Overview over our proposed method (left-hand side) and example of its systematic application to fix a single defect (right-hand side). The numbers in parenthesis in the example refer to the steps of the overview they represent. In particular steps 4 and 5 are applied iteratively. (Color figure online)

is abandoned. If, in addition, during that cycle there is at least one scenario that requests an event that *must* occur, and that event *does not* occur during the cycle, a liveness violation is indicated for the states of that cycle.

The goal at this stage is limited to finding *at least one* failure which the environment could force on the system. The findings of this step will be the input to the subsequent steps, whose goal is to pinpoint and *understand* the problem towards manual repair by a human engineer (for automated repair of scenario-based programs see, e.g. [15]. Once such a problem is repaired or bypassed, the process can repeat, starting again with formal analysis.

In a variation on the formal methods approach for obtaining failed executions, one can identify failures by creating a collection of traces using multiple random (possibly parameterized) runs, in which undesired emergent properties are observed automatically (see, e.g. [8]), or by a human.

5.2   Generating Sets of Failing Traces

Developers commonly work with one trace at a time, reflecting one way to reach the problem state. The methods we propose enhance this kind of work, and also augment it with tools for working with sets of traces. This adds features that are common across multiple failing traces and behaviors that are unique to certain failing traces to the analysis. Naturally, many failing execution traces come from failed test runs and from problem reports. To these we suggest to add the following. Once a bad system state is identified as described in the formal analysis step, do not suffice with a single counterexample run that violates the specification or manifests some desired behavior. Instead collect *multiple* such paths in the model's state graph.

Depending on the nature of the portion of the state graph leading to the bad state, it may be possible to generate *all* bad execution traces (this is the case in our preliminary results). Alternatively, the number of traces can be reduced systematically using heuristics, such as,

- Partial order reduction: One specifies sets of events the order of which the engineer believes will not affect their understanding of the problem.
- Event filtering: Eliminate events from the trace that are deemed irrelevant. E.g., environment events that are listed and logged but do not affect the outcome. Some of these can be detected automatically, based on the logic of the scenarios involved. Or, one may filter events based on the apparent relevance of scenarios that requested them to the issue being studied.
- Random trace selection: Create the traces using random sampling of the possible branches in the state graph.

5.3   Enhancing the Traces

Whether in the development lab or in the field, we propose that classical event traces be augmented. In our experiments, we enhanced the classical trace of state labels and transition events with an extensive snapshot including:

- a list of active scenarios (ideally, this would include their respective local states)
- the enabled events (metaphorically, the 'roads not chosen', at any given state), and,
- selected objects (e.g., cars) and their states (i.e., property values).

While such richly-labeled traces can become unwieldy in large systems, we observe and propose that extensive logging can be a game-changer in SE in general, regarding the ability of a system to be adaptive in real time to changes in the environment and to the results of its own behavior (see also [16]). Hence, developing fast automated offline and run-time techniques for compressing and filtering extensive traces would be an important enabler not only for problem detection, as in the present research, but for other purposes as well.

5.4   Ad-hoc Tool Validation

Whenever one relies on a tool to diagnose problem (especially in the case of a new tool, or a first time use by a novice user) there is a need to confirm, time and again, that the tool does not miss important problems, and does not generate false alarms, as may happen due to incorrect application of the tool, major errors in the original specification (e.g., a logically bad assertion that makes all runs into good ones), or bugs in the tool itself.

While SBP offers advantages in incremental development, our preliminary experiments show that it is also advantageous in doing the opposite: incremental removal of features, or isolated insertion of well-specified undesired behaviors. These can then be used to make sure that the tool indeed works as expected.

In the car-to-x SBP model described in Sect. 2 we have experimentally modified (or have removed altogether) individual specification scenarios (both individually and several together), and checked whether the proposed techniques can help identify the root cause of problems. We propose that when analyzing the root cause of a particular behavior (e.g., a hard-to-solve, hard-to-recreate customer-reported problem), we also modify the specification intentionally to generate similar external symptoms, and keep enhancing our tools until they are able to automatically detect the new known (synthetic) root cause. Then, we can more safely apply the same tools to the traces from the customer problem at hand.

5.5   A Rich Trace-Processing API

In our experiments we externalized a rich and growing library of filtering and validation functions to end-users and to higher-level scripts. This enables the easy creation and modification of chains of trace-processing functions suited to the task at hand. Often, engineers gain additional insights while closely examining a defect, thus they need to be able to easily incorporate these new insights into the trace analysis, both via ad-hoc queries regarding a problem being studies and via automating future trace-set analysis.

The trace-processing tools should also allow engineers to readily incorporate any heuristics they develop, as a method to be readily accessible in all future analyses, for the entire community.

For example, our proof-of-concept APIs include, among others:

- generating all traces induced by a model or specification that exhibit interesting properties, such as:
  - traces which lead from one particular state to another particular state (our experiments are a special case of this: the traces lead from the initial state of the system to a violating state),
  - traces that visit a particular state
  - traces that have certain length
  - traces that contain a particular event or sequence of events
  - traces during which a certain scenario is active
  - traces that begin with a particular setting and configuration of the objects in the environment (e.g., in our case, initial location of all cars and initial state of the obstacle controller.

Such APIs enable engineers to describe the case-specific properties that the selected traces should have, e.g., only traces which lead to a collision of two cars, and to collect traces for any interesting observed behavior, even one which does not yet violate the specification. For this purpose one may also add scenarios, that look for certain conditions at run time, to the specification and generate additional events which are then referenced in pruning the trace generation process.

- filtering a given sets of traces based on the same properties and conditions which can also be used for collecting traces in the first place. This feature enables engineers to quickly modify the set of traces they work with offline without the need to run full system simulations.
- computing the intersection of traces. For example, one approach we used is to treat each trace as a set of events, compute the intersection of these sets, and then choose a trace, and filter it to show only those events that are common to all traces in the set. Assuming that all traces in the entire set fail in the same or similar way, this may help pinpoint the elements that are essential to the failure.
- compute the complements of such intersections, in search for properties that are unique to individual traces or to particular (sub)sets of traces. For example, filter a trace such that the result shows only events that are not common to *all* traces in the set being studied. By contrast to the previous element, if analyzing commonalities does not help pinpointing the problem, perhaps analyzing the way by which each trace is different from all others (or many others) may provide the desired insights (Tolstoy's Anna Karenina opening

sentence "All happy families are alike; every unhappy family is unhappy in its own way." may explain some of the rationale for this approach, though in our case all traces in the set are failed ones).

- retrieving or filtering sets of traces according to properties of the trace itself. A key property which we found useful is the scenario (or scenarios) being violated, and the identity of the violating event. Other properties can include order and correlation of events or properties of individual trace entries.
- quantitative analysis (e.g., producing histograms) of trace properties (within a set of traces) and of entry properties (within a trace or set of traces). This can be helpful for identifying properties that may not occur in all traces but may still occur in many traces and point towards the cause of a problem.
- trace transformation, especially according to specification properties. Traces may contain superfluous information which the engineer may want to remove, e.g., in our car-2-x example, information about a third and fourth car when investigating the collision of two cars, or removing the most frequent or most infrequent events in preparation for quantitative analysis or for anomaly detection.
- specification manipulation API. When narrowing down a problem, it is often necessary to modify the original specification, such as adding simplifying assumption, removing irrelevant scenarios, etc. One may also mark certain 'bad' states as 'good' in order to bypass certain problems and allow otherwise hard-to-obtain traces to proceed past that point for further analysis. On the one hand, the scenario-based approach simplifies this kind of analysis, allowing the engineers to test a variety of combination of scenarios, adding and removing them to create different specification configuration, in a way that is much easier than is commonly possible with ordinary procedural code, using, say, special test scaffolding, method-call stubs and mock objects. On the other hand, managing manual modification, even when done in a well-controlled source/version management system would be risky, especially as it would be combined by the actual incremental repair. Hence a specification-control system with allowance of temporary addition and removal of scenario is desired. Such an API can be seen as a partial manifestation of the concept of reactive specification [16], where the specification itself is a reactive system in its own right, adapting, in this particular case, to changes in the requirements, as opposed to changes in the runtime environment.

The right-hand side of Fig. 4 illustrates a systematic process how an engineer could use the methodology and the proposed API to find and fix a defect in a specification. All steps in blue boxes with black borders are steps directly supported by our proposed API whereas all other steps require manual, creative effort by a human engineer. First, the engineers collect all traces from the state graph induced by a scenario-based specification that exhibit some undesirable behavior, e.g., all simple paths leading from the initial state to a state in which any safety violation occurs. As there may be multiple defects in the specification, they then group these traces by violated scenario (or set of violated scenarios) and the violating event (i.e., the last event in each path). After choosing a group to investigate next, based, e.g., on severity of the symptoms they take a closer look at the violated scenario to find out whether this scenario itself may be wrong. If, as is often the case, the violation is only the symptom of a defect, with the actual cause being somewhere else in the specification, the engineers enter an iterative process in order to gain understanding of the actual cause of the defect. In each iteration they filter and transform the traces from the group being investigated, based on insights on the defect's cause they have already gained so far. For example, irrelevant events such as ones representing the movement of a far-away car when investigating a collision that does not involve it all. Additionally, they filter and query the trace (using the above API), and modify the original specification in various ways to gain additional information and insight.

6 Preliminary Results

6.1 The Specification

In this section we describe an experiment we conducted to develop and exercise the proposed methodology. We also describe additional reflections and insights gained in the process, which have methodological implications for software development and associated tools, that are applicable to a broader context, beyond debugging with sets of traces.

In the experiment, we created an SML specification [4–6] of the example from Sect. 2. This specification defined the behavior of an obstacle controller which tells approaching cars when they must wait and when they may enter the single available lane, so that cars approaching from opposite directions can pass the obstacle without colliding with each other.

The specification contained three conceptual kinds, or categories, of scenarios, each kind modeling a different aspect of the system, or of the design process. A similar distinction is, of course, applicable in other contexts as well, but the scenario-based approach allows tying it to executable parts of the code. The categories are:

(A) Assumptions about the environment's behavior. E.g., in our case, how the cars and drivers behave, the layout of the road, etc., which are the environment in which the obstacle controller system exists and behaves.

(B) Rules guiding the behavior of the system. E.g., in our case, what the obstacle controller must or must not do following certain events or when certain conditions hold.

(C) Requirements that the final behavior of the obstacle controller must fulfill given its environment. E.g., in our case, that collisions are not allowed. This reflects the purpose of the system and overall constraints not covered by the first two categories.

Note: The general problem in formal program synthesis is to produce category (B) specifications (in the form of an automaton, a procedural program or a scenario-based program) given only category (A) and category (C) specifications. Further the boundary between categories (B) and (C) is not crisply defined, and keeps moving with the development of the ever higher abstractions available in programming languages and in synthesis capabilities.

In the present specific context of scenario-based programs, and in particular, as the execution is often driven by *play-out* rather than by running synthesized programs, the scenarios of category (C) serve multiple purposes: First, they enable underspecification in scenarios of category (B), leaving the system more options to choose from at run time. The category (C) scenarios actively participate in the play-out, and are consulted as guards and constraints during event selection. Second, category (C) scenarios can guide smart play-out (i.e., execution with lookahead) or program synthesis so that the proper choices can be made. Finally, when the category (B) scenarios define the system's behavior fully and deterministically, the category (C) scenarios serve as a separate, nearly independent alternative specification of the properties that the system should be tested against.

6.2   Inserting Defects

We made the following modifications to the specifications in our experiments:

1. We changed an obstacle controller scenario to have an "off-by-one" error - where when only one car is passing in the narrow area, cars arriving from the other direction are not signaled to stop. When two or more cars occupy the narrow area, the signal works correctly.
2. We removed the (often forgotten) environment assumption that drivers obey the stop/go signal on their dashboard.
3. We omitted the scenario that, as soon as the narrow area becomes free, allows the passing of cars that were previously told to wait.
4. We introduced a copy&paste error in the scenario describing the requirement that car collisions must be avoided.

These modifications reflect commonly made mistakes such as "off-by-one" errors, errors resulting from using copy&paste incorrectly, or forgetting to specify important aspects of the system. The modifications in our experiments also covered all three categories of scenarios.

6.3   Systematic Analysis of Traces to Identify Defects

We used a prototype of our aforementioned trace-processing tools and API to analyze traces induced by our modified specifications. Initially, we created a version of the specification that contained the first three modifications and collected all traces leading from the initial state of the system to a state violating the specification. This initial set of traces occupied 78MB. It contained about 5000 traces of about 20 events each. The three modifications we picked all represented defects in (A) or (B) kind scenarios.

Clearly one or few of these small traces could have been analyzed manually using traditional techniques, but in our initial experimentation we were able to execute the following partially automated analysis of the entire set as follows. In the first batch of steps:

1. We extracted all traces that lead to a safety violation of the specification.
2. We created a list of all events that trigger a violation.
3. We (manually for now) observed in this list that violations occur upon the event of a car reaching the obstacle or the event of a car passing the obstacle.
4. We used this observation to narrow our set of traces to all those in which the event `carB1.obstacleReached` is the cause of a violation. (such choice can emanate from, say, a customer complaint—that after certain actions certain undesired conditions emerged). This yielded 670 traces, all with the same violated scenario, the one named `CarReceivesAnswerBeforeReachingObstacle` (where the name is self explanatory).
5. We checked a failed trace against this scenario and saw that the above event occurred out of order and the expected event (of reaching the obstacle) has not arrived yet at that point.
6. We checked all scenarios which can emit this event. This yielded (in this case) just a single scenario. Finding the "off-by-one" bug in this small scenario was then straightforward.

While some of these steps are similar to classical debugging, one should note that some of the answers apply to a multitude of test runs and not just to one, providing a greater generality to the analysis and to the proposed solution.

We then pursued a second batch of steps as follows:

1. We fixed the bug we have found above.
2. We collected new traces from the specification now presumably containing only defects 2 and 3.
3. We verified that the first problem was indeed fixed, i.e., the previously observed undesirable behavior of having cars reach the obstacle without being signaled whether they should wait or may pass was indeed gone. The events triggering a safety violation now only included events of cars that are trying to pass the obstacle.
4. Again, we narrowed down the set of traces under investigations to those in which a particular event, `carB1.passingObstacle`, triggers the violation. This resulted in a set of 3640 traces.
5. We investigated which scenarios were violated, and found 4200 violations of the scenario specifying that car collisions must be avoided.
6. We inspected these violations and noticed that `carB1` can collide with two other cars, `carA1` and `carA2`. Sometimes even with both at the same time, thus triggering two violations with one event.
7. We went back to the set of traces under investigation and used our API to filter it some more. We removed all traces that include `carA2` to focus on collisions between the other two cars.

8. We used the intersection feature of our API to find the common behavior among all these remaining traces and found the following:

```
env -> carA1.approachingObstacle()
carA1 -> obstacle.register()
env -> carB1.approachingObstacle()
carB1 -> obstacle.register()
env -> carA1.passingObstacle()
env -> carB1.passingObstacle()
```

and two kinds of complements of the intersection, namely six traces containing

```
obstacle -> carA1.allowPassage()     // may pass
obstacle -> carB1.disallowPassage() // must wait
```

and four traces containing

```
obstacle -> carB1.allowPassage()
obstacle -> carA1.disallowPassage()
```

This suggested that the cars simply ignored the signals they were sent. Both cars tried to pass the obstacle at the same time despite one car having received a wait signal.

9. We examined the entire specification looking for a specification that forbids events associated with a car's progression between getting events associated with disallowing passage and events associated with allowing passage. We could not find any such scenarios (granted, one does not always know *exactly* what one is looking for in such cases as some of the desired effect may be only indirectly implied from well-thought-out specifications). We concluded that a specification of the assumption that cars obey the signals that are sent to them was missing.

We were able to reach the same conclusion about the root cause of the problem (cars ignore the signals from the obstacle controller) using our API also with different analysis steps, this time quantitative ones, as follows:

1. We created a histogram of the number of occurrences of all pairs and triplets of consecutive events in all the traces.
2. We observed that the triplet (and its analogue for the other cars)

```
obstacle->carB1.disallowPassage()
 env->carB1.obstacleReached()
 env->carB1.passingObstacle()
```

occurred many times.
3. In a slightly different quantitative analysis, using our API to create three transformations of each trace, each transformation only containing the events involving one particular car, we could show that each trace contained at least one offending triplet, i.e., at least one car ignored its wait signal.

We then fixed the problem we just identified, i.e., we added (back) the assumption that cars obey the signals, and proceeded with the partially-automated analysis as follows:

1. We used the API to generate the state graph and look for violations. This showed that there are no safety violations, only liveness violations. The specific property that was violated was that each car eventually goes past the narrow area.
2. We collected a set of traces leading to the liveness violation.
3. After several filtering operations similar to the above, we observed that the last event received by `carB1` prior to entering a cycle in which a car never goes past the narrow area, is `carB1.disallowPassage()`, and that no `allowPassage()` is sent to it after that event, despite all cars that drive in the opposite direction being conspicuously past the narrow area (e.g., the location of `carA1` is `BehindObstacle`).

In this experiment we showed that using multiple traces instead of just one single example, can significantly help the process of understanding of the cause of a problem. Note that while the observed violations were all in the requirements scenarios, (i.e., some property encoded in a category (C) scenario did not hold), the actual causes of the problems were elsewhere, and trace analysis helped to understand and pinpoint the causes, even though the problematic sequence of events may have occurred much earlier than the actual violation. Even in cases in which entire scenarios where missing this approach worked well and it works for both safety and liveness violations.

6.4   Defects in the Requirements

During this first experiment we noticed that all three mutations of our specifications relied on the presence of category (C) scenarios. The latter forced the defective category (A) and (B) scenarios to cause violations. This leads to two questions:

1. How should one handle user reports of an issue that does not cause a violation (e.g., because the respective category (C) scenario encoding the user's expectation is missing)?
2. What happens if there is a defect in one of the category (C) scenarios?

One answer to the first question is that the proposed API needs to support the collection of traces fulfilling arbitrary user-defined properties. Collecting all traces from the initial state to a violating state is a special case of an engineer wanting to inspect all traces which lead from one specific state in which the system is still known to be in a good state, to another specific state, where the engineers know the target state or paths between the two are undesirable. Our API now includes support for such trace collection request. Extending this to sets of source states and sets of target states, as defined by some properties is left as future work.

The answer to the second question has two parts. First, if the defective category (C) scenario is indeed violated by an otherwise valid trace, this can be discovered immediately when examining the violated scenario upon encountering such a violation. In scenario-based specifications, where program modules are usually short and refer to one sentence or a short paragraph in the requirements as conceived by stakeholders and engineers, it is often easy to notice the error in the way a requirement is specified which causes it to be unduly violated. This became apparent in a second, smaller-scale iteration of our experiment in which we tried to apply our proposed methodology to a mutated version of our example specification which contained the fourth defect of those listed in Sect. 6.2. Throughout our experiments, when intended and unintended defects caused the defective scenario itself to manifest a violation, discovering and fixing the defect was straightforward.

In order to be able to discover problems in category (C) scenarios which are not manifested by their violation, we propose a somewhat different approach. For each category (C) scenario, one should prepare a setup that violates it. For example, such a setup can be a single test scenario that requests a sequence of events that should violate the property at hand. As part of initial testing (perhaps immediately when the category (C) scenario for the property is first written) any other existing scenarios which may prevent the violation should be disabled or removed and the test scenario be executed alongside with the tested property. Then one should confirm that either the property is violated, or that the property scenario causes the test scenario to be stuck, or to terminate prematurely.

Thus, the main strength of the trace analysis approach described in Sect. 5 lies in helping to identify defects in which the cause lies at a different point in time than the observed undesirable behavior.

6.5 Support for Demonstrating Relevant Properties

The debugging tools and methodology presented above, can also be used for a different purpose: demonstrating desired properties in specifications and sets of traces. Consider for example a request by a reviewer of the system to see a demonstration 'proving' that the obstacle controller sends a `disallowPassage` signal to approaching cars whenever there are other cars occupying the narrow area in the opposite direction. We assume also that this has not been and cannot be added as a separate category (C) scenario, and must be implied by other, existing scenarios. Note also that a straightforward formal verification that this property holds in the specification may even be misleading, e.g., if due to other modeling errors it turns out that cars rarely, or even never, arrive at the obstacle from opposite directions at the same time. Of course, a single test run would be a nice, but insufficient demonstration. This is what often happens in real system demos. However, a more powerful demonstration would be to show statistics indicating that in an extensive collection of runs, triples like

```
env->carA1.passingObstacle()
obstacle->carB1.disallowPassage()
env->carB1.obstacleReached()
```

occurred thousands of times, repeatedly, and in distinct traces. This feature of the entire approach also serves as a reminder that a particular trace or set thereof may possess multiple relevant properties, and engineers may be interested in different properties at different times. E.g., during our analysis of collisions in pursuing the second defect, the automated trace analysis informed us, without us asking explicitly, that the obstacle sent the required signals correctly in all possible runs.

7   Conclusion

We presented a method for the analysis of large sets of long execution traces which are obtained from scenario-based specifications. We demonstrated how an engineer can extract useful knowledge for debugging from such a set of traces by iteratively applying functions, e.g., filtering, from a rich trace analysis API. In each iteration, the engineer narrows down on the actual root cause of the problem under investigation until they finally understand why the system does not behave as expected. The scenario-based nature of the specifications then makes it easy for them to fix any faulty scenarios or add any missing scenarios.

7.1   Future Work

There are several areas in which we would like to improve our method to support engineers even further.

One is expanding our trace analysis API to allow even richer queries, e.g., "from which set of alternative events did the system choose when it picked event E1 and are there traces in which the alternatives where picked?". Also, queries regarding strategies may help engineers: some undesirable behavior may be avoidable by the system when it follows a certain strategy. In such cases engineers may want to know whether some behavior is avoidable (i.e., if a variant of the strategy exists), and if it is, under what circumstances this will be possible.

Currently, our method relies on an engineer making decisions on how to use the proposed trace analysis API to narrow down on the cause of a problem. We want to expand our method, e.g., through heuristics, to help engineers with these decisions by proposing new queries based on past iterations that may guide the engineer towards his or her goal.

Also, we would like to develop stronger tools which support determining the causality of events: event A occurred and thus it was unavoidable that event B eventually happens ($A \implies B$). If the distance between an event, that ultimately causes a violation, and the violation itself is rather larger, building chains of causality can help determine where exactly changes in the specification are necessary. Also, knowing which events are not part of the chain can be used as a filtering mechanism.

Augmenting traces with additional information, especially traces which are logs of an actual system running in the real world, can help engineers make informed decisions. In the Introduction we described, as an example, a near-collision between two cars. Suppose the aggressively driving car (C_2) actually was an ambulance with sirens on, the engineers may decide on different changes to the specifications: how to behave in an emergency situation vs. how to behave when dealing with a driver not adhering to the rules.

Currently, we work with formal languages (formal models and formal queries). In the future, a natural language interface could provide many benefits: bug reports from users could be investigated more easily, useful documentation which does more than describe mere interfaces can be generated automatically, interactions with professional customers can be made easier, and maybe more.

Acknowledgements. This work has been funded in part by grants from the German-Israeli Foundation for Scientific Research and Development (GIF), from the Minerva foundation, and from the Israel Science Foundation (ISF).

References

1. Greenyer, J., Gritzner, D., Harel, D., Marron, A.: Towards systematic and automatic handling of execution traces associated with scenario-based models. In: Proceedings of the 6th International Conference on Model-Driven Engineering and Software Development (MODELSWARD), pp. 560–566 (2018)
2. Damm, W., Harel, D.: LSCs: breathing life into message sequence charts. Formal Methods Syst. Des. **19**, 45–80 (2001)
3. Harel, D., Marelly, R.: Come, Let's Play: Scenario-Based Programming Using LSCs and the Play-Engine. Springer, Heidelberg (2003). https://doi.org/10.1007/978-3-642-19029-2
4. Greenyer, J., et al.: Scenarios@run.time - distributed execution of specifications on IoT-connected robots. In: 10th International Workshop on Models@Run.Time (MRT), Co-located with MODELS 2015, CEUR Workshop Proceedings (2015)
5. Greenyer, J., Gritzner, D., Katz, G., Marron, A.: Scenario-based modeling and synthesis for reactive systems with dynamic system structure in scenariotools. In: Proceedings of the MoDELS 2016 Demo and Poster Sessions, Co-located with ACM/IEEE 19th International Conference on Model Driven Engineering Languages and Systems (MoDELS), CEUR (2016)
6. Gritzner, D., Greenyer, J.: Controller synthesis and PCL code generation from scenario-based GR (1) robot specifications. In: Proceedings of the 4th Workshop on Model-Driven Robot Software Engineering (MORSE 2017), Co-located with Software Technologies: Applications and Foundations (STAF) (2017)
7. Harel, D., Marron, A., Weiss, G.: Behavioral programming. Commun. ACM **55**, 99–100 (2012)
8. Harel, D., Katz, G., Marelly, R., Marron, A.: An initial wise development environment for behavioral models. In: Proceedings of the 4th International Conference on Model-Driven Engineering and Software Development (MODELSWARD), pp. 600–612 (2016)
9. Hamou-Lhadj, A., Lethbridge, T.: Summarizing the content of large traces to facilitate the understanding of the behaviour of a software system. In: 14th IEEE International Conference on Program Comprehension (ICPC), pp. 181–190. IEEE (2006)

10. Braun, E., Amyot, D., Lethbridge, T.C.: Generating software documentation in use case maps from filtered execution traces. In: Fischer, J., Scheidgen, M., Schieferdecker, I., Reed, R. (eds.) SDL 2015. LNCS, vol. 9369, pp. 177–192. Springer, Cham (2015). https://doi.org/10.1007/978-3-319-24912-4_13
11. Noda, K., Kobayashi, T., Toda, T., Atsumi, N.: Identifying core objects for trace summarization using reference relations and access analysis. In: 2017 IEEE 41st Annual Computer Software and Applications Conference (COMPSAC). IEEE (2017)
12. Bertero, C., Roy, M., Sauvanaud, C., Trédan, G.: Experience report: log mining using natural language processing and application to anomaly detection. In: 28th International Symposium on Software Reliability Engineering (ISSRE) (2017)
13. Weimer, W., Forrest, S., Le Goues, C., Nguyen, T.: Automatic program repair with evolutionary computation. Commun. ACM 53, 109–116 (2010)
14. Clarke, E., Grumberg, O., Jha, S., Lu, Y., Veith, H.: Counterexample-guided abstraction refinement for symbolic model checking. J. ACM (JACM) 50, 752–794 (2003)
15. Harel, D., Katz, G., Marron, A., Weiss, G.: Non-intrusive repair of safety and liveness violations in reactive programs. Trans. Comput. Collect. Intell. (TCCI) 16, 1–33 (2014)
16. Marron, A.: A reactive specification formalism for enhancing system development, analysis and adaptivity. In: 15th ACM-IEEE International Conference on Formal Methods and Models for System Design (MEMCODE) (2017)

A Textual Notation for Modeling
and Generating Code for Composite Structure

Mahmoud Husseini Orabi[✉], Ahmed Husseini Orabi[✉],
and Timothy C. Lethbridge[✉]

University of Ottawa, Ottawa, Canada
{mhuss092, ahuss045, timothy.lethbridge}@uottawa.ca

Abstract. Models of the composite structure of a software system describe its components, how they are connected or contain each other, and how they communicate using ports and connectors. Although composite structure is one of the UML diagram types, it tends to be complex to use, or requires particular library support, or suffers from weak code generation, particularly in open source tools. Our previous work has shown that software modelers can benefit from a textual notation for UML concepts as well as from high-quality code generation, both of which we have implemented in Umple. This paper explains our extensions to Umple in order create a simple textual notation and comprehensive code generation for composite structure. A particular feature of our approach is that developers do not always need to explicitly encode protocols as they can be in many cases inferred. We present case studies of the composite structure of several systems designed using Umple, and demonstrate how the volume of code and cyclomatic complexity faced by developers is far lower than if they tried to program such systems directly in C++.

Keywords: Umple · Active object · Composite structure · UML

1 Introduction

A system modelled using *composite structure* has a set of components that run concurrently, and interact or communicate via *ports* and *connectors* [1]. Some components contain (are composed of) others, while additional components can be distributed on a network. Composite structure is one of the key diagram types of UML; advances in composite structure development such as those outlined in this paper will help in the development of connected embedded devices.

In UML, components interact by sending each other messages and signals, which can be one-way (asynchronous) with no immediate results returned or blocking while waiting for a response (synchronous). Typically, when an event message is received, an event-handler method is invoked. Event handling is often performed in a component's state machine.

Handling message flow among ports and components is typically managed using protocols. In a normal workflow, defining a protocol involves careful engineering, and some redundancy in the specifications since outgoing and incoming message types and sequences must correspond. This adds complexity to the development process.

© Springer Nature Switzerland AG 2019
S. Hammoudi et al. (Eds.): MODELSWARD 2018, CCIS 991, pp. 355–379, 2019.
https://doi.org/10.1007/978-3-030-11030-7_16

Open-source tools such as eTrice and ArgoUml do not support all the major features of composite structure [1]. On the other hand, commercial tools that provide strong support for composite structure typically restrict users to certain libraries, such as Connexis, which is tightly integrated with RSARTE [2].

Motivated by the above, we show how we extend Umple, an open-source tool that has been actively developed since 2008, to support composite structure and overcome such limitations.

Umple is a textual modelling language that looks like a programming language, and allows embedding of code from multiple C-family programming languages. UML Diagrams are, for the most part, *generated* as the developer edits the Umple code, although Umple also provides a capability to edit parts of the resulting diagrams in order to modify the text in real time. The Umple compiler can take system written in Umple and produce a full executable system in languages such as C++, Java, and PHP [3–5]. Our previous research has shown that using Umple can be considerably easier for developers than coding or using diagrams.

Umple implements the core features of UML, such as state machines, associations, and attributes. In addition, Umple provides other features to ease development such as traits, mixins, and aspect-orientation. The selected target language in this paper is C++. Umple can be tried online using the UmpleOnline website (http://try.umple.org), but has an Eclipse plugin and a command-line interface too.

This paper describes how we have enhanced Umple to support specification and design of systems with composite structure using a simple syntax. Umple generates code for many types of ports and connections among components. In particular, Umple allows developers to avoid having to specify protocols in many situations: The necessary protocols can be inferred from the ports, connectors and components, with the requisite protocol code being generated. Umple thus enables developing using a protocol-free approach.

Umple's current generated code for composite structure supports TCP/UDP communication and JSON as a message interchange format, although additional options can be added in the future. It uses the *active object* pattern [6, 7] to extend and enable the request-scheduling mechanism.

In Sect. 2 of this paper we discuss existing technologies for modelling with components. Section 3 outlines Umple's syntax and semantics of composite structure, with Sect. 4 focusing on port types. Section 5 presents case studies, and Sect. 6 discusses how an Umple system can save considerable coding. Section 7 concludes the paper.

This paper is a significant extension of the our previous MODELSWARD conference paper [8] providing much greater detail, additional case studies, and more evaluation. Specifically:

- We discuss common component-based modelling features, as well as their related languages and standards.
- We highlight major inconsistencies typically associated with such features, and show how Umple addresses them.

- We discuss different settings of port and connector implementation, including forward or inverse. We explain this by examples and case studies. This includes port redefinition and reusability through interfaces.
- We explain the implementation of port multiplicity in Umple. Umple uses port multiplicity to enforce connection constraints, and to maintain referential integrity. We provide examples that explain different usages of port multiplicity and associations.
- We show how our implementation can work for distributed applications without restricting users to particular network paradigms or transport data formats.
- We include additional case studies encompassing many features such as ports, constraints, redefinition, and peer-to-peer communication. We discuss the implementation of an embedded case study: Light control.

2 Languages and Standards for Component-Based Modelling

Many modeling languages and methods support component-based modeling. These include UML [9], SysML [10], Specification and Description Language (SDL), Real-time Object-Oriented Modelling (ROOM) [11], UML-RT, MARTE [12], and AUTOSAR.

UML profiles and system models can become complex; SysML can facilitate simpler modelling of a wider range of system types using lightweight profiles, incorporating stereotypes, constraints, and tagged values. SysML has nine diagram types (Fig. 1), while UML has seven (Fig. 2). UML class and component (composite) diagrams are referred to in SysML as block definitions and internal blocks respectively.

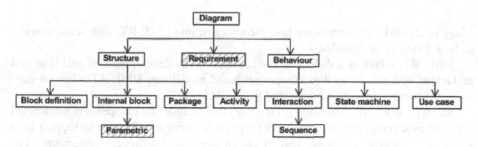

Fig. 1. SysML diagram types. Additional SysML diagrams, as compared to UML are highlighted [8].

SDL has been commonly used for the modelling of real-time and communication systems. It has similar functionality to UML and SysML but with different notations (Table 1), which are mainly aimed at being unambiguous [13].

ROOM, which was developed by ObjectTime [4] allowed for hierarchal modelling and incremental refinement of complex behaviour. The ROOM language used *actors* as the primary elements communicating with other elements via port interfaces. A port is an instance of a protocol class, which is used to define communication among actors.

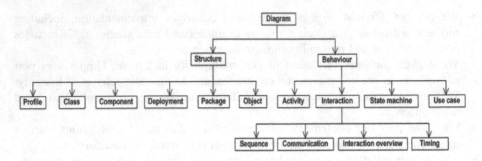

Fig. 2. UML diagram types [8].

Table 1. UML to SDL term mapping [8].

UML	SDL
Class	Type
Interface	Interface
Associations	Channels
Operations	Signal list
Variable	Attribute
Sub	Block
Abstract	Abstract
Implementation	Process
Type	Gate
Inheritance	Inheritance

Many of ROOM's concepts were later incorporated into UML-RT, with actors coming to be referred to as capsules.

UML-RT, which is a dialect of UML, supports the development of real-time and embedded systems, as well as component-based modelling. UML-RT relies on *capsules* for communication via ports and protocols [14].

MARTE is a UML extension [9] (profile) that includes an independent metamodel defining its specialized concepts. MARTE provides some key features to support non-functional property modeling, and to enrich time and resource management. The generic component modeling (GCM) sub-profile of MARTE defines the core concepts of component-based, real-time and embedded systems. MARTE also integrates SysML concepts such as block diagrams and flow ports. The common ports used in MARTE include FlowPort and MessagePort [12].

AUTOSAR is a standard architecture and UML profile used to support the development of component-based, distributed, and hardware-independent automotive applications [12]. It aims to ease the integration of different manufacturers' components via well-defined interfaces. Ports in AUTOSAR are defined as interfaces, which can be *provided* (P-Port) or *required* (R-Port). AUTOSAR enables interactions through *runnable entities*, *tasks*, or *operations*.

Our work takes in consideration future integration with AUTOSAR, so it can be used in the automotive industry.

3 Composite Structure in Umple

Composite structure is used to define the structural implementation of an object, while state machines are widely used to define that object's behaviour.

The main elements of composite structure are components, ports, and connectors. In Umple, a component is an active object that has a unique identifier (UID) and runs within its own thread of control in order to encapsulate behaviour.

Communication among components is based on protocols, ports and connectors. Protocols are used to define the communication rules among ports. In Umple, protocols are internally generated in order to reduce complexity.

Table 2. Selected OMG issues related to component-based modeling [15, 16].

Related Issues	Description
UMLR-107	Behavioural and non-behavioural ports have inconsistencies related to request handling and realization of their provided interfaces **Umple resolution:** The active methods are used with behavioural and non-behavioural ports (Sect. 4), which helps maintain consistent request handling and realization
UMLR-106	Limited capabilities to interact with and specify parts bound with the connector ends **Umple resolution:** Umple provides semantics to allow for wired and unwired bindings (Sect. 4)
SYSML12-9, SYSML11-66, SYSML12-5, and SYSML11-117	Limitations related to port decomposition (complex port or sub-ports), provided interface realization, and data flow These issues have been addressed by loosening UML constraints on connectors **Umple resolution:** Umple supports port decomposition (Sect. 3.2)
SYSML16-10, SYSML16-54	Limited binding semantics related to multiplicity **Umple Resolution:** Umple provides advanced options to handle port multiplicity (Sect. 3.4), as well as the number of the allowed part instances
SYSML16-48	Limited decomposition support, since connector bindings cannot be typed by an association **Umple Resolution:** Umple provides rich semantics to handle different variations of associations, which are used closely with ports and connectors (Sects. 3.2 and 3.4)

A component has a public interface, connection type, and transport data format, as well as an internal router that is used to manage components in distributed environments.

A public interface defines the methods that are used for communication, which can be asynchronous, synchronous, or future asynchronous. Asynchronous communication uses port interface methods, while synchronous communication uses standard methods. On the other hand, *future* asynchronous communication is a special case, in which an active (asynchronous) method has a return value that can be used later to retrieve the response.

The internal routing table handles the mechanisms of send, reply, and scheduling requests between component's internal methods and respondents.

A communication stack defines the connection mechanism as well as the data interchange format. The default connection mechanism and data interchange format used in Umple are TCP/IP and JSON respectively. However, Umple is extendible so it could be adapted to support other connection mechanisms such as UDP and Bluetooth, or data interchange formats such as XML.

A component by default is local. When a component listens to other components, it acts as a server, and when it initiates communication with another component, it acts as a client; in both cases, this component becomes distributable. In Umple, there is no restriction to specific network arrangements such as client/server or peer-to-peer. A component handles both remote method invocation (RMI) and inter-process communication (IPC).

In our code generation, we use template meta-programming (TMP) in order to reduce the amount of code to be written by users, avoid writing repetitive code stubs, and make the communication stack extensible [17, 18]. A method is represented as a generic template proxy that is used by the internal router in a publish-subscribe pattern.

Several issues that have been reported to OMG highlighting the inconsistencies of UML-RT and SysML component-based semantics (Table 2). We show how Umple resolves such issues.

```
1   class A { // A component                              Umple
2       active method1 {
3       cout <<"Method without parameters"
4          << endl;
5       }
6   }
7
8       class B {
9       active method2 (int someParam) {
10      cout << " Parameter value"" <<
11         someParam <<endl;
12      }
13  }
14
15      class C {
16         A a;
17         B b;
18  }
```

Snippet 1. An example of a component definition [8].

3.1 Components and Parts

In Umple, a component is a class that has at least one active method, port, or connector.

An active method is defined the same manner as a regular method, but it is proceeded by the *active* keyword (Snippet 2 - Lines 2 and 9). An active method executes within its own thread; i.e. asynchronously.

An instance of a component is referred to as a part or subcomponent. Parts are owned by a component and represented by the composite structure of that component.

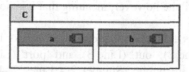

Fig. 3. SysML diagram types. Additional SysML diagrams, as compared to UML are highlighted [8].

A component can own a part of its type similarly to many programming patterns. Parts can be specified in the class definition, alongside the definition of constructors, attributes, state machines and associations

```
1   class Component{                                    Umple
2       in Integer inPort;
3       out Integer outPort;
4       port Integer dualPort;
5       internal in Integer privatePort;
6       in SomeClass someComplexPort;
7       port CompoundPort compoundPort;
8       CompoundPort
9           active compoundPort_ActiveMethods(){
10              [someInPort]
11              active void handleDefaultDirection(){}
12                  ->handleConjugatedDirection(){
13              // CompoundPort inversion is as below
14              //out Integer someInPort;
15              //int Integer someOutPort;
16          }
17      }
18
19      void active someMethod(){
20          stateEvent(pIn1 + 1);
21      }
22
23      pIn1Statemachine{
24          receive{
25              stateEvent(int val) /{cout<< val;} ->done;
26          }
27          done {}
28      }
29  }
30  class SomeClass{}
31  class CompoundPort{
32      in Integer someInPort;
33      out Integer someOutPort;
34  }
```

Snippet 2. Port examples [8].

A composite component (Fig. 3 – see C) is a component that owns multiple parts (see a and b that are instances of A and B). Subcomponents can be also composite.

A component has a composition relationship to the class types of the parts that this component owns. For instance, C in Fig. 3 has a composition relationship to A and B, since it owns two instances of them, a and b.

3.2 Ports

In Umple, a port is defined as an attribute (Snippet 2 - Lines 2–4). To use Umple's terminology it is a *lazy* attribute however, meaning that it is not initialized via its class's constructor.

Additionally, a port has a direction that can be *in*, *out*, or both (dual), for which we use the keywords 'in' (Line 2), 'out' (Line 3), and 'port' (Line 4) respectively.

By default, attributes are public (Snippet 2 - Lines 2–4). We use the 'internal' keyword (Line 5) to set the visibility to private. Private ports, or attributes in general, are only accessible by their owning components.

A port can be *simple*, *complex*, or *compound* based on its type. It is considered simple if it is typed by a simple type such as string or Double (Snippet 2 - Lines 2–4); otherwise, it is considered complex. There is no restriction on the port type.

A *compound* port consists of subports encompassing multiple events (Lines 7, 8, and 30–33).

The relationships among components are defined using associations (Snippet 3), which also define their multiplicity (Line 7); i.e. minimum and maximum numbers of components [19].

```
1     class Client{                                                    Umple
2         in String cp;
3     }
4
5     class Server{
6         out String sp;
7         * -- * Client;  //Many to many association
8     }
9
10    class Sys{
11        Client c;
12        Server s;
13        s.sp-> c.cp;
14
15        public static void main(int argc, char *argv[]){
16           Server* server= new Server();
17           Client* c1= new Client();
18           Client* c2= new Client();
19           Client* c3= new Client();
20           server ->addClient(c1);
21           server -> addClient (c2);
22           server -> addClient (c3);
23           s->sp("Broadcast a message to all instances");
24        }
25    }
```

Snippet 3. Basic active objects in Umple [8].

3.3   Connectors

A connector establishes a communication channel for data transmission between two ports. A class becomes a component if it has a connector defined, even if it does not contain active methods or ports (Sect. 3.1).

Similarly to associations, we use the operator "->" to define a connector between two ports, such that the source and target are on the left and right sides respectively. The ports can be in the same component (Snippet 4 - Line 8) or different components (Lines 24 and 25). Figure 4 shows the composite structure generated by UmpleOnline of the component "D" defined in Snippet 4.

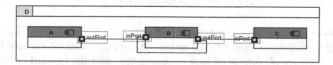

Fig. 4. Composite structure of connected components [8].

The operator "->" is the same as the C++ pointer syntax (Snippet 4 - Line 21). However, the context in which it is used for relationships (associations and connectors) is syntactically quite distinct, so no confusion should result.

A connector can only connect ports if they have compatible in terms of their directions and types. Regarding direction, it must be an in port with an out port, a dual port with an in port, a dual port with an out port, or a dual port with another dual port. Types must be compatible too: one cannot connect a port typed as a String to a port typed as an Integer, for instance.

Connectors are related to associations. Upon sending a message via a port (Snippet 3 - Line 23), it will be propagated to all instances in an association (Lines 20–22).

```
1    class A{                                              Umple
2       out Integer outPort;
3    }
4
5    class B{
6       in Integer inPort ;
7       out Integer outPort;
8       inPort -> outPort;
9    }
10
11   class C{
12      in Integer inPort;
13   }
14
15   class D{
16      A a;
17      B b;
18      C c;
19
20      void active someMethod(){
21         a->outPort(120); // Send a signal of 120
22      }
23
24      a.outPort->b.inPort;
25      b.outPort->c.inPort;
26   }
```

Snippet 4. Connector examples [8].

Table 3. Forward versus inverse implementations.

Defined ports at source	Defined ports at target	Connectors	Source	Target
port ComplexPort source	port ComplexPort target	None	Forward	Forward
By default, the forward implementations are used when no connectors are defined					
port ComplexPort source	conjugated port ComplexPort target	None	Forward	Inverse
If no connector exists, and a port is defined with the conjugated keyword, the inverse implementation is used (see target). Otherwise, the forward implementation is used (see source)					
port ComplexPort source; port ComplexPort otherSource	port ComplexPort target; conjugated port ComplexPort target	None	Forward	Both
Multiple instances of the same complex port can be defined in a class. If there is at least a base and conjugated ports defined, both forward and inverse implementations are used (see target). If the multiple ports are all defined as base or conjugated, only the forward or inverse implementations are used respectively (see source)					
port ComplexPort source	port ComplexPort target	source-> target	Forward	Inverse
If a connector exists from a source to target, and both ports to not use the conjugated keywords, the source will use the forward implementations, and the target will use the inverse implementation					
conjugated port ComplexPort source	conjugated port ComplexPort target	source-> target	Both	Inverse
A connector guarantees that a source will have the forward implementation, and a target will use the inverse implementation. If a target uses the conjugated keyword, nothing will change, since it is already assigned to use the inverse implementation (see target). If a source uses the conjugated keyword, it will use the inverse implementation as well as the forward implementation it is already assigned (see source)					
port ComplexPort source	port ComplexPort target	source-> target target-> source	Both	Both
Multiple connectors can exist between a source and target. If a connector exists from the source to target, we mentioned that the source and target will be assigned forward and inverse implementations respectively. If another connector exists from the target to source, inverse and forward implementations will be assigned to source and target respectively. This means that both source and target will use both implementations					

3.4 Port Multiplicity

Port multiplicity defines the number of port instances that can be created within a port's owning component.

We use class associations to create and link component instances, and to specify port multiplicity (Snippet 3 - Line 7). Multiplicity enforces connection constraints and maintains referential integrity. Relying on associations can help reduce difficulties surrounding connections and the integrity of multiplicity constraints [19].

Typically, there are two types of multiplicity, port and connector multiplicities. Port multiplicity is optional and is used for design purposes in order to specify the minimum and maximum number of component instances. On the other hand, connector multiplicity is used to enforce multiplicity on the port ends; i.e. source and target.

We support connector multiplicity for code generation. We support port multiplicity at the model level only, since associations are enough to manage part and port instances [19].

In many modelling tools, port multiplicity is used for design purposes while giving the possibility to dynamically change size. For instance, in UML-RT, the method resize () is used to allocate more space for incoming connections [14]. This will not be required in Umple as the association semantics is rich; i.e. users can specify all possible UML multiplicity constraints, and the code generation ensures these constraints are enforced.

3.5 Protocols and Our Protocol-Free Approach

A protocol-based approach involves many steps to define the communication among different components. These steps include the creation of sequence, activity, composite structure, and state machine diagrams. A protocol is restricted in some tools to be an interface that only contains of void method with void parameters to ease the interaction through method invocations. However, such design disables scenarios that require synchronous communication, as well as data propagation. It is also difficult to decompose a port into subports, which require specialized profiles.

We took a different direction in order to support simple, complex, and compound ports at early design stages. A developer can create an interface with different return types and parameters. They can also use other communication patterns such as scheduled asynchronous calls. Developers are able to build predefined compound ports, which have redefinition support.

In our approach, developers do not need to define protocols at the model level; i.e. see Snippet 8. Typically, an active method uses port attaches to listen to port events (Snippet 8 - Line 13, 21, and 38). In our protocol-free approach, a port attachment holds the information about incoming and outgoing ports, which makes it possible to generate protocols based on such information.

In terms of code generation, a protocol class is generated to handle communication for each component via its ports. When a port type is complex, we apply an appropriate serialization/deserialization technique. A port value is serialized into an intermediary object transmitted in the form of messages. When messages transmitted are received, they are deserialized back to the original object form.

Data is sent through connectors as *signals*. A port is expected to be able to receive signals simultaneously from different connectors. This means that there must be a queue mechanism to handle signals appropriately based on their priority and/or receiving order.

In our implementation, we provide a priority FIFO queue, in which requests are ordered based on their priorities (i.e. Snippet 4 - Line 21), and then based on their receiving order.

At the level of the generated code, queuing depends on an internally generated helper class, MessageService. The utility class MessageService is also generated when processing any Umple model that uses composite structure features.

Communicating components can exist in different applications or locations. Hence, it was important to support buffered message transmission. This is handled using a generic API MessageDescriptor we implemented, which is also generated as needed. MessageDescriptor follows a publisher-subscriber pattern. MessageDescriptor and MessageService APIs are generated for any Umple model that has ports or connectors defined.

By default, the maximum size of a transfer request is 512 Kilobytes. If a message to be transmitted exceeds this maximum size, it will be divided into a number of smaller chunks, such that each chunk size will not exceed that size. When all chunks are received, they will be assembled into a message, which will be deserialized into the form of the object data originally sent. We selected a small maximum size in order to make sure that it will not exceed the maximum transmission unit (MTU) of a network, such that it will take less memory and execute rapidly. As future work, we will experiment with other values to see which can be better, and investigate whether we can adjust the value at the model level.

MessageService works closely with the publisher-subscriber API existing in MessageDescriptor. Upon receiving incoming events, new messages will be created based on a subscriber list, which contains the active methods subscribed. The created messages will be added to the message queue using the MessageService API.

4 Port Types

A port has a type that can be either *conjugated* or *base*. By default, a port is base (Snippet 2 - Lines 2–6). A conjugated port (Lines 11 and 12) can be alternatively referred to as an *invert* port. For instance, a conjugated in port also acts as an out port, and a conjugated out port also acts as an in port. Conjugation is only used with compound ports. When a port is compound, its conjugated version will have all of the subports inverted, as commented in (Snippet 2 - Lines 13–15).

An in or dual port can additionally be a relay or end port. Relay and end ports are called external ports. Any out port is a relay port (Snippet 4 - Lines 2 and 7). Ports that propagate signals to other ports are considered relay ports (Line 6). Signal propagation stops at end ports (Lines 12).

The process of signal propagation changes whether a port is a service or nonservice port, and whether it is a behaviour or nonbehaviour port.

A service port expects to receive inputs from, or send outputs to, its environment. Service ports are drawn on the boundary of its owning part. In Umple, public ports are considered service ports (i.e. Snippet 2 - Lines 2–4).

On the other hand, nonservice ports are only visible within its part, and thus they are drawn within the internal region of its part. In Umple, private ports are considered nonservice (Snippet 2 - Line 5).

A nonservice port can still receive or send signals to or from other components via another relay port, which will act as an intermediary port.

When a port triggers a state machine event, it is considered a behaviour port (i.e. Snippet 2 - Lines 19–28).

A port cannot be nonservice and nonbehaviour at the same time. On the other hand, a service port can possibly be a behaviour or nonbehaviour port.

Associations are typically used to manage the number of port instances in a class (Sect. 3.4). A replicated port means that this port can have multiple instances. When a port is connected to other ports, it is referred to as a wired port. An unwired port can still connect dynamically to other ports at runtime.

Table 2 summarizes the different types of ports. Figure 5 shows ports of different types visualized using UmpleOnline. We follow the notations in specifications such as UML [20] and AUTOSAR [21].

When a port is a service port, it is drawn on the boundary of the composite structure; otherwise, it is drawn within the composite. Hence, all ports in Fig. 5 are service ports, since they are all drawn on the boundary of their owning component.

We recognize wired ports if they are connected to other ports via connectors; Fig. 4 for instance.

We distinguish between in and out ports using the crescent symbol, such that the open end of the crescent refers to the out port, and the closed end refers to the in port [1].

At the moment, we do not visually distinguish between behaviour and nonbehaviour ports, since this will require parsing users' method code to check whether there are invocations to state events (Snippet 2 - Line 20). For future work, we will assess the necessity of supporting this feature.

4.1 Port Implementation

Forward or inverse implementation depends on port directions as well as the connectors defined. By default, if no connector exists, we assume that a class will use the forward implementation. A user can use the keyword conjugated to use the inverse implementation instead. Table 3 shows the common variations involved to decide whether to use forward implementation, inverse implementation, or both. In Table 3, there is a ComplexPort used by two classes, Source and Target, such that a number of variations exist when defining connectors among ports or using the conjugated keyword. The forward implementation, inverse implementation, or both are used based on such variations (Fig. 6 and Table 4).

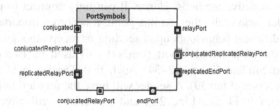

Fig. 5. Visualization of different port types using Umple [8].

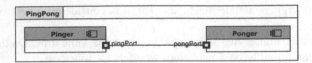

Fig. 6. Structure diagram of the ping-pong example [8].

Table 4. Port types [8].

Type	Description
Behavior	Triggers state machine events
Nonbehaviour	Does not propagates signals via state machines
Complex	Encompasses a number of attributes rather than a single attribute as in simple ports
Base	A port designed to send out signals
Conjugated	A port that also defines an inverse port that operates in the reverse manner
Service	Used to communicate between ports in its environment and ports in other environments; i.e. public or external
Nonservice	Only visible within its part; i.e. private
Replicated	Can have multiple instances
In	Provides a service for other ports. It can be conjugated, replicated, or service
Out	Requires a service from other ports. It can be conjugated, replicated, or service
Wired	Means that a port is connected to other ports at the model level
Unwired	Means that a port is not connected to other ports at the model level, but possibly can still connect at runtime

5 Case Studies

In this section, we present case studies that demonstrate component-based and event driven programming in Umple.

These case studies encompass many features reported in this paper, such as compound ports, complex ports, constraints, redefinition, and peer-to-peer communication.

5.1 Math Question

A complex port is typically used as a template encompassing a number of attributes (Sect. 3.2) as well as active methods. Hence, it can only connect to ports of its type, since they can understand each other. At this point, it becomes important that an active method will have different behaviours upon sending or receiving signals. For instance, in Snippet 5, we define a complex port (Lines 1–26) used by two classes, Teacher (Lines 28–30) and Student (Lines 32–34), such that Teacher acts as a sender and Student acts as a receiver (Line 39). A sender will have the forward implementations of active objects (Lines 9–11 and Line 22), and a receiver will have the conjugated implementations, which come after the -> operator (Lines 13–16 and Line 24). Teacher and Student have one-to-many associations (Line 40).

An active method is used with a number of parameters that match the ports it listens to (Snippet 5 - Lines 7 and 20). For instance, a teacher can ask a simple parameterized math question (Snippet 5 - Line 45), which consists of two numbers and an operator (Lines 2–4). A student has to answer the question (Line 5). Each parameter value is transmitted via its subport accordingly. Once parameter signals are received, the inverse method will be invoked (Line 13–16). A new signal is sent via the solution port (Lines 14 and 16), which is handled forwardly by Teacher (Line 22) and inversely by Student (24).

In terms of the code generation, we inject the forward and inverse implementations into Teacher and Student respectively. We make sure to propagate forward signals to all associated instances right after executing the base active content. We do not do the same for inverse active methods, since they do not need to notify the forward active methods; otherwise, we will have infinite notifications.

```
1     class MathQuestion{                                    Umple
2        out Integer num1;
3        out Integer num2;
4        out String op;
5        in Integer solution;
6
7        [num1, num2, op]
8        void active ask(int num1, int num2, String op) {
9           cout<< num1;
10          cout<< num2;
11          cout<< op;
12       }->answer {
13          if(op== "+"){
14             solution(num1+num2);
15          }elseif(op== "-"){
16             solution(num1-num2);
17          }
18       }
19
20       [solution]
21       void active receive{
22          cout<<"Answer provided is " + solution;
23       }-> logOut{
24          cout<<"Answer sent to out port is " + solution;
25       }
26    }
27
28    class Teacher{
29       port MathQuestionquestion;
30    }
31
32    class Student{
33       port MathQuestion answer;
34    }
35
36    class System{
37       Student s;
38       Teacher t;
39       t.question -> s.answer;
40       0..1 -- * Student student;
41       public static void main(int argc, char *argv[]){
42          Student* student= new Student();
43          Teacher* teacher= new Teacher();
44          teacher->addStudent(student);
45          teacher->ask(4, 11, "+");
46       }
47    }
48    association { * Student students -- * Teacher teachers;}
```

Snippet 5. The math question case study.

We as well notify associated instances when receiving signals via a port. This time, notifications are defined at the out ports as well, which are assumed to be used by inverse methods, since we allow for the assumption that a signal may start directly from a port in case a user decided not to invoke an active method directly (Snippet 5 - Lines 14 and 16).

Notifying an association depends on its ends, which can either be one or many. For the first case, we directly propagate signals to the single instance. If an association end is optional, we make sure to check for null. For the many case, we loop through each instance, and notify it.

5.2 Port Redefinition

The implementations of forward and inverse active methods at a complex port have default implementations. A component that uses a complex port can redefine such methods (Snippet 6 - Lines 3–5 and Lines 11–13). In terms of the code generation, a component implementation is placed after a default complex port implementation (Snippet 6 - Lines 6 and 20).

```
1   class Student{                                              Umple
2       port MathQuestion answer;
3       void receive(int num1, int num2, string op){
4           cout <<"Answering a question";
5       }
6   }
7
8   class Teacher{
9       port MathQuestion question;
10      1 -- * Student;
11      void ask(int num1, int num2, string op){
12          cout <<"Asking a question";
13      }
14  }
```

Snippet 6. An updated portion of Snippet 5 (with method redefinition).

5.3 Ports with Interfaces

Ports are usually defined as interfaces specifying the communication design among protocol layers [22]. In our implementation, we do not restrict users to certain interfaces as a way to improve usability and code readability. However, users can still enforce certain specifications if required. Snippet 7 shows an updated version of Snippet 5, where we define two interfaces, ISender (Lines 1–4) and IReceiver (Lines 6–9), specifying the methods to be implemented; i.e. communication specifications. Senders (Line 28) and receivers (Line 16) will need to implement both interfaces in order to initiate an appropriate communication.

5.4   Ping-Pong

In Snippet 8, we show a simple ping-pong example. There are two peers denoted as Pinger (Lines 30–33) and Ponger (Lines 35–42). Both components are contained in another component (Lines 44–54), which will send an initial message via a port (pIn1) to get the communication started (Line 51).

In Snippet 8, we use the complex port feature (Lines 9–28), such that there are two interfaces, IPinger (Lines 1–3) and IPonger (Lines 5–7).

Pinger does not redefine the ping port, meaning that the basic implementation defined in the complex port will be used (Line 15). On the other hand, Ponger redefines the pong port (Lines 38–40), by adding a constraint to ensure that the message propagation will go back and forth between Pinger and Ponger instances, until the count reaches 10 (Line 38).

The communication paradigm is almost solely peer-to-peer (P2P), except for the fact that Pinger starts communication, hence it could be considered a super peer. The communication is initialized between a single Pinger and Ponger.

```
1    interface ISender{                                        Umple
2        ask(Integer num1, Integer num2, String op);
3        receive(Integer solution);
4    }
5
6    interface IReceiver{
7        answer(Integer num1, Integer num2, String op);
8        logOut(Integer solution);
9    }
10
11   class MathQuestion{
12       .....
13   }
14
15   class Student{
16       isA IReceiver;
17       port MathQuestion answer;
18       void answer(int num1, int num2, string op){
19           cout << "Answering a question";
20       }
21
22       void logOut(int solution){
23           cout << "Question answered";
24       }
25   }
26
27   class Teacher{
28       isA ISender;
29       port MathQuestion question;
30       void ask(int num1, int num2, string op){
31           cout << "Asking a question";
32       }
33
34       void receive(int solution){
35           cout << "Answer received";
36       }
37   }
```

Snippet 7. An updated portion of Snippet 5 (with interfaces).

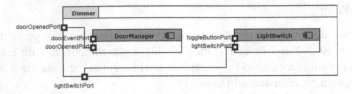

Fig. 7. The composite structure of Snippet 9.

```
1    interface IPinger{                                    Umple
2        void ping(int pIn);
3        }
4
5      interface IPonger{
6        void pong(int pOut);
7      }
8
9      class PingPongPort{
10       public out Integer pingPort;  // require port
11       public in Integer pongPort;   // provide port
12
13        [pingPort]
14        active void ping(int num) {
15          pongPort(num + 1);
16        }->void logPortData {
17         cout <<"CMP 1 : Ping Out data = "
18            << pOut1 << endl;
19        }
20
21        [pongPort]
22        active void pong(int num) {
23          pingPort(num + 1);
24        }->void logPortData {
25         cout <<"CMP 1 : Pong Out data = "
26            << pOut1 << endl;
27        }
28      }
29
30      class Pinger {
31        isA IPinger;
32        port PingPongPort pingPort;
33      }
34
35      class Ponger {
36        isA IPonger;
37        port PingPongPort pongPort;
38        [pongPort, num < 10]
39        active void pong(int num) {
40          pingPort( num + 1);
41        }
42      }
43
44      class PingPong {
45        Pinger cmp1;
46        Ponger cmp2;
47        Integer startValue;
48
49        after constructor {
50          // Initiates communication in the constructor
51          cmp1->ping(startValue);
52        }
53        cmp1.pingPort -> cmp2.pongPort;
54  }
```

Snippet 8. Ping-pong case study [8].

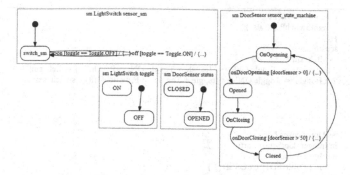

Fig. 8. The state machines of Snippet 9.

5.5 Light Control Case Study (An Automotive Example)

Interior light control is standard in modern cars. When a car door is open, the interior lights will be automatically switched on to warn the driver. The lights will stay on as long as a door is still open.

DoorManager is responsible for sending signals when a car's door has been opened or closed. This depends on the sensors attached to each door. *LightSwitch* simply receives signals when someone, in the car, toggles the interior lights.

The out signals of both DoorManager and LightSwitch are sent to the *Dimmer* component, which handles the communication between those two components and LightActuator. Dimmer is the composite component in this case study (Fig. 8).

When DoorManager sends signals to Dimmer that a door has been opened, Dimmer will send a signal to LightActuator to turn the interior lights on.

When all doors become closed, Dimmer will send a signal to LightActuator to turn the lights off. However, if the lights were already switched on before one the doors were opened, Dimmer will not request the lights to be switched off.

Note that this example does not contain the full action code, nor hardware and sensor configurations. As a result, it is only intended to provide an additional example of the applicability of our work.

```
1    class LightSwitch{                          Umple
2        in Integer toggleButtonPort;
3        out Boolean lightSwitchPort;
4        toggle { OFF{} ON{} }
5
6        [toggleButtonPort]
7        void active receiveToggleButtonPort{
8            if(toggleButtonPort > 0) {
9                on();
10           } else {
11               off();
12           }
13       }
14       void switchOn() {
15           lightSwitchPort(true);
16       }
```

Snippet 9. Light control case study.

```
17        void switchOff() {
18          lightSwitchPort(false);
19        }
20        sensor_sm {
21          switch_sm {
22            on [toggle == Toggle.OFF]-> / {toggle = Toggle.ON; switchOn(); } switch_sm;
23            off [toggle == Toggle.ON]-> / {toggle = Toggle.OFF; switchOff();} switch_sm;
24          }
25        }
26      }
27
28      class DoorSensor {
29        in Integer doorSensorPort;
30        out Integer doorEventPort;
31        status { OPENED{} CLOSED{} }
32
33        [doorSensorPort]
34        void active receiveSensorData{
35          if(doorSensorPort > 10 && doorSensorPort < 40) {
36            onDoorOpenning(doorSensorPort);
37          }else{
38            onDoorClosing(doorSensorPort);
39          }
40        }
41
42        void DoorOpened() {
43          doorEventPort(1);
44        }
45        void DoorClosed() {
46          doorEventPort(0);
47        }
48        sensor_state_machine {
49          OnOpenning {
50            onDoorOpenning[doorSensor > 0] ->/ {status = Status.OPENED;}
51            Opened;
52          }
53          Opened {
54            entry /{ DoorOpened(); }
55            ->OnClosing;
56          }
57          Closed {
58            entry /{ DoorClosed(); }
59            ->OnOpenning;
60          }
61          OnClosing {
62            onDoorClosing[doorSensor > 50] ->/ {status = Status.CLOSED;}
63            Closed;
64          }
65        }
66      }
67
68
69      class DoorManager {
70        in Integer doorEventPort;
71        out Boolean doorOpenedPort;
72        0..1 -- 4 DoorSensor door;
73
74        [doorSensorPort]
```

Snippet 9. (*continued*)

```
75          void active onDoorOpenedEvent{
76              doorOpenedPort(doorSensorPort > 1);
77          }
78
79          door.doorEventPort -> doorEventPort;
80      }
81
82      class Dimmer {
83          in Boolean doorOpenedPort;
84          in Boolean lightSwitchPort;
85          DoorManager dm;
86          LightSwitch ls;
87          Boolean doorOpened;
88          Boolean lightSwitched;
89
90          void dimLight(Boolean light) {
91              //communicate with LightActuator
92          }
93          // ignore off switch in case of opened door
94          [lightSwitchPort, !isDoorOpened()]
95          void active onLightSwitchEvent{
96              setLightSwitch(lightSwitchPort);
97              dimLight(lightSwitchPort);
98          }
99
100         [doorOpenedPort]
101         void active onDoorOpenedEvent{
102             setDoorOpened(doorOpenedPort);
103             if(doorOpenedPort) {
104                 dimLight(true);
105             } else if( !doorOpenedPort && !isLightSwitched()) {
106                 dimLight(false);
107             }
108         }
109
110         dm.doorOpenedPort -> doorOpenedPort;
111         ls.lightSwitchPort -> lightSwitchPort;
112     }
```

Snippet 9. (*continued*)

6 Evaluation of Umple's Ability to Allow Concise Specification of Composite Structure

In this section, we evaluate the above-mentioned case studies, along with the same models discussed in [8, 18] (Fig. 9). We use two evaluation metrics, McCabe cyclomatic complexity [23] and lines of code (LOC).

6.1 Computations

Cyclomatic complexity is used to measure the understandability of code in terms of its complexity. This in turn allows assessment of its maintainability, and hence technical debt. Cyclomatic complexity describes the possible independent execution paths of a piece of code by counting logical conditions. A high number of paths indicates high cognitive effort would be required to understand and change it.

LOC is a widely-used metric that focuses on code size; the more code to read, the more time and effort are required to understand it.

We calculate cyclomatic complexity ratio as $100 - (MCabe_U/McCabe_G) \times 100$. $McCabe_G$ is the conventional McCabe calculation based on generated C++ code.

$MCabe_U$ is computed from the input Umple code/model as follows:

- Guards and other constraints are evaluated based on Boolean operators. A transition with a simple Boolean guard is weighted as two because of having two paths, TRUE and FALSE.
- For associations, we compute the score based on the multiplicity of association ends. In most cases, associations are weighted as two, except for Umple association definitions [19], which weight four when the involved classes are more than one.
- For state machines, an event is weighted in the same manner a Boolean condition. Each additional event is considered as another choice path.
- For action code (embedded C++ methods, transition actions, entry actions, exit actions and activities) the conventional McCabe calculation is used.

We use the LocMetrics tool [24] to calculate the cyclomatic complexity and LOC of the generated code and the embedded C++ methods.

The generated code of an Umple model provides a builtin lightweight library that supports many features such as distributed communication and multi-threading. We exclude the generated code of this library in order to avoid evaluation bias. This code is a constant and is the same across all platforms; excluding this is similar to not including the complexity of standard libraries or virtual machines – a developer would never have to code these aspects, but would just use them.

6.2   Results

The average reduction in lines of code that the developer need to write when using Umple as opposed to directly creating a system in C++ is 96.5%. For the 10 systems we evaluated, the absolute reduction in lines of code averages 1086. There is a high statistical significant ($p < 0.0001$ and $t = 8.49$) in terms of lines of code reduction between Umple models and the generated C++ code (Fig. 7).

The reduction in percentage for ten Umple test models is shown in Fig. 8. More details about the models used in our evaluation are in [18].

The reduction of cyclomatic complexity averages about 93.6%. Figure 9 is a doughnut chart showing the cyclomatic complexity differences between C++ generated code and Umple in the case study models. Note that for three of the models, the cyclomatic complexity of the Umple code is zero.

A threat to validity of our evaluation is that hand-written C++ code will clearly be different from the code generated by Umple. Some developers may argue that they may be able to come up with C++ code that is more compact. However, compact code might in fact be more obfuscated leading to even greater complexity (Figs. 10 and 11).

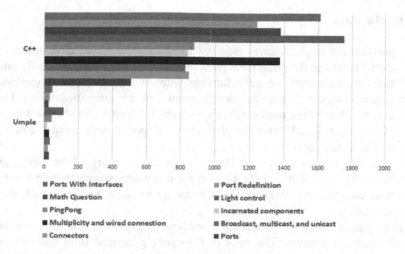

Fig. 9. LOC comparison.

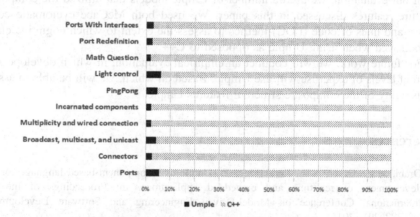

Fig. 10. LOC comparison by percentage.

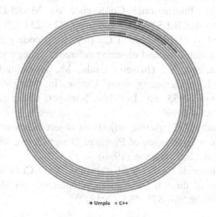

Fig. 11. Cyclomatic complexity doughnut.

7 Conclusions

Umple provides the major features required for component-based development, in a simple textual language designed for typical programmers to assimilate easily and use with C-like languages they are most familiar with. Our focus in this paper was on showing how composite structure development can be simplified using Umple. Specifically, we showed our protocol-free approach, in which protocols and the code to manage them are inferred from the definitions of ports, components, connectors, interfaces, and state events.

We discussed how we extended Umple to overcome many of the limitations in existing modeling tools that lack the support for many composite structure features or tend to have complicated workflows [1] due to, for instance, needing to additionally define protocols.

We showed a component-interface-based case study, which used a number of composite structure features. The lines of C++ code generated from this use case is more than 2700, as compared to the Umple model that consists of only 54 lines.

In our evaluation, we used a number of Umple models that utilized the composite structure features discussed in this paper. We used both McCabe cyclomatic complexity and lines of code (LOC) metrics to assess the extent to which cognitive effort can be saved when using Umple as opposed to C++.

For future work, we will conduct an empirical evaluation, in which developers of different levels of expertise will use Umple. Based on which, we will be able to assess the usability of the composite structure features Umple.

References

1. Orabi, M.H., Orabi, A.H., Lethbridge, T.: Umple as a component-based language for the development of real-time and embedded applications. In: Proceedings of the 4th International Conference on Model-Driven Engineering and Software Development, pp. 282–291 (2016)
2. Lakkimsetti, S.K.: Rational Software Architect Community: Connexis User Guide (2014)
3. Badreddin, O., Lethbridge, T.C., Forward, A.: A test-driven approach for developing software languages. In: International Conference on Model-Driven Engineering and Software Development, MODELSWARD 2014, pp. 225–234 (2014)
4. Badreddin, O., Forward, A., Lethbridge, T.C.: Improving code generation for associations: enforcing multiplicity constraints and ensuring referential integrity, vol. 430 (2014)
5. Lethbridge, T.C., Abdelzad, V., Husseini Orabi, M., Husseini Orabi, A., Adesina, O.: Merging modeling and programming using Umple. In: Margaria, T., Steffen, B. (eds.) ISoLA 2016. LNCS, vol. 9953, pp. 187–197. Springer, Cham (2016). https://doi.org/10. 1007/978-3-319-47169-3_14
6. Lavender, R.G., Schmidt, D.C.: Active object: an object behavioral pattern for concurrent programming. In: Pattern Languages of Program Design 2, pp. 483–499. Addison-Wesley Longman Publishing Co., Inc., Boston (1996)
7. Husseini Orabi, M., Husseini Orabi, A., Lethbridge, T.C.: Concurrent programming using Umple. In: Proceedings of the 6th International Conference on Model-Driven Engineering and Software Development, pp. 575–585 (2018)

8. Husseini Orabi, M., Husseini Orabi, A., Lethbridge, T.C.: Component-based modeling in Umple. In: Proceedings of the 6th International Conference on Model-Driven Engineering and Software Development, pp. 247–255 (2018)
9. OMG: UML Profile for MARTE: Modeling and Analysis of Real-Time Embedded Systems (2011)
10. Mallet, F., Peraldi-Frati, M.A., André, C.: Marte CCSL to execute east-ADL timing requirements. In: Proceedings of the 2009 IEEE International Symposium on Object/Component/Service-Oriented Real-Time Distributed Computing, ISORC 2009, pp. 249–253 (2009)
11. Selic, B.: Real-Time Object-Oriented Modeling (ROOM). In: Proceedings of the 2nd IEEE Real-Time Technology and Applications Symposium (RTAS 1996), p. 214 (1996)
12. Espinoza, H., Gérard, S., Lönn, H., Kolagari, R.T.: Harmonizing MARTE, EAST-ADL2, and AUTOSAR to improve the modelling of automotive systems. In: The Workshop Standard, AUTOSAR (2009)
13. Olsen, A., Færgemand, O., Møller-Pedersen, B., Smith, J.R.W., Reed, R.: Systems Engineering Using SDL-92, North Holland, 28 September 1994
14. Mohlin, M.: Rational Software Architect Community: Modeling Real-Time Applications in RSARTE (2015)
15. OMG: OMG SysML Open Issues. https://issues.omg.org/issues/lists/sysml-rtf?view=OPEN. Accessed 20 Apr 2018
16. OMG: OMG UML Open Issues. https://issues.omg.org/issues/spec/UML/2.5?view=OPEN. Accessed 20 Apr 2018
17. Smaragdakis, Y., Batory, D.S.: Mixin-based programming in C++. In: Proceedings of the Second International Symposium on Generative and Component-Based Software Engineering-Revised Papers, GCSE 2000, pp. 163–177 (2000)
18. Orabi, M.H.: Facilitating the representation of composite structure, active objects, code generation, and software component descriptions in the Umple model-oriented programming language (Ph.D. thesis), University of Ottawa (2017)
19. Forward, "The Convergence of Modeling and Programming: Facilitating the Representation of Attributes and Associations in the Umple Model-Oriented Programming Language (PhD Thesis)," University of Ottawa, 2010
20. OMG: UML Superstructure Specification, v2.4.1 (2011). http://www.omg.org/spec/UML/2.4.1/Superstructure/PDF/. Accessed 01 May 2015
21. AUTOSAR: Release 4.2 Overview and Revision History (2014). https://www.autosar.org/documents/. Accessed 01 Jan 2016
22. Douglass, B.P.: Real Time UML: Advances in the UML for Real-Time Systems (2004)
23. Kan, S.H.: Metrics and Models in Software Quality Engineering. Addison-Wesley, Reading (2003)
24. LocMetrics: LocMetrics - C#, C++, Java, and SQL. http://www.locmetrics.com/. Accessed 19 Apr 2018

Application of a Process-Oriented Build Tool for Flight Controller Development Along a DO-178C/DO-331 Process

Markus Hochstrasser[1(✉)], Stephan Myschik[2], and Florian Holzapfel[1]

[1] Institute of Flight System Dynamics, TU München, Munich, Germany
markus.hochstrasser@tum.de
[2] Chair of Flight Mechanics and Flight Control,
Universität der Bundeswehr München, Neubiberg, Germany

Abstract. Growing software size and complexity paired with its application in increasingly safety-critical environments requires to follow strict software development processes. They demand extensive documented development and verification activities as well as the creation and management of a huge number of artefacts. This paper presents a monolithic, process-oriented build tool for model-based development in MATLAB, Simulink, and Stateflow as well as its application and adaption for the implementation of a flight control algorithm in the light of RTCA DO-178C/DO-331, the accepted standard for airborne software certification. Beyond classical build automation functionality, the tool accelerates achieving a software design compliant to standards and evaluates completeness of process artefacts, their consistency, and correctness at a central place.

Keywords: Build automation · Workflow management system ·
Software development process · Model standards · Model scaffolding ·
Continuous integration · DO-178C · DO-331

1 Introduction

Safety critical software has an increasing impact in all industry markets. Algorithms rapidly grow in size and complexity [1], development cycles become shorter and at the same time, the software has to fulfill higher safety and security standards due to the evolved tasks it takes over. In addition, software development in safety critical contexts suffers from the "big freeze" problem[1]. Introducing changes after certification causes significant effort and costs, since a fine-grained impact is hard to identify.

In 2010, the National Research Council (U.S.) thus stated that "assurance is facilitated by advances in diverse aspects of software engineering and technology, including modeling, analysis, tools and environments, traceability programming

---

[1] http://open-do.org [Accessed on 2018/27/04].

© Springer Nature Switzerland AG 2019
S. Hammoudi et al. (Eds.): MODELSWARD 2018, CCIS 991, pp. 380–405, 2019.
https://doi.org/10.1007/978-3-030-11030-7_17

languages, and process support. Advances focused on simultaneous creation of assurance-related evidence with ongoing development effort have high potential to improve the overall assurance of systems ([2] Finding 4-2)".

Nowadays, model-based development (MBD) is a frequently applied technique, but requires "an established development process" [3] as well as a high degree of scalability and automation of tasks to fulfill objectives [4]. A recent review of MBD workflows in [5] according to a described framework comes to the conclusion, that no MBD workflow provides more than 20% DO-178C process coverage and consistent traceability is a commonly observed gap.

In addition, the long-term experience of the authors in developing safety-critical flight control algorithms at the Institute of Flight System Dynamics at TU München [6–9] showed that significant difficulties exist in communicating and realizing a planned process due to the extensive documentation, large number of artefacts, and dependencies that have to be managed manually.

Assessment of process conformance, consistency, and cleanliness of the software project, especially after changes, is still manual work and linked to enormous effort. Every tool has its own report format and justification workflow. Model reviews are intensively used by a majority of companies [3], but sophisticated tool support is missing.

In former work, Hochstrasser et al. [10] presented a *process-oriented build tool* supporting safety-critical, model-based software development in MATLAB, Simulink, and Stateflow[2] (SL/SF) throughout various phases. Focus was on the functionality and the backend implementation of the build tool.

This paper is an extension to the previously published work, which in addition elaborates and demonstrates setup and application of the tool for a DO-178C/DO331 process [11,12] based on Design Models in SL/SF (Release 2017b) with automatic code generation (ACG) as applicable for various domains [13–17]. Demonstration example is a quadrocoptor controller - a use case from a rapidly growing industry, in which especially small companies are active. They are often faced with steadily increasing safety requirements, but are lacking of personnel and long-term experience to establish heavy development processes. The build tool may offer high benefit in such scenarios.

The process-oriented build tool is specifically designed for MBD in high-integrity applications. In general, build tools allow modeling of a dependency network of tasks and their execution in an ordered and optimized way (cf. [18–20]). The presented tool enhances these known capabilities. The introduced term *process-oriented* emphasizes on the one hand the interaction with a traceability graph in contrast to task- and product-oriented tools [19]. On the other hand, features are added to improve process conformance, guidance, and the resolution of the previously stated challenges in a safety-critical context.

---

[2] Product of The MathWorks Inc. for model-based simulation and software development.

A configured tool supports the model-based software development by

- predicting required artefacts and tasks to do based on the current set of development artefacts (High-Level Requirements, Design Model, Source Code).
- checking the completeness and consistency of required artefacts (for example, whether a report matches to the SL model it has been generated form).
- checking the cleanliness of projects (search for orphaned artefacts).
- providing fine-grained control of acceptable verification results.
- supporting internal and external review workflows.
- summarizing the project status.
- assembling traceability in situ with the build for impact analysis.

Section 2 gives a short overview of the build tool, its application workflow, and some technical details with emphasis on parts, which have been less considered in [10]. Section 3 then discusses a concrete application example, which is the main contribution of this work. The software process and its context are presented in Sect. 3.2, before a build tool configuration is derived. Application of the configured build tool on a controller is demonstrated in Sects. 3.3 (development) and 3.4 (verification). Finally, related work and future considerations are discussed in Sect. 4, before a conclusion is drawn.

2   Build Tool Overview

This section presents the usage workflow, features, and technical concepts of the developed build tool based on [10].

2.1   Workflow

The build tool promotes modular software development. *Software modules* are self-contained parts of the software with artefacts passing the development and verification process together. In a DO-178C project, they would be treated as separate Configuration Item. Modules can reference other software modules as dependencies.

Figure 1 depicts the underlying MBD workflow for a single software module. Involved are three roles, a Process Manager, a Developer, and an Assessor. Developer and Assessor may be the same person depending on the required independence of the process.

Recent studies showed that build tools are well accepted, if they do not hinder usual work style, are customizable, and fit into existing workflows [21]. The presented tool thus accompanies the whole software development workflow without preventing developers to use existing, familiar routines at the same time.

The process starts with a planning phase (1) led by the Process Manager, in which activities and tools are chosen, tool configurations set up, modeling rules defined, as well as checklists written. The process-oriented build tool provides an environment to schematize design artefact classes and wrap procedures or checklists into a dynamic build workflow.

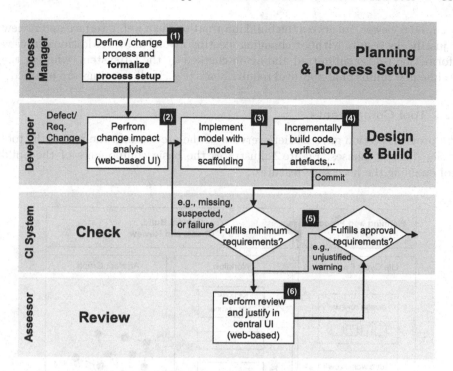

Fig. 1. Change workflow with build tool support and CI system from [10].

This formalized setup is passed to the Developer and integrated into the software module prior to software development (3). After that, the tool exposes several automatic and semi-automatic methods to rapidly scaffold the software model according to standards and guidelines along the design schema. This accelerates model creation and leads to models, which are compliant to standards by construction.

As soon as the design has been updated, various artefacts have to be generated spanning code generation, verification, and simulation (4). The definition of the tasks is part of the build workflow.

Along with the build, the tool automatically creates and maintains detailed traceability. This close interaction between build steps and traceability is a key aspect of the tool, as it relieves developers from manually updating traceability information (except traceability between development artefacts).

In case of a change, impact analysis is performed prior to the actual modification of the design (2). Traceability information of a previous build can be accessed via a web interface and is useful to estimate the impact of a change in advance.

Finally, the changed software module is submitted to the version control system and passes through a double-stage checking process. A CI system retrieves status information from the build tool and verifies, whether the minimum requirements of a successful build are fulfilled and the stored build information is up-to-date (5) (i.e. if all artefacts exist hand tasks have pass status). If everything is up-to-date, a manual reviewer can access the build information via a web interface and review or justify the results without changing existing artefacts (6). Additional review information is also submitted and again checked by the CI system, whether the module now fulfills final approval requirements (e.g., if all warnings are justified).

2.2   Tool Components

The previous section gave a brief overview of the process and the role of the tool in the different phases. Figure 2 illustrates the basic components of the build tool enabling the necessary features.

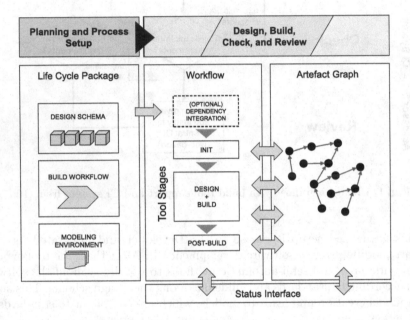

Fig. 2. Build tool components.

In the Planning and Process Setup phase, the Process Manager creates a so-called *Life Cycle Package*. The package is a self-contained set of customizations for the tool related to a specific process. A Life Cycle Package linked to a software module provides the basic information for the workflow component. In five sequential stages, the tool exposes the workflow and further features for the Developer, Assessor, or CI system. The status interface provides access to the project condition. Backbone is an artefact graph storing dependency information of all existing and various expected artefacts.

Life Cycle Package. According to Fig. 2, the Life Cycle Package can roughly be divided into the *design schema*, the *build workflow*, and the *modeling environment*. None of the three parts can be considered isolated, there are strong couplings between all of them. To leverage configuration control independence of the actually developed software, the build tool allows loading the Life Cycle Package from a separate version control repository.

The *design schema* defines classes of design artefacts including rules, how they can be created, identified, validated, initialized, or decomposed. Design artefacts are files and objects used by SL/SF like Simulink Parameters objects[3]. The design schema serves as foundation for the artefact graph, but at the same time enables *model scaffolding*. Many tasks, like writing initialization scripts or creating model data objects according to the modeling rules, are time-consuming, error-prone, and regularly repeated by every developer. Iterating to compliant model and model data with checks[4] is both a reverse and time-wasting workflow. Model scaffolding provides methods to quickly create artefacts based on the principle "Convention over Configuration" as further elaborated in [10].

The *build workflow* is a set of *jobs* organized in an hierarchical structure. Each job provides means to control

- the prerequisites to be executed (i.e., other job dependencies)
- whether it is executed iteratively (and on which artefacts) or just once
- input dependencies (artefacts)
- expected outputs (artefacts)
- the work done during execution
- exception handling and logging during execution
- methods to evaluate the output results.

Jobs are implemented in derived MATLAB classes and organized in an XML specification, which is converted to an acyclic, directed dependency graph. Dependent jobs are checked and re-executed prior to the called job in an organized manner derived from the execution graph.

The third part is the *modeling environment* containing various resources to configure tools along the development and verification process [7, 22, 23].

Software Module. Previously, the term *software module* has been introduced. In the scope of the build tool, any model-based software module at least consists of a single Simulink Projects[5] instance, a Simulink Data Dictionary[6] to store data supplemental to models, and a XML module description. The XML description

---

[3] https://www.mathworks.com/help/releases/R2017b/simulink/slref/parameter.html.

[4] Jaffry, David, 2014, http://de.mathworks.com/company/newsletters/articles/best-practices-for-implementing-modeling-guidelines-in-simulink.html [Accessed on 2017/27/07].

[5] Simulink Projects is a MathWorks toolbox for team collaboration and to manage models, https://www.mathworks.com/discovery/simulink-projects.html [Accessed on 2018/28/04].

[6] Persistent repository of data for modeling in SL/SF, https://www.mathworks.com/help/releases/R2017b/simulink/ug/what-is-a-data-dictionary.html [Accessed on 2018/27/04].

is the basic information source of the module and defines a unique ID, a name of the module, other module dependencies that shall be loaded, and the Life Cycle Package that applies to the module.

Stages. Modules created with the build tool and linked to a Life Cycle Package provide functionality along stages. Four stages are given by the tool and cannot be changed. Into each stage, phases and jobs can be hooked.

In the *Dependency Integration Stage*, the tool supports integration of other modules and transitive dependency resolution. Thereby, version conflicts are detected and reported. Life Cycle Packages are handled like software modules, too. Thereby it is avoided that dependent modules link to different revisions of the Life Cycle Package (this is a common problem when using, for example, GIT with submodules as source control approach).

The *Init Stage* loads the Life Cycle Packages, sets up the environment, and auto-initializes artefacts of the current module and linked modules. Build jobs, which must be executed prior to design stage, can be hooked into this stage. This is beneficial, if, for example, the software environment shall be checked or customizations be registered in SL/SF in advance.

In the *Design and Build Stage*, the Developer actually develops the model, simulation test cases, or requirement linking, and calls the majority of build jobs. In contrast to previous implementations [10], design and build have been merged into one stage. In consequence, the developer can start a build sequence at any time during design development. The tool instantaneously updates the artefact graph for the current design. The workflows are basically unconstrained in this stage, but support is given by model scaffolding.

The *Post-Build Stage* presupposes that all build jobs have been executed at least once and traceability has been established as far as possible. Basic intention of this stage is to compose a single, holistic artefact graph and store it for future impact analysis. Besides, orphaned files, which are not in the artefact graph and are in consequence suspected to have no functionality in the module, can be identified and optionally be removed.

Status Interface. Via the status interface, the condition of the software module, i.e., the completeness, correctness, and up-to-dateness of activities, can be retrieved at any time. Such a status scan is "silent", it does not modify any artefact of the module, but detects changes and outdated artefacts.

Important is to mention that the status of artefacts can only be assessed in the context of a job. An artefact itself does not have a status. For example, a source code file may be up-to-date from the viewpoint of the auto-code generation job, since it has been currently regenerated, but it may be deprecated from the viewpoint of the static code analysis.

Each element in the build workflow has a status according to Fig. 3.

Core data container of the status interface is a *status object*, which, beside the actual state (Fig. 3), stores detailed formatted descriptions. Furthermore, it holds justification information, e.g., whether the status can be justified, whether

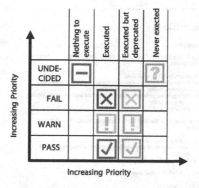

Fig. 3. Execution status types based on [10].

it is justified, and optionally a rationale. Nested status objects can represent arbitrary hierarchies of results.

The status interface provides cumulated status information in different formats (e.g., JUnit Test format) via a MATLAB API pluggable to CI systems[7].

In addition, all status information is available via a web-based interface. The architecture is depicted in Fig. 4. Design goal was to support a read-only scenario, in which no running MATLAB session is required, as well as a scenario, in which the web interface is fully interactive and closely connected to MATLAB.

Therefore, any status and traceability information change is directly written to persistent XML files. A client browser can request this data via a Jetty HTTP server[8]. The client page is programmed with JavaScript. Calls and callbacks to and from MATLAB are realized by a Jetty servlet extension and the MATLAB API for Java. Data is exchanged in the JSON format.

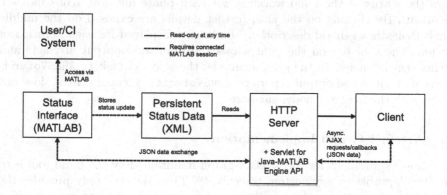

Fig. 4. Architecture of status and web-based interface.

---

[7] https://blogs.mathworks.com/developer/2015/01/20/the-other-kind-of-continuous-integration [Accessed on 2018/27/04].

[8] https://www.eclipse.org/jetty [Accessed on 2018/27/04].

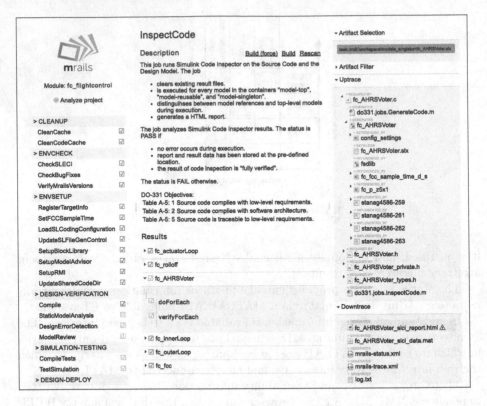

Fig. 5. Graphical user interface of the build tool from [10].

Figure 5 shows the screen capture of a job status page. The left panel displays the status of the build workflow for each phase and job. Icons indicate the status. By clicking on the jobs, further details are exposed on the middle panel. Beneath a general description, results are displayed for each iteration of the job. The tool bar on the right shows the input and output artefacts and further dependencies. In the given example, the selected task fc_AHRSVoter is deprecated, since the output report fc_AHRSVoter_slci_report.html does not match with the existing model anymore.

2.3   Artefact Graph Implementation

The main requirement for the artefact graph maintained by the build tool is to keep it adaptable to any custom traceability. Thus the tool only provides the infrastructure to store, relate, update, and query meta data of artefacts in a directed graph, not the rules to establish traces.

Rules are specified in the design schema and build jobs. The rule-based approach provides the most flexibility and can cope with the heterogeneity of artefacts [24]. Furthermore, this method supports the definition of *candidate traces*, which are traces that finally must exist, but are not created yet. They are required to display missing artefacts.

Traces are definable between any type of software artefact, from informal to formal (cf. [25]), in-memory, or on the file system. Also the type of link, by [25] and [26] categorized under hard (explicit) references, soft (implicit) references, and semantic connections, is unrestricted.

To efficiently handle artefact meta data and artefact graphs, an optimised data model is required. Especially the repeated calculation of checksums and the high number of artefact graphs (cf. [10]) must remain manageable. The implementation consists of three core elements as shown in the UML diagram in [10]: An Artefact Pool, multiple Artefact Trees, and Meta-Artefacts.

Meta-Artefacts are the main element. They store (at minimum) a unique ID, a name, information about existence, and the current checksum. A Meta-Artefact is not necessarily bound to a tangible software artefact, but can be created for every element whose existence and checksum can be identified. For example, Meta-Artefacts may be created for different kinds of files, but also for objects in the memory of MATLAB, like Simulink Parameters or model subsystems.

All artefacts are managed an Artefact Pool, which is a central collections of artefacts without relations between artefacts. Main function of the pool is to centralize access and checking for deprecation. Artefact Pools ensure that artefact meta data is just computed once per run (unless explicitly enforced otherwise).

Artefacts plus their trace links are organized in artefact graphs. Each artefact graph consists of a set of connected or unconnected directed graphs. It provides efficient methods to query artefacts with customized selectors, traverse the graphs, as well as serialize them. Important is that artefact graphs only organize the relations and do not store the Meta-Artefacts. This keeps the graph algorithms slim and efficient.

That performance and accessibility of the arefact graph is a major challenge shows the example given in [10]. For a relatively small software project and a simple workflow, the artefact tree already consists of 237 artefacts and 592 traces (cf. Fig. 6). The huge amount of dependencies gives an impression of the effort required to maintain consistency between artefacts in a safety-critical process.

3 Process Coverage Demonstration

This section presents parts of an example application. The build tool is used to support a software development process along DO-178C/DO-331. The tool itself does not claim any certification credit and does not release from manually reviewing the consistency, correctness, and completeness of artefacts. In a first step, the software under development is discussed. Afterwards, configuration of the build tool for the chosen process framework is presented. Finally, the application of the tool both during development and verification is summarized.

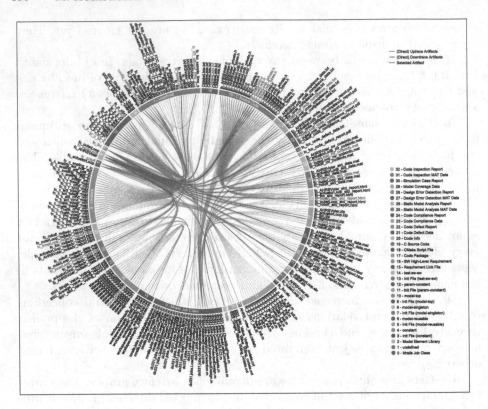

Fig. 6. Full artefact graph for a simple example from [10] arranged using hierarchical edge bundling [27].

3.1   Software Under Development

The application to be covered with the build tool is a flight control algorithm for a quadrotor testbed as shown in Fig. 7, which is equipped with an embedded microprocessor to run the software developed during the process. Information about the current flight state of the vehicle is collected by an array of sensors including a microelectromechanical interial measurement unit (MEMS IMU), a barometric pressure sensor, and a GPS module. Accurate position and attitude information are obtained through sensor data fusion with an extended Kalman filter.

Although the software for this testbed will never have to undergo certification according to DO-178C, it is a realistic use case. Especially in the market of lightweight UAVs, various small- and medium-size companies are faced with increasing safety requirements (especially if the products get larger and heavier), but do not have longstanding experience in safety-critical software development. A process-oriented build tool may be of high benefit for them.

The structure of the flight control system (FCS) is depicted in Fig. 8. It comprises two feedback loops of which the inner-loop is responsible for stabilizing

Fig. 7. Quadrotor flying testbed.

the unstable dynamics of the quadrocopter using rate feedback of the body-fixed angular velocities. The outer-loop controls the vehicle's attitude and allows the operator to control the direction of flight. This type of cascaded control structure based on proportional-integral feedback loops for each axis is well described in the relevant literature and will only be discussed briefly here [28].

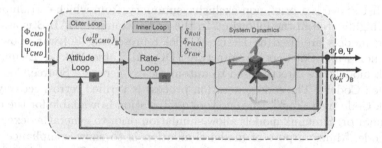

Fig. 8. Flight control system structure.

For the whole system exists a simulation model. It consists of a 6-DoF model of the quadrocopter flight dynamics, mathematical models of the available sensors, and a representation of the actuators as well as the propulsion system. Closed-loop simulation of both the simulation and software controller model leverages validation of requirements and design, assessment of functional correctness, and effects of parameter variations in an early development stage.

3.2 Build Tool Configuration

Prerequisites. In a DO-178C/DO-331 process, the setup of the Life Cycle Package is implemented at the end of the software planning process. Being able to setup the Life Cycle Package of the regarded project requires the following prerequisites:

1. The DO-178C/DO-331 process framework has been tailored for the given project. The Software Level (DAL) as well as interfaces to other processes (system, hardware) have been defined, a Software Life Cycle has been chosen, and the role of models and simulation has been clarified. Additional considerations of DO-178C have been regarded (e.g., use of Parameter Data Items).
2. Development and verification activities as well as the related tool chain have been planned to fulfill the objectives of DO-331 Appendix MB.A. Proceedings for activities have been written describing the inputs, outputs, settings/customizations, configuration management, checklists, and interpretation of results.
3. A detailed traceability information model as been created clarifying bidirectional traceability required by DO-178C from requirements over models to code as well as to test cases.
4. The configuration management process has been planned specifying issue tracking, configuration management (or version control) systems, impact analysis, change management process, and archival.
5. Design, modeling, and coding rules have been defined. In a DO-331 project, rules are documented in respective Design, Model, and Code Standards.

The list above is a brief, non-exclusive summary, from which certain aspects shall be highlighted in the following. In the given example, DAL B is assumed. Simulink models are used as Design Model representing Software Low-Level Requirements and Software Architecture (DO-331 Table MB.1-1 Example 4). Simulink models are directly used to automatically generate Source Code with Embedded Coder[9]. The code generation process is verified retrospectively with Simulink Code Inspector[10], since no tool qualification is available for the chosen code generator. Simulink models allow simulation prior to generating executable object code. Main purpose of model simulation is to show compliance of the Software Design with Software High-Level Requirements. The developed simulation cases are reused for testing of the executable object code. The process is similar but not identical to the process proposed in [29].

Design Schema Setup. Table 1 introduces a few design artefact classes derived from the Design and Model Standard. The classes describe model elements with particular settings and for a special purpose. For each class, functions to identify, create, initialize, or decompose instances are implemented.

Various further classes beyond those listed in Table 1 exist, e.g., for further models types, parameters, signals, enums, or simulation cases.

---

[9] Product of The MathWorks Inc. for code generation out of SL/SF, https://de.mathworks.com/products/embedded-coder.html [Accessed on 2018/27/04].
[10] Product of The MathWorks Inc. to prove structural equivalence of models and thereof generated code, https://www.mathworks.com/products/simulink-code-inspector.html [Accessed on 2018/27/04].

Table 1. Example artefact classes.

Artefact class	Description
model-top	Simulink model, which is the root of the model hierarchy. It cannot not be referenced in other models (except model test harnesses). External interfaces differ from those of other models. A separate configuration set is applied
model-singleton	Models, which can only be referenced once in a model hierarchy (in contrast to model-reusable). Exported global signals can be used, Simulink global signals not
param-data-item	Simulink Parameter object configured with a storage class to introduce a Parameter Data Item in the sense of DO-178C. A Parameter Data Item underlies full robustness testing and must be linked to requirements
bus-exported	Simulink Bus objects specially configured as interface to the software framework in top-level models

Build Workflow. The applied build workflow is listed in Table 2. Although the table represents a flat list, execution dependencies between jobs exist. For example, prior to "Model Coverage Analysis", the "Simulation Case Execution" must have been successfully performed.

Each job specifies input and expected artefacts and how the jobs are actually executed. The interpretation of results after execution is defined detailedly, too. Two examples are given in Tables 3 and 4. The first table maps static model analysis results of Simulink Model Advisor to the generalized build tool status based on check categorization derived from the criticality of the respective rules as described in [7]. Table 4 derives the execution status from Polyspace Bug Finder results representing the compliance to MISRA C:2012 [30], which is a common standard to restrict the C language to a sufficiently safe subset.

Modeling Environment Setup. The modeling environment for SL/SF contains tool configurations, custom checks, templates, shared code, and various artefacts required along the build workflow. A detailed description is provided in [7].

3.3 Example Implementation

Simulation framework and flight control algorithm design are kept separately in two software modules in a separate GIT repository. Only the latter is developed under DO-178C/DO-331. The flight controller module is referenced by the simulation framework as a dependency in the build tool, which also manages the whole integration.

Figure 9 shows the architectural design of the flight control software as it is realized in Simulink. The inner loop is represented by the component fc_rateloop and the outer-loop by fc_attloop. Both units are developed separately and are referenced by the top-level architecture model fc_main.

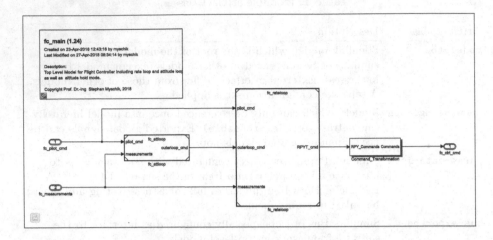

Fig. 9. Flight controller top-level architecture (`fc_main`).

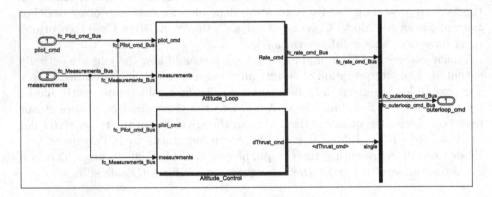

Fig. 10. Attitude controller and altitude-hold autopilot (`fc_attloop`).

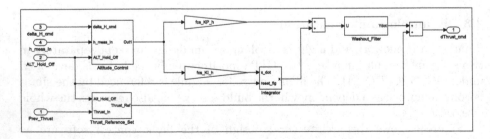

Fig. 11. Altitude-hold autopilot (`fc_rateloop`).

Table 2. Example DO-178C/DO-331 build workflow. Reviews tagged with * are not integrated into the tool yet.

Build workflow	Tool	DO-331 Ref. (Tables MB-A)
Cleanup		
Clean simulation cache	Custom	n/a
Clean code cache	Custom	n/a
Environment check		
Check SLECI	Custom	n/a
Check bug fixes	Custom	n/a
Environment setup		
Register target info	Custom	n/a
Setup block library	Custom	n/a
[...]		
Design verification		
Static model analysis	SL model advisor (customized)	4-3, 4-5, 4-12
Design error detection	SL design verifier	5-2, 5-7, 5-9
Traceability review	Checklists by build tool	4-1, 4-6
Model review	Checklists by build tool	4-3, 4-5, 4-6, 4-10, 4-12
Simulation testing		
Compile simulation cases	Custom	n/a
Simulation case execution	SL Test	4-1, 4-2, 4-4, 4-7, 4-8, 4-9, 4-11
Requirement coverage review*	Checklists by build tool	7-3 (assumes reuse of simulation cases as test cases)
Simulation case review*	Checklists by build tool	4-4, 4-11, 4-14, 4-15
Model coverage analysis	SL coverage	4-1, 4-4, 4-11, 7-4 (assumes reuse of simulation cases as test cases)
Code generation		
Shared code gen	Embedded coder (customized)	2-6
Code generation	Embedded coder	2-6
Code verification		
Auto code review	SL code inspector	5-1, 5-2, 5-5
Code compliance analysis	Polyspace bug finder	5-4, 5-6
Code defect analysis	Polyspace bug finder	5-4, 5-6
Code proving	Polyspace code prover	5-6
Documentation		
Code review*	Checklists by build tool	5-4
Reviewed report generation	Custom	n/a

Table 3. Status derivation for "Static Model Analysis" (categorization according [7]).

SL model advisor check violation	Check category	Derived build tool status	Deviation handling	Comment
Failure	Any	FAIL	Not allowed	Returned check result indicates abnormal exit, e.g., caused by a non-compilable model or a bug in the check. Rework or bugfix is required
Warning	Safety	FAIL	Not allowed	Violations may have high impact on safety and thus not justifiable
	Compatibility	WARN	Justifiable	Violation may cause incompatibility and rework in the subsequent tool chain, but any safety impact is reliably detected by other qualified tools
	Quality	PASS	Documented	No impact on safety

Table 4. Status derivation for "Check Code Compliance" (MISRA C:2012 [30] for auto-generated code).

MISRA violation category	Derived build tool status	Deviation handling	Comment
Mandatory	FAIL	Not allowed	Violations of mandatory MISRA rules and directives are not justifiable according to the standard ([30] Sect. 6.2.1)
Required	WARN	Justifiable	Required violations can be justified with by following the formal deviation procedure. ([30] Sect. 6.2.2))
Advisory	PASS	Documented	Advisory violations do not have to be formally justified, but are documented instead ([30] Sect. 6.2.3))

The in- and output ports of fc_main define the interfaces of flight control software to the integration framework. Pilot commands and sensor measurements are provided to the software units by the input ports. Motor speed commands are exchanged with the software framework via the output port. The interfaces are realized using Simulink Bus objects of class bus-exported, which are later converted to C structure type definitions and global C variables during ACG.

All three models are considered as Design Models and follow the Design and Modeling Standard as outlined in [7]. Used is only a restricted blockset compatible with the verification tool chain.

Figure 10 provides a closer look at the architecture of the fc_attloop software unit. It comprises two sub-components. The attitude-loop is responsible for controlling the vehicles orientation and therefore allowing the pilot to control the direction of flight. The second component realizes an altitude-hold functionality, which alleviates the operation of the system significantly by keeping it at a constant altitude if activated. Without this functionality the operator would have to adjust the throttle setting constantly, especially during maneuvers.

Upon activation of the autopilot, which is displayed in Fig. 11, the current flying altitude is set as a reference value for a control loop which compensates for deviations in altitude by adjusting the thrust command to the propulsion system accordingly. In addition to holding a constant altitude, it is also possible to change the reference value of the altitude in order to climb or descent using the throttle setting on the remote control. Realizing this functionality requires logical elements to account for discrete events (activation / deactivation), which also increases the importance of testing on model and code level to ensure the absence of unintended functionality.

3.4 Example Verification

This section presents some results and artefacts gathered in the application of the build-tool during the development of the flight control application example.

Static Model Analysis. DO-331 Table MB.A-4 Objectives 5 and 12 require to ensure conformance of the Design Model with rules defined in the Design and Model Standard. According to Table 2, this is achieved by the job "Static Model Analysis".

Figure 12 shows, how the build tool presents check results after executing a pre-configured subset of safety-relevant checks from the modeling environment. The results are directly inlined, and, if possible, direct links into the model are given. Justification is possible in the build tool UI (internal review workflow). In the given case, one check throws a warning. Since the respective MAAD guideline [31] is categorized under "safety", no justification possibilities are offered and rework is necessary.

The Uptrace section of the panel on the right-hand side lists input artefacts. Note that every customized check and the Model Advisor configuration file are listed as dependency. Any change would be recognized by the tool.

Fig. 12. Results of job "Static Model Analysis".

Model Coverage Analysis. In the given process, model coverage is measured based on the execution of simulation cases derived from Software High-Level Requirements. Model coverage is used to assess verifiability of the Software Design (DO-331 Table MB.A-4 Objectives 4 and 11) and to show that all low-level requirements are covered. If latter is the case, low-level testing can be omitted (DO-178C note in Sect. 6.4), presumed that the (derived) high-level test cases achieve sufficient structural test coverage (cf. [29]). Evaluated is decision coverage only, since this is the structural coverage required for DAL B software, too.

Figure 13 presents model coverage results for the altitude-hold function obtained with the available functional simulation cases for the flight control algorithm. These results show that based on the simulation cases, only 80% decision coverage can be achieved. Additional simulation cases helped to increase the coverage, but failed to reach 100% decision coverage. The reason therefore was found in the code defect analysis later on.

Auto Code Review. Central part of the MathWorks tool chain is automatic code review with Simulink Code Inspector. It retrospectively verifies structural equivalence between generated Source Code and the Design Model, and provides detailed traceability (DO-331 Table MB.A-5 Objectives 1, 2, 5). The Simulink Code Inspector is an independent verification tool that can be qualified under TQL-4 in an DO-178C compliant development process to eliminate manual code reviews [13, 29, 32, 33].

In Fig. 14 the results of the analysis performed by the Simulink Code Inspector are presented. Since the status is PASS, structural equivalence between the Source Code and the Simulink models has been proven. Any partial traceability results would not be accepted by the build tool.

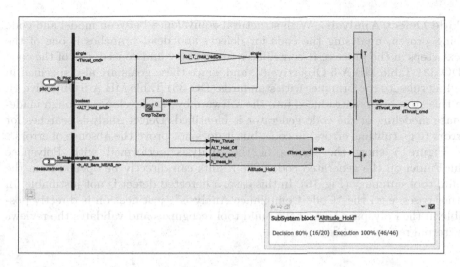

Fig. 13. Results of job "Model Coverage Analysis".

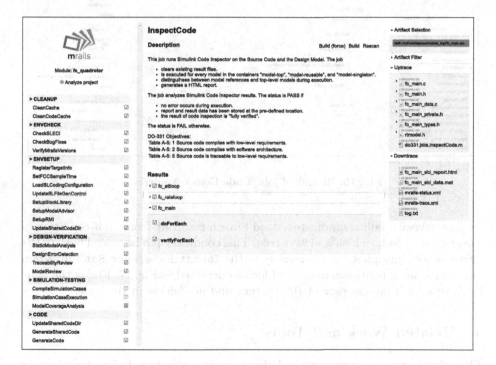

Fig. 14. Results of job "Auto Code Review".

Code Defect Analysis. With structural equivalence between model and code being proven, analysing the code for defects and dead branches is one of the next steps in the process. It contributes to accuracy and consistency of the code (DO-331 Table MB.A-5 Objective 6), and, since these goals are also specified in coding rules, to conformance with standards (DO-331 Table MB.A-5 Objective 4). In this step, errors introduced into the software by the developer through inadequate modeling or the code generator is identified. Defect analysis searches for errors (e.g., runtime errors) in code, but it does not prove the absence of errors.

Figure 15 show the results of the analysis performed with Polyspace BugFinder on the generated code. The results can directly be opened from the build tool summary (Fig. 16). In this case, a detected defect is not justifiable. In other cases, e.g., the "Code Compliance Analysis", justification is directly possible in the Polyspace UI and the build tool recognizes and validates the reviews (external review workflow).

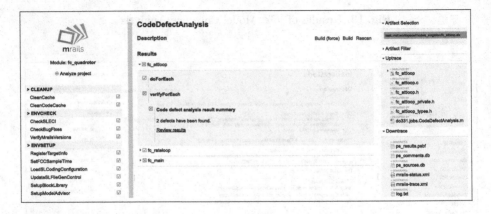

Fig. 15. Results of job "Code Defect Analysis".

The revealed failures indicate a dead branch resulting from an if-condition in the generated code, which is always true. This condition can be traced back to the altitude-hold autopilot, more precisely to the `Thrust_Reference_Set` subsystem and a misplaced relational operator block as depicted in Fig. 17. Fixing the issue leads to a decision coverage of 100 percent and no defects in the code.

4 Related Work and Tools

This section gives an overview of existing approaches and related tools and works out the differences. For the separate disciplines combined in the presented tool, a variety of alternatives could be listed. However, they rarely integrate with SL/SF in the depth as the presented tool does, and no tool provides a similar seamless approach.

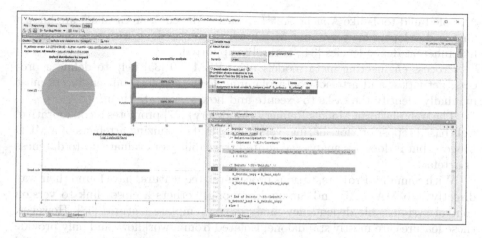

Fig. 16. Polyspace BugFinder analysis results.

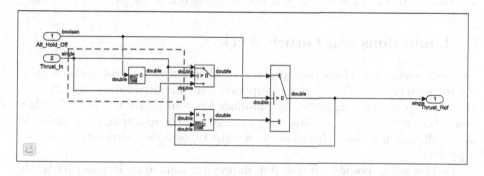

Fig. 17. Origin of dead-code in Simulink model in the `Thrust_Reference_Set` subsystem.

Closest to the presented tool are application life cycle management solutions like VeroTrace[11], PTC Integrity[12], BTC EmbeddedPlatorm[13], or SQUORing[14]. However, they either do not deeply integrate with MBD in SL/SF or use custom modeling and coder solutions.

Tools like Reqtify[15] or Yakindu Traceability[16] provide powerful traceability features, but are not integrated with build automation and mainly focus on retrospective traceability capture.

[11] http://www.verocel.com/tools/lifecycle-management/ [Accessed on 2018/27/04].

[12] https://www.ptc.com/de/products/plm/plm-products/integrity [Accessed on 2018/27/04].

[13] https://www.btc-es.de/de/ [Accessed on 2018/27/04].

[14] https://www.squoring.com/en/ [Accessed on 2018/27/04].

[15] Traceability management tool of Dassault Systems, https://www.3ds.com/products-services/catia/products/reqtify/ [Accessed on 2018/27/04].

[16] Traceability management solution of itemis AG, https://www.itemis.com/en/yakindu/traceability/ [Accessed on 2018/27/04].

Sole build tools like Apache Ant[17], Apache Maven[18], or Gradle[19] are known among developers for years, but MBD, which comes along with new challenges like inherent dependencies [34], is rarely supported.

Process engineering meta models like SPEM 2.0 [35] help to define a process, activities, and artefacts on a planning level (cf. [36]), but engineers must manually identify the tasks to execute and how to execute them.

The web platform Models Refinery (Modelery) [37] promotes a collaborative, web-based repository for sharing, versioning, and organizing artefacts of a MBD process, but it does not analyse generated traceability or evaluate up-to-dateness of artefacts.

With Simulink Projects, various process-related features have found their way directly into MATLAB and Simulink, amongst others a closer link to version control systems, file dependency analyses, or template features [38]. However, these features are mostly standalone, isolated from a workflow, and only provide a subset of the functionality used in the demonstrated tool. Of course, any build structure can be implemented by investing time and money, but an infrastructure as provided by the presented tool is not available out of the box.

5   Limitations and Future Work

Different assumptions have been necessary to implement the tool in the scope of the research project. The build tool supports only a limited subset of features in SL/SF, mainly those supported by Simulink Code Inspector (cf. [33]). Furthermore, the tool bases on various design decisions. For example, it assumes the usage of Simulink Data Dictionaries as data repositories, alternatives are not supported.

Further work should be invested in improving scalability. In many parts, the software implementation follows a conservative, but resource-costly approach to manage dependencies and perform up-to-date checking in the background. Although it is much faster than manual review, performance updates should be considered.

Future research may also focus on a stronger interaction with SL/SF. Instead of manually triggering a rescan of the project, events might be used to automatically update the status of jobs in the background *in situ*, whenever a model or object has been changed.

The presented build workflow does not cover the full DO-178C/DO-331 process, although to a high degree. In future work, the missing review checklists shall be added to the tool with more sophisticated dynamic capabilities. In addition,

---

[17] Apache Ant is a Java library to setup build processes, http://ant.apache.org [Accessed on 2018/27/04].

[18] Apache Maven is a project management and comprehension tool, https://maven.apache.org, [Accessed on 2018/27/04].

[19] Gradle is a build management and automation tool, https://gradle.org [Accessed on 2018/24/04].

jobs for Software-, as well as Proccessor-In-the-Loop simulation/testing shall be integrated.

A commonly requested feature is the ability to import existing model-based designs into a design schema. Plans exist to implement an import assistant, proposing the closest artefact classes and reorganizing the project.

Last but not least, since the full status of the project and relations to all artefacts are known, documentation like parts of a Software Accomplishment Summary (DO-178C 11.20) may be generated automatically.

6 Conclusions

The paper has introduced a build tool for MBD, which seamlessly integrates process-oriented features to improve standard compliance and standardisation throughout major parts of the software development and serves as central platform to monitor and summarize the status of certification evidence.

In an example application, the tool has been customized for a DO-178C/ DO-331 workflow. Therefore, the prerequisites have been discussed in detail and excerpts of the design artefact classes as well as the build workflow have been given. Afterwards, the applicability for flight controller development has been shown. The discussion of related work has highlighted the difference to existing solutions. Finally, a summary of limitations coming along with the build tool and future enhancement plans has been provided.

The presented tool has the ability to solve problems of different process participants. With the Life Cycle Package, the Process Manager is able to distribute workflows, standards, checklists, and procedures in a new level of detail. The work of developers is eased by model scaffolding, which improves conformance of design artefacts to the standard by construction and releases them from reading exceeding documentation. Fine-grained traceability does not have to be created retrospectively or manually, but is implicitly captured during build. Various methods to evaluate completeness of artefacts, conformance to standards, correctness, consistency, and cleanliness support Assessors in their daily work or are pluggable to other build automation systems, like a CI server.

References

1. Basagiannis, S.: Software certification of airborne cyber-physical systems under DO-178C. In: Proceedings of 2016 International Workshop on Symbolic and Numerical Methods for Reachability Analysis (SNR), pp. 1–6. IEEE (2016)
2. National Research Council (U.S.), National Academies Press (U.S.): Critical Code: Software Producibility for Defense. National Academies Press, Washington, D.C. (2010)
3. Broy, M., Kirstan, S., Krcmar, H., Schätz, B.: What is the benefit of a model-based design of embedded software systems in the car industry? In: IR Management Association (ed.) Software Design and Development, pp. 310–334. IGI Global (2014)

4. Bhatt, D., Madl, G., Oglesby, D., Schloegel, K.: Towards scalable verification of commercial avionics software. In: AIAA (ed.) Proceedings of AIAA Infotech@Aerospace 2010 (2010)
5. Paz, A., El Boussaidi, G.: On the exploration of model-based support for DO-178C-compliant avionics software development and certification. In: Proceedings of 2016 IEEE International Symposium on Software Reliability Engineering Workshops (ISSREW), pp. 229–236. IEEE (2016)
6. Hochstrasser, M., Hornauer, M., Holzapfel, F.: Formal Verification of Flight Control Applications along a Model-Based Development Process: A Case Study, 05 October 2016
7. Hochstrasser, M., Schatz, S.P., Nürnberger, K., Hornauer, M., Myschik, S., Holzapfel, F.: Aspects of a consistent modeling environment for DO-331 design model development of flight control algorithms. In: Dołęga, B., Głębocki, R., Kordos, D., Żugaj, M. (eds.) Advances in Aerospace Guidance, Navigation and Control, pp. 69–86. Springer, Cham (2018). https://doi.org/10.1007/978-3-319-65283-2_4
8. Schatz, S.P., et al.: Flightplan flight tests of an experimental DA42 generation aviation aircraft. In: IEEE Control Systems Society (ed.) Proceedings of 14th International Conference on Control, Automation, Robotics and Vision (2016)
9. Nürnberger, K., Hochstrasser, M., Holzapfel, F.: Execution time analysis and optimisation techniques in the model-based development of a flight control software. IET Cyber-Phys. Syst.: Theory Appl. 2(2), 57–64 (2017). https://doi.org/10.1049/iet-cps.2016.0046
10. Hochstrasser, M., Myschik, S., Holzapfel, F.: A process-oriented build tool for safety-critical model-based software development. In: Proceedings of the 6th International Conference on Model-Driven Engineering and Software Development, pp. 191–202. SCITEPRESS - Science and Technology Publications (2018)
11. RTCA: DO-178C - Software Considerations in Airborne Systems and Equipment Certification (2011)
12. RTCA: DO-331 - Model-Based Development and Verification Supplement to DO-178C and DO-278A (2011)
13. Conrad, M., et al.: Automating code reviews with simulink code inspector. In: Dagstuhl (ed.) Proceedings of VIII Dagstuhl-Workshop, München, fortiss GmbH (2012)
14. Conrad, M., Friedman, J., Sandmann, G.: Verification and validation according to IEC 61508: a workflow to facilitate the development of high-integrity applications. SAE Int. J. Commercial Veh. 2, 272–279 (2009)
15. Erkinnen, T., Potter, B.: Model-based design for DO-178B with qualified tools. In: AIAA Modeling and Simulation Technologies Conference and Exhibit. American Institute of Aeronautics and Astronautics Inc, Hyatt Regency McCormick Place, Chicago (2009)
16. Marques, J.C., Yelisetty, S.M.H., Dias, L.A.V., da Cunha, A.M.: Using model-based development as software low-level requirements to achieve airborne software certification. In: Proceedings of 2012 Ninth International Conference on Information Technology - New Generations, pp. 431–436. IEEE (2012)
17. Potter, B.: Complying with DO-178C and DO-331 using Model-Based Design (2012)
18. Berglund, T., McCullough, M.: Building and Testing with Gradle. O'Reilly, Beijing and Sebastopol (2011)
19. Humble, J., Farley, D.: Continuous Delivery: Reliable Software Releases Through Build, Test, and Deployment Automation. Tenth printing edn. A Martin Fowler Signature Book. Addison-Wesley, Upper Saddle River (2015)

20. Sonatype Company: Maven: The Definitive Guide. O'Reilly, Cambridge (2008)
21. Rahman, A., Partho, A., Meder, D., Williams, L.: Which factors influence practitioners' usage of build automation tools? In: Proceedings of 2017 IEEE/ACM 3rd International Workshop on Rapid Continuous Software Engineering (RCoSE), pp. 20–26. IEEE (2017)
22. Dillaber, E., Kendrick, L., Jin, W., Reddy, V. (eds.) Pragmatic Strategies for Adopting Model-Based Design for Embedded Applications. SAE International (2010)
23. Estrada, R.G., Sasaki, G., Dillaber, E.: Best practices for developing DO-178 compliant software using Model-Based Design. AIAA Infotech@Aerospace, Boston (2013)
24. Zisman, A.: Using rules for traceability creation. In: Cleland-Huang, J., Gotel, O., Zisman, A. (eds.) Software and Systems Traceability, pp. 147–170. Springer, London (2012). https://doi.org/10.1007/978-1-4471-2239-5_7
25. Seibel, A., Hebig, R., Giese, H.: Traceability in model-driven engineering: efficient and scalable traceability maintenance. In: Cleland-Huang, J., Gotel, O., Zisman, A. (eds.) Software and Systems Traceability, pp. 215–240. Springer, London (2012). https://doi.org/10.1007/978-1-4471-2239-5_10
26. Lochmann, H., Hessellund, A.: An integrated view on modeling with multi domain-specific languages. In: Proceedings of the IASTED International Conference Software Engineering (2009)
27. Holten, D.: Hierarchical edge bundles: visualization of adjacency relations in hierarchical data. IEEE Trans. Vis. Comput. Graph. 12, 741–748 (2006)
28. Quan, Q.: Introduction to Multicopter Design and Control. Springer, Singapore (2017). https://doi.org/10.1007/978-981-10-3382-7
29. The MathWorks Inc.: DO Qualification R2017b: Model-Based Design Workflow for DO-178C (2017)
30. The Motor Industry Software Reliability Association: MISRA-C:2012 - Guidelines for the use of C language in critical systems, March 2013
31. The MathWorks Automotive Advisory Board: MathWorks Automotive Advisory Board Control Algorithm Modeling Guidelines Using MATLAB, Simulink, and Stateflow: R2016b (2017)
32. The MathWorks Inc.: DO Qualification Kit - Simulink Code Inspector Tool Operational Requirements: R2017b (2017)
33. The MathWorks Inc.: Simulink Code Inspector Reference: R2017b, Natick, MA, USA (2017)
34. Seibel, A., Neumann, S., Giese, H.: Dynamic hierarchical mega models: comprehensive traceability and its efficient maintenance. Softw. Syst. Model. 9, 493–528 (2010)
35. OMG Object Management Group: Software & System Process Engineering Meta-Models Specification (SPEM 2.0), April 2008
36. Gallina, B.: A model-driven safety certification method for process compliance. In: Proceedings of 2014 IEEE International Symposium on Software Reliability Engineering Workshops, pp. 204–209. IEEE (2014)
37. Couto, R., Ribeiro, A.N., Campos, J.C.: The modelery: a collaborative web based repository. In: Murgante, B., et al. (eds.) ICCSA 2014. LNCS, vol. 8584, pp. 1–16. Springer, Cham (2014). https://doi.org/10.1007/978-3-319-09153-2_1
38. Mahapatra, S., Ghidella, J., Walker, G.: Team-based collaboration in model-based design. In: AIAA Modeling and Simulation Technologies Conference. American Institute of Aeronautics and Astronautics, Reston (2012)

A Methodology for Generating Tests for Evaluating User-Centric Performance of Mobile Streaming Applications

Mustafa Al-tekreeti[1](✉), Kshirasagar Naik[1], Atef Abdrabou[2], Marzia Zaman[3], and Pradeep Srivastava[3]

[1] University of Waterloo, Waterloo, ON, Canada
{mmaltekr,snaik}@uwaterloo.ca
[2] UAE University, Al-Ain, UAE
atef.abdrabou@uaeu.ac.ae
[3] Technologie Sanstream, Gatineau, QC, Canada
{mzaman,psrivastava}@sansteam.ca

Abstract. Compared to other platforms, mobile apps' quality assurance is more challenging, since their functionality is affected by the surrounding environment. In literature, a considerable volume of research has been devoted to develop frameworks that facilitate conducting performance analysis during the development life cycle. However, less attention has been given to test generation and test selection criteria for performance evaluation. In this work, a model based test generation methodology is proposed to evaluate the impact of the interaction of the environment, the wireless network, and the app configurations on the performance of a mobile streaming app and thereby on the experience of the end user. The methodology steps, inputs, and outputs are explained using an app example. The methodology assumes that the app has a network access through a WiFi access point. We evaluate the effectiveness of the methodology by comparing the time cost to design a test suite with random testing. The obtained results are very promising.

Keywords: Performance · Testing · Software · Coverage criteria

1 Introduction

Performance is one of the important non-functional properties of software systems, having a vital impact on the user's experience. In the mobile systems domain, the main theme of hand-held devices is being context sensitive [20, 41], imposing extra requirements on mobile software development. Being able to communicate with many network types ranging from Near Field Communication (NFC) to global communication using cellular networks necessitates testing whether the application (app) will perform as required under different environmental and contextual scenarios [22]. Another important aspect of mobile devices is the emphasis on the user experience. Therefore, there is a need for performance

© Springer Nature Switzerland AG 2019
S. Hammoudi et al. (Eds.): MODELSWARD 2018, CCIS 991, pp. 406–429, 2019.
https://doi.org/10.1007/978-3-030-11030-7_18

testing methodologies that take into account both the network behaviour and the quality of end-user experience [45].

Figure 1 depicts the main elements of the system model. The objective is to evaluate the interaction of network operating parameters (NOPs) and app configuration parameters (ACPs) on the end user experience. The app is assumed to be functionally correct. NOPs are a set of parameters that model the wireless network condition, such as data rate. NOPs can be identified at different layers along the network stack. ACPs represent a set of configuration settings of the app that have an impact on the performance metric under consideration, such as the size of the receiving buffer. Because the number of interactions can grow up exponentially to unmanageable limits, an effective set of interactions is chosen as follows. First, end user experience is characterised by few specific categories (normally 3 to 5). Then, given the performance levels that correspond to the identified categories of end user experience, test inputs (the values of ACPs and NOPs) are determined. In fact, determining the test input that leads to a certain performance behaviour is a sort of solving the *inversion* problem [38]. It is quite similar to solving program predicates in white-box approach to determine the test input that leads to the execution of certain program paths.

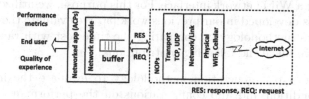

Fig. 1. System model of the app under test.

Since performance metrics are statistical measures, test execution parameters (TEPs) are required. TEPs encompass all the necessary information to efficiently execute test cases. From the statistical point of view, each test case is an experiment. Therefore, we need to know how many times the experiment should be repeated, or for how long it should be executed, so that the output is statistically reliable. Hence, the objective is to design a set of test cases where each test case is basically a set of ACPs, NOPs, TEPs and the expected performance level. In other words, if the SUT is executed with the determined parameters in the three sets (ACPs, NOPs, and TEPs), then the observed performance level is statistically equivalent to the expected performance level if and only if the SUT is correctly implemented from the performance point of view. Because performance metrics are mainly continuous, infinite number of performance levels and test cases are anticipated. Therefore, some test selection strategies need to be applied to generate an efficient suite of performance test cases.

The testing methodology is realized by a procedure of three main steps. We adopt a system level black-box model-based testing (MBT) approach [3,51,52]. We target an important category of networked mobile apps, which is real-time mobile apps, such as voice-over-ip, streaming, video conferencing, and on-line gaming [56]. In the first step, two performance models (mathematical and simulation) to capture the interactions between the SUT and the network are developed using the Markovian framework. In the second step, generating tests to evaluate the end-user experience is formulated as an inversion problem and solved as an optimization problem. In the third step, TEPs are inferred using the simulation model. To enhance the quality of the generated test cases, two test coverage criteria are proposed: user experience (UE) and user experience and input interaction (UEII). In UE, test cases are generated to fully cover the identified categories of end-user experience. In UEII, test cases are generated to cover the categories of end-user experience and the interaction of the input parameters (ACPs and NOPs) simultaneously. Input parameters interactions are explored using combinatorial criteria [46]. Because the network model constrains NOPs by non-linear constraints, state of art combinatorial test generation tools are not applicable directly. To overcome this problem, we constrain the input space first. Then, we apply the combinatorial testing criterion to generate test cases. The generated test cases are validated using the performance simulation model. Using a case study of a mobile multimedia streaming application, we explain the different steps of the proposed methodology. The mobile app is assumed to have network access through a WiFi network interface. For this purpose, we utilize the network model that was developed in our previous work [5]. We evaluate the effectiveness of the proposed methodology by comparing the time cost with random testing. In summary, we make the following contributions:

- We propose a test generation methodology to evaluate the interaction of network condition and app configurations on the performance of a mobile networked application;
- We propose two performance testing coverage criteria to enhance the quality of the generated test cases; and
- We show by means of a procedure how TEPs are inferred using performance simulation models.

The paper is organized as follows. In Sect. 2, related works are reviewed. In Sect. 3, we introduce the proposed test generation methodology. In Sect. 4, the main steps of the methodology are illustrated using an app example. In Sect. 5, we evaluate the effectiveness of the approach. In Sect. 6, the main challenges of applying the proposed methodology are discussed. Finally, in Sect. 7, the work is concluded and pointers to the future works are outlined.

2   Related Works

In this section, we survey the published works that are related to the contributions of the paper. In general, software testing can be invoked at any step during the design process. It can be performed at the unit, integration, or system level. In literature, considerable efforts have been made on integrating performance analysis with the development life cycle. In this approach, different software design artefacts are augmented with performance values and then transformed into stochastic models, such as Petri nets, simulation models, or queueing networks. A comprehensive summary can be found in [37] and [7]. The main objective in this research is to conduct performance analysis to evaluate design alternatives while the software is still in the development process, whereas our objective is to generate test cases to test the SUT after its implementation. They assume that the performance requirements are available so that they can annotate the design diagrams with performance values, whereas in our work, performance requirements are elicited as one of the by-products of the model-based testing process. In fact, our approach is orthogonal to theirs, but complementary to the early-stage performance testing phase.

Frequently, performance testing is viewed as load testing. Load testing is used to test large-scale multi-user transaction based software systems, such as web sites and database systems. In contrast, we target software applications that are developed for mobile devices, where network access is accomplished via wireless technologies. This difference in scope leads to a core distinction between our work and the model-based load testing. The developed models in load testing is network-technology independent, while our approach models explicitly the network technology. In addition, test input for load testing can be generated simultaneously while the real SUT executes (on-line) or independently (off-line). In the off-line approach, test loads are designed from the source code using static analysis techniques such as data flow analysis [57] and symbolic execution [61,62], using the operational profile (workload characterization) [6,55], or using design models annotated with statistics derived from the operational profile and past data, such as UML use-case diagrams [16,19], Markov chains [23,47,54], and probabilistic time automata [2]. In the on-line approach, there is a feedback from the real system to the test generation process to refine the test loads. Different techniques are used to enhance the test loads, such as machine learning [28], linear programs [59,60], Bayesian estimation [26], hill climbing [9,10], and genetic algorithms [21,30]. A comprehensive survey of load testing is given in [34]. Our testing methodology can share some of the concepts with load testing, however, the approach and scope of our work are distinct. Our approach is off-line, yet casting the test generation as an inversion problem resembles the feedback in on-line load testing.

In the mobile domain, because of the short development cycle compared to other software domains, most of the performance testing activities are conducted after implementations [35]. Another observation is that most testing frameworks follow a white-box approach due to many reasons. First, most applications are of small to moderate sizes (tens to hundreds of lines of code). Second, many mobile applications are developed by non-professional software developers which increases the probability of code level mistakes. Third, black-box testing needs special skills in order to develop different types of models. Although a white-box approach in mobile testing has its own advantages, it does not facilitate a systematic consideration of the environment in the testing process [51].

In spite of the much research efforts going into performance testing in the mobile software domain, test generation to evaluate the network impact on app performance has not received much attention [41]. In this regard, we conduct a survey targeting any published work in test generation for networked (wired or wireless) software systems. We observe that the main focus is on testing for functional requirements. For example in [50], a model checking approach is used to verify UDP-based software systems. Since UDP protocol does not implement any mechanism to ensure data integrity, a tool is provided to check for faults in the software part that is responsible for networking. The tool can introduce three types of errors in communication: packet duplication, packet loss, and packet reordering. In another work [53], networked software systems are checked for violations in functional specifications using fuzz testing and model refinement. In both, the main focus is on the functional requirements.

In trying to enable mobile software developers to debug their apps for communication errors, a software profiler is provided in [22]. It analyses the communication link and generate metrics to capture different aspects, such as connectivity and power consumption. It also allows for doing measurements correlation to pinpoint the error. This work belong to the efforts of conducting performance analysis early in the development process, while our objective is designing test suites to be used after implementation.

Providing test execution beds to evaluate the performance of networked apps is very important. In [49], an emulator based test bed is designed to evaluate the impact of physical mobility and hands-over in 4G networks on the operation of wireless mobile apps. It does not address how test scenarios are designed and what is the coverage criterion to use.

In terms of the end-user quality of experience, the work reported in [13] had developed a test bench to automate end-user QOE capturing for Android apps. Thus, it is meant to facilitate test execution, while in our work, we utilize QOE characterization to guide test selection process to evaluate the performance from the end-user point of view and to minimize the size of the test suites.

In software engineering, simulation models have been widely used in different software development activities. However, the emphasis is on using simulation models to evaluate alternative design choices [8,36], or to design test cases to verify software systems represented as simulation models [11,43]. In our work, test execution parameters are inferred from simulation models. In addition, we provide a procedure based on two statistical methods, while in literature, statistical techniques, such as hypothesis testing, are mainly used to verify the output of test execution [31,32].

3   The Proposed Test Generation Methodology

In this section, our test generation methodology is introduced. Figure 2 shows the main steps, the inputs, and the expected output of the methodology. We start by discussing the methodology input requirements. Then, we explain the methodology steps. In Sect. 4, the methodology is illustrated by means of an app example.

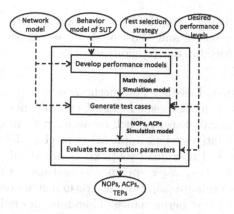

Fig. 2. The main steps of the methodology [5].

3.1 Inputs to the Methodology

The methodology requires four different artefacts as inputs. In this section, we describe them briefly:

Behaviour Model of the SUT. This model should describe how the app-network interactions impact the performance metric under consideration. According to the system model, the app-network interactions are clearly observed in the buffering behaviour. Thus, the behaviour model of the SUT should explicitly feature the buffer dynamics. In literature, different diagrams are used to model software dynamics. For example, using UML diagrams, the de facto software modelling language, software behaviours are commonly described using state diagrams, activity diagrams, and/or collaboration diagrams. In this work, we use activity diagrams to describe this model. The outcomes of this task are the behaviour model of the SUT and the set of app configuration parameters (ACPs) that affect the considered performance metric. In Sect. 4.1, an example of how to develop a behaviour model for a mobile streaming app is shown.

Network Model. This model should capture how the wireless network affects the considered performance metric. In general, network model development is mainly determined by the technology (WiFi or cellular) and the transport protocol (TCP or UDP). According to the system model, the app interacts with the network through a basic *request-response* (REQ-RES) mechanism. Thus, the network's impact can be captured by modelling the RES inter-arrival time delay, which is modelled as a random variable. The expected outcomes of network modelling are the probability distribution of this random variable, the network operating parameters (NOPs), and any assumptions and/or conditions that are made during model development. Those conditions and assumptions are required in the second step of the methodology. To obtain the distribution, we employ distribution fitting using the first two moments: the mean and variance [4]. Assuming UDP protocol and WiFi network access, we utilize the network model that was developed in our previous work [5].

Desired Performance Levels. The methodology requires a set of levels of the performance metric under consideration. Generally, performance metrics are evaluated using statistical measures such as mean, percentage, and probability. In this work, we are interested in application level performance metrics that directly relate to the end user quality of experience (QOE) [24]. For example, the user experience of file transfer apps is assessed using two metrics: goodput and transfer time performance [33]. Both are ratio metrics on a scale from 0 to 1, where 1 represents the best performance. Therefore, desired performance levels are merely numerical values sampled from the interval $[0, 1]$. How many levels are needed and how they are chosen are addressed in test selection strategies.

Test Selection Strategies. In general, a test selection strategy encodes the main objectives of the testing process. In black-box testing, all testing activities are carried out in terms of software (or software model) inputs and outputs. In this methodology, we propose two coverage criteria. Initially, we need to introduce some notations. The sets of NOPs and ACPs are denoted as S_{NOP} and S_{ACP} with cardinality numbers as n and m, respectively. Thus, the input parameter set is $S_{INP} = S_{NOP} \cup S_{ACP}$. Therefore, we have $n + m$ input parameters $p_1, p_2, \ldots, p_{n+m}$. To generate a test case, we assign a specific value vp_i to each parameter p_i, where $vp_i \in Vp_i$, the set of permissible values of the parameter p_i, $1 \leq i \leq n + m$. Thus, a test case t_j is basically a set of the form $(vp_1^j, vp_2^j, \ldots, vp_{n+m}^j, l_j)$, where l_j is the expected performance level.

(i) User Experience (UE) Coverage Criterion. Herein, the objective is to generate test cases to cover the whole spectrum of the considered performance metric. However, since the performance spectrum is most likely to be continuous, an infinite number of test cases are needed. To generate a minimal set of test cases, partition testing [29] is applied. This technique is mainly used to generate test cases from input space models for functional testing. The idea is to partition the parameter space into multiple regions where all the points of the same region are equivalent from the testing point of view. In this work, we apply partition testing to performance metrics, utilizing the fact that the end-user experience is not linearly proportional with the performance behaviour and it can be characterized by few specific categories called QOE categories. Given R categories, we divide the performance spectrum W into R non-overlapped regions $r_1, r_2, \ldots, r_R$ such that $W = \bigcup_i^R r_i$. The number of QOE categories are app type dependent. It also depends on the available resources for the testing process, because test suite size directly relates with R. Then, a performance level l_i is selected for each region such that $l_i \in r_i$, $1 \leq i \leq R$. Thereafter, the corresponding test input $vp_1^i, vp_2^i, \ldots, vp_{n+m}^i$ for l_i is determined. As an example, we can divide the interval $[0,1]$ of the goodput metric according to the end-user QOE into (say) three regions: if goodput is between 0.9 and 1 ($r_1 = [1, 0.9]$), the quality is *excellent*; between 0.9 and 0.7 ($r_2 = (0.9, 0.7]$), the quality is *good*; and less than 0.7 ($r_3 = (0.7, 0]$), the quality is *poor*. Then, three performance levels are picked, e.g., $l_1 = 0.95$, $l_2 = 0.85$, and $l_3 = 0.5$, to represent the identified categories. The following procedure summarizes the steps needed to generate test cases that satisfy this criterion:

- **Procedure 1:** Test selection strategy to achieve the UE coverage criterion
- **Inputs:** The number of QOE categories R
- **Outputs:** A test suite T of R test cases
  S1: Partition the performance metric spectrum W into R regions $r_1, r_2, \ldots, r_R$;
  S2: Select a set of performance levels $S_l = \{l_j : l_j \in r_j, 1 \leq j \leq R\}$;
  S3: Generate a test input $vp_1^j, vp_2^j, \ldots, vp_{n+m}^j$ for each desired performance level $l_j \in S_l$.

Step 3 of this procedure is further explained in the next section. This criterion is achieved if at least one desired performance level from each QOE category is within the generated test cases.

(ii) User Experience and Input Interaction (UEII) Coverage Criterion.

It may be noted that the UE coverage criterion is an output based criterion. However, satisfying this criterion is not enough to assure the quality of the app, because the designed test suite does not adequately cover the input space of the SUT. In combinatorial testing, it is emphasized that the effectiveness of the generated test cases increases as the coverage of the interactions of the input parameters increases [58]. Therefore, in this criterion, we are interested in generating test cases that satisfy both aspects of the SUT: the input space and the performance behaviour. For this purpose, we extend the procedure of the UE coverage criterion. First, we generate a set of R seed test cases T_S using "Procedure 1". This set does cover the whole performance spectrum. Then, to enhance input space coverage, we use the seed tests to generate follow-up test cases so that a combinatorial metric is satisfied. The combinatorial metric is applied on subsets $g_1, g_2, \ldots, g_G$ of the S_{INP} set, where $G \geq 1$. These subsets are constructed such that the parameters in which their interactions are important to cover are grouped into a subset. For example, one may partition the S_{INP} set into two subsets ($G = 2$): $g_1 = S_{ACP}$ and $g_2 = S_{NOP}$. A set of follow-up test cases T_{ij} is generated for every subset g_j and seed test s_i. The parameters' values $vp_1, vp_2, \ldots, vp_{n+m}$ of the follow-up test cases are determined as follows. The values of the parameters of the g_j subset are determined using a combinatorial coverage metric. The remaining parameters $\{p : p \in S_{INP} - g_j\}$ are assigned the same values of the parameters of the seed test case s_i.

The input space is constrained by conditions imposed by the network, the SUT, and by the condition that the expected performance levels for the follow-up test cases should remain within the same region of the performance. That is, given the sets T_S, $S_G = \{g_1, g_2, \ldots, g_G\}$, X (the set of constraints), and a combinatorial metric b, $T_{ij} = Pert(g_j, s_i, X, b)$, $1 \leq j \leq G$, $1 \leq i \leq R$, where $Pert$ realizes the follow-up test generation using the combinatorial coverage metric b. Therefore, test generation to satisfy this criterion is basically a combinatorial test generation with constrained parameters. The generated test suite T is the union of the follow-up test sets T_{ij} and the seed test cases T_S. The main steps to satisfy this criterion are summarized as follows:

- **Procedure 2:** Test selection strategy to achieve the UEII coverage criterion
- **Inputs:** R, G, X, and b
- **Outputs:** A test suite T
  S1: Generate the set T_S of R seed test cases using "Procedure 1";
  S2: Create the set $S_G = \{g_j : g_j \subset S_{INP}, 1 \leq j \leq G\}$;
  S3: $\forall j, i$, and given the set X and the metric b, $T_{ij} = Pert(g_j, s_i, X, b)$. The test suite is $T = \bigcup_{i,j} T_{ij} \bigcup T_S$.

The UEII criterion subsumes the UE criterion. In Sect. 4.3, we give the implementation details of test generation using both criteria.

3.2   The Methodology Procedure

The methodology's three steps as shown in Fig. 2 are:

Develop Performance Models. The performance model is any mathematical representation that quantitatively captures the impact of the interaction of the network operating parameters (NOPs) and the app configuration parameters (ACPs) on the performance of the SUT. In literature, many stochastic notations have been used to develop software performance models, such as simulation models, stochastic Petri nets, and queueing networks [15]. Furthermore, different model transformation frameworks have been proposed to guide performance model generation from UML based software design models [12]. In this work, we employ the Markovian modelling framework to develop the performance models. This framework is appropriate especially when the system state is defined by the buffering behaviour of the SUT. We use supplementary variable technique (SVT) [17,18] to solve the model. This technique is used if the stochastic process is not Markovian, allowing for more practical interactions between the SUT and the network to be modelled. In this methodology, two performance models are developed: mathematical and simulation. The simulation model is used to verify the mathematical model and in the test generation process as well. This step requires the network model and behaviour model of the SUT.

Generate Test Cases. The network and SUT configuration parameters are found by formulating test generation as solving the inversion problem. In order to determine the input that leads to a certain output, an inverse relationship should be derived. For most mathematical models, deducing a closed form for the inverse relationship may not be feasible. Furthermore, the structure of some mathematical models are unknown as in simulation models. Therefore, we cast the inversion problem as a root finding problem. Given the desired performance level $l_i \in S_l$, the test input is basically the root that satisfies the relationship [5]:

$$Perf\_model(p_1, p_2, \ldots, p_{n+m}) - l_i = 0 \tag{1}$$

where $Perf\_model(\ldots)$ represents the performance model. The roots (NOPs and ACPs values) can be found by reformulating the previous equation as a minimization problem as follows [5]:

$$\textbf{Minimize} \quad |Perf\_model(p_1, p_2, \ldots, p_{n+m}) - l_i| \tag{2}$$

where $|.|$ is the absolute value operator. We minimize the absolute of the difference to force the solver that the required minimum is zero. In this work, we use the mathematical performance model as the objective function, although the simulation model can also be used. The minimization problem is constrained by the conditions imposed by the network model and the semantics of the SUT behaviour. The constraints should be formulated in terms of the chosen input parameters. Beside the performance model, this task requires the network model and the desired performance levels. The following procedure summarizes the steps needed to determine ACPs and NOPs:

- **Procedure 3:** Determine the test inputs
- **Inputs:** The performance model, the network model, and the desired performance level l_j
- **Outputs:** Test input values $vp_1^j, vp_2^j, \ldots, vp_{n+m}^j$ and the constraints set X
  S1: Define the constraints in terms of input parameters $p_1, p_2, \ldots, p_{n+m}$;
  S2: Solve the minimization problem of Eq. 2.

In Sect. 4.3, we explain this procedure by means of a concrete example.

Determining TEPs. We employ the performance simulation model to determine the TEPs. We determine the parameters by two stages. First, we estimate the mean test execution time using a univariate sequential procedure called Law and Carson (abbreviated as L&C) [39]. We estimate the mean run length for the simulation model to reach steady-state and use this value as an estimate for the mean test case execution time. We build a point estimator and a confidence interval so that the estimated value for the considered performance metric is within a pre-specified error from the true value. Then, the rest of TEPs are inferred simultaneously by utilizing the Bonferroni inequality [14]. This inequality provides a lower bound for the overall confidence level $(1 - \zeta)$ given that the overall significant level ζ is equal to the sum of the individual significant levels $(\zeta_1, \zeta_2, \ldots, \zeta_k)$ for the remaining k TEPs. We construct individual confidence intervals using the Independent Replication Sequential procedure [39]. The precision of estimation is controlled by a tunable parameter γ, called the *relative error* in estimation. The following procedure summarizes this step:

- **Procedure 4:** Determine TEPs using the performance simulation model
- **Inputs:** The test case $(vp_1^j, vp_2^j, \ldots, vp_{n+m}^j, l_j)$, γ, ζ, and the number of replications
- **Outputs:** The corresponding TEPs values
  S1: Invoke the L&C procedure to obtain the estimated mean of the test case execution time $\hat{T}_x$ and the confidence interval $CI(\hat{T}_x)$;
  S2: Choose the values for $\zeta_1, \zeta_2, \ldots, \zeta_k$ so that $\sum_{i=1}^{k} \zeta_i = \zeta$;
  S3: Invoke the Independent Replication Sequential procedure to obtain the estimated mean and the confidence interval for the remaining TEPs.

4   Using the Proposed Methodology

In this section, we apply the proposed methodology on an example of a multimedia streaming app running on a mobile device. The considered performance quality is the smoothness of the streaming as seen by the end user. We assume the app utilizes UDP as a transport protocol and the last hop to the end user is through a wireless connection using a WiFi hotspot that implements the IEEE 802.11 protocol. We start this section by defining the behaviour model of the SUT and the network model. Then, we apply the proposed methodology to generate test cases using both test selection strategies.

4.1   Behaviour Model of the SUT

The dynamics of streaming apps are captured if the buffering behaviour is modelled. In this app example, we assume that the SUT implements a *progressive* streaming mechanism in which both frame downloading and decoding (playing) are interleaved [42]. The app behaviour is modelled by two main components: a *downloader* and a *player*. Both components interact with each other through a buffer known as a *playback buffer*. Figure 3 shows the desired behaviour of the SUT. At the beginning, the application is in the *Buffering* phase. In this phase, the downloader starts fetching media frames from the network and queues them in the buffer, while the player is still off. The application remains in this phase until the data level in the playback buffer reaches a certain limit usually known as a *high watermark* (M). This level determines the length of the buffering phase and thereby the length of the time period the user has to wait before the player starts playing. Also, this level determines when the app stops asking for new frames. The downloader resumes fetching media frames whenever data level drops below a certain limit known as a *low watermark* (L). This level represents the minimum amount of data in the buffer to ensure smooth continuous playback. In multimedia streaming, many performance metrics are proposed to capture end-user experience. In this work, we consider *the frequency of rebuffering events* as the performance metric [44]. This metric has a direct relationship with the frequency of visiting the *Empty Buffer* state. The SUT behaviour is characterised by three configuration parameters (ACPs): playback buffer size B, M, and L. The "state" in this diagram represents the activity in which the software is currently running. The text on the arrow from state x to state y, represents the condition that triggers a transition from state x to state y.

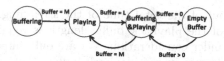

Fig. 3. The behaviour model of the app example [5].

4.2   Wireless Network Model

The end-user is streaming via a WiFi hotspot. We assume all the fluctuations in the wireless channel and the queueing effects of the different routers along the path from the server to the client device manifest as a time delay. That is, packet loss is negligible. The probability distribution of the frame inter-arrival time delay is matched with a Hyper-Erlang distribution [5]. The network impact is captured by three operating parameters (NOPs): data rate (D), the mean rate of frame arrival into the access point (λ) per user, and the number of end users (N) connected to the AP.

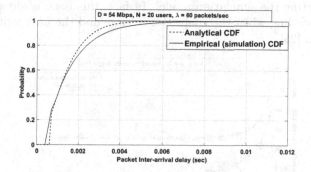

Fig. 4. The empirical and analytical CDFs [5].

To validate the distribution fitting process, we conduct simulation experiments using the Network Simulator NS2 tool. The simulated scenario is a file downloading, where a number of users are simultaneously downloading a large file through the access point (AP). Figure 4 shows both the empirical CDF that is generated from the simulation and the matched CDF for a specific scenario.

4.3   Test Generation for the Running Application Example

Given the network model and the behaviour model of the SUT, we can start applying the methodology procedure:

Performance Models. In this step, we develop two performance models: mathematical and simulation. Since the performance metric under consideration is a long-run metric, the buffering phase is not included in the performance models. The performance metric correlates with the fraction of time of being in the

Empty Buffer state out of the total time of the streaming. Therefore, the stationary distribution of the playback buffer length is required to evaluate the performance metric under consideration. We are only interested in the probability of having zero frames in the playback buffer. To facilitate the modelling process, we assume that the frame decoding rate is exponentially distributed. Nevertheless, the stochastic process is still not Markovian, as the frame arrivals are not exponentially distributed. To use the Markovian framework, we develop and solve the model using the supplementary variable technique. The details are shown in [5]. The end product of this task is the performance model.

To verify the performance modelling process, Fig. 5 shows the probability of empty playback buffer state (π_0) with different buffer sizes and for both simulation and mathematical models, where μ represents the mean rate of frame decoding and f is a tunable parameter to control the relation between the frame arrival rate and the decoding rate. In the simulation model, we simulate a streaming session of 30 min. Each simulation experiment is repeated 50 times. An important point to mention, as playback buffer size increases, the time overhead of evaluating the mathematical model becomes comparable with the time overhead of evaluating the simulation model. In fact, this issue is already observed in Markov modelling when the chain size is large and the underlying process is not Markovian [25].

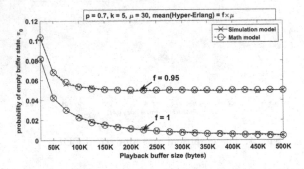

Fig. 5. The considered performance metric versus playback buffer size [5].

Test Generation. We apply Procedure 3 to determine the test input. In **Procedure 3.S2**, to determine the objective function, the desired performance levels l_i's should be specified. This task is part of the test selection criteria and we tackle it in **Procedure 1 and 2**. In **Procedure 3.S2**, the constraints and bounds of input parameters are defined. The ACPs (B, M, and L) are defined as an integer number of multimedia frames. The semantics of the SUT introduce the following two constraints [5]:

$$M \leq B,$$
$$L \leq M - 1. \tag{3}$$

The high watermark cannot be higher than the buffer size, and the low watermark cannot be equal or higher than the high watermark. For the NOPs, data rate D according to the IEEE 802.11 a/g standard can be in one of the following values: 6, 9, 12, 18, 24, 32, 48, or 54 Mbps. It mainly relates to the quality of the wireless connection between the AP and the end user. Regarding the number of users N, the network model is validated with the number of mobile devices that ranges from 4 to 30. The parameter λ is the only continuous. Using the upper and lower bounds of N and D and the constraints imposed by the network, we bound λ between 10 and $416\,packet/sec$. Therefore, the optimization problem is a constrained mixed non-linear problem.

In multimedia streaming, the mean encoding rate at the server is set according to the end-user device characteristics. To simplify the analysis, it is often assumed that the mean arrival rate to the end user $1/E_r$ is equal to the mean decoding rate (μ) [40]. That is [5]:

$$\mu = \frac{1}{E_r} \tag{4}$$

Solving Eq. (4) in terms of NOPs (λ, N, and D), a non-linear equality constraint is obtained. Since most optimization solvers do not easily accommodate non-linear equality constraints, we assume that the mean of the packet inter-arrival time delay falls in a closed interval around $1/\mu$. Thus [5]:

$$\frac{k1}{\mu} \le E_r \le \frac{k2}{\mu} \tag{5}$$

where $k1$ and $k2$ are parameters introduced to control the width of the closed interval around $1/\mu$. By doing so, we relax the non-linear equality constraint to two non-linear inequalities that are easier to deal with (if $k1$ and $k2$ are both set to 1, the equality constraint (4) is reproduced). Another constraint that should be taken into consideration is that the traffic intensity ρ at the AP should be less than 1. Otherwise, the buffer at the AP will build up infinitely [5]:

$$\rho < 1 \tag{6}$$

Therefore, the optimization problem has five constraints given by Eqs. (3), (5), and (6). Now, we show how test cases are generated using the two proposed coverage criteria:

(i) Test Input Generation Using UE Coverage Criterion. In **Procedure 1.S1**, the performance spectrum is partitioned according to the end-user QOE categories. In multimedia streaming and using the probability of empty buffer state as a performance metric, three different end-user experiences are reported ($R = 3$) [44]. If the probability of empty buffer state is less than 2%, the video quality is high; between 2% and 15%, the quality is medium; and for more than 15%, the quality is considered poor. Therefore, we divide the performance behaviour according to the reported three regions. Then, we select a desired level for each region $\{l_1 = 0.01, l_2 = 0.05, l_3 = 0.2\}$. Solving the minimization problem for each performance level (**Procedure 3.S2**), the corresponding network and SUT parameters' values are determined as shown in Table 1. The buffer size B is bounded between 10 and 40 frames, the mean of the decoding rate μ is 30 fps, and the parameters $k1$ and $k2$ are assigned as 0.75 and 1.25, respectively.

Table 1. Test cases to satisfy UE coverage criterion. D is in Mbps.

l_i	B	M	L	D	λ	N
0.01	34	34	4	18	131.965	7
0.05	38	31	7	32	162.8702	8
0.2	24	7	2	6	98.9693	4

(ii) Test Input Generation Using the UEII Coverage Criterion. We consider the three generated test cases that are listed in Table 1 as test seeds T_S (**Procedure 2.S1**). We utilize the combinatorial coverage metric *each-choice* [29] to enhance the input space coverage. We represent the only continuous parameter λ by the following 42 discrete values $[10, 20, 30, \dots, 410, 416]$. For **Procedure 2.S2**, we choose to cover the interaction of S_{ACP} and S_{NOP} independently (i.e., $G = 2$ and $g_1 = S_{ACP}$, $g_2 = S_{NOP}$). For g_1 subset, we apply each-choice coverage for high watermark (M) and low watermark (L) only, since the playback buffer size (B) does not directly affect the system output. That is, the parameters B, D, λ, and N are kept fixed on seed' values. The same procedure is applied for g_2 subset.

To automate the process, we can benefit from the available combinatorial test generation tools. Unfortunately, we cannot use anyone of them directly, because the type of constraints in our case is more complex than what is supported in the available tools. To mitigate this issue, we first find out the permissible parameter values that satisfy the constraints and then we apply the combinatorial testing criterion. This approach enables us to use the available tools without any modifications, but sometimes, it might be expensive. The combinatorial tool ACTS v3 [1] is used in this process.

Applying the procedure for the g_1 subset, we get 9 (T_{11}), 40 (T_{12}), and 33 (T_{13}) test cases for the performance regions $(0.15, 1]$, $(0.02, 0.15]$, and $[0, 0.02]$, respectively:

$$T_{11} = \{(10,5), (11,1), (12,1), (13,1), (8,7), (6,4), (5,3), (9,6), (7,2)\}$$

$$\begin{aligned} T_{12} = \{&(6,5), (7,6), (8,6), (9,4), (38,37), (38,36), (38,35), (37,34), (38,33), \\ &(33,32), (34,31), (38,30), (30,29), (29,28), (28,27), (27,26), (26,25), \\ &(25,24), (24,23), (23,22), (22,21), (21,20), (20,19), (19,18), (18,17), \\ &(17,16), (16,15), (15,14), (14,13), (13,12), (12,11), (11,10), (10,9), \\ &(38,8), (37,6), (36,5), (35,4), (35,4), (34,3), (33,2), (32,1), (31,7)\} \end{aligned}$$

$$\begin{aligned} T_{13} = \{&(10,9), (11,10), (12,11), (13,12), (14,13), (15,14), (16,15), (17,16), \\ &(18,17), (19,18), (20,19), (21,20), (22,21), (23,22), (24,23), (25,24), \\ &(26,25), (27,26), (32,27), (33,28), (30,29), (33,30), (34,31), (33,32), \\ &(34,33), (33,8), (32,7), (31,6), (30,5), (29,3), (28,2), (34,1), (34,4)\} \end{aligned}$$

The first element of each tuple is M and the second is L. The remaining parameters' values are fixed on test seed values. For the g_2 subset, using the same procedure and test seeds, we get 5 (T_{21}), 3 (T_{22}), and 3 (T_{23}) test cases for the regions $[0, 0.02]$, $(0.02, 0.15]$, and $(0.15, 1]$, respectively:

$$T_{21} = \{(6M, 30, 13), (32M, 50, 26), (32M, 100, 13), (32M, 130, 10), (32M, 260, 5)\}$$

$$T_{22} = \{(54M, 110, 15), (54M, 150, 11), (54M, 330, 5)\}$$

$$T_{23} = \{(54M, 110, 15), (54M, 150, 11), (54M, 330, 5)\}$$

The first element of each tuple is D, the second is λ, and the third is N. The remaining parameters' (B, M, and L) values are fixed on test seed values. Therefore, the designed test suite T according to the UEII criterion is the union of the sets T_{11}, T_{12}, T_{13}, T_{21}, T_{22}, T_{23}, and the seed test cases T_S.

Table 2. The set T_S augmented with TEPs. $\hat{T}_x$ is in seconds and $\hat{F}_s$ is in MB.

l_i	$\hat{T}_x$	$CI(\hat{T}_x)$	$\hat{F}_s$	$CI(\hat{F}_s)$
0.01	9.5573×10^3	$[8.7231 \times 10^3, 1.0392 \times 10^4]$	425.8	$[425.32, 426.28]$
0.05	6.5536×10^3	$[4.4497 \times 10^3, 8.6575 \times 10^3]$	280.2018	$[279.77, 280.63]$
0.2	384	$[279.0665, 488.9335]$	13.8505	$[13.780, 13.921]$

Determining TEPs. In the third step, test case execution parameters (TEPs) are determined. For the running example, each test case is a streaming session with certain configuration parameters. To efficiently execute each test case, the length of the streaming session and the size of the multimedia file should be determined. We cannot conclude the file size from the streaming session time length, since the player rate is not deterministic. Since we have two TEPs parameters only, we do the estimations without the need to use Bonferroni inequality (**Procedure 4.S2**). The used values for γ, ζ, and the number of replications are 0.075, 0.1, and 10, respectively. We build a point estimator and a confidence interval independently for the mean test case execution time $\hat{T}_x$ (**Procedure 4.S1**) and the mean file size $\hat{F}_s$ (**Procedure 4.S3**) so that the estimated probability of the empty playback buffer state ($\hat{l}$) is within a pre-specified error from the true value. We estimate $\hat{T}_x$ and $\hat{F}_s$ for the three test cases listed in Table 1. The augmented test cases are shown in Table 2. As shown, the confidence interval for the test execution time $CI(\hat{T}_x)$ is somewhat wide. It can be narrowed by increasing the number of replications. We gauge the adequacy of the estimated simulation time by controlling the width of the confidence interval $CI(\hat{l})$ through the parameter γ. As expected, test case execution time is test case dependent. Moreover, as l increases, the required time to reach steady-state decreases.

5   The Evaluation of the Approach

We use random testing as a baseline to evaluate the effectiveness of the proposed test generation methodology. Figure 6 shows how random testing is normally used to generate test cases, where R is the number of performance regions, Q is the number of the required test cases per region, and C is the coverage criterion. The set S holds the generated test cases. In this section, we use the phrases test configurations and test cases interchangeably. The test configuration t_c is basically a set of values of ACPs and NOPs. Because the implementation of the SUT is not available, the shown procedure is not directly applicable. Therefore, we modify the procedure as shown in Fig. 7. We use the developed performance model to evaluate the performance behaviour l_c of the configuration t_c. To anticipate the incurred cost of random test generation, we keep track of the following types of test configurations:

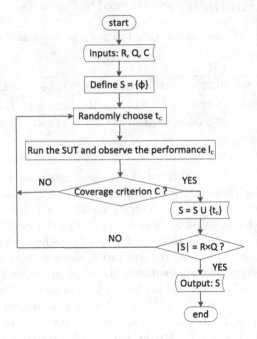

Fig. 6. The flowchart of test generation using random testing.

- Invalid executable test configurations (IETCs),
- Invalid non-executable test configurations (INTCs),
- Valid-and-useful test configurations (VTCs),
- Valid-but-not-useful test configurations (VNTCs).

The test configuration t_c is invalid if the chosen parameters' values do not satisfy the constraints imposed by the network model, SUT, or both. If t_c does not satisfy the network requirements only (invalid NOPs), the SUT can still

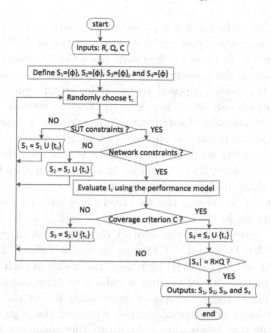

Fig. 7. The modified flowchart of test generation using random testing. The sets S_1, S_2, S_3, and S_4 are the sets of INTCs, IETCs, VNTCs, and VTCs, respectively [5].

execute, while if t_c does not satisfy the constraints imposed by the SUT (invalid ACPs) or both the network and SUT (invalid NOPs and ACPs), the configuration is not executable. We assume the SUT implements the necessary logic to catch out inconsistent ACPs. Therefore, we have two types of invalid test configurations: executable (IETCs) and non-executable (INTCs). It is important to differentiate between them because IETCs are more expensive than INTCs from the time cost point of view. If t_c satisfies all the imposed constraints, it is a valid configuration. Moreover, if this valid configuration increases the coverage of the designed test suite so far, it is considered as a valid-and-useful configuration. Otherwise, it is considered a valid-but-not-useful test configuration.

To estimate the incurred cost of generating a test suite of size $R \times Q$ using random testing, we design an experiment with R and Q can take values from one to three. Thus, we have in total nine test generation scenarios. We repeat the experiment for each scenario 10 times. The obtained results for UE criterion are shown in Table 3. The results are basically the median of 10 repetitions. For example, to randomly generate a test suite with one test case ($R = 1$, $Q = 1$), the incurred time cost is approximately the sum of the time cost of running 566 IETCs and one VTCs, while in our framework, we need to execute the SUT with one VTC only. Since performance metrics are mostly statistical, the time needed to observe the performance behaviour l_c of the real system is not trivial. As we employ a heuristics based optimization formulation which solely depends on function (performance model) evaluations to find the optimal point (test case), random testing can be better than ours if the performance model evaluation is more expensive than running the real SUT and/or if the employed optimizer needs more model evaluations than random testing. For the first condition, even if the performance is modelled using a simulation model, many techniques has been proposed to speed up simulation executions, while real system executions cannot be accelerated. For the second condition, many heuristics based optimization formulations are available in literature that can perform better than the employed optimizer (genetic algorithm). Indeed, within the same algorithm, many strategies can be used to fine tune the performance of the algorithm. In summary, there is still much room to enhance the performance of our framework compared to random testing.

In addition, as R increases, the incurred time cost increases and reaches astronomical limits as in the case with $R = 3$ and $Q = 3$. In this scenario, the time cost is approximately the sum of the time cost of running 1.0785×10^5 IETCs, 178.5 VNTCs, and 9 VTCs as shown in Table 3. In theory, as the number of performance regions (R) increases, the width of each region decreases and thereby the probability of getting a valid test case using random testing decreases. In contrast, the time cost of generating a test case by solving the inversion problem does not depend on the width of the region. Compared to random search, our test generation framework (optimization based approach) employs a guided search to figure out the valid test configuration. These results also apply for UEII coverage criterion since it builds on UE criterion.

Table 3. The cost of random testing for different scenarios [5].

R	Q	Suite size	IETCs	INTCs	VNTCs	VTCs
1	1	1	566	1795.5	0	1
1	2	2	1471	5016	0	2
1	3	3	1849.5	6149	0	3
2	1	2	3193	10317	3	2
2	2	4	4817	15966	6.5	4
2	3	6	11472	38262	14.5	6
3	1	3	18290	60399	29.5	3
3	2	6	40018	1.3266×10^5	66.5	6
3	3	9	1.0785×10^5	3.5653×10^5	178.5	9

6   Applicability of the Methodology

In general, performance degradation can be due to an error in the SUT or an error in the environment (network). As the SUT is assumed to be functionally correct, an error in the SUT may happen due to lacking the necessary resources, such as CPU and memory. Therefore, this methodology is proposed to generate test cases to evaluate the impact of the network on the performance of a real-time mobile app under different configuration settings. A real-time app is any networked app in which user perceived performance is sensitive the to network condition. Because of the semantic gap between software design models and stochastic notations, introducing several frameworks to test different app categories is inevitable.

The main observation was the high cost of the mathematical model evaluations compared to the simulation model when the buffer size increases beyond certain limits. To mitigate this issue, we can offload model expensive evaluations to the cloud, or we can employ the simulation model in solving the inversion problem. In literature, there is an increasing interest in using simulation models in optimization problems [27,48]. For real complex systems, it may not be possible to develop any type of mathematical models. For such cases, simulation based approach is the only way to do the analysis.

In this regard, it is worthy to indicate that using simulation models to predict performance measures is not seamless. In the app example, we used the simulation model to infer about test case execution time and multimedia file size. We noticed that as the performance metric under consideration became very small, the required simulation run length became very long that in some cases led to out of memory errors. In brief, most statistical procedures depend on covariance evaluations of the performance metric to determine weather the simulation model has reached the steady-state or not. If the performance level is close to zero, the covariance value is not defined. Therefore, it is not recommended to assign performance levels that are close to zero.

To enhance the quality of the generated test cases, we proposed a UEII coverage criterion to cover the performance spectrum and the input space at the same time. Indeed, network side had imposed more complicated constraints than what state of art combinatorial testing tools can support. To overcome this issue, we exhaustively checked all combinations for the imposed constraints. Then, we applied the combinatorial criterion on the combinations that had satisfied the constraints. However, this approach might be very expensive in terms of execution time, especially for systems with a large number of parameters and/or parameter values which indicates the need for more powerful mechanisms to address such scenarios.

7   Conclusions

In this paper, a model based test generation methodology was proposed to evaluate the impact of the interaction of the app configuration parameters (ACPs) and the network operating parameters (NOPs) on the performance of a mobile multimedia streaming app and on the experience of the end-user. Test generation was formulated as an inversion problem and solved as a minimization problem. The methodology required four different artefacts as inputs: the behaviour model of the SUT, the network model, the desired performance levels, and the test selection strategies. It was realized by three steps: performance model development test generation, and estimation of test execution parameters. We used both simulation and mathematical performance models in the methodology. To generate effective test cases, two coverage criteria were proposed: user experience (UE) and user experience and input interaction (UEII). In UE, the objective was to generate test cases that cover the performance behaviours as characterized by the end-user. In UEII, the objective was to generate test cases that simultaneously cover both the main performance behaviours and the input parameters' interactions. We applied the proposed methodology to generate test cases to evaluate the performance of an example of a mobile multimedia streaming app. To account for more practical interactions between the app and the network, the mathematical performance model was developed using the Markovian framework and solved using the supplementary variable technique. The mobile app is assumed to have network access via WiFi AP that implements IEEE 802.11 protocol. The methodology efficacy was evaluated and the obtained results are very promising.

For the future, we have many directions to complete the work. We want to show the applicability of the methodology to other real-time mobile apps. Another point, simulation models are more flexible than mathematical models. We want to generate test cases using performance simulation models. Also, we are interested to apply the proposed methodology to test the performance of applications that utilize TCP protocol. Moreover, we would like to test for other performance metrics, such as power consumption and wireless bandwidth. Last, mobile applications can access network resources via different technologies. We are interested to develop network models for cellular networks.

References

1. Advanced combinatorial testing system (acts) (2016). http://csrc.nist.gov/groups/SNS/acts/
2. Abbors, F., Ahmad, T., Truscan, D., Porres, I.: Model-based performance testing in the cloud using the mbpet tool. In: Proceedings of the 4th ACM/SPEC International Conference on Performance Engineering, pp. 423–424. ACM (2013)
3. Abbors, F., Can, D.T.: Approaching performance testing from a model-based testing perspective. In: 2010 Second International Conference on Advances in System Testing and Validation Lifecycle (VALID), pp. 125–128. IEEE (2010)
4. Adan, I., Resing, J.: Queueing Theory. Department of Mathematics and Computing Science, Eindhoven University of Technology, Eindhoven (2001)
5. Al-tekreeti, M., Naik, K., Abdrabou, A., Zaman, M., Srivastava, P.: Test generation for performance evaluation of mobile multimedia streaming applications. In: Proceedings of the 6th International Conference on Model-Driven Engineering and Software Development, vol. 1, pp. 225–236. SciTePress (2018)
6. Avritzer, A., Kondek, J., Liu, D., Weyuker, E.J.: Software performance testing based on workload characterization. In: Proceedings of the 3rd International Workshop on Software and Performance, pp. 17–24. ACM (2002)
7. Balsamo, S., Marco, A.D., Inverardi, P., Simeoni, M.: Model-based performance prediction in software development: a survey. IEEE Trans. Softw. Eng. **30**(5), 295–310 (2004)
8. Balsamo, S., Marzolla, M.: A simulation-based approach to software performance modeling. In: ACM SIGSOFT Software Engineering Notes, vol. 28, pp. 363–366. ACM (2003)

9. Barna, C., Litoiu, M., Ghanbari, H.: Autonomic load-testing framework. In: Proceedings of the 8th ACM International Conference on Autonomic Computing, pp. 91–100. ACM (2011)

10. Barna, C., Litoiu, M., Ghanbari, H.: Model-based performance testing (NIER track). In: Proceedings of the 33rd International Conference on Software Engineering, pp. 872–875. ACM (2011)

11. Briand, L., Nejati, S., Sabetzadeh, M., Bianculli, D.: Testing the untestable: model testing of complex software-intensive systems. In: Proceedings of the 38th International Conference on Software Engineering Companion, pp. 789–792. ACM (2016)

12. Brosig, F., Meier, P., Becker, S., et al.: Quantitative evaluation of model-driven performance analysis and simulation of component-based architectures. IEEE Trans. Softw. Eng. 41(2), 157–175 (2015)

13. Canfora, G., Mercaldo, F., Visaggio, C.A., DAngelo, M., Furno, A., Manganelli, C.: A case study of automating user experience-oriented performance testing on smartphones. In: 2013 IEEE Sixth International Conference on Software Testing, Verification and Validation, pp. 66–69. IEEE (2013)

14. Charnes, J.M.: Analyzing multivariate output. In: Proceedings of the 27th Conference on Winter Simulation, pp. 201–208. IEEE Computer Society (1995)

15. Cortellessa, V., Di Marco, A., Inverardi, P.: Model-Based Software Performance Analysis. Springer, Heidelberg (2011). https://doi.org/10.1007/978-3-642-13621-4

16. Costa, L.T., Czekster, R.M., de Oliveira, F.M., Rodrigues, E.d.M., da Silveira, M.B., Zorzo, A.F.: Generating performance test scripts and scenarios based on abstract intermediate models. In: SEKE, pp. 112–117 (2012)

17. Cox, D.R.: The analysis of non-Markovian stochastic processes by the inclusion of supplementary variables. In: Mathematical Proceedings of the Cambridge Philosophical Society, vol. 51, pp. 433–441. Cambridge University Press (1955)

18. Cox, D.R., Miller, H.D.: The Theory of Stochastic Processes. CRC Press, Boca Raton (1977)

19. Da Silveira, M.B., Rodrigues, E.d.M., Zorzo, A.F., Costa, L.T., Vieira, H.V., De Oliveira, F.M.: Generation of scripts for performance testing based on UML models. In: SEKE, pp. 258–263 (2011)

20. Dantas, V.L.L., Marinho, F.G., da Costa, A.L., Andrade, R.M.: Testing requirements for mobile applications. In: 24th International Symposium on Computer and Information Sciences, ISCIS 2009, pp. 555–560. IEEE (2009)

21. Di Penta, M., Canfora, G., Esposito, G., Mazza, V., Bruno, M.: Search-based testing of service level agreements. In: Proceedings of the 9th Annual Conference on Genetic and Evolutionary Computation, pp. 1090–1097. ACM (2007)

22. Diaz, A., Merino, P., Rivas, F.J.: Mobile application profiling for connected mobile devices. IEEE Pervasive Comput. 9(1), 54–61 (2010)

23. Doerner, K., Gutjahr, W.J.: Extracting test sequences from a Markov software usage model by ACO. In: Cantú-Paz, E., et al. (eds.) GECCO 2003. LNCS, vol. 2724, pp. 2465–2476. Springer, Heidelberg (2003). https://doi.org/10.1007/3-540-45110-2_150

24. Fiedler, M., Hossfeld, T., Tran-Gia, P.: A generic quantitative relationship between quality of experience and quality of service. IEEE Netw. 24(2), 36–41 (2010)

25. German, R.: Performance Analysis of Communication Systems with Non-Markovian Stochastic Petri Nets. Wiley, Hoboken (2000)

26. Gias, A.U., Sakib, K.: An adaptive Bayesian approach for URL selection to test performance of large scale web-based systems. In: Companion Proceedings of the 36th International Conference on Software Engineering, pp. 608–609. ACM (2014)

27. Gosavi, A.: Simulation-Based Optimization: Parametric Optimization Techniques and Reinforcement. ORSIS, vol. 55. Springer, Boston (2015). https://doi.org/10.1007/978-1-4899-7491-4
28. Grechanik, M., Fu, C., Xie, Q.: Automatically finding performance problems with feedback-directed learning software testing. In: 2012 34th International Conference on Software Engineering (ICSE), pp. 156–166. IEEE (2012)
29. Grindal, M., Offutt, J., Andler, S.F.: Combination testing strategies: a survey. Softw. Test. Verif. Reliab. **15**(3), 167–199 (2005)
30. Gu, Y., Ge, Y.: Search-based performance testing of applications with composite services. In: International Conference on Web Information Systems and Mining, WISM 2009, pp. 320–324. IEEE (2009)
31. Guderlei, R., Mayer, J.: Statistical metamorphic testing: testing programs with random output by means of statistical hypothesis tests and metamorphic testing. In: 7th International Conference on Quality Software (QSIC), pp. 404–409. IEEE (2007)
32. Guderlei, R., Mayer, J., Schneckenburger, C., Fleischer, F.: Testing randomized software by means of statistical hypothesis tests. In: Fourth International Workshop on Software Quality Assurance: in Conjunction with the 6th ESEC/FSE Joint Meeting, pp. 46–54. ACM (2007)
33. Ivanovici, M., Beuran, R.: Correlating quality of experience and quality of service for network applications, chap. 15. In: Adibi, S. (ed.) Quality of Service Architectures for Wireless Networks: Performance Metrics and Management, pp. 326–351. IGI Global, Hershey (2010)
34. Jiang, Z., Hassan, A.: A survey on load testing of large-scale software systems. IEEE Trans. Softw. Eng. **41**(11), 1091–1118 (2015)
35. Joorabchi, M.E., Mesbah, A., Kruchten, P.: Real challenges in mobile app development. In: 2013 ACM/IEEE International Symposium on Empirical Software Engineering and Measurement, pp. 15–24. IEEE (2013)
36. Kim, Y., Choi, O., Kim, M., Baik, J., Kim, T.H.: Validating software reliability early through statistical model checking. IEEE Softw. **30**(3), 35–41 (2013)
37. Koziolek, H.: Performance evaluation of component-based software systems: a survey. Perform. Eval. **67**(8), 634–658 (2010)
38. Kumar, R., Tomkins, A., Vassilvitskii, S., Vee, E.: Inverting a steady-state. In: Proceedings of the Eighth ACM International Conference on Web Search and Data Mining, pp. 359–368. ACM (2015)
39. Law, A.M.: Simulation Modeling and Analysis, 5th edn. McGraw-Hill, New York (2015)
40. Li, M., Claypool, M., Kinicki, R.: Playout buffer and rate optimization for streaming over IEEE 802.11 wireless networks. ACM Trans. Multimed. Comput. Commun. Appl. (TOMM) **5**(3), 26 (2009)
41. Liu, Y., Xu, C., Cheung, S.C.: Diagnosing energy efficiency and performance for mobile internetware applications. IEEE Softw. **32**(1), 67–75 (2015)
42. Ma, K.J., Bartos, R., Bhatia, S., Nair, R.: Mobile video delivery with HTTP. IEEE Commun. Mag. **49**(4), 166–175 (2011)
43. Matinnejad, R., Nejati, S., Briand, L.C., Bruckmann, T.: Automated test suite generation for time-continuous Simulink models. In: Proceedings of the 38th International Conference on Software Engineering, pp. 595–606. ACM (2016)
44. Mok, R.K., Chan, E.W., Chang, R.K.: Measuring the quality of experience of HTTP video streaming. In: 12th IFIP/IEEE International Symposium on Integrated Network Management (IM 2011) and Workshops, pp. 485–492. IEEE (2011)

45. Nayebi, F., Desharnais, J.M., Abran, A.: The state of the art of mobile application usability evaluation. In: CCECE, pp. 1–4 (2012)
46. Nie, C., Leung, H.: A survey of combinatorial testing. ACM Comput. Surv. (CSUR) **43**(2), 11 (2011)
47. Prowell, S.J.: Using Markov chain usage models to test complex systems. In: Proceedings of the 38th Annual Hawaii International Conference on System Sciences, HICSS 2005, p. 318c. IEEE (2005)
48. Rios, L.M., Sahinidis, N.V.: Derivative-free optimization: a review of algorithms and comparison of software implementations. J. Glob. Optim. **56**(3), 1247–1293 (2013)
49. Satoh, I.: Software testing for wireless mobile computing. IEEE Wirel. Commun. **11**(5), 58–64 (2004)
50. Sebih, N., Weitl, F., Artho, C., Hagiya, M., Tanabe, Y., Yamamoto, M.: Software model checking of UDP-based distributed applications. In: 2014 Second International Symposium on Computing and Networking, pp. 96–105. IEEE (2014)
51. Siavashi, F., Truscan, D.: Environment modeling in model-based testing: concepts, prospects and research challenges: a systematic literature review. In: Proceedings of the 19th International Conference on Evaluation and Assessment in Software Engineering, p. 30. ACM (2015)
52. Utting, M., Pretschner, A., Legeard, B.: A taxonomy of model-based testing approaches. Softw. Test. Verif. Reliab. **22**(5), 297–312 (2012)
53. Walls, R.J., Brun, Y., Liberatore, M., Levine, B.N.: Discovering specification violations in networked software systems. In: 2015 IEEE 26th International Symposium on Software Reliability Engineering (ISSRE), pp. 496–506. IEEE (2015)
54. Walton, G.H., Poore, J.H.: Generating transition probabilities to support model-based software testing. Softw.: Pract. Exp **30**(10), 1095–1106 (2000)
55. Weyuker, E.J., Vokolos, F.I.: Experience with performance testing of software systems: issues, an approach, and case study. IEEE Trans. Softw. Eng. **12**, 1147–1156 (2000)
56. Xu, Q., Mehrotra, S., Mao, Z., Li, J.: PROTEUS: network performance forecast for real-time, interactive mobile applications. In: Proceedings of the 11th Annual International Conference on Mobile Systems, Applications, and Services, pp. 347–360. ACM (2013)
57. Yang, C.S.D., Pollock, L.L.: Towards a structural load testing tool. In: ACM SIGSOFT Software Engineering Notes, vol. 21, pp. 201–208. ACM (1996)
58. Yılmaz, C., Fouche, S., Cohen, M.B., Porter, A., Demiröz, G., Koç, U.: Moving forward with combinatorial interaction testing. Computer **47**(2), 37–45 (2014)
59. Zhang, J., Cheung, S.C.: Automated test case generation for the stress testing of multimedia systems. Softw.: Pract. Exp. **32**(15), 1411–1435 (2002)
60. Zhang, J., Cheung, S.C., Chanson, S.T.: Stress testing of distributed multimedia software systems. In: Proceedings of the IFIP TC6 WG6.1 Joint International Conference on Formal Description Techniques for Distributed Systems and Communication Protocols and Protocol Specification, Testing and Verification, pp. 119–133. Kluwer, BV (1999)
61. Zhang, P., Elbaum, S., Dwyer, M.B.: Automatic generation of load tests. In: Proceedings of the 2011 26th IEEE/ACM International Conference on Automated Software Engineering, pp. 43–52. IEEE Computer Society (2011)
62. Zhang, P., Elbaum, S., Dwyer, M.B.: Compositional load test generation for software pipelines. In: Proceedings of the 2012 International Symposium on Software Testing and Analysis, pp. 89–99. ACM (2012)

Combining Model-Driven Architecture and Software Product Line Engineering: Reuse of Platform-Specific Assets

Frédéric Verdier[1,2]([✉]), Abdelhak-Djamel Seriai[1], and Raoul Taffo Tiam[2]

[1] LIRMM, University of Montpellier, CNRS, 161 rue Ada,
34095 Montpellier, France
seriai@lirmm.fr
[2] Acelys Informatique, Pôle Eureka,
418 rue du Mas Verchant, 34000 Montpellier, France
{frederic.verdier,raoultaffo.tiam}@acelys-info.fr

Abstract. Reuse automation is a main concern of software engineering to produce high quality applications in a faster and cheaper manner. Some approaches define cross-platform model-driven software product lines to systematically and automatically reuse generic assets in software development. They improve the product line assets reusability by designing them according to the Model-Driven Architecture specifications. However, their reuse of platform-specific assets is limited due to an inefficient platform-specific variability management. This issue interfere with gains in productivity provided by reuse.

In this paper, we define platform-specific variability by identifying variation points in different software concerns based on the well-known "4+1" view model categorization. Then, we fully manage platform-specific variability by structuring the Platform-Specific Model using two sub-models: the Cross-Cutting Model, obtained by transformation of the Platform-Independent Model; and the Application Structure Model, obtained by reuse of variable platform-specific assets. This structure is supported by a framework, based on a Domain-Specific Modeling Language, helping developers to build an application model. Experiments on three concrete applications confirmed that our approach significantly improves product lines productivity.

Keywords: Reuse · Model-Driven Architecture ·
Software product line · Variability · Platform-Specific Model ·
Domain Specific Modeling Language

1 Introduction

In software engineering, systematic reuse is a way to improve productivity by designing more reliable products in a faster and cheaper manner [1]. Several approaches favor systematic reuse in software development by addressing the

© Springer Nature Switzerland AG 2019
S. Hammoudi et al. (Eds.): MODELSWARD 2018, CCIS 991, pp. 430–454, 2019.
https://doi.org/10.1007/978-3-030-11030-7_19

two main dimensions of reuse: development for reuse and development by reuse. On the one hand, development for reuse consists in the specification, realization and organization of assets that will be reused in future application developments. Design patterns [2], software libraries, component-based software engineering [3], aspect-oriented programming [4] and Model-Driven Engineering (MDE) [5] are approaches favoring development of assets for reuse. On the other hand, development by reuse consists in maximizing the integration of reusable assets already defined in previous projects in the development of new products. Software Product Line Engineering (SPLE) [6] is an approach favoring development by reuse thanks to its systematic selection and integration of reusable assets in new software realizations.

Model-driven software product line engineering is a recent trend which favors reuse in both dimensions. It combines MDE which favors development for reuse, and SPLE, favoring development of new software by reuse. MDE helps developers to design more reusable assets than source code sections by improving their genericity. MDE consists in designing an application with models which are abstractions of a system. Models are managed using model transformation operations to target another abstraction level producing another model or source code. Software Product Line Engineering (SPLE) permits to systematically identify, organize then select and integrate assets of any nature in new applications depending on the customer's needs.

More specifically, some approaches [7,8] propose cross-platform model-driven software product lines by combining SPLE with Model-Driven Architecture [9], the famous MDE approach proposed by the Object Management Group (OMG). MDA defines a separation of concerns for assets based on different abstraction levels. Assets in high abstraction levels are independent of any platform or technology that can be involved in the application development. Then, platform specificities are added by lowering the abstraction level using MDE model transformation operations until obtaining the product source code.

Nevertheless, existing MDA and SPLE combinations focus primarily on reuse of platform-independent assets of high abstraction levels, not on platform-specific ones which are obtained through model transformation. In fact, platform-specific variability is handled in model transformation operations. Therefore, the complexity of those operations increases with the addition of new platform-specific implementation variants to consider. Consequently, transformation operations are difficult to maintain knowing that any variation point evolution implies to modify transformation operations. That is why the majority of approaches either ignore or only partially manage platform-specific variability [10]. In this case, the produced source code can contain unwanted implementation patterns caused by ignored variants and must be modified manually. Those issues interfere with gains in productivity provided by reuse (in terms of cost reduction, quality, etc.).

In this paper, we propose to improve productivity by fully managing platform-specific variability. We believe that variability should be managed in dedicated operations which are independent from model refinement operations. That is why we propose to build the Platform-Specific Model (PSM), responsible to represent the application realization including platform specificities, as a combination of two sub-models: one obtained by transformation of the higher abstraction levels; and the other one obtained by reuse of variable platform-specific assets defined in the domain engineering. To do so, we first identify how platform-specific variability impacts the software implementation. Then, we propose to structure the PSM to distinguish assets obtained through model transformation and those obtained by derivation (e.g. by direct selection and integration through variability management of reusable assets). Platform-specific reusable assets are organized according to platform-specific variability. A part of this work was presented in [11].

We go further in this paper by describing how the approach is supported by a framework based on a Domain Specific Modeling Language (DSML). This framework assists developers in the realization of an application PSM by reuse of variable platform-specific assets. Moreover, we detail how we extended our analysis and experiments to compare our proposal with a wider range of existing approaches on the production of three concrete applications using this DSML.

The remaining of the paper is structured as follows. Firstly, we define main concepts and provide an overview of the state of the art regarding platform-specific variability in Sect. 2. Then, the proposed structure of the PSM is explained in Sect. 3. Section 4 describes how the framework supports our approach with a DSML. Section 5 details how our solution has been validated. Lastly, we conclude in Sect. 6.

2   Platform-Specific Variability: Context and Presentation

In this section, we describe the main principles of combining MDA and SPLE before providing a better understanding of the platform-specific variability nature and its influence on reuse.

2.1   MDA and SPLE

MDA and SPLE are two famous software engineering approaches favoring reuse. In this perspective, they complement each other and overcome their limits [7].

Model-Driven Architecture (MDA). MDA [9] is an MDE approach which permits developers to produce an application for different platforms. It defines a separation of concerns based on the evolution pace of development assets. This separation of concerns consists of three abstraction levels:

Computation-Independent Model (CIM)
    The CIM describes the application business domain without describing how the application is realized. In UML [12], use case, workflow and sometimes class diagrams fit to this abstraction level.
Platform-Independent Model (PIM)
    The PIM represents the application realization without including the targeted platform specificities. In UML, component, state machine and sequence diagrams fit to this abstraction level.

Platform-Specific Model (PSM)

The PSM represents the application realization including the targeted platform specificities. It consists of a refinement of the PIM to include those specificities. For example, entity-relationship diagrams [13] fit to this abstraction level knowing their content depends on the targeted database management system.

The three abstraction levels are supported in the MDA transformation process (cf. Fig. 1). This development process starts by modeling the targeted application business domain in the CIM. Then the CIM is transformed using MDE transformation operations into the PIM. The PIM is refined into the application PSM to include the platform specificities using a transformation operation dedicated to this platform. This PIM to PSM refinement can be repeated several times to iteratively add more platform specificities. Then, the PSM is transformed into the application source code.

For example, to produce a bank management system, its CIM is realized to describe the business domain concepts and uses cases with UML workflow and class diagrams. The CIM is then transformed into the PIM. The latter refines the workflow general tasks in smaller atomic tasks with a sequence diagram while describing the application's architecture with a component diagram. Then, depending on the targeted database management system, the PIM is transformed into a different PSM containing a description of the persisted data structure as an entity-relationship diagram. The PSM is further refined to add security specificities required by the targeted bank infrastructure. Finally, the PSM is transformed into source code which conforms to the PSM specifications.

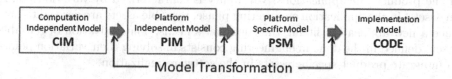

Fig. 1. The MDA transformation process (adapted from [14]).

In this way, assets of each abstraction level evolve independently of lower levels assets. For example, the CIM and PIM do not vary from a platform to another one. Depending on the targeted platform, a specific PIM to PSM transformation operation is used which produces a different PSM.

Software Product Line Engineering (SPLE). While MDA permits developers to design highly reusable assets, Software Product Line Engineering (SPLE) permits to systematically identify, organize then select and integrate assets of any nature in new applications depending on the client's needs.

A Software Product Line is a "set of software-intensive systems that share a common, managed set of features satisfying the specific needs of a particular

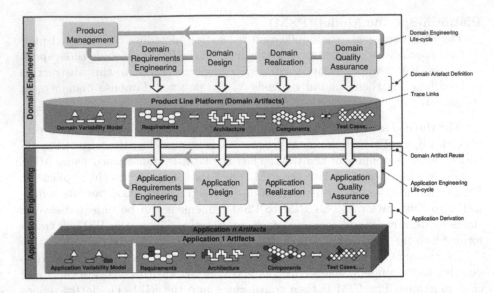

Fig. 2. SPLE parallel development processes [15].

market segment or mission and that are developed from a common set of core assets in a prescribed way" [6].

SPLE defines two parallel development processes [16] as depicted in Fig. 2. The domain engineering phase focuses on the identification and design of reusable core assets which are organized according to the commonalities and variabilities of the product line applications. Variability is characterized by variation points on assets. In the application engineering phase, reusable assets are derived to produce a new application fitting the customer's needs. The derivation of reusable assets defined in the domain engineering consists in solving their variation points to integrate product-specific assets in the software realization.

Combining MDA and SPLE. SPLE and MDA complement each other [7,8]. Their combination results in a cross-platform model-driven software product line. The latter is a software product line in which reuses assets designed according to the MDA specifications.

In the application engineering, applications are produced according to the MDA development process. An application model is progressively refined from the CIM to the source code by transformation operations which integrate reused assets defined in the domain engineering.

In this paper, we focus on reuse at the PSM abstraction level and how platform-specific variability is managed.

2.2   Platform-Specific Variability

In this section, we define what is platform-specific variability and its impacts on reuse before giving an overview of existing approach capabilities to manage it.

What Is Platform-Specific Variability? Platform-specific variability consists of variation points that appear only when a specific platform or technology is selected. Each variation point represents a decision impacting the source code related to the use of the selected platforms.

Platform-specific variation points can influence numerous parts of a software realization. To describe the impacts of platform-specific variability on an application implementation, we identified platform-specific variation points in different parts of a system. Those parts are based on the "4+1" view model [17]. This model is composed of 5 views defining the different parts of a system: the logical view, the process view, the physical view, the development view and the scenario view.

In the following, we focus on views in which we identified platform-specific variation points:

Platform-Specific Variability in the Process View. The process view describes how the main blocks of system functionalities interact with each other. This view captures concurrency, inter-process communication, distribution of blocks, etc.

One of the elements the process view can describe is the messaging system between the software and some distant system.

For example, a messaging system design can vary entirely from a framework to another. For example, a system implementation using RabbitMq[1] describes the map of the message exchanges while a system implementation using Kafka[2] describes the structure of messages without managing how those messages are sent. For each platform, the different possible configurations can be reused and organized with a variation point specific to this platform.

Platform-Specific Variability in the Physical View. The physical view describes the infrastructure of the system and how it is deployed.

Then, the physical view can describe the hardware peripherals the software interacts with. For example, mobile applications often interact with different captors which can be specific to the device they are deployed on and the operating system. The heterogeneity of hardware devices in mobile applications is identified in [18]. But this variety of devices is different in each operating system. Consequently, this variation point cannot be included in the PIM without adding platform specificities.

---

[1] https://www.rabbitmq.com/.
[2] https://kafka.apache.org/.

Platform-Specific Variability in the Development View. The development view describes how functional blocks are implemented (using layer, component or class diagrams for example).

One of the elements the development view can describe is the persisted data structure in the system using a database management system.

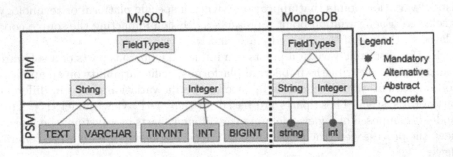

Fig. 3. Variability of field types depending on the database management system used (initially presented in [11]).

Some database management systems like MySQL in Fig. 3 can encode generic primitive types (like *String*) with different concrete types (*VARCHAR* and *TEXT*). Those types differ in their length to fit different use cases. The available types differ from a technology to another one. In fact, MongoDB provides only one concrete type to encode string fields. Consequently, the PIM cannot be responsible to solve those variation points without including platform specificities in the model. Then, by selecting MySQL, a new platform-specific variation point is included for each field corresponding to the variety of available types.

We identified platform-specific variability in three concerns of the software design. It is now possible to understand what are the impacts of platform-specific variability on reuse.

Impacts of Platform-Specific Variability on Reuse. In MDA and SPLE combinations, platform-specific variability influence on reuse is not as visible as impacts of variability in higher abstraction levels.

In fact, if platform-specific variability is ignored, only one platform-specific asset variant is always selected. In our example, ignoring the *String* variation point for MySQL implies that only one concrete type is always selected such as *TEXT*. Then, the code must be manually modified to use the right concrete type for each field.

However, according to [19], it is preferable to produce source code from only one source of information to be able to identify how a source code section is produced (through code generation or manual development). In this way, it is possible to produce the application source code incrementally (e.g. after multiple iterations of code generation). Moreover, modifying generated source code can be expensive. In fact, developers must manually identify where corrections are required. Some modifications can have large impacts on the application implementation. In our example, changing the concrete type of a field modifies the database structure implementation as well as functional data validation rules implementation. Impacts can also vary depending on how MySQL is combined with other technologies. For example, if an Object Relational Mapping is used like the Hibernate framework [20], the mapping logic is also impacted.

Similarly, if platform-specific variability is partially managed, some platform-specific asset variants are ignored. Then, it leads to the same consequences previously mentioned.

Therefore, platform-specific variability is impactful on productivity. With our definition of platform-specific variability, we can determine capabilities of existing MDA and SPLE combinations to manage platform-specific variability.

State of the Art. We evaluate previous works which have addressed the problem of handling platform-specific variability following their capabilities to handle, partially handle or not handle each case of platform-specific variation points identified in the "4+1" view model listed in Sect. 2.2. Table 1 summaries the result of the comparison of these works.

Table 1. Capabilities of existing approaches to handle platform-specific variability aligned on the "4+1" view model.

Approaches	Platform variability	Platform-specific variability		
		Process view	Physical view	Development view
Deelstra et al.[7]	✓	✗	✗	✗
Czarnecki et al.[21]	✓	!	!	!
Hamed and Colomb[22]	✓	!	!	!
Dageförde et al.[10]	✓	✓	✗	✗
Usman et al.[18]	✓	✗	✓	✗

Legend: ✓ Handled   ! Inefficiently handled   ✗ Not handled

Reusing MDA models in a software product line is an idea introduced by Deelstra et al. [7]. However, only platform variability is addressed in this paper. But the variability of platforms is not platform-specific variability. In fact, platform variability consists of the set of available platforms which can address a specific problem. For example, to implement a software, the different programming languages are platform variants, all addressing the problem of implementing the system.

Alternatively, Czarnecki et al. [21] proposed a staged configuration process in which variability is represented in several feature models. Each feature model represents the system features or a subsystem features to correspond to the abstraction level of a development team. Then, an application is designed by selecting features from the highest abstraction level model. Selected features are refined into specific feature models in lower abstraction levels. Once the staged configuration is complete, core assets are automatically selected and integrated in the system to produce. The staged configuration process can be adapted to our problem using the MDA abstraction levels. Thus, platform-specific variability can be managed. However, it is necessary to design core assets for each platform or technology possible because they realize the lowest abstraction level features which are specific to platforms. Then, the staged configurations approach using MDA abstraction levels does not scale up with the addition of new platforms.

Hamed and Colomb [22] identified the problem of platform-specific variability lack of management in existing approaches. This approach addresses the problem of handling Non-Functional Requirements (NFR). NFRs are client's requirements that are not related to the application functionalities or business domain such as the quality requirements (performance, maintainability). Depending on the chosen NFRs, platform-specific design variants are selected by integrating variation points in PIM to PSM transformation operations. Consequently, those operations complexity increases quickly with the addition of new design variants because each alternative has to be described in its dedicated transformation rule. Moreover, NFRs are global features often related to quality criteria. Therefore, some selected implementation variants are applied without considering the application specific use cases.

Dageförde et al. [10] proposed to use a MDA and SPLE combination to realize a cross-platform mobile product line. It extends the model-driven cross-platform framework MD2 to adapt it to a SPLE context. MD2 describes an application using a textual Domain Specific Modeling Language. The application is designed by deriving a variable workflow of tasks similar to the Business Process Model and Notation [23]. The approach permits to produce applications that can collaborate with each others thanks to the expressiveness of MD2. Managing the variability with modification of the workflow implies that only high abstraction variability is handled. In fact, workflow models are coarse grained models using tasks as basic elements. Consequently, the workflow describes the application behavior but not its architecture. Therefore, it is not possible to select an alternative platform-specific implementation pattern such as a different architecture (physical and development views). Modifying the application design to satisfy a non-functional requirement would require to be able to choose between different model transformation operations automatically.

Usman et al. [18] proposed an MD-SPLE approach which combines MDA and SPLE for mobile development context. This approach addresses the problem of using product lines in the mobile development context with its extensive use of different platforms and hardware devices. It uses UML2 models. The approach integrates platform variability by using UML profiles. Those profiles specialize PIM elements to add platform specificities. They can be seen as a Platform Description Models (PDM) which describe platform specificities. However, variation points are related to features or hardware choices (physical view) and not to implementation choices (development view). Similarly to [10], modifying the application design is hard because the approach relies on a common architecture implicitly described in model to text transformation operations. Consequently, variability related to the process view is not managed. Moreover, PDMs modify uniformly every elements of a targeted kind. Therefore, it is not possible to select different variants for different elements in the same model.

3 Separating Transformation and Derivation Operations: A New PSM Structure

In order to efficiently reuse platform-specific implementation patterns, we propose a way to capitalize on SPLE techniques to manage platform-specific variability. Assets defined at the PSM abstraction level are considered as variable core assets similarly to assets defined in higher abstraction levels.

To do so, the PSM is first structured to distinguish its elements obtained by transformation of the PIM from those obtained by derivation of platform-specific core assets. Then, two different mechanisms are used to represent platform-specific variability. Finally, assets are composed to obtain the application engineering PSM.

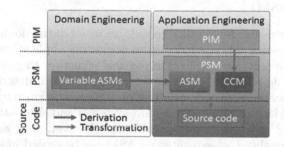

Fig. 4. Content of the PSM and how it is obtained (initially presented in [11]).

As depicted in Fig. 4, the content of an application engineering PSM is composed of more fine-grained models: the Cross-Cutting Models (CCM), which are resulting of the PIM transformation, and the Application Structure Models (ASM), which are obtained by deriving reusable models of the same nature.

3.1 PSM Obtained by Transformation: The Cross-Cutting Model (CCM)

The CCM is obtained by transformation of the PIM. Consequently, CCMs do not contain reusable assets and so, are not produced in the domain engineering.

A CCM describes the application realization including the business domain, functionalities, graphical user interfaces as well as cross-domain features such as security management protocols.

Section 2 showed that PIM to PSM transformation operations could not manage platform-specific variability efficiently. That is why they must not define any platform-specific reusable asset. This implies that those operations are responsible to translate PIM information to the PSM formalism but must not add information that is not described in the PIM. In this way, generic concepts in the PIM are translated to platform-specific concepts.

For example, a string field in a PIM class diagram is transformed into a class diagram field in PSM typed as *String* if Java is used or *string* if C# is selected. However, PIM to PSM transformation operations cannot add new information like the database architecture.

Therefore, a CCM is similar to the PIM it comes from. Its formalism can change in different development contexts. In fact, different companies can use different diagrams to model their softwares. For example, the CCM can be composed of different UML diagrams such as component, class and sequence diagrams. An excerpt of CCM using a class diagram is depicted in Fig. 5.

Similar to the PIM, the CCM cross-cuts the source code. Thus, it is necessary to bridge the gap between source code and Cross-Cutting Models. This bridge is realized by ASMs.

3.2   PSM Obtained by Derivation: The Application Structure Model (ASM)

ASMs are platform-specific reusable models designed in the domain engineering as variable core assets. They are reused to design the application PSM.

An ASM represents an application physical structure to generate. Variable ASMs are reusable physical structure patterns. A pattern describes the use of a platform, for defined concerns, as a tree of implementation structure elements (such as files, folders, libraries and distant systems) and sub-patterns.

Therefore, ASMs are specific to platforms. However, they are independent from business domains. Consequently, an ASM can be reused in several product lines to produce applications using the described set of technologies.

ASM elements define the concrete implementation by referencing the PSM to text transformation operations to use for each file to generate. In this way, those operations can have well defined and separated responsibilities:

- An operation produces the implementation of using a specific platform for a defined concern.
- An operation produces local implementation sections such as the content of a method, a single file or a set of similar files.
- An operation can use intermediate PSM to PSM refinement operations if required. Those operations refine the PSM with the addition of new information (for example, the description of the database architecture).

Then, ASMs promote the use of template-based approaches [24] to realize PSM to text transformations. In fact, a template is responsible to describe the code to produce for a source code section such as a method or a file.

Domain engineering ASMs can describe how any platform is used with its generic formalism. In fact, an application implementation is always structured using elements such as files and folders.

An application engineering ASM represents the software physical structure to generate for an application. It is built as a composition of derived domain engineering ASMs. It reuses and modify the physical structure of the product line applications and, therefore, its architectural components that are related to specific platforms.

For example, an excerpt of an absence demand scheduler software PSM is depicted in Fig. 5. Elements with the stereotype *Pattern* are ASMs. The ASM named *MySQLDatabase* describes how a MySQL database is implemented. It defines a subtree composed of two sub-patterns (*DomainDefinition* and *MySQL-Database*). In this way, if the content of a sub-pattern evolves, the content of *MySQLDatabase* is also impacted. Elements with the stereotype *File* represent a file to generate. The element named *DomainClass* references a generation template. The latter produces a file implementing a C# class for each class defined in the CCMs.

Domain engineering ASMs are variable. Their variation points constitute the platform-specific variability.

3.3 Realizing Platform-Specific Variability

Representing the variability in the PSM abstraction level lets developers choose which platform-specific reusable solution to integrate among several variants. In this way, it is possible to reuse more efficiently a wider range of platform-specific assets by using variability management to organize them.

We distinguish two mechanisms to realize variability in models:

Asset Variants. Those variation points provide choices between different variants which we commonly see in SPLE approaches.

In Fig. 5, applications can use a specific MySQL database or use an already existing database. Both cases are handled with specific variants (*ApplicationDatabaseMigrations* and *ExternalDatabaseMapping* assets) of the ASM *MySQLMigration*.

Asset Attributes. Models are configurable as recommended in [7]. In this way, their genericity is improved. Those variation points can have an uncountable number of solutions unlike asset variants.

Figure 5 provides an example of model attribute related to the variability of MySQL types described in Sect. 2.2. A default variant is chosen for each type. In this way, string fields are by default typed by *VARCHAR* and integer fields are typed by *INT*. However, *VARCHAR* have a limited length that does not fit to long string like descriptions. That is why the *description* field of *AbsenceDemand* is typed as *TEXT* which has an unlimited length.

In the application engineering, CCM and ASM parts of the PSM are produced separately. Those parts are composed to produce the PSM of an application.

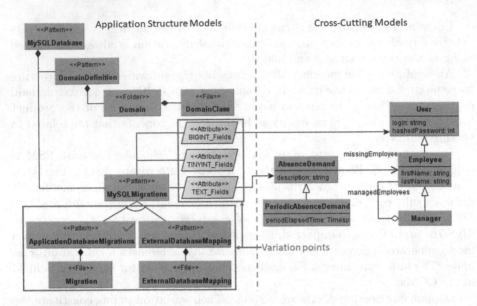

Fig. 5. PSM of the absence demand scheduler (initially presented in [11]).

3.4   Composing CCM and ASM Sub-models

The application PSM is obtained by composing the CCM (obtained by transformation of the PIM) with reused ASMs (obtained by derivation of domain engineering ASMs). CCMs and ASMs are loosely coupled to simplify the PSM construction. This is possible for two reasons.

On the one hand, CCMs cross-cut the source code. They do not rely on specific source code areas. Thus, their definition is independent from ASMs which define the source code structure.

On the other hand, only model attributes (refer to Sect. 3.3) may induce relations between ASM and CCM assets. Then, in application engineering, solving the ASM dependencies consists in solving its model attributes. Although this resolution is manual, dependencies are organized and identified with specific variation points.

An example of CCM and ASM composition is depicted in Fig. 5. Only the resolution of model attributes is creating relations between ASM and CCM elements. This resolution is realized by the application engineering development team.

Our approach is realized in a framework based on a Domain-Specific Modeling Language (DSML). This framework is described in the following section.

4   A Framework for Platform-Specific Reuse Based on a Domain Specific Modeling Language (DSML)

To ensure a better adoption of our proposition by development teams, the approach is supported by a framework based on a graphic DSML. This DSML translates MDA and SPLE vocabulary to the development team one at the PSM abstraction level. In this way, the learning curve of the approach is softened.

Moreover, the DSML allows us to better manage the granularity of the manipulated assets than generic modeling languages (such as UML) can. In fact, we want developers to manipulate reusable assets and their variation points. Although a generic modeling language would be able to model the different concerns handled by the DSML, it does not permit us to choose the granularity of PSM elements.

Finally, depending on the development context, modeled concerns can differ. Therefore, the PSM meta-model can vary to focus on different parts of the realization. For example, web applications are strongly data-oriented and contain graphical user interfaces. In contrary, avionic applications are mainly composed of logical components with no graphical interfaces but focus on safety and performances. Consequently, a PSM meta-model fitting the web design development context would not fit well for an avionic development context and vice-versa.

The DSML encompasses all the different concerns of the approach to assist developers during application engineering phases. In the following, we describe a DSML designed for our partner's development context.

4.1   Case Study: The Absence Demand Management System

To illustrate our approach, we provide examples based on one of our case studies located in our industrial partner's product line. The latter is an application named *Absence Manager* which manages a company's human resources and their absence demands.

The company's employees have absence credits based on the country's laws and their employment contract. They can create absence demands which spend those credits to manage their holidays. An absence demand is described by a start and end date as well as a description of the demand motive. After their creation, absence demands are either validated or refused by their creator's manager. Managers are notified via an email when they have new absence demands to validate are created by their managed employees.

This Software as a Service application relies on a server implemented in C#.NET which exposes a RESTful API.

4.2   CCMs in the DSML

CCMs, obtained by transformation, are represented with graphical elements linked by relations. Different viewpoints constitute the application CCM:

- the data viewpoint models the business concepts manipulated in the application similarly to a class diagram as entities. Business rules, named validation constraints, can be added to those concepts to ensure the data coherence.

    For example, in Fig. 6, the case studies concepts are described with *Entity* and *DomainEnumeration* elements. To ensure that absence demands end date are posterior to their start date, the *AbsenceDemand* entity describing the absence demand concept declares a validation constraint on its *StartDate* and *EndDate* fields. This constraint, named *IsLowerThan*, ensures that the start date is lower than the end date.
- the functional viewpoint represents the different application functionalities as tasks. Tasks may require clearances that users must possess to be able to perform a task.

    For example, in Fig. 6, creating an absence demand is a task named *CreateAbsenceDemand* that can be performed by employees. Users identified as employees have the *Employee* profile. Validating or refusing an absence demand is a task named *ValidateAbsenceDemand*. This task can be performed by the absence demand creator's manager. This clearance depends on the using context (a manager cannot validate absence demands of employees he does not manage). In our partner's development team, contextual clearances are named roles. That is why this clearance is modeled with the role named *EmployeeValidator*.
- the graphical user interface viewpoint models the different application views.

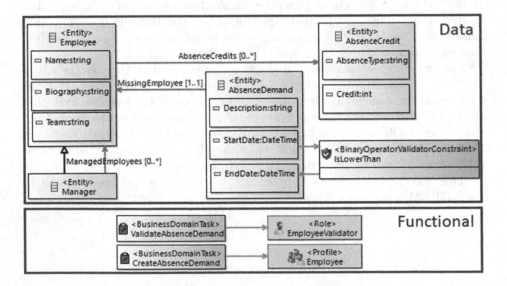

Fig. 6. CCM excerpt of the *Absence Manager* case study displayed in the DSML.

4.3 ASMs in the DSML

Application engineering ASMs are obtained by derivation of platform-specific assets realized in the domain engineering. The latter are registered in a database and organized according to their commonalities and variabilities. In Fig. 7, *Pattern* elements are reused ASMs obtained by derivation of domain engineering assets. Each pattern describes the implementation of an architectural concern using specific technologies. In this way, *NHibernate_Domain* describes the implementation of domain description in C#.NET using the NHibernate framework [20] while *MySQLDatabase* describes the implementation of a MySQL database in C#.NET.

In the PSM, the ASM is a forest graph of projects, folders and files. Each file represents one or several similar source code files. Their content is described by a reference to the PSM to text transformation operation that produces it. In the ASM of our case study (depicted in Fig. 7), the file named *DomainClasses* describes a set of files implementing the different classes representing the business domain concepts.

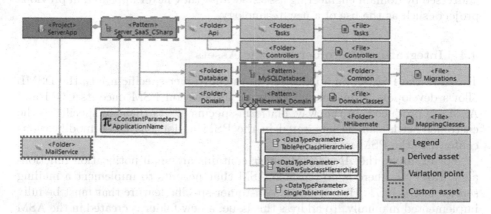

Fig. 7. ASM excerpt of the *Absence Manager* case study displayed in the DSML.

Depending on the software architecture and the involved technologies, domain engineering variable ASMs are automatically selected and composed.

Domain engineering ASMs variation points (refer to Sect. 3.3) are solved in two different instants of the PSM realization:

- Variants are solved when the assets to reuse are selected. This resolution is performed before their integration in the application engineering PSM. Therefore, ASM variants are not represented in the DSML.
- Attributes are solved after the integration of the reused assets in the application engineering PSM. The DSML graphically represents the attributes to solve as parameters and assists developers during the resolution by providing a list of possible values.

In Fig. 7, *TablePerClassHierarchies*, *TablePerSubclassHierarchies* and *SingleTableHierarchies* are attributes specific to the NHibernate framework. NHibernate is an ORM which administrates a relational database similarly to an object-oriented database. It creates a mapping between the business domain entities and the database architecture. Because of the lack of inheritance relationship in relational databases, NHibernate provides three strategies to realize such relations. Each strategy has advantages and drawbacks making it suitable to specific use cases. In fact, it is possible to use different strategies in the same application for different persisted concepts. Each attribute corresponds to an available strategy and references the inheritance trees in the CCM that are realized with it.

Hence, the DSML helps developers to solve ASM variation points and by this way, helps them to compose the ASM and CCM parts of the PSM (refer to Sect. 3.4).

Although ASMs can be entirely obtained by derivation of reusable platform-specific assets, it is not guaranteed that available assets are enough to obtain the application PSM. In fact, customers might express requirements that cannot be addressed by domain engineering assets because they never appeared in previous projects such as the use of a new technology.

4.4 Integrating Customer-Specific Assets

To adapt the PSM of an application to the customer-specific needs, the DSML allows developers to manually modify an application PSM once its CCM and ASM are produced. In this way, platform-specific assets that are specific to the customer needs can be integrated in the PSM as long as those modifications conform to the PSM meta-model.

For example, the *Absence Manager* contains an email notification functionality. However, there is no reusable ASM that permits to implement a mailing service in C#.NET. Hence, this is a customer-specific feature that must be fully implemented manually. To address this issue, a new folder is created in the ASM to identify where the specific implementation will be located. Then, it will be easy to extract the newly developed assets during the next domain engineering to improve the product line capabilities.

4.5 The DSML Realization

The DSML is realized using the framework Sirius[3] which is based on the Eclipse Modeling Framework (EMF) [25]. Sirius provides tools to design graphical domain-specific languages consisting in a mapping between semantic concepts described in a meta-model (conforming to Ecore) and syntactic graphical elements.

Sirius permits us to capitalize on the EMF capabilities regarding Model-Driven Engineering techniques. In fact, EMF provides a wide variety of tools for

---

[3] Sirius website: http://www.eclipse.org/sirius/.

MDE such as model transformation languages like ATL (ATLAS Transformation Language) [26] or Eclipse QVTo[4].

With the DSML, we could experiment our approach on three concrete cases in collaboration with the development team.

5 Validation

The following describes how the approach has been validated.

5.1 Research Questions

In order to measure the efficiency of the proposal, we conducted experiments on three concrete applications to answer the following questions:

Q1. Does the proposal permit reusing variable platform-specific assets?
  - **Q1.1:** Can the proposal model variable platform-specific reusable assets?
  - **Q1.2:** Can the proposal integrate platform-specific reusable assets in new applications?

Q2. Does the proposal improve productivity?
  - **Q2.1:** Does the proposal improve the management of platform-specific variability?
  - **Q2.2:** Does the proposal reduce development efforts for new applications?

5.2 Data Collection

We studied two product lines already used in our industrial partner's production. Both product lines contain client-server applications implemented in C#.NET. The first one consists in several applications sharing a common data-oriented architecture. The second one is composed of applications providing digital solutions for cities.

Table 2. Statistics of 2 case studies applications.

Application	Lines of code	PSM variation points		Nb. functionalities	Project cost[a] (realization)
		Variants	Model attributes		
Absence Manager	20861	5	14	81	40 M/D
Mobility Advisor	11348	3	14	31	32.5 M/D
City Community	16296	10	12	80	62 M/D

[a]Estimated costs measured in Man/Day (M/D).

---

[4] Eclipse QVT Operational: https://projects.eclipse.org/projects/mo\discretionary-del\discretionary-ing.mmt.qvt-oml.

Three applications of those product lines were selected as case studies (described in Table 2). The first application (*Absence Manager*) manages a company's human resources and their absence demands. The second application (*Mobility Advisor*) provides tools to manage users' travels with routing optimization advices. The third application (*City Community*) is a social network for city inhabitants.

5.3   Experiment Protocol

In the following, we detail how each research question is answered by our experiments.

How to Answer Q1. A domain engineering phase has been performed to identify reusable platform-specific assets in the server part of several client-server applications from diverse product lines using a similar set of technologies. In this way, we ensure that identified assets are platform-specific and independent from business domains.

Then, the development team of the case studies (described in Table 2) modeled their application engineering PSM with our help. Those applications use a similar set of technologies.

How to Answer Q2. We developed a tool which helps the development team to design an application engineering PSM that reuses domain engineering ASMs and creates CCMs. In this way, we implemented the composition of reused ASMs with CCMs and we also observed how the tool was used to create the case studies PSM by the development team. Moreover, we developed PSM to text transformation operations corresponding to the identified platform-specific assets. Those operations were realized as templates for a template engine used by our industrial partner.

The applications PSMs have been transformed into source code using the developed PSM to text transformation operations. The obtained source code has been compared to their hand-crafted version. With this comparison, we could analyze the ratio of generated source code that we could obtain and evaluate the ability of the proposal to handle platform-specific variation points. In fact, when a variant is ignored or inefficiently managed, the produced implementation is different from the expected one. To compare our solution results with related works, we looked for generic approaches that could use similar PSM to text transformation operations. To compare our solution results with related works, we looked for generic approaches that could use similar PIM to PSM and PSM to text transformation operations. Among them, we selected [10] as an operational approach and [22] as a generic approach that can address more kinds of variation points (refer to Sect. 2.2).

We estimated the amount of gained time on the applications realization obtained by using the proposal compared to the time needed to implement them manually. We also estimated the amount of gained time obtained by using

[10] and [22]. These estimations were compared to the real cost of the application overall project including all development phases (**Project cost** in Table 2). Knowing that our estimations concerned the gained time obtained in the realization phase (through code generation), we also compared our results to the real server realization phase costs (**Server realization cost** in Table 2).

5.4 Direct Results

Obtained results are described in Table 3. We use the following metrics to evaluate our results:

- Correctly generated code: ratio of the application source code successfully generated for the server part.
- Generated code requiring corrections: ratio of the application generated source code that required additional manual modifications for the server part.
- Gained time (realization phase): estimation of time that could be gained with the code generation.

Table 3. Results of using the studied solutions on the case studies.

Application	Approach	Generated code		Gained time
		Correctly	With errors	(realization)[a]
Absence Manager	Dageförde et al. [10]	71%	14%	16 M/D (40%)
	Hamed and Colomb [22]	73%	12%	19 M/D (47.5%)
	Our approach	80%	5%	25 M/D (62.5%)
Mobility Advisor	Dageförde et al. [10]	70%	11%	4 M/D (12.3%)
	Hamed and Colomb [22]	71%	10%	6 M/D (18.5%)
	Our approach	78%	3%	10 M/D (30.7%)
City Community	Dageförde et al. [10]	-	-	-
	Hamed and Colomb [22]	61%	22%	16 M/D (25.8%)
	Our approach	79%	4%	35 M/D (56.4%)

[a]Estimated costs measured in Man/Day (M/D).

During the domain engineering phase, we identified ASMs from applications with similar technologies. In Table 2, **PSM variation points** display the count of variation points solved to produce each application (*Q1.1*).

All approaches were able to generate the same source code amount. However, our approach generates sounder source code with a lower ratio of faulty source code.

Moreover, our approach significantly reduces costs more efficiently in the realization phase than existing solutions do.

Using these results, it is now possible to answer to the previously mentioned questions.

5.5   Interpretation and Discussions

Answering Q1. During the domain engineering phase, we identified ASMs from applications related to different product lines with similar technologies. They could be organized following their commonalities and variabilities. We identified variation points related to each software concern mentioned in Sect. 3.3. The obtained product line realized the platform-specific variability using the two mechanisms described in Sect. 3.3. In Table 2, **Nb. PSM variation points** represents the count of variation points solved to produce each application (*Q1.1*).

Results show that with a single domain engineering phase, we were able to generate a significant amount of source code correctly by reusing numerous variable ASMs identified in the domain engineering phase. Experimented cases are related to different business domains. Therefore, those assets are reusable in different product lines (*Q1.2*).

Thus, the proposal permits reusing variable cross-domain platform-specific assets.

Answering Q2. The development team successfully realized each case study application engineering PSM. During the experiments, the produced PSM did not require manual corrections. This was possible thanks to our separation between transformation and derivation operations.

Firstly, we fully automated the creation of the CCM with simple PIM to PSM transformation operations implemented in ATL.

Then, the integration of reused PSM assets was successfully automated by using the PIM application architecture design and their traceability links with the available ASMs. In fact, results show how the PIM architecture design impacts the PSM content. [10] could not produce a correct PSM for the third application because of its different architecture. In contrast, our approach and [22] were able to produce a sound PSM with their management architecture variability (*Q2.1*).

Consequently, we could obtain similar performances as we measured in our previous work at the PSM abstraction level but for a wider range of applications. In fact, we were able to generate a significant amount of source code correctly by reusing numerous PIM and PSM assets.

Moreover, less additional manual corrections were needed in the source code produced by our proposal than in source code produced using [10] or [22]. In fact, these approaches could not generate platform-specific implementation variants which had large impacts on the source code.

The estimated gained time difference between existing approaches and the proposed one is explained by the required manual correction ratio difference between the experimented solutions. In fact, additional manual efforts are required in existing solutions for code sections that have a large impact on the application implementation. Thus, using existing approaches, it is sometimes preferable to not generate source code sections that can vary depending on a technical variation point instead of generating them.

The estimated gained time over real realization cost ratio was lower than the ratio of successfully generated source code. In fact, for a given source code section, it is slower to manually modify generated source code sections than to produce the same entire sections manually. Some modifications involved different parts of the software and were difficult to perform. However, most of the required modifications on the source code produced using our approach could be handled with automatic tools provided by any IDE.

Although the estimated gained time in our experiments involves only the realization phase, we believe that the proposed solution can reduce the amount of time required in other development phases. For example, costs in project management are reduced because we lower human resource costs in the realization phase. Moreover, after the realization phase, the produced application must be tested before being released to the customer. The cost of this qualification phase is variable. It depends on several factors such as the requirements about the product quality, the application complexity or even the testing process reliability. By reusing assets tested in previous projects, we reduce the application complexity by providing standardization. We can also improve the testing process reliability because a large amount of the source code is obtained by reusing assets that are linked to features. Therefore, it is possible to provide test scenarios, designed in previous applications containing the same features, to help testers in the qualification phase (*Q2.2*).

Therefore, our approach improves productivity more efficiently than existing MDA and SPLE combinations.

5.6 Conclusions and Threats to Validity

Experiments confirmed that our approach improves productivity compared to existing MDA and SPLE combinations thanks to its ability to fully support platform-specific variability.

However, we identified some threats to our experiments validity.

External Threats. Firstly, the comparison between our proposition and the existing approaches is limited. In fact, we could compare our results to only one solution. Furthermore, estimations involving the existing approach are theoretical and not obtained by measuring results using a concrete tool. These estimations rely on the estimations of the development team regarding specific implementation and correction tasks.

Moreover, the tested applications have a similar architecture (client-server) to experiment variable ASMs reuse. The size of tested applications is small because their architecture improved reuse of components "on the shelf". Therefore, the application source code focuses only on domain-specific behaviors and connections between components implementations. Consequently, the proposal applicability in a more generic context is not guaranteed.

Finally, adoption in an industrial context is a main concern for both model-driven engineering and software product line approaches. In our case, we believe that this threat is reduced by the maturity of available MDE tools and by the fact that the approach ensures that code can be generated by template engines.

Internal Threat. A potential limitation of the proposal is that the PIM and PSM meta-models must evolve alongside the evolution of the product line. But those meta-models' evolutions can be difficult because they impact other reusable assets like model transformation operations meaning those assets might have to evolve too. This threat is reduced by the large amount of existing MDE solutions addressing the problem of the meta-model evolution [27].

6   Conclusions

In this paper, we proposed a generic solution which goes further in the combination of MDA and SPLE that consider MDA models as configurable core assets of a product line. The proposal improves productivity regarding existing MDA and SPLE combinations by enhancing reuse of platform-specific assets and fully managing platform-specific variability.

Firstly, we provided a definition of platform-specific variability by identifying platform-specific variation points in different concerns of the software design. These concerns were defined accordingly to the "4+1" view model which is a well-known categorization of a system concerns. We also showed that platform-specific variability has a not negligible impact on the reuse capabilities of the product line.

Then we proposed a new PSM structure based on a composition of two sub-models. On the one hand, the Cross-Cutting Model (CCM) is obtained by transformation of the PIM which defines the application conception. On the other hand, the Application Structure Model (ASM) is obtained by reuse of variable models of the same nature defined in domain engineering.

Platform-specific variability is represented on ASMs with two mechanisms: asset variants which permit to replace an ASM with one of its variants and model attributes which permit to configure the assets to reuse. In this way, domain engineering ASMs are generic configurable assets organized by their commonalities and variabilities.

To support the approach, we developed a framework based on a Domain Specific Modeling Language (DSML) to translate MDA and SPLE concepts in our partner's development teams' vocabulary. The framework assists developers when they reuse variable assets by providing tools to identify variation points and their possible resolutions.

With the DSML, we could experiment our proposal to produce three concrete applications. The obtained results confirmed that fully handling platform-specific variability significantly increases the productivity of a product line. In fact, the generated code could vary according to business-independent, platform-specific variation points.

Finally, we analyzed the capabilities of existing approaches addressing the problem of managing platform-specific variability. Results have shown that platform-specific variability is either ignored, only partially managed or fully managed but implying shortcomings in terms of maintainability of the product line.

The presented work involved only the PSM abstraction level. We expect that the proposed PSM definition could impact the CIM and PIM contents. Our future works will address impacts on higher abstraction levels to integrate the proposal in a full approach involving all MDA abstraction levels. We plan to work on two main axes.

Firstly, further works will be required to understand how the selection of CIM and PIM abstraction level assets can impact the selection of PSM abstraction level ones. We expect that the selection of ASMs will be motivated by two criteria: the non-functional requirements expressed by the client represented in the CIM and the software architecture design of the PIM.

Then, the proposal core assets organization is managed by a feature model. This model purpose is to represent coarse-grained features. However, PSM reusable assets can be fine-grained models. Integrating Common Variability Language [28] is a promising solution that might help us organize more fine-grained assets.

Acknowledgments. We would like to thank the National Association of Research and Technology (ANRT in French) for its contribution to this research.

References

1. Jacobson, I., Griss, M., Jonsson, P.: Software Reuse: Architecture Process and Organization for Business Success. ACM Press, New York (1997)
2. Gamma, E., Helm, R., Johnson, R., Vlissides, J.: Design Patterns: Elements of Reusable Object-oriented Software. Addison-Wesley Longman Publishing Co., Inc., Boston (1995)
3. Vale, T., Crnkovic, I., De Almeida, E.S., Neto, P.A.D.M.S., Cavalcanti, Y.C., de Lemos Meira, S.R.: Twenty-eight years of component-based software engineering. J. Syst. Softw. **111**, 128–148 (2016)
4. Filman, R.E., Elrad, T., Clarke, S., Aksit, M. (eds.): Aspect-Oriented Software Development. Addison Wesley, Boston (2004)
5. Schmidt, D.C.: Model-driven engineering. Computer **39**, 25 (2006)
6. Clements, P., Northrop, L.: Software Product Lines: Practices and Patterns. ddison-Wesley Professional, Reading (2001)
7. Deelstra, S., Sinnema, M., van Gurp, J., Bosch, J.: Model driven architecture as approach to manage variability in software product families. ResearchGate (2003)
8. Kim, S.D., Min, H.G., Her, J.S., Chang, S.H.: Dream : a practical product line engineering using model driven architecture. In: Proceedings of the Third International Conference on Information Technology and Applications (ICITA 2005) (2005)
9. Miller, J., Mukerji, J.: MDA guide. Object Management Group (2003)
10. Dageförde, J.C., Reischmann, T., Majchrzak, T.A., Ernsting, J.: Generating app product lines in a model-driven cross-platform development approach. In: 49th Hawaii International Conference on System Sciences (HICSS) (2016)

11. Verdier, F., Seriai, A.D., Tiam, R.T.: Reusing platform-specific models in model-driven architecture for software product lines. In: Proceedings of the 6th International Conference on Model-Driven Engineering and Software Development, pp. 106–116 (2018)
12. Object Management Group: OMG unified modeling language (2015)
13. Frantiska, J.: Entity-relationship diagrams. In: Frantiska, J. (ed.) Visualization Tools for Learning Environment Development. SECT, pp. 21–30. Springer, Cham (2018). https://doi.org/10.1007/978-3-319-67440-7_4
14. Kardoš, M., Drozdová, M.: Analytical method of CIM to PIM transformation in model driven architecture (MDA). J. Inf. Organ. Sci. **34**, 89–99 (2010)
15. Pohl, K., Metzger, A.: Variability management in software product line engineering. In: Proceedings of the 28th International Conference on Software Engineering, ICSE 2006, pp. 1046–1050. ACM (2006)
16. Pohl, K., Böckle, G., van der Linden, F.J.: Software Product Line Engineering: Foundations, Principles and Techniques. Springer, New York (2005). https://doi.org/10.1007/3-540-28901-1
17. Kruchten, P.B.: The 4+1 view model of architecture. IEEE Softw. **12**, 42–50 (1995)
18. Usman, M., Iqbal, M.Z., Khan, M.U.: A product-line model-driven engineering approach for generating feature-based mobile applications. J. Syst. Softw. **123**, 1–32 (2017)
19. Brambilla, M., Cabot, J., Wimmer, M.: Model-driven software engineering in practice, 2nd edn. Synthesis Lectures on Software Engineering. Morgan & Claypool Publishers (2017)
20. O'Neil, E.J.: Object/relational mapping 2008: hibernate and the entity data model (edm). In: Proceedings of the 2008 ACM SIGMOD International Conference on Management of Data, SIGMOD 2008. ACM, pp. 1351–1356 (2008)
21. Czarnecki, K., Helsen, S., Eisenecker, U.: Staged configuration using feature models. In: Nord, R.L. (ed.) SPLC 2004. LNCS, vol. 3154, pp. 266–283. Springer, Heidelberg (2004). https://doi.org/10.1007/978-3-540-28630-1_17
22. Hamed, A., Colomb, R.M.: End to end development engineering. J. Softw. Eng. Appl. **4**, 195–216 (2014)
23. Object Management Group: Business Process Model and Notation. Version 2.0. (2011)
24. Czarnecki, K., Helsen, S.: Classification of model transformation approaches. In: Proceedings of the 2nd OOPSLA Workshop on Generative Techniques in the Context of the Model Driven Architecture, pp. 1–17 (2003)
25. Steinberg, D., Budinsky, F., Paternostro, M., Merks, E.: EMF: Eclipse Modeling Framework, 2nd edn. Addison-Wesley Professional, Reading (2009)
26. Jouault, F., Allilaire, F., Bézivin, J., Kurtev, I., Valduriez, P.: ATL: a QVT-like transformation language. In: Companion to the 21st ACM SIGPLAN Symposium on Object-Oriented Programming Systems, Languages, and Applications, pp. 719–720. ACM (2006)
27. Paige, R.F., Matragkas, N., Rose, L.M.: Evolving models in model-driven engineering: state-of-the-art and future challenges. J. Syst. Softw. **111**, 272–280 (2016)
28. Haugen, O., Wasowski, A., Czarnecki, K.: CVL: common variability language. In: Proceedings of the 17th International Software Product Line Conference, SPLC 2013, pp. 277–277. ACM (2013)

A Test Specification Language
for Information Systems Based on Data
Entities, Use Cases and State Machines

Alberto Rodrigues da Silva[1], Ana C. R. Paiva[2,3]([✉]), and Valter E. R. da Silva[2]

[1] INESC-ID, Instituto Superior Técnico, Universidade de Lisboa, Lisboa, Portugal
alberto.silva@tecnico.ulisboa.pt
[2] Faculdade de Engenharia da Universidade do Porto, Porto, Portugal
apaiva@fe.up.pt, svalter.ribeiro@gmail.com
[3] INESC TEC, Rua Dr. Roberto Frias, s/n, 4200-465 Porto, Portugal

Abstract. Testing is one of the most important activities to ensure the quality of a software system. This paper proposes and discusses the TSL (Test Specification Language) that adopts a model-based testing approach for both human-readable and computer-executable specifications of test cases. TSL is strongly inspired on the grammar, nomenclature and writing style as defined by the RSLingo RSL, which is a rigorous requirements specification language. Both RSL and TSL are controlled natural languages that share common concepts such as data entities, use cases and state machines. However, by applying black-box functional testing design techniques, TSL includes and supports four complementary testing strategies, namely: domain analysis testing; use case tests; state machine testing; and acceptance criteria. This paper focuses on the first three testing strategies of TSL. Finally, a simple but effective case study illustrates the overall approach and supports the discussion.

Keywords: Test Specification Language (TSL) ·
Test case specification · Model based Testing (MBT) ·
Test case generation

1 Introduction

One of the most important activities to increase the quality of software systems is software testing. It is known that up to 50% of the total development costs are related to testing [3] and that about 30 to 60% of the total effort within a project is spent on testing [7].

Model-based testing (MBT) is one technique that systematizes and automates more of the testing process [11,18,27,35–38,42]. Test cases are generated from a model of a given Software System. These models or specifications vary in nature: they can be more or less abstract and represented textually [12] and/or graphically [10]; they can describe the functionalities and other qualities or goals [16] of the system. However, often these models do not exist, which demand they

© Springer Nature Switzerland AG 2019
S. Hammoudi et al. (Eds.): MODELSWARD 2018, CCIS 991, pp. 455–474, 2019.
https://doi.org/10.1007/978-3-030-11030-7_20

have to be developed from scratch; or, if they exist, they are described in a very informal way, which does not allow to derivate automatically test cases from it. Also, write system and acceptance tests manually is ineffective since tests are hard to write and costly to maintain. Hence, the existence of requirements specification, defined with controlled natural languages, may enable the derivation of test cases directly from such specifications. So, leveraging domain specific languages (DSLs) for functional testing can provide several benefits. For example, Robin Buuren recognizes in his work "Domain-Specific Language Testing Framework" three major quality aspects [2]: (i) Effectiveness, because it reduces the time of test development, since tests can be generated from a model; (ii) Usability, because it is easier to produce such test specification, considering the support provided by the work environment; and (iii) Correctness, because it makes system tests clearer by giving testers programmatic and strictly defined rules, leading to fewer errors.

This research proposes and discusses the TSL (Test Specification Language) that adopts a model-based testing approach for both human-readable and computer-executable specification of test cases. TSL is strongly inspired on the grammar, nomenclature and writing style as defined by the RSLingo RSL, which is a rigorous requirements specification language [24,25]. TSL applies black-box functional testing design techniques and includes and supports four complementary testing strategies, namely, (i) domain analysis testing: a testing strategy that uses techniques such as equivalence partitioning and boundary value analysis for the definition of structural data values; (ii) use case tests: a testing strategy that defines tests based on the scenarios defined for each use case; (iii) state machine testing: a testing strategy that traverses the state machine expressed in RSL according to different coverage criteria, e.g., cover all states; and (iv) acceptance criteria: a more general testing strategy based on the BDD (Behavior Driven Development) approach and very popular with user stories. This paper focus on the first three testing strategies.

To illustrate the overall TSL approach we use a fictitious information system (the "BillingSystem") that is partially described as a variety of informal requirements. That description is to some extent deliberately incomplete, vague and inconsistent as it is common in real-world situations. From that description, RSL requirements are defined and afterwards some TSL tests are derived and/or manually defined. The TSL definition of test cases for data entities, use cases and state machines and the corresponding generated Gherkin specifications are presented.

This paper updates and extends the one presented in [32] that introduced the general idea and architecture of the TSL language. This paper restructures that former paper describing first the overall approach in a more general way, and then further presenting and discussing the language based on an illustrative example. Furthermore this paper describes in more detail the constructs Data Entities, Use Cases and State Machines, and originally discusses the respective test strategies, namely the domain analysis testing (based on the construct *DataEntityTestCase*); use case testing (based on the construct *UseCaseTestCase*); and state machine testing (based on the construct *StateMachineTestCase*). Finally, this paper also adds the description of the TSL for specifying tests based on use cases and it extends the illustrative case study with TSL test cases based on use cases, and so, showing the strong relation between these three constructs at both requirement and testing levels.

This paper is organized in 6 sections. Section 2 introduces and overviews the RSL language, by introducing its bi-dimensional multi-view architecture, based on abstraction levels and concerns. Section 3 gives a very short introduction to the concepts of Cucumber and Gherkin. Section 4 presents and discusses the TSL constructs and views, namely tests based on data entities use cases and state machines. Section 5 presents a case study to illustrate the overall approach. Finally, Sect. 6 presents the conclusion and identifies issues for future work.

2   RSL Overview

It is known that natural language, although the most used notation in the requirements documents, it is prone to produce ambiguities and inconsistencies that are difficult to validate or transform automatically [9,19]. RSLingo is a long-term research initiative that proposed an approach to use simplified natural language processing techniques as well as human-driven techniques for capturing relevant information from ad-hoc natural language requirements specifications and then applying lightweight parsing techniques to extract domain knowledge encoded within them [4]. This was achieved through the use of two original languages: the RSL-PL (Pattern Language) [5], designed for encoding RE-specific linguistic patterns, and RSL-IL (Intermediate Language), a domain specific language designed to address RE concerns [6]. Based on these two languages and the mapping between them, it is possible to extract, analyze and convert the initial written knowledge in natural language into a more structured format, reducing its original ambiguity and creating a more rigorous SRS (System Requirements Specification) document [23,28].

Based on the former languages [5,6,14,15,17,18,21,22,29,30], Silva et al. designed, more recently, a broader and more consistent language, called "RSLingo's RSL" (or just "RSL" for the sake of brevity). RSL is a control natural language to help the production of SRSs in a systematic, rigorous and consistent way [24,25]. RSL is a process- and tool-independent language, i.e., it can be used and adapted by different users and organizations with different processes/methodologies and supported by multiple types of software tools.

RSL provides several constructs that are logically arranged into views according to two viewpoints: the abstraction level (Levels) and the specific RE concerns (Concerns) they address. These views are organized according to two abstraction levels: business and system levels; and to five concerns: context, active structure, behavior, passive structure and requirements (Fig. 1).

At the business level, RSL supports the specification of the following business-related concerns: (1) the people and organizations that can influence or will be affected by the system; (2) business processes, events, and flows that might help

Concerns		Context	Active Structure	Behavior	Passive Structure	Requirements
Levels	Package		(Subjects)	(Verbs. Actions)	(Objects)	
Business	package-business	Business SystemRelation BusinessElement Relation	Stakeholder	BusinessProcess (BusinessEvent, BusinessFlows)	GlossaryTerm	BusinessGoal
System	package-system	System Requirement Relation	Actor	StateMachine (State, Transition, Action)	DataEntity DataEntityView	SystemGoal QR Constraint FR UseCase UserStory

Fig. 1. RSL levels and concerns [24, 25, 32].

to describe the business behavior; (3) the common terms used in that business domain; and (4) the general business goals of stakeholders regarding the value that the business as well the system will bring. Considering these concerns, RSL business level comprises respectively the following views: *Stakeholders* (active structure concern), *BusinessProcesses* (behavior concern), *Glossary* (passive structure concern), and *BusinessGoals* (requirements concern). In addition, the references to the systems used by the business, as well as their relationships, can also be defined at this level (context concern).

On the other hand, at the system level, RSL supports the specification of multiple RE specific concerns, namely by the adoption of the following constructs: (1) to describe the actors that interact with the system; (2) to describe the behavior of some system's data entities, namely based on state machines; (3) to describe the structure of the system, namely based on data entities and data entity views; and (4) several to specify the requirements of the system according different styles. Considering these concerns, the system level respectively comprises the following views: *Actors* (active structure concern); *StateMachines* (behaviour concern); *DataEntities* and *DataEntityViews* (passive structure concern); and multiple types of Requirements such as *SystemGoals*, *QualityRequirements* (QRs), *Constraints*, *FunctionalRequirements* (FRs), *UseCases*, and *UserStories* (requirements concern). In addition, all these elements and views should be defined in the context of a defined *System* (context concern).

The following subsections give some detail regarding the RSL elements that are then used (in Sect. 4) to support the TSL tests specifications.

2.1   Data Entities

A *DataEntity* in RSL (see Spec. 1) denotes an individual structural entity that might include the specification of attributes, foreign keys and other (check) data constraints. A *DataEntity* is classified by a type and an optional subtype.

An Attribute denotes a particular structural property of the respective *DataEntity*. An attribute has an *id*, *name*, *type* (e.g., Integer, Double, String, Date) and optionally the specification of its *multiplicity*, *default value* (i.e., the value assigned by default in its creation time), *values* (i.e., a list of possible values, e.g., enumeration values separately by semicolons), and *is not null* and *is unique* constraints.

2.2   Use Cases

UseCases view in RSL defines the uses cases of a system under study (see Spec. 2). Traditionally a use case means a sequence of actions that one or more actors perform in a system to obtain a particular result [33]. However, the RSL's *Use-Case* construct extends such general and vague definition considering some additional aspects, namely [20, 25]:

```
'dataEntity' name=ID ':' type=DataEntityType (':' subType=DataEntitySubType)?'['
            ('name' nameAlias=STRING)
            ('isA' super=[DataEntity])?
            (attributes+=Attribute)+
            (primaryKey=PrimaryKey)?
            (foreignKeys+=ForeignKey)*
            (checks+=Check)*
            ('description' description=STRING)?
']';

'attribute' name=ID ':' type=AttributeType ('(' size = DoubleOrInt ')')? '['
            ('name' nameAlias=STRING)
            ('multiplicity' multiplicity=Multiplicity)?
            ('defaultValue' defaultValue=STRING)?
            ('values' values=STRING)?
            (notNull='NotNull')?
            (unique='Unique')?
            ('description' description=STRING)?
']';
```

Spec. 1. Definition of Data Entities in RSL.

- A use case shall be classified by a set of use case types;
- A use case can be applicable to a cluster of data entities, called *DataEntityView*;
- A use case shall define at least the actor that initiates it and, optionally, other actors that might participate; these actors can be end-users, external systems or even timers;
- A use case can define pre-conditions and post-conditions;
- A use case can define several actions that may occur in its context;
- A use case can define "includes" relations to other use cases;
- A use case can define several extensions points available in its context;
- A use case can extend the behavior of other use case (the target use case) in its specific extension point;
- The behavior of a use case can be detailed by a set of scenarios that are also classified as main, alternative or exception scenario; by definition a use case can only have one main scenario and zero or more alternative and exception scenarios;
- A use case scenario is defined by a set of sequential or parallel steps;
- A use case step is classified by a set of types and defined as simple or complex step;

```
'useCase' name=ID ':' type=UseCaseType '['
  ('name' nameAlias=STRING)
  ('actorInitiates' actorInitiates=[Actor])
  ('actorParticipates' actorParticipates+=RefActor)?
  ('dataEntityView' dEntityView=[DataEntityView])?

  ('precondition' precondition=STRING)?
  ('postcondition' postcondition=STRING)?

  (actions= UCActions)?
  (extensionPoints= UCExtensionPoints)?

  (includes= UCIncludes)?
  (extends+= UCExtends)*

  ('stakeholder' stakeholder=[Stakeholder])?
  ('priority' priority=PriorityType)?
  ('description' description=STRING)?

  scenarios+=Scenario*
']';

'scenario' name=ID ':' type=ScenarioType '['
  ('name' nameAlias=STRING)
  ('executionMode' mode=('Sequential'|'Parallel'))?
  ('description' description=STRING)?
  (steps+=Step*)
']';

'step' name=ID ':' type=StepOperationType (':' subType=StepOperationSubType )?'['
  (simpleStep= SimpleStep | subSteps+= Step+ | ifSteps+= IfStep* )
']';
```

Spec. 2. Definition of Use Cases in RSL.

```
'stateMachine' name=ID ':' type=StateMachineType '['
  'name' nameAlias=STRING
  'dataEntity' entity= [DataEntity]
  ('description' description=STRING)?
  states= States
']';


State:
'state' name=ID
  (isInitial ?= 'isInitial')?
  (isFinal ?= 'isFinal')?
  ('onEntry' onEntry= STRING)?
  ('onExit' onExit= STRING)?
  (':' (actions+= RefUCAction))? (actions += RefUCAction)* ;

RefUCAction:
  ('useCaseAction' action= [UCAction] ('nextState' nextstate= [State])?);
```

Spec. 3. Definition of State Machines in RSL.

2.3   State Machines

The *StateMachines* view in RSL defines the behavior of *DataEntities* in their relationships with use cases (see Spec. 3). A *StateMachine* is necessarily assigned to just one *DataEntity* and classified as simple or complex depending on the number of states and transitions involved (e.g., a *StateMachine* with more than 4 states might be classified as Complex). A *StateMachine* includes several states corresponding to the situations that a *DataEntity* may be find itself during its life cycle (e.g., as shown in Spec. 11 states like *Pending, Approved, Rejected*). In addition, a state can be defined as initial (*isInitial*) or final (*isFinal*). Several actions can be defined when a *DataEntity* enters (*onEntry*) or exits (*onExit*) the respective state. Moreover, several use case's actions (*actions*) can occur on the *DataEntity* when it is in a given state, and the occurrence of these actions can optionally imply a state transition (*nextState*).

3   Gherkin and Cucumber Overview

Behavior-Driven Development (BDD) is a software development methodology in which a software application is specified and designed describing how its behavior should appear to an external observer [26]. In BDD, acceptance tests are first written describing the behavior of the system from a user's point of view, and then these acceptance tests are reviewed and approved so that code development can begin.

Acceptance tests written in a behavior-driven style can be executed by the testing tool Cucumber [39]. Cucumber reads the acceptance tests and validates that the software does what is expected. Because tests are automatically executed by Cucumber, it is easy to maintain the specifications up-to-date.

Gherkin [40] is a simple language that Cucumber is able to understand. Gherkin allows to define tests in an easily readable format. Gherkin tests are organized into features. Each feature is made up of a collection of scenarios defined by a sequence of steps and following a Given-When-Then (GWT) rule. A simple example is illustrated in Spec. 4, more information can be obtained, for example, in [40].

```
Feature: Login Action
Scenario: Successful Login with Valid Credentials
       Given User is on Home Page
       When User Navigate to LogIn Page
       And User enters UserName
       And Password
       Then Message displayed Login Successfully
```

Spec. 4. Simple Test Case Example in Gherkin.

4   TSL Approach and Language

The original goal of this research is to develop an approach to support the specification and generation (whenever relevant) of software tests defined in TSL, directly from requirements specifications originally defined in RSL. It is intended to achieve the following goals: (i) extend the RSLingo approach with the support for testing activities; (ii) define a set of strategies that would allow generating test cases from the RSL constructs; and (iii) automate the test case generation process.

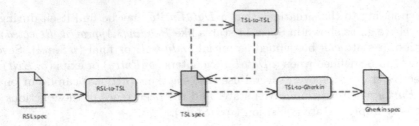

Fig. 2. TSL based approach [32].

Figure 2 suggests the proposed approach. First, RSL requirements specifications are the input for the RSL-to-TSL transformation that generates TSL specifications. Second, based on predefined strategies, these TSL specs can be expanded and generated into other TSL specs (e.g., for increasing the system testing domain with more test cases). Third, the TSL specs are the input for the TSL-to-Gherkin transformation that generates Gherkin specifications, and ultimately these specs can be used for documentation purposes or even for testing execution.

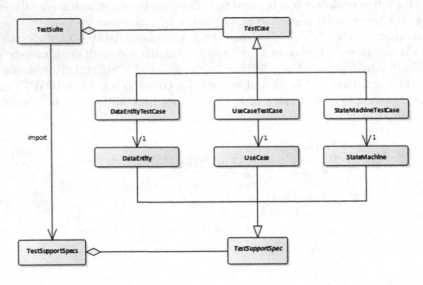

Fig. 3. Metamodel of the TSL general architecture (partial view) [32].

As illustrated in Fig. 3, a TSL specification is a combination of two different types of elements. First, the *TestSupportSpecs* package includes *TestSupportSpec* elements such as *DataEntities*, or *StateMachines*. These elements are a simplified version of the equivalent elements supported by the RSL language (e.g., the TSL *DataEntity* element is a simplified version of the RSL *DataEntity*). These TSL *TestSupportSpec* elements can be authored manually but usually shall be generated from the RSL specs.

Second, the *TestSuite* package includes *TestCase* elements such as *DataEntity TestCase*, *UseCase TestCase* or *StateMachine TestCase*. Each *TestCase* shall be defined as *Valid* or *Invalid* and shall have a dependency to a respective *TestSupportSpec*, e.g., a *StateMachine TestCase* has a dependency to the respective *StateMachine*. These *TestCase* elements can be generated by the RSL-to-TSL and TSL-to-TSL transformations, but usually shall be also authored and refined by the software testers.

TSL allows specifying various black-box test cases in a syntactic manner similar to that expressed by RSL. In addition, TSL allows to systematize the test developing process with both Xtext-based and Excel RSL formats. Xtext based format is handled with the integration of the Eclipse IDE [1]. This environment provides an editor for test construction, covering most important features concerning IDE, granting TSL a semi-automated way to formally specify test cases. This Eclipse-based tool provides great assist for composing tests, namely comprehends a syntax-aware editor with features like immediate feedback, incremental syntax checking, suggested corrections, and auto-completion. On the other hand, the RSL/TSL Excel template [34] is extended with the creation of some Excel sheets, arranged in a tabular way, for each of the provided test types. This grants a broader usage, since testers with no IT background can specify tests using a general tool as MS-Excel. On the other hand, it loses part of the rigor and formality inherent to formal grammar defined in Xtext.

TSL supports the specification of the following tests:

– *DataEntity TestCases* can be defined by applying equivalence class partitioning and boundary value analysis [31] over RSL *DataEntities*;
– *UseCase TestCase* can be defined by exploring multiple sequences of steps defined in RSL use cases' scenarios, and also by associating data values to the involved data entities;
– *StateMachine TestCases* can be defined by applying different algorithms to traverse the state machine defined in RSL, so that it shall be possible to build different test cases that correspond to different paths through the state machine.

4.1 Data Entity Test Cases

Data Entity test cases are based on classic input domain analysis test design techniques known as "equivalence class partitioning" and "boundary value analysis" [31].

Since most of the times it is unfeasible to test all possible values of an input domain, equivalent class partitioning divides the input domain into classes (or data entities in the RSL/TSL terminology) assuming that the behavior of the software is the same for any value inside a class. Hence, the test cases are designed so as to test one randomly chosen value of each class.

Knowing that the probability of finding failures is higher for boundary values, boundary value analysis chooses the boundaries of the classes for test input data instead of randomly chosen values.

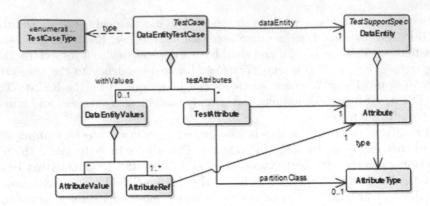

Fig. 4. Metamodel of the TSL DataEntityTestCase definition (partial view) [32].

As shown in Fig. 4, a *DataEntity* keeps information about a specific data entity and its attributes; for each attribute it keeps information about its type, size, among others. Based on this information, it is possible to define equivalence classes and test input data. For example, consider an entity with an attribute A of type real and with one decimal place within [2.3, 25.4], according to equivalence class partitioning, the tester should test valid and invalid input values. So, for this particular case, the tester could define a valid input inside the interval, e.g., 15.2, and invalid inputs outside the interval, e.g., 1.2 and 30.3.

The benefit of the TSL is that it builds a view with all the entities and attributes for which the tester should define test input data. In case of sequential attribute values (such has numbers), it is also possible to apply boundary value analysis to define test input data. For instance, considering the same attribute A between [2.3, 25.4] the tester should define test input data for the boundaries: 2.2, 2.3, 2.4 (for one boundary) and 25.3, 25.4, 25.5 (for the other boundary).

As illustrated in Fig. 4, a *DataEntityTestCase* refers to just one *DataEntity* and defines a combination of values that are associated to its respective attributes. These values can be defined individually at an attribute basis (using the *TestAttribute* object) or as a table of values associated to multiple attributes (using the *Values* object). Each *DataEntityTestCase* shall be defined as *Valid* or *Invalid* type depending on the validity of such values.

4.2 Use Case Test Cases

A use case is a description of a particular use of the system by an actor (a user of the system). It helps defining the functional system software requirements by illustrating a process flow of the actual real use of the system. For each use case there is, usually, at least one basic scenario (or main scenario) and zero or more alternative/exceptional flows.

Use Case tests (Fig. 5) are derived from the various process flows expressed by a RSL Use Case. TSL defines Use Cases Tests from the RSL System-level view

Actors and *UseCases*. Each test contains multiple scenarios, which are derived from the various flows of each RSL Use Case. A scenario encompasses of a group of steps and must be executed by an actor, which are also derived from the RSL System-level view.

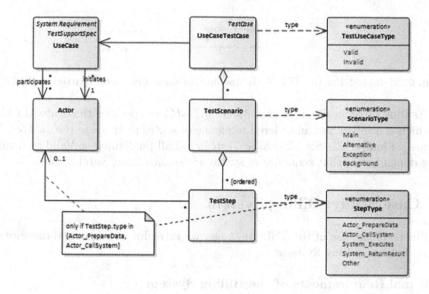

Fig. 5. Metamodel of the TSL UseCaseTests definition (partial view).

This construct begins by defining the test set, including *ID*, *name* and the use case *type*. Then it encompasses the references keys [UseCase] indicating the Use Case in which the test is proceeding, background [UseCase] in the circumstances of prevailing event flow that take place before the current Use Case, [DataEntity] referring to a possible data entity that is managed throughout the action flow. For each test case multiple scenarios can be defined. For each of these scenarios it is specified a *name*, the scenario *Type* (Main, Alternative or Exception flow), and the *set of steps* needed to be performed. For each step, it shall be indicated the actor who performs it [Actor], or alternatively the system responsible for it and a step definition, informally describing the action step executed.

4.3   State Machine Test Cases

A state machine is a model that describes the behavior of a system as a whole or more commonly of a given data entity (or object) throughout its life-cycle. A RSL state machine allows to represent the behavior of a data entity as a set of event-driven actions from a state to another when triggered by a given use case action. In addition, from a state machine defined in RSL, it is possible to apply different algorithms that traverse the state machine according to different test coverage criteria, such as, all states or all transitions or others [41].

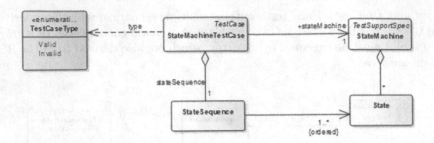

Fig. 6. Metamodel of the TSL StateMachineTestCase definition (partial view) [32].

As illustrated in Fig. 6, a *StateMachineTestCase* specifies the State Machine to which is applied and an ordered sequence of states to traverse (i.e., a *StateSequence*). Finally, this *StateMachine TestCase* shall be defined as Valid or Invalid type depending if that sequence of states are semantically valid or not.

5 Case Study: Billing System

To illustrate the use of the TSL language, we introduce an informal description of the fictions Billing System.

Informal Requirements of the Billing System
BillingSystem is a system that allows users to manage customers, products and invoices. A user of the system is someone that has a user account and is assigned to one or more user roles, such as user, user-operator, user-manager and user-administrator [...].

User-operator is responsible for managing customers and invoices. System shall allow user-operator to create/update information related to customers and invoices [...].

The creation of invoices is a shared task performed by the user-operator and the user-manager. System shall allow user-operator to create new invoices (with respective invoice details). Before sending an invoice to a customer, the invoice shall be formally approved by a user-manager. Only after such approval, the user-operator shall issue and send that invoice electronically by e-mail and by regular post. In addition, for each invoice, the user-operator needs to keep track if it is paid or not [...].

User-manager shall be responsible for approving invoices before they are issued and sent to their customers. User-manager shall allow monitoring the process of creating, approving and payments invoices. User-manager shall approve or reject invoices [...].

5.1   TSL: Data Entity Tests

An invoice is a commercial document related to a sale transaction between a seller and a buyer (customer). For each invoice the system shall indicate the products, quantities, agreed prices for products or services the seller had provided to the buyer. Each product has a price with and without the respective VAT. The VAT (value-added tax) is a type of general consumption tax that is collected incrementally, based on the surplus value, added to the price on the work or the product at each stage of production. Specification in Spec. 5 shows a TSL specification of some of these entities, namely the e_VAT, e_Product and e_Customer data entities.

```
DataEntity e_VAT "VAT Category" : Reference [
    attribute VATCode "VAT Code" : Regex [isNotNull isUnique]
    attribute VATName "VAT Class Name" : String(30) [isNotNull]
    attribute VATValue "VAT Class Value" : Decimal(2.1) [isNotNull]
    primaryKey (VATCode)
    description "VAT Categories"]

DataEntity e_Product "Product" : Master [
    attribute ID "Product ID" : Integer [isNotNull isUnique]
    attribute Name "Name" : String(50) [multiplicity "1..2" description "Product Name"]
    attribute valueWithoutVAT "Price Without VAT" : Decimal(16.2) [isNotNull ]
    attribute valueWithVAT "Price With VAT" : Decimal(16.2) [isNotNull ]
    attribute VATCode "VAT Code" : Integer [isNotNull]
    attribute VATValue "VAT Value" : Decimal(2.2) [isNotNull]
    primaryKey (ID)
    foreignKey e_VAT(VATCode)
    description "Products"]

DataEntity e_Customer "Customer" : Master [
    isEncrypted
    attribute ID "Customer ID" : Integer [isNotNull isUnique]
    attribute Name "Name" : String(50) [isNotNull isUnique]
    attribute fiscalID "Fiscal ID" : String(12) [isNotNull isUnique]
    attribute BankID "Bank ID" : Regex
    attribute phone "Phone #" : String(12) [isNotNull isUnique]
    attribute image "Image" : Image
    primaryKey (ID)
    check ck_Customer1 "ValidFiscalID(fiscalID)"
    description "Customers"]
```

Spec. 5. Example of a TSL (partial) specification of data entities.

Based on this data entities' specification it is possible to define and also to generate some data entity test cases. Spec. 6 shows some of these tests defined for the *e_VAT* data entity. First, *detVAT1* is defined as a valid test case and defines two *testAttributes*, which both define a partition class check, valid values, and for the *e_VAT.VATCode* attribute a uniqueness constraint. Second, *detVAT2* is defined as a valid test case but shows a set of relevant attributes with valid values in a table format; this representation is usually the most practical and convenient approach to define such values. In addition, *detVAT2* also defines three *testAttributes*. Third, *detVAT3* is defined as an invalid test case and involves the definition of two *testAttributes*, both with problems referred by their respective messages (i.e., "Incorrect VAT values" and "Incorrect *VATValue* PartitionClass").

Spec. 7 shows the equivalent data entity test case in the Gherkin language.

```
DataEntityTestCase detVAT1 : Valid [
    dataEntity e_VAT
    testAttribute VATCode (partitionClass Integer values "0;1;2;3" isUnique)
    testAttribute VATValue (partitionClass Decimal(2.2)  values "0; 0,06; 0,13; 0,23" )
    message "Correct VAT values (1)" ]

DataEntityTestCase detVAT2 "detVAT2" : Valid [
    dataEntity e_VAT  withValues (
    | VATCode          | VATValue        | VATValue   +|
    | 0                | "NO-VAT"        | 0          +|
    | 1                | "Reduced"       | 0.06       +|
    | 2                | "Intermediate"  | 0.13       +|
    | 3                | "Normal"        | 0.23       +| )
    testAttribute VATCode (partitionClass Integer values "0, 1")
    testAttribute VATName (partitionClass String)
    testAttribute VATValue (partitionClass Decimal(2.2))
    message "Correct VAT values (2)" ]

DataEntityTestCase  detVAT3 "detVAT3" : Invalid [
    dataEntity e_VAT
    testAttribute VATValue (values "0,08; 0,25" message "Incorrect VAT values")
    testAttribute VATValue (partitionClass Integer message "Incorrect VATValue PartitionClass") ]
```

Spec. 6. Example of a TSL (partial) specification of data entity tests.

```
Feature: Management of VAT data entity

Scenario: Valid VAT (1)
Given dataEntity VAT
When e_VAT.VATCode partitionClass is Integer
 And e_VAT.VATCode values are "0;1;2;3;"
 And e_VAT.VATValue partitionClass is Decimal(2.2)
 And e_VAT.VATValue values are "0; 0,06; 0,13; 0,23"
Then Output Correct VAT values (1)

Scenario: Valid VAT (2)
Given dataEntity VAT with values:
    | e_VAT.VATCode   | e_VAT.VATName     | e_VAT.VATValue  |
    | 0               | "No-VAT"          | 0               |
    | 1               | "Reduced"         | 0.06            |
    | 2               | "Intermediate"    | 0.13            |
    | 3               | "Normal"          | 0.23            |
When e_VAT.VATCode partitionClass is Integer
 And e_VAT.VATName partitionClass is String
 And e_VAT.VATValue partitionClass is Decimal(2.2)
 And e_VAT.VATName values are <e_VAT.VATName>
 And e_VAT.VATValue values are <e_VAT.VATValue>
Then Output Correct VAT values (2)


Scenario: Invalid VAT (1)
Given dataEntity VAT
When e_VAT.VATValue values are "0,08; 0,25"
Then message "Incorrect VAT values"

Scenario: Invalid VAT (2)
Given dataEntity VAT
When e_VAT.VATValue partitionClass is Integer
Then message "Incorrect VATValue PartitionClass"
```

Spec. 7. Example of a Gherkin (partial) specification of data entity tests.

5.2   TSL: Use Case Tests

Use case tests are derived from various use cases (Spec. 8) expressed by RSL. TSL defines Use Cases Test Cases (Spec. 9) from the RSL system-level view *Actors* and *UseCases*. Each test contains multiple test scenarios, which are derived from the various flows of each use case. A test scenario encompasses of a group of test steps and shall be executed by an actor, which are also derived from the RSL.

```
UseCase uc_2_ManageCustomers "Manage Customers" : EntitiesManage [
    actorInitiates aU_Operator
    dataEntity ec_Customer
    actions aClose, aSearch, aFilter, aCreate, aRead, aUpdate, aDelete, aPrint_Customer
    extensionPoints Create, Read, Update, Delete, Print_Customer, Print_Customers]

UseCase uc_2_1_CreateCustomer "Create Customer" : EntityCreate [
    actorInitiates aU_Operator
    dataEntity ec_Customer
    actions aSave, aCancel
    extends uc_2_ManageCustomers onExtensionPoint Create]

UseCase uc_2_2_ConsultCustomer "Consult Customer" : EntityRead [□

UseCase uc_2_3_UpdateCustomer "Update Customer" : EntityUpdate [□

UseCase uc_2_4_DeleteCustomer "Delete Customer" : EntityDelete [
    actorInitiates aU_Operator
    dataEntity ec_Customer
    actions aDelete, aCancel
    extends uc_2_ManageCustomers onExtensionPoint Delete]
```

Spec. 8. Example of a TSL (partial) specification of Use Cases.

```
UseCaseTestCase t_uc_2_1_CreateCustomer "Create Customer" : Valid [
    useCase uc_2_1_CreateCustomer
    actorInitiates aU_Operator

    testScenario CreateCustomer_Generic :Main [
        isAbstract
        testStep s1:System_Execute:ShowData ["The System shows a CreateCustomer form"]
        testStep s2:Actor_PrepareData ["The Operator fills the fields Name and FiscalID"]
        testStep s3:Actor_CallSystem ["The Operator click the Save button"]
        testStep s4:System_Execute ["The System check if the Name and FiscalID are unique"]
        testStep s5:System_ReturnResult ["The System shows a successful notification message"] ]

    testScenario CreateCustomer_Concrete :Alternative [
        isConcrete
        testStep s1:System_Execute:ShowData ["The System shows a CreateCustomer form"]
        testStep s2:Actor_PrepareData ["The Operator fills the fields with the following data:"
            dataEntity e_Customer withValues (
            |  e_Customer.Name  |  e_Customer.fiscalID      +|
            |  "Mary White"     |  "999 997 688"            +|
            )]
        testStep s3:Actor_CallSystem ["The Operator click the Save button"]
        testStep s4:System_Execute ["The System check that Name and FiscalID are unique"]
        testStep s5:System_ReturnResult ["The System shows a successful notification message"] ]

    testScenario CreateCustomer_Exception :Exception [
        testStep s1:System_Execute:ShowData ["The System shows a CreateCustomer form"]
        testStep s2:Actor_PrepareData ["The Operator fills the fields Name and FiscalID"]
        testStep s3:Actor_CallSystem ["The Operator click the Save button"]
        testStep s4:System_Execute ["The System check if the Name and FiscalID are unique,
                            and if they exist already the System does not save the data"]
        testStep s5:System_ReturnResult ["The System shows a error notification message!"] ]
]
```

Spec. 9. Example of a TSL (partial) specification of Use Case tests.

The UseCaseTestCase construct begins by defining the test set, including *ID*, *name* and the use case *type*. Then it encompasses the references keys [UseCase] indicating the Use Case in which the test is proceeding, background [UseCase] in the circumstances of prevailing event flow that take place before the current Use Case, [DataEntity] referring to a possible data entity that is managed.

For each scenario, it is specified a *name*, the scenario *Type* (Main, Alternative or Exception flow, respectively), and the *set of steps* involved. For each test step, it must be indicated the *actor* who performs it [Actor], a reference to the equivalent *use case step* [Step] if relevant, and an informal step *definition*, that describes the action executed. The equivalent Gherkin specification of the TSL Use Case tests is illustrated in Spec. 10.

```
Feature: Use Case: Create Customer

Scenario: CreateCustomer_Generic
        given "I'm in the role of Operator"
        when "I select the Create Customer option"
        and "The System shows a Create Customer form with the following fields:
            Name, FiscalID"
        and "I fill the fields Name and FiscalID"
        and "I click the Save button"
        then "The System check if the Name and FiscalID are unique, and saves the data"
        and "The System shows a successful notification message"

Scenario: CreateCustomer_Concrete
        given "I'm Peter Brown in the role of Operator"
        when "I select the Create Customer option"
        and "The System shows a Create Customer form with the following fields:
            Name, FiscalID"
        and "I fill the fields Name and FiscalID"
        and   dataEntity Customer with values:
            |   e_Customer.Name     |   e_Customer.FiscalID   |
            |   "Mary White"        |   "999 997 688"         |
        and "I click the Save button"
        then "The System check if the Name and FiscalID are unique, and saves the data"
        and "The System shows a successful notification message"

Scenario: CreateCustomer_Generic
        given "I'm in the role of Operator"
        when "I select the Create Customer option"
        and "The System shows a Create Customer form with the following fields: Name, FiscalID"
        and "I fill the fields Name and FiscalID"
        and "I click the Save button"
        then "The System check if the Name and FiscalID are unique, and if they exist already
            the System does not save the data"
        and "he System shows a error notification message: The customer data already exist!"
```

Spec. 10. Example of a Gherkin (partial) specification of Use Case tests.

5.3   TSL: State Machines Tests

Spec. 12 shows some examples of *StateMachineTestCase* associated to the *e_Invoice*'s s_m_e_invoice state machine (see Spec. 11).

```
StateMachine sm_e_Invoice "StateMachine_Invoice" : Complex [
    dataEntity e_Invoice
    description "StateMachine of entity Invoice"
    state StateInitial isInitial onEntry "In creation"
        useCase uc_1_1_CreateInvoice action aCreate nextState PendingState
    state PendingState onEntry "e.state= 'Pending'; e.isApproved= False"
    state ApprovedState onEntry "e.state= 'Approved'; e.isApproved= True"
    state RejectedState onEntry "e.state= 'Rejected'; e.isApproved= False"
    state PaidState isFinal onEntry "e.state= 'Paid'"
    state DeletedState isFinal onEntry "e.state= 'Deleted'"]
```

Spec. 11. Example of a TSL (partial) specification of state machine.

```
StateMachineTestCase tsm1_SM_E_Invoice "tsm1_SM_E_Invoice Invalid" : Invalid [
    stateMachine sm_e_Invoice
    stateSequence PendingState, PaidState, RejectedState
    message "(SM_E_Invoice) Invalid State Sequence"]

StateMachineTestCase tsm2_SM_E_Invoice "tsm2_SM_E_Invoice Valid" : Valid [
    stateMachine sm_e_Invoice
    stateSequence PendingState, RejectedState, DeletedState
    message "(SM_E_Invoice) Valid State Sequence - Rejected Invoice"]

StateMachineTestCase tsm3_SM_E_Invoice "tsm3_SM_E_Invoice Valid" : Valid [
    stateMachine sm_e_Invoice
    stateSequence PendingState, ApprovedState, PaidState
    message "(SM_E_Invoice) Valid State Sequence - Approved Invoice"]
```

Spec. 12. Example of a TSL (partial) specification of state machine tests.

```
Feature: Management of Invoice data entity

Scenario: tsm1_SM_E_Invoice Invalid
Given stateMachine sm_e_Invoice
When stateSequence Initial > Pending > Paid > Rejected
Then Output "(SM_E_Invoice) Invalid State Sequence"

Scenario: tsm2_SM_E_Invoice Valid
Given stateMachine sm_e_Invoice
When stateSequence Initial > Pending > Rejected > Deleted> Archived
Then Output "(SM_E_Invoice) Valid State Sequence - Rejected Invoice"

Scenario: tsm3_SM_E_Invoice Valid
Given stateMachine sm_e_Invoice
When stateSequence Initial > Pending > Approved > Paid
Then Output "(SM_E_Invoice) Valid State Sequence - Approved Invoice"
```

Spec. 13. Example of a Gherkin (partial) specification of state machine tests.

The first (i.e., *tsm1_SME_Invoice*) is an invalid test case because it defines an invalid sequence of states (namely, *Initial, Pending, Paid*). The second (i.e., *tsm2_SME_Invoice*) is a valid test case because it defines a valid sequence of states related with a reject situation (namely involving the following sequence of states: *Initial, Pending, Rejected, Deleted, Archive*); the third (i.e., *tsm3_SM_E_Invoice*) is also a valid test case but it defines a valid sequence of states related with an approved and paid situation.

Spec. 13 shows the equivalent specification of these state machine test cases in the Gherkin language.

6   Conclusion

This paper describes the TSL language and the companion model-based testing approach where test cases are derived from RSL constructs that describe the system behavior, such as *Actor* view, *DataEntity* view, *UseCase* view and *StateMachine* view. Based on a black-box approach and from these views, it is possible to define three main test constructs: data entity tests, state machine tests and use case tests.

The approach is illustrated based on a fictitious informal specification of an invoice management application, the "Billing System". It shows how the test cases constructs may be represented and demonstrates that by using executable requirements specifications, functional tests can be easy to "read, write, execute, debug, validate, and maintain" [8].

As future work, we intend to explore and implement test case input data generation techniques (e.g., through domain analysis and resolution of constraints on attribute values) and implement other algorithms for generating test cases from state machines based on other coverage criteria, for example, Switch-1 or Switch-2. Also, we aim to extract test scenarios based on the varies flows expressed by Use Cases and extend the language to also support user story test cases. In addition, we aim to automate the TSL test case generation processes that may be based on the following transformations: generate TSL test cases from equivalent RSL requirements specifications; and directly from existent systems and databases, namely adopting model-driven reverse engineering techniques like we researched recently [13].

Finally, we aim to automate even further the whole process by using test frameworks like Cucumber or Specflow which enable to execute automatically test cases written in Gherkin.

Acknowledgments. This work was partially supported by national funds under FCT project UID/CEC/50021/2019.

References

1. Bettini, L.: Implementing Domain-Specific Languages with Xtext and Xtend. Packt Publishing Ltd., Birmingham (2016)
2. Ten Buuren, R.A.: Domain-Specific Language Testing Framework. Master of Science, University of Twente, Enschede (2015)
3. Fagan, M.E.: Advances in software inspections. In: Broy, M., Denert, E. (eds.) Pioneers and Their Contributions to Software Engineering. Springer, Heidelberg (2001). https://doi.org/10.1007/978-3-642-48354-7_14

4. Ferreira, D., Silva, A.R.: RSLingo: an information extraction approach toward formal requirements specifications. In: Proceedings of MoDRE 2012. IEEE CS (2012)

5. Ferreira, D., Silva, A.R.: RSL-PL: a linguistic pattern language for documenting software requirements. In: Proceedings of RePa 2013. IEEE CS (2013)

6. Ferreira, D., Silva, A.R.: RSL-IL: an interlingua for formally documenting requirements. In: Proceedings of the of Third IEEE International Workshop on Model Driven Requirements Engineering. IEEE CS (2013a)

7. Ibe, M.: Decomposition of test cases in model-based testing. In: CEUR Workshop Proceedings (2013)

8. King, T.: Functional testing with domain-specific languages (2014)

9. Kovitz, B.: Practical Software Requirements: Manual of Content and Style. Manning, Shelter Island (1998)

10. Monteiro, T., Paiva, A.C.R.: Pattern based GUI testing modeling environment. In: Sixth International Conference on Software Testing, Verification and Validation (ICST) Workshops Proceedings (2013)

11. Morgado, I., Paiva, A.C.R.: Mobile GUI testing. Softw. Qual. J. **26**, 1–18 (2017)

12. Paiva, A.C.R.: Automated specification-based testing of graphical user interfaces, Ph.D. thesis, Faculty of Engineering, Porto University, Porto, Portugal (1997)

13. Reis, A., Silva, A.R.: XIS-Reverse: a model-driven reverse engineering approach for legacy information systems. In: Proceedings of MODELSWARD 2017. SCITEPRESS (2017)

14. Ribeiro, A., Silva, A.R.: XIS-mobile: a DSL for mobile applications. In: Proceedings of the 29th Annual ACM Symposium on Applied Computing (SAC) (2014)

15. Ribeiro, A., Silva, A.R.: Evaluation of XIS-mobile, a domain specific language for mobile application development. J. Softw. Eng. Appl. **7**(11), 906–919 (2014a)

16. Moreira, R.M.L.M., Paiva, A.C.R., Nabuco, M., Memon, A.: Pattern-based GUI testing: bridging the gap between design and quality assurance. Softw. Test. Verif. Reliab. J. **27**(3), e1629 (2017)

17. Savic, D., et al.: SilabMDD: a use case model driven approach. In: ICIST 2015 5th International Conference on Information Society and Technology (2015)

18. Silva, A.R.: Model-driven engineering: a survey supported by a unified conceptual model. Comput. Lang. Syst. Struct. **43**(C), 139–155 (2015)

19. Silva, A.R.: SpecQua: towards a framework for requirements specifications with increased quality. In: Cordeiro, J., Hammoudi, S., Maciaszek, L., Camp, O., Filipe, J. (eds.) ICEIS 2014. LNBIP, vol. 227, pp. 265–281. Springer, Cham (2015). https://doi.org/10.1007/978-3-319-22348-3_15

20. Silva, A.R., et al.: A pattern language for use cases specification. In: Proceedings of EuroPLOP 2015. ACM (2015)

21. Silva, A.R., Saraiva, J., Ferreira, D., Silva, R., Videira, C.: Integration of RE and MDE paradigms: the ProjectIT approach and tools. IET Softw. **1**(6), 294–314 (2007)

22. Silva, A.R., Saraiva, J., Silva, R., Martins, C.: XIS - UML profile for eXtreme modeling interactive systems. In: Proceedings of MOMPES 2007. IEEE Computer Society (2007)

23. Silva, A.R., Verelst, J., Mannaert, H., Ferreira, D., Huysmans, P.: Towards a system requirements specification template that minimizes combinatorial effects. In: Proceedings of QUATIC 2014 Conference. IEEE CS (2014)

24. Silva, A.R.: Linguistic patterns and linguistic styles for requirements specification (i): an application case with the rigorous RSL/business-level language. In: Proceedings of EuroPLOP2017. ACM (2017)

25. Silva, A.R.: A rigorous requirement specification language for information systems: focus on RSL's use cases, data entities and state machines, INESC-ID Technical Report (2017)

26. Solis, C., Wang, X.: A study of the characteristics of behaviour driven development. In: 37th EUROMICRO Conference on Software Engineering and Advanced Applications (SEAA), pp. 383–387. IEEE (2011)

27. Stahl, T., Volter, M.: Model-Driven Software Development. Wiley, Hoboken (2005)

28. Verelst, J., Silva, A.R., Mannaert, H., Ferreira, D.A., Huysmans, P.: Identifying combinatorial effects in requirements engineering. In: Proper, H.A., Aveiro, D., Gaaloul, K. (eds.) EEWC 2013. LNBIP, vol. 146, pp. 88–102. Springer, Heidelberg (2013). https://doi.org/10.1007/978-3-642-38117-1_7

29. Videira, C., Silva, A.R.: Patterns and metamodel for a natural-language-based requirements specification language. In: CAiSE Short Paper Proceedings (2005)

30. Videira, C., Ferreira, D., Silva, A.R.: A linguistic patterns approach for requirements specification. In: Proceedings 32nd Euromicro Conference on Software Engineering and Advanced Applications, Euromicro 2006. IEEE Computer Society (2006)

31. Bhat, A., Quadri, S.M.K.: Equivalence class partitioning and boundary value analysis - a review. In: 2nd International Conference on Computing for Sustainable Global Development (INDIACom) (2015)

32. Silva, A.R., Paiva, A.C.R., Silva, V.E.R.: Towards a test specification language for information systems: focus on data entity and state machine tests. In: The 6th International Conference on Model-Driven Engineering and Software Development (2018)

33. Jacobson, I., et al.: Object oriented Software engineering: A Use Case Driven Approach. Addison- Wesley, Boston (1992)

34. Silva, A.R.: RSLingo RSL Excel Template, v4.0, October 2017. https://www.researchgate.net/publication/320256323_RSLingo_RSL_Excel_Template_v40 (2017)

35. Neto, A.C.D., Subramanyan, R., Vieira, M., Travassos, G.H.: A survey on model-based testing approaches: a systematic review. In: Proceedings of the 1st ACM International Workshop on Empirical Assessment of Software Engineering Languages and Technologies: Held in Conjunction with the 22nd IEEE/ACM International Conference on Automated Software Engineering (2007)

36. Hasling, B., Goetz. H., Beetz, K.: Model based testing of system requirements using UML use case models. In: 1st International Conference on IEEE Software Testing, Verification, and Validation (2008)

37. Utting, M., Pretschner, A., Legeard, B.: A taxonomy of model-based testing approaches. Softw. Test. Verif. Reliab. **22**(5), 297–312 (2012)

38. Broy, M., Jonsson, B., Katoen, J.-P., Leucker, M., Pretschner, A. (eds.): Model-Based Testing of Reactive Systems. LNCS, vol. 3472. Springer, Heidelberg (2005). https://doi.org/10.1007/b137241

39. Wynne, M., Hellesoy, A., Tooke, S.: The Cucumber Book: Behaviour-Driven Development for Testers and Developers. Pragmatic Bookshelf, Raleigh (2017)

40. Cucumber & Gherkin. https://cucumber.io/docs/reference. Accessed March 2018

41. Paiva, A.C.R., Vilela, L.: Multidimensional test coverage analysis: PARADIGM-COV tool. Cluster Comput.-J. Netw. Softw. Tools Appl. **20**, 633–649 (2017)

42. Nabuco, M., Paiva, A.C.R.: Model-based test case generation for web applications. In: Murgante, B., et al. (eds.) ICCSA 2014. LNCS, vol. 8584, pp. 248–262. Springer, Cham (2014). https://doi.org/10.1007/978-3-319-09153-2_19

Synchronizing Heuristics for Weakly Connected Automata with Various Topologies

Berk Cirisci[✉], Barış Sevilmiş, Emre Yasin Sivri,
Poyraz Kıvanç Karaçam, Kamer Kaya, and Hüsnü Yenigün

Computer Science and Engineering, Faculty of Engineering and Natural
Sciences, Sabancı University, Istanbul, Turkey
{berkcirisci, barissevilmis, emreyasinsivri, karacam,
kaya, yenigun}@sabanciuniv.edu

Abstract. Since the problem of finding a shortest synchronizing sequence for an automaton is known to be NP-hard, heuristics algorithms are used to find synchronizing sequences. There are several heuristic algorithms in the literature for this purpose. However, even the most efficient heuristic algorithm in the literature has a quadratic complexity in terms of the number of states of the automaton, and therefore can only scale up to a couple of thousands of states. It was also shown before that if an automaton is not strongly connected, then these heuristic algorithms can be used on each strongly connected component separately. This approach speeds up these heuristic algorithms and allows them to scale to much larger number of states easily. In this paper, we investigate the effect of the topology of the automaton on the performance increase obtained by these heuristic algorithms. To this end, we consider various topologies and provide an extensive experimental study on the performance increase obtained on the existing heuristic algorithms. Depending on the size and the number of components, we obtain speed-up values as high as 10000x and more.

Keywords: Finite state automata · Synchronizing sequences ·
Strongly connected component

1 Introduction

A *synchronizing sequence* w for an automaton A is a sequence of inputs such that without knowing the current state of A, when w is applied to A, A reaches to a particular final state, regardless of its initial state. If an automaton A has a synchronizing sequence, A is called as *synchronizing automaton*.

Synchronizing automata and synchronizing sequences have various applications. One example area of application is the model-based testing, in particular Finite State Machine (FSM) based testing. When the abstract behavior of an interactive system is modeled by using an FSM, there are various methods to derive test sequences with high fault coverage [2, 4, 7]. These methods construct a test sequence to be applied when the implementation under test is at a certain state. Therefore, it is required to bring the implementation under test to this particular state, regardless of the initial state of the

S. Hammoudi et al. (Eds.): MODELSWARD 2018, CCIS 991, pp. 475–493, 2019.
https://doi.org/10.1007/978-3-030-11030-7_21

implementation, which can be accomplished by using a synchronizing sequence. Even when the implementation has a reset input for this purpose, there are cases where using a synchronizing sequence is preferred [5]. For more examples of application areas of synchronizing sequences and for an overview of the theoretical results related to synchronizing sequences please see [11].

For practical purposes, e.g. the use of a synchronizing sequence in model-based testing, one is interested in finding synchronizing sequences as short as possible. However, finding a shortest synchronizing sequence is known to be a NP-hard problem [3]. Therefore, heuristic algorithms, known as synchronizing heuristics, are used to find short synchronizing sequences. Among such heuristics are Greedy [3], Cycle [10], SynchroP [8], and SynchroPL [6]. In this paper, we consider using the structure of an automaton while applying a synchronizing heuristic to speed up the execution of these heuristics. Namely, we consider the connectedness of automata.

An automaton is called *strongly connected* if every state is reachable from every other state by traversing the edges (only in the direction they point). An automaton is called *weakly connected* if one can reach any state starting from any other state by traversing the edges in some direction (i.e., not necessarily in the direction they point). To be synchronizing, an automaton needs to be at least weakly connected. When an automaton A is not strongly connected, it can be represented as a union of strongly connected automata. These automata are called as *strongly connected components* (*SCCs*) of A. In [1], given a weakly connected automaton A, a method is suggested to build a synchronizing sequence for A by using the synchronizing sequences of the SCCs of A. We will call the method suggested by [1] as *the SCC method*.

In [1], the SCC method has been experimented on randomly generated automata. Both Greedy and SynchroP algorithms have been applied to the strongly connected components of the automaton. The SCC method has proven itself by improving running time greatly in both algorithms. In [1], our aim was to find if taking the SCCs into account yields a better, faster heuristic, however we lacked variety in graph generation.

In this work, we focus on the performance of the SCC method further. We carefully construct our experimental testbed and connected the SCCs in various ways to generate different topologies. To have a control on the overall topology, we first assume a DAG of SCCs that can be either; (1) Linear, (2) All-To-One, (3) Tree, (4) Complete, (5) Random. Each vertex in the DAG corresponds to a single SCC of the automata. These DAG structures are described in more detail later in the text. While we connect the SCCs, we respect the chosen DAG and do not allow any other connections between SCCs. Our main interest is on the possible improvements on the sequence length and running time on the above-mentioned DAG types. To analyze the method's performance further, we also experiment on the ratio of the number of the edges connecting SCC's.

The rest of the paper is organized as follows. In Sect. 2, we introduce the notation and briefly give the required background. In Sect. 3, we introduce our approach. In Sect. 4, we talk about the synchronizing heuristics that we have worked on and their integration to our approach. In Sect. 5, we compare the proposed approach with the traditional one that performs synchronization heuristics on full automata. In Sect. 6, we conclude the paper and provide some future directions for our work.

2 Background and Notation

A (deterministic) *automaton* is defined by a tuple $A = (S, \Sigma, D, \delta)$ where S is a finite set of n states, Σ is a finite alphabet consisting of p input letters (or simply *letters*). $D \subseteq S \times \Sigma$ is the called the *domain* and $\delta \colon D \to S$ is a transition function. When $D = S \times \Sigma$, then A is called *complete*, otherwise A is called *partial*. Below, we consider only complete automata, unless otherwise stated.

An element of the set Σ^* is called an *input sequence* or simply *a sequence*. For a sequence $w \in \Sigma^*$, we use $|w|$ to denote the length of w, and ε is the empty sequence of length 0. For a complete automaton, we extend the transition function δ to a set of states and to a sequence in the usual way. For a state $s \in S$, we have $\delta(s, \varepsilon) = s$, and for a sequence $w \in \Sigma^*$ and a letter $x \in \Sigma$, we have $\delta(s, xw) = \delta(\delta(s, x), w)$. For a set of states $C \subseteq S$, we have $\delta(C, w) = \{\delta(s, w) \mid s \in C\}$.

For a set of states $C \subseteq S$, let $C^2 = \{\{s, s'\} \mid s, s' \in C\}$ be the set of all *multisets* with cardinality 2 with elements from C, i.e. C^2 is the set of all subsets of C *with* cardinality 2, where repetition is allowed. An element $\{s, s'\} \in C^2$ is called a *pair*. Furthermore, it is called *a singleton pair* (or *an s–pair*, or simply a *singleton*) if $s = s'$, otherwise it is called *a different pair* (or *a d–pair*). The set of s–pairs and d–pairs in C^2 are denoted by C_s^2 and C_d^2 respectively. A sequence w is said to be a *merging sequence for a pair* $\{s, s'\} \in S^2$ if $\delta(\{s, s'\}, w)$ is singleton. For an s-pair $\{s, s\}$, every sequence (including ε) is a merging sequence. For a given automaton $A = (S, \Sigma, S \times \Sigma, \delta)$ and a subset of states $S' \subseteq S$, a sequence w is called an *S'-synchronizing sequence for A* if $\delta(S', w)$ is singleton. When $S' = S$, w is simply called a *synchronizing sequence for A*. An automaton A is called *S'-synchronizing* if there exists an S'-synchronizing sequence for A. An automaton A is called *synchronizing* if there exists a synchronizing sequence for A.

In this paper, we only consider synchronizing automata. As shown by Eppstein [3], deciding if an automaton is synchronizing can be performed in time $O(pn^2)$ by checking if there exists a merging sequence for $\{s, s'\}$, for all $\{s, s'\} \in S^2$.

We use $\delta^{-1}(s, x)$ to denote the set of those states with a transition to state s with letter x. Formally, $\delta^{-1}(s, x) = \{s' \in S \mid \delta(s', x) = s\}$. For pairs, we also define $\delta^{-1}(\{s, s'\}, x) = \{\{p, p'\} \mid p \in \delta^{-1}(s, x) \wedge p' \in \delta^{-1}(s', x)\}$.

An automaton $A = (S, \Sigma, S \times \Sigma, \delta)$ is said to be *strongly connected* if for every pair of states $s, s' \in S$, there exists a sequence $w \in \Sigma^*$ such that $\delta(s, w) = s'$. Given an automaton $A = (S, \Sigma, S \times \Sigma, \delta)$ and another automaton $B = (S', \Sigma, D, \delta')$, B is said to be a *sub-automaton* of A if (i) $S' \subseteq S$, (ii) $D = \{(s, x) \in S' \times \Sigma \mid \exists s' \in S' \text{ s.t. } \delta(s, x) = s'\}$, and (iii) $\forall (s, x) \in D$, $\delta'(s, x) = \delta(s, x)$. Intuitively, the states of B consist of a subset of states of A. Every transition in A from a B state to a B state is preserved, and all the other transitions are deleted.

A *strongly connected component* (SCC) of a given automaton $A = (S, \Sigma, S \times \Sigma, \delta)$, is a sub-automaton $B = (S', \Sigma, D, \delta')$ of A such that B is strongly connected, and there does not exist another strongly connected sub-automaton C of A, where B is a sub-automaton of C. When one considers an automaton A as a directed graph (by representing the states of A as the nodes, and the transition between the states as the edges of the graph), B simply corresponds to a SCC of the directed graph of A.

For a set of SCCs $\{A_1, A_2, ..., A_k\}$, where $A_i = (S_i, \Sigma, D_i, \delta_i)$, $1 \leq i \leq k$, we have $S_i \cap S_j = \emptyset$ when $i \neq j$, and $S_1 \cup S_2 \cup ... \cup S_k = S$. Please note here that $k = 1$ if and only if A is strongly connected. In Fig. 1, a weakly connected automaton and its SCCs are given.

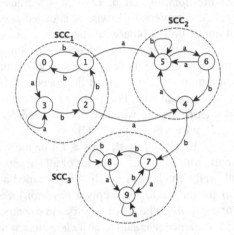

Fig. 1. An automaton with 10 states, 2 inputs and 3 SCCs. (Source: [1])

An SCC $A_i = (S_i, \Sigma, D_i, \delta_i)$ is called a sink component if $D_i = S_i \times \Sigma$. In other words, for a sink component, all the transitions of the states in S_i in A are preserved in A_i. Therefore, if $A_i = (S_i, \Sigma, D_i, \delta_i)$ is not a sink component, then some transitions of some states will be missing. For this reason, A_i is a complete automaton if and only if A_i is a sink component. For the automaton given in Fig. 1, SCC3 is the only sink component.

Given a partial automaton, we consider the completion of this automaton by introducing a new state and adding the missing transitions of states to this new state. Formally for a partial automaton $A = (S, \Sigma, D, \delta)$ such that $D \subset S \times \Sigma$, we define *the completion of A* as $A' = (S \cup \{*\}, \Sigma, S \times \Sigma, \delta')$, where (i) the star state * is a new state which does not exist in S, (ii) $\forall (s, x) \in D$, $\delta'(s, x) = \delta(s, x)$, (iii) $\forall (s, x) \notin D$, $\delta'(s, x) = *$, (iv) $\forall x \in \Sigma$, $\delta'(*, x) = *$. Any SCC that is not a sink component will be a partial automaton. In Fig. 2, the completion of the SCC1 of the automaton of Fig. 1 is given.

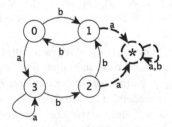

Fig. 2. SCC$_1$(A$_1$) with additional star state. * is the synchronizing state. (Source: [1])

3 Sequences for Weakly Connected Automata

To keep the paper self-contained, we explain the SCC method given in [1]. Consider an automaton $A = (S, \Sigma, S \times \Sigma, \delta)$ and its SCC decomposition $\{A_1, A_2, ..., A_k\}$.

Lemma 1: A is synchronizing iff there exists only one sink component in A_i in $\{A_1, A_2, ..., A_k\}$ and A_i is synchronizing.

Proof: If there are multiple sink components A_i and A_j, a state s_i and A_i and a state s_j in A_j cannot be merged, hence A is not synchronizing. If A_i is the only sink component of A and A_i is not synchronizing, A is not synchronizing as well.

Similar to the topological sorting of strongly connected components of a graph, we consider the topological sorting of SCCs of an automaton. Let $A = (S, \Sigma, S \times \Sigma, \delta)$ be an automaton and $\{A_1, A_2, ..., A_k\}$ be the SCCs of A. We consider the SCCs of A sorted as $\langle A_1, A_2, ..., A_k \rangle$ such that for any $1 \leq i < j \leq k$, there do not exist $s_i \in S_i$, $s_j \in S_j$, $w \in \Sigma^*$ where $\delta(s_j, w) = s_i$. Note that in this case A_k must be a sink component. From this point on, we consider $A = (S, \Sigma, S \times \Sigma, \delta)$ to be an automaton which is not strongly connected, and we consider $\langle A_1, A_2, ..., A_k \rangle$ to be the topologically sorted SCCs of A, where $A_i = (S_i, \Sigma, D_i, \delta_i)$. We have the following result.

Lemma 2: For any sequence $w \in \Sigma^*$ and for a state $s \in S_i$, $1 \leq i \leq k$, we have $\delta(s, w) \in (S_i \cup S_{i+1} \cup ... \cup S_k)$.

Proof: Since the components are topologically sorted, states in A_i can only move to a state in A_i, or to a state in $A_{i+1}, A_{i+2}, ..., A_k$.

Lemma 3: Let A_i be an SCC of an automaton which is not a sink component. Then the completion A'_i of A_i is a synchronizing automaton.

Proof: When A_i is not a sink component, then A_i is a partial automaton. In this case the completion A'_i of A_i, is an automaton with a unique sink-state (the star state), which is known to be synchronizing [9, 12].

3.1 An Initial Approach to Use SCCs

We now explain an idea to form a synchronizing sequence for an automaton A by using synchronizing sequences of the SCCs of A. For $1 \leq i < k$, let β_i be a synchronizing sequence for the completion A'_i of $A_i = (S_i, \Sigma, D_i, \delta_i)$. Based on Lemma 3, one can always find a synchronizing sequence for A'_i, $1 \leq i < k$. Let β_k be a synchronizing sequence for A_k. Lemma 1 suggests that A_k always has a synchronizing sequence if A is synchronizing.

We first claim that the sequence $\beta_1\beta_2...\beta_k$ is a synchronizing sequence for A. In order to see this, it is sufficient to observe the following.

Lemma 4: For any $0 \leq i < k$ we have $\delta(S, \beta_1\beta_2...\beta_i) \subseteq (S_{i+1} \cup S_{i+2} \cup ... \cup S_k)$.

Proof: We will use induction; the base case, $i = 0$, holds trivially. Assume that the claim holds for $i - 1$, i.e. $\delta(S, \beta_1\beta_2...\beta_{i-1}) \subseteq (S_i \cup S_{i+1} \cup ... \cup S_k)$. For a state $s \in \delta(S, \beta_1\beta_2...\beta_{i-1})$ such that $s \in (S_{i+1} \cup S_{i+2} \cup ... \cup S_k)$, then $\delta(s, \beta_i)$ will also belong to

$(S_{i+1} \cup S_{i+2} \cup \ldots \cup S_k)$ based on Lemma 2. Therefore it remains to show that for any state $s \in \delta(S, \beta_1\beta_2\ldots\beta_{i-1})$ such that $s \in S_i$, $\delta(s, \beta_i)$ is not in S_i. The sequence β_i is a synchronizing sequence for the completion A'_i of SCC A_i. Since the star state of A'_i is the only state in which the states of A'_i can be synched, we must have $\delta'_i(S_i, \beta_i) = \{*\}$. Note that the star state in A'_i represents the states $S \backslash S_i$ for A_i. Hence the sequence β_i is in fact a sequence that pushes all the states in S_i to the states in the other components, i.e., $\delta(S_i, \beta_i) = \varnothing$. This implies that for a state $s \in \delta(S, \beta_1\beta_2\ldots\beta_{i-1})$ such that $s \in S_i$, $\delta(s, \beta_i)$ is not in S_i. Finally, we can state the following result.

Theorem 5: Let β_i be a synchronizing sequence for the completion A'_i of A_i, $1 \leq i < k$, and let β_k be a synchronizing sequence for A_k. The sequence $\beta_1\beta_2\ldots\beta_k$ is a synchronizing sequence for A.

Proof: Using Lemma 4, we have $\delta(S, \beta_1\beta_2\ldots\beta_{k-1}) \subseteq S_k$. Since β_k is a synchronizing sequence for A_k, $\delta(S_k, \beta_k)$ is singleton. Combining these two results, we have $\delta(\delta(S, \beta_1\beta_2\ldots\beta_{k-1}), \beta_k) = \delta(S, \beta_1\beta_2\ldots\beta_{k-1}\beta_k)$ singleton as well.

3.2   An Improvement on the Initial Approach

Theorem 5 implies a trivial algorithm for constructing a synchronizing sequence for an automaton A based on its SCCs. As one may notice, though, the length of the sequence to be constructed can be reduced based on the following observation. Consider a sequence β_i, for some $1 < i \leq k$, used in the sequence $\beta_1\beta_2\ldots\beta_{k-1}\beta_k$. The sequence β_i is constructed to push all the states in A_i out of the component A_i. However, the sequence $\beta_1\beta_2\ldots\beta_{i-1}$ applied before β_i can already push some of the states in A_i out of A_i. On the other hand, the sequence $\beta_1\beta_2\ldots\beta_{i-1}$ can also move some of the states in the components $A_1, A_2, \ldots, A_{i-1}$ to a state in A_i. Therefore, a more careful approach can be taken considering which states in A_i must be moved out of A_i when constructing the sequence to handle the component A_i.

To take this observation into account, we define the following sequences recursively. For the base cases, we define $\alpha_0 = \varepsilon$ and $\sigma_0 = \varepsilon$. For $1 \leq i < k$, let $S'_i = S_i \cap \delta(S, \sigma_{i-1})$ and let α_i be a S'_i-synchronizing sequence for A'_i. For $1 \leq i < k$, let $\sigma_i = \sigma_{i-1}\alpha_i$.

Lemma 6: For $0 \leq i < k, \delta(S, \sigma_i) \subseteq S_{i+1} \cup S_{i+2} \cup \ldots \cup S_k$.

Proof: For the base case $i = 0$ we have $\delta(S, \sigma_0) = \delta(S, \varepsilon) = S = S_1 \cup S_2 \cup \ldots \cup S_k$, so it trivially holds. $\delta(S, \sigma_i) = \delta(S, \sigma_{i-1}\alpha_i) = \delta(\delta(S, \sigma_{i-1}), \alpha_i)$ and using the induction hypothesis we have $\delta(S, \sigma_{i-1}) \subseteq S_i \cup S_{i+1} \cup \ldots \cup S_k$. α_i is a S'_i-synchronizing sequence for A'_i, where $S'_i = S_i \cap \delta(S, \sigma_{i-1})$. Therefore, α_i merges all the states in S'_i in the star state of A_i, which means $\delta(S'_i, \alpha_i) = \varnothing$. Therefore $\delta(\delta(S, \sigma_{i-1}), \alpha_i) \subseteq S_{i+1} \cup S_{i+2} \cup \ldots \cup S_k$.

Theorem 7: Let $S'_k = S_k \cap \delta(S, \sigma_{k-1})$ and α_k be a S'_k-synchronizing sequence for A_k. Then $\sigma_{k-1}\alpha_k$ is a synchronizing sequence for A.

Proof: If α_k is a S'_k-synchronizing sequence for A_k, $\delta(S'_k, \alpha_k)$ is a singleton. Using Lemma 6, we have $\delta(S, \sigma_{k-1}) \subseteq S_k$. Therefore $S'_k = S_k \cap \delta(S, \sigma_{k-1}) = \delta(S, \sigma_{k-1})$. Then we have $\delta(S, \sigma_{k-1}\alpha_k) = \delta(\delta(S, \sigma_{k-1}), \alpha_k) = \delta(S'_k, \alpha_k)$, which is a singleton.

Based on Theorem 7, the algorithm given in Fig. 3 can be used to construct a synchronizing sequence for an automaton A. This algorithm uses a synchronizing heuristic to find a synchronizing sequence for SCCs. Any synchronizing heuristic can be used for this step. In the next section, we explain two different algorithms from the literature that we used in our experiments.

```
Input:     An automaton A = (S,Σ,D,δ)
Output: A synchronizing sequence for A

C = S; // All states are active initially
Γ = ε ;  // Γ: synch. sequence to be constructed,
             // initially empty
<A₁, A₂,…, Aₖ> = find/sort SCCs of A
foreach i in {1, 2, …, k} do
    // Consider Aᵢ = (Sᵢ,Σ,Dᵢ,δᵢ)
    S'ᵢ = C ∩ Sᵢ; // find active states of Aᵢ
    Γᵢ = Heuristic(A'ᵢ,S'ᵢ); // find S'ᵢ sync. sequence
                                   // of completion A'ᵢ of Aᵢ
    Γ = Γ Γᵢ; // append Γᵢ to sync. seq.
    C = δ(C, Γᵢ ); // Update active states
return Γ ;
```

Fig. 3. SCC algorithm to compute synchronizing sequences. (Source: [1])

4 Synchronizing Heuristics

There exist various synchronizing heuristics in the literature where we experimented with two of these heuristics, *Greedy* and *SynchroP*. Both of these heuristics have two phases. Phase 1 is common in these heuristics and given in Fig. 4 below.

```
Input:   An automaton A = (S,Σ,D,δ)
Output: A merging sequence for all
           {i,j} ∈ S²

let Q be an initially empty queue // Q: BFS frontier
P = ∅ // P: keeps the set of nodes in the BFS forest constructed so far
foreach {i,j} ∈ S²ₛ do
    push {i,j} onto Q
    insert {i,j} into P
    set τ(i,j) = ε;

while P ≠ S² do
    {i,j}= pop next item from Q;
    foreach x ∈ Σ do
        foreach {k,l} ∈ δ⁻¹({i,j},x) do
            if {k,l} ∉ P then
                τ(k,l)=x τ(i,j);
                push {k,l} onto Q;
                P = P ∪ {{k,l}};
```

Fig. 4. Phase 1 of Greedy and SynchroP. (Source: [1])

In Phase 1 of the synchronizing heuristics, a shortest merging sequence $\tau(i, j)$ for each $\{i, j\} \in S^2$ is computed by using a breadth first search. Note that in the algorithm, $\tau(i,j)$ is not unique.

Figure 4 performs a breadth first search (BFS), and therefore constructs a BFS forest, rooted at s–pairs $\{i, i\} \in S_s^2$, where these s–pair nodes are the nodes at level 0 of the BFS forest. A d–pair $\{i, j\}$ appears at level k of the BFS forest if $|\tau\{i,j\}| = k$. The first phase requires $\Omega(n^2)$ time since each $\{i, j\} \in S^2$ is pushed to Q exactly once.

4.1   The Greedy Heuristic

Greedy's Phase 2 (given in Fig. 5 below) constructs a synchronizing sequence by using the information from Phase 1. Its main loop can iterate at most $n - 1$ times, since in each iteration $|C|$ is reduced by at least one. The min operation at line 4 requires $O(n^2)$ time and line 5 takes constant time. Line 6 can normally be handled in $O(n^3)$ time, but using the information precomputed by the intermediate stage between Phase 1 and Phase 2 [3], line 6 can be handled in $O(n)$ time. Therefore, Phase 2 of Greedy requires $O(n^3)$ time. Note that Phase 2 of Greedy finds an S-synchronizing sequence for a given complete automaton $A = (S, \Sigma, S \times \Sigma, \delta)$. However, we need to find an S'-synchronizing sequence for a given subset $S' \subseteq S$ of states.

```
Input: An automaton A = (S,Σ,D,δ), τ(i,j) for all {i,j} ∈S²ₛ, S' to be
synchronized
Output: An S'-synch. sequence Γ for A

C = S'    // C: current state set
Γ = ε     // Γ: synch. sequence to be constructed, initially empty

while |C| > 1 do  // still not a singleton
    {i,j} = arg min<k,l>∈C²d|τ(k,l)|; // decide the d-pair to be
                                      // merged
    Γ = Γ τ(i,j); // append τ(i,j) to the synchronizing sequence
    C= δ(C, τ(i,j));     //update current state set with τ(i,j)
```

Fig. 5. Phase 2 of Greedy. (Source: [1])

4.2   The SynchroP Heuristic

Similar to Greedy, the second phase of SynchroP constructs a synchronizing sequence iteratively. It keeps track of the current set C of states, which is initially the entire set of states S. In each iteration, the cardinality of C is reduced at least by one. This is accomplished by picking a d-pair $\{i, j\} \in C_d^2$ in each iteration, and considering $\delta(C, \tau(i, j))$ as the current set in the next iteration. Since $\tau(i, j)$ is a merging sequence for the states i and j, the cardinality of $\delta(C, \tau(i, j))$ is guaranteed to be smaller than that of C. For a set of states $C \subseteq S$, let the cost $\varphi(C)$ of C be defined as

$$\varphi(C) = \sum_{i,j \in C} |\tau(i,j)| \tag{1}$$

where $\varphi(C)$ is a heuristic indication of how hard it is to bring the set C to a singleton. The intuition here is that, the larger the cost $\varphi(C)$ is, the longer a synchronizing sequence would be required to bring C to a singleton set.

During the iterations of SynchroP, the selection of $\{i, j\} \in C_d^2$ that will be used is performed by considering the cost of the set $\delta(C, \tau(i, j))$. Based on this cost function, the second phase of SynchroP is given in Fig. 6. As in Greedy with the SCC method, we also use a slightly modified version of the second phase of SynchroP algorithm to find S'-synchronizing sequence.

```
Input:   An atomaton A = (S,Σ,D,δ), τ(i,j) for all {i,j} ∈ S²ₛ, S' to
be synchronized
Output: An S'-synch. sequence Γ for A

C = S'    // C: current state set
Γ = ε     // Γ: synchronizing sequence to be constructed,
          // initially empty
while |C| > 1 do // still not a singleton
    minCost = ∞
    foreach d-pair {i,j} ∈ C²d do
        thisPairCost = Φ(δ(C,τ(i,j)))
        if thisPairCost < minCost then
            minCost = thisPairCost
            τ' = τ(i,j)

    Γ = Γ τ';   // append τ' to the synch. sequence
    C= δ(C, τ'); //update current state set with τ'
```

Fig. 6. Phase 2 of SynchroP. (Source: [1])

5 Experimental Results

The experiments were performed on a machine with Intel Xeon E5-2620 CPU and 64 GB of memory, using Ubuntu 16.04.2. The code was written in C/C++ and compiled using gcc with -O3 option enabled.

In order to evaluate the performance of the SCC method, we generated automata with 5 different DAG types, $nSCC \in \{32, 64, 128\}$ states for each SCC, $p \in \{2, 4, 8\}$ inputs, $d \in \{0.25, 0.5, 0.75\}$ (edge distribution factor), $k \in \{2, 4, 8\}$ SCC's for four DAG types ($t \in \{$All-to-One, Linear, Complete, Random$\}$) and $k \in \{3, 7, 15\}$ SCC's for one DAG type ($t =$ Tree). To construct an automaton A with the given parameters, we first construct k different strongly connected automata $A_1, A_2, ..., A_k$, where each A_i has $nSCC$ states, p inputs. To construct an automaton A_i, we consider each state s in A_i and each input x, and assign $\delta(s, x)$ to be one of the states in A_i randomly. If A_i is not strongly connected after the initial random assignment, we reassign $\delta(s, x)$ for some of the states and inputs randomly again, keep repeating this process until A_i becomes strongly connected. Once we have A_i strongly connected, we identify those state s and input x pairs in A_i (except for the last SCC A_k) such that A_i stays strongly connected even without using the transition of the state s and with the input x. For these state/input pairs in A_i, we reassign $\delta(s, x)$ to be one of the states in the automata $A_{i+1}, A_{i+2}, ..., A_k$

according to the DAG type that we select. We used the distribution factor parameter $d \in \{0.25, 0.5, 0.75\}$ as follows: after finding M transitions that can be reassigned safely without making A_i not strongly connected, we use at most $(d \times M)$ of them to connect the current SCC to the other SCCs based on the chosen DAG type t.

For Linear automata, we connect each SCC A_i to the SCC A_{i+1} except A_k as shown in Fig. 7. For Complete automata, all SCC A_i to SCC A_j connections are established for $i < j$. For Random automata, each transition reassignment for SCC A_i is performed randomly to an SCC A_j where $i < j$. In All-to-one automata, all the reassignments are performed to $SCC\ A_k$, the sink component. For Tree automata, we connect each SCC A_i to its parent in a (complete binary) tree. In this automata type, $k \in \{3, 7, 15\}$ since we aim to generate complete trees.

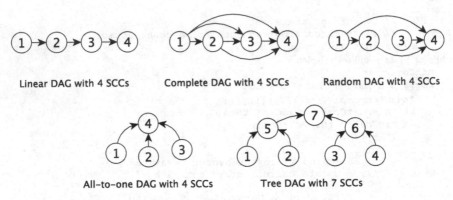

Fig. 7. Example DAGs with 4 SCCs for the types Linear, Complete, Random and All-to-one, and 7 SCCs for the type Tree.

In general, for each $nSCC$-p-d-k-t combination we created 50 automata. However, due to the complexity of SynchroP, for automata with $nSCC = 128$, $p \in \{2, 4, 8\}$ inputs, $d \in \{0.25, 0.5, 0.75\}$, $k = 15$ and $t = $ Tree, we created only 20 automata rather than 50.

For an automaton $A = (S, \Sigma, S \times \Sigma, \delta)$ with $nSCC$ states for each SCC, p inputs and k SCCs $\langle A_1, A_2, \dots, A_k \rangle$ where $A_i = (S_i, \Sigma, D_i, \delta_i)$, $1 \leq i \leq k$, we find a synchronizing (i.e. S-synchronizing) sequence for A by using Greedy and SynchroP algorithms given in Figs. 5 and 6, respectively. We also find a synchronizing sequence for A by using the SCC method given in Fig. 3, where for each $A_i = (S_i, \Sigma, D_i, \delta_i)$, we use Greedy and SynchroP to find S'_i-synchronizing sequence as explained in Sect. 3.

Figure 8 shows the performance improvements in terms of time and sequence length due to the SCC method over the original Greedy algorithm. We measured the ratios of the execution time and sequence length of original Greedy to those of Greedy with SCC method and report the averages of these metrics. The first three columns in each block of Fig. 8 present the improvements over time, i.e., speedups, whereas the last three columns do the same for average sequence length. As the figure shows, for all DAG types, the SCC method is more than 6x faster than the original Greedy for automata with 8 SCCs. For binary-tree DAGs, the speedups look more; however, one

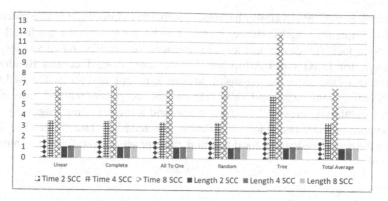

Fig. 8. Greedy/SCC Method Time Ratio (Speedup) and Sequence Length Ratio Results for Automata with 2, 4 and 8 SCC's and 5 DAG types (3,7 and 15 SCC's for Tree DAGs).

should note that for tree DAGs, the results are given for 3,7 and 15 SCCs (instead of 2, 4 and 8). Hence for tree DAGs, the proposed method yields 12x speedup for automata with 15 SCCs. This also confirms that the speedups tend to increase with the number of SCCs. As the figure shows, the SCC method reduces the sequence lengths on average. Furthermore, similar to the average execution time, the amount of the reduction on sequence lengths tends to increase with the number of SCCs. We present a more detailed result set in Tables 1, 2, 3, 4, 5 and 6.

Compared to Greedy, SynchroP is a slower heuristic. Hence, we expect that the impact of the SCC method over SynchroP will be more. Figure 9 confirms our expectations. As the figure shows, the proposed method can make SynchroP around 10x, 100x and 1000x faster on automata with 2, 4 and 8 SCCs, respectively. For tree DAGs, the improvement is 10000x on average for 15 SCCs. Thus, similar to the Greedy, one can say that the improvement on runtime tends to increase with the number of SCCs. However, it slightly decreases when the number of inputs, i.e., the alphabet size, increases.

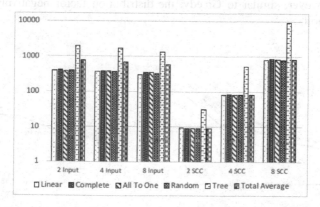

Fig. 9. SynchroP/SCC Method Time Ratio (Speedup) Results for Automata with 2, 4 and 8 inputs and 5 DAG types in logarithmic scale (3, 7 and 15 SCC's for Tree DAGs).

Although SynchroP is a slower heuristic, compared to Greedy, it is also much better in terms of sequence lengths. Hence, it should be harder to improve the length of the sequences. In fact, one can expect longer sequences for the SCC-based variant. In our experiments, for DAG types All-to-one, Linear, Complete, Tree and Random, the average ratios of the sequence lengths of original SynchroP and the SCC-based variant are 0.95, 1.04, 0.96, 0.95 and 0.98. Hence, the proposed method increases the sequences length only around 2.4% on average, and it improves the lengths by 4% for weakly connected automata whose SCCs are connected like a binary tree. The detailed results on the sequence lengths for different parameter sets can be found in Tables 1, 2, 3, 4, 5 and 6.

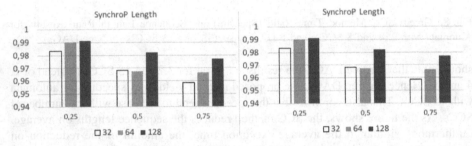

Fig. 10. SynchroP/SCC Method and Greedy/SCC Method Sequence Length Ratio with Distribution Factors 0,25, 0,5, 0,75 and nSCCs 32, 64, 128.

To visualize the results on sequence lengths more clearly, Fig. 10 presents the trends for varying distribution factors and number of SCCs used to generate the automata. As shown in the figure, for Greedy, the improvement on the sequence length decreases both with increasing number of states in each SCC (bottom legends in the figure) and increasing distribution factor. That being said, even in the worst pair of parameters the improvement is 8% on average. The results with SynchroP are different: when the number of SCCs increases, the SCC-based variant gets closer to original SynchroP. However, similar to Greedy, the distribution factor negatively affects the proposed method.

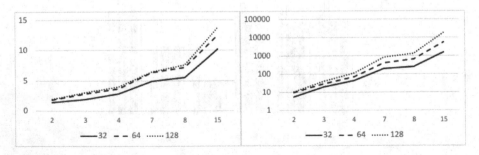

Fig. 11. Greedy/SCC Method and SynchroP/SCC Method Time Ratio (Speedup) with 2, 3, 4, 7, 8 and 15 SCC's and 32, 64 and 128 nSCCs.

Figure 11 shows the trend on with different number of SCCs and nSCCs. Similar to the figures above, the speedups increase with the number of SCCs. They also increase with the number of states in a single SCC. This is expected since the automata get larger and the heuristics become more costly.

Table 1. Experimental results for all to one automata.

Number of states for each SCC	Number of SCCs	Number of inputs	Greedy vs SCC method		SynchroP vs SCC method	
			Time ratio	Length ratio	Time ratio	length ratio
32	2	2	0,74	1,04	4,87	1
		4	1,35	1,07	5,48	0,99
		8	1,5	1,08	5,57	0,99
	4	2	2,56	1,11	53,57	0,94
		4	2,97	1,14	47,89	0,94
		8	2,96	1,12	39,03	0,91
	8	2	5,32	1,11	318,62	0,94
		4	5,47	1,14	267,33	0,92
		8	5,4	1,15	209,87	0,84
64	2	2	1,78	1,02	10,22	0,98
		4	1,68	1,07	10,36	1,01
		8	1,91	1,06	7,9	1,01
	4	2	3,44	1,06	86,74	0,96
		4	3,63	1,11	77,65	0,96
		8	3,7	1,12	60,84	0,92
	8	2	6,93	1,06	851,08	0,93
		4	6,73	1,13	606,1	0,91
		8	7,16	1,14	542,36	0,86
128	2	2	1,96	1,04	9,72	0,99
		4	1,98	1,05	10,11	1,01
		8	1,93	1,06	9,94	1,01
	4	2	3,88	1,04	103,49	0,97
		4	3,8	1,13	113,04	0,95
		8	3,96	1,1	115,95	0,95
	8	2	7,46	1,08	1297,94	0,94
		4	7,1	1,16	1427,74	0,91
		8	7,63	1,12	1414,44	0,9

Table 2. Experimental results for linear automata.

Number of states for each SCC	Number of SCCs	Number of inputs	Greedy vs SCC method		SynchroP vs SCC method	
			Time ratio	Length ratio	Time ratio	Length ratio
32	2	2	1,09	1,04	6,07	1
		4	1,24	1,07	5,88	0,99
		8	1,98	1,08	5,7	0,99
	4	2	2,49	1,14	51,37	1,01
		4	2,69	1,17	43,92	1,02
		8	3,06	1,09	36,31	1,07
	8	2	4,93	1,18	337,16	1,03
		4	5,31	1,15	246,47	1,11
		8	5,93	1,09	190,13	1,14
64	2	2	1,89	1,02	10,86	0,98
		4	1,5	1,07	10,4	1,01
		8	1,84	1,06	7,86	1,01
	4	2	3,54	1,11	82,46	0,98
		4	3,56	1,14	76,65	1,06
		8	3,85	1,1	59,64	1,05
	8	2	6,69	1,17	898,92	1
		4	6,84	1,15	603,7	1,1
		8	7,51	1,07	532,77	1,14
128	2	2	1,89	1,04	9,88	0,99
		4	1,86	1,05	10,68	1,01
		8	1,93	1,06	9,6	1,01
	4	2	3,95	1,08	107,72	0,99
		4	3,72	1,14	116,89	1,04
		8	4,01	1,09	107,85	1,05
	8	2	7,22	1,15	1320,74	1,02
		4	6,86	1,16	1366,23	1,1
		8	8,19	1,07	1163,29	1,12

Table 3. Experimental results for complete automata.

Number of states for each SCC	Number of SCCs	Number of inputs	Greedy vs SCC method		SynchroP vs SCC method	
			Time ratio	Length ratio	Time ratio	Length ratio
32	2	2	1,48	1,04	5,26	1
		4	1,48	1,07	5,59	0,99
		8	1,4	1,08	5,87	0,99
	4	2	2,47	1,11	55,03	0,97
		4	3	1,14	48,5	0,99
		8	2,85	1,09	38,61	0,95
	8	2	5,43	1,11	335,4	0,92
		4	5,28	1,15	271,77	0,92
		8	5,76	1,12	215,82	0,87
64	2	2	1,6	1,02	10,53	0,98
		4	1,62	1,07	10,39	1,01
		8	1,78	1,06	7,74	1,01
	4	2	3,63	1,05	88,12	0,98
		4	3,68	1,12	78,49	0,98
		8	3,77	1,09	64,21	0,94
	8	2	7,28	1,11	920,73	0,94
		4	7,05	1,13	647,01	0,93
		8	7,45	1,11	633,61	0,89
128	2	2	1,91	1,04	9,62	0,99
		4	1,94	1,05	10,04	1,01
		8	1,9	1,06	10,1	1,01
	4	2	4,02	1,06	108,14	0,96
		4	3,83	1,13	119,44	0,99
		8	4	1,1	115,12	0,97
	8	2	7,52	1,11	1395,27	0,95
		4	7,3	1,16	1428,9	0,94
		8	8,01	1,12	1407,34	0,92

Table 4. Experimental results for tree automata.

Number of states for each SCC	Number of SCCs	Number of inputs	Greedy vs SCC method		SynchroP vs SCC method	
			Time ratio	Length ratio	Time ratio	Length ratio
32	3	2	1,67	1,07	19,11	0,97
		4	1,81	1,12	20,08	0,98
		8	2,12	1,11	17,82	0,93
	7	2	4,68	1,14	251,53	0,94
		4	4,89	1,16	210,9	0,94
		8	5,02	1,18	150,54	0,93
	15	2	9,73	1,17	1898,79	0,96
		4	10,04	1,22	1591,15	0,94
		8	10,58	1,2	1299,54	0,94
64	3	2	6,13	1,13	481,43	0,95
		4	5,95	1,18	446,86	0,96
		8	6,66	1,15	340,69	0,97
	7	2	6,13	1,13	481,43	0,95
		4	5,95	1,18	446,86	0,96
		8	6,66	1,15	340,69	0,97
	15	2	12,45	1,17	7360,79	0,96
		4	11,85	1,22	5763,36	0,95
		8	12,97	1,19	4320,21	0,94
128	3	2	2,99	1,06	40,28	0,95
		4	2,99	1,12	40,22	0,98
		8	3,11	1,08	40,56	0,97
	7	2	6,55	1,11	799,83	0,95
		4	6,23	1,2	861,5	0,98
		8	6,59	1,14	809,63	0,97
	15	2	13,38	1,13	21815,24	0,94
		4	12,53	1,23	20093,27	0,93
		8	14,54	1,16	16178,07	0,96

Table 5. Experimental results for random automata.

Number of states for each SCC	Number of SCCs	Number of inputs	Greedy vs SCC method		SynchroP vs SCC method	
			Time ratio	Length ratio	Time ratio	Length ratio
32	2	2	1,21	1,04	5,61	1
		4	1,54	1,07	5,77	0,99
		8	1,45	1,08	5,73	0,99
	4	2	2,48	1,11	54,68	0,96
		4	2,7	1,13	45,33	0,97
		8	2,99	1,1	36,38	0,98
	8	2	5,41	1,17	334,1	0,95
		4	5,81	1,15	258,82	0,97
		8	5,97	1,16	199,64	0,96
64	2	2	1,64	1,02	10,22	0,98
		4	1,78	1,07	10,36	1,01
		8	1,8	1,06	7,9	1,01
	4	2	3,57	1,09	86,74	0,98
		4	3,43	1,14	77,65	0,99
		8	3,8	1,11	60,84	0,98
	8	2	6,96	1,13	851,08	0,95
		4	6,9	1,15	606,1	0,98
		8	7,7	1,14	542,36	0,97
128	2	2	1,98	1,04	9,55	0,99
		4	1,9	1,05	10,42	1,01
		8	1,91	1,06	9,91	1,01
	4	2	3,88	1,07	107,13	0,98
		4	3,73	1,13	115,24	1
		8	4,06	1,1	111,98	1
	8	2	7,25	1,12	1326,64	0,97
		4	7,28	1,17	1392,2	1
		8	8,23	1,14	1284,89	0,99

6 Conclusions

This work is an extension of a previous study [1] on the use of synchronizing heuristics on the strongly connected components separately, which is called the SCC method. It was shown before that the SCC method can be used with any synchronizing heuristic to make it run faster on weakly connected automata. In this paper, we focused on the effect of the topology of the automaton on the performance increase obtained by the application of the SCC method.

Five different topologies are considered as explained in Sect. 5. In addition to the topology, we also considered the effect of the ratio of the number of transitions outgoing from strongly connected components. The detailed analysis of the experimental results is given in Sect. 5 as well. To summarize these findings, Table 6 presents the average of all the experiments in all topology classes considered.

Table 6. Summary of experimental results.

Topology	Greedy vs SCC method		SynchroP vs SCC method	
	Time ratio	Length ratio	Time ratio	Length ratio
All to one	3,89	1,09	285,48	0,95
Linear	3,91	1,10	274,78	1,04
Complete	3,98	1,09	298,02	0,96
Tree	7,19	1,15	3189,64	0,95
Random	3,98	1,10	280,27	0,98

Like the results obtained in the original study given in [1], we see that Greedy when used with the SCC method improves both the running time and the length of the synchronizing sequence obtained. The improvement obtained is independent of the topology of the automaton. Although the Tree topology gives better improvements, this is mainly related to the fact that number of SCCs used in the experiments for the Tree topology is higher.

SynchroP heuristic with the SCC method yields a much higher improvement in time as expected. Similar to the case of Greedy, we see that the improvement obtained in the time performance is independent of the topology of the automaton. As in [1], the synchronizing sequences obtained by using SynchroP with the SCC method are slightly longer than the ones obtained by the direct application of SynchroP. Only in the Linear topology, we see that SynchroP with the SCC method gives shorter synchronizing sequences.

For future work, one direction is to improve our synchronizing sequence lengths for the SCC method when used with SynchroP. Among the topologies considered in this paper, the Linear topology is the only one in which the use of SynchroP with the SCC method gives shorter synchronizing sequences. Therefore, a deeper investigation of the behavior of SynchroP algorithm under the Linear topology case can provide hints to improve the synchronizing sequence lengths for the other topologies.

Finally, both in [1] and in this paper, an automaton is decomposed into the strongly connected components. Another direction of research can be to find other decompositions for an automaton, in such a way that the components can be analyzed separately to compute a synchronizing sequence for the original automaton.

Acknowledgments. This work was supported by The Scientific and Technological Research Council of Turkey (TUBITAK) [grant number 114E569].

References

1. Cirisci, B., Kahraman, M.K., Yildirimoglu, C.U., Kaya, K., Yenigun, H.: Using structure of automata for faster synchronizing heuristics. In: Proceedings of the 6th International Conference on Model-Driven Engineering and Software Development, MODELSWARD 2018, Funchal, Madeira - Portugal, pp. 544–551 (2018)
2. Chow, T.S.: Testing software design modelled by finite state machines. IEEE Trans. Softw. Eng. **4**, 178–187 (1978)
3. Eppstein, D.: Reset sequences for monotonic automata. SIAM J. Comput. **19**(3), 500–510 (1990)
4. Hierons, R.M., Ural, H.: Optimizing the length of checking sequences. IEEE Trans. Comput. **55**(5), 618–629 (2006)
5. Jourdan, G.V., Ural, H., Yenigün, H.: Reduced checking sequences using unreliable reset. Inf. Process. Lett. **115**(5), 532–535 (2015)
6. Kudlacik, R., Roman, A., Wagner, H.: Effective synchronizing algorithms. Expert Syst. Appl. **39**(14), 11746–11757 (2012)
7. Lee, D., Yannakakis, M.: Principles and methods of testing finite state machines-a survey. Proc. IEEE **84**(8), 1090–1123 (1996)
8. Roman, A., Szykula, M.: Forward and backward synchronizing algorithms. Expert Syst. Appl. **42**(24), 9512–9527 (2015)
9. Rystsov, I.: Reset words for commutative and solvable automata. Theoret. Comput. Sci. **172**(1–2), 273–279 (1997)
10. Trahtman, A.N.: Some results of implemented algorithms of synchronization. In: 10th Journees Montoises d'Inform (2004)
11. Volkov, M.V.: Synchronizing automata and the Černý conjecture. In: Martín-Vide, C., Otto, F., Fernau, H. (eds.) LATA 2008. LNCS, vol. 5196, pp. 11–27. Springer, Heidelberg (2008). https://doi.org/10.1007/978-3-540-88282-4_4
12. Volkov, M.V.: Synchronizing automata preserving a chain of partial orders. Theoret. Comput. Sci. **410**(37), 3513–3519 (2009)

Author Index

Printed in the United States
By Bookmasters